VERTICAL AGREEMENTS IN EC COMPETITION LAW

VERTICAL AGREEMENTS IN EC COMPETITION LAW

FRANK WIJCKMANS
FILIP TUYTSCHAEVER
ALAIN VANDERELST

OXFORD
UNIVERSITY PRESS

OXFORD
UNIVERSITY PRESS

Great Clarendon Street, Oxford OX2 6DP

Oxford University Press is a department of the University of Oxford.
It furthers the University's objective of excellence in research, scholarship,
and education by publishing worldwide in

Oxford New York

Auckland Cape Town Dar es Salaam Hong Kong Karachi
Kuala Lumpur Madrid Melbourne Mexico City Nairobi
New Delhi Shanghai Taipei Toronto

With offices in

Argentina Austria Brazil Chile Czech Republic France Greece
Guatemala Hungary Italy Japan Poland Portugal Singapore
South Korea Switzerland Thailand Turkey Ukraine Vietnam

Oxford is a registered trade mark of Oxford University Press
in the UK and in certain other countries

Published in the United States
by Oxford University Press Inc., New York

British Library Cataloguing in Publication Data

Data available

Library of Congress Cataloging-in-Publication Data
Wijckmans, Frank.
  Vertical agreements in EC competition law / Frank Wijckmans, Filip Tuytschaever,
Alain Vanderelst.
    p. cm.
  ISBN-13: 978–0–19–928581–5 (alk. paper)
  ISBN-10: 0–19–928581–0 (alk. paper)
  1. Exclusive contracts—European Union countries. 2. Distributors (Commerce)—
Legal status, laws, etc.—European Union countries. 3. Restraint of trade—European
Union countries. I. Tuytschaever, Filip. II. Vanderelst, Alain. III. Title.
  KJE6478.W55 2006
  343.24'0721—dc22   2006010269

Typeset by Newgen Imaging Systems (P) Ltd., Chennai, India
Printed in Great Britain
on acid-free paper by
Antony Rowe Limited, Chippenham, Wiltshire

ISBN 0–19–928581–0   978–0–19–928581–5

1 3 5 7 9 10 8 6 4 2

ACKNOWLEDGEMENTS

We are enormously grateful to many people who have given us assistance at various stages of the writing of this book. Our special thanks goes to Sofie de Keer, whose help in all stages of the writing has been invaluable. We are also particularly grateful to Mieke Beeuwsaert, Maaike Visser, Gerrit van Gassen, Tom Antonissen, Lot Goris, Louise Dancet, Herlinde Burez, and Matthias Debroyer. Jim Timms has done a great job as our language editor. This book would not have been possible without the support and encouragement from Anne Knops and Pascale van Houtte of Larcier. Last but not least, Chris Rycroft, Katarina Wihlborg, Annette Lord, Louise Kavanagh, and Kirsty Asher of Oxford University Press have seen the manuscript through the publishing process with wonderful efficiency.

This book reflects the law as it stood on 1 November 2005.

CONTENTS—SUMMARY

CONTENTS

I INTRODUCTORY

1. General Introduction

Contents

IV MOTOR VEHICLE DISTRIBUTION UNDER REGULATION 1400/2002

11. The Motor Vehicle Distribution Block Exemption

TABLE OF CASES AND DECISIONS

EUROPEAN COURT OF FIRST INSTANCE

EUROPEAN COMMISSION DECISIONS

NATIONAL CASES

Belgium

France

Netherlands

TABLE OF TREATIES AND LEGISLATION

Part I

INTRODUCTORY

1

GENERAL INTRODUCTION

A. Scope, Methodology, and Plan

This book analyses the European Community ('EC') competition rules **1.01**. applying to vertical agreements which fall both in and outside the scope of Commission Regulation (EC) No 2790/99 of 22 December 1999 on the application of Article 81(3) of the Treaty to categories of vertical agreements and concerted practices ('Regulation 2790/99' or 'the Regulation')[1] and Commission Regulation (EC) No 1400/2002 of 31 July 2002 on the application of Article 81(3) of the Treaty to categories of vertical agreements and concerted practices in the motor vehicle sector ('Regulation 1400/2002').[2]

The term 'vertical agreements' covers a wide range of supply and distribution **1.02**. agreements (exclusive and selective distribution, franchising, agency, etc). In a brochure specifically on vertical agreements, the European Commission ('the Commission'), having emphasized the importance of this type of agreement given that almost all goods reach the final customer via a distribution channel, describes vertical agreements as:

> Agreements for the sale and purchase of goods or services which are entered into between companies operating at different levels of the production or distribution chain. Distribution agreements between manufacturers and wholesalers or retailers are typical examples of vertical agreements. However, an industrial supply agreement between a manufacturer of a component and a producer of a product using that component is also a vertical agreement.[3]

Business practice, in other words, is filled with vertical agreements, and sooner **1.03**. or later any practising lawyer is likely to be asked to advise on the admissibility of certain restrictions of competition which are frequently included in such agreements. To do so, Regulation 2790/99, which is the umbrella block

---

[1] [1999] OJ L336/25.   [2] [2002] OJ L203/30.
[3] European Commission, *Competition Policy in Europe. The Competition Rules for Supply and Distribution Agreements* (OOPEC, 2002) 7.

exemption regulation for vertical agreements, is likely to be the starting point for any such analysis. Regulation 2790/99 applies if and when no other, more specific, block exemption regime applies. For motor vehicle distribution however, such a specific block exemption exists, namely Regulation 1400/2002. Technology transfer agreements, which concern the licensing of technology, are also vertical agreements for which a specific block exemption regime has been created, namely Commission Regulation (EC) No 772/2004 of 27 April 2004 on the application of Article 81(3) of the Treaty to categories of technology transfer agreements.[4] Technology transfer agreements and the block exemption regime of Regulation 772/2004 are dealt with only in passing in this book, as the focus is on distribution (rather than production) agreements. Technology transfer agreements are the subject of a number of separate specific studies.[5]

1.04. This book is written from a practitioner's perspective and aims to provide the reader with a practical tool for the analysis of vertical agreements and the various competition restraints which may arise in that context. Where relevant, the book incorporates the informal views we have received from officials of the Competition Directorate-General ('DG COMP') of the Commission. While we have our own opinions on the Commission's policy on vertical restraints, in this book we take the law as its stands as a starting point rather than exhibiting our personal views.

1.05. This book is divided into four parts. Part I provides a sketch of the overall legal background of the EC competition law treatment of vertical restraints. Part II contains a detailed analysis of the scope and the conditions for the application of Regulation 2790/99 to a given vertical agreement. Part III discusses the EC competition law analysis of vertical agreements which are not covered by, or

---

[4] [2004] OJ L123/11.

[5] M Monti, *The New EU policy on Technology Transfer Agreements*, Speech 04/19, 16 January 2004; V Korah, 'Draft Block Exemption for Technology Transfer' [2004] ECLR 247; RC Lind and P Muysert, 'The European Commission's Draft Technology Transfer Block Exemption Regulation and Guidelines: A Significant Departure from Accepted Competition Policy Principles' [2004] ECLR 181; M Dolmans and A Piilola, 'The New Technology Transfer Block Exemption. A Welcome Reform, After All' (2004) 3 World Competition 351; M Hansen and O Shah, 'The New EU Technology Transfer Regime—Out of the Straightjacket into the Safe Harbour?' [2004] ECLR 465; C Ritter, 'The New Technology Transfer Block Exemption under EC Competition Law' (2004) 31 Legal Issues of European Integration 161; E Vollebregt, 'The Changes in the New Technology Transfer Block Exemption Compared to the Draft' [2004] ECLR 660; L Peeperkorn, L Kjolbye, and D Woods, 'Commission Adopts New Safe Harbour for Licensing of Patents, Know-How and Software Copyright' (2004) 2 EC Competition Policy Newsletter 14; S Anderman and J Kallaugher, *Technology Transfer and the New EU Competition Rules. Intellectual Property Licensing after Modernization* (OUP, 2006); M Lubitz, 'Die neue Technologietransfer-Gruppenfreistellungsverordnung' (2004) 15 Europäische Zeitschrift für Wirtschaftsrecht 652; PM Louis, 'Le nouveau réglement d'exemption par catégorie des accords de transfert de technologie: une modernisation et une simplification' [2004] CDE 377; and P Vos, 'De nieuwe technologievrijstelling' (2004) Nederlands Tijdschrift voor Europees Recht 211.

do not comply with the conditions of, Regulation 2790/99. Finally, Part IV focuses on Regulation 1400/2002.

The horizontal issues which are addressed in this Part I (Chapter 1) are the general principles of the implementation, and the (public and private) enforcement, of Articles 81 and 82 EC before and after the entry into force of Council Regulation (EC) No 1/2003 of 16 December 2002 on the implementation of rules on competition laid down in Articles 81 and 82 of the Treaty ('Regulation 1/2003'),[6] the historical background of Regulation 2790/99 and Regulation 1400/2002, as well as the nature and legal and practical consequences of soft EC competition law (eg notices, guidelines) as opposed to hard EC competition law (provisions of primary and secondary EC law). **1.06**.

Part II (Chapters 2 to 9) discusses the application of Regulation 2790/99 to vertical agreements. The various chapters of Part II cover the following topics: **1.07**.

— Chapters 2, 3, and 4 deal, respectively, with the material scope of application of Regulation 2790/99 (*ratione materiae*), its territorial scope of application (*ratione loci*), and its application in time (*ratione temporis*).
— Chapters 5 and 6 follow the structure of Regulation 2790/99 in order to discuss, respectively, the blacklisted clauses and the conditions which non-compete obligations must comply with to be covered by the safe harbour of Regulation 2790/99.
— Chapter 7 summarizes the discussion of Chapters 2 to 6. It takes a number of frequently used distribution formulas as a starting point and then checks the admissibility of certain vertical restraints used in the context of those formulas under Regulation 2790/99. The frequently used distribution formulas are:
  • exclusive and non-exclusive distribution;
  • selective distribution;
  • franchising; and
  • agency.
For each one of these distribution formulas, the following vertical restraints are checked:
  • territorial protection of the buyer;
  • territorial restrictions imposed on the buyer;
  • customer restrictions imposed on the buyer;
  • non-compete obligations; and
  • exclusive purchasing requirements.
The approach adopted in Chapter 7 results, so to speak, in a 'Regulation 2790/99 checklist' for each of the frequently used distribution formulas.

---

[6] [2003] OJ L1/1.

— Chapter 8 addresses a specific type of vertical agreements, namely sub-contracting agreements, which over the course of the years have come to lie at the crossroads of various legal instruments. As a consequence, any practitioner will confirm that it is a challenge to advise on the competition law permissibility of certain restrictions of competition in a subcontracting agreement (whether it be between competing companies or not). Chapter 8 attempts to systematize the competition law assessment of subcontracting, and in particular the EC competition law treatment of exclusive supply-back obligations (ie the obligation on the part of the subcontractor to supply the relevant products to only one particular customer, being the contractor).

— Finally, Chapter 9 discusses the circumstances in which the safe harbour of Regulation 2790/99 can be disapplied or withdrawn.

1.08. Part III (Chapter 10) discusses the EC competition law assessment of vertical agreements which are not covered by, or do not comply with the conditions of, Regulation 2790/99. There is no presumption of illegality of a vertical agreement which is outside the scope of Regulation 2790/99. Whether or not an agreement which falls outside this scope is illegal will therefore depend on the reason for not being covered. The competition law assessment does indeed vary depending on whether the reason is that the market share of the parties to the agreement exceeds the limit of Regulation 2790/99 or whether the agreement contains one or several severe infringements of the competition rules. Chapter 10 approaches this issue from the same two angles which are applied in Chapter 7: on the one hand, from the angle of the frequently used distribution formulas and, on the other hand, from the angle of the individual restrictions of competition.

1.09. Finally, Part IV (Chapter 11) analyses the specific regime of Regulation 1400/2002 on motor vehicle distribution. This regime is substantially stricter than that contained in Regulation 2790/99 and reflects the Commission's wish to regulate, in considerable detail, how the motor vehicle market should function. Regulation 1400/2002 is undoubtedly one of the most complex block exemptions ever to be adopted.

B. Articles 81 and 82 EC

(1) General

1.10. One of the EC's activities is to establish a system that ensures that competition in the internal market is not distorted (Article 3(1)(g) EC) and to this end, the EC Treaty contains a chapter (Chapter I of Title IV) on competition. This chapter contains a section on 'rules applying to undertakings' (Articles 81 to

86 EC), and this section, in particular Article 81 (ex-Article 85) and Article 82 (ex-Article 86) EC serve as the general legal background of any EC competition law handbook.

Article 81 EC concerns restrictive practices between companies, while Article 82   **1.11**. EC concerns the abuse of a dominant position. Article 81 EC consists of three paragraphs: Article 81(1) EC prohibits agreements between undertakings, decisions by associations of undertakings, and concerted practices which may affect trade between Member States and have as their object or effect the prevention, restriction, or distortion of competition; Article 81(2) EC states one particular consequence of the infringement of this prohibition, which is automatic nullity; Article 81(3) EC lists the cumulative conditions which must be fulfilled for the prohibition of Article 81(1) EC to be declared inapplicable. As opposed to Article 81 EC, Article 82 EC applies to a company's (or several companies') unilateral conduct, on condition that this company or these companies hold a dominant position (single or collective dominance). Article 82 EC does not prohibit the creation of dominance as such, but instead the abuse of such a dominant position.

(2) Article 81 EC

Article 81 EC provides: **1.12**.

1. The following shall be prohibited as incompatible with the common market: all agreements between undertakings, decisions by associations of undertakings and concerted practices which may affect trade between Member States and which have as their object or effect the prevention, restriction or distortion of competition within the common market, and in particular those which:
   (a) directly or indirectly fix purchase or selling prices or any other trading conditions;
   (b) limit or control production, markets, technical development, or investment;
   (c) share markets or sources of supply;
   (d) apply dissimilar conditions to equivalent transactions with other trading parties, thereby placing them at a competitive disadvantage;
   (e) make the conclusion of contracts subject to acceptance by the other parties of supplementary obligations which, by their nature or according to commercial usage, have no connection with the subject of such contracts.
2. Any agreements or decisions prohibited pursuant to this article shall be automatically void.
3. The provisions of paragraph 1 may, however, be declared inapplicable in the case of:
   — any agreement or category of agreements between undertakings,
   — any decision or category of decisions by associations of undertakings,
   — any concerted practice or category of concerted practices,

which contributes to improving the production or distribution of goods or to promoting technical or economic progress, while allowing consumers a fair share of the resulting benefit, and which does not:
 (a) impose on the undertakings concerned restrictions which are not indispensable to the attainment of these objectives;
 (b) afford such undertakings the possibility of eliminating competition in respect of a substantial part of the products in question.

1.13. Article 81(3) EC therefore contains four cumulative conditions for the prohibition of Article 81(1) EC to be declared inapplicable. Two of these are positive conditions, and two are negative conditions:

— the agreement must contribute to improving the production or distribution of goods or contribute to promoting technical or economic progress;
— consumers must receive a fair share of the resulting benefits;
— the agreement must not impose restrictions which are not indispensable to the attainment of these objectives; and
— the agreement must not afford the parties the possibility of eliminating competition in respect of a substantial part of the products in question.

The four conditions are discussed at length in the Commission Notice— Guidelines on the application of Article 81(3) of the Treaty.[7]

(3) *Article 82 EC*

1.14. Article 82 EC reads:

Any abuse by one or more undertakings of a dominant position within the common market or in a substantial part of it shall be prohibited as incompatible with the common market in so far as it may affect trade between Member States.

Such abuse may, in particular, consist in:
 (a) directly or indirectly imposing unfair purchase or selling prices or other unfair trading conditions;
 (b) limiting production, markets or technical development to the prejudice of consumers;
 (c) applying dissimilar conditions to equivalent transactions with other trading parties, thereby placing them at a competitive disadvantage;
 (d) making the conclusion of contracts subject to acceptance by the other parties of supplementary obligations which, by their nature or according to commercial usage, have no connection with the subject of such contracts.

1.15. As opposed to Article 81(2) EC, Article 82 EC does not state the consequences of the abuse of a dominant position. The same principles as Article 81(2) EC nonetheless apply to infringements of Article 82 EC.[8] Also as opposed to Article 81 EC, Article 82 EC does not contain a provision corresponding to

---

[7] [2004] OJ C101/97, paras 38 *et seq* (hereafter 'Guidelines on the application of Art 81(3)').
[8] Paras 1.71 and 1.72 below.

Article 81(3) EC. There is indeed no possibility of an exemption from the prohibition to abuse a dominant position. The prohibition to abuse a dominant position is therefore absolute.

(4) Relation between Articles 81 and 82 EC[9]

Articles 81 and 82 EC operate independently from one another. This means **1.16**. that the application of Article 81 EC cannot prevent the application of Article 82 EC and vice versa. This principle also implies that Articles 81 and 82 EC can be applied simultaneously to the same agreement or conduct.[10] The possibility of the parallel application of Articles 81 and 82 EC also implies that an agreement which falls within the scope of Article 81(1) EC, but qualifies for the application of Article 81(3) EC, may nonetheless be an abuse of dominant position in the sense of Article 82 EC. This is unlikely to occur if the Commission has individually exempted the agreement on the basis of Article 81(3) EC. It may be assumed that the investigation which the Commission pursues in accordance with Article 81(3) EC will not lead to the exemption of an agreement which infringes, or may in the future infringe, Article 82 EC. The situation is different for agreements covered by, and complying with the conditions of, a block exemption regulation. Article 81(3) EC applies to these agreements without individual investigation by the Commission.[11] In the absence of such an individual investigation, the safe harbour created by a block exemption regulation cannot therefore offer the same guarantees as an individual exemption as witnessed in the *Tetra Pak I* judgment.[12]

This is noteworthy because the regime which currently implements Articles 81 **1.17**. and 82 EC, to which we will now turn our attention, no longer provides for a possibility to request an individual exemption from the prohibition of Article 81(1) EC to the Commission,[13] but instead requires that companies self-assess the compliance of their agreements with EC competition law, including, if they

---

[9] eg J Faull and A Nikpay, *The EC Law of Competition* (OUP, 1999) paras 3.334–3.343; DG Goyder, *EC Competition Law* (OUP, 2003) Ch 16; and PM Roth (ed), *Bellamy and Child. European Community Law of Competition* (5th edn, Sweet & Maxwell, 2001) paras 9.005–9.007.

[10] See in particular, the case law on the abuse of collective dominance: eg Joined Cases T–68/89, T–77/89, and T–78/89 *Società Italiana Vetro SpA, Fabbrica Pisana SpA and PPG Vernante Pennitalia SpA v Commission (Italian Flat Glass)* [1992] ECR II–1403; Case C–393/92 *Almelo* [1994] ECR I–1477; and Joined Cases C–395/96P and C–396/96P *Compagnie Maritime Belge Transports SA, Compagnie Maritime Belge SA & Dafra Lines A/S v Commission* [2000] ECR I–1365. For an overview, DG Goyder (n 9 above) 327–31.

[11] More generally on the technique of block exemption regulations, see para 1.22 below.

[12] Case T–51/89 *TetraPak I* [1990] ECR II–309.

[13] It is only if the Commission has issued a 'finding of inapplicability' under Reg 1/2003, Art 10, that a company would have similar guarantees to an individual exemption. A finding of inapplicability will only be adopted in 'exceptional cases where the public interest of the Community so requires' (Reg 1/2003, recital 14). On Reg 1/2003, Art 10, see also para 1.68 below.

fall within the scope of Article 81(1) EC, whether they comply with the conditions of Article 81(3) EC.

C. Implementation of Articles 81 and 82 EC

1.18. Article 83 (ex-Article 87) EC empowers the Council to implement Articles 81 and 82 EC. Presently, the implementation of Articles 81 and 82 EC is governed by Regulation 1/2003. In order to understand the relevance of Regulation 1/2003, it is useful first to briefly recall the guiding principles of the regime existing before it, namely the regime of Regulation (EEC) No 17/62 First Regulation implementing Articles 85 and 86 of the Treaty ('Regulation 17')[14] which governed the implementation of Articles 81 and 82 EC for approximately four decades.

(1) Implementation of Articles 81 and 82 EC according to Regulation 17

Centralized notification and authorization system

1.19. Regulation 17 created a system based on a combination of the direct applicability of the prohibition rule of Article 81(1) EC and the prior notification of agreements for exemption by the Commission under Article 81(3) EC. Accordingly, while the Commission, national courts, and national authorities could apply Article 81(1) EC, the Commission had a monopoly on the application of Article 81(3) EC. In short, Regulation 17 created a centralized notification and authorization system.[15]

1.20. Specifically, notification was foreseen by Article 4(1) of Regulation 17, which stated that '[a]greements, decisions and concerted practices of the kind described in Article [81(1)] of the Treaty which come into existence after the entry into force of this Regulation and in respect of which the parties seek application of Article [81(3)] must be notified to the Commission'. According to Article 6(1) of Regulation 17, Commission decisions pursuant to Article 81(3) EC could not take effect earlier than the date of notification. Certain categories of (relatively unimportant)[16] agreements were exempted from the duty of prior

---

[14] [1962] OJ 13, p 204/62.

[15] The regime of Reg 17/62, as well as the pros and cons of such a regime, are discussed in the European Commission, *White Paper on Modernisation of the Rules Implementing Articles 85 and 86 of the EC Treaty (Commission Programme no 99/027)*, approved on 28 April 1999, available at http://europa.eu.int/comm/competition/antitrust/wp_modern_en.pdf.

[16] It was only from 18 June 1999 onwards that Reg 17, Art 4(2) was revised to include all vertical agreements: see para 1.54 below.

notification. However, for these and other agreements, the Commission had the sole power to declare Article 81(1) EC inapplicable pursuant to Article 81(3) EC.[17]

Consequences of the centralized notification and authorization system

The consequences of the centralized notification and authorization system are **1.21**. well-known. In the Commission's own words, '[t]he ex ante control mechanism inherent in the authorisation system set up by Regulation No 17 resulted in undertakings systematically notifying their restrictive practices to the Commission which, with limited administrative resources, was very soon faced with the impossibility of dealing by formal decision with the thousand of cases submitted',[18] and 'as early as 1967, the Commission was faced with a mass of 37,450 cases that has accumulated since the entry into force of the Regulation four years earlier'.[19]

Adjustments to the centralized notification and authorization system

In the course of the years, the Commission has sought to reduce the number of **1.22**. notifications. It has done so at least in three complementary ways, which continue to exist to the present day. Two of these concern the interpretation of Article 81(1) EC (in particular how to limit the scope of the prohibition of Article 81(1) EC),[20] and a third concerns Article 81(3) EC:[21]

— *De minimis agreements.* First, as regards Article 81(1) EC, the Commission sought to remove minor cases from the scope of Article 81(1) EC by reading an appreciability criterion into Article 81(1) EC. Accordingly, agreements would only be covered by Article 81(1) EC if they restricted competition in an appreciable way. This approach, which was rubberstamped by the Court in the landmark case of *Völk v Vervaecke*,[22] led the Commission to adopt its

---

[17] Reg 17, Art 9(1).   [18] European Commission (n 15 above) para 24.
[19] ibid, para 25.
[20] On the Commission's over-broad interpretation of the scope of Art 81(1) EC, see BE Hawk, 'System Failure: Vertical Restraints and EC Competition Law' [1995] CML Rev 973. A list of other academic critiques on the catch-all approach to Art 81(1) EC can be found in R Whish, *Competition Law* (5th edn, LexisNexis, 2005) 107. On the broad interpretation of the scope of Art 81(1) EC, see paras 2.65–2.85 below.
[21] The administrative practice of issuing so-called 'comfort letters', which informed undertakings that the agreement which they notified to the Commission, based on the information provided in the notification, either did not meet the conditions for the application of Art 81(1) EC (negative clearance) or qualified for an Art 81(3) EC exemption (exemption letter), speeded up the processing of notifications, but was not instrumental in reducing the number of notifications. Even so, by the time the Commission adopted its White Paper on Modernization in 1999, 90% of the notifications were closed informally by comfort letter or were filed without further action (European Commission (n 15 above) para 34).
[22] Case 5/69 *Völk v Vervaecke* [1969] ECR 295.

first Notice on agreements of minor importance which do not appreciably restrict competition under Article 81(1) EC (also: *De Minimis* Notice).[23] The currently applicable version of the *De Minimis* Notice is discussed in detail in paragraphs 2.125–2.136.

— *General notices.* Second, also with respect to Article 81(1) EC, the Commission started publishing other general notices to clarify which categories of agreements are not normally covered by the scope of Article 81(1) EC.[24] An example of such a notice, which is discussed in this book and which continues to apply to the present day, is the Commission Notice of 18 December 1978 concerning its assessment of certain subcontracting agreements in relation to Article 85(1) [now 81(1)] EC.[25]

— *Block exemption regulations.* Third, Article 83 EC grants the Council the power to adopt any appropriate regulation in order to give effect to the principles as set out in Articles 81 and 82 EC. Based on this power, the Council adopted (specifically in the field of vertical agreements) an enabling regulation—Regulation 19/65[26]—which empowered the Commission to declare the prohibition of Article 81(1) EC inapplicable to certain categories of vertical agreements.[27] In other words, a block exemption regulation is a regulation by means of which the Commission, authorized by the Council, creates a rebuttable presumption that certain categories of agreements as defined in the block exemption fulfil the conditions of Article 81(3) EC. Agreements which comply with the provisions of the block exemption regulation no longer need to be notified to the Commission for authorization.

1.23. In spite of its (successful) attempts to decrease the number of individual notifications, the notification and authorization system of Regulation 17 continued to weigh on the Commission's enforcement priorities. Notification-related work continued to consume about half of the resources of the DG COMP divisions that were not dealing with mergers and state aid.[28] In addition to this, the most serious restrictions of competition were never notified. As a witness to

---

[23] [1970] OJ Spec Ed C64/1.
[24] In so doing, a corpus of what can be referred to as 'soft EC competition law' gradually came into being. The relation of this soft law to the EC competition law provisions of primary and secondary EC law is discussed below in paras 1.81–1.96.   [25] [1979] OJ C1/2.
[26] Regulation (EEC) No 19/65 of 2 March 1965 on the application of Article 85(3) of the Treaty to certain categories of agreements and concerted practices [1965] OJ Spec Ed C36/533.
[27] Other enabling regulations were Regulation (EEC) No 2821/71 of the Council of 20 December 1971 on the application of Article 85(3) of the Treaty to categories of agreements, decisions and concerted practices [1971] OJ L285/46 (for research and development agreements, as well as specialization agreements) and Council Regulation (EEC) No 1534/91 of 31 May 1991 on the application of Article 85(3) of the Treaty to certain categories of agreements, decisions and concerted practices in the insurance sector [1991] OJ L143/1.
[28] W Wils, *Principles of European Antitrust Enforcement* (Hart Publishing, 2005) para 33.

that, notifications hardly ever led to prohibition decisions. In 1999, at the time of the adoption of its White Paper on Modernization, when Regulation 17 had been in force for about thirty-five years, the Commission had only adopted nine decisions in which a notified agreement was prohibited without a complaint having been lodged against it.[29]

(2) Implementation of Articles 81 and 82 EC according to Regulation 1/2003

General

In its White Paper on Modernization, the Commission proposed to end the centralized notification and authorization system created by Regulation 17 (instead of trying to improve it) and to switch to a directly applicable exception system: Article 81(3) EC would become directly applicable and restrictive practices prohibited by Article 81(1) EC, but meeting the conditions of Article 81(3) EC, would be lawful as from their conclusion, without the need for prior notification and authorization by the Commission. **1.24.**

The result of the public and institutional debate which the Commission launched by means of its 1999 White Paper is Regulation 1/2003. This Regulation applies from 1 May 2004 and does indeed embrace a directly applicable exception system. Article 1(2) explicitly provides that 'Agreements, decisions and concerted practices caught by Article 81(1) of the Treaty which satisfy the conditions of Article 81(3) of the Treaty shall not be prohibited, no prior decision to that effect being required.' **1.25.**

In addition to Regulation 1/2003, the so-called 'modernisation package' consists of a regulation laying down rules concerning the initiation of proceedings by the Commission as well as the handling of complaints and the hearing of the parties concerned[30] and of six general notices. Two of these six notices are notices on substantive EC competition law. They are directly relevant to our topic and are discussed elsewhere in this book, namely: **1.26.**

(1) Commission Notice—Guidelines on the effect on trade concept contained in Articles 81 and 82 of the Treaty,[31] discussed in Chapter 2 (paragraphs 2.31–2.59); and
(2) Commission Notice—Guidelines on the application of Article 81(3) of the Treaty,[32] incorporated in the discussion on the EC competition

---

[29] European Commission (n 15 above) para 77.
[30] Commission Regulation (EC) No 773/2004 of 7 April 2004 relating to the conduct of proceedings by the Commission pursuant to Articles 81 and 82 of the EC Treaty [2004] OJ L123/18.   [31] [2004] OJ C101/81.
[32] [2004] OJ C101/97.

law assessment of vertical agreements outside Regulation 2790/99 in Chapter 10.[33]

1.27. The main features of the implementation of Articles 81 and 82 EC by Regulation 1/2003 are the abolition of the notification requirement (paragraph 1.28 below) and the abandonment of the exemption monopoly (ie the decentralized application of EC competition law) (paragraphs 1.29–1.31).[34] We would also like to recall the importance of the effect on trade concept (paragraphs 1.32 and 1.33), as well as the rules which Regulation 1/2003 contains regarding the relationship between EC and national competition law (paragraphs 1.34–1.46), and the uniform application of EC competition law by the Commission and the national authorities (paragraph 1.47). Finally, it is useful to recall the continued relevance of block exemption regulations in a directly applicable exception system (paragraph 1.48).

Abolition of the notification requirement

1.28. Regulation 1/2003 frees parties from the requirement to notify their agreements to the Commission in order to benefit from the exemption provided by Article 81(3) EC. This would tend to imply that the practice of seeking legal certainty by way of a notification now belongs in the past. Accordingly, the abolition of the notification requirement has, as a minimum, two immediate consequences:

— First, with the freedom of no longer having to notify agreements to the Commission comes the responsibility for companies to self-assess their

---

[33] The other four notices of the modernization package are notices which deal mainly with various procedural aspects of the EC competition law enforcement rules of Reg 1/2003: Commission Notice on co-operation within the network of competition authorities [2004] OJ C101/43; Commission Notice on the co-operation between the Commission and the courts of the EU Member States in the application of Articles 81 and 82 EC [2004] OJ C101/54; Commission Notice on the handling of complaints by the Commission under Articles 81 and 82 of the EC Treaty [2004] OJ C101/65; Commission Notice on informal guidance relating to novel questions concerning Articles 81 and 82 of the EC Treaty that arise in individual cases (guidance letters) [2004] OJ C101/78.

[34] Some insiders' views on the implementation of Arts 81 and 82 EC by Reg 1/2003 can be found in: C Gauer, D Dalheimer, L Kjolbye, and E de Smijter, 'Regulation 1/2003: A Modernised Application of EC Competition Rules' (2003) 1 EC Competition Policy Newsletter 3; E Paulis and C Gauer, 'La réforme des règles d'application des articles 81 et 82 du Traité' [2003] Journal des tribunaux droit européen 65; W Wils (n 28 above) 1–59. Other contributions of interest are: CD Ehlermann, 'The Modernization of EC Antitrust Policy: A Legal and Cultural Revolution' [2000] CML Rev 537; H Gilliams, 'Modernisation: from Policy to Practice' [2003] ELR 451; L Idot, 'Le nouveau système communautaire de mise en oeuvre des articles 81 et 82 CE (règlement 1/2003 et projets de texts d'application)' [2003] CDE 283; A Riley, 'EC Antitrust Modernisation: The Commission Does Very Nicely—Thank You! Part One: Regulation 1 and the Notification Burden' [2003] ECLR 604; A Riley, 'EC Antitrust Modernisation: The Commission Does Very Nicely—Thank You! Part Two: Between the Idea and the Reality: Decentralisation under Regulation 1' [2003] ECLR 657; and J Venit, 'Brave New World: The Modernization and Decentralization of Enforcement under Articles 81 and 82 of the EC Treaty' [2003] CML Rev 545.

agreements. This is particularly the case for those agreements or clauses in agreements which may raise competition issues (eg non-compete obligations with a duration of more than five years).[35] As opposed to the system of Regulation 17, undertakings can no longer notify such agreements to the Commission to ask for a negative clearance or an individual exemption from Article 81(3) EC in order to have *ex ante* legal certainty that the agreement concerned is not void (and hence will be enforceable) and also to have certainty that they are immune from fines with effect from the date of notification onwards.[36]

—As a consequence, it is only *ex post*, at a time when they are confronted with questions from a competition authority or when a contracting party questions the enforceability of certain contractual provisions, that undertakings will now know for sure whether or not they have correctly performed their self-assessment.[37] In order to assist companies in their self-assessment, the Commission, as stated above (paragraph 1.26), accompanied Regulation 1/2003 with a set of general notices. Because these notices are not directly legally binding on third parties, including national competition authorities ('NCAs') and national courts,[38] the abolition of the notification requirement will undoubtedly lead companies, where possible (eg if they do not exceed the market share limit), to opt for legal certainty and to draft their agreements so that they qualify for the safe harbour created by a block exemption regulation. Block exemption regulations, originally meant to reduce the number of notifications to the Commission, therefore remain a useful instrument of EC competition law policy under the regime of Regulation 1/2003.[39]

Decentralized application of EC competition law

The modernization of the EC competition law enforcement rules not only **1.29.** increases the responsibility of companies, but also that of the NCAs and the

---

[35] On non-compete obligations, see Ch 6 below.

[36] A small opening for *ex ante* advice is left by Reg 1/2003, recital 38, which reads as follows: '[l]egal certainty for undertakings operating under the Community competition rules contributes to the promotion of innovation and investment. Where cases give rise to genuine uncertainty because they present novel or unresolved questions for the application of these rules, individual undertakings may wish to seek informal guidance from the Commission. This Regulation is without prejudice to the ability of the Commission to issue such informal guidance'. Para 38 is given more flesh on the bone in a Commission Notice on informal guidance relating to novel questions concerning Articles 81 and 82 of the EC Treaty that arise in individual cases (guidance letters) [2004] OJ C101/78.

[37] If the company wants to rely on Art 81(3) EC, it carries the burden of proof. In this respect, Reg 1/2003, Art 2 provides that '[t]he undertaking or association of undertakings claiming the benefit of Article 81(3) of the Treaty shall bear the burden of proving that the conditions of that paragraph are fulfilled.' [38] Paras 1.89–1.95 below.

[39] For the role of block exemption regulations in the post–Reg 1/2003 era, see para 1.48 below.

national courts. Under the new regime, all these have to apply Article 81(3) EC directly. To this end, Regulation 1/2003 provides for mutual assistance to occur between the Commission and the national authorities.

Decentralized application by NCAs

1.30. Together with the Commission, the NCAs form the European Competition Network ('ECN'). The principles of the close co-operation between the Commission and the NCAs in the context of the ECN are laid down in Articles 11 to 14 of Regulation 1/2003, and they are further developed in the Commission Notice on co-operation within the Network of Competition Authorities.[40] The close co-operation between the Commission and the NCAs essentially concerns the allocation of cases,[41] and the exchange of information,[42] including the exchange and use of confidential information in the ECN.[43] *Sensu lato*, it also concerns the rules applying to the parallel application of EC and national competition law, as well as the consecutive application of EC competition law by the Commission and the NCAs.[44]

Decentralized application by national courts[45]

1.31. National courts may be called upon to apply Articles 81 and 82 EC in litigation between private parties (contractual litigation; action for damages).[46] The co-operation between the national courts and the Commission in the context of such lawsuits is provided for in Article 15 of Regulation 1/2003 and further developed in the Commission Notice on the co-operation between the Commission and the courts of the EU Member States in the application of Articles 81 and 82 EC.[47] The co-operation between the Commission and the national courts is reciprocal: on the one hand, the Commission serves as *amicus curiae*; on the other hand, the national courts facilitate the Commission's role to enforce EC competition law:

— In relation to the Commission being *amicus curiae*, Article 15(1) of Regulation 1/2003 provides that the national courts may ask the Commission to transmit to them information in its possession or its opinion on questions

---

[40] [2004] OJ C101/43. [41] ibid, paras 5–15.
[42] Reg 1/2003, Art 11 and Commission Notice on co-operation within the Network of Competition Authorities (n 40 above) paras 16–19.
[43] Reg 1/2003, Art 12 and Commission Notice on co-operation within the Network of Competition Authorities (n 40 above) paras 26–8. [44] Paras 1.34–1.48 below.
[45] A comprehensive overview of the impact of Reg 1/2003 on the judiciary can be found in K Lenaerts and D Gerard, 'Decentralisation of EC Competition Law Enforcement: Judges in the Frontline' (2004) 3 World Competition 313.
[46] On private enforcement of Arts 81 and 82 EC, see paras 1.69–1.80 below.
[47] [2004] OJ C101/54.

concerning the application of EC competition law.[48] At its own initiative, the Commission may submit written observations to a national court in the case where the coherent application of Articles 81 or 82 EC so requires. The Commission may also make oral observations if the national court so permits (Article 15(3)).[49]

— In relation to the national court's facilitation of the Commission's role in enforcing EC competition law, Regulation 1/2003 provides for the transmission of judgments applying Articles 81 or 82 EC to the Commission (Article 15(2)), as well as the transmission of documents necessary for the assessment of a case in which the Commission would like to submit its observations (Article 15(3)).[50] Article 20(6) and (8) furthermore highlight the role of national courts in the context of an investigation by the Commission.[51] *Sensu lato*, the co-operation between the Commission and the national courts also concerns the rules which apply to the parallel application of EC and national competition law, as well as to the consecutive application of EC competition law by the Commission and the national courts.[52]

The importance of the 'effect on trade' concept

Each time an NCA or national court applies national competition law, it must, **1.32**. under the regime of Regulation 1/2003, ask itself if Articles 81 or 82 EC also apply. In this respect, the first question which the NCA or national court will have to address is whether or not the agreement or conduct may appreciably affect trade between the Member States. If not, EC competition law does not apply and the NCA or national court must decide the case exclusively on the basis of national competition law. Conversely, if there is an appreciable effect on trade between the Member States, Article 3(1) of Regulation 1/2003 requires that the NCA or national court apply Articles 81 and 82 EC alongside national competition law:

> Where the competition authorities of the Member States or national courts apply national competition law to agreements, decisions by associations of undertakings or concerted practices within the meaning of Article 81(1) of the Treaty which may affect trade between Member States within the meaning of that provision, they shall also apply Article 81 of the Treaty to such agreements, decisions or concerted practices. Where the competition authorities of the Member States or

---

[48] In the Notice on the co-operation between the Commission and the courts of the EU Member States in the application of Articles 81 and 82 EC (n 47 above), the Commission stated that it 'will endeavour to provide the national court with the requested opinion within four months from the date it receives the request' (para 28). The duty to transmit information and the request for an opinion are further dealt with in the Notice, respectively, paras 21–6 and 27–30.

[49] Notice on the co-operation between the Commission and the courts of the EU Member States in the application of Articles 81 and 82 EC, paras 31–5.   [50] ibid, para 36.

[51] ibid, paras 38–41.   [52] Paras 1.34–1.48 below.

national courts apply national competition law to any abuse prohibited by Article 82 of the Treaty, they shall also apply Article 82 of the Treaty.[53]

1.33. Logically, there has been a revival of the effect on trade concept. Traditionally, the concept had little practical relevance given that it was interpreted very broadly and therefore was considered as being easily fulfilled. Nowadays, under the regime of Regulation 1/2003, the analysis has become more than a mere formality. In this book, the effect on trade concept is discussed in more detail as one of the steps which must be considered when determining the application of Regulation 2790/99 (paragraphs 2.27–2.60).

Relationship between EC and national competition law

The convergence rule

1.34. When a national authority investigates a restrictive practice within the meaning of Article 81(1) EC which may affect trade between the Member States, or an abuse prohibited by Article 82 EC,[54] and must apply EC and national competition law in parallel, then Regulation 1/2003 imposes restrictions on the way in which that national authority can apply national competition law.[55]

1.35. These restrictions are stated in the convergence rule of Article 3(2) of Regulation 1/2003, which reads:

> The application of national competition law may not lead to the prohibition of agreements, decisions by associations of undertakings or concerted practices which may affect trade between Member States but which do not restrict competition within the meaning of Article 81(1) of the Treaty, or which fulfil the conditions of Article 81(3) of the Treaty or which are covered by a Regulation for the

---

[53] Originally, the Commission wanted EC competition law to apply to the exclusion of national competition law in the case of an appreciable effect on inter-state trade. In its proposal of what would later become Reg 1/2003 (COM(2000)582 final [2000] OJ C3653/284), Art 3 read: 'Where an agreement, a decision by an association of undertakings or a concerted practice within the meaning of Article 81 of the Treaty or the abuse of a dominant position within the meaning of Article 82 may affect trade between Member States, Community competition law shall apply to the exclusion of national competition laws'.

[54] It follows from the wording of Art 82 EC that it only applies if inter-state trade is affected: 'Any abuse . . . shall be prohibited as incompatible with the common market in so far as it may affect trade between Member States'.

[55] Reg 1/2003, Art 3(3) clarifies that the restrictions do not apply when the national authorities apply national merger control laws nor do they preclude the application of provisions of national law that predominantly pursue an objective different from that pursued by Arts 81 and 82 EC. As regards the latter, Reg 1/2003, recital 9 refers to acts of unfair trade practice. According to Reg 1/2003, recital 8, *in fine*, the Regulation also 'does not apply to national laws which impose criminal sanctions on national persons except to the extent that such sanctions are the means whereby competition rules applying to undertakings are enforced'. In the Member States that impose such criminal sanctions, there is uncertainty regarding the meaning of this sentence. An attempt to interpret its meaning, as well as references to other such attempts, can be found in Wils (n 28 above) paras 153–7.

application of Article 81(3) of the Treaty. Member States shall not under this Regulation be precluded from adopting and applying on their territory stricter national laws which prohibit or sanction unilateral conduct engaged in by undertakings.

In line with the wording of Article 3(2) of Regulation 1/2003, a distinction must **1.36**. be made between, on the one hand, restrictive practices within the meaning of Article 81(1) EC (agreements, decisions by associations of undertakings, or concerted practices) and, on the other, unilateral behaviour (including Article 82 EC).

Convergence and Article 81 EC

With regard to the parallel application of Article 81 EC and national compe- **1.37**. tition law, there is total convergence: an NCA or national court may not prohibit, on the basis of national competition law, a restrictive practice which is not prohibited by Article 81 EC. The reason why the restrictive practice is not prohibited is irrelevant: it may be because there is no (appreciable) restriction of competition in the sense of Article 81(1) EC[56] or because the restrictive practice fulfils the conditions of Article 81(3) EC on the basis of an individual exemption or a block exemption regulation (eg Regulation 2790/99 or Regulation 1400/2002). So if an NCA or national court finds that a restrictive practice does appreciably affect inter-State trade but that it does not appreciably affect competition in the sense of Article 81(1) EC (eg because it is covered by the *De Minimis* Notice), it may no longer prohibit the practice on the basis of national competition law. Inversely, if trade is not appreciably affected, then EC competition law does not apply and the national authority is entitled to fully and exclusively apply its national competition legislation.

The opposite is also true. National authorities cannot authorize a restrictive **1.38**. practice under national competition law if it is prohibited under Article 81 EC. This is not mentioned in Article 3(2) of Regulation 1/2003, but is a straight-forward application of the general principle of the primacy of EC law.

As regards the relationship between Article 81 EC and national competition **1.39**. law, Article 3(2) of Regulation 1/2003 innovates in one respect, when compared to the situation that existed before Regulation 1/2003, namely that the application of national competition law may no longer lead to the prohibition of a restrictive practice which may affect trade between Member States but does not restrict competition within the meaning of Article 81(1) EC (eg because it is an agreement of minor importance in the sense of the *De Minimis* Notice). Prior to Regulation 1/2003, a national authority was entitled to prohibit such a

---

[56] For a survey of the reasons why a restrictive practice may not be covered by Art 81(1) EC, see para 2.124 below.

restrictive practice on the basis of national competition law.[57] Now, under the regime of Regulation 1/2003, the convergence rule no longer allows this.

1.40. In this respect, it must be noted that several Member States continue to require the notification of agreements which are restrictive of competition. To the extent that these notifications involve agreements which have an appreciable effect on trade between the Member States, Article 3(1) and (2) of Regulation 1/2003 imply that the NCA is required to apply Article 81 EC and national competition law in parallel and may not prohibit, on the basis of national competition law, that which is authorized under Article 81 EC. If an agreement qualifies for an exemption according to Article 81(3) EC, this results in the fact that an NCA may no longer prohibit an agreement according to national competition law, irrespective of whether or not notification has taken place. Under these circumstances, notification in itself becomes redundant.

Convergence and unilateral behaviour (including Article 82 EC)

1.41. **Concept 'unilateral conduct'.** Pursuant to Article 3(2), *in fine*, of Regulation 1/2003, Member States shall not be precluded from adopting and applying on their territory stricter national laws which prohibit or sanction unilateral conduct engaged in by undertakings.

1.42. For obvious reasons, the concept of 'unilateral conduct' has been linked to behaviour which is caught by Article 82 EC.[58] In our opinion, however, the concept refers in the first place to behaviour which is outside the scope of Article 81 EC. Put differently, we believe that the scope of the concept must be linked to the scope of Article 81 EC rather than to that of Article 82 EC. This approach is in line with the system of convergence under Regulation 1/2003: Article 81 EC does not apply to genuinely unilateral conduct of undertakings. Therefore, the rule that there must be total convergence in the case of the parallel application of Article 81 EC and national competition law is not endangered if a national authority applies stricter national laws[59] to such genuinely unilateral conduct.

1.43. In order to determine where the borderline lies between an 'agreement' in the sense of Article 81 EC and unilateral conduct outside the scope of Article 81 EC, consideration should be given to the discussion of the relevant case law in paragraphs 2.65–2.85. It follows from this case law that, for example, a non-compete obligation that a dominant undertaking imposes in a supply or

---

[57] For a discussion with references, see R Wesseling, *The Modernisation of EC Antitrust Law* (Hart Publishing, 2000) 119.

[58] eg Gilliams (n 34 above) footnote 39; Riley (n 34 above); and Venit (n 34 above) footnote 7.

[59] We assume that 'laws' must be understood in a broad sense of the word and also encompasses any instrument which is legally binding within the territory of a Member State (eg royal or ministerial decrees).

distribution agreement which is within the scope of Article 81 EC, can no longer be prohibited by a national authority on the basis of its powers to apply stricter national laws to unilateral conduct. The agreement concerned is an agreement within the scope of Article 81 EC and so there must be total convergence in the relationship between the national competition law and Article 81 EC. It seems to us that the fact that the non-compete obligation is applied by a dominant player and is not prohibited under Article 82 EC[60] is irrelevant in this context. It is indeed not because of the fact that it is not prohibited under Article 82 EC that it must be considered as unilateral conduct in the sense of Article 3(2) of Regulation 1/2003, which continues to be subject to the application of stricter national laws.

1.44. In respect of the application of stricter national laws to unilateral conduct, it is also important to note that Article 3(2) of Regulation 1/2003 does not distinguish between dominant and non-dominant undertakings. The possibility for a national authority to apply stricter national laws therefore applies to unilateral conduct by dominant as well as by non-dominant undertakings.

1.45. **Dominant undertakings.** In respect of dominant undertakings, recital 8 of Regulation 1/2003 says that stricter national laws 'may include provisions which prohibit or impose sanctions on abusive behaviour toward economically dependent undertakings'. In other words, as regards unilateral conduct, national competition law may be more strict than Article 82 EC. If unilateral behaviour amounts to an abuse in the sense of Article 82 EC, a national authority must respect the general principle of primacy of EC law and cannot authorize the conduct purely on the basis of national law. Conversely, if the conduct is not abuse in the sense of Article 82 EC, the national authority may apply stricter national laws.

1.46. **Non-dominant undertakings.** Aside from dominant undertakings, non-dominant undertakings may also pursue unilateral conduct (eg refusal to sell) which is, by definition, outside the scope of Article 82 EC. Given that such unilateral conduct is equally outside the scope of Article 81 EC, Article 3(2) of Regulation 1/2003 allows a national authority to apply stricter national law.

Uniform application of EC competition law

1.47. Specifically in order to assure the uniform application of EC competition law, Regulation 1/2003 contains the following provisions:

—*Article 11(4), as read in combination with Article 11(6).* Pursuant to Article 11(4), an NCA must communicate draft negative decisions to the Commission no later than thirty days before their adoption. If necessary, the

---

[60] See paras 1.16–1.17 above for the parallel application of Arts 81 and 82 EC.

Commission has the power, pursuant to Article 11(6) of Regulation 1/2003, to relieve the NCA of its competence to apply Articles 81 and 82 EC by initiating proceedings itself. In the Joint Statement of the Council and the Commission on the functioning of the Network of Competition Authorities,[61] the Commission indeed lists as one of the situations in which it will use its power according to Article 11(6): 'Network members envisage a decision which is obviously in conflict with consolidated case law'.[62]

—*Article 15(2).* Member States shall forward to the Commission a copy of any written judgment of the national court's decisions on the application of Articles 81 or 82 EC without delay after the full written judgment has been notified to the parties. This will enable the Commission 'to become aware in a timely fashion of cases for which it might be appropriate to submit observations where one of the parties lodges an appeal against the judgement'.[63]

—*Article 16.* This provision, which is self-explanatory, guarantees the uniform application of EC competition law in the case of its successive application by the Commission and by the national authorities:

1. When national courts rule on agreements, decisions or practices under Article 81 or Article 82 of the Treaty which are already the subject of a Commission decision, they cannot take decisions running counter to the decision adopted by the Commission. They must also avoid giving decisions which would conflict with a decision contemplated by the Commission in proceedings it has initiated. To that effect, the national court may assess whether it is necessary to stay its proceedings. This obligation is without prejudice to the rights and obligations under Article 234 of the Treaty.[64]

2. When competition authorities of the Member States rule on agreements, decisions or practices under Article 81 or Article 82 of the Treaty which are already the subject of a Commission decision, they cannot take decisions which would run counter to the decision adopted by the Commission.[65]

Relevance of block exemption regulations

1.48. The implementation of Articles 81 and 82 EC according to Regulation 1/2003 changes the rationale of block exemption regulations, but does not change their legal nature or consequences. Block exemption regulations were, and still are, directly applicable general legislative acts which create a rebuttable presumption that certain categories of agreements fulfil the conditions of Article 81(3) EC. However, because Regulation 1/2003 abolished the notification requirement,

---

[61] Council document 15435/02 ADD 1, 10 December 2002. [62] ibid, para 21.

[63] Notice on the co-operation between the Commission and the courts of the EU Member States in the application of Articles 81 and 82 EC (n 47 above) para 37.

[64] Art 234 EC is the preliminary rulings procedure whereby national courts can (and in some circumstances must) seek guidance on the validity and interpretation of EC law from the European Court of Justice.

[65] Art 16(2) must be read in light of Art 11(6) by means of which the Commission can relieve an NCA of its competence to apply Art 81 and 82 EC.

their rationale has changed. They no longer serve to reduce the number of notifications to the Commission. Instead, they are an important, if not the most important (because they are legally binding) tool for companies and their advisors to perform a self-assessment under Article 81(3) EC. The Commission already emphasized this in its White Paper on Modernization, where it stated: 'In a directly applicable exception system, the legislative framework is of primary importance. The application of the rules must be sufficiently reliable and consistent to allow business to assess whether their restrictive practices are lawful. The Commission would keep the sole right to propose legislative texts . . . to ensure consistency and uniformity in the application of the competition rules. Block exemptions are the first of these legislative texts'.[66] This principle has been incorporated into the convergence rule of Article 3(2) of Regulation 1/2003: If an agreement is covered by, and complies with the conditions of, a block exemption regulation, then it benefits from Article 81(3) EC and can also no longer be challenged on the basis of national competition law.[67]

D. Regulations 2790/99 and 1400/2002

(1) Introduction

This section briefly outlines the coming into being of the two block exemption regulations which are discussed in detail in this book, ie Regulations 2790/99 and 1400/2002. The latter Regulation replaced Regulation 1475/95 which, in its turn, had replaced the first block exemption regulation that specifically addressed distribution in the motor vehicle sector, Regulation 123/85. For its part, Regulation 2790/99 replaced three existing block exemption regulations:

1.49.

—Commission Regulation (EEC) No 1983/83 of 22 June 1983 on the application of Article 85(3) of the Treaty to categories of exclusive distribution agreements:[68]

---

[66] White Paper on Modernisation (n 15 above) paras 84–85.

[67] In this respect, block exemption regulations are a mechanism to save on enforcement costs. As Wouter Wils puts it: 'for any category of agreements (i) which are very frequently concluded in business practice, (ii) for which a full individual assessment would in the overwhelming majority of cases lead to the conclusion that the conditions of Article 81(3) are fulfilled, and (iii) which can be sufficiently clearly defined, the cost saving, including the reduction of risk, at the level of self-assessment by the undertakings when concluding these agreements as well as at the level of ex post litigation is likely to outweigh the cost of adopting the block exemption regulation', Wils (n 28 above) para 72.

[68] [1983] OJ L173/1. The date of expiry of the regulation was extended from 31 December 1997 to 31 December 1999 by Commission Regulation (EC) No 1582/97 of 30 July 1997 amending Regulations (EEC) No 1983/83 and No 1984/83 on the application of Article 85(3) of the Treaty to categories of exclusive distribution agreements and exclusive purchasing agreements respectively [1997] OJ L214/27, Art 1.

— Commission Regulation (EEC) No 1984/83 of 22 June 1983 on the application of Article 85(3) of the Treaty to categories of exclusive purchasing agreements;[69] and

— Commission Regulation (EEC) No 4087/88 of 30 November 1988 on the application of Article 85(3) of the Treaty to categories of franchise agreements.[70]

1.50. The overall policy objective of Regulations 2790/99 and 1400/2002 was to adopt a more economic and less prescriptive approach. Prior to these Regulations, block exemption regulations had a so-called straitjacket effect. They did not confine themselves just to defining the categories of agreements to which they applied and to specifying the restrictions or clauses which were not to be contained in the agreements, but they also listed the exempted clauses. This approach, which forced the parties to a vertical agreement to paraphrase the wordings of the applicable block exemption regulation to benefit from its safe harbour, resulted in more or less standardized distribution agreements. The cornerstone of the Commission's new approach was the introduction of market share limits (so that individual control would be limited to vertical agreements involving at least one company with market power) and the adoption of a blacklist approach (so that everything would be allowed that is not prohibited, instead of everything being prohibited that is not expressly allowed). Given that the scope of the existing block exemption regulations was considered as being too narrow, the Commission's objective was also to broaden the scope of application of the block exemption regulation; that is, to introduce an umbrella block exemption regulation applicable to a wide array of vertical agreements.

(2) Background to Regulation 2790/99

1.51. The coming into being of Regulation 2790/99 must be seen against the background of the 1997 Green Paper on Vertical Restraints in Community Competition Policy.[71] In this Green Paper, the Commission identified a number of shortcomings in its then existing policy on vertical restraints:

— existing block exemption regulations were comprised of rather strict form-based requirements (every restriction of competition which is not expressly allowed, is prohibited) and hence were considered to be too legalistic and to operate as a straitjacket;

— existing block exemption regulations did not contain any market share limit. Accordingly, they were form-based instead of effect-based, and companies

---

[69] [1983] OJ L173/5. The date of expiry of the regulation was extended from 31 December 1997 to 31 December 1999 by Commission Regulation 1582/97 (n 68 above) Art 2.
[70] [1988] OJ L359/46.   [71] COM(96)721 final, 22 January 1997.

which had significant market power could benefit from them. The sanction of withdrawal of the benefit of block exemption was not considered as a real deterrent because it only worked with effect in the future; and

— existing block exemption regulations only covered vertical agreements concerning the resale of final goods and not of intermediate goods or, aside from Regulation 4087/88 (franchising), services. Therefore, a significant percentage of all vertical agreements were outside of the existing block exemption regulations, even when the parties involved did not have any market power.[72]

The Green Paper was the subject of an opinion from the Committee of the Regions[73] and the Economic and Social Committee,[74] as well as a Report of the European Parliament's Committee on Economic and Monetary Affairs and Industrial Policy,[75] and a Resolution of the European Parliament adopted on the basis of this report.[76] In addition, the Commission received 227 written submissions to its Green Paper. The majority of these reactions (64%) came from companies and trade associations, whose principal concern was legal certainty.[77] A summary of the submissions was published in a November 1998 Follow-up to the Green Paper.[78]   **1.52**.

Based on these reactions, the Follow-up to the Green Paper concluded that the new policy on vertical restraints would be aimed at, first, creating more efficient protection of competition by allowing the competition authorities to concentrate their efforts on those cases involving market power and, second, doing away with the straitjacket effect. In line with this, the two pillars of the new policy would be (i) one broad umbrella block exemption regulation applying to both goods and services, with market share thresholds and a blacklist approach, and (ii) the publication of guidelines detailing the policy above the thresholds.[79]   **1.53**.

In addition to the drafting of the umbrella block exemption regulation and its accompanying guidelines, the new policy also required extensive revision of two   **1.54**.

---

[72] These shortcomings are listed in European Commission, *Communication from the Commission on the application of the Community competition rules to vertical restraints (Follow-up to the Green Paper on Vertical Restraints)* [1998] OJ C365/3.

[73] Committee of the Regions, *Opinion on the 'Green Paper on vertical restraints in EC competition policy'* [1997] OJ C244/38.

[74] Economic and Social Committee, *Opinion on the 'Green Paper on vertical restraints in EC competition policy'* [1997] OJ C296/19.

[75] European Parliament—Committee on Economic and Monetary Affairs and Industrial Policy, *Report on the 'Green Paper on vertical restraints in EC competition policy'* A4-0242/97, 4 July 1997 [1997] OJ C286/8.

[76] Resolution on the Commission's Green Paper on vertical restraints and EU competition policy (COM(96)721–C4-0053/97), 18 July 1997.

[77] European Commission (n 72 above) 5.   [78] ibid.

[79] For an early overview of the contents of the Regulation, see J Nazerali and D Cowan, 'Reforming EU Distribution Rules—Has the Commission Found Vertical Reality?' [1999] ECLR 159; and J Nazerali and D Cowan, 'Unlocking EU Distribution Rules—Has the European Commission Found the Right Keys?' [2000] ECLR 50.

Council regulations, ie Regulation (EEC) No 19/65 of 2 March 1965 on application of Article 85(3) of the Treaty to certain categories of agreements and concerted practices[80] and Regulation 17/62:[81]

— Regulation 19/65 is the enabling regulation for the Commission to adopt block exemption regulations. It had to be revised in at least two respects. First, Regulation 19/65 excluded the adoption of a block exemption regulation covering vertical agreements between more than two undertakings, selective distribution agreements, agreements concerning services, and agreements concerning the supply or purchase, or both, of goods or services intended for processing or incorporation. So, its scope of application had to be extended considerably to accommodate the Commission's anticipated reform of its policy on vertical restraints. Second, Regulation 19/65 also had to be revised because it required block exemption regulations to list the clauses which must be contained in the vertical agreements. In this respect, Regulation 19/65 lay at the very basis of the straitjacket approach. Regulation 19/65 was revised in June 1999 by Council Regulation (EC) No 1215/1999 of 10 June 1999 amending Regulation No 19/65/EEC on the application of Article 81(3) of the Treaty to certain categories of agreements and concerted practices.[82]

— Next, the scope of application of Article 4(2) of Regulation 17 had to be extended. Article 4(2) dispensed with the requirement of notification prior to exemption for certain agreements, but not vertical agreements. By means of Regulation 1216/99,[83] the scope of Article 4(2) of Regulation 17 was extended and all vertical agreements were also dispensed from the requirement of notification prior to exemption. Prior to the entry into force of Regulation 1/2003, this revision made it possible that vertical agreements which were not covered by the block exemption regulation (eg because the parties misjudged their market share), but had not been notified to the Commission, qualified for retroactive individual exemption from the prohibition of Article 81(1) EC. In the absence of this revision, such agreements would only have qualified for exemption from the day of notification onwards.

1.55. Once these legislative amendments had been adopted, work on the finalization of the new regulation proceeded quickly. A draft regulation and guidelines were published on 24 September 1999. Interested parties were given one month to comment on the draft regulation and two months to comment on the draft guidelines. Regulation 2790/99 was finally adopted on 22 December 1999 and

---

[80] [1965] OJ Spec Ed 36/533.   [81] [1962] OJ 13, p 204/62.
[82] [1999] OJ L148/1.
[83] Council Regulation (EC) No 1216/1999 of 10 June 1999 amending Regulation No 17: first Regulation implementing Articles 81 and 82 of the Treaty [1999] OJ L148/5.

it entered into force on 1 January 2000. The Guidelines on Vertical Restraints ('the Guidelines') were published some ten months later, on 13 October 2000.[84]

(3) Background to Regulation 1400/2002

From the outset, the motor vehicle sector has been governed by a specific competition law regime.[85] The foundations of this regime were laid in the Commission's 1974 *BMW* decision.[86] This decision was designed as a landmark case[87] and 'it was hoped that manufacturers would adapt their distribution systems accordingly'.[88] The most significant feature of the *BMW* decision was that it endorsed a combination of exclusive and selective distribution. For decades, it has been this combination that has distinguished motor vehicle distribution from the distribution of other products.[89]   **1.56.**

The *BMW* decision did not produce the desired effect of bringing motor vehicle distribution agreements into line, as many manufacturers continued to submit notifications with the aim of obtaining an individual exemption for the types of agreement that were specifically used by them.[90] It was against this background that the Commission decided to adopt a sector-specific block exemption. Regulation 123/85[91] remained in force from 1 July 1985 until 30 June 1995 and essentially codified the principal holdings found in the *BMW* decision.   **1.57.**

Regulation 123/85 was succeeded by Regulation 1475/95,[92] which remained in force until 30 September 2002. This new Regulation did not differ substantially   **1.58.**

---

[84] Commission Notice—Guidelines on Vertical Restraints [2000] OJ C291/1 (hereafter 'Guidelines').

[85] For an interesting comparison between the position in the US and the EU, see D Gerard, ' "Regulated Competition" in the Automobile Distribution Sector: A Comparative Analysis of the Car Distribution System in the US and the EU' [2003] ECLR 518.

[86] *Bayerische Motoren Werke AG* [1975] OJ L29/1.

[87] European Commission, *IVth Report on Competition Policy (1974)*, para 86.

[88] European Commission, *Report on the Evaluation of Regulation (EC) No 1475/95 on the application of Article 85(3) of the Treaty to certain categories of motor vehicle distribution and servicing agreements*, 15 November 2000, COM(2000)743 final, 149, para 28, available at http://europa.eu.int/eur-lex/en/com/rpt/2000/com2000_0743en01.pdf (hereafter the 'Evaluation Report').

[89] This feature has also been cited as the main problem that has caused the single market for cars not to function properly: E van Ginderachter, 'Concurrence: Les nouvelles règles applicables au secteur automobile' [2002] Journal des Tribunaux Droit Européen 233, 235; and L Idot, 'Le nouveau règlement d'exemption relatif à la distribution automobile' (2002) 50 JCP–La Semaine Juridique Entreprises et Affaires, 2000, 2002.

[90] A Hermel, 'La distribution automobile: les problèmes actuels, les réponses à venir' (2002) 59 Petites Affiches 6; and K Stöver, 'Les règlements d'exemption catégorielle relatifs à la distribution des voitures et aux stations-service', Speech delivered at the University of Liège, 4 June 1986, mimeo.

[91] Commission Regulation (EEC) No 123/85 on the application of Article 85(3) of the Treaty to certain categories of motor vehicle distribution and servicing agreements [1985] OJ L15/16.

[92] Commission Regulation (EC) No 1475/95 on the application of Article 85(3) of the Treaty to certain categories of motor vehicle distribution and servicing agreements [1995] OJ L145/25.

from its predecessor, and the concept of combined exclusive and selective distribution was kept intact. The main changes included the requirement that dealers had to be allowed to handle multiple brands (albeit that strict conditions could be imposed by the supplier)[93] and also the mandatory access to certain technical information by independent repairers so as to increase their ability to compete on the after-sales market with the authorized network.[94] In order to facilitate the use of Regulation 1475/95, the Commission issued a so-called Explanatory Brochure.[95]

1.59. The preparation of the current block exemption, Regulation 1400/2002, was, in contrast, an elaborate exercise. The first step was the publication of the Evaluation Report in November 2000. This Report was provided for in Article 11(3) of Regulation 1475/95. The overall tone of the Evaluation Report was fairly pessimistic and clearly set the scene for a major reform. The suggestion that a radical change was called for was strengthened by a series of cases brought by the Commission against leading car producers. These cases[96] concerned serious infringements of the competition rules (ie unjustified restrictions on lawful cross-border trade and resale price maintenance) and, given their timing, clearly served to underscore the deficiencies of the existing regime.

1.60. A number of studies were commissioned in order to obtain advice from independent consultants on major aspects of the review.[97] The Commission organized a hearing[98] in February 2001 to discuss the findings of the Evaluation

---

[93] Reg 1475/95, Art 3(3).   [94] Reg 1475/95, Art 6(12).

[95] Available at http://europa.eu.int/comm/competition/car_sector/distribution/explanatory_reg_1475_95_en.pdf (hereafter the 'Explanatory Brochure').

[96] *Volkswagen I* [1998] OJ L124/60; *Opel* [2001] OJ L59/1; *Volkswagen II* [2001] OJ L262/14; *DaimlerChrysler* [2002] OJ L257/1; and Case T–325/01 *DaimlerChrysler v Commission*, judgment of 15 September 2005, not yet reported.

[97] Andersen, *Study on the impact of possible future legislative scenarios for motor vehicle distribution on all parties concerned*, 3 December 2001, available at http://europa.eu.int/comm/competition/car_sector/distribution/eval_reg_1475_95/studies/impact_legislative_scenarios/ (hereafter the 'Andersen Report'); H Degryse and F Verboven, *Car Price Differentials in the European Union: An Economic Analysis*, November 2000, Catholic University Leuven and CEPR 176, available at http://europa.eu.int/comm/competition/car_sector/distribution/eval_reg_1475_95/studies/car_price_differentials.pdf; R Lademann, *Customer Preferences for Existing and Potential Sales and Servicing Alternatives in Automotive Distribution*, 21 December 2001, Dr Lademann & Partner Gesellschaft für Unternehmens und Kommunalberatung mbH, 81, available at http://europa.eu.int/comm/competition/car_sector/distribution/eval_reg_1475_95/studies/customer_preferences.pdf; F Verboven, *Quantitative Study on the Demand for New Cars to Define the Relevant Market in the Passenger Car Sector*, 17 September 2002, Catholic University Leuven 43, available at http://europa.eu.int/comm/competition/car_sector/distribution/eval_reg_1475_95/studies/study01.pdf (hereafter the 'Verboven Report'); J Wormald and V Gardner, *The Natural Link between Sales and Service*, November 2000, Autopolis 63, available at http://europa.eu.int/comm/competition/car_sector/distribution/eval_reg_1475_95/studies/sales_and_service.pdf.

[98] N Navarro Blanco and C Dussart, 'Auditions des 13 et 14 Février 2001 concernant le Rapport d'évaluation du Règlement (CE) n° 1475/95 de la Commission sur la distribution

Report, as well as those of the first independent studies that had become available. A draft of the new regulation was adopted by the Commission on 5 February 2002[99] and some 350 reactions from interested parties were received by the Commission in relation to the draft. The Commission consulted with the Advisory Committee on Restrictive Practices and Dominant Positions and received the opinions of both the European Parliament[100] and the Economic and Social Committee.[101] The Commission adopted Regulation 1400/2002 on 31 July 2002, which entered into force on 1 October 2002.

Guidance on the manner in which DG COMP proposes to apply Regulation 1400/2002 can be found in an Explanatory Brochure[102] that was issued immediately prior to the entry into force of the Regulation. In order to address the many questions that were triggered by the application of the new approach, DG COMP subsequently issued an additional document, entitled 'Frequently Asked Questions'.[103] **1.61**.

E. Enforcement of Articles 81 and 82 EC

Thus far, we have outlined the guiding principles of the implementation of Articles 81 and 82 EC under Regulation 1/2003. In that context, we have pointed out the continued relevance of block exemption regulations, and have briefly set out the precedents and the coming into being of Regulations 2790/99 and 1400/2002. In this section we add a dimension, namely the public and private enforcement in cases of the infringement of Articles 81 and 82 EC. In **1.62**.

---

automobile' (2001) 2 EC Competition Policy Newsletter 38; Commission Press Release IP/01/204, 14 February 2001; and Presentation slides and speaking notes of the participants available at http://europa.eu.int/comm/competition/car_sector/distribution/eval_reg_1475_95/report/hearing/#02_13.

[99] European Commission, *Draft Commission Regulation (EC) on the application of Article 81(3) of the Treaty to categories of vertical agreements and concerted practices in the motor vehicle industry* [2002] OJ C67/2; L Tsoraklidis, 'Towards a New Motor Vehicle Block Exemption—Commission Proposal for Motor Vehicle Distribution, adopted on 5 February 2002' (2002) 2 EC Competition Policy Newsletter 31.

[100] European Parliament, *Resolution on the draft Commission regulation on the application of article 81(3) of the Treaty to categories of vertical agreements and concerted practices in the motor vehicle industry* [2003] OJ C187E/149.

[101] Economic and Social Committee, *Opinion of the Economic and Social Committee of 29 May 2002 on the Draft Commission Regulation on the application of article 81(3) of the Treaty to categories of vertical agreements and concerted practices in the motor vehicle industry* [2002] OJ C221/10. [102] Explanatory Brochure (n 95 above).

[103] European Commission—Directorate General Competition, *Frequently Asked Questions*, available at http://europa.eu.int/comm/competition/car_sector/distribution/faq_en.pdf (hereafter 'Frequently Asked Questions'). DG COMP has specified that the Frequently Asked Questions are intended to complement and not to replace the Explanatory Brochure (Frequently Asked Questions, opening paragraph).

this respect, an overall distinction must be made between the public enforce-ment of Articles 81 and 82 EC (ie their enforcement by the Commission and the NCAs) and the private enforcement of Articles 81 and 82 EC (ie their enforcement by private parties in private litigation).

(1) Public enforcement

1.63. The guiding principle of public enforcement which underpins Regulation 1/2003 is that the Commission and the NCAs together form a network of public authorities which apply the EC competition rules in close co-operation.[104] To this end, it is obviously a requirement that the NCAs must be competent to apply Articles 81 and 82 EC. Before Regulation 1/2003 came into force, this was not always the case (about half of the NCAs were only able to apply national competition law). However, Regulation 1/2003 now explicitly requires that the Member States must designate and empower authorities to apply Articles 81 and 82 EC.[105]

1.64. The Commission and the NCAs can uncover infringements during *ex officio* investigations or as a consequence of complaints. Given that any person showing a legitimate interest can lodge a complaint, private parties play an important role in the public enforcement of competition law. The moder-nization package contains a special notice on complaints, ie the Commission Notice on the handling of complaints by the Commission under Articles 81 and 82 of the EC Treaty.[106] The purpose of the directly applicable exception system established by Regulation 1/2003 is to liberate sufficient resources for *ex officio* investigations into serious infringements of competition (ie hardcore cartels such as horizontal price fixing or market sharing).[107] In addition to *ex officio* investigations and complaints, a third way of uncovering cartels is to provide for the immunity or the reduction of fines for those companies that are involved in a cartel but denounce it to the competition authorities. At the EC level, this type of leniency is governed by the Commission Notice on immunity from fines and reduction of fines in cartel cases.[108] Whilst the 'Leniency Notice' has generally been a success,[109] given that it only applies to horizontal cartels between

---

[104] Reg 1/2003, recital 15.   [105] ibid, recital 35 and Art 35.   [106] n 33 above.
[107] 'The Commission will in future concentrate on pro-actively investigating serious infrin-gements, following complaints or on its own initiative', C Gauer, D Dalheimer, L Kjolbye, and E De Smijter (n 34 above) 3.   [108] [2002] OJ C45/3.
[109] Some figures are given in B van Barlingen, 'The European Commission's 2002 Leniency Notice after One Year of Operation' (2003) 2 EC Competition Policy Newsletter 16; JF Bellis, 'La détermination des amendes pour infraction au droit communautaire de la concurrence—Bilan de cinq années d'application des lignes directrices de 1998' [2003] CDE 377; M Schneider, *Kronzeugenregelung im EG-Kartellrecht: Die Praxis der Europäischen Union beim Erlaß und der Ermäßigung von Geldbußen in Kartellsachen unter Einbeziehung der 'Leniency Notice' des*

competitors,[110] it is of little relevance in the context of the discussion of this book and will not be discussed at any length.

The powers which Regulation 1/2003 has given to the Commission and to the **1.65**. NCAs for the public prosecution of infringements of Articles 81 and 82 EC are as follows.

Public enforcement by NCAs

According to Article 5 of Regulation 1/2003, the NCAs have the power, acting **1.66**. on their own initiative or on a complaint, to take the following decisions:

— requiring that an infringement be brought to an end,
— ordering interim measures,
— accepting commitments,
— imposing fines, periodic penalty payments or any other penalty provided for in their national law.

Where on the basis of the information in their possession the conditions for prohibition are not met they may likewise decide that there are no grounds for action on their part.

Public enforcement by the Commission

The Commission can adopt the same decisions as the NCAs: **1.67**.

— finding and termination of an infringement (Article 7);
— interim measures (Article 8);
— commitments, in case the Commission intends to adopt a decision under Article 7 and the undertakings concerned offer commitments expressed to them by the Commission in its preliminary assessment (Article 9); and
— fines, with a maximum of 10% of a company's total turnover in the preceding business year (Article 23), as well as periodic penalty fines (Article 24).

Exceptionally,[111] the Commission can also, acting on its own initiative, adopt **1.68** a 'finding of non-applicability' in accordance with Article 10 of Regulation 1/2003. A 'finding of non-applicability' is a Commission decision in which the Commission finds that the prohibition of Article 81 EC is not applicable, either because the conditions of Article 81(1) EC are not fulfilled, or because the conditions of Article 81(3) EC are satisfied. The Commission may likewise reach such a finding with reference to Article 82 EC.

US-Department of Justice und der 'Bonusregelung' des Bundeskartellamtes (Peter Lang, 2004). Specifically on leniency post–Reg 1/2003, see eg S Blake and D Schnichels, 'Leniency Following Modernisation: Safeguarding Europe's Leniency Programmes' (2004) 2 EC Competition Policy Newsletter 7; and C Swaak and MR Mollica, Leniency Applicants Face to Modernisation of EC Competition Law [2005] ECLR 507.

[110] Leniency Notice, para 1: 'This notice concerns secret cartels between two or more competitors aimed at fixing prices, production or sales quotas, sharing markets including bid-rigging or restricting imports or exports'. [111] ibid, para 14.

(2) Private enforcement

1.69. Recently, the private enforcement of Articles 81 and 82 EC before national courts has taken centre-stage. Private enforcement of competition law rules via litigation before the national courts is generally considered to have a number of advantages when compared to public enforcement. A number of these perceived advantages are listed in the Commission Notice on the handling of complaints by the Commission under Articles 81 and 82 of the Treaty. They are:

— National courts may award damages for loss suffered as a result of an infringement of Article 81 or 82.
— National courts may rule on claims for payment or contractual obligations based on an agreement that they examine under Article 81.
— It is for the national courts to apply the civil sanction of nullity of Article 81(2) in contractual relationships between individuals. They can in particular assess, in the light of the applicable national law, the scope and consequences of the nullity of certain contractual provisions under Article 81(2), with particular regard to all the other matters covered by the agreement.
— National courts are usually better placed than the Commission to adopt interim measures.
— Before national courts, it is possible to combine a claim under Community competition law with other claims under national law.
— Courts normally have the power to award legal costs to the successful applicant. This is never possible in an administrative procedure before the Commission.[112]

Direct effect of Articles 81 and 82 EC

1.70. A prerequisite for the private enforcement of Articles 81 and 82 EC is that they must have direct effect so that they can be applied by the national courts. This direct effect was recognized by the Court of Justice a long time ago, in the 1974 *BRT v SABAM* case: 'As the prohibitions of Articles [81(1)] and [82] tend by their very nature to produce direct effects in relations between individuals, these Articles create direct rights in respect of the individuals concerned which the national courts must safeguard'.[113]

Consequences of infringement of Article 81 (and 82) EC according to Article 81(2) EC

1.71. According to Article 81(2) EC, any agreement or decision which is prohibited by Article 81(1) EC and which cannot be exempted on the basis of Article 81(3) EC

---

[112] [2004] OJ C101/65, para 16. Also M Monti, 'Private Litigation as a Key Complement to Public Enforcement of Competition Rules and the First Conclusions on the Implementation of the New Merger Regulation', Speech 04/403, 17 September 2004. For a dissonant voice in the discussion on the advantages of private enforcement: W Wils, 'Should Private Antitrust Enforcement Be Encouraged in Europe?' (2003) 3 World Competition 1; and the reaction by CA Jones, 'Private Antitrust Enforcement in Europe: A Policy Analysis and Reality Check' (2004) 1 World Competition 13.   [113] Case 127/73 *BRT v SABAM* [1974] ECR 51, para 16.

is automatically void. Article 82 EC does not contain a provision which is equivalent to Article 81(2) EC but, given the direct effect of Article 82 EC as confirmed in *BRT v SABAM*, agreements infringing that provision are unenforceable. There is no further provision in the EC Treaty concerning the consequences of the infringement of Articles 81 and 82 EC.

Consequences of infringement of Article 81 (and 82) EC according to national law

From the case law of the Court of Justice, it would seem that the consequences **1.72**. of the infringement of Articles 81 and 82 EC are, by and large, a matter of national law:[114]

> 11. In its judgment of 25 November 1971 in Case 22/71 (*Béguelin Import Company and others v S.A.G.L. Import Export and others* (1971) ECR 949), the Court ruled that an agreement falling under the prohibition imposed by Article [81(1)] of the Treaty is void and that, since the nullity is absolute, the agreement has no effect as between the contracting parties. It also follows from previous judgments of the Court, and in particular from the judgment of 30 June 1966 in Case 56/65 (*Société Technique Minière v. Machinenbau Ulm* (1966) ECR 235), that the automatic nullity decreed by Article [81(2)] applies only to those contractual provisions which are incompatible with Article [81(1)]. The consequences of such nullity for other parts of the agreement are not a matter for Community law . . .
> 12. The . . . automatic nullity decreed by Article [81(2)] of the Treaty applies only to those contractual provisions which are incompatible with Article [81(1)]. The consequences of such nullity for other parts of the agreement, and for any orders and deliveries made on the basis of the agreement, and the resulting financial obligations are not a matter for Community law. Those consequences are to be determined by the national court according to its own law.

Private enforcement as a 'shield' and a 'sword'

In terms of the consequences of the automatic nullity of restrictive practices and **1.73**. conduct incompatible with Articles 81 and 82 EC, which are thus governed by national law, a distinction is often made between the use of Articles 81 and 82 EC as a shield or as a sword.[115]

---

[114] Case 319/82 *Kerpen & Kerpen* [1983] ECR 4173. Reference can also be made to Case 10/86 *VAG France SA* [1986] ECR 4071, paras 14–15. On *Kerpen & Kerpen*, reference can also be made to paras 6.42 *et seq*.

[115] The distinction has been made by FG Jacobs and T Diesenhofer, 'Procedural Aspects of the Effective Private Enforcement of EC Competition Rules: A Community Perspective' in CD Ehlermann and I Atanasiu (eds), *European Competition Law Annual 2001: Effective Private Enforcement of EC Antitrust Law* (Hart Publishing, 2003) 189–90; also Venit (n 34 above) 570–1.

Private enforcement as a 'shield'

1.74. Articles 81 and 82 EC are used as a shield when the infringement of either one of them is invoked before a national court as a defence in order to defeat a contractual obligation (eg a non-compete obligation or a territorial or customer restriction imposed on a distributor) or to counter a claim for damages.[116]

1.75. Regulation 1/2003 improves the conditions for the use of Article 81 EC as a shield. Following Regulation 1/2003, national courts have the power to apply Article 81 EC in its entirety, including Article 81(3) EC.[117] This implies that national proceedings no longer need to be suspended to await the outcome of the Commission's decision on the applicability of Article 81(3) EC to the agreement in dispute. For Article 82 EC, nothing changes: national courts were and remain competent to apply Article 82 EC directly.

1.76. As stated above, the consequences of the nullity provided for by Article 81(2) EC are, by and large, a matter of national law. It is therefore in accordance with national law that the national courts will decide on, for example, the extent and the temporal effect of nullity between the parties of the agreement and third parties. Block exemption regulations, including Regulations 2790/99 and 1400/2002, are an exception to this rule in so far as they usually contain language which governs the extent of the nullity, ie the question of severability. Non-compliance with the conditions of a block exemption regulation may either affect all of the provisions which fall within Article 81(1) EC or it may be severable from such other provisions. Traditionally, if an agreement contains a *hardcore restriction*, it will not be possible to sever that restriction to allow the remainder of the agreement to benefit from the safe harbour of the block exemption regulation.[118] Conversely, if an agreement infringes a block exemption's *conditions*, this will not, as a rule, entail the loss of the safe harbour of the block exemption for other provisions of the agreement that are within Article 81(1) EC.[119]

1.77. It follows from the above considerations that nullity may have a tremendous impact on the parties to a supply or distribution agreement. The restrictions of competition which they contain are often crucial to their existence. If they have not been drafted in accordance with applicable competition law, the parties (or

---

[116] Other examples are given in Roth (n 9 above) para 10–030. For practical applications, F Randolph and A Robertson, 'The First Claims for Damages in the Competition Appeal Tribunal' [2005] ECLR 365.

[117] Reg 1/2003, Art 6 ('National courts shall have the power to apply Articles 81 and 82 of the Treaty').

[118] Reg 2790/99, Art 4 (Ch 5 below); Reg 1400/2002, Art 4 (paras 11.19 and 11.109–11.160 below).

[119] Reg 2790/99, Art 5 (paras 6.41–6.45 below); Reg 1400/2002, Art 5 (paras 11.20 and 11.177–11.211 below).

at the very least one of them) may be stuck with a binding deal but with unenforceable prices, non-compete obligations, etc.

Private enforcement as a 'sword'

Articles 81 and 82 EC are used as a sword principally when they are invoked in support of an action for damages before the national courts. In *Courage v Crehan*, the Court of Justice explicitly recognized the existence of a Community right to damages between private parties when it stated that '[t]he full effectiveness of Article [81 EC], in particular, the practical effect of the prohibition laid down in Article [81(1)] would be put at risk if it were not open to any individual to claim damages for loss caused to him by a contract or by conduct liable to restrict or distort competition'.[120] In the context of a distribution agreement, damages may become an issue when the distributor is of the opinion, for example, that the supplier has abused its dominant position by asking excessive prices and the distributor therefore wants to introduce a claim for the excessive prices he paid and/or for the loss caused to his business. Similarly, a distributor may want to claim damages for the absolute territorial restrictions imposed by his supplier. **1.78**.

In the past, the private enforcement of Articles 81 and 82 EC has not been, to say the least, a success. A study commissioned by DG COMP on the conditions for claims for damages in cases of infringement of EC competition rules concluded that there was an underdevelopment of actions for damages for breach of EC competition law, and that there exists an astonishing diversity of approaches taken by the Member States. Specifically, it identified only twelve successful damages awards for breach of EC competition law since the entry into force of Regulation 17 in 1962.[121] **1.79**.

At the time of writing, the Commission is looking at the conditions under which private parties can bring an action for damages before the national courts of the Member States for breach of the EC competition rules and adopted a Green Paper on the private enforcement of EC competition law.[122] **1.80**.

---

[120] Case C–453/99 *Courage v Crehan* [2001] ECR I–6297, para 26. On *Courage v Crehan*: eg A Anastasia, 'Individual Tort Liability for Infringements of Community Law' [2002] LIEI 177; A Jones and D Beard, 'Co-contractor, Damages and Article 81: The ECJ Finally Speaks' [2002] ECLR 246; AP Komninos, 'New Prospects for Private Enforcement of EC Competition Law: *Courage v Crehan* and the Community Right to Damages' [2002] CML Rev 447; O Odudu and J Edelman, 'Compensatory Damages for breach of Article 81' [2002] ELR 327; T Tridimas, 'Liability for Breach of Community Law: Growing Up or Mellowing Down?' [2001] CML Rev 301; and W van Gerven, 'Of Rights, Remedies and Procedures' [2000] CML Rev 501.

[121] The study is available at http://europa.eu.int/comm/competition/antitrust/others/private_enforcement/index_en.html.

[122] The Green Paper is available at <http://europa.eu.int/com/competition/antitrust/others/actions_for_damage/gp.html>. A bird's eye view of existing case law and of the obstacles to increased private enforcement can be found in D Woods, A Sinclair, and D Ashton, 'Private Enforcement of Community Competition Law: Modernisation and the Road Ahead' (2004) 2 EC Competition Policy Newsletter 31.

F. Hard v Soft EC Competition Law

(1) General

1.81. A final horizontal issue which we would like to address in this introductory chapter concerns the relation between hard and soft EC competition law. In this context, 'hard law' stands for the rules of primary and secondary EC competition law (Articles 81 and 82 EC, the block exemption regulations) while 'soft law' stands for a variety of 'quasi-legal measures'[123] or 'rules of conduct which, in principle have no legally binding force but which nevertheless may have practical effects'.[124] The use of soft law as a means to develop Community policy is expressly recognized in Article 249 EC in the form of non-binding 'recommendations' and 'opinions'. Apart from these recommendations and opinions, soft law has in the meanwhile taken on a variety of different forms, including resolutions, green papers, white papers, notices, guidelines, 'frameworks' (eg in the field of State aid), codes of conduct, and inter-institutional agreements.

1.82. Any competition law practitioner will acknowledge that nowadays when responding to competition law questions in many cases it involves references to soft law instruments. For vertical restraints, reference can be made to the Guidelines (Regulation 2790/99) and to the Explanatory Brochure and the Frequently Asked Questions (Regulation 1400/2002). First, we will address the question of the legal nature of the Guidelines (paragraphs 1.83–1.86), as well as their legal and practical consequences (paragraphs 1.87–1.95). Subsequently, we will transpose our findings to the Explanatory Brochure and the Frequently Asked Questions (paragraph 1.96).

(2) The legal nature of the Guidelines

1.83. According to the Commission, the Guidelines set out the principles for the assessment of vertical agreements under Article 81 EC.[125] While the Guidelines are without prejudice to the possible parallel application of Article 82 EC to vertical agreements, they do not provide the reader with any specific guidance on the said application.[126] As to Article 81 EC, then, the Commission's

---

[123] H Cosma and R Whish, 'Soft Law in the Field of EU Competition Policy' [2003] European Business Law Review 25, 53.

[124] F Snyder, 'Soft Law and Institutional Practice in the European Community' in S Martin, *The Construction of Europe. Essays in Honour of Emile Noël* (Kluwer, 1994) 197. In line with its increased use, studies on EC soft law have been on the rise. An extensive list of references to such studies can be found in D Trubek, P Cottrell, and M Nance, ' "Soft Law", "Hard Law" and European Integration: Towards a Theory of Hybridity', available at http://www.wisc.edu/wage/pubs/papers/Hybridity%20Paper%20April%202005.pdf.   [125] Guidelines, para 1.

[126] On the application of Art 82 EC to vertical agreements, see Guidelines, para 1. There are limited exceptions to the rule that the Guidelines do not deal with Art 82 EC. They contain a

objective with the Guidelines is to help companies to make their own EC competition law assessment of their vertical agreements.[127] The Commission rules out a mechanical application of the Guidelines, and considers that each case must be evaluated in the light of its own facts, and that it will apply the Guidelines reasonably and flexibly.[128]

While the Commission's objective can be encouraged, in reality matters are nonetheless much more complex. The reason for this is that the Guidelines also contain a section (Section III, paragraphs 21–70) which 'comments' on the application of Regulation 2790/99. On closer analysis, it appears that the term 'to comment' must be taken with a pinch of salt, given that the Guidelines on several occasions add extra conditions for the block exemption to apply or interpret the Regulation in a way which is hard to reconcile with its express wording.   **1.84.**

One of the most telling examples of this concerns one of the Regulation's blacklisted clauses. Pursuant to Article 4(b), first indent, of Regulation 2790/99, an active sales restriction can be imposed with regard to territories or customers which are exclusively reserved to the supplier or exclusively allocated by the supplier to another dealer. The Guidelines (paragraph 50), however, add to this that the exclusive dealer must be protected against active sales in his territory 'by the supplier and all other buyers of the supplier inside the Community'. If a supplier omits to impose the latter condition in his distribution agreements, this would mean, according to the Guidelines at least, that those agreements contain a hardcore restriction and consequently, that the benefit of the block exemption would be lost to the agreements in their entirety.[129] The question regarding the legal nature of the Guidelines is therefore not merely theoretical but is instead directly relevant for the practitioner.   **1.85.**

The answer to the question of the legal nature is a short one. It clearly follows from the case law of the Court that instruments of soft law, such as the Guidelines, are not legally binding as such. Whilst they may clarify the terms of Regulation 2790/99 and indicate the Commission's approach, they cannot alter the scope of the Regulation as a matter of law.[130] Legally speaking, the provisions of the Regulation prevail over any conflicting statement in the Guidelines.   **1.86.**

---

number of general statements on the assessment under Art 82 EC of non-compete obligations (para 141), fidelity rebate schemes (para 152), and tying (para 215). For more details on the application of Art 82 EC to vertical agreements, reference is made to Pt III of this book.

[127] Guidelines, para 3.   [128] ibid.

[129] This example has been developed in F Wijckmans and F Tuytschaever, 'Active Sales Restrictions Revisited' [2004] ECLR 104. It is also dealt with below in paras 5.61–5.85.

[130] Roth (n 9 above) para 3–079. For instance, in C–226/94 *Grand Garage Albigeois and others* [1996] ECR I–651, para 21; and Case C–309/94 *Nissan France and others* [1996] ECR I–677, para 22, the Court ruled in regard of the Commission Notice of 4 December 1991

(3) The consequences of the Guidelines (Regulation 2790/99)

1.87. The fact that the Guidelines cannot alter the scope of Regulation 2790/99 does not mean that they are by definition void of any legal, let alone any practical, consequences. To briefly consider these effects, a distinction must be made between the effects for the institution which adopted it—in this case, the Commission—and the effects for third parties.

For the Commission

1.88. For the Commission, the Guidelines provide a structure for the margin of discretion which it enjoys in the context of its vertical restraints policy. They are meant to enhance the degree of legal certainty and to result in a more uniform application of the rules.[131] In line with the Court, the Commission is bound by the Guidelines on the basis of the principle *patere legem quam ipse fecisti*.[132] Should this not be the case, the Commission would be entitled to breach the legitimate expectations of those who rely on the Guidelines to assess whether or not their vertical agreement may enjoy the block exemption contained in the Regulation. Since the respect of the principle of legitimate expectations is a general principle of EC law,[133] this cannot be allowed.

For third parties

1.89. In order to appreciate the legal effects of the Guidelines for third parties, a distinction must be made between the Community courts, the national courts, the NCAs, and finally the individual market players.

Community courts

1.90. The Guidelines explicitly state:

> These Guidelines are without prejudice to the interpretation that may be given by the Court of First Instance and the Court of Justice of the European Communities in relation to the application of Article 81 EC Treaty.[134]

---

entitled 'Clarification of the Activities of Motor Vehicle Intermediaries' ([1991] OJ C329/20), that 'its purpose is merely to clarify certain terms used in the regulation and it cannot therefore alter the scope of the regulation'. Reference is also made to the case law cited in V Korah and D O'Sullivan, *Distribution Agreements Under the EC Competition Rules* (Hart Publishing, 2002) 127.

[131] In general, Cosma and Whish (n 123 above) 50.

[132] eg Case T–105/95 *WWF UK v Commission* [1997] ECR II–313, para 55 (as regards the Commission's code of conduct on access to documents, which meanwhile has been replaced), where the Court ruled that the Commission had to comply with a series of obligations it had voluntarily accepted.

[133] eg K Lenaerts and P van Nuffel, *Constitutional Law of the European Union* (Sweet & Maxwell, 2005) 714, para 17–069 with references; and Korah and O'Sullivan (n 130 above) 125.

[134] Guidelines, para 4. A similar statement can be found in the Commission Notice—Guidelines on the applicability of Article 81 of the EC Treaty to horizontal cooperation agreements, para 16; as well as in a number of notices accompanying Regulation 1/2003, eg Guidelines on the application of Art 81(3) EC (n 7 above) para 7 and the Guidelines on the effect on trade

The Guidelines therefore only have interpretative force for the Community **1.91**.
courts: the Community judge may interpret EC law on the basis of certain
declarations from the institutions, as long as the content of those declarations is
publicly available.[135] However, the Community courts are not bound by the
Guidelines and may allow their own views to prevail over those of the Commission. A Court judgment is binding upon the Commission.

NCAs and national courts

In respect of the national authorities (NCAs or national courts), the Guidelines **1.92**.
are not, as such, legally binding and Article 10 EC (the 'loyalty clause') cannot
be invoked against them (because the Commission issued the Guidelines
autonomously).[136] The application of the Guidelines by the Commission
nevertheless entails (different) legal consequences for the NCAs and the national
courts. This can be illustrated by way of a statement taken from the Commission's White Paper on Modernization:

> [Guidelines] might not be binding on national authorities, but they would make a
> valuable contribution to the consistent application of Community law, because in
> its decisions in individual cases the Commission would confirm the approach they
> set out. Provided those individual decisions were upheld by the Court of Justice,
> then, notices and guidelines would come to form part of the rules that must be
> applied by national authorities.[137]

This statement confirms that the Guidelines do not have a binding legal **1.93**.
character, but that their application in Commission decisions may have legal
effects for the NCAs and national courts:

— Both for NCAs and national courts, the direct legal effects of a Commission
  decision are governed by Article 16 of Regulation 1/2003: Both may no longer,
  on the basis of national competition law, arrive at a different conclusion
  than the Commission for the agreements, decisions, or practices 'which are
  already the subject of a Commission decision'. The application of the
  Guidelines in a Commission decision therefore does not entail direct legal
  effects for agreements, decisions, or practices which are not the subject of the
  decision concerned.
— For NCAs, the legal effects of a Commission decision which applies
  the Guidelines may extend beyond its factual context by means of the

---

concept contained in Articles 81 and 82 of the Treaty [2004] OJ C101/81, para 5. On the judicial
review of Art 81 EC, D Bailey, 'Scope of Judicial Review under Article 81 EC' [2004] CML
Rev 1327.

[135] Case C–292/89 *Antonissen* [1991] ECR I–745, para 18; Case C–25/94 *Commission v
Council* [1996] ECR I–1469; and Case C–329/95 *Länsratten I Stockholms Län* [1997] ECR
I–2675, para 23.

[136] Binding force for decisions *sui generis* exists only when there exists a formal agreement
between the Commission and all of the Member States, eg European Commission, *Competition
Law in the EC—Volume IIB. Explanation of rules applicable to state aid* (OOPEC, 1997) 15.

[137] White Paper on Modernisation (n 15 above) para 86.

Commission's use of Article 11(6) of Regulation 1/2003 (ie the initiation of a procedure which relieves the NCAs of their competence to apply Articles 81 and 82 EC). This may occur in particular if the Commission's viewpoint has been supported by the Community courts. In this respect, the Joint Statement of the Council and the Commission on the functioning of the Network of Competition Authorities is relevant. It confirms that the type of situations which justify the Commission's initiation of a procedure (and the corresponding impossibility for an NCA to apply Articles 81 and 82 EC to a given case) includes situations in which an NCA may want to go against 'previous decisions': 'Network members envisage a decision which is obviously in conflict with consolidated case law; the standards defined in the judgements of the Community courts and in previous decisions and regulations of the Commission should serve as a yardstick'.[138]

— In view of the principle of the separation of powers, there is no counterpart to Article 11(6) of Regulation 1/2003 for national courts. If a national court is confronted with a case which is similar to a case in which the Commission has already applied the Guidelines to a specific situation, and the national court has questions on that application, it may want to take advantage of the Commission's role as *amicus curiae* to ask its opinion. In addition, and in accordance with Article 234 EC, it can always refer one or several preliminary questions to the Court of Justice.

Market players

1.94 Market players are first and foremost bound by the wording of the Regulation. Where a supplier's distribution policy is questioned on a matter where the Guidelines deviate from the Regulation, the supplier, in its turn, is entitled to question the Guidelines. In other cases, the supplier may want to show that, in spite of its apparent infringement of the Guidelines, in reality, it complies with the conditions to enjoy a safe harbour under the Regulation.

1.95 The practical consequences of the Guidelines for the market players however are undeniable. A lawyer advising a client on the legality of its vertical agreements simply cannot ignore the Commission's views on the application of its own Regulation, as expressed in the Guidelines. As a consequence, when confronted with an inconsistency between the Guidelines and the Regulation, it is always advisable to contact DG COMP.

(4) The legal and practical effects of the Explanatory Brochure and the Frequently Asked Questions (Regulation 1400/2002)

1.96 The above observations in respect of the Guidelines are equally applicable to the Explanatory Brochure and the Frequently Asked Questions which accompany

---

[138] Joint Statement of the Council and the Commission on the functioning of the Network of Competition Authorities (n 61 above) para 21.

the motor vehicle block exemption regulation. The most essential points are the following:

— The Commission expressly states that the Explanatory Brochure is not legally binding.[139] A member of the so-called Block Exemption Regulation Team of DG COMP expressed it as follows: 'Although the Brochure is intended as a legally non-binding guide to the Regulation, experience shows indeed that this kind of information tools are instrumental in clarifying each party's responsibilities, hence contributing to avoiding or quickly resolving disputes'.[140]

— Whilst the Explanatory Brochure and the Frequently Asked Questions do not bind the Community Courts, the NCAs, the national courts (save from the effects identified in paragraph 1.93 above), or the sector (eg producers, dealers, independent traders), the same is not true for the Commission. For the reasons, and under the conditions set out, above (paragraph 1.88), the Commission is bound by its interpretation of Regulation 1400/2002 as laid down in the Explanatory Brochure and the Frequently Asked Questions.[141]

— Both the Explanatory Brochure and the Frequently Asked Questions provide interpretations and clarifications of provisions of Regulation 1400/2002 which are not necessarily covered by the wording of the block exemption regulation.[142] To the extent that such interpretations and clarifications in these documents go beyond the parameters set forth in the Regulation, they are invalid as a matter of law. Indeed, non-binding guidelines are not the correct legal instrument to broaden the scope of restrictions or conditions that are contained in a Commission regulation.

---

[139] Explanatory Brochure (n 95 above) 9; P Arhel, '104 questions/réponses sur le nouveau règlement automobile (la brochure explicative)' [2002] 237 Petites Affiches 7.

[140] M Martinez Lopez, 'New explanatory Brochure on Commission Block Exemption Regulation No 1400/2002 on the motor vehicle sector: bringing competition rules closer to consumers and market operators' (2003) 1 EC Competition Policy Newsletter 59.

[141] This opinion would seem not to be shared by M Malaurie-Vignal, 'Présentation et commentaire du Règlement 1400/2002 du 31 juillet 2002' [2002] 239 Petites Affiches 3, 5.

[142] ibid, 5.

PART II

VERTICAL AGREEMENTS UNDER REGULATION 2790/99

2

MATERIAL SCOPE OF
APPLICATION OF REGULATION 2790/99

A. Introduction

The material scope of application of Regulation 2790/99[1] is more extensive **2.01**.
than that of any other previous block exemption regulation applicable to vertical
restraints.[2] It is defined in the five paragraphs that make up Article 2 of that
Regulation. The principle of the broad scope of application of the block
exemption regulation is reflected in Article 2(1). Article 2(2) to (5) then go on
to revise and refine that principle in the following respects:

— Article 2(2) limits the scope of application to certain agreements between an
  association of undertakings and its members or its suppliers;
— Article 2(4) does the same as regards agreements between competitors;
— Article 2(3) addresses the Regulation's (limited) application to vertical agreements containing provisions on intellectual property rights ('IPRs'); and
— Article 2(5) concerns the interaction between Regulation 2790/99 and other
  block exemption regulations.

This Chapter provides practical guidance on the analysis of the Regulation's **2.02**.
material scope of application. It sets out to do this by posing a set of questions
which allow a more systematic approach to the matter, and then taking an
overview of the practical relevance of each of those questions. Subsequently,
each question is addressed separately in more detail.

---

[1] Commission Regulation (EC) No 2790/1999 of 22 December 1999 on the application of
Article 81(3) of the Treaty to categories of vertical agreements and concerted practices [1999] OJ
L336/21.
[2] Reg 2790/99 has therefore been dubbed an 'umbrella' block exemption regulation:
JM Schultze, S Pautke, and D Wagener, *Die Gruppenfreistellungsverordnung für vertikale Ver-
einbarungen* (Verlag Recht und Wirtschaft GmbH, 2001) para 204; M Mendelsohn and S Rose,
Guide to the EC Block Exemption for Vertical Restraints (Kluwer Law International, 2002) 43; A
Jones and B Sufrin, *EC Competition Law, Text, Cases and Materials* (2nd edn, OUP, 2004) 655
and 659; and J Nazerali and D Cowan, 'Reforming E.U. Distribution Rules—Has the Commission Found Vertical Reality?' [1999] ECLR 59.

B. Methodology: Seven Key Questions

2.03. Practically speaking, in order to determine whether or not a given agreement falls within the scope of application of the Regulation, the following seven questions need to be answered:

1. Does the agreement affect trade between the Member States in the sense of Article 81 EC?
2. Is there a vertical agreement in the sense of Article 81(1) EC?
3. Does the vertical agreement contain vertical restraints in the sense of Article 81(1) EC?
4. Is the vertical agreement covered by another block exemption regulation?
5. Does the supplier's (or the buyer's) market share exceed 30%?
6. Does the vertical agreement contain provisions on IPR and, if it does, are they ancillary?
7. Is the agreement between competitors, between an association of undertakings and its members, or between an association of undertakings and its suppliers?

2.04. The relevance of each of these questions to the material scope of application of Regulation 2790/99 is summarized below (at paragraphs 2.06–2.24). It is on the basis of these summaries that the specific issues can be determined that, in a given case, require a more in-depth review in order to decide whether or not the agreement falls within the scope of application of the Regulation.

2.05. It must be remembered that the result of the review of these seven key questions is not that it will determine that the agreement concerned is actually block exempted under Regulation 2790/99. The review only determines whether or not the agreement falls within the (material) scope of application of the Regulation. It is only following a second stage that it will be possible to decide whether the agreement effectively benefits from the block exemption. To this end, it must be assessed whether or not it contains provisions which run counter to the blacklist contained in Article 4 of the Regulation or which do not comply with the conditions (imposed, for example, on non-compete obligations) of Article 5 of the Regulation. This assessment is discussed later in Chapters 5 and 6, respectively.

(1) First question: 'effect on trade' between Member States

2.06. The 'effect on trade' concept is central to determining whether the EC competition rules apply:

— If such effect is not present, the vertical agreement concerned is not caught by the material scope of EC competition law and, therefore, not by Regulation 2790/99. Accordingly, the restraints of competition that the vertical agreement contains will have to be assessed exclusively from the perspective of national competition law.

— If there is an appreciable effect on inter-State trade, then EC competition law will apply to the restraints of competition that the vertical agreement contains.

In the latter case, the convergence rule enters into play. This rule requires that **2.07.** the outcome of the assessment of vertical restraints under national competition rules may not contradict the results of their review on the basis of Article 81 EC. In other words, if a vertical agreement is compatible with Article 81 EC (either because it is not caught by the prohibition of Article 81(1) EC or because it benefits from an exemption pursuant to Article 81(3) EC), it cannot be prohibited on the basis of national competition rules. The convergence theory also functions the other way round: if an agreement is incompatible with Article 81 EC, it will not be possible to rely on national competition law to allow the vertical restraints concerned. The first question is therefore critical, not only in determining whether EC competition law applies, but also in order to define the role and importance of national competition law.

The following aspects of the first question are important and are discussed in **2.08.** more detail elsewhere in this book:

— The assessment of whether the required effect on trade between Member States is present is discussed in paragraphs 2.27–2.60.
— The convergence rule is discussed in Chapter 1 (paragraphs 1.34–1.46).

(2) Second question: vertical agreements

The second question concerns the presence of a 'vertical agreement', which is a **2.09.** Regulation-specific concept: Article 2(1) of the Regulation makes it clear that the Regulation applies exclusively to this type of agreement.

In the context of the second question, there are two separate issues that need to **2.10.** be addressed. First, whether or not there is an agreement; second, if there is, whether or not the agreement is a vertical agreement.

Usually these issues will not create problems. If two independent companies **2.11.** enter into a distribution agreement (which is probably the most common example of a case covered by the Regulation), hardly any time needs to be spent on considering this second question. By definition, a distribution agreement, whether it is formalized or not, qualifies as a vertical agreement.

The following issues do, however, require a more careful review: **2.12.**

— While the concept of 'agreement' in Article 2(1) of the Regulation encompasses not only agreements as such, but also concerted practices, it does not cover unilateral conduct. In borderline cases, where there is doubt as to whether the conduct qualifies as an agreement or as a concerted practice, or whether it must be characterized as unilateral, a more in-depth review of the second question is required.

— The vertical agreement must be entered into between 'undertakings'. A distribution agreement entered into between two commercial companies will, in principle, be a vertical agreement between 'undertakings', but a more careful review is necessary in the case where public bodies or organizations acting in the context of social solidarity are involved.

— The concept of 'agreement' requires that two 'independent' undertakings are involved. Intra-group agreements may not meet this test and hence will fall outside the scope of application of Article 81(1) EC. Therefore, if vertical agreements between related parties are involved it will be necessary to check, in relation to the second question, whether the intra-group theory is applicable or not.

— The agreement will be deemed as 'vertical' if, for the purposes of the agreement, the parties act at a different level in the production or distribution chain and the agreement relates to the purchase, sale, or resale of goods and/or services. This requirement will only pose a problem in the case of rent or lease agreements, or where it is unclear whether the restrictions included in the agreement do actually all relate to the purchasing, selling, or reselling of goods or services.

2.13. The following aspects of the second question are addressed in greater detail below:

— the concepts of 'agreement' and 'concerted practice', as opposed to 'unilateral conduct', at paragraphs 2.65–2.90;
— the concept of 'undertaking' at paragraphs 2.91–2.103;
— the intra-group theory (or the concept of 'independent' undertaking) at paragraphs 2.104–2.111;
— the concept of 'vertical' agreement at paragraphs 2.112–2.122.

(3) Third question: vertical restraints

2.14. Regulation 2790/99 grants a block exemption; that is an exemption from the prohibition contained in Article 81(1) EC. Logically, therefore, the Regulation is only relevant to cases where the vertical agreement in question contains restrictions within the scope of Article 81(1) EC. As the second sentence of Article 2(1) states: '[The] exemption shall apply to the extent that such agreements contain restrictions of competition falling within the scope of Article 81(1) ("vertical restraints")'.

The following tools, which serve the purpose of identifying whether a given **2.15.** vertical agreement contains such vertical restraints or not, must be applied in the context of the third question:

— the Commission's *De Minimis* Notice at paragraphs 2.125–2.136;
— ad hoc economic analysis at paragraphs 2.137–2.54;
— the ancillary restraints doctrine at paragraphs 2.155–2.160.

(4) Fourth question: applicability of other block exemption regulations

Even if a vertical agreement passes the hurdles raised by the first three questions, **2.16.** it will still fall outside the material scope of application of the Regulation if its subject matter is within the scope of another block exemption regulation. The fourth question therefore aims to identify whether any other such block exemption regulation applies. It is important to note that it is irrelevant, for the purposes of the fourth question, whether the agreement effectively benefits from another block exemption regulation. If the subject matter of the agreement is within the scope of application of another block exemption regulation, Regulation 2790/99 does not apply, and this is irrespective of whether the agreement may contain a clause that is blacklisted under the other block exemption regulation or is not covered by that block exemption for some other reason (eg high market share).

In this context, the applicability of the following block exemption regulations **2.17.** must be checked:

— Regulation 1400/2002 concerning the purchase, sale, or resale of new motor vehicles, spare parts for such vehicles and repair and maintenance services pertaining to such vehicles at paragraphs 2.206–2.208, as well as more generally, Chapter 11;
— Regulation 2658/2000 concerning specialization agreements at paragraphs 2.180–2.188;
— Regulation 2659/2000 concerning R & D agreements at paragraphs 2.189–2.194;
— Regulation 772/2004 concerning technology transfer agreements at paragraphs 2.195–2.205.

(5) Fifth question: market share limit of 30%

The material scope of application of the Regulation is confined to cases where the **2.18.** supplier's market share does not exceed 30%. If the vertical agreement contains an exclusive supply obligation (ie an obligation which causes the supplier to sell the goods or services specified in the vertical agreement only to one buyer inside the Community for the purposes of a specific use or resale), it is the buyer's, instead of the supplier's, market share that shall not exceed 30%. In this case, the buyer's share is calculated on the basis of the buyer's purchases on the relevant purchase market. This is the same market as the one on which the supplier's market share would have been calculated if there had been no exclusive supply obligation.

2.19. More detailed guidance is given below on the following issues:

— absence of the need to calculate market shares for new products or in case of the penetration of new geographic markets at paragraph 2.253;
— the situation where the market share temporarily exceeds 30% at paragraphs 2.212–2.219 and 2.261–2.266;
— the definition of the relevant markets on which the market share must be measured at paragraphs 2.220–2.247;
— the technique of market share calculation at paragraphs 2.248–2.260.

(6) Sixth question: intellectual property rights

2.20. Vertical agreements which include the assignment of IPRs are not necessarily outside the material scope of application of the Regulation. However, pursuant to Article 2(3) of the Regulation, such agreements only fall within the material scope of application of the block exemption regulation if the following five cumulative conditions are met:

— the IPRs must be part of a vertical agreement, ie an agreement reflecting the conditions under which the parties may purchase, sell, or resell certain goods or services;
— the IPRs must be assigned to, or for the use of, the buyer;
— the IPRs must not constitute the primary object of the agreement;
— the IPRs must be directly related to the use, sale, or resale of goods or services by the buyer or his customers; and
— the IPRs, in relation to the contract goods or services, must not contain restrictions of competition having the same object or effect as vertical restraints which are not exempted.

2.21. As regards vertical agreements containing provisions relating to the assignment of IPRs, more detailed guidance is provided on the following topics:

— the five conditions for the application of Regulation 2790/99 to vertical agreements containing IPR provisions at paragraphs 2.271–2.283;
— trademarks at paragraph 2.285;
— copyright at paragraphs 2.286–2.287;
— know-how at paragraphs 2.288–2.290.

(7) Seventh question: involvement of competitors or associations of undertakings

As a general rule, vertical agreements entered into between actual or potential **2.22**. competitors are outside the material scope of Regulation 2790/99. As an exception to this, Article 2(4) of the Regulation provides that the block exemption applies where competitors enter into a non-reciprocal vertical agreement which complies with any of the following three conditions:

— the buyer has a total annual turnover not exceeding € 100 million; or
— the supplier is a manufacturer and a distributor of goods, while the buyer is a distributor not manufacturing goods competing with the contract goods; or
— the supplier is a provider of services at several levels of trade, while the buyer does not provide competing services at the level of trade where it purchases the contract services.

Provided that certain conditions are fulfilled, Regulation 2790/99 applies to **2.23**. vertical agreements between an association of undertakings and its members or between such an association and its suppliers. In such a case the cumulative conditions to be fulfilled for such application are defined in Article 2(2) of the Regulation, as follows:

— all the association's members are retailers of goods (ie not retailers of services); and
— no individual member of the association, together with its connected undertakings, has a total annual turnover exceeding € 50 million.

Below, more detailed guidance is given in regard to both vertical agreements **2.24**. between competitors (paragraphs 2.292–2.301) and vertical agreements involving associations of undertakings (paragraphs 2.302–2.305).

(8) The outcome of the review of the seven key questions

If a given agreement passes each of the hurdles raised by the seven key questions, **2.25**. then it will fall within the material scope of application of Regulation 2790/99. As a second stage, it must then be assessed on the basis of the applicability of the blacklist (Article 4) and the conditions (Article 5) of the Regulation as to whether it can enjoy the safe harbour of the block exemption.

If the agreement however, does not pass one of these hurdles, the consequences **2.26**. will be as follows:

— First question: If the required effect on inter-State trade is absent, then the agreement will have to be reviewed exclusively under the applicable national competition law.

— Second question: There are several scenarios that are possible if no vertical agreement is found to exist. If only unilateral conduct, rather than an agreement, is involved, such conduct will have to be assessed on the basis of Article 82 EC (abuse of dominant position) and not on the basis of Article 81 EC. Another possibility is that the unilateral conduct is assessed on the basis of national competition law that is stricter than Article 82 EC.[3] If the agreement turns out to be an intra-group agreement (in other words, if there are not at least two independent undertakings), then Article 81 EC will also not apply. Finally, if the agreement is horizontal instead of vertical, then Article 81 EC may be applicable, but Regulation 2790/99 will not be the proper legal instrument to use to assess whether the agreement may be block exempted. Other block exemption regulations may be relevant (for example: specialization, R & D) or a self-assessment in accordance with the principles of the Horizontal Guidelines may be required.

— Third question: If there are no vertical restraints, the prohibition of Article 81(1) EC will not apply and there will be no need to assess whether the agreement in question qualifies for an individual or block exemption.

— Fourth question: If the agreement comes within the scope of application of another block exemption regulation, it must be reviewed in light of the provisions of that regulation. If the agreement does not qualify for block exemption, a self-assessment will have to be undertaken to determine whether or not the agreement is eligible for an (individual) exemption pursuant to Article 81(3) EC.

— Fifth question: If the market share is exceeded, the vertical agreement must be assessed on the basis of the Vertical Guidelines[4] in order to determine whether it meets the conditions for an (individual) exemption pursuant to Article 81(3) EC.

— Sixth question: If the agreement's IPR provisions prevent the applicability of the block exemption of Regulation 2790/99 and the subject matter of the agreement does not come within the scope of application of another block exemption regulation (see question 4), then a self-assessment of the agreement will be required on the basis of the Horizontal Guidelines, the Vertical Guidelines, the TTBER Guidelines, or the Subcontracting Notice.

— Seventh question: If competitors or associations of undertakings are involved, and neither Regulation 2790/99 nor any other block exemption regulation is applicable, then a self-assessment of the agreement will have to be conducted on the basis of the Horizontal Guidelines and possibly on the basis of the Vertical Guidelines.

---

[3] Paras 1.41–1.146 above. See also Art 82 EC.
[4] Commission Notice, Guidelines on Vertical Restraints [2000] OJ C291/1 (hereafter 'Vertical Guidelines' or 'Guidelines').

C. First Question: Effect on Trade Criterion

(1) Introduction

First and foremost, the question of whether there is an effect on trade in the **2.27.**
sense of Articles 81 and 82 EC must be discussed. If there is no such effect, EC
competition law does not apply and only national competition law has to be
taken into account. As the Commission puts it in the Guidelines on the effect
on trade concept contained in Articles 81 and 82 of the Treaty:

> The effect on trade criterion is an autonomous Community law criterion, which
> must be assessed separately in each case. It is a jurisdictional criterion, which
> defines the scope of application of Community competition law. Community
> competition law is not applicable to agreements and practices that are not capable
> of appreciably affecting trade between Member States.[5]

The requirement that Article 81(1) EC only applies to agreements or concerted **2.28.**
practices which are capable of affecting inter-State trade in an appreciable way,
was of limited practical relevance in the past. Prior to the Regulation 1/2003
era, the Court and, in its wake, the Commission interpreted this criterion in a
broad way so that it was easily fulfilled. Sometimes, the Commission even
turned its investigation immediately towards establishing whether or not
competition was restricted in the sense of Article 81(1) EC, effectively skipping
the initial question of its competence. If this was found not to be the case, it
then merely observed that it was therefore not necessary to examine whether
trade between Member States could be affected.[6]

It has been argued that the existing case law on the effect on inter-State trade has **2.29.**
not been neutral but instead biased in favour of finding such an effect.[7] As a
result, the number of cases in which EC competition law entered into play
multiplied. Undoubtedly, there is some truth in this. However, account must
be taken of the fact that the Court's case law, as well as concomitant Commission decision-making practice, came about at a time when several Member
States had not yet enacted national competition legislation.[8] Accordingly, the
choice was often either between applying EC competition rules or not applying
any competition rules at all. This may explain the propensity towards the
broadening of the effect on inter-State trade concept.

---

[5] Guidelines on the effect on trade concept contained in Articles 81 and 82 of the Treaty
[2004] OJ C101/81, para 12 (hereafter 'Guidelines on the effect on trade concept').
[6] *Villeroy & Boch* [1985] OJ L376/15, para 39; *Elopak/Metal Box–Odin* [1990] OJ L209/15,
para 37.
[7] R Wesseling, *The Modernisation of EC Antitrust Law* (Hart Publishing, 2000) 116 *et seq.*
[8] eg A Fiebig, *Modernization of European Competition Law as a Form of Convergence* (2004)
Jean Monnet/Robert Schuman Paper Series, available at http://www.miami.edu/eucenter/
fiebigfinal.pdf.

(2) Regulation 1/2003 and the 'effect on trade' concept

2.30. The question of the effect on inter-State trade took on a new dimension following the entry into force of Regulation 1/2003 and the publication of a Commission Notice specifically addressing the matter.[9] It seems that this resulted in two immediate consequences for the issue under consideration.

— First, the modernization exercise has prompted the Commission to take stock of the existing case law and decision-making practice and, interestingly, to add new elements (in particular an attempt to quantify the concept of appreciability). This attempt is demonstrated most clearly in the Commission's definitions of two presumptions, one negative and one positive, on knowing when there is an effect on trade in the sense of Article 81(1) EC or not.[10]

— Second, there is the convergence rule of Article 3(1) of Regulation 1/2003.[11] This rule requires NCAs and national courts which apply national competition law to agreements, decisions by associations of undertakings or concerted practices which may affect trade between Member States, also to apply Article 81 EC. In addition, NCAs and national courts which apply national competition law to any abuse prohibited by Article 82 EC, must also apply Article 82 EC. It is obvious that, as a result of the convergence theory, both the role and the importance of the effect on trade criterion have increased dramatically. In the years to come, it will be interesting to see what impact the modernization package will have on the NCAs' and national courts' decisions on the effect on trade concept; what evidence they will require in order to determine whether or not trade between the Member States is affected in an appreciable way; and to what extent their views will impact on the scope of application of the EC competition rules. This point is acknowledged in the Guidelines, which, seeking convergence, state that although they are not binding upon them, they 'also intend to give guidance to the courts and authorities of the Member States in their application of the effect on trade concept contained in Articles 81 and 82'.[12]

(3) Guidelines on the 'effect on trade' concept

2.31. Aside from an introduction, the Commission's Guidelines on the effect on trade concept principally consists of two parts, dealing respectively with 'the effect on trade criterion' and 'the application of the above principles to common types of

---

[9] [2004] OJ C101/81.   [10] Paras 2.49–2.59 below.
[11] For further details on the convergence rule, paras 1.34–1.46 above.
[12] Guidelines on the effect on trade concept, para 3.

agreements and abuses'. The guiding principles of each of these two parts will be discussed hereafter, to the extent that they concern vertical agreements and their possible effect on inter-State trade.

Effect measured at the level of the agreement as a whole

Whether or not an agreement has an effect on trade must be measured at the **2.32**. level of the agreement as a whole. There is no requirement that each individual part of the agreement, including any restriction of competition flowing from it, must be capable of affecting inter-State trade: if the agreement as a whole is capable of affecting trade between Member States, there is Community law jurisdiction in respect of the entire agreement.[13] If an agreement covers several activities, the activities must be directly linked and form an integral part of the same overall business arrangement for them to belong to the same agreement. If they do not, then each activity constitutes a separate agreement.[14]

Similarly, for Article 82 EC to apply, the abuse as a whole must be capable of **2.33**. affecting trade. It is not necessary that each element of the unilateral behaviour of the dominant undertaking does so.[15]

Whether or not the participation of a particular undertaking in the agreement **2.34**. has an appreciable effect on trade between Member States is immaterial. An undertaking cannot escape Community law jurisdiction just because its own contribution to an agreement, which itself is capable of affecting trade between Member States, is insignificant.[16]

No link with a restriction of competition required

In order to establish Community law jurisdiction it is not necessary to establish **2.35**. a link between an alleged restriction of competition and the capacity of the agreement to affect trade between Member States. Agreements which are non-restrictive of competition may still affect trade between Member States. For instance, a selective distribution agreement which is based on purely qualitative selection criteria, justified by the nature of the products, is generally deemed as not being restrictive of competition within the meaning of Article 81(1) EC.[17] Notwithstanding this, it may still affect trade between Member States.

---

[13] ibid, para 14 (with reference to Case 193/83 *Windsurfing International v Commission* [1986] ECR 611, para 96; and Case T–77/94 *Vereniging van Groothandelaren in Bloemkwekerijproducten and others v Commission* [1997] ECR II–759, para 126).
[14] Guidelines on the effect on trade concept, para 14.   [15] ibid, para 17.
[16] ibid, para 15; and Case T–141/89 *Tréfileurope Sales Sarl v Commission* [1995] ECR II–791, para 122 (with reference to Case T–6/89 *Enichem Anic v Commission* [1991] ECR II–1623, paras 216 and 224).   [17] para 7.25 below.

'May affect'

Definition

2.36. The Court of Justice's established view of the notion of 'may affect' is:

> that it must be possible to foresee with a sufficient degree of probability on the basis of a set of objective factors of law or fact that the agreement or practice may have an influence, direct or indirect, actual or potential, on the pattern of trade between Member States.[18]

2.37. This case law definition contains three elements, and thus in order for inter-State trade to be affected, there must be:

    (i) a sufficient degree of probability on the basis of a set of objective factors of law or fact;

    (ii) an influence on the pattern of trade between Member States; and

    (iii) a direct or indirect, actual or potential influence on the pattern of trade.

2.38. In addition to these factors, which are briefly discussed below, the legal and factual background of the agreement must also be taken into account. For instance, legal barriers to cross-border trade may preclude any effect of the agreement on such trade.

Sufficient degree of probability

2.39. Based on the existing case law, there is no requirement to show that the agreement or practice 'will actually have or has had an effect on trade between Member States'. Rather, it is sufficient that the agreement or practice is 'capable' of having such an effect.[19] In order to determine the probability of effect on trade between Member States, the Commission puts forward a three-pronged test where regard must be given to:

    (i) the nature of the agreement;

    (ii) the nature of the products covered by the agreement; and

    (iii) the position and importance of the undertakings concerned.

2.40. It transpires from the Guidelines on the effect on trade concept that particular attention needs to be paid to the nature of the agreement. The Commission for instance mentions that some agreements and practices are 'by their very nature' capable of affecting trade between Member States.[20] As will be seen

---

[18] Case 42/84 *Remia and others v Commission* [1985] ECR 2545, para 22; and Case C–359/01P *British Sugar v Commission* [2004] ECR I–4933, para 27 (with references). See also the cases referred to in the Guidelines on the effect on trade concept, footnote 15.

[19] Guidelines on the effect on trade concept, para 26 (with reference to Case T–228/97 *Irish Sugar* [1999] ECR II–2969, para 170; and Case 19/77 *Miller* [1978] ECR 131, para 15).

[20] The need for further clarification between actions that 'by their own nature' affect trade between Member States and those which do not, has been emphasized by the International Bar Association ('IBA'), *Comments on Communication from the Commission. Draft Notice Guidelines*

below,[21] these types of agreements are subject to a so-called 'positive presumption' that they affect trade between Member States. In the Guidelines on the effect on trade concept, the Commission identifies the following agreements, which may be vertical agreements, as being 'by their very nature' capable of affecting trade between Member States:

— distribution agreements prohibiting exports (paragraph 16);
— cross-border cartels (paragraph 29) and specifically, cartel agreements 'such as those involving price fixing and market sharing covering several Member States' (paragraph 64);
— agreements which concern imports or exports (paragraph 48);
— agreements which cover several Member States, at least 'in almost all cases' (paragraphs 48 and 53);[22]
— agreements that impose restrictions on active and passive sales[23] and resale by buyers to customers in other Member States (paragraph 63);
— joint ventures which engage in activities in two or more Member States or which produce an output that is sold by the parents in two or more Member States (paragraph 67);
— agreements between suppliers and distributors which provide for resale price maintenance and which cover two or more Member States (paragraph 72).

Influence on the pattern of trade between Member States

In line with the examples given above, the Guidelines on the effect on trade concept confirm that it can generally be assumed that there will be an influence on the pattern of trade between Member States where a vertical agreement contains territorial restrictions on sales in other Member States.[24] **2.41.**

Direct or indirect influence on the pattern of trade

There will be a direct effect, for instance, if a supplier limits the rebates granted to distributors for products sold within the Member State in which the distributors are established. This increases the relative price of products destined for export and renders export sales less attractive, therefore making them less competitive.[25] There will be an indirect effect where a manufacturer limits **2.42.**

---

on the Effect on Trade Concept Contained in Articles 81 and 82 of the Treaty, available at http://europa.eu.int/comm/competition/antitrust/legislation/procedural_rules/comments/iba_28074_en.pdf.

[21] Para 2.58.

[22] The latter two categories are also mentioned in tandem, as follows: 'agreements between undertakings in two or more Member States that concern imports and exports are by their very nature capable of affecting trade between Member States' (para 62).

[23] On the distinction between 'active' and 'passive' sales, see paras 5.46–5.53 below.

[24] cf Guidelines on the effect on trade concept, para 27.

[25] ibid, para 37. As to the influence on the pattern of trade, the term 'pattern of trade'. It is neutral and therefore not required that trade must be restricted or reduced. It is particularly useful

warranties to products sold by distributors within their Member State of establishment. This creates disincentives for consumers from other Member States to buy the products because they will not be able to invoke the warranty.[26] Indirect effects can also occur in respect of intermediate products; for instance, if a supplier restricts its buyer's ability to sell components, supplied for the purposes of incorporation, to customers who would use them to manufacture the same type of goods as those produced by the supplier.[27]

Actual or potential influence on the pattern of trade

2.43. Actual effects will occur in the case of an agreement between a supplier and a distributor within the same Member State which prohibits exports to other Member States: Without the agreement, the distributor would have been free to engage in export sales.[28] Potential effects are those that may occur in the future, with a sufficient degree of probability: in *AEG Telefunken*, the Court of Justice for instance, rejected AEG's argument that trade between the Member States could not be affected as follows:

> the mere fact at a certain time traders applying for admission to a distribution network or who have already been admitted are not engaged in intra-Community trade cannot suffice to exclude the possibility that restrictions on their freedom of action may impede intra-Community trade, since the situation may change from one year to another in terms of alterations in the conditions or composition of the market both in the common market as a whole and in the individual national markets.[29]

2.44. Presumably, the practical consequences of the above can best be understood by taking the alternative point of view, namely that only remote, hypothetical, or speculative effects are excluded from the potential reach of the 'may affect' notion.[30]

'May affect appreciably'

General

2.45. It is not sufficient for an agreement to (be capable of) affect(ing) inter-State trade. For EC competition law to apply, it must in addition be (capable of) doing so in an appreciable manner. In this respect, it must be remembered that the notion of appreciable effect on trade must be distinguished from the notion of appreciable restriction of competition. The Guidelines on the effect on trade

---

to recall this for Dutch readers as the Dutch version of Arts 81(1) and 82 EC continues to state that trade must be 'negatively affected'.

[26] Guidelines on the effect on trade concept, para 39.
[27] On Reg 2790/99, Art 4(b), fourth indent, see paras 5.102–5.108 below.
[28] This can be implied from the Guidelines on the effect on trade concept, para 40.
[29] Case 107/82 *AEG Telefunken v Commission* [1983] ECR 3151, para 60.
[30] Guidelines on the effect on trade concept, para 43.

concept only deal with the former; the latter is dealt with later in the context of the agreements of minor importance or under the so-called *De Minimis* rule.[31]

Quantification of appreciability: SMEs

The Guidelines refer to the *De Minimis* Notice[32] to the extent that they **2.46**. transpose the Commission's approach regarding agreements between small-and medium-sized undertakings ('SMEs') to the effect on inter-State trade.

According to Commission Recommendation (EC) No 2003/361 of 6 May **2.47**. 2003 concerning the definition of micro, small and medium-sized enterprises,[33] applicable from 1 January 2005, SMEs are defined as:

> enterprises which employ fewer than 250 persons and which have an annual turnover not exceeding € 50 million, and/or an annual balance sheet total not exceeding € 43 million.[34]

Agreements between SMEs are normally not considered as being capable of **2.48**. affecting trade between Member States. The reason for this is that the activities of SMEs are normally local or, at most, regional in nature. However, SMEs may be subject to Community law jurisdiction where they engage in cross-border economic activity.[35] The general reference to 'Community law jurisdiction' must be taken to refer to agreements in the sense of Article 81 EC but also, albeit rather exceptionally in the case of SMEs, to abusive practices in the sense of Article 82 EC.

Quantification of appreciability: presumptions

The Guidelines extend beyond the Court's existing case law and innovate by **2.49**. quantifying the notion of appreciability. They do this by creating two rebuttable presumptions, one negative and one positive. By the creation of the negative presumption, the Commission seeks to establish an across-the-board so-called NAAT rule ('non-appreciable affectation of trade rule'), in addition to that applicable to SMEs. Inversely, by means of the positive presumption, it seeks to identify those agreements which are presumed to appreciably affect inter-State trade.

Quantification of appreciability: negative presumption

The negative presumption does not apply to abuses in the sense of Article 82 **2.50**. EC, but only to agreements.

---

[31] Paras 2.125–2.136.
[32] Commission Notice on agreements of minor importance which do not appreciably restrict competition under Article 81(1) of the Treaty establishing the European Community [2001] OJ C368/13 (hereafter '*De Minimis* Notice').   [33] [2003] OJ L124/36.
[34] Recommendation's Annex [2003] OJ L124/36, Title 1, Art 1.
[35] Guidelines on the effect on trade concept, para 50.

2.51. According to the negative rebuttable presumption, the NAAT rule will apply to the vertical agreements if both of the following conditions are fulfilled:

— the aggregate market share of the parties on any relevant market within the Community affected by the agreement does not exceed 5%; and

— the aggregate Community turnover during the previous financial year of the supplier in the products covered by the agreement does not exceed € 40 million.

2.52. For vertical agreements, the aggregate annual Community turnover is, as stated above, the turnover of the supplier. However, for purchase agreements concluded between a buyer and several suppliers, the relevant turnover is the buyer's combined purchases of the contract products.[36] Where a supplier has concluded a network of agreements with different distributors, sales made through the entire network must be taken into account in order to calculate the relevant market share.[37]

2.53. In line with the Guidelines on the effect on trade concept (paragraphs 54–5), the threshold of € 40 million must be calculated on the basis of total Community sales, excluding tax, during the previous financial year by the undertakings concerned, of the products covered by the agreement (the contract products). Sales between entities which form part of the same undertaking are excluded.[38] The market share on the relevant product and geographic markets[39] must be calculated on the basis of sales or purchase value data (the latter in the case where the buyer's purchases are the relevant reference point). If value data are not available, estimates based on other reliable market information (including volume data) may be used instead.

2.54. The 'safe harbour' created by the negative presumption continues to apply, much in the same way as Regulations 2790/99 and 1400/2002 do,[40] where during two successive calendar years the turnover and market share thresholds are not exceeded by more than a given limit. In the case of the Guidelines, the turnover may not be exceeded by more than 10% (hence, the supplier's turnover may be € 44 million at most), or the market share by more than 2 percentage points (hence, the parties' combined market share may be 7% at most).[41]

2.55. The Commission will apply the negative presumption to all agreements within the meaning of Article 81(1) EC, irrespective of the nature of the restrictions

---

[36] ibid, para 52.   [37] ibid, para 56.
[38] The term 'undertakings concerned' must be understood in the sense of para 12.2 of the *De Minimis* Notice; see Guidelines on the effect on trade concept, footnote 39.
[39] On these concepts, see paras 2.220–2.247 below.
[40] See respectively, paras 2.212 and 11.66 *infine*.
[41] Guidelines on the effect on trade concept, para 52.

contained in the agreement, including restrictions that have been identified as hardcore restrictions in block exemption regulations. This is a logical extension of the fact that the Court has ruled on several occasions that even an agreement which contains hardcore restrictions (eg an agreement imposing absolute territorial protection) escapes the prohibition laid down in Article 81(1) EC if it only affects inter-State trade in an insignificant way, regard being had to the weak position of the persons concerned on the market of the products in question.[42]

2.56. Practically speaking, the Commission will not normally initiate proceedings (either upon application or upon its own initiative) in respect of agreements qualifying for the NAAT rule. If it does do so, because it has been shown that in spite of the presumption, trade between the Member States is nonetheless appreciably affected, it will not impose fines where the undertakings concerned have assumed in good faith that they were covered by the presumption.[43]

2.57. As regards the instances in which trade may be appreciably affected, even though the NAAT rule is complied with, the Guidelines on the effect on trade concept offer at least two examples: first, where it concerns an agreement which by its very nature is capable of affecting trade; second, where the agreement forms part of a parallel network of agreements which, when taken as a whole, may appreciably affect trade.[44]

Quantification of appreciability: positive presumption

2.58. The Guidelines also create a positive presumption that an agreement is capable of appreciably affecting inter-State trade where the following conditions are met:

— the agreement is, by its very nature, capable of affecting inter-State trade;[45] and
— the aggregate Community turnover during the previous financial year of the undertakings concerned in the products covered by the agreement exceeds € 40 million; or
— the aggregate market share of the parties on any relevant market within the Community affected by the agreement exceeds 5%,

unless the agreement covers only part of a Member State.[46]

---

[42] Case 5/69 *Völk v Vervaecke* [1969] ECR 295, para 7; Joined Cases 100/80 to 103/80 *Musique Diffusion Française and others v Commission* [1983] ECR 1825, para 85; Case C–306/96 *Javico* [1998] ECR I–1983, para 17; Case T–119/02 *Royal Philips Electronics NV v Commission* [2003] ECR II–1433; and Case T–114/02 *BaByLiss v Commission* [2003] ECR II–1279, para 423.   [43] Guidelines on the effect on trade concept, para 50.
[44] ibid, para 49.   [45] For a list, see para 2.40 above.
[46] Guidelines on the effect on trade concept, para 53.

Case-by-case assessment

2.59. Just because an agreement does not comply with the criteria of the negative presumption does not mean that it will automatically be considered as an agreement capable of appreciably affecting inter-State trade. A case-by-case analysis is required to determine that this is actually the case.[47]

(4) *Summary overview of the effect of vertical agreements on inter-State trade*

2.60. The following criteria can be isolated in order to determine whether or not a vertical agreement may appreciably affect inter-State trade in the sense of Article 81(1) EC:

— As a rule, vertical agreements concluded between SMEs with locally based business or with business which is, at most, regional will not appreciably affect inter-State trade.

— The same rule applies to vertical agreements concluded between SMEs with cross-border business and between companies which are not SMEs, but remain within the thresholds of the NAAT rule. To be on the safe side, an additional check as to whether there are any special circumstances which may lead to the conclusion that inter-State trade is appreciably affected even though the NAAT rule is complied with is useful in these cases. Special circumstances may, for example, be that it concerns an agreement which by its very nature is capable of affecting trade (eg because it concerns imports or exports or covers several Member States) or that the agreement forms part of a parallel network of agreements which, when taken as a whole, appreciably affects trade.

— If the criteria laid out in the NAAT rule are exceeded, the first question will be whether the vertical agreement concerned is covered by the positive presumption:

• if it is, then the burden of proof that EC competition law does not apply because the agreement is not of the kind to appreciably affect inter-State trade lies with the parties to the agreement;

• if it is not, then the parties will have to assess themselves in good faith, on the basis of an analysis of the type of agreement as well as the restrictions of competition it contains, whether or not their agreement is covered by EC competition law because it is capable of appreciably affecting inter-State trade.

---

[47] ibid, para 51.

D. Second Question: Vertical Agreements

(1) Introduction

Article 81(1) EC and vertical agreements

Since the Court's judgments in the 1966 *Société Technique Minière v Machinenbau*   **2.61**.
Ulm[48] and *Consten and Grundig*[49] cases,[50] it is no longer disputed that vertical
agreements may come within the scope of the prohibition of Article 81(1) EC. In
Consten and Grundig, the applicants still submitted that the prohibition in Article
81(1) EC applied only to so-called horizontal agreements. The Italian Government,
intervening in support of Consten and Grundig, argued furthermore that sole
distributorship contracts did not constitute 'agreements between undertakings'
within the meaning of that provision, since the parties were not on an equal footing.
With regard to these contracts, freedom of competition could, according to the
opinion of the Italian Government, only be protected by virtue of Article 82 EC.

The Court rejected these arguments and upheld the possibility for Article 81(1)   **2.62**.
EC to apply to vertical agreements. The Court reasoned as follows:

— Article 81 EC refers in a general way to all agreements that distort competition within the common market and does not lay down any distinction
 between those made between competitors operating at the same level in
 the economic process or those made between non-competing economic
 operators. In *Société Technique Minière v Maschinebau Ulm*, the Court
 adopted the same stance in stating that:

> In order to fall within this prohibition, an agreement must have been made
> between undertakings. Article [81(1)] makes no distinction as to whether the
> parties are at the same level in the economy (so-called 'horizontal' agreements),
> or at different levels (so-called 'vertical' agreements). Therefore an agreement
> containing a clause 'granting an exclusive right of sale' may fulfil this condition.[51]

— The possible application of Article 81(1) EC to a sole distributorship contract
 cannot be excluded merely because the supplier and the distributor are not
 competitors *inter se* and are not on an equal footing. Not only are agreements
 limiting competition between the parties covered by Article 81(1) EC, but also
 agreements which may prevent or restrict the competition between one of them
 and third parties. For this purpose, it is irrelevant whether or not the parties to
 the agreement are on an equal footing with regard to their position and function
 in the economy. This applies all the more since, by such an agreement the parties
 could, by preventing or limiting the competition of third parties in respect of the

---

[48] Case 56/65 *Société Technique Minière v Machinenbau Ulm* [1966] ECR 235.
[49] Joined Cases 56 and 58/64 *Consten and Grundig v Commission* [1966] ECR 339–40.
[50] More recently confirmed by eg Case 306/96 *Javico* [1998] ECR I–1983, para 11.
[51] Case 56/65 *Société Technique Minière v Maschinebau Ulm* [1966] ECR 235, 248.

products, seek to create or obtain for themselves, an unjustified advantage at the expense of the consumer or user, contrary to the general aims of Article 81 EC.
— An agreement between a producer and a distributor could re-establish national divisions in trade between Member States and, in so doing, frustrate the most fundamental objectives of the EC. The Treaty, which seeks to achieve the opposite of this and in several of its provisions displays a stern attitude with regard to the reappearance of trade barriers, could not allow undertakings to re-establish such barriers. Article 81 EC is designed therefore to pursue this aim, even in the case of agreements between undertakings situated at different levels within the economic process.

It is therefore possible that, without involving an abuse of a dominant position, an agreement between economic operators at different levels, may affect trade between Member States and at the same time have as its object or its effect the prevention, restriction, or distortion of competition, and therefore be caught by the prohibition of Article 81(1) EC. So, while the 'horizontal' or 'vertical' nature of the agreement may be relevant for the purposes of the analysis to be conducted under Article 81 EC, it is irrelevant for the application of Article 81 EC as such.

Regulation 2790/99 and vertical agreements

2.63. Unlike the other definitions in Regulation 2790/99, the definition of 'vertical agreement' is to be found in Article 2(1) and not in Article 1. Article 2(1) provides that pursuant to Article 81(3) EC and subject to the provisions of Regulation 2790/99, Article 81(1) EC shall not apply:

> to agreements or concerted practices entered into between two or more undertakings each of which operates, for the purposes of the agreement, at a different level of the production or distribution chain, and relating to the conditions under which the parties may purchase, sell or resell certain goods or services.

2.64. This definition contains four components and all four must be present in order to bring Regulation 2790/99 into play:

— Two of the components are closely related to the application of Article 81(1) EC in general, namely that:
  (i) Regulation 2790/99 applies both to agreements and concerted practices (see paragraphs 2.65–2.90); and
  (ii) the agreement or concerted practice must be between two or more undertakings (see paragraphs 2.91–2.111).
— The other two components apply specifically to vertical relationships, namely that:
  (iii) for purposes of the agreement, the undertakings involved must operate at a different level of the production or distribution chain (see paragraphs 2.112–2.114); and

(iv) the agreement or concerted practice must relate to the conditions under which the parties may purchase, sell or resell certain goods or services (see paragraphs 2.115–2.122).

(2) *First component: agreements and concerted practices*

General

In respect of most vertical restraints, there is no need for discussion that they are **2.65**. included in an agreement. For instance, a formalized distribution agreement is a textbook example of a vertical agreement. In such a case the first component of the second question will not require any in-depth analysis at all. It is only in more complex scenarios that the first component of the second question may require a more detailed review; for example, when the vertical co-operation is not formalized or when certain conduct could be characterized as unilateral (see paragraphs 2.66–2.85). In addition it should also be noted that Regulation 2790/99, like Article 81 EC, applies not only to agreements but also to concerted practices, which are further discussed in paragraphs 2.86–2.90.

Agreements

Broad interpretation of the concept 'agreement'

Article 81 EC does not apply to unilateral measures of undertakings. Unilateral **2.66**. measures, including those in a vertical relationship, may be caught by Article 82 EC on the condition that the existence of a dominant position, as well as an abuse, is demonstrated. When read in combination, Articles 81 and 82 EC therefore do not prohibit the unilateral measures of a supplier that does not have a dominant position. The convergence theory contained in Article 3 of Regulation 1/2003 does not exclude the prohibition of such unilateral measures on the basis of national competition law.

In an attempt to fill this 'lacuna', the Community institutions have interpreted **2.67**. Articles 81 and 82 EC in a broad manner. As part of this practice, the concept 'agreement' stated in Article 81(1) EC has been construed widely. According to the Court of First Instance, it is for instance sufficient for the purposes of Article 81(1) EC that the undertakings in question have expressed their joint intention to conduct themselves on the market in a specific way.[52] In other words, the concept of agreement centres on the existence of a concurrence of wills between at least two parties. In this respect, as the Commission observed in *Nintendo*, the Court 'does not make a distinction between horizontal and vertical infringements'.[53]

---

[52] Case T–41/96 *Bayer AG v Commission* [2000] ECR II–3383, para 67 (with references); and Case T–325/01 *DaimlerChrysler AG v Commission*, not yet published, para 83.

[53] *Nintendo* [2003] OJ L255/33, para 323.

Concurrence of wills— irrelevance of the form of the agreement

2.68. In its turn, the term concurrence of wills has also been widely drawn. The Court of First Instance has confirmed that the form in which the concurrence of wills is actually manifested is unimportant, as long as it constitutes the faithful expression of the parties' common intention.[54] For its part, the Commission considers that an agreement can be said to exist:

> when the parties adhere to a common plan which limits or is likely to limit their individual commercial conduct by determining the lines of their mutual action or abstention from action in the market. The agreement need not be made in writing, no formalities are necessary, and no contractual penalties or enforcement measures are required. The fact of agreement may be express or implicit in the behaviour of the parties.[55]

Concurrence of wills—irrelevance of implementation

2.69. The non-implementation of an agreement which restricts competition is not sufficient to conclude that no such agreement exists.[56]

Concurrence of wills—agreement by tacit acquiescence

2.70. Roughly speaking, from the 1979 *BMW Belgium* case onwards,[57] the Court of Justice has held that measures which are adopted or imposed in an apparently unilateral manner can also constitute an agreement within the meaning of Article 81(1) EC. The Court has done this by distinguishing between those instances in which an undertaking has adopted a genuinely unilateral measure and those in which the unilateral character of the measure is merely apparent. Whilst the former measures are outside of the scope of Article 81(1) EC because the undertaking acts without the express or implied participation of another undertaking, the latter measures are deemed to reveal an agreement between

---

[54] eg Case T–41/96 *Bayer AG v Commission* [2000] ECR II–3383, para 69; Case T–141/89 *Tréfileurope Sales Sarl v Commission* [1995] ECR II–791, para 96; Case T–9/99 *HFB and others v Commission* [2002] ECR II–1487, para 200; and Case T–56/02 *Bayerische Hypo- und Vereinsbank* [2004] OJ C314/14, para 61.   [55] eg *Nintendo* [2003] OJ L255/33, para 247.

[56] Case T–67/01 *JCB Service v Commission* [2004] OJ C85/23, para 103; Case 86/82 *Hasselblad v Commission* [1984] ECR 883, para 46; Joined Cases C–89/85, C–104/85, C–114/85, C–116/85, C–117/85, and C–125/85 to C–129/85 *Ahlström Osakeyhtiö and others v Commission* [1993] ECR I–1307, para 175; and Case T–77/92 *Parker Pen v Commission* [1994] ECR II–549, para 55. In a like manner, a party to an agreement that infringes Art 81 EC does not cease to be a party to that agreement merely because its subsequent behaviour is not in all respects in line with the anti-competitive agreement; eg Case T–9/89 *Hüls v Commission* [1992] ECR II–499, paras 126–7.

[57] Joined Cases 32/78, 36/78 to 82/78 *BMW Belgium and others v Commission* [1979] ECR 2435, paras 28–30. The case law has been confirmed in later cases; eg Case 107/82 *AEG v Commission* [1983] ECR 3151, para 38; Joined Cases 25 and 26/84 *Ford-Werke and Ford of Europe Inc v Commission* [1985] ECR 2575, para 21; Case T–43/92, *Dunlop Slazenger v Commission* [1994] ECR II–441, para 54; and Case T–325/01 *DaimlerChrysler AG v Commission*, not yet published, para 84.

undertakings and may fall within the scope of Article 81(1) EC.[58] Specifically, in the context of vertical agreements, it concerns practices and measures in restraint of competition which, although they are apparently adopted uni-laterally by the manufacturer within the context of its contractual relations with its dealers, nevertheless receive at least the tacit acquiescence of those dealers.[59]

Where, in the course of an investigation, the Commission or an NCA is of the opinion that unilateral conduct in reality forms the basis of an agreement between undertakings, it lies with the Commission or the NCA to establish that there is, at the very least, tacit acquiescence.[60] This is in line with Article 2 of Regulation 1/2003, which provides that the burden of proving an infringement of the competition rules rests with the party or authority alleging the infringement.[61] **2.71**.

In 2003–4, the Community judiciary was, in a number of cases, called to rule on the requisite legal standard in order to establish the existence of tacit acquiescence in a vertical relationship. In this respect, reference is made in particular to *Volkswagen I* (Court of Justice),[62] *Volkswagen II* (Court of First Instance),[63] as well as to *Bayer (Adalat)* (Court of Justice).[64] **2.72**.

Volkswagen I and II

In *Volkswagen I*, the Court of Justice had to rule on an appeal introduced by Volkswagen against a judgment of the Court of First Instance partially upholding a Commission decision. The decision in question imposed a fine on Volkswagen for having entered into agreements with the Italian dealers in its distribution network to prohibit or restrict re-exports, ie sales to final consumers coming from another Member State.[65] According to Volkswagen, the supply quotas which the dealership contracts provided for the Italian market did not constitute agreements for the purposes of Article 81(1) EC. Under the contracts, distributors were free to sell the vehicles delivered by Volkswagen to **2.73**.

---

[58] Case T–41/96 *Bayer AG v Commission* [2000] ECR II–3383, paras 70–1 (with references).
[59] ibid.
[60] Joined Cases 32/78, 36/78 to 82/78 *BMW Belgium and others v Commission* [1979] ECR 2435, paras 28–30; Case 107/82 *AEG v Commission* [1983] ECR 3151, para 38; Joined Cases 25 and 26/82 *Ford-Werke and Ford of Europe Inc v Commission* [1985] ECR 2575, para 21; Case C–277/87 *Sandoz Prodotti Farmaceutici v Commission* [1990] ECR I–45, paras 7–12; Case T–41/96 *Bayer v Commission* [2000] ECR II–3383, para 72; and Case T–208/01 *Volkswagen AG v Commission* [2003] ECR II–5141, para 36.
[61] As confirmed in Joined Cases C–204/00P, C–205/00P, C–211/00P, C–213/00P, C–217/00P, and C–219/00P *Aalborg Portland v Commission* [2004] ECR I–123, paras 78 and 79.
[62] Case C–338/00P *Volkswagen AG v Commission* [2003] ECR I–9189.
[63] Case T–208/01 *Volkswagen AG v Commission* [2003] ECR II–5141.
[64] Joined Cases C–2/01P and C–3/01P *Adalat* [2004] ECR I–23. On *Volkswagen* and *Adalat*, see also SB Völcker, 'Developments in EC Competition Law in 2003: An Overview' [2004] CML Rev 1031–3; and Jones and Sufrin (n 2 above) 138–46.   [65] *Volkswagen* [1998] OJ L124/60.

both foreign end-users and to other dealers. Accordingly, the restrictions were not desired by dealers because they rejected reductions in supplies and such restrictions had, in so far as they existed, the character of a unilateral measure falling outside the scope of Article 81(1) EC.[66]

2.74. The Court of Justice did not accept these arguments. It found that the limitation on re-exports, which was the objective that was pursued by Volkswagen, also resulted from the business conduct of the Italian dealers, as influenced by Volkswagen. Furthermore, the means employed in order to arrive at the limitation of re-exports, and in particular the restricted supply of vehicles, resulted from clauses in the dealership contract and therefore received the agreement of the dealers.[67]

2.75. In *Volkswagen II*, similar questions arose as to the concept of 'agreement' in Article 81(1) EC. The difference between this and *Volkswagen I* was that in *Volkswagen II*, the Court of First Instance was not asked to rule on clauses in the dealership contracts and their consequences, but on a number of circulars issued by Volkswagen subsequent to the signing of the dealership contracts. Specifically, in a number of circulars, Volkswagen had urged its German dealers to maintain a price discipline for the new VW Passat model and hence not to offer it for sale below the recommended retail price. Following an investigation, the Commission had fined Volkswagen for retail price maintenance for the VW Passat on the German market.[68] The Court of First Instance was called upon to rule on the legality of the Commission's decision. The Commission was of the opinion that the admission to a distribution network implied that a dealer, either explicitly or implicitly, accepted the distribution policy of the manufacturer concerned. Therefore, it considered that the circulars had become part and parcel of the agreements between Volkswagen and its authorized dealers. As a result they had to be regarded as part of a set of continuous business relations based on an existing general agreement, namely the dealer agreement. Opposing this, Volkswagen argued that the measures objected to were unilateral actions which were outside the scope of Article 81(1) EC.

2.76. In its judgment, the Court of First Instance concurred with Volkswagen. It did not accept the Commission's view that a dealer who signed a dealership agreement which complies with competition law must be deemed, upon and by such signature, to have accepted in advance a later unlawful variation of that contract. The Court of First Instance therefore refuted that acquiescence, and hence an agreement on unlawful variations, can be regarded as having been established as a matter of principle by the mere fact that a dealer has entered a distribution network.[69] It

---

[66] Case C–338/00P *Volkswagen AG v Commission* [2003] ECR I–9189, paras 52–5.
[67] ibid, para 67.   [68] *Volkswagen* [2001] OJ L262/14.
[69] Case T–208/01 *Volkswagen AG v Commission* [2003] ECR II–5141, paras 43–45 and 55.

annulled the Commission's decision. The Commission has appealed the Court of First Instance's judgment (Case C-74/04P) and it argues that the Court of First Instance overlooked the peculiarities of selective distribution systems, which are based upon a framework agreement. The fact that such an agreement is not itself unlawful at a certain time does not preclude it from becoming so at a later date. According to the Commission, the dealer's general interest is in retaining their position as members of the distribution system. Accordingly, the Commission puts forward the view that it cannot be assumed that, upon the conclusion of the contract, they systematically reject all later requirements which may prove to be unlawful.

Bayer (Adalat)

In *Bayer*, the Court of First Instance was called upon to pronounce itself on **2.77.** appeal on the legality of a Commission decision which fined Bayer for an overt change in its supply policy whereby it no longer met orders placed by Spanish and French wholesalers for a pharmaceutical product called 'Adalat'. The reason for the change of supply policy was that in the period between 1989 and 1993 the prices charged for Adalat in France and Spain were about 40% lower than those charged in the United Kingdom. This led to significant parallel exports of Adalat from Spanish and French wholesalers to the United Kingdom. As a result these exports caused a significant loss of turnover for Bayer's British subsidiary.

Bayer applied to the Court of First Instance to annul the Commission decision **2.78.** on the ground that the allegedly infringing conduct was, in fact, unilateral conduct: In the absence of any agreement between itself and its wholesalers, relating to the export of Adalat to the United Kingdom, the conduct did not fall within the scope of Article 81(1) EC. Bayer contended that it had adopted a unilateral policy of limited delivery in order to make parallel exports more difficult, and that, far from agreeing to such a policy, the wholesalers had opposed it. Accordingly, the requisite 'concurrence of wills' was plainly lacking, and without such concurrence, Article 81(1) EC could not apply.

The Commission, on the other hand, contended that there was an agreement **2.79.** between Bayer and the Spanish and French wholesalers in relation to the export of Adalat to other Member States. Its case was that Bayer's delivery policy amounted to an export ban, to which the wholesalers had consented, in the knowledge that if they did not do so their orders would be further restricted. According to the Commission, the actions of the wholesalers showed that they had aligned their own conduct in relation to the export ban because they limited their orders from Bayer purely to their domestic requirements. Supplies intended for exports were obtained from elsewhere (for example, from non-supervised wholesalers).

2.80. Based on the facts of the case, the Court of First Instance did not accept the Commission's view. According to it, the Commission had not proved to the requisite legal standard:

    (i) that Bayer imposed an export ban on its wholesalers, or

    (ii) that Bayer established a systematic monitoring of the actual final destination of the packets of Adalat supplied after the adoption of its new supply policy, or

    (iii) that Bayer applied a policy of threats and penalties against exporting wholesalers, or

    (iv) that it made supplies of that product conditional upon compliance with the alleged export ban.

In the Court of First Instance's view, the documents reproduced in the contested Commission decision also did not show that Bayer sought to obtain any form of agreement from the wholesalers concerning the implementation of its policy designed to reduce parallel imports.[70]

2.81. On appeal, the Court of Justice, sitting in plenary session, confirmed the Court of First Instance's judgment and thereby confirmed that, under the given circumstances no agreement in the sense of Article 81(1) EC could exist. The Court of Justice's ruling in *Bayer* is innovative to the extent that, on the specific issue of the existence of an agreement in the sense of Article 81(1) EC, it ruled that for an agreement to be capable of being regarded as having been concluded by tacit acceptance:

> it is necessary that the manifestation of the wish of one of the contracting parties to achieve an anti-competitive goal must constitute an invitation to the other party, whether express or implied, to fulfil that goal jointly, and that applies all the more where . . . such an agreement is not at first sight in the interest of the other party, namely the wholesalers.[71]

2.82. On previous occasions, the Court of Justice had already touched upon what it considers to be an express or implied invitation. In *Sandoz*, for instance, the Court of Justice confirmed the Commission's view that if a customer continues to place orders for products and, without protest, pays the prices indicated on the invoices, where those invoices bear the words 'Export Prohibited', this constitutes tacit acquiescence on the part of the customer. Specifically, the Court of Justice agreed that the existence of a prohibited agreement does not rest on the simple fact that a customer continues to obtain supplies from a manufacturer which had shown its intention to prevent exports, but on the fact that an export ban had been imposed by the manufacturer and tacitly accepted

---

[70] Case T–41/96 *Bayer v Commission* [2000] ECR II–3383, paras 109–10. On the importance of the case, see R Whish, *Competition Law* (5th edn, LexisNexis, 2005) 106.

[71] Joined Cases C–2/01P and C–3/01P *Adalat* [2004] ECR I–23, para 102.

by the wholesalers.[72] In *Bayer*, a similar situation did not occur because Bayer's change of supply policy could be carried out without the co-operation of the wholesalers. The fact that Bayer's policy had the same effect on the national market as an export restriction could not, in the Court of Justice's view, lead to any other result: A hindrance to parallel imports is not, in and of itself, sufficient to demonstrate the existence of an agreement in the sense of Article 81(1) EC.[73]

Summary

As stated at the beginning of this section, the question of whether or not there is an **2.83.** agreement in the sense of Article 81 EC will, in most cases, raise no particular issues. In the bulk of cases, questions on the applicability of the block exemption under Regulation 2790/99 will be in respect of formalized agreements (typically distribution, supply, or purchase agreements) between two or more undertakings.

Vertical agreements which are not formalized will also be able to benefit from **2.84.** the block exemption under Regulation 2790/99 as long as there is a concurrence of wills, which can take the form of tacit acquiescence.

Finally, if tacit acquiescence is not in the interest of the buyer, what can be **2.85.** referred to as the 'invitation theory' must be applied. The mere fact that a measure adopted by an undertaking falls within the context of on-going business relations is not sufficient.[74] Instead, it is a necessary prerequisite for an agreement to exist in the sense of Article 81 EC, that there has been an invitation from the side of the other party or parties to achieve an anti-competitive goal. In the absence of such an invitation, the measures concerned are unilateral and are therefore outside the scope of Article 81 EC.

Concerted practice

In addition to agreements, Article 2(1) of Regulation 2790/99 also encompasses **2.86.** concerted practices. The preamble (paragraph 3) of Regulation 2790/99 states: 'the term "vertical agreements" includes the corresponding concerted practices'.

Definition

According to the Court of Justice, a concerted practice refers to: **2.87.**

> a form of co-ordination between undertakings which knowingly substitutes for the risks of competition practical co-operation between them, without however having been taken to a stage where an agreement properly so-called has been concluded.[75]

---

[72] Case 277/87 *Sandoz Prodotti Farmaceutici SpA v Commission* [1990] ECR I–45.

[73] Joined Cases C–2/01P and C–3/01P *Adalat* [2004] ECR I–23, para 110. For a comment, see C Brown, '*Bayer v Commission*: the ECJ Agrees' [2004] ECLR 386.

[74] Guidelines on the application of Article 81(3) of the Treaty [2004] OJ C101/97, para 15 (hereafter 'Guidelines on the application of Art 81(3) EC').

[75] Case C–199/92P *Hüls AG v Commission* [1999] ECR I–4287, para 158 (with reference to the Court of Justice's judgment *par excellence* on concerted practices, namely Joined Cases 40/73

2.88. According to the Court of Justice, the criteria of 'co-ordination' and 'co-operation' must be understood in the light of the concept inherent in the Treaty's competition provisions, namely that each undertaking must independently determine the policy which it intends to adopt on the market. This does not deprive undertakings of the right to adapt themselves intelligently to the existing or anticipated conduct of their competitors. However, it does preclude any direct or indirect contact that occurs between them in order to influence the conduct on the market of an actual or potential competitor or to disclose to such a competitor the course of conduct which they themselves have decided to adopt or are contemplating adopting on the market, where the object or effect of such a contact is to create conditions of competition which do not correspond to the normal conditions of the market in question.[76]

Application to vertical relations

2.89. In *Pioneer*, the Court of Justice confirmed that a concerted practice can exist in the vertical relation between a manufacturer and its distributors.[77] Even though in *Pioneer* the concerted practices had anti-competitive effects, the Court of Justice confirmed that a concerted practice may still be caught by Article 81(1) EC in the absence of anti-competitive effects on the market. Like agreements between undertakings, concerted practices are prohibited, regardless of their effect, when they have an anti-competitive object.[78]

2.90. The above confirms once more that the absence of a formal agreement is irrelevant for the purposes of the application of Article 81(1) EC and hence Regulation 2790/99. The Regulation also applies to non-formalized conduct of undertakings implementing a practice which prevents, restricts, or distorts competition. Obviously this is a double-edged sword. On the one hand, parties will be able to enjoy the benefit of the block exemption for non-formalized practices which comply with Regulation 2790/99; whilst on the other hand they may lose the benefit of the block exemption for an infringement of a hardcore restriction,[79] even though the formalized agreement does not contain such a

---

to 48/73, 50/73, 54/73 to 56/73, 111/73, 113/73, and 114/73 *Suiker Unie and others v Commission* [1975] ECR 1663, para 26).

[76] eg Case C–199/92P *Hüls AG v Commission* [1999] ECR I–4287, paras 159–60 (with references); Cases T–5/00 and T–6/00 *Nederlandse Federatieve Vereniging voor de Groothandel op Elektrotechnisch Gebied* [2003] ECR II–5761, para 286 (with references); and *PO/Interbrew and Alken-Maes* (COMP/M3289) [2003] OJ L200/1, para 220 (with reference to case law).

[77] Case 100/80 *Musique Diffusion Française v Commission* [1983] ECR 1825, paras 72–80.

[78] Case C–199/92P *Hüls AG v Commission* [1999] ECR I–4287, paras 163–5; for the Court of First Instance, Cases T–5/00 and T–6/00 *Nederlandse Federatieve Vereniging voor de Groothandel op Elektrotechnisch Gebied* [2003] ECR II–5761, para 275 (with references to Case C– 219/95 P *Ferriere Nord v Commission* [1997] ECR I–4411, paras 14 and 15; and Case C–235/92 P *Montecatini v Commission* [1999] ECR I–4539, para 122).

[79] On hardcore restrictions under Reg 2790/99, see Ch 5 below.

restriction. For example, the absence of, say, a vertical price-fixing clause in a distribution agreement does not necessarily safeguard the application of the block exemption if there is a concerted practice to charge fixed prices.

(3) Second component: two or more undertakings

General

Regulation 2790/99 only applies to vertical agreements concluded between two **2.91**. or more undertakings. In respect of this there are two issues which must be clarified: first, the concept of 'undertaking' (see paragraphs 2.92–2.103) and, second, the fact that it must concern two or more independent undertakings and that intra-group agreements are therefore excluded from the scope of application of the Regulation (see paragraphs 2.105–2.111).

The concept of 'undertaking'[80]

Definition

The concept of 'undertaking' is not defined in the EC Treaty. In accordance with **2.92**. the settled case law, an undertaking for the purposes of EC competition law means 'any entity engaged in an economic activity, regardless of its legal status and the way in which it is financed'.[81] The Court of First Instance put it thus:

> Article 81(1) of the Treaty is aimed at economic units which consist of a unitary organisation of personal, tangible and intangible elements, which pursues a specific economic aim on a long-term basis and can contribute to the commission of an infringement of the kind referred to in that provision.[82]

In its Recommendation on the definition of micro, small and medium-sized **2.93**. enterprises, the Commission defined the concept 'enterprise',[83] parallel to that of an 'undertaking', as follows:

> An enterprise is considered to be any entity engaged in an economic activity, irrespective of its legal form. This includes, in particular, self-employed persons

---

[80] The concept is dealt with extensively in V Louri, ' "Undertaking" as a Jurisdictional Element for the Application of EC Competition Rules' [2002] LIEI 143.

[81] eg Case C–41/90 *Höfner v Macrotron* [1991] ECR I–1979, para 21; Joined Cases C–159/91 and C–160/91 *Poucet and Pistre* [1993] ECR I–637, para 17; Case C–244/94 *Fédération française des sociétés d'assurances* [1995] ECR I–4013, para 14; Case C–55/96 *Job Centre* [1997] ECR I–7119, para 21; and Case C–309/99 *Wouters* [2002] ECR I–1577, para 46.

[82] Case T–9/99 *HFB and others v Commission* [2002] ECR II–1487, para 54; Case T–352/94 *Mo Och Domsjö AB v Commission* [1998] ECR II–1989, para 87; and Case T–11/89 *Shell v Commission* [1992] ECR II–757, para 311. For the Commission, eg *Nintendo* [2003] OJ L255/33, para 243.

[83] 'Entreprise' is also the concept used in the French version of the EC Treaty.

and family businesses engaged in craft or other activities, and partnerships or associations regularly engaged in an economic activity.[84]

Hence, the assessment whether or not a given entity or person qualifies as an undertaking in the sense of Article 81 EC is determined by the application of a functional test, ie whether or not the entity or person performs an economic activity.

The performance of an economic activity

2.94. The performance of an economic activity in the context of the EC competition rules is defined by reference to the entity's output: an 'economic activity' is 'any activity consisting of offering goods and services on a given market'.[85]

2.95. For that reason agreements with final consumers are only excluded from the scope of Article 81(1) EC if the final consumers in question do not operate as an undertaking.[86] If a company purchases products for which it is the final consumer (eg lubricants for production machinery), but also offers goods on the market, then the agreement with its supplier(s) will be covered by Article 81(1) EC if it is restrictive of competition. As opposed to this, agreements with final consumers who buy goods for their own private consumption but who do not offer goods or services on a given market (and hence are not undertakings) are agreements outside the scope of Article 81(1) EC.

2.96. In line with the above considerations, the Court of First Instance has excluded the application of the competition rules to an organization which purchases goods—even if in great quantity—which are not for the purpose of offering goods and services as part of an economic activity, but in order to use them in the context of a different activity, such as their use for a purely social nature.[87] Services such as national education systems are also excluded from the application of the EC competition rules, as the State, in establishing and maintaining such a system, is not seeking to engage in a gainful activity but is fulfilling its duty towards its own population in the social, cultural and educational fields.[88]

---

[84] Commission Recommendation (EC) No 2003/61 of 6 May 2003 concerning the definition of micro, small and medium-sized enterprises [2003] OJ L124/36.

[85] eg Case T–128/98 *Aéroports de Paris v Commission* [2000] ECR II–3929, para 107; Case C–82/01 *Aéroports de Paris v Commission* [2002] ECR I–9297, para 75; and Case T–319/99 *Fenin v Commission* [2003] ECR II–357, para 35. Winterstein puts it thus: 'On the face of it, the Court considers that an activity is of an economic nature if it faces actual or potential competition by private companies, thus establishing a strong presumption for the economic character of any activity', A Winterstein, 'Nailing the Jellyfish: Social Security and Competition Law' [1999] ECLR 324 (also available at http://europa.eu.int/comm/competition/speeches/text/sp2001_029_en.pdf). [86] This is stated in so many words in the Guidelines, para 24.

[87] Case T–319/99 *Fenin v Commission* [2003] ECR II–357, para 37.

[88] Case 263/86 *Belgian State v Humbel* [1988] ECR I–5365, para 18.

No need for legal incorporation

It follows from the above that the concept of 'undertaking' does not centre on **2.97**. organizational features, such as legal status. Therefore, not only companies, but also self-employed persons (eg lawyers)[89] and associations, insofar as their own activities or those of the undertakings which belong to them are intended to produce the results to which Article 81 EC refers,[90] can be undertakings for the purposes of EC competition law. The application of EC competition law rules in general, and Regulation 2790/99 in particular, to commercial agents is discussed in more detail below.[91]

Public bodies

Public bodies are not always necessarily excluded from the scope of the concept **2.98**. of 'undertaking'. In cases involving public bodies, a distinction must be drawn between the State acting in the exercise of its official authority and the State carrying out economic activities.

Public bodies in the exercise of official authority (*'imperium'*). If a public **2.99**. body acts in the exercise of official authority, the activity concerned forms part of the essential functions of the State. Such activity is therefore not considered to be subject to EC competition law for lack of an economic nature. Such cases relate to a 'public authority' proper. The Court of Justice has, for example, ruled that the powers relating to the control and supervision of air space are typically those of a public authority,[92] as well as those concerning anti-pollution surveillance and, more generally, the protection of the environment.[93] Other activities that are intrinsically prerogatives of the State are the assurance of internal and external security, the administration of justice, and the conduct of foreign relations.[94]

---

[89] Case C–309/99 *Wouters* [2002] ECR I–1577, para 49. On the other hand, employees are not undertakings when they act in their capacity of employees: Case C–22/98 *Bécu* [2001] ECR I–5665, para 26: 'It must therefore be concluded that the employment relationship which recognised dockers have with the undertakings for which they perform dock work is characterised by the fact that they perform the work in question for and under the direction of each of those undertakings, so that they must be regarded as "workers" within the meaning of Article 48 of the EC Treaty (now, after amendment, Article 39 EC), as interpreted by the case-law of the Court . . . Since they are, for the duration of that relationship, incorporated into the undertakings concerned and thus form an economic unit with each of them, dockers do not therefore in themselves constitute "undertakings" within the meaning of Community competition law'.

[90] Case 71/74 *FRUBO v Commission* [1975] ECR 563, paras 28–32. A summary of the Court's case law on the matter can also be found in the Court's Digest of Community Law, to be consulted (in French) on its website http://curia.eu.int/. It includes case law, for example, on trade unions, professional associations, sporting bodies and trade associations proper. See also Louri (n 80 above) 154–9.   [91] Paras 7.52 *et seq* below.

[92] Case C–364/92 *Eurocontrol* [1994] ECR I–43, para 17.

[93] Case C–343/95 *Diego Calì & Figli* [1997] ECR I–1547, paras 22 and 23.

[94] Communication from the Commission—Services of general interest in Europe [2001] OJ C17/4, para 28.

2.100. **Public bodies engaging in an economic activity.** To the extent that they engage in an economic activity, public bodies are subject to the competition rules. For example, the Court of Justice held that the Federal German employment agency was an undertaking as the service that it provided, employment procurement, was an economic activity.[95] Similarly, it held that the French National Institute for Agricultural Research engaged in an economic activity to the extent that it concluded a series of contracts whose principal subject matter was the marketing and sale to farmers of maize seed developed by the Institute following research activity.[96]

Services of general economic interest

2.101. As opposed to the exercise of *imperium*, which is by definition a non-economic activity, a service of general economic interest is an economic activity with only a relative immunity from the application of EC competition law. Services of general economic interest are services (in sectors such as public transport, tele-communication, postal services, or energy) which the State considers are needed to be provided, even where the market is not sufficiently profitable for the supply of such services. The concern therefore is to ensure that a quality service is provided at an affordable price everywhere and for everyone. These services can be provided either by public undertakings or by private under-takings to which the State has granted special or exclusive rights.

2.102. Pursuant to Article 86(2) EC, the rules on competition apply here in so far as they do not obstruct the performance, in law or in fact, of the particular tasks that are assigned to those undertakings. Article 86(2) EC is an exception and so it must be invoked either by the government or by the undertaking wishing to rely upon it.[97] If an undertaking entrusted with a service of general economic interest is a party to a vertical agreement falling within the material scope of application of Regulation 2790/99, there will of course be no issues regarding the agreement's compatibility with EC competition law rules if the agreement complies with the substantive rules of the Regulation. If it does so, the agreement will benefit from the block exemption. If this is not the case, a self-assessment will have to be performed to demonstrate whether or not an exemption, pursuant to Article 81(3) EC, is possible. Article 86(2) EC may then be relied upon in this context.[98]

Non-undertakings on the basis of the solidarity principle

2.103. In a more recent set of judgments, the Court of Justice has excluded from the application of EC competition law health, pension, and other insurance services

---

[95] Case C–41/90 *Höfner v Macrotron* [1991] ECR I–1979, para 23.
[96] Case 258/78 *Nungesser v Commission* [1982] ECR 2015, para 9.
[97] eg *La Poste* [2002] L120/19, para 95; and *New postal services in Italy* [2001] L63/59, para 30.
[98] J Faull and A Nikpay, *The EC Law of Competition* (OUP, 1999) para 5.155 (with references).

rendered by social security schemes to which affiliation is compulsory. Specifically, it has held that organizations managing health funds are not undertakings for the purposes of Article 81 EC, given (and on condition) that (i) they fulfil an exclusively social function, (ii) their activity is based on the principle of national solidarity, and (iii) they are non-profit-making, the benefits paid out being statutory benefits that bear no relation to the level of the contributions made.[99]

The requirement of more than one undertaking

General

Regulation 2790/99 only applies if at least two independent undertakings are involved and therefore intra-group agreements may fail to meet this test of independence (see paragraphs 2.105–2.110). Regulation 2790/99 does not, however, limit the number of undertakings concerned (see paragraph 2.111).   **2.104.**

Intra-group agreements

Since at least two undertakings must be party to the agreement or concerted practice, Article 81 EC does not, pursuant to what is referred to as 'the single economic entity doctrine',[100] apply in the case of intra-group agreements. As far back as 1964 this was confirmed by the Court of Justice when, in *Consten and Grundig*, it stated: 'The wording of Article [81 EC] causes the prohibition to apply, provided that the other conditions are met, to an agreement between several undertakings. Thus it does not apply where a sole undertaking integrates its own distribution network into its business organization'.[101] In the 1974 *Centrafarm v Sterling Drug* case, the Court of Justice held that Article 81 EC: **2.105.**

> is not concerned with agreements or concerted practices between undertakings belonging to the same concern and having the status of parent company and subsidiary, if the undertakings form an economic unit within which the subsidiary has no real freedom to determine its course of action on the market, and if the agreements or practices are concerned merely with the internal allocation of tasks as between the undertakings.[102]

---

[99] Joined Cases C–159/91 and C–160/91 *Poucet and Pistre* [1993] ECR I–637, paras 18–19; also Case C–218/00 *INAIL* [2002] ECR I–691, paras 31–46 (INAIL has the task of operating, on behalf of the State and under its supervision, a system of compulsory insurance for workers against accidents at work and occupational diseases; the amount of the benefits and of the contributions was, in the last resort, fixed by the State); and Joined Cases C–264/01, C–306/01, C–354/01, and C–355/01 *AOK Bundesverband* [2004] ECR I–2493, paras 45–66 (as regards groups of sickness funds); for a comment, see KPE Lasok, 'When is an Undertaking not an Undertaking?' [2004] ECLR 383. For the same view, but a different conclusion, Case C–244/94 *Fédération française des sociétés d'assurances and others* [1995] ECR I–4013, paras 15–16; and Case C–67/96 *Albany* [1999] ECR I–5751, para 78. Winterstein (n 85 above) discusses this series of cases in detail.
[100] On the single economic entity doctrine, eg Jones and Sufrin (n 2 above) 123.
[101] Joined Cases 56 and 58/64 *Consten and Grundig v Commission* [1966] ECR 339.
[102] Case 15/74 *Centrafarm BV v Sterling Drug Inc* [1974] ECR 1147, para 41.

2.106. This test, which can also be found in *Bodson*,[103] is slightly confusing given the single economic entity doctrine. If only agreements which concern the internal allocation of tasks are outside the scope of Article 81(1) EC, then this means that a whole realm of other agreements are not. Resale price maintenance, for instance, can hardly be said to concern the internal allocation of tasks.

2.107. Interestingly, in more recent cases, the third criterion is no longer mentioned.[104] The Court of First Instance at a certain point even ruled squarely against it by stating:

> It does not therefore avail the applicant to argue that the agreements at issue infringe Article [81(1)] on the ground that they exceed an internal allocation of tasks within the group. It is apparent from its very terms that Article [81(1)] does not apply to conduct which is in reality performed by an economic unit. It is not for the Court, on the pretext that certain conduct, such as that to which the applicant objects, may fall outside the competition rules, to apply Article [81] to circumstances for which it is not intended in order to fill a gap which may exist in the system of regulation laid down by the Treaty.[105]

2.108. Meanwhile, the Commission also seems to have adopted the latter line of thinking. For example, in *Nintendo* it stated very matter-of-factly that 'Article 81(1) EC Treaty does not apply to relationships within a single economic unit or undertaking, such as those between a parent company and its dependent subsidiaries'.[106]

2.109. Therefore, adopting a reasonable view of the issue, the single economic entity doctrine will apply to all agreements and practices within that unit.

2.110. As regards the concept of the 'single economic entity' itself, the concept will not raise problems as long as it concerns agreements between a parent company and its 100% wholly-owned subsidiaries, or agreements between 100% wholly-owned subsidiaries, or between a parent company and its subsidiaries in which it holds a majority share. Sometimes, however, matters are less clear-cut. The formal separation between companies, resulting from their separate legal personality, may sometimes not outweigh the unity of their conduct on the market for the purposes of applying the rules on competition.[107] Where legally distinct natural or legal persons constitute an economic unit, they must indeed be treated as a single undertaking for the purpose of applying the Community

---

[103] Case 30/87 *Bodson* [1988] ECR 2479. It has also been invoked by the Commission in Case T–141/89 *Tréfileurope Sales Sarl v Commission* [1995] ECR II–791, para 125.

[104] Case T–141/89 *Tréfileurope Sales Sarl v Commission* [1995] ECR II–791; Case 66/86 *Ahmed Saeed Flugreisen and Silver Line Reisebüro* [1989] ECR 803, para 35; and Case C–73/95P *Viho* v *Commission* [1996] ECR I–5457, para 16.

[105] Case T–102/92 *Viho v Commission* [1995] ECR II–17, para 54.

[106] *Nintendo* [2003] OJ L255/33, para 245.

[107] Case 46/69 *ICI v Commission* [1972] ECR 619, para 140.

competition rules.[108] In Chapter 7 (paragraphs 7.52 *et seq*), the practical relevance of this matter will be discussed in the context of the relationship between a company and its commercial agents. Questions of this type may also arise in the context of agreements between two undertakings, one of which holds a minority participation in the other. It is generally accepted that agreements between such companies may be caught by Article 81(1) EC, unless it can be shown that the minority stake gives the minority shareholder a level of control that enables it to determine the strategic commercial behaviour of the company in which it holds the stake. What is and what is not to be considered as control is dealt with extensively under the EC merger control regime.[109] In light of a consistent application of the concept of 'control' in EC competition law, the authors believe that the same substantive test should apply across-the-board. In our view, this implies that control need not actually be exercised, but that control is merely 'the possibility of exercising decisive influence'.[110]

No limit on the number of contracting undertakings

As opposed to earlier block exemption regulations on vertical agreements, in particular Regulation 1983/83 (exclusive distribution) and Regulation 1984/83 (exclusive purchasing), the scope of application of Regulation 2790/99 is no longer limited to agreements between two undertakings. As long as there are two or more, the number of contracting undertakings is now irrelevant in the assessment of the applicability of the Regulation. **2.111.**

(4) Third component: undertakings operating at a different level of the production or distribution chain

In addition to being an agreement or concerted practice between two or more undertakings, a 'vertical agreement' in the sense of Regulation 2790/99 must also be between parties in a vertical relationship. Such a relationship is present in standard distribution agreements in which a supplier supplies a product to a reseller, and in purchase agreements between one party, who supplies components, and another party selling the products which incorporate the components purchased from the supplier. The same goes for agreements between three parties, the first being a manufacturer, the second a wholesaler, and the third a retailer.[111] **2.112.**

---

[108] Case 170/83 *Hydrotherm* [1984] ECR 2999, para 11; and Case T–234/95 *DSG v Commission* [2000] ECR II–2603, para 124.

[109] Commission Notice on the concept of concentration under Regulation (EEC) No 4064/89 on the control of concentrations between undertakings [1998] OJ C66/5.

[110] Council Regulation (EC) No 139/2004 of 20 January 2004 on the control of concentrations between undertakings (the EC Merger Regulation) [2004] L24/1, Art 3(2). It is noteworthy that a book on EC competition law written by Commission officials applies the same principle and also refers to the merger control regime: Faull and Nikpay (n 98 above) paras 2.37 *et seq*.

[111] Guidelines, para 24, second indent.

2.113. The definition of a vertical agreement in Article 2(1) of Regulation 2790/99 confirms that a vertical relationship must exist only 'for the purposes of the agreement'. Accordingly, agreements involving undertakings which operate at the same level in the production or distribution chain are not, by definition, excluded. The only criterion that matters is that the vertical relationship exists for the purposes of the agreement to which Regulation 2790/99 is applied. So the application of the block exemption contained in that Regulation to an import agreement for cookware is not endangered if the appointed importer also produces cookware. The fact that, for the purposes of the agreement, the other party acts as producer and supplier, while the second party acts as importer and buyer, is sufficient to make the agreement of a vertical nature.

2.114. In addition, Regulation 2790/99 is not excluded in cases of dual distribution, whereby a manufacturer sells his products to end-users on the one hand (possibly via wholly-owned distributors) and on the other hand via independent distributors.[112] The question of whether or not the undertakings concerned operate at a different level within the production or distribution chain need not be answered with respect to the whole scope of activities exercised by an undertaking, but only with respect to those activities addressed in the agreement concerned. Accordingly, it is possible for an agreement between competitors to be a vertical agreement in the sense of Regulation 2790/99.

(5) Fourth component: agreements or concerted practices which relate to the conditions under which the parties may purchase, sell, or resell certain goods or services

2.115. As regards the type and subject matter of the agreements or concerted practices to which the block exemption regulation applies, a comparison of the regime existing prior to Regulation 2790/99 with the regime existing now, shows that the latter has a much broader scope.

Vertical agreements covered by block exemptions prior to Regulation 2790/99

2.116. Regulation 1983/83 (exclusive distribution) only applied to:

agreements to which only two undertakings are party and whereby one party agrees with the other to supply certain goods for resale within the whole or a defined area of the common market only to that other (Article 1).

2.117. In the same vein, Regulation 1984/83 (exclusive purchasing) only applied to:

agreements to which only two undertakings are party and whereby one party, the reseller, agrees with the other, the supplier, to purchase certain goods specified in

---

[112] On dual distribution, see paras 2.258 and 2.300–2.301 below.

the agreement for resale only from the supplier or from a connected undertaking or from another undertaking which the supplier has entrusted with the sale of his goods (Article 1).

As a consequence, Regulations 1983/83 and 1984/83 excluded from their scope **2.118**. of application certain types of agreements, such as agreements on services and agreements on the supply or purchase of goods and services used as an input for the production of the buyer's own goods and services. This was confirmed in the Commission's Notice on both regulations:[113]

> The notion of resale requires that the goods concerned be disposed of by the purchasing party to others in return for consideration. Agreements on the supply or purchase of goods which the purchasing party transforms or processes into other goods or uses or consumes in manufacturing other goods are not agreements for resale. The same applies to the supply of components which are combined with other components into a different product. The criterion is that the goods distributed by the reseller are the same as those the other party has supplied to him for that purpose. The economic identity of the goods is not affected if the reseller merely breaks up and packs the goods into other packages before resale.

Vertical agreements covered by Regulation 2790/99

Regulation 2790/99 abandons these limits on the scope of application of **2.119**. Regulations 1983/83 and 1984/83 and it applies to all intermediate and final goods and services, with the exception of certain goods and services in the motor vehicle sector[114] which are covered by a separate block exemption regulation.[115] The goods and services provided by the supplier may be resold or may be used as an input by the buyer to produce his own goods or services.[116]

In addition, Regulation 2790/99 also applies to sales and purchase agreements **2.120**. which are not distribution agreements, and to all 'agreements which concern the conditions for the purchase, sale or resale of the goods or services supplied by the supplier and/or which concern the conditions for the sale by the buyer of the goods or services which incorporate these goods or services'.[117]

Since they do not involve the purchase, sale, or resale of a product or service, **2.121**. Regulation 2790/99 does not, therefore, apply to rental and lease agreements. However, it does apply to goods that are sold and purchased for renting to

---

[113] Commission Notice concerning Commission Regulations (EEC) No 1983/83 and (EEC) No 1984/83 of 22 June 1983 on the application of Article 85(3) of the Treaty to categories of exclusive distribution and exclusive purchasing agreements [1983] C355/7, and republished in [1984] OJ C102/2.

[114] Hence, the possible explanation for the use of the word 'certain' preceding 'goods or services' in Reg 2790/99, Art 2(1). See also Mendelsohn and Rose (n 2 above) 50.

[115] This block exemption regulation on motor vehicle distribution, Reg 1400/2002, is discussed in Part IV.   [116] Guidelines, paras 2 and 24, third indent.

[117] ibid, para 24, third indent.

third parties.[118] In the latter case, the agreement continues to be a purchase agreement. The fact that a purchaser buys the goods or services in order to rent them out to third parties afterwards, is irrelevant for purposes of the application of the Regulation.

2.122. As stated above, the application of the Regulation is limited to 'the conditions for the purchase, sale or resale of the goods or services'. The Regulation therefore does not cover conditions—the Commission refers specifically to restrictions and obligations not conditions[119]—that do not relate to the purchase, sale or resale, 'such as an obligation preventing parties from carrying out independent research and development which the parties may have included in an otherwise vertical agreement'.[120] This is not tantamount to saying that agreements which contain these types of restrictions and obligations cannot be covered by Regulation 2790/99 but instead is saying that these restrictions and obligations, which are not conditions for the purchase, sale or resale of the goods and services in question, will not be able to benefit from the block exemption contained in the Regulation.

E. Third Question: Vertical Restraints

(1) Introduction

2.123. Regulation 2790/99 does not apply to agreements that are not capable of appreciably restricting competition by object or effect in the sense of Article 81(1) EC. In this respect the last sentence of Article 2(1) of this Regulation states that the exemption it contains only applies 'to the extent that such agreements contain restrictions of competition falling within the scope of Article 81(1) ("vertical restraints")'. This is logical given that the need for an exemption (be it an individual or a block exemption) only occurs with respect to practices that are caught by the prohibition of Article 81(1) EC. If the prohibition does not apply, then there is no need for an exemption.

2.124. In our discussion below, we propose to approach the third question from the opposite angle and to identify those agreements and provisions of agreements which, although they appreciably affect inter-State trade, actually fall outside the scope of Article 81(1) EC and hence need no exemption. Generally the provisions and agreements in question are four-fold:

— First, restrictions of competition do not fall within the scope of Article 81(1) EC if they are covered by the Commission's *De Minimis* Notice[121] and are

---

[118] ibid, para 25.   [119] ibid.   [120] ibid.
[121] *De Minimis* Notice. The Guidelines (para 8) state that they are without prejudice to the application of the present or any future *De Minimis* Notice.

thus considered to be of minor importance (see paragraphs 2.125–2.136). In this Notice, the Commission quantifies, with the help of market share thresholds, what it considers not to be appreciable restrictions of competition in the sense of Article 81(1) EC.

— Second, even if an agreement does not qualify for the application of the *De Minimis* Notice, the agreement will not be automatically considered as an agreement that appreciably restricts competition in the sense of Article 81(1) EC. For this to be so a market analysis must show that the agreement has the object or effect of restricting competition and if this is found to be the case, that it does so in an appreciable way (see paragraphs 2.137–2.154).

— Third, restrictions of competition which are directly related and necessary to the implementation of a main, non-restrictive commercial transaction and are proportionate to it—that is, ancillary restraints—are also not caught by Article 81(1) EC (see paragraphs 2.155–2.160).[122]

— Finally, even if the main agreement is restrictive to competition, it would appear that certain (intra-brand) restrictions of competition may be outside Article 81(1) EC if they are objectively justified (see paragraphs 2.161–2.172).

(2) De Minimis *Notice*

Market share thresholds

Definition

According to the Commission, an agreement does not appreciably restrict competition in the sense of Article 81(1) EC: **2.125**.

(a) if the aggregate market share held by the parties to the agreement does not exceed 10% on any of the relevant markets affected by the agreement, where the agreement is made between undertakings which are actual or potential competitors on any of these markets (agreements between competitors); or

(b) if the market share held by each of the parties to the agreement does not exceed 15% on any of the relevant markets affected by the agreement, where the agreement is made between undertakings which are not actual or potential competitors on any of these markets (agreements between non-competitors).[123]

---

[122] In the present context, we will not discuss 'ancillarity' in the sense of the Court of Justice's judgment in Case C–309/99 *Wouters* [2002] ECR I–1577, as that case did not concern a commercial but rather a regulatory ancillarity: Whish (n 70 above) 120–4.

[123] *De Minimis* Notice, para 7.

2.126. In addition to agreements, the *De Minimis* Notice also applies to decisions by associations of undertakings and to concerted practices.[124] As a result, where the term 'agreement' is used hereafter, it can be taken to include such decisions and concerted practices.

Different approaches towards the appreciability concept

2.127. The Commission adopts a different appreciability standard in the Guidelines on the effect on trade concept than in the *De Minimis* Notice. It does this in two different respects.

— First, the *De Minimis* Notice, unlike the Guidelines on the effect on trade concept, does not distinguish between horizontal and vertical agreements but between agreements between competitors and agreements between non-competitors. These notions do not necessarily overlap as a vertical agreement can be concluded between competitors.

— Second, the presumptions created by the *De Minimis* Notice rely exclusively on market share thresholds, whilst those introduced by the Guidelines on the effect on trade concept rely not only on market share thresholds but also on turnover. While there is undeniably a difference between, on the one hand, appreciability in the context of the effect on trade concept and, on the other hand, appreciability in the context of the restrictive impact on competition, the reasons for this different approach (especially why a turnover threshold would adequately express this difference) remain unclear.

Combined market share for competitors and individual market shares for non-competitors

2.128. The market share threshold introduced by the *De Minimis* Notice is a combined market share threshold (of 10%) for agreements between competitors and an individual market share threshold (of 15%) for agreements between non-competitors. As vertical agreements are frequently concluded between non-competitors, such agreements, even if it has been shown that they appreciably affect inter-State trade, will not be caught by Article 81(1) EC if the supplier's and the buyer's individual market share does not exceed 15% on any of the relevant markets affected by the agreement.[125]

2.129. In cases where it is difficult to classify the agreement as either an agreement between competitors or an agreement between non-competitors the 10% threshold is applicable.[126]

---

[124] ibid, para 5.
[125] A non-competing undertaking is an undertaking which is neither an actual nor a potential competitor. These concepts are addressed in paras 2.292–2.295 below.
[126] *De Minimis* Notice, para 7.

Cumulative foreclosure effects

Competition on a given relevant market may be restricted because of the **2.130.** cumulative effect of vertical agreements for the sale of goods or services entered into by different suppliers or distributors. Where such cumulative foreclosure effects occur—generally beginning where there is a coverage of 30% or more of the relevant market by parallel (networks of) agreements—the market share threshold for the purposes of the application of the *De Minimis* Notice is reduced to 5% for agreements between competitors as well as for agreements between non-competitors. Individual suppliers or distributors with a market share that does not exceed 5% are generally not considered to contribute significantly to a cumulative foreclosure effect,[127] and their agreements will be able to continue to benefit from the *De Minimis* Notice.

In the past, the existence of cumulative foreclosure effects has been dealt with in **2.131.** the context of beer supply agreements,[128] the supply of ice-cream,[129] as well as in the context of petrol-service station agreements.[130]

Temporary crossing of market share thresholds

Undertakings can continue to rely on the *De Minimis* Notice as long as their **2.132.** market share does not exceed the applicable threshold by more than 2 percentage points during any two successive calendar years; in other words, if their aggregate market share does not exceed 12% (for agreements between competitors) or their individual market share does not exceed 17% (agreements between non-competitors) during two successive calendar years. Where the relevant market is characterized by the presence of cumulative foreclosure effects, the *De Minimis* Notice will continue to apply for agreements between suppliers and distributors with a market share which does not exceed 7% for a period of two successive years.[131]

In cases covered by the *De Minimis* Notice, the Commission will not institute **2.133.** proceedings either upon application or at its own initiative. Where undertakings assume, in good faith, that an agreement is covered by the *De Minimis* Notice, the Commission will not impose fines. This is a matter of Commission policy and has no bearing on the convergence rule under Regulation 1/2003. In other words, if an NCA, as opposed to the Commission, is of the opinion that the imposition of a fine is nevertheless called for, it can do so without breaching the convergence principles.

---

[127] ibid, para 8.

[128] Case C–234/89 *Delimitis v Henninger Bräu* [1991] ECR I–935; and Case T–25/99 *Colin Arthur Roberts and Valérie Ann Roberts v Commission* [2001] ECR II–1881.

[129] Case T–7/93 *Langnese-Iglo v Commission* [1995] ECR II–1533; and Case C–275/95P *Langnese Iglo v Commission* [1998] ECR I–5609.

[130] Case C–214/99 *Neste* [2000] ECR I–11121.   [131] *De Minimis* Notice, para 9.

Hardcore restrictions

2.134. Irrespective of the market share of the undertakings concerned, the *De Minimis* Notice does not apply to agreements which contain the hardcore restrictions that are stated in the Notice.[132] A comparison shows that the hardcore restrictions listed in the *De Minimis* Notice are identical to those stated in Regulation 2790/99. Practically speaking this means that these hardcore restrictions, which are discussed later in Chapter 5, are almost by way of definition banned by EC competition law: The Commission assumes that they always restrict competition in the sense of Article 81(1) EC (and that it is therefore not possible to justify them solely with a reference to the *De Minimis* Notice); they do not qualify for block exemption under Regulation 2790/99; and, given the Commission's Guidelines on the application of Article 81(3) of the Treaty,[133] they are also unlikely to qualify for application of Article 81(3) EC.[134]

2.135. Yet, while they are assumed to affect competition in the sense of Article 81(1) EC, hardcore restrictions do not necessarily always appreciably affect trade between Member States. As stated above (paragraph 2.55), the Commission states in its Guidelines on the effect on trade concept that it will apply the Guidelines' negative presumption—that is, the presumption that a given agreement does not come within the scope of Article 81(1) EC for lack of appreciable effect on the inter-State trade—irrespective of the nature of the restrictions that are contained in the agreement. EC competition law will therefore not necessarily need to be considered if an agreement contains one or several hardcore restrictions.

2.136. The actual practical relevance of this observation is probably small. In all likelihood, it will be difficult to convince an NCA or national court to exempt an agreement containing one or several restrictions which, at the EC level, are hardcore restrictions and which the NCA or national court, had there been an appreciable effect on inter-State trade, would in any case have had to prohibit in light of the convergence rule.

(3) Case-by-case assessment of the restrictive object or effect

2.137. An agreement which exceeds the market share thresholds as laid down in the *De Minimis* Notice is not automatically considered as an agreement which appreciably restricts competition in the sense of Article 81(1) EC.[135] Such an

---

[132] ibid, para 11. [133] [2004] OJ C101/97.

[134] Guidelines on the application of Article 81(3) EC, para 46.

[135] *De Minimis* Notice, para 2. The statement is illustrated by such judgments as Case T–7/93 *Langnese-Iglo v Commission* [1995] ECR II–1533, para 98; and Cases T–374/94, T–375/94, T–384/94, and T–388/94 *European Night Services v Commission* [1998] ECR II–3141, para 102.

agreement may still be outside the scope of Article 81(1) EC either because it does not have the restriction of competition as its object or effect (see paragraphs 2.138–2.141) or because it does not in itself appreciably restrict competition (see paragraphs 2.142–2.154). In this context, the restriction of competition refers both to the restriction of inter-brand competition (ie competition between suppliers of competing brands) and of intra-brand competition (ie competition between distributors of the same brand). Article 81(1) EC prohibits both.[136] A test to examine whether an agreement restricts either inter-brand or intra-brand competition or both is given in the Commission's Guidelines on the application of Article 81(3) EC, paragraph 18.

Restrictive object or effect

To determine whether an agreement which is not covered by the *De Minimis* Notice contains vertical restraints in the sense of Regulation 2790/99, it must first be checked whether or not it has restriction of competition as its object or effect. Once it has been established that an agreement (or concerted practice)[137] has restriction of intra- or inter-brand competition as its object, there is no longer any need to demonstrate the agreement's actual effects on the market.[138]   **2.138**.

Restrictions by object are restrictions which are assumed, by their very nature, to have the potential of restricting competition. Hardcore restrictions (which by definition do not qualify for the application of the *De Minimis* Notice) are generally considered as being restrictive by object. Specifically as regards vertical agreements, it concerns, for example fixed and minimum resale price maintenance; and restrictions providing absolute territorial protection, including restrictions on passive sales.[139]   **2.139**.

If an agreement is not restrictive of competition by object, it must be examined whether it has any actual or potential restrictive effects on competition. This will be the case if it entails, with a sufficient degree of probability, negative effects on prices, output, innovation, or the variety or quality of goods or services.[140]   **2.140**.

While it may sometimes be possible to show negative effects directly, it will often be necessary to resort to proxies.[141] For instance, pursuant to the Guidelines on   **2.141**.

---

[136] Joined Cases 56/64 and 58/66 *Consten and Grundig* [1966] ECR 429.

[137] Joined Cases T–5/00 and T–6/00 *Nederlandse Federatieve Vereniging voor de Groothandel op Elektrotechnisch Gebied* [2003] ECR II–5761, para 287.

[138] Guidelines on the application of Art 81(3) EC, para 20. More details on the distinction between 'restrictive object' and 'restrictive effect' are given in paras 5.01–5.09.

[139] ibid, para 23. It will be recalled that hardcore restrictions involving two or more Member States, or covering the whole territory of a Member State, are also restrictions which 'by their very nature' affect trade between Member States: see para 2.40.

[140] Guidelines on the application of Art 81(3) EC, paras 25–6.

[141] L Kjølbye, 'The New Commission Guidelines on the Application of Article 81(3): An Economic Approach to Article 81' [2004] ECLR 566, 570.

the application of Article 81(3) EC, the likelihood that an agreement brings about negative effects on the market increases if the parties have, or obtain, a degree of market power and the agreement in question contributes to the creation, maintenance, or strengthening of market power or allows the parties to exploit such market power. The same Guidelines describe 'market power' as 'the ability to maintain prices above competitive levels for a significant period of time or to maintain output in term of product quantities, product quality and variety or innovation below competitive level for a significant period of time',[142] and also state that the degree of market power necessary for the finding of an infringement of Article 81(1) EC is less than that for the finding of dominance under Article 82 EC.[143]

Appreciable restriction of competition

2.142. If an agreement is shown to have the restriction of competition as its object or effect (and if it is not of minor importance in the sense of the *De Minimis* Notice), then it must be ascertained that the restriction of competition is appreciable. If this is not the case, it is not caught by Article 81(1) EC and the safe harbour created by Regulation 2790/99 does not come into play.

2.143. This condition that competition must be restricted in an appreciable way applies to vertical agreements which have the restriction of competition as their object as well as to those which have such restriction as their effect. In *Société Technique Minière*, the Court stated the following on both:

> Where ... an analysis of said clauses [ie the clauses as to the purpose of the agreement] does not reveal the effect on competition to be *sufficiently* deleterious, the consequences of the agreement should then be considered and for it to be caught by the prohibition it is then necessary to find that those factors are present which show that competition has in fact been prevented or restricted or distorted *to an appreciable extent* [emphasis added].[144]

Appreciable restriction of competition by object

2.144. Specifically with regard to vertical agreements which have the restriction of competition as their object, the requirement that the restriction must be appreciable has been confirmed by the Court of Justice subsequent to *Société Technique Minière* in the case of *Völk v Vervaecke*[145] as well as in a number of other cases.[146] *Völk v Vervaecke* concerned a vertical agreement which was clearly restrictive by object: Völk had given absolute territorial protection to

---

[142] Guidelines on the application of Art 81(3) EC, para 25.   [143] ibid, para 26.
[144] Case 56/65 *Société Technique Minière v Machinenbau Ulm* [1966] ECR 235, 249.
[145] Case 5/69 *Völk v Vervaecke* [1969] ECR 295.
[146] eg Joined Cases 100 to 103/80 *SA Musique Diffusion Française* [1983] ECR 1825, para 85; and C–306/96 *Javico* [1998] ECR I–1983, para 17 (on *Javico*, see paras 3.07–3.14 below).

Vervaecke, its exclusive dealer in Belgium and Luxembourg. The Court of Justice ruled as follows:

> an agreement falls outside the prohibition in Article [81] when it has only an insignificant effect on the markets, taking into account the weak position which the persons concerned have on the market of the product in question. Thus an exclusive dealing agreement, even with absolute territorial protection, may, having regard to the weak position of the persons concerned on the market in the products in question in the area covered by the absolute protection, escape the prohibition laid down in Article [81(1)].

On vertical agreements which have the restriction of competition as their object, **2.145.** the Commission's policy seems to be to informally apply the *De Minimis* Notice, and this is in spite of the Notice's wording, namely, that it excludes hardcore restrictions from its scope of application. In a book written by officials of DG COMP, the rationale which is given for this approach is that, in economic terms,

> the impact of the most restrictive agreements would be muted at low market share levels and the allocation of resources to such agreements would, it is submitted, be questionable. If the Commission did challenge such agreements, the most likely reason for doing so would be pedagogical—to help ensure that a 'competition culture' was developed or maintained in particular sector of the economy.[147]

Appreciable restriction of competition by effect

For vertical agreements which are not restrictive of competition by object but **2.146.** only by effect, it becomes much more difficult, if not impossible, to provide a general rule for determining when they may restrict competition in an appreciable way. The reasons for this are at least two-fold.

First, any competition analysis necessarily depends on the facts of the case. For **2.147.** vertical agreements, the various factors which the Commission takes into account to determine whether the agreement brings about an appreciable restriction of competition in the sense of Article 81(1) EC are listed in the Guidelines (paragraphs 121–33). These factors include:[148]

— the **market position of the supplier** (the higher its market share, the higher its market power and therefore the more risk for negative effects);
— the **market position of the competitors** (the higher their market share and the greater their number, the less risk there is for market foreclosure and associated reduction of inter-brand competition);
— the **market position of the buyer** (the greater the buying power, the greater the possibility of negative effects in the case of distribution systems based

---

[147] Faull and Nikpay (n 98 above) para 2.70.
[148] These factors are discussed in Ch 10 below.

on exclusive supply,[149] exclusive distribution,[150] or quantitative selective distribution);

— **entry barriers** (low entry barriers are better for competition than high entry barriers; if prices above the competitive level are likely to attract entry within one or two years, then entry barriers are low);

— the **maturity of the market** (mature markets are more prone to negative effects than dynamic markets);

— the **level of trade** (negative effects are generally less likely for intermediate than for final goods or services);

— the **nature of the product** (when the product is more heterogeneous, less expensive, and resembles more of a one-off purchase, vertical restraints are more likely to have negative effects).

2.148. Second, in addition to the fact that the importance of the various factors, as well as their inter-relationship, changes from one case to another, there continues to be discussion on the scope for economic analysis under Article 81(1) EC to determine whether or not an agreement or clauses contained in an agreement appreciably restrict competition. The current position on this matter appears to be as follows:

— On the one hand, it is established case law that any economic analysis under Article 81(1) EC must stop short of a so-called 'rule of reason' approach. Pursuant to such an approach, the pro- and anti-competitive effects of an agreement must be weighed to determine whether it is caught by the prohibition of that article. Such approach is not embraced under Article 81(1) EC. In *Métropole Télévision*, the Court of First Instance rejected it and ruled that it is within the context of Article 81(3) EC that the pro- and anti-competitive aspects of a restriction must be weighed.[151]

— On the other hand, the Court of First Instance stated, in the same judgment, that:

> in assessing the applicability of Article [81(1) EC] to an agreement, account should be taken of the actual conditions in which it functions, in particular the economic context in which the undertakings operate, the products or services covered by the agreement and the actual structure of the market concerned... That interpretation, while observing the substantive scheme of Article [81 EC] and, in particular, preserving the effectiveness of Article [81(3) EC], makes it possible to prevent the prohibition in Article [81(1)] from

---

[149] An 'exclusive supply obligation' is defined in Reg 2790/99, Art 1(c), as 'any direct or indirect obligation causing the supplier to sell the good or services specified in the agreement only to one buyer inside the Community for the purposes of a specific use or for resale'.

[150] 'Exclusive distribution' is an agreement whereby the supplier agrees to sell its products to only one distributor for resale in a particular territory (Guidelines, paras 161 *et seq*).

[151] Case T–112/99 *Métropole Télévision (M6) v Commission* [2001] ECR II–2459, paras 72–80.

extending wholly abstractly and without distinction to all agreements whose effect is to restrict the freedom of action of one or more of the parties.[152]

It is probably best to illustrate the Article 81(1) EC economic analysis to which **2.149**. this may give rise by way of a practical example.[153] In respect of this, reference can be made to the decision of 28 May 2002 by the Dutch Competition Authority (the 'Nederlandse Mededingingsautoriteit' or 'NMa') in the *Heineken* case.[154] This decision is of particular interest because the NMa came to the conclusion that, notwithstanding Heineken's significant market power, its agreements with the horeca (short for 'hotels, restaurants and cafés'; hereafter referred to as 'on-premise outlets') did not appreciably restrict competition.

Prior to the entry into force of Regulation 2790/99, and under the regime of **2.150**. Regulation 1984/83, Heineken's existing supply agreements for on-premise outlets were long-term (five or ten years) exclusive supply agreements covering all types of beer (on draught, in bottles, or in cans). Following the entry into force of Regulation 2790/99 and given that its market share substantially exceeds 30% (it is between 50 and 60%), Heineken's supply agreements for on-premise outlets were no longer block exempted. Heineken notified the NMa of a new set of agreements. The main features of these new agreements were that financial support was provided to the outlet concerned in return for exclusivity in respect of the supply of draught beer. On the condition of the repayment of the loan, the outlet could terminate the supply agreement at any time, whilst Heineken had to respect a two months' notice period. The loan agreement could also be terminated with a two months' notice period. There was no penalty due for termination

The NMa investigated Heineken's new supply agreement and corresponding **2.151**. loan agreement under Article 6 of the Dutch Competition Act (ie the Dutch counterpart of Article 81 EC), which it applied in conformity with the Guidelines. Initially, the NMa stated that the position of Heineken on the relevant market was of importance: the stronger that position, the more important the risk of anti-competitive effects. However, it added to this that the question of whether Heineken had a dominant position (and, if so, whether exclusivity was objectively justified)[155] is relevant only if it can be established that the agreements may result in the appreciable restriction of competition; in other words, if they are covered by Article 6(1) of the Dutch Competition Act, ie Article 81(1) EC.

---

[152] ibid, para 77.
[153] A list of examples of EC cases in which agreements containing restrictions were found not to have anti-competitive effects can be found in Whish (n 70 above) 117–19.
[154] The case is available (in Dutch only) at http://www.nmanet.nl/nederlands/home/besluiten/besluiten_2002/2036.asp. It is discussed by S Bishop, 'Pro-Competitive Exclusive Supply Agreements: How Refreshing!' [2003] ECLR 229.
[155] On the concept of 'objective justification', see paras 2.161–2.162 below.

2.152. According to the NMa, this was not the case. Despite Heineken's significant market position and the corresponding risk for the restriction of competition, the NMa concluded that Heineken's supply agreements did not lead to appreciable restriction of competition. The NMa's investigation focused on determining whether the exclusive supply agreement for draught beer could lead to foreclosure of the market for competing brewers. The economic assessment performed by the NMa relied mainly on the following factors to conclude that this was not the case:[156]

— First, 60% of the Dutch on-premise outlets (22,000 out of a total of 45,000) either have exclusive ties with a brewer or are owned by one. Therefore, 40% of the outlets remain open to competition between all brewers.

— Second, given the nature of the exclusivity, the NMa did not consider that the supply agreements could seal the market. Under the old supply agreements, it had been established that a significant number of outlets switched supplier at the time of contract renewal. Pursuant to the new supply agreement, the outlet could switch at any time. In the absence of any notice period of significance, the outlets with Heineken exclusivity were continually open to competition from competing brewers. The opposite is however not the case: all competing brewers are covered by Regulation 2790/99 and may therefore impose, in accordance with that block exemption regulation, a non-compete obligation for a maximum period of five years.[157]

— Third, in the course of the procedure before the NMa, Heineken had made two additional concessions. It had agreed that it would, once a year, expressly point out to the outlets the possibility of termination and the absence of any sanction should they choose to switch. It also agreed to limit the extent of exclusivity solely to draught beer. Accordingly, on-premise outlets are entitled to purchase bottles from competing brewers ('bottles free'). These represent approximately 20% of the volume of beer sold via on-premise outlets.

— Fourth, consumer research has shown that pilsner is a commodity. Customers typically do not specify a brand when they order pilsner beer, and also outlets which are not subject to exclusivity agreements tend to stock only one brand of beer. In this respect too, the new supply agreement did not appreciably foreclose the market (in particular inter-brand competition) within one and the same on-premise outlet.

2.153. Based on these considerations, the NMa concluded that the exclusivity of the new supply agreements did not foreclose the market and did not appreciably restrict competition in the sense of Article 6 of the Dutch Competition Act.

---

[156] Some of these parameters are also to be found in the landmark *Delimitis* case of the Court of Justice, which is discussed in paras 6.35–6.40 below.

[157] On non-compete obligations within the framework of Reg 2790/99, see Ch 6 below.

The NMa's economic analysis under Article 6 of the Dutch Competition Act can **2.154.** be transposed to that under Article 81(1) EC. It shows that for vertical agreements outside the scope of Regulation 2790/99 (here, because of the supplier's market share), undertakings should not immediately jump to checking whether their agreements fulfil the conditions required for an individual exemption under Article 81(3) EC. Instead, they would be well advised to first check the applicability of Article 81(1) EC to the agreements concerned. As the *Heineken* case shows, competition authorities may be willing to perform a detailed assessment of the appreciability of the anti-competitive effects of a given agreement. This may lead to real exclusivity provisions being found to be outside the scope of Article 81(1) EC.

(4) Ancillary restraints

The concept of ancillary restraints

Finally, in order to determine whether or not an agreement contains vertical **2.155.** restraints in the sense of Article 81(1) EC, it is also necessary to consider whether or not certain restrictions qualify as so-called 'ancillary restraints'. The rule of thumb is as follows: once it has been concluded that the main transaction covered by an agreement (which may affect trade between Member States) is not restrictive of competition in the sense of Article 81(1) EC, it should be examined whether or not individual restraints contained within the agreement are ancillary to the main non-restrictive transaction. If they are, then they also fall outside the scope of Article 81(1) EC.[158]

Conditions for the ancillary nature of certain restraints

An alleged restriction of competition must be directly related to and necessary **2.156.** for the implementation of a main non-restrictive transaction for it to qualify as an ancillary restraint. Being 'directly related' to the implementation of a non-restrictive transaction means that the restriction must be subordinate to the implementation of the transaction, whilst being inseparably linked to it; being 'necessary' that it must be objectively necessary for the implementation of the main transaction and be proportionate to it.[159] In practice, this test is generally performed by determining whether or not the implementation of the main non-restrictive agreement would be difficult or even impossible without the restriction(s) in question.[160]

---

[158] Guidelines on the application of Art 81(3) EC, para 28 (where the Commission discusses ancillary restraints as 'individual restraints...compatible with Article 81(1)', whereas in the following paras 29 and 31, the Commission correctly considers ancillary restraints to 'fall outside Article 81(1)').   [159] ibid, para 29.
[160] cf ibid, para 31.

Ancillary restraints v Article 81(3) EC analysis

2.157. In its Guidelines on the application of Article 81(3) EC, the Commission reiterates that the application of the ancillary restraints concept must be distinguished from the application of the defence under Article 81(3) EC. The latter relates to certain economic benefits resulting from restrictive agreements (which are balanced against the restrictive effects of the agreements). The former does not involve any weighing of pro- and anti-competitive effects.[161] As soon as it has been established that the main transaction is restrictive of competition in the sense of Article 81(1) EC, then the ancillary restraints doctrine is no longer relevant and the restrictions can only be exempted from the prohibition of Article 81(1) EC by way of an individual Article 81(3) EC exemption or via the safe harbour of a block exemption regulation such as Regulation 2790/99.[162]

Ancillary vertical restraints in a horizontal or a purely vertical context

2.158. The question of ancillary (vertical) restraints may arise in the context of a horizontal agreement (most notably a concentration between undertakings, including the creation of a joint venture) or in a purely vertical context:[163]

— As regards the competition law assessment of the former, reference can be made to the guidance which can be found in the Commission Notice on restrictions directly related and necessary to concentrations.[164]

— As regards the latter, the Guidelines on the application of Article 81(3) EC refer to the 1986 *Pronuptia* judgment to illustrate the point that if the main object of a franchise agreement does not restrict competition, then restrictions necessary for the proper functioning of the agreement, such as obligations aimed at protecting the uniformity and reputation of the franchise system, also fall outside of Article 81(1) EC.

2.159. In *Pronuptia*, a dispute had arisen between Pronuptia de Paris GmbH (the franchisor) and one of its franchisees concerning the latter's obligation to pay arrears or royalties. In order to avoid payment of the arrears, the franchisee

---

[161] ibid, para 30.

[162] This is not to say that there are no similarities between the analyses conducted under Art 81(1) and Art 81(3) EC; there are. In particular, the parallel between ancillary restrictions and the indispensability test for restrictive clauses under the third condition of Art 81(3) EC has been called striking: L Gyselen, 'The Substantive Legality Test under Article 81(3) EC Treaty Revisited in Light of the Commission's Modernisation Initiative' in A von Bogdandy *et al* (eds), *European Integration and International Co-operation. Studies in Transnational Economic Law in Honour of Claus-Dieter Ehlermann* (Kluwer Law International, 2002) 181–97.

[163] For a critique on the application of the ancillary restraints doctrine to vertical restraints, see P Lugard and L Hancher, 'Honey, I Shrunk the Article! A Critical Assessment of the Commission's Notice on Article 81(3) of the EC Treaty' [2004] ECLR 410, 415–17.

[164] [2001] OJ C188/5.

claimed that its contract was contrary to Article 81(1) EC and did not qualify for exemption under Regulation 67/67, which was the prevailing block exemption regulation on certain categories of exclusive dealing agreements at that time. Initially, the franchisee was successful as the national court considered that the agreements did indeed contain certain mutual obligations of exclusivity which infringed Article 81(1) EC and were not covered by Regulation 67/67. On appeal, the national court referred a number of preliminary questions to the Court on the scope of application of Article 81(1) EC in relation to 'distribution franchises'; that is, franchises under which the franchisee, for a fee, sells certain products in a shop which bears the franchisor's business name or symbol. According to the Court, distribution franchises (the main agreement in question) do not, in themselves, interfere with competition. Such franchises, in order to function properly, may furthermore include certain (ancillary) restrictions which are not restrictions of competition in the sense of Article 81(1) EC. In *Pronuptia*, these concerned:

— on the one hand, restrictions which are strictly necessary to ensure that the know-how and assistance provided by the franchisor do not benefit competitors, namely:
  • a prohibition on the franchisee, during and for a reasonable period after the expiry of the agreement, from opening a shop of the same or of a similar nature within the territory allotted to him;
  • a prohibition imposed on the franchisee from transferring its shop to another party without the prior approval of the franchisor.
— on the other hand, restrictions which establish the control strictly necessary for maintaining the identity and reputation of the franchise network, namely:
  • the obligation to apply the business methods developed by the franchisor (such as advertising, the establishment and decoration of the shop, staff training, sales techniques);
  • the obligation to sell only products supplied by the franchisor or by suppliers selected by him, as long as this obligation does not prevent the franchisee from obtaining those products from other franchisees; and finally also,
  • price recommendations, as long as there is no concerted practice for the actual application of such prices.[165]

---

[165] Case 191/84 *Pronuptia* [1986] ECR 353. For more on *Pronuptia* and its implications for the ancillary restraints doctrine, see F Wijckmans, 'Franchising en het EEG-kartelrecht: een plotselinge verliefdheid of een duurzaam huwelijk' [1988] Rechtskundig Weekblad 1008; J Venit, 'Pronuptia: Ancillary Restraints or Unholy Alliances' [1986] ELR 217; V Korah, 'Pronuptia Franchising: The Marriage of Reason and the EEC Competition Rules' [1986] European Intellectual Property Review 102; and V Korah and D O'Sullivan, *Distribution Agreements under the EC Competition Rules* (Hart Publishing, 2002) 98.

2.160. It follows from the Guidelines (paragraph 44) that similar principles to those laid down by the Court in *Pronuptia* continue to apply to the present day.[166] The following obligations fall outside of the scope of Article 81(1) EC, to the extent that they are necessary in order to protect the franchisor's IPRs:

— an obligation on the franchisee not to engage in, either directly or indirectly, any similar business;

— an obligation on the franchisee not to acquire financial interests in the capital of a competing undertaking if such an acquisition would give the franchisee sufficient power to be able to influence the economic conduct of the competing undertaking;

— an obligation on the franchisee not to disclose to third parties the know-how provided to them by the franchisor, for as long as this know-how is not in the public domain;

— an obligation on the franchisee to communicate to the franchisor any experience gained in exploiting the franchise and to grant it and other franchisees a non-exclusive licence for the know-how resulting from that experience;

— an obligation on the franchisee to inform the franchisor of infringements of licensed IPRs, to take legal action against infringers or to assist the franchisor in any legal actions taken against infringers;

— an obligation on the franchisee not to use the know-how licensed by the franchisor for purposes other than the exploitation of the franchise; and

— an obligation on the franchisee not to assign the rights and obligations under the franchise agreement without the franchisor's consent.

(5) Objective justification

Concept of objective justification

2.161. Let us assume that a distribution agreement, which is itself restrictive of competition, contains a hardcore restriction (for example, a prohibition on passive sales outside the territory).[167] Bearing in mind what was said above, this means, first, that the *De Minimis* Notice does not apply (as it concerns a hardcore restriction) and second, that the restriction cannot be outside the scope of Article 81(1) EC by application of the ancillary restraints doctrine (as it is part of a main agreement which is restrictive of competition). Notwithstanding this, it still seems possible for the restriction to be outside the scope of Article 81(1) EC. In this respect, reference can be made to the Guidelines on the application

---

[166] On franchising and Reg 2790/99, see also Ch 7, paras 7.38–7.51 below.

[167] On passive sales, which pursuant to Reg 2790/99 must at all times be permitted, see para 5.48 below.

of Article 81(3) EC, which (at paragraph 18(2)) states the following on intra-brand restrictions of competition:

> [C]ertain restrictions may in certain cases not be caught by Article 81(1) when the restraint is objectively necessary for the existence of an agreement of that type or that nature . . . The question is not whether the parties in their particular situation would not have accepted to conclude a less restrictive agreement, but whether given the nature of the agreement and the characteristics of the market a less restrictive agreement would not have been concluded by undertakings in a similar setting.

It follows from this that certain intra-brand restrictions of competition, irre- **2.162**. spective of whether they are part of a main agreement which is restrictive or non-restrictive of competition in the sense of Article 81(1) EC, may still be outside the scope of Article 81(1) EC because they are objectively justified. Given that the main agreement may be restrictive of competition this is then an extension of the ancillary restraints doctrine. This doctrine applies exclusively to restrictions which form a part of main non-restrictive agreements.

Scope and conditions of objective justification

As stated above, the scope of application of the objective justification test is **2.163**. limited to restrictions of intra-brand competition (ie restrictions of competition between distributors of the same brand).

The conditions for its application are similar, but not identical, to those of the **2.164**. ancillary restraints doctrine. As previously stated, for the latter doctrine to apply, a restriction of competition must be directly related and necessary to the implementation of a main non-restrictive transaction. This means that it would be difficult or even impossible to implement without the restriction. For a restriction of intra-brand competition to be outside of Article 81(1) EC on account of an objective justification, the Guidelines provide for a different test, namely that it must be checked whether, in light of the nature of the agreement as well as the characteristics of the markets, the parties would not have concluded the agreement without the restriction concerned.

Some examples given by the Commission are as follows: **2.165**.

— Territorial restraints in an agreement between a supplier and a distributor, even though they are normally considered to be hardcore restrictions, may, for a certain period of time, fall outside the scope of Article 81(1) EC if the restraints are objectively necessary for the distributor in order to penetrate a new market. In this respect, the Guidelines (paragraph 119(10)) state that in the case of the entry in a new geographic market, restrictions on active as well as passive sales are not caught by Article 81(1) EC if they are imposed on the direct buyers of the supplier located in other markets to intermediaries in the new market as well as limited to a period of two years after first putting the product on the market.[168] So with the exception of passive sales directly made to end-users, active and passive sales can be prevented because this is objectively necessary to penetrate a new geographic market.

— The Guidelines on the application of Article 81(3) EC (paragraph 18(2)) consider that a prohibition imposed on all distributors not to sell to certain categories of end-users may not be restrictive of competition in the sense of Article 81(1) EC if such a restraint results from external factors and is objectively necessary for reasons of safety or health, related to the dangerous nature of the product in question.[169]

2.166. In summary, if certain intra-brand restrictions of competition are objectively necessary for the existence of a vertical agreement, and the agreement does not affect inter-brand competition, Article 81(1) EC does not apply. As a consequence, Article 81(1) EC applies if the agreement does not affect inter-brand competition but does include intra-brand restrictions which go beyond what is objectively necessary for the agreement to exist. For instance, Article 81(1) EC will apply if a distribution agreement grants territorial protection of, for example, five years to a distributor penetrating a new market if there are objective factors which lead to the conclusion that the parties would also have concluded the agreement with a territorial protection limited to a period of, for example, three years.[170] Also, agreements that restrict inter-brand competition 'do not escape Art 81(1) EC merely because in the absence of a restraint, the agreement would not have been concluded. From a competition perspective it may be preferable that the agreement does not occur at all'.[171]

Objective justification and dominance

2.167. The objective justification test takes on an altogether different dimension in the context of the application of Article 81(3) EC to vertical agreements concluded by dominant undertakings. In this context, the Guidelines state (paragraph 135):

> Where an undertaking is dominant or becoming dominant as a consequence of the vertical agreement, a vertical restraint that has appreciable anti-competitive effects can in principle not be exempted. The vertical agreement may however fall outside

---

[168] It would appear that the principle relies upon the Court of Justice's ruling in Case 56/65 *Société Technique Minière* [1966] ECR 235, 250, where it stated that 'it may be doubted whether there is an interference with competition if the said agreement [granting "an exclusive right of sale"] seems really necessary for the penetration of a new area by an undertaking'. A similar approach can be found in Case 258/78 *Nungesser* [1982] ECR 2015, paras 44 *et seq.*

[169] The Vertical Guidelines (para 49) add to this that the justification will only withstand scrutiny if the supplier also accepts to refrain from selling the products concerned to the relevant categories of customers (see also para 5.42). Other examples of what is referred to as 'qualitative restrictions based on objective criteria' can be found in PM Roth (ed), *Bellamy & Child. European Community Law of Competition* (5th edn, Sweet & Maxwell, 2001) para 2–113.

[170] Lugard and Hancher (n 163 above) 413–14. [171] Kjølbye (n 141 above) 568–9.

Article 81(1) if there is an objective justification, for instance if it is necessary for the protection of relationship-specific investments or for the transfer of substantial know-how without which the supply or purchase of certain goods or services would not take place.

Based on this language, it appeared that DG COMP's view on vertical agree- **2.168**. ments concluded by dominant companies was that those agreements should not contain restrictions which appreciably restrict competition.[172] This view was apparently further confirmed by an official of DG COMP who wrote that if they did, they do not qualify for application of Article 81(3) EC:

> Dominant companies should compete on the merits only and should avoid behaving anti-competitively. Unless a restriction of competition can be objectively justified, dominant companies should refrain from such restrictions. This is why, for instance, dominant companies should in general refrain from imposing non-compete obligations or applying loyalty rebates.[173]

As a consequence of this approach, the competition law analysis of the beha- **2.169**. viour of dominant undertakings in respect of their vertical relationships seemed to be focused exclusively on Article 81(1) EC, and Article 81(3) EC no longer seemed to come into play. In other words, the approach was that vertical restraints agreed between a dominant company and its suppliers or customers seemed to be permissible under EC competition law only if they were ancillary (which would imply that the main agreement was not restrictive of competition) or objectively justified.

Another official of DG COMP explains that the reason for this approach is that **2.170**. the Commission took the view that elimination of competition could be equated with dominance:

> However, in recent case law the CFI has held that elimination of competition is not the same as dominance [ie Joined Cases 1–191/98, 212/98 and 214/98 *Atlantic Container Line (TACA)* [2003] ECR II–3275, para 939 and Case T–395/ 94 *Atlantic Container Line* [2002] ECR II–875, para 330]. As a consequence, the Guidelines [ie the Guidelines on the application of Article 81(3) EC] do not exclude the application of Art 81(3) to dominant undertakings.[174]

In the Guidelines on the application of Article 81(3) EC, published in 2004, the **2.171**. Commission indeed revisited its view and emphasized that for the application of Article 82 EC, there must at all times be an abuse. In paragraph 106 of this Notice, the Commission states that 'since Articles 81 and 82 both pursue the aim of maintaining effective competition on the market, consistency requires

---

[172] For a critique, see S Bishop and D Ridyard, 'E.C. Vertical Restraints Guidelines: Effects-based or Per se Policy?' [2002] ECLR 35.

[173] L Peeperkorn, a DG COMP official closely involved in the drafting of Reg 2790/99 and the Guidelines, in a reaction to the article cited in the previous footnote ('E.C. Vertical Restraints Guidelines: Effects-based or Per se Policy?—A Reply' [2002] ECLR 38, 41).

[174] Kjølbye (n 141 above) 576.

that Article 81(3) be interpreted as precluding *any application of this provision to restrictive agreements that constitute an abuse of a dominant position*' [emphasis added]. A footnote is added to this, which reads: 'This is how paragraph 135 of the Guidelines on vertical restraints . . . ,should be understood when they state that in principle restrictive agreements concluded by dominant undertakings cannot be exempted'.

2.172. It would therefore seem that, given the Commission's most recent statements on vertical agreements concluded by dominant undertakings which contain vertical restraints, these restraints are permissible under EC competition law if they are ancillary (which implies a non-restrictive main agreement) or if they are objectively justified, in which case the restraints do not fall under Article 81(1) EC. If they do, exemption under Article 81(3) EC remains possible as long as the vertical restraints do not amount to an abuse of dominant position. Article 81(3) EC cannot prevent the application of Article 82 EC.[175]

F. Fourth Question: The Applicability of Other Block Exemption Regulations

(1) Introduction

2.173. The relationship between Regulation 2790/99 and other block exemption regulations is generally dealt with by Article 2(5) of Regulation 2790/99, which reads 'This Regulation shall not apply to vertical agreements the subject matter of which falls within the scope of any other block exemption regulation'.

2.174. The Guidelines (paragraph 45) explain that this means that Regulation 2790/99:

> does not apply to agreements covered by Commission Regulation (EC) No 240/96 on technology transfer, Regulation (EC) No 1475/199[5] for car distribution or Regulations (EEC) No 417/85 and (EEC) No 418/85 exempting vertical agreements concluded in connection with horizontal agreements, as last amended by Regulation (EC) No 2236/97 or any future regulations of that kind.

2.175. This does not mean that Regulation 2790/99 does not apply when an agreement or practice benefits from an exemption under any of the other block exemption regulations. The meaning of Article 2(5) of Regulation 2790/99 is different from that. It states that an agreement whose subject matter comes within the scope of application of another block exemption regulation will not be able to use Regulation 2790/99 as a lifebuoy. If such an agreement does not fulfil the criteria of the applicable block exemption regulation, then Article 2(5) prevents that agreement

---

[175] Guidelines, para 106 (with references). See also the discussion in Pt III on the EC competition law analysis of vertical agreements outside Reg 2790/99.

from being block exempted under Regulation 2790/99.[176] So, for instance, a practice which is blacklisted under Regulation 1400/2002 on motor vehicle distribution, but not under Regulation 2790/99, can no longer be exempted under the latter block exemption if the agreement in which the practice is contained is within the scope of Regulation 1400/2002. Similarly, if an agreement is covered by Regulation 772/2004 (ie the current technology transfer agreements block exemption regulation), but does not qualify for block exemption under that Regulation (eg because a market share limit is exceeded), then the agreement concerned cannot enjoy a 'safe harbour' under Regulation 2790/99.

Therefore, the fourth question that needs to be addressed is whether the subject matter of a given vertical agreement falls within the scope of application of any other block exemption regulation. If it does, then Regulation 2790/99 does not apply. If it does not, the fourth question does not provide a hurdle to the application of the block exemption contained in Regulation 2790/99. As will be seen below, matters are not as black and white as they are presented here. The substance of a given vertical agreement may indeed be mixed and it may therefore require some analysis before it is possible to determine the commercial focus of the agreement as well as the relevant block exemption regulation. **2.176.**

The block exemption regulations, that are in force at the time of writing and that are relevant to the fourth question as they may apply to vertical restraints, are the following: **2.177.**

— Horizontal co-operation agreements:

- Regulation 2658/2000 (specialization agreements) (paragraphs 2.180–2.188)
- Regulation 2659/2000 (research and development agreements) (paragraphs 2.189–2.194)
- Regulation 772/2004 (technology transfer agreements) (paragraphs 2.195–2.205)
- Regulation 1400/2002 (motor vehicle distribution) (paragraphs 2.206–2.208).

(2) The relationship with the block exemption regulations on horizontal co-operation agreements

General

Horizontal co-operation agreements are entered into between companies operating at the same level(s) in the market and therefore may be concluded **2.178.**

---

[176] cf R Whish, 'Regulation 2790/99: The Commission's "New Style" Block Exemption for Vertical Agreements' [2000] CML Rev 907; Korah and O'Sullivan (n 165 above) 140–2.

between competitors.[177] There are two block exemption regulations which currently apply to this type of agreement:

— Commission Regulation (EC) No 2658/2000 of 29 November 2000 on the application of Article 81(3) of the Treaty to categories of specialization agreements;[178] and
— Commission Regulation (EC) No 2659/2000 of 29 November 2000 on the application of Article 81(3) of the Treaty to categories of research and development agreements.[179]

2.179. Both Regulations entered into force on 1 January 2001 and are due to lapse on 31 December 2010.[180]

The relation between Regulations 2658/2000 and 2790/99

The limits to the scope of application of Regulation 2790/99

2.180. On the basis of Article 2(5) of Regulation 2790/99, when read in conjunction with the Guidelines (paragraph 45), the block exemption of Regulation 2790/99 does not apply to vertical agreements covered by Regulation 2658/2000.

The scope of application of Regulation 2658/2000

2.181. In addition to applying to (horizontal) specialization agreements (paragraphs 2.182–2.184), Regulation 2658/2000 also applies to certain vertical obligations and arrangements concluded in connection with specialization agreements (paragraphs 2.185–2.188).

2.182. **Specialization agreements.** Recital 10 of Regulation 2658/2000 recalls that 'unilateral specialisation agreements between non-competitors may benefit from the block exemption provided by [Regulation 2790/99]' and that therefore 'the application of the present Regulation [that is, Regulation 2658/2000] to unilateral specialisation agreements should be limited to agreements between competitors'. Recital 11 continues: 'All other agreements entered into between undertakings relating to the conditions under which they specialise in the production of goods and/or services [ie specialization agreements][181] should fall within the scope of this Regulation'.

2.183. The fact that all specialization agreements, aside from unilateral specialization agreements between non-competitors, fall within the scope of application of

---

[177] Commission Notice—Guidelines on the applicability of Article 81 of the EC Treaty to horizontal cooperation agreements [2001] OJ C3/02, para 1 (hereafter 'Horizontal Guidelines').
[178] [2000] OJ L304/3.   [179] [2000] OJ C304/7.
[180] Reg 2658/2000, Art 9; and Reg 2659/2000, Art 9.
[181] For the definition, see Reg 2658/2000, Art 1(1).

Regulation 2658/2000 is reflected in Article 1(1) of that Regulation. According to this provision, Article 81(1) EC does not apply to the following three categories of specialization agreement:

(a) unilateral specialisation agreements, by virtue of which one party agrees to cease production of certain products or to refrain from producing those products and to purchase them from a competing undertaking, while the competing under-taking agrees to produce and supply those products; or
(b) reciprocal specialisation agreements, by virtue of which two or more parties on a reciprocal basis agree to cease or refrain from producing certain but different products and to purchase these products from the other party or parties, who agree to supply them; or
(c) joint production agreements, by virtue of which two or more parties agree to produce certain products jointly.

2.184. According to recital 11 of Regulation 2658/2000, the block exemption on specialization agreements 'should also apply to provisions contained in spe-cialisation agreements which do not constitute the primary object of such agreements, but are directly related to and necessary for their implementation, and to certain related purchasing and marketing arrangements'. The latter category (purchasing and marketing arrangements) is addressed in Article 3 of Regulation 2658/2000 (paragraph 2.185). The other category (provisions which do not constitute the primary object of specialization agreements, but are directly related to and necessary for their implementation) is addressed in Article 1(2) (paragraphs 2.186–2.188).

Purchasing and marketing obligations in connection with specialization agreements

2.185. *Supply and purchase obligations.* It follows from the definitions given above that both unilateral and reciprocal specialization agreements are covered by the block exemption of Regulation 2658/2000 if (and only if) they include a vertical dimension. They must not only concern the production, but also the supply of the products concerned. The reason for this is that the Commis-sion wishes to avoid the possibility of specialization agreements leading to market sharing. This follows in so many words from recital 12 of Regulation 2658/2000, which reads:

> To ensure that the benefits of specialisation will materialise without one party leaving the market downstream of production, unilateral and reciprocal agreements should only be covered by this Regulation where they provide for supply and purchase obligations.

The recital continues that 'the supply and purchase obligations may, but do not have to, be of an exclusive nature'. In line with this, Article 3(a) provides that the block exemption will continue to apply to the specialization agreement concerned if 'the parties accept an exclusive purchase and/or exclusive supply obligation in the context of a unilateral or reciprocal specialisation agreement or a joint production agreement'.

— *Marketing obligations.* In respect of certain marketing obligations, Article 3(b) of Regulation 2658/2000 provides that the block exemption will continue to apply where the parties do not sell the products that are the subject of the specialization agreement independently, but provide for joint distribution. In the context of a joint production agreement, they may also agree to appoint a third party distributor on an exclusive or a non-exclusive basis, provided that the third party is not a competing undertaking.

2.186. **Provisions which do not constitute the primary object of specialization agreements, but which are directly related to and necessary for their implementation.** Specialization agreements will continue to be covered by the block exemption of Regulation 2658/2000 if they contain certain marketing arrangements. In this respect, Article 1(2) provides that the exemption also applies to 'provisions . . . which do not constitute the primary object of such agreements, but are directly related to and necessary for their implementation, such as those concerning the assignment or use of intellectual property rights'.

2.187. An example of the type of IPR provisions contained in a specialization agreement is where a producer of, for example, construction equipment, who also manufactures merchandise (sweatshirts, outerwear, etc), and a sportswear manufacturer, agree that the former will stop manufacturing the merchandise and will procure these from the latter, who will receive a licence to use the trademark of the former to print it on the merchandise. While the trademark licence is directly related to and necessary for the implementation of the production agreement, the manufacture of the merchandise is the primary object of the specialization agreement. The trademark licence will therefore be covered by the exemption of Regulation 2658/2000.

2.188. In conclusion, if one is dealing with a specialization agreement, it must first be determined whether it is a unilateral specialization agreement between non-competitors. If it is, then it is covered by the scope of application of Regulation 2790/99. If it is not, it is covered by Regulation 2658/2000, even if (and, in some cases, on condition that) the specialization agreement concerned contains non-exclusive or exclusive vertical arrangements between the parties to the agreement.

The relation between Regulations 2659/2000 and 2790/99

The limits to the scope of application of Regulation 2790/99

2.189. As with Regulation 2658/2000 on specialization agreements, the block exemption of Regulation 2790/99 does not, according to Article 2(5) of Regulation 2790/99, when read in conjunction with the Guidelines (paragraph 45), apply to vertical agreements covered by Regulation 2659/2000.

The scope of application of Regulation 2659/2000

In addition to R & D agreements (see paragraph 2.191), Regulation 2659/2000 **2.190.** also applies to certain vertical agreements concluded in connection with R & D agreements (see paragraphs 2.192–2.194).

R & D agreements.   In accordance with Article 1(1) of Regulation 2659/ **2.191.** 2000, R & D agreements are entered into between two or more undertakings and relate to the conditions under which those undertakings pursue, as follows:

(a) joint research and development of products or processes and joint exploitation of the results of that research and development,
(b) joint exploitation of the results of research and development of products or processes jointly carried out pursuant to a prior agreement between the same parties, or
(c) joint research and development of products or processes excluding joint exploitation of the results.

Vertical agreements in connection with R & D agreements ('joint exploitation **2.192.** **of R & D results').**   The above definition of R & D agreements means that the block exemption of Regulation 2659/2000 covers 'the joint exploitation of the results'. This notion is defined in Article 2(8) of Regulation 2659/2000 as including, for example, the distribution of the contract products:

> the production or distribution of the contract products or the application of the contract processes or the assignment or licensing of intellectual property rights or the communication of know-how required for such manufacture or application.

According to Article 2(11), the exploitation of results is carried out 'jointly' **2.193.** where the work involved is:

(a) carried out by a joint team, organization, or undertaking,
(b) jointly entrusted to a third party, or
(c) allocated between the parties by way of specialization in research, development, production, or distribution.

It follows from these various provisions that vertical agreements (including for **2.194.** example supply, purchase, and distribution agreements) concluded between the parties (or between the parties and a third party) which concern the joint exploitation of the results of their R & D, which they had previously agreed to perform within the context of an R & D agreement, is covered by Regulation 2659/2000 and is therefore outside the scope of Regulation 2790/99.

(3) The relation with the technology transfer block exemption regulation

General

2.195. The technology transfer block exemption regulation ('TTBER')—Regulation 772/2004[182]—entered into force on 1 May 2004 and is due to expire on 30 April 2014.[183] The relation between Regulation 2790/99 and the TTBER is addressed both in the TTBER itself and in the Guidelines on the application of Article 81 of the EC Treaty to technology transfer agreements ('the TTBER Guidelines').[184]

The relation between Regulations 772/2004 and 2790/99

The limits to the scope of application of Regulation 2790/99

2.196. On the basis of Article 2(5) of Regulation 2790/99, as read in conjunction with the Guidelines (paragraph 45), the block exemption of Regulation 2790/99 does not apply to 'vertical agreements covered by Commission Regulation [772/2004] on technology transfer'.

The scope of application of Regulation 772/2004

2.197. **Technology transfer agreements.** Article 2 of the TTBER covers 'technology transfer agreements entered into between two undertakings permitting the production of contract products'. In its turn, a 'technology transfer agreement' is defined in Article 1(1)(b) of the TTBER as:

> A patent licensing agreement, a know-how licensing agreement, a software copyright licensing agreement or a mixed patent, know-how or software copyright licensing agreement, including any such agreement containing provisions which relate to the sale and purchase of products or which relate to the licensing of other intellectual property rights or the assignment of intellectual property rights, provided that those provisions do not constitute the primary object of the agreement and are directly related to the production of the contract product.

2.198. It is important for the relation between the TTBER and Regulation 2790/99 that the TTBER also applies to sale and purchase provisions contained in technology transfer agreements (see paragraph 2.199) as well as to the licensing of other IPRs, such as trademarks and copyright other than software copyright licensing (see paragraphs 2.200–2.201), each time on the condition that these do not constitute the primary object of the agreement and that they are directly related to the production of the contract product.

---

[182] Commission Regulation (EC) No 772/2004 on the application of Article 81(3) of the Treaty to categories of technology transfer agreements [2004] OJ L123/11.

[183] Reg 772/2004, Art 11.

[184] Commission Notice—Guidelines on the application of Article 81 of the EC Treaty to technology transfer agreements [2004] OJ C101/2 (hereafter 'TTBER Guidelines').

Sale and purchase provisions which do not constitute the primary object of a **2.199** **technology transfer agreement, but are directly related to and necessary for its implementation.**   In this respect, the meaning of the concepts 'tying product' and 'tied product' are important: the tying product is the licensed technology, and the tied product is the product which the licensee is required to buy from the licensor or someone designated by him to obtain the tying product.[185] Pursuant to the TTBER Guidelines (paragraph 49), the TTBER is most likely to apply if the tied products take the form of equipment or process inputs which are specifically tailored to efficiently exploit the tying product (eg specific tooling for the manufacture of the products incorporating the licensed technology). Conversely, where the tied products are simply another input into the final product, it will have to be carefully examined whether the licensed technology does indeed constitute the primary object of the agreement:

— If the licensee already manufactures a final product on the basis of another technology, the technology licence will need to lead to a significant improvement of the licensee's production process, exceeding the value of the product purchased from the licensor. If it does not, then the TTBER will not apply.[186]
— The TTBER does not cover the purchase of tied products that have no relation with the products incorporating the licensed technology. For instance, where the tied product is not intended to be used with the licensed product, but is related to an activity on a separate market, then the TTBER will again not apply.[187]

Licensing of other IPRs, which do not constitute the primary object of a **2.200** **technology transfer agreement, but are directly related to, and necessary for, its implementation.**   The licensing of other IPRs (such as trademarks and copyrights, other than software copyright licensing), and the extent to which that licensing may be covered by the TTBER, is addressed in paragraphs 50–3 of the TTBER Guidelines. At paragraph 53, the TTBER Guidelines confirm that the TTBER does not cover trademark licensing:

> Trademark licensing often occurs in the context of distribution and resale of goods and services and is generally more akin to distribution agreements than to technology licensing. Where a trademark license is directly related to the use, sale or resale of goods or services and does not constitute the primary object of the agreement, the license agreement is covered by [Regulation 2790/99].

Put simply, it follows from the above considerations that the primary objective of **2.201** agreements covered by Regulation 2790/99 must be the sale or purchase of goods or services, while the primary objective of agreements covered by the TTBER must be the transfer of technology. IPR provisions which are part of an agreement

---

[185] TTBER Guidelines, para 191.   [186] ibid, para 49.   [187] ibid.

on the sale and purchase of goods or services are also covered by Regulation 2790/99, as long as they do not constitute the primary object of the agreement and they are directly related to the use, sale, or resale of goods or services by the buyer or his customers.[188] Inversely, provisions on the sale or purchase of goods or services which are part of a technology transfer agreement are covered by the TTBER, as long as these provisions do not constitute the primary object of the agreement and are directly related to the production of the contract products.

Agreements concerning different levels of trade

2.202. The TTBER states in recital 19:

> This Regulation should cover only technology transfer agreements between a licensor and a licensee. It should cover such agreements even if conditions are stipulated for more than one level of trade, by, for instance, requiring the licensee to set up a particular distribution system and specifying the obligations the licensee must or may impose on resellers of the products produced under the licence. However, such conditions and obligations should comply with the competition rules applicable to supply and distribution agreements. Supply and distribution agreements concluded between a licensee and its buyers should not be exempted by this Regulation.

2.203. The TTBER Guidelines (paragraphs 39 and 106) confirm this by stating that the TTBER:

> covers licence agreements whereby the licensor imposes obligations which the licensee must or may impose on his buyers, including distributors. However, these obligations must comply with the competition rules applicable to supply and distribution agreements. Since the TTBER is limited to agreements between two parties the agreements concluded between the licensee and his buyers implementing such obligations are not covered by the TTBER. Such agreements are only block exempted when they comply with Regulation 2790/99.[189]

2.204. As a consequence of this, the TTBER (which only applies to agreements between two parties) makes a distinction between technology transfer agreements concluded between the licensor and the licensee at one level of trade and those agreements concluded between the licensee and the buyers at a subsequent level of trade. The former agreements must comply with the TTBER to be block exempted, whilst the latter must comply with Regulation 2790/99. More guidance on this distinction can be found in the TTBER Guidelines (paragraph 63). The TTBER does not prevent a licensor from imposing within a technology transfer agreement, certain obligations on the licensee relating to the distribution of the products that incorporate the licensed technology (eg that the licensee must establish an exclusive or selective distribution system). This does not imply, however, that the distribution agreements concluded between the licensee and the buyers are automatically block exempted under Regulation

---

[188] Paras 2.267–2.283 below.   [189] TTBER Guidelines, para 106.

2790/99. To be so exempted, these agreements must comply with the conditions of the latter.[190]

If a licensor licenses technology to different licensees for the production of their **2.205.** own products, which they then subsequently sell to their distributors, the freedom of the distributors of one licensee to sell actively and passively in territories which are covered by the distribution systems of other licensees may not normally be restricted. The reason for this is that, for the purposes of Regulation 2790/99, each licensee is considered to be a separate supplier.[191] Therefore, agreements on the territories in which their respective distributors are entitled to sell their products will amount to illegal market sharing. The TTBER Guidelines however clarify that, in the case where the products incorporating the licensed technology are sold under a common brand belonging to the licensor, similar restraints between licensees' distribution systems may be agreed as within a single vertical distribution system.[192]

(4) The relation with the motor vehicle distribution block exemption regulation

The scope of application of Regulation 1400/2002 concerns vertical agreements **2.206.** 'where they relate to the conditions under which the parties may purchase, sell or resell new motor vehicles, spare parts for motor vehicles or repair and maintenance services for motor vehicles'.[193] A 'motor vehicle' is defined as 'a self propelled vehicle intended for use on public roads and having three or more road wheels'.[194] Accordingly, Regulation 1400/2002 applies to the distribution and services of new passenger cars, light commercial vehicles, trucks, buses, and touring coaches. It does not apply to the distribution of tractors and vehicles used in the construction industry (bulldozers, cranes, etc). Nor does it apply to second-hand vehicles.

As regards the previous motor vehicle block exemption regulations, the Court **2.207.** confirmed this in the *JCB* case.[195] JCB argued that its construction machinery equipment could be used and was intended to be used as both road vehicles and non-road vehicles. The Court replied to this that:

> according to the wording of its Article 1 in the 1984 version, that regulation concerns: certain motor vehicles intended for use on public roads and having three or more road wheels, and the 1995 Regulation stipulates additionally that such vehicles must be new. Moreover, regulations on block exemption must be interpreted narrowly (Case C–234/89 *Delimitis* [1991] ECR I–935, paragraphs 36, 37 and 46). It is clear that the construction site machinery produced by JCB is intended for earthmoving and construction and that, although it may be used on

---

[190] ibid, para 63.   [191] On active and passive sales, see paras 5.46–5.53 below.
[192] These restraints are discussed in Chs 5 and 6.   [193] Reg 1400/2002, Art 2(1).
[194] ibid, Art 1(1)(n).
[195] Case T–67/01 *JCB Service v Commission* [2004] OJ C85/23, paras 163–4.

public roads it is not intended for such use within the meaning of the exemption regulation in question. The products manufactured by JCB are therefore not covered by that regulation which cannot be applied by analogy to categories of vehicles other than those to which it relates.

2.208. Regulation 1400/2002, which, with the exception of one provision, entered into force on 1 October 2002 and is due to expire on 31 May 2010,[196] is discussed in detail below in Chapter 11.

G. Fifth Question: Market Share Limit

(1) Introduction

2.209. The fifth step in our analysis of the scope of application of Regulation 2790/99 concerns its market share limit. The across-the-board rules relating to the market share limit are set out in this introduction. In the subsequent sections, more details are provided on the way to determine the relevant (product and geographic) market (*section 2*) and on the calculation of the market share (*section 3*). Finally, *section 4* concludes by providing some case studies.

2.210. This fifth step centres around the question of whether or not the supplier's (or in certain cases, the buyer's) market share exceeds 30%. In this respect, Article 3 of Regulation 2790/99 provides:

1. Subject to paragraph 2 of this Article, the exemption provided for in Article 2 shall apply on condition that the market share held by the supplier does not exceed 30% of the relevant market on which it sells the contract goods or services.
2. In the case of vertical agreements containing exclusive supply obligations, the exemption provided for in Article 2 shall apply on condition that the market share held by the buyer does not exceed 30% of the relevant market on which it purchases the contract goods or services.

2.211. The material scope of application of Regulation 2790/99 is thus limited to those cases where the supplier (or, for exclusive supply obligations, the buyer) has a market share which does not exceed 30% of the relevant market. In accordance with the *De Minimis* Notice, vertical agreements are not covered by Article 81(1) EC if they do not contain hardcore restrictions and if the parties' market share does not exceed certain limits. For agreements between non-competitors, the level set is an individual market share of 15% of the relevant market; and for agreements between competitors, it is set at a combined market share of 10% of the relevant market. If the market is foreclosed by the application of parallel networks of similar vertical agreements by several companies,

---

[196] Reg 1400/2002, Art 12.

the *de minimis* limit is reduced to 5%.[197] As a consequence, in the absence of cumulative foreclosure effects Regulation 2790/99 essentially applies to vertical agreements between non-competitors with a market share of between 15% and 30% of the relevant market and for competitors with a market share ranging between 10% and 30% of the relevant market.[198]

One should not be misguided by this seemingly limited scope of application. **2.212.** Just as it has done with other block exemption regulations, the Commission has injected a degree of dynamics into the market share limit test of Regulation 2790/99. Specifically, the safe harbour under Regulation 2790/99 continues to apply if the market share limit is exceeded only temporarily. That is, if the market share is initially not more than 30% but subsequently rises above that level, but without exceeding 35%, the exemption will continue to apply for a period of two consecutive calendar years following the year in which the 30% market share limit was first exceeded.[199] In the situation where the market share is initially not more than 30% but subsequently rises above 35%, then the exemption provided continues to apply for one calendar year following the year in which the level of 35% was first exceeded.[200] This benefit given by Article 9(2)(c) and (d) may not be combined so as to exceed a period of two calendar years.[201] To put this differently, a vertical agreement will not be able to benefit from the block exemption of Regulation 2790/99 in the next calendar year if the market share of the supplier (or the buyer) (a) exceeded 35% in the previous calendar year; or (b) exceeded 30% in the previous two calendar years.

Schematically the application in time of Regulation 2790/99 pursuant to **2.213.** Article 9 can be represented as follows:[202]

'Initially' %	Previous calendar year (−2) %	Previous calendar year (−1) %	Current calendar year	Next calendar year	Applicable provision
n.a.	n.a.	≤ 30	✓	✓	Article 3
≤ 30	≤ 30	>30/ ≤ 35	✓	✓	Article 9(2)(c)
≤ 30	≤ 30	>35	✓	−	Article 9(2)(d)
≤ 30	>30/ ≤ 35	>30	✓	−	Article 9(2)(c)
≤ 30	>35	>30	−	−	Article 9(2)(d)
>30	>30	>30	−	−	Article 3

A number of practical examples of the principles laid down in Article 9 of Regulation 2790/99 are discussed below.

---

[197] *De Minimis* Notice, para 7 and paras 2.125–2.133 above.
[198] Vertical agreements between competitors must also comply with the conditions set out in Reg 2790/99, Art 2(4), as discussed in paras 2.291–2.305 below. [199] Reg 2790/99, Art 9(2)(c).
[200] ibid, Art 2(1)(d).   [201] ibid, Art 2(1)(e).
[202] See also Schultze, Pautke, and Wagener (n 2 above) para 306.

2.214. According to Article 11(1) of Regulation 2790/99, the terms 'undertaking', 'supplier', and 'buyer' shall include their respective connected undertakings.[203] The market share on the relevant market therefore includes the market share of such connected undertakings. This is logical. In the alternative, it would be possible to circumvent the market share limit by concluding vertical agreements via group companies—'special purpose vehicles'—which only have a minimal presence on the relevant market. In a like manner, the market share must be calculated across brands: if a company or group of companies owns several brands on a relevant market, all of those brands must be taken into account when calculating the market share.

2.215. In accordance with Article 3, Regulation 2790/99 only takes account of the market share of the supplier or the buyer, as the case may be, on the market on which both the supplier and the buyer are involved. In the Guidelines (paragraph 22), the Commission states that it realizes that this is a simplified approach as, from an economic point of view, a vertical agreement may have effects 'not only on the market between supplier and buyer but also on markets downstream of the buyer'. Clearly, a vertical agreement may have a competitive impact on upstream markets as well. For instance, a vertical agreement on after-sales services (including the supply of spare parts) may lead to restrictions of competition for the primary product, particularly where the availability and quality of the after-sales services are elements which contribute to the purchase of the primary product.

2.216. The reasons why the Commission considers that the simplified approach is justified are that below the threshold of 30% the effects on downstream markets will in general be limited, that it makes the application of Regulation 2790/99 easier and that it enhances the level of legal certainty. Should problems on related markets arise, the Commission points at the possibility to use the instrument of withdrawal.[204] Apart from the fact that experience has shown that the instrument of withdrawal is actually applied very rarely, the motives of the Commission can be approved of. In many cases, Regulation 2790/99 would indeed fail to produce its intended effect if the parties first have to calculate their market share on related markets.

2.217. The introduction of a market share limit is one of the major innovations of Regulation 2790/99. It is an innovation which in the meantime has been transposed to the other 'new style' block exemption regulations, and which was first suggested in the Commission's Green Paper on Vertical Restraints in EC Competition Policy.[205] In Chapter VIII of the Green Paper, entitled 'Options',

---

[203] For the definition of 'connected undertakings' see para 2.255 below.
[204] On withdrawal, see ch 9 below.   [205] COM(96)721 final, 22 January 1997.

the Commission had initially suggested two market share limits, of 20% and 40%.[206] In the Follow-up to the Green Paper on Vertical Restraints,[207] it nevertheless appeared that a large majority of companies, consumer organizations, associations of undertakings, and law firms opposed the introduction of a market share limit. Most support (46.2% in favour; 23.3% not in favour) went to the option of a wider block exemption without a market share cap. The options with a market share limit attracted much less support:

— more focused block exemptions with a market share cap of 40%: 6.7% in favour; 59.6% not in favour;
— negative clearance presumption up to 20% and above wider block exemptions without a market share cap: 20.2% in favour; 59.5% not in favour; and
— negative clearance presumption up to 20% and above wider block exemptions with market share cap of 40%: 8.1% in favour; 82.4% not in favour.[208]

The negative reactions mostly related to the fact that the introduction of a market share limit would bring an element of uncertainty in its wake. However, contrary to the opinions of the market participants, Member States were much less opposed to the introduction of a market share limit, and it was in the course of the consultation process after the Green Paper, that a consensus grew between the Commission and the Member States regarding the introduction of one broad block exemption regulation with one or two market share limits.[209] The Commission was able to build a solid basis for this approach with the Member States essentially because the market participants, in their reactions to the Green Paper, had been unable to suggest any better indicator to measure relative market power than guidelines that would make it possible to use the full set of market factors for the assessment of vertical restraints. However, the Commission (supported by the Member States) considered that this would have represented too radical a change and would have afforded industry a lower level of legal certainty than the use of a block exemption with market share limits.[210] This explains why Regulation 2790/99 contains a market share limit even though this was opposed by a large majority of market participants. **2.218**.

In the event market share tests were to be introduced, the market participants had asked the Commission to provide as many flanking measures as possible to protect legal certainty. In particular, it was suggested that the Commission **2.219**.

---

[206] F O'Toole, 'The EC Green Paper on Vertical Restraints: Option IV Defended' (1999) ECLR 5; and J Nazerali and D Cowan, 'Reforming E.U. Distribution Rules—Has the Commission Found Vertical Reality?' (1999) ECLR 159.
[207] [1998] OJ C365/3.
[208] Communication from the the Commission on the application of the Community Competition rules to vertical restraints—Follow-up to the Green Paper on Vertical Restraints, 8 available at http://www.europa.eu.int/comm/competition/antitrust/com1998544_en.pdf.
[209] ibid, 12.   [210] ibid, 22.

should provide guidelines on the application of the rules above the market share limits and solve the problem of automatic nullity under Article 81(2) EC in the case where a company had failed to notify because it incorrectly assessed its market share.[211] The first request explains why the Guidelines, in addition to a discussion on the application of Regulation 2790/99, also contain an extensive amount of information on the Commission's enforcement policy in individual cases. The second request may help to explain the revision of Regulation 17/62[212] and also as to why the Commission states in the Guidelines that, where undertakings have failed to notify an agreement because they assumed in good faith that they did not exceed the market share limit of Regulation 2790/99, it will not impose fines.[213]

(2) Relevant markets

Definition of the relevant product and geographic market

2.220. The definition of the relevant market is a prerequisite to the performance of the calculation of market shares. The relevant market consists of the relevant product and the relevant geographic markets. The concepts are elaborated in the Commission's Notice on the definition of the relevant market for the purposes of Community competition law:[214]

> A relevant product market comprises all those products and/or services which are regarded as interchangeable or substitutable by the consumer, by reason of the products' characteristics, their prices and their intended use (paragraph 7).

> The relevant geographic market comprises the area in which the undertakings concerned are involved in the supply and demand of products or services, in which the conditions of competition are sufficiently homogeneous and which can be distinguished from neighbouring areas because the conditions of competition are appreciably different in those areas (paragraph 9).

2.221. In what follows, the discussion of the relevant (product and geographic) market is centred on vertical agreements. More general provisions of the Commission's Notice are only dealt with in passing. Suffice it to say that the method which the Notice propounds in order to determine substitutability is the so-called 'SSNIP test' (which stands for 'small but significant non-transitory increase in price'):

> Conceptually, this approach means that, starting from the type of products that the undertakings involved sell and the area in which they sell them, additional products and areas will be included in, or excluded from, the market definition

---

[211] ibid, 10.   [212] Para 1.54 above.

[213] Guidelines, para 65, in fine. It goes without saying that this language became obsolete following the entry into force of Reg 1/2003 which abolished the notification requirement.

[214] [1997] OJ C372/5.

depending on whether competition from these other products and areas affect or restrain sufficiently the pricing of the parties' products in the short term.

The question to be answered is whether the parties' customers would switch to readily available substitutes or to suppliers located elsewhere in response to a hypothetical small (in the range 5% to 10%) but permanent relative price increase in the products and areas being considered. If substitution were enough to make the price increase unprofitable because of the resulting loss of sales, additional substitutes and areas are included in the relevant market. This would be done until the set of products and geographical areas is such that small, permanent increases in relative prices would be profitable.[215]

Practically speaking, the SSNIP test is performed as follows: **2.222**.

— If a price increase of 5 to 10% of product A in area X leads a certain number of buyers to switch to product B and a certain number of other buyers to buy product A in area Y, and the resulting loss of sales of product A in area X makes the price increase unprofitable, then products A and B will belong to the same product market and areas X and Y to the same geographic market.
— If a price increase of products A and B in areas X and Y leads a number of buyers to buy products A and B in area Z, and the resulting loss of sales of products A and B makes the price increase of A and B unprofitable, then areas X, Y, and Z belong to the same geographic market.
— Finally, if a further increase of price of products A and B in areas X, Y, and Z is profitable, then the relevant product and geographic market have been determined.

Relevant market—market share of the supplier

General

According to the rule in Article 3(1) of Regulation 2790/99, the supplier's   **2.223**. market share determines the application of the block exemption. The broader the product and geographic markets on which the supplier operates, the lower his market share on those markets is likely to be. In the case where the vertical agreements are concluded between an association of retailers and individual members, the association is considered as the supplier and its market share must be taken as the starting point of the analysis.[216]

The market share of a supplier is his share of the relevant product and geo-   **2.224**. graphic market on which he sells to his buyers (distributors). The definition of the relevant product and geographic market are addressed in the Guidelines (paragraph 91), and are discussed hereafter.

---

[215] Notice on the definition of the relevant market for the purposes of Community competition law, paras 16–17. See also M Monti, *Market Definition as a Cornerstone of EU Competition Policy*, Speech 01/439, 5 October 2003.   [216] Guidelines, para 89.

Relevant product market rule (1): substitutability for input products from a buyer's perspective

2.225. The relevant product market of the supplier depends in the first place on substitutability from a buyer's perspective. Accordingly, the definition of the relevant product market for vertical agreements under Regulation 2790/99 differs from that of the Notice on the definition of the relevant market for the purposes of Community competition law. Under the latter Notice, the relevant product market is defined from the viewpoint of the consumer. Regulation 2790/99 however does not apply to vertical agreements with end-consumers,[217] but only to those with buyers, often distributors, who resell the goods (possibly after having incorporated them into a final product) and services to end-consumers.

2.226. Substitutability from a buyer's perspective is relatively easy to determine if the buyer uses the products (eg components) as an input in order to produce other products and is therefore the end-user of the products concerned. Normally, these input products are not recognizable in the end product or the customers of the buyers do not have strong preferences about the input used by the buyer. As a result, the product market can be defined exclusively on the basis of the direct buyers' preferences. In the Guidelines, the Commission seems to suggest that the situation may only be different in cases where vertical restraints agreed between the supplier and the buyer relate not only to the sale and purchase of the intermediate product, but also to the sale of the resulting product. In those cases, account may have to be taken of the preferences of the final consumers, much in the same way as is discussed hereafter.

Relevant product market rule (2): substitutability for final products from a final consumer's perspective

2.227. In the case of the distribution of final products, the issue of substitutability will be influenced or determined by the final consumers' preferences. As a reseller, a distributor cannot ignore the final consumers' preferences. Accordingly, the relevant product market must be determined at the level of the final consumer. This is all the more so because, at the distribution level, the vertical restraints concern not only the sale of products between suppliers, but also their resale.

Exception to relevant product market rule (2): substitutability for a portfolio of final products from a buyer's perspective

2.228. Where suppliers sell a portfolio of products, the entire portfolio may determine the product market when the portfolios, and not the individual products, are regarded as substitutes by the buyers. Two examples that can be given are shoes

---

[217] Para 2.95 above.

and clothing. Generally an assortment of shoes or a collection of clothes from a given supplier may be considered to belong to the same product market, and no further distinction should be made between the different types of shoes or clothes.

Relevant product market rule (3): as a rule, the distribution form is irrelevant

Because different forms of distribution usually compete, they do not as a rule **2.229**. define the product market. In other words, if a product (eg white goods) is distributed both in supermarkets and via more specialized outlets, no distinction should be made between these two forms of distribution in order to determine the relevant market.

In the past, the Commission has adopted several decisions in which it has **2.230**. decided that there is a separate market in food retailing which embraces all retailers (supermarkets and hypermarkets) which carry a range of food and non-food products which is typical of the food-retailing trade (excluding, that is, specialized outlets such as butchers and bakers).[218]

Relevant geographic market

In order to determine the relevant geographic market, account must be taken of **2.231**. the fact that Regulation 2790/99 does not apply to vertical agreements with final consumers, but only to such agreements concluded with professional buyers. These professional buyers are repeat players with more purchasing experience (and power) than the average consumer. In order to maximize their profitability they will usually seek to benchmark several suppliers, both at home and abroad. The relevant geographic market for professional buyers is therefore likely to be wider than the market where the product is resold to final consumers. Typically, this will lead to the definition of at least national, or wider, geographic markets.[219]

Relevant market—market share of the buyer

The exception to the rule that the market share of the supplier determines the **2.232**. applicability of Regulation 2790/99 is in relation to exclusive supply arrangements. For this type of arrangement, it is the buyer's market share that is decisive. In this context, it is important to recall the definition of 'exclusive supply obligation' contained in Article 1(c), namely

> Any direct or indirect obligation causing the supplier to sell the goods or services specified in the agreement only to one buyer inside the Community for the purposes of a specific use or for resale.

---

[218] *Rewe/Meinl* (Case IV/M1221) [1999] OJ L274/1; also *Rewe/Billa* (Case IV/M803) [1996] OJ C306/4; *Spar/Pro* (Case IV/M1071) [1998] OJ C49/13; and *ICA Ahold/Dansk Supermarked* (COMP/M2604) [2001] OJ C342/17, para 10.   [219] Guidelines, para 91.

Exclusive supply, therefore, is the extreme form of limited distribution in as far as the limit on the number of buyers is concerned: there is only one buyer for the final products inside the Community.[220] As soon as the supplier sells its final products to more than one buyer inside the Community, then the market share of the supplier, and only that market share, is the decisive factor for the application of Regulation 2790/99. For intermediate products, the Guidelines (paragraph 202) contain an exception to this rule. For such products, the buyer's market share will be relevant if there is only one buyer in the Community *or* if there is only one buyer inside the Community for purposes of a specific use.[221]

2.233. In case of exclusive supply, the Guidelines (paragraph 92) clarify that the buyer's market share is 'his share of all purchases on the relevant purchase market'. As a practical example, reference is made to what was said above about the existence of a single food-retailing market from the supplier's side (paragraph 2.230). Account must be taken of the fact that such a uniform purchase market for food-retailing trade does not exist from the buyer's side, because it is not possible for a buyer to obtain a complete range of goods from one and the same producer. Producers generally produce a single product or category of products (such as dairy products, bread, and pastries) and are unable to switch readily to making other products. Accordingly, these product categories (ranging from meat and sausages, fruit and vegetables to wine and spirits, and baby food) will constitute different relevant purchase markets.[222]

2.234. The rule that the relevant market share is the market share of the buyer applies to all agreements with an exclusive supply obligation, irrespective of whether such obligations are mirrored by an exclusive purchase commitment.

Relevant market—multi-party agreement at different levels of trade

2.235. If a vertical agreement involves three or more parties operating at two different levels of trade, then the Guidelines (paragraph 93) state that the parties' market shares must be below 30% at both levels in order to benefit from the block exemption under Regulation 2790/99. For a vertical agreement which restricts competition and is concluded between a manufacturer, a wholesaler

---

[220] Also: Guidelines, para 202.

[221] In our opinion, this passage from the Guidelines exclusively concerns the question of whose market share is relevant to determine the application of the block exemption regulation (ie that of the supplier or that of the buyer(s)). In other words, the passage does not (and, given the fact that it is not legally binding, cannot) derogate from the hardcore restrictions stated in Reg 2790/99, Art 4 (which includes, eg customer and territorial restrictions). If a supplier appoints several buyers, each for one specific use of an intermediate product, the agreements concerned will still have to comply with Art 4.

[222] *Rewe/Meinl* (Case IV/M1221) [1999] OJ L274/1, paras 76–7; *Carrefour/Promodes* (COMP/M1684) [2000] OJ C164/5, paras 14 *et seq*.

(or association of retailers) and a retailer in order to qualify for block exemption under Regulation 2790/99, the market share of both the manufacturer and the wholesaler therefore may not exceed 30%.

The rationale of this approach, and in particular why multi-party agreements **2.236**. must be treated differently than two separate agreements, is unclear. Let us assume a manufacturer (with a market share of 35%), several wholesalers—one of them with a market share of say 15%—and its retailers. According to the Commission, a multi-party agreement between the manufacturer, the wholesaler, and one of its retailers, which imposes a number of restrictions of competition on the latter (eg a non-compete obligation which is in line with Article 5 of Regulation 2790/99), is not covered by Regulation 2790/99 on account of the size of the manufacturer's market share. As opposed to this, if the wholesaler (having a market share of 15%) concludes a separate agreement with its retailers, containing the same non-compete obligation as the multi-party agreement, that obligation can benefit from the block exemption.

If this is correct, and the Commission is intent on enforcing what appears to be **2.237**. a formalistic approach, the parties will have no other choice than to conclude separate agreements.

Relevant market—portfolio of products distributed through the same distribution system

If a supplier uses the same distribution agreement to distribute several types of **2.238**. goods or services, some of these may remain below the market share limit and will therefore be covered by the block exemption under Regulation 2790/99, whilst others may not. In that case, the block exemption continues to apply to those goods and services for which the limit is not exceeded.[223] It will be recalled that these conditions may continue to be fulfilled in the case where the market share limit is only temporarily exceeded.

Even though the Guidelines do not mention this expressly, it is reasonable to **2.239**. assume that the same applies to the situation where different types of goods or services are, in accordance with the same distribution agreement, supplied exclusively to one buyer in the Community. In that case, the block exemption will apply to those goods and services for which the buyer does not have a 30% share of the relevant purchase market.

Relevant market—secondary products

The definition of the relevant market for secondary products, ie spare parts and, **2.240**. by extension, accessories and consumables, is complex and warrants a cautious

---

[223] Guidelines, para 68.

approach. The main reason for this is that the Commission has adopted a case-by-case approach to the argument that is often used by producers of primary equipment, namely that an overarching market for primary and secondary products exists and that the producer's market share in the primary market must therefore necessarily be more or less the same as its share of the after-market.

2.241. The fact that the Commission has never succumbed entirely to this argument is reflected in the Guidelines (paragraph 94), where it states:

> Where a supplier produces both original equipment and the repair or replacement parts for this equipment, the supplier will often be the only or the major supplier on the after-market for repair and replacement parts. This may also arise where the supplier (OEM supplier) subcontracts the manufacturing of the repair or replacement parts. The relevant market for application of [Regulation 2790/99] may be the original equipment market including the spare parts or a separate original equipment market and after-market depending on the circumstances of the case, such as the effects of the restrictions involved, the lifetime of the equipment and importance of the repair and replacement costs.

2.242. A similarly cautious approach can also be found in the Notice on the definition of the relevant market for the purposes of Community competition law (paragraph 56):[224]

> The method to define markets [ie primary and secondary markets] is the same, ie to assess the responses of customers based on their purchasing decisions to relative price changes, but taking into account as well constraints on substitution imposed by conditions in the connected markets. A narrow definition of the market for secondary products, for instance, spare parts, may result when compatibility with the primary product is important. Problems of finding compatible secondary products together with the existence of high prices and a long life time of the primary products may render relative price increases of secondary products profitable. A different market definition may result if significant substitution between secondary products is possible or if the characteristics of the primary products make quick and direct consumer responses to relative price increases of the secondary products feasible.

2.243. In short, the Commission has not actually committed itself to one position or the other.[225] Instead, it offers a set of relatively open-ended criteria, namely that one must consider (i) the effects of the restrictions; (ii) the lifetime of the primary product; (iii) the importance of repair/replacement costs; (iv) the possibility to substitute between spare parts; and (v) the possibility to react quickly and directly to price increases of the secondary products.

2.244. As a consequence, an OEM (eg an inkjet printer manufacturer), who also manufactures secondary products (eg inkjet cartridges) will not be able to

---

[224] [1997] OJ C372/5.
[225] The same is true for the Commission's approach to spare parts in the motor vehicle sector: see para 11.54 below.

assume automatically that both products belong to the same product market and therefore that its market share for the original equipment will also be that for the secondary products. The Commission could adopt the opposite view, which could lead to Regulation 2790/99 being applicable to the original equipment, but not to the secondary products or vice versa.

Given the above, it is difficult to provide more general guidance on the relevant **2.245.** product market for secondary products. A cautious approach is therefore warranted. It goes without saying that this is specifically the case if no alternative source of supply for the secondary product(s) concerned is available. If there are alternatives, then these will, by definition, be included in the relevant product market. If there is no alternative source of supply, the OEM risks being dominant, unless account can be taken of potential competition (supply-side substitutability) or unless there are good reasons to assume that there is a solid case for an overarching market of primary and secondary products:

— Pursuant to the Notice on the definition of the relevant market for purposes of Community competition law (paragraph 20), potential competition requires that suppliers are able to switch production to the relevant secondary products and to market them in the short term without incurring significant additional costs or risks in response to small and permanent changes in relative prices. In the past, DG COMP has informally indicated to us that it may be willing to take potential competition for secondary products into consideration and thus be able to extend the relevant product market to include the potential substitutes. In our example, for instance, the market for ink cartridges specifically manufactured by the OEM for its inkjet printers would be extended to take into account the position of other inkjet cartridge suppliers which may be able, in the short term, to provide a substitute for our OEM's cartridges.

— It is difficult, if not impossible, to provide more guidance on the cases in which it will be possible to present a solid case for the existence of an overarching primary and secondary market. This will depend on the branch of industry and the type of customer. For instance, in the case of motor vehicles, the Commission, in its Explanatory Brochure (footnote 185),[226] states that the issue to be decided is

> whether a significant proportion of buyers make their choice taking into account the lifetime costs of the vehicle or not. Buying behaviour may significantly differ, for instance, between buyers of trucks who purchase and operate a fleet which take into account maintenance costs at the moment of purchasing the vehicle (eg bundled purchase and use contracts of trucks billed on price per km) and buyers of individual vehicles.

---

[226] Para 11.56 below.

2.246. To the present day, neither the Commission's decision-making practice nor the Court's case law provides a definitive answer to the question of whether or not the market for secondary products of a given product can or must be further subdivided; that is, whether all secondary products of a product are the relevant product market or whether a distinction can be made between different markets according to the secondary products involved. For spare parts, the former approach was adopted by the Court in, for example, *Hugin*,[227] where the Court considered the market for spare parts in cash registers as a single relevant product market. Conversely, in *Hilti*,[228] the Court of First Instance took the view that nail guns, cartridge strips, and nails constituted three separate specific product markets. Since cartridge strips and nails are specifically manufactured, and purchased by users, for a single brand of gun, the Court of First Instance concluded that each of them was subject to competition on the market and hence constituted a separate product market. While cartridge strips and nails are to be qualified as accessories or consumables, rather than spare parts, the analysis may be assumed to also be relevant to spare parts.

2.247. As regards the relevant geographic market, bearing in mind what was said in paragraph 2.231 above, a cautious and pragmatic approach is to rely on national territories.

(3) Calculation of market shares

2.248. In what follows, attention will first be given to the market share calculation of the supplier. However, the same rules apply, vice versa, to the market share calculation of the buyer in the case of an exclusive supply obligation in the sense of Article 1(c) of Regulation 2790/99.

Market share in value and market share in volume

2.249. Once the relevant product and geographic market have been defined, the market share of the supplier can then be calculated. This calculation must be done in accordance with Article 9 of Regulation 2790/99, which distinguishes between market share in value and market share in volume.

Market share in value

2.250. The rule is that the market share calculation needs to be based in principle on value figures.[229] Specifically, it must be based on the market sales value of the goods or services sold in the preceding calendar year by the supplier on the relevant market.[230] To be clear, the market share of the supplier is calculated not

---

[227] Case 22/78 *Hugin v Commission* [1979] ECR 1869.
[228] Case T–30/89 *Hilti v Commission* [1991] ECR II–1439.   [229] Guidelines, para 97.
[230] Reg 2790/99, Art 9(1) read in combination with Art 9(2)(a). The same calculation method is used in the context of non-compete obligations (para 6.10 below).

only on the basis of its sales of contract goods and services, but also on the basis of all of its sales of goods and services on the relevant market; that is, including sales of other goods or services which are regarded as interchangeable or substitutable by the buyer, due to the products' characteristics, their prices, and their intended use.

Market share in volume

As an exception to this rule, if no value data are available, substantiated esti- **2.251**. mates can be made on the basis of other reliable market information such as volume figures,[231] that is the volume of sales and purchases on the relevant market in the preceding calendar year.

Market data relating to the preceding calendar year

The fact that the market share calculation must, following Article 9(2)(a) of **2.252**. Regulation 2790/99, be based on data relating to the preceding calendar year (in contrast to the preceding fiscal year) may have peculiar consequences. While more details are given below, let us for present purposes assume that a supplier has a market share of 40% in year X and that, due to a sharp increase in competition (eg successful market entry of a competitor) or, in a tender-driven market, due to the loss of a number of important tenders, its market share drops to 16% in year X + 1. In accordance with Article 9(2)(a), the supplier will no longer be able to enjoy the benefit of the block exemption under Regulation 2790/99 in year X + 1, although its market share in that year is only 16%. Of course, this does not prevent the supplier's vertical agreements from being enforceable on the basis of the direct effect of Article 81(3) EC.

Taken together with Article 9(2)(c) to (e) on the continued application of the **2.253**. block exemption in the case where the market share limit is only temporarily exceeded, Article 9(2)(a) also entails that a start-up company will, as a rule, be able to benefit from the block exemption in the first three years after its start-up. The only exception to this rule would be if the start-up company acquires a share in excess of 35% of the relevant market in its first two years following its start-up. Even so, the prohibition of Article 81(1) EC will not apply for a period of two years after first putting the product on to the market if the introduction of new products or the penetration of new geographic markets is done in accordance with the Guidelines, paragraph 119(10):

> In the case of a new product, or where an existing product is sold for the first time on a different geographic market, it may be difficult for the company to define the market or its market share may be very high. However, this should not be considered a major problem, as vertical restraints linked to opening up new product or geographic markets in general do not restrict competition. This rule holds,

---

[231] Guidelines, para 97.

irrespective of the market share of the company, for two years after the first putting on the market of the product. It applies to all non-hardcore vertical restraints and, in the case of a new geographic market, to restrictions on active and passive sales imposed on the direct buyers of the supplier located in other markets to intermediaries in the new market. In the case of genuine testing of a new product in a limited territory or with a limited customer group, the distributors appointed to sell the new product on the test market can be restricted in their active selling outside the test market for a maximum period of 1 year without being caught by Article 81(1).[232]

Market share of connected undertakings, joint ventures, cases of dual distribution, and intra-group sales

Connected undertakings

2.254. Pursuant to Article 11, sales of connected undertakings must be included for the purposes of the market share calculation.

2.255. 'Connected undertakings' are defined in Article 11(2) of Regulation 2790/99 as:

(a) undertakings in which a party to the agreement, directly or indirectly:
   — has the power to exercise more than half the voting rights, or
   — has the power to appoint more than half the members of the supervisory board, board of management or bodies legally representing the undertaking, or
   — has the right to manage the undertaking's affairs;
(b) undertakings which directly or indirectly have, over a party to the agreement, the rights or powers listed in (a);
(c) undertakings in which an undertaking referred to in (b) has, directly or indirectly, the rights or powers listed in (a);
(d) undertakings in which a party to the agreement together with one or more of the undertakings referred to in (a), (b) or (c), or in which two or more of the latter undertakings, jointly have the rights or powers listed in (a);
(e) undertakings in which the rights or the powers listed in (a) are jointly held by:
   — parties to the agreement or their respective connected undertakings referred to in (a) to (d), or
   — one or more of the parties to the agreement or one or more of their connected undertakings referred to in (a) to (d) and one or more third parties.

2.256. Accordingly, the definition of connected undertakings includes the supplier's subsidiaries (under (a)), its parent companies (under (b) and (c)), as well as sister companies, including joint ventures with other undertakings (under (d) and (e)).

---

[232] On 'hardcore restrictions', as well as the concepts of 'active' and 'passive sales', see Ch 5.

Joint ventures

As regards joint ventures, Article 11(3) of Regulation 2790/99 provides that **2.257**.
the market share held by them must be apportioned equally to each parent
company.

Dual distribution

Dual distribution occurs when a producer of final goods (eg sportswear) acts as a **2.258**.
distributor in competition with independent distributors.[233] In such cases, the
market definition and market share calculation must include the goods sold by
the producer through its own shops (also referred to as the integrated distributors). This follows on logically from the fact that integrated distributors
are connected undertakings in the sense of Article 11 of Regulation 2790/99.
Sales via agents must also be included.

Intra-group sales

Sales between the supplier and its connected undertakings, as well as sales **2.259**.
between connected undertakings are not taken into account.[234]

Market share and captive or in-house production[235]

In-house production means the production of an intermediate product for one's **2.260**.
own use in the final product. The more in-house production of intermediate
products there is, the more vertically integrated a company is. In-house production is important as a source of potential competition[236] and to accentuate
the market position of a company. Notwithstanding this, for the purpose of
market definition and the market share calculation for intermediate goods and
services, in-house production is not taken into account at all. The reason for this
is very clear: in-house production is 'consumed' internally and is therefore not
marketed to compete with similar products.

(4) Practical examples

What follows are a number of practical examples of the interaction between **2.261**.
Articles 3, 9(1), and 9(2)(c) to (e) of Regulation 2790/99. As a brief reminder:

—Article 3 establishes the market share limit of 30%;
—Article 9(1) states that the market share calculation must be based on the data
   of the preceding calendar year; and

---

[233] On 'dual distribution', see Guidelines, paras 27 and 99.
[234] Reg 2790/99, Art 10(1), *in fine*.   [235] Guidelines, para 98.
[236] eg *ArvinMeritor/Volvo (Assets)* (COMP/M3351), as well as Commission Press Release,
IP/04/1170, 4 October 2004.

—Article 9(2)(c) to (e) inserts a dose of dynamics into the application of the market share limit (and hence the block exemption on the whole) by stating that a company may continue to benefit from the block exemption for a limited period of time in cases where it temporarily oversteps the threshold.[237]

Example 1

Calendar year	−3	−2	−1	0	1	2	3
Market share %	37	32	29	35	43	38	34
Block exemption	n.a.	−	−	✓	✓	✓	−

2.262. Contrary to what one would expect, this first example shows that a combination of Articles 3 and 9 of the Regulation results in the situation that the block exemption does not only apply to the scenario where the market share of the supplier (or the buyer) does not exceed 30%. Article 9 may result in the fact that the block exemption continues to apply to a supplier's or a buyer's vertical agreements in a year where their market share is considerably higher than 30%.

2.263. In the example above, the block exemption does not apply in calendar year −2 because the market share in calendar year −3 is higher than 30% (Article 3 read in combination with Article 9(1)). In the next calendar year (−1), the same rule prevents the application of the block exemption (that is, in calendar year −2, which is the reference year, the market share was more than 30%). During the present calendar year (year 0), however, the agreements concerned may benefit from the block exemption under Regulation 2790/99: the market share in the previous calendar year was less than 30% (Article 3 read in combination with Article 9(1)). The block exemption continues to apply in calendar year 1, although the company's share has meanwhile risen to 43%. Article 9(2)(c) states that if the market share is initially not more than 30% (ie 29%), but subsequently rises above that level without exceeding 35% (ie the present calendar year with a share of 35%), the exemption continues to apply for a period of two consecutive calendar years following the year in which the 30% market share was first exceeded. For the same reason, the block exemption applies in calendar year 2. Finally, in calendar year 3 (34%), the block exemption does not apply because of the general rule of Article 3 (in combination with Article 9(1)).

2.264. The second example (see overleaf) also illustrates the sometimes surprising consequences of Article 9 of Regulation 2790/99. Here the block exemption applies in the current calendar year (in spite of a 36% market share) and the next calendar year (in spite of a 32% market share); it does not apply in calendar

---

[237] Another set of practical examples can be found in Schultze, Pautke, and Wagener (n 2 above) paras 307–8.

Example 2

Calendar year	−3	−2	−1	0	1	2	3
Market share %	28	31	29	36	32	30	42
Block exemption	n.a.	✓	✓	✓	✓	−	✓

year 2 (although the market share does not exceed 30% in that year) but applies again in calendar year 3 (although the market share is 42%). In the current year 0, the agreements concerned enjoy the block exemption on the basis of Article 3 of Regulation 2790/99, bearing in mind that, according to its Article 9(2), the point of reference is the market share in the previous calendar year (namely 29%), which is below the 30% threshold. In calendar year 1, the block exemption continues to apply because of the rule of Article 9(2)(d), namely: if the market share is initially not more than 30% (ie 29%), but subsequently rises to exceed 35% (ie the present calendar year with a share of 36%), then the exemption continues to apply in the calendar year following the year in which the 30% market share was first exceeded (so following year 0). This explains why the block exemption applies in year 1, but not in year 2. In year 3, finally, the agreement benefits from the block exemption because the reference market share (ie the market share in year 2) does not exceed 30%.

Example 3

Calendar year	−3	−2	−1	0	1	2	3
Market share %	22	27	32	37	42	47	52
Block exemption	n.a.	✓	✓	✓	✓	−	−

This third example shows that the interplay of the above provisions may result **2.265.** in the scenario that a very successful company may have acquired a share of 47% (thus considerably exceeding the market share limit of 30%) before its distribution agreements will no longer be block exempted under Regulation 2790/99. The exemption in the current calendar year 0 and year 1 are based on the rule of Article 9(2)(c) of Regulation 2790/99: the market share is initially not more than 30% (ie 27%), but subsequently rises above that level without exceeding 35% (ie 32% in year −1), so the exemption continues to apply for a period of two consecutive calendar years following the year in which the 30% market share was first exceeded. The block exemption therefore continues to apply in the current calendar year 0 and year 1. This is no longer the case for calendar years 2 and 3, where Article 3 read in combination with Article 9(1) excludes the application of the block exemption.

Example 4

Calendar year	−3	−2	−1	0	1	2	3
Market share %	7	40	12	48	42	22	8
Block exemption	n.a.	✓	✓	✓	✓	−	✓

2.266. This fourth and final example mirrors the previous ones in that it concerns a company with heavy market share losses, first in a period of a year and then subsequently over a period of three years. It is important to note that market share fluctuations may occur for example in tender-driven markets. In calendar year −2 the distribution agreements are block exempted on the basis of the general rule of Article 3 read in combination with Article 9(1): the market share in the previous calendar year (year –3) is 7%, so the block exemption applies in year −2. In the previous calendar year (year −1) the exemption continues to apply because of the rule of Article 9(1)(d): if the market share is initially not more than 30% (ie 7%), but subsequently rises to exceed 35% (ie 40%), the exemption continues to apply in the calendar year following the year in which the 30% market share was first exceeded (so following year −2). In the current calendar year, the agreements concerned will nevertheless be able to enjoy the benefit of the block exemption because the market share in the previous calendar year did not exceed 30% (it was only 12%). In year 1, the block exemption continues to apply because of the rule of Article 9(1)(d). The same rule further results in the situation that in year 2, the agreements do not qualify for block exemption even though the market share has dropped to 22% in the meantime. Finally, in year 3, the block exemption applies once again in accordance with Article 3 read in combination with Article 9(1) of Regulation 2790/99.

H. Sixth Question: The Role of Intellectual Property Rights

(1) Introduction

2.267. Article 2(3) states that Regulation 2790/99 applies to:

> Vertical agreements containing provisions which relate to the assignment to the buyer or use by the buyer of intellectual property rights, provided that those provisions do not constitute the primary object of such agreements and are directly related to the use, sale or resale of goods or services by the buyer or its customers. The exemption applies on condition that, in relation to the contract goods or services, those provisions do not contain restrictions of competition having the same object or effect as vertical restraints which are not exempted under this Regulation.

Article 1(e) of Regulation 2790/99 states that the concept 'IPRs' includes **2.268.** 'industrial property rights, copyright and neighbouring rights'.[238]

In view of Article 2(3), the role assumed by IPRs in a vertical agreement must be **2.269.** carefully assessed in order to determine whether the presence of the IPRs prevents the application of Regulation 2790/99. Article 2(3) effectively limits the scope of application of Regulation 2790/99 in that, if a vertical agreement contains IPR provisions, the agreement can only be covered by the block exemption if a certain number of conditions are fulfilled. These conditions (as stated in the Guidelines in paragraph 30) are as follows:

— the IPRs must be part of a vertical agreement;
— the IPRs must be assigned to, or for use by, the buyer;
— the IPRs must not constitute the primary object of the agreement;
— the IPRs must be directly related to the use, sale, or resale of goods or services by the buyer or his customers; and
— the IPRs, in relation to the contract goods or services, must not contain restrictions of competition having the same object or effect as vertical restraints which are not exempted.

The purpose of these conditions is to ensure that the block exemption of **2.270.** Regulation 2790/99 applies to vertical agreements where the use, sale, or resale of goods or services can take place more effectively because of the fact that IPRs are assigned to or transferred for use by the buyer. Each of these five required conditions are discussed hereafter (paragraphs 2.271–2.283). In addition, given the fact that the wording of the Regulation and that of the Guidelines do not overlap entirely, specific attention will be given to the content of the IPRs which are covered by the Regulation (paragraphs 2.284–2.285).

(2) First condition: IPRs as part of a vertical agreement

In order to qualify for the application of Regulation 2790/99, the IPR provisions **2.271.** must first and foremost be part of a vertical agreement; that is an agreement with conditions under which the parties may purchase, sell, or resell certain goods or services. Accordingly, IPR provisions which are part of a lease agreement will not be able to enjoy the safe harbour of Regulation 2790/99 because lease agreements are not vertical agreements in the sense of Article 2(1) of the Regulation.

The Guidelines (paragraph 32) are slightly confusing in this respect. They read **2.272.** as follows:

> The first condition makes clear that the context in which the IPRs are provided is
> an agreement to purchase or distribute goods or an agreement to purchase or

---

[238] The use of the word 'includes' shows that the list of IPRs should not be regarded as exhaustive, Mendelsohn and Rose (n 2 above) 47.

provide services and not an agreement concerning the assignment or licensing of IPRs for the manufacture of goods, nor a pure licensing agreement. The Block Exemption Regulation does not cover for instance:

— agreements where a party provides another party with a recipe and licenses the other party to produce a drink with this recipe;
— agreements under which one party provides another party with a mould or master copy and licenses the other party to produce and distribute copies;
— the pure licence of a trade mark or sign for purpose of merchandising;
— sponsorship contracts concerning the right to advertise oneself as being an official sponsor of an event;
— copyright licensing such as broadcasting contracts concerning the right to record and/or the right to broadcast an event.

2.273. It would seem that this language, which concerns 'the context in which the IPRs are provided', relates more to the other conditions of Article 2(3) than it does to the first condition that the IPR provisions must be part of a vertical agreement. For instance, the examples that Regulation 2790/99 neither covers 'the pure licence of a trade mark or sign for purpose of merchandising' nor sponsorship contracts or copyright licensing, does not specifically relate to the first condition. Pure licensing agreements, as well as sponsorship contracts and copyright licence agreements, can very well be 'vertical agreements' in the sense of Article 2(1) of the Regulation. The reason why they are not covered by Regulation 2790/99 is quite different. For pure licensing agreements, for instance, it is because the IPRs must not constitute the primary object of the agreement (the third condition).

2.274. In our opinion, the analysis required by the first condition coincides with that of the second question of our analysis on the material scope of application of Regulation 2790/99, discussed in paragraphs 2.61–2.122 above ('Vertical Agreements').[239]

(3) Second condition: IPRs assigned to, or for use by, the buyer

2.275 The second condition concerns the direction of the assignment of or the right to use the IPRs: they must be assigned to the buyer or be for use by the buyer. Regulation 2790/99 therefore does not apply to situations where the buyer provides the IPRs to the supplier/manufacturer, no matter whether the IPRs concern the manner of manufacture or the manner of distribution. So an agreement relating to the transfer of IPRs to the supplier, and containing possible restrictions on the sales made by the supplier, is not covered by Regulation 2790/99. In practice, this scenario may occur in the context of subcontracting agreements: a buyer concludes an agreement with a

---

[239] The Commission's approach to the first condition is also questioned in Korah and O'Sullivan (n 165 above) paras 3.4.9.1 and 3.4.9.2.

subcontractor on the manufacture and supply of a component and, in that context, the buyer supplies the subcontractor with the IPR which enables the manufacturing to occur. Given that the IPRs go from the buyer to the supplier, the application of the block exemption contained in Regulation 2790/99 is excluded.[240]

(4) *Third condition: IPRs which do not constitute the primary object of the agreement*

2.276. The third condition for the application of Regulation 2790/99 in this context is that the IPR provisions may not constitute the primary object of the agreement. In addition to Article 2(3), this condition is also reflected in recital 3 of the Regulation, which states that one of the categories of vertical agreements which can be regarded as normally satisfying the conditions laid down in Article 81(3) EC includes 'vertical agreements containing ancillary provisions on the assignment or use of intellectual property rights'. Therefore, in order to be covered by the block exemption, the primary object of the agreement must not be the assignment of licensing of IPRs. The primary object must be the purchase or distribution of goods or services and the IPR provisions must serve the implementation of the vertical agreement.[241]

2.277. For instance, suppose that the holder of a well-known brand grants a licence to affix its brand to all sorts of gadgets and that, in the framework of this licensing agreement, the licensee agrees to purchase T-shirts and pens from the licensor. The sale of the T-shirts and pens is clearly an ancillary element in the business relationship between the licensor and the licensee. At the centre of that relationship stands the licensee's right to use the brand. Therefore, as a consequence, the block exemption of Regulation 2790/99 will not apply to this relationship.

(5) *Fourth condition: IPRs which are directly related to the use, sale, or resale of goods or services*

2.278. As a fourth condition, the IPR provisions must be directly related to the use, sale, or resale of goods or services by the buyer or his customers. In the Guidelines (paragraph 35), the Commission states that these provisions will normally be related to the marketing of goods or services.

2.279. The Commission gives two examples. First, of a franchise agreement where the franchisor sells to the franchisee goods for resale and in addition licenses the franchisee to use its trademark and (commercial) know-how in order to market

---

[240] See also Guidelines, para 33. Subcontracting is discussed separately in Ch 8 below.
[241] Guidelines, para 34.

the goods (eg McDonald's). Such IPR provisions are, according to the Commission, covered by Regulation 2790/99. Second, it gives the example of a supplier of a concentrated extract who licenses the buyer to dilute and bottle the extract before selling it as a drink.[242] It can be seen that in respect of this scenario the IPRs are directly related to the resale of goods.

2.280. The fourth condition continues to be fulfilled if a licensee purchases the goods or services for use or resale from a third supplier and not directly from the licensor.[243]

(6) Fifth condition: IPRs which do not contain restrictions of competition having the same object or effect as vertical restraints which are not exempted

2.281. The final condition for the application of Regulation 2790/99 to vertical agreements with IPR provisions is that these provisions may not impose restrictions regarding the contract goods or services which have the same object or effect as vertical restraints which are not exempted. This means that the provisions in question cannot have the same object or effect as either one of the hardcore restrictions of Article 4 of Regulation 2790/99[244] or as one of the restrictions mentioned in Article 5 of Regulation 2790/99 to which the block exemption does not apply.[245]

2.282. It is clear that IPR provisions on the granting of a licence for the manufacture and marketing of certain products or services may not result in territorial protection which is incompatible with Article 4(b) of Regulation 2790/99. For instance, passive sales (that is, sales resulting from unsolicited requests)[246] outside a distributor's territory must, as a rule, always be permitted. A licence granted to the distributor for the sale of the contract products or services may therefore not be invoked against the distributor to prohibit such passive sales, for example, because the territorial scope of the licence has been limited to the distributor's territory. If this were so, then the block exemption would be lost for the agreement in its entirety.

2.283. The consequences of the fact that a vertical agreement contains IPR provisions having the same object or effect as vertical restraints which are not exempted are

---

[242] This is confirmed in the TTBER Guidelines, para 53: 'Where a trademark license is directly related to the use, sale or resale of goods and services and does not constitute the primary object of the agreement, the license agreement is covered by [Regulation 2790/99]'.
[243] Guidelines, para 35.   [244] Ch 5 below.   [245] Ch 6 below.
[246] For the definition of 'passive sales', see para 5.48 below.

somewhat peculiar and mean that care needs to be taken in the drafting of the IPR provisions. There are two reasons for this:

— First, it must be borne in mind that Article 2(3) concerns IPR provisions which have as their object *or* effect a vertical restraint which is not exempted under Regulation 2790/99. As discussed in more detail in paragraphs 5.01–5.09, only agreements which have as their object (and not as their effect) the infringement of one of the hardcore restrictions of Article 4 of Regulation 2790/99 lose the benefit of the block exemption for the agreement in its entirety. With regard to the wording of Article 2(3) of Regulation 2790/99, it must be understood that this is different if the agreement contains IPR provisions and if these provisions do not have the object, but do have the effect, of infringing one of the hardcore restrictions. In such a case, Article 2(3), on a literal reading, would exclude the application of the block exemption to the vertical agreement concerned. The reason for this difference in treatment is unclear.

— Second, with respect to what is meant by 'vertical restraints which are not exempted under this Regulation', the Commission refers both to the hardcore restrictions under Article 4 and to the restrictions excluded from the coverage of the block exemption by Article 5.[247] As will be seen below, Article 5 concerns non-compete obligations. Specifically, it sets out those conditions which a non-compete obligation must fulfil in order to be block exempted. The rule of severability applies to Article 5; that is to say, if a non-compete obligation does not comply with the conditions mentioned in Article 5, then the block exemption will not apply to that obligation, but will continue to apply to the other restrictions of competition which the agreement contains, as long as those restrictions are not hardcore infringements.[248]

It seems somewhat odd to notice that this would not be the case if the IPR provisions of the agreement infringed Article 5. As it is explained by the Commission in its Guidelines, the fifth condition of Article 2(3) of Regulation 2790/99 must be taken to imply that an infringement of Article 5 by the IPR provisions of a vertical agreement entails that the block exemption no longer applies to the agreement in its entirety. The authors are of the opinion that this difference in treatment is difficult to substantiate, and argue that an infringement of Article 5, whether it be by the IPR provisions of a vertical agreement or not, should only have the non-enforceability of the non-compete obligation as its consequence. It should leave the other restrictions of competition intact as long as they are not hardcore restrictions.

---

[247] Guidelines, para 36.
[248] On severability under Reg 2790/99, Art 5, see paras 6.33–6.34 below.

(7) Trademarks, copyright, and know-how

2.284. The Commission's objective by the block exempting of vertical agreements with IPR provisions under Regulation 2790/99 is to ensure that the use, sale, or resale of goods or services can be performed more effectively on account of the assignment or the transfer for use of IPRs to the buyer. In the Guidelines (paragraph 37), the Commission states that it is of the opinion that there are three categories of IPRs which serve this purpose:

> Intellectual property rights which may be considered to serve the implementation of vertical agreements within the meaning of Article 2(3) of the Block Exemption Regulation generally concern three main areas: trademarks, copyright and know-how.

Each of these is briefly considered below.

Trademarks

2.285. A trademark licence granted to a distributor may be related to the distribution of the licensor's products in a particular territory. If it is an exclusive licence, then the agreement amounts to exclusive distribution.[249]

Copyright

2.286. A copyright holder may oblige the resellers of goods which are covered by copyright (eg books or CDs) only to resell the goods on the condition that the buyer (ie a reseller or end-user) shall not infringe the copyright. Where such an obligation falls within the scope of Article 81(1) EC, it is covered by the block exemption.

2.287. The Guidelines (paragraphs 40 and 41) treat copyright on software separately:

— First, in the light of the involvement of three parties (the copyright owner, the reseller, and the user of the software), the Guidelines (paragraph 40) state that an agreement according to which hard copies of software are supplied for resale by the copyright owner to a reseller, and according to which the latter only has a right to resell the hard copies and does not acquire a licence over the software, is regarded an agreement for the supply of goods for resale in the sense of Regulation 2790/99. Under these circumstances, the licence is given directly by the copyright owner to the software user, and the reseller merely acts as an intermediary. A practical example of this type of software agreement is in the case of a so-called 'shrink wrap' licence, where a set of conditions is included in the package of the hard copy of the software and where the user is deemed as accepting the conditions of that license by the act of opening the package.

---

[249] Guidelines, para 38.

— Second, according to the Guidelines (paragraph 41), a copyright holder may oblige a buyer of hardware which incorporates copyright-protected software not to infringe the copyright (eg not to make copies and resell the software or not to make copies and use the software in combination with other hardware). Where such an obligation falls within the scope of Article 81(1) EC, it is covered by the block exemption.

Know-how

As shown above, the Guidelines (paragraph 37) expressly include know-how as a third category of IPR which may facilitate the implementation of a vertical agreement. The approach of the Regulation is however somewhat different. The Regulation distinguishes between 'know-how' and 'IPRs' and, further, contains a separate definition for each. **2.288**.

— Article 1(e) defines 'intellectual property rights' as including 'industrial property rights, copyright and neighbouring rights';
— Article 1(f) defines 'know-how' separately as 'a package of non-patented practical information resulting from experience and testing by the supplier, which is secret, substantial and identified'.[250]

This contradiction is not without some practical relevance: if know-how must be treated separately from IPRs, then the conditions that the IPR provisions in a vertical agreement must fulfil, pursuant to Article 2(3) of Regulation 2790/99 so that the agreement may be block exempted, do not apply to the provisions on know-how of the vertical agreement. **2.289**.

In all likelihood the reason for this confusion is that a distinction can be made between, on the one hand, commercial know-how and, on the other hand, technical know-how. The definition which Article 1(f) of Regulation 2790/99 contains is taken directly from the definition of know-how contained in Article 1(f) of Regulation 4087/88, the former franchise block exemption regulation, which only related to commercial (and not to technical) know-how. In other words, for commercial know-how, the conditions which Article 2(3) of Regulation 2790/99 imposes on the application of the block exemption regulation do not apply. Conversely, technical know-how can be seen as an IPR and it is probably this type of know-how which led the Commission to include know-how as a third category of IPRs in the **2.290**.

---

[250] On 'secret, substantial and identified': Art 1(f) continues to state that ' "secret" means that the know-how, as a body or in the precise configuration and assembly of its components, is not generally known or easily accessible; "substantial" means that the know-how includes information which is indispensable to the buyer for the use, sale or resale of the contract goods or services; "identified" means that the know-how must be described in a sufficiently comprehensive manner so as to make it possible to verify that it fulfils the criteria of secrecy and substantiality'.

Guidelines.[251] In so doing, technical know-how is covered by the definition of IPRs in Article 1(e) of Regulation 2790/99 and a vertical agreement which contains provisions on purely technical know-how will be able to benefit from the block exemption only if it complies with the conditions of Article 2(3).

I. Seventh Question: Agreements Between Competitors and Agreements Entered into by an Association of Undertakings

2.291. The seventh and final question concerns the applicability of Regulation 2790/99 to vertical agreements between competitors and vertical agreements entered into by an association of undertakings. It should be noted that Regulation 2790/99 covers these agreements only if they comply with certain conditions. These conditions are discussed below for agreements between competitors (paragraphs 2.292–2.301) and agreements entered into by an association of undertakings (paragraphs 2.302–2.305).

(1) Agreements between competitors

The rule: exclusion from the scope of Regulation 2790/99

2.292. In principle, the block exemption of Regulation 2790/99 does not cover agreements between competitors. In Article 1(a) of Regulation 2790/99, 'competing undertakings' are defined as:

> actual or potential suppliers in the same product market; the product market includes goods or services which are regarded by the buyer as interchangeable with or substitutable for the contract goods or services, by reason of the products' characteristics, their prices and their intended use.

2.293. An undertaking is considered to be an actual competitor if it is either active on the same relevant product market or if an immediate supply-side substitutability exists; that is, if in the absence of an agreement with its competitors, the undertaking concerned is able to switch its production to the relevant products and then to market them in the short term without incurring significant additional costs or risks, in response to a small, permanent increase in relative prices (in the range of 5 to 10%). When supply-side substitutability entails the need to significantly adjust existing tangible and intangible assets, to make additional investments, to take strategic decisions or to incur time delays, an

---

[251] An additional indication of this direction is that Reg 772/2004, Art 1(g) defines 'intellectual property rights' as 'industrial property rights, know-how, copyright and neighbouring rights', thus expressly including know-how in the definition of IPRs. Given the language of Art 1(g) and the TTBER Guidelines (para 47) the know-how that is included in the definition of IPRs is technical know-how.

undertaking will not be treated as an actual competitor but possibly as a potential competitor.[252]

A potential competitor is an undertaking that does not actually produce a **2.294.** competing product but could, and would, be likely to undertake the necessary investments or other costs relating to switching production so that it could enter the relevant market in response to a small, permanent increase in relative prices. Traditionally, this is taken to mean that it must be realistic, not merely theoretical, to assume that the undertaking would be able to and would be likely to undertake the necessary additional investments and supply the market within one year.[253] However, in individual cases, longer time periods can be taken into account. The time period needed by companies that are already active on the market to adjust their capacities can be used as a yardstick to determine this period.[254]

The non-applicability in principle of the block exemption of Regulation **2.295.** 2790/99 to (actual or potential) competitors applies irrespective of whether or not the suppliers are competitors on the same geographic market.[255]

The exception: agreements between competitors within the scope of Regulation 2790/99

Conditions

Pursuant to Article 2(4) of Regulation 2790/99, the block exemption applies to **2.296.** the situation where competitors enter into a non-reciprocal vertical agreement which complies with any one of the following three conditions:

— the buyer has a total annual turnover not exceeding € 100 million;[256] or
— the supplier is a manufacturer and a distributor of goods, while the buyer is a distributor not manufacturing goods competing with the contract goods; or
— the supplier is a provider of services at several levels of trade, while the buyer does not provide competing services at the level of trade where it purchases the contract services.

Accordingly, only vertical agreements which are non-reciprocal and further **2.297.** comply with any one of the three conditions cited may be block exempted

---

[252] Commission Notice on the definition of the relevant market for the purposes of Community competition law [1997] OJ C372/5, paras 20–3; Horizontal Guidelines, para 9; and (Vertical) Guidelines, para 26.

[253] Commission Notice on the definition of the relevant market for the purposes of Community competition law [1997] OJ C372/5, para 24; Horizontal Guidelines, para 9; and (Vertical) Guidelines, para 26. On the concepts of 'product' and 'geographic market', see paras 2.220–2.222 above. [254] Horizontal Guidelines, footnote 9.

[255] Guidelines, para 26.

[256] A similar provision can be found in Art 3(b) of Commission Regs 1983/83 (exclusive distribution) and 1984/83 (exclusive purchasing agreements) (with the exception of the fact that under that article, each party could have a turnover of no more than 100 million ECU).

under Regulation 2790/99. As to non-reciprocity, the Guidelines (paragraph 26) give the example 'that while one manufacturer becomes the distributor of the products of another manufacturer, the latter does not become the distributor of the products of the first manufacturer'. In this respect, the question can be asked whether the condition of non-reciprocity applies to competing as well as to non-competing products. Put differently, can two local producers of alcohol enter into a distribution agreement pursuant to which one competitor will distribute the alcohol produced by the other party, and the latter will distribute eg ceramic tiles which the former manufactures? Neither Article 2(4) nor the Guidelines address this issue. Clearly, the agreement is a reciprocal agreement between competing undertakings and, on a literal reading, is excluded from the application of Article 2(4). However, given that such an agreement does not concern competing products, there appears to be little fear that the agreement will lead to collusion as to the parties' competitive behaviour with regard to the market on which they are both active (which in all likelihood is the Commission's concern). In our opinion, this type of agreement should be able to benefit from the block exemption, provided that the parties otherwise qualify for the application of Article 2(4).

Turnover limit

2.298. **Calculation.** The turnover threshold of the first condition must be calculated in accordance with Article 10(1) of Regulation 2790/99, namely on the basis of the turnover achieved during the previous financial year by the buyer (and its 'connected undertakings')[257] in respect of all goods and services, excluding all taxes and other duties. For this purpose, no account is to be taken of intra-group sales, which are those dealings between the party to the vertical agreement and its connected undertakings or between its connected undertakings.

2.299. **Temporarily overstepping the turnover limit.** According to Article 10(2) of Regulation 2790/99, the exemption remains applicable where, for any period of two consecutive financial years, the total annual turnover threshold is exceeded by no more than 10% (ie that the buyer's total annual turnover does not exceed € 110 million).

Dual distribution

2.300. The second and third exceptions to the rule that agreements between competitors fall outside the scope of Regulation 2790/99 concern instances of dual distribution, where a manufacturer of particular goods (or services) also acts as a distributor of the goods (or services) in competition with independent distributors.[258] To put it differently, this says that the block exemption of

---

[257] On 'connected undertakings', see para 2.255 above.
[258] Guidelines, paras 27 and 99.

Regulation 2790/99 may apply where the undertakings are not competing manufacturers, but are competing distributors. For instance, the exception may apply to agreements where a clothes manufacturer, with its own sales outlets, also markets its goods via independent shops. Or, more generally, in cases of dual distribution via franchises and company owned outlets.

Dual distribution is also relevant in the context of subcontracting. Later, in **2.301**. Chapter 8, it will be shown that if a contractor fails to completely outsource the manufacture of the input, and therefore remains a manufacturer competing with its supplier/subcontractor, then the agreement does not qualify for the application of any block exemption but must be assessed in accordance with the Horizontal Guidelines. In this respect, it is interesting to note that the (Vertical) Guidelines (paragraph 27) state that '[a] distributor who provides specifications to a manufacturer to produce particular goods under the distributor's brand name is not to be considered a manufacturer of such own-brand goods'. So a subcontracting agreement between a distributor (as contractor) and a manufacturer is an agreement between non-competitors, and the appropriate legal framework for the analysis of the subcontracting agreement (pursuant to which no IPRs or know-how, but merely specifications, are transferred) is Regulation 2790/99.

(2) Agreements entered into by an association of undertakings

In addition to agreements and concerted practices, a third category of situations **2.302**. covered by Article 81(1) EC is decisions of associations of undertakings. In principle, decisions of associations of undertakings are horizontal in nature. This is probably most likely the reason why there is no reference to such decisions in Regulation 2790/99, or in its empowering regulation, Regulation 19/65.[259] However, in the context of an association of undertakings, the possibility of the conclusion of vertical agreements—between the association and its members or between the association and its suppliers—cannot be excluded. Such vertical agreements are covered by Regulation 2790/99 if they comply with the conditions of Article 2(2) of Regulation 2790/99, as follows:

— all the association's members are retailers of goods (ie not retailers of services; not wholesalers); and
— if no individual member of the association, together with its connected undertakings, has a total annual turnover exceeding € 50 million.

The turnover is calculated in accordance with Article 10(1) of Regulation **2.303**. 2790/99, as described above (paragraph 2.298). In this respect too, the

---

[259] Regulation No 19/65 of 2 March of the Council on application of Article 85(3) of the Treaty to certain categories of agreements and concerted practices [1965] OJ Spec Ed 36/533.

exemption is retained where, for any period of two consecutive financial years, the total annual turnover threshold is exceeded by no more than 10% (ie if the total annual turnover of any member of the association does not exceed € 55 million) (Article 10(2)). The Guidelines (paragraph 28) nevertheless add to this that if 'a limited number of the members of the association have a turnover not significantly exceeding the € 50 million threshold, this will normally not change the assessment under Article 81'. The reader is left to muse on what the Commission would consider to be 'a limited number of members' and 'a turnover not significantly exceeding the € 50 million threshold'.

2.304. Because both horizontal and vertical agreements can be concluded in the framework of an association of undertakings, a double form of control applies. In this respect, Article 2(2), of Regulation 2790/99 reads *in fine* that 'vertical agreements entered into by such associations shall be covered by [Regulation 2790/99] without prejudice to the application of Article 81 to horizontal agreements concluded between the members of the association or decisions adopted by the association'.

2.305. Pursuant to the Guidelines (paragraph 29), the way to undertake the double control is as follows:

> Horizontal agreements concluded between the members of the association or decisions adopted by the association, such as the decision to require the members to purchase from the association or the decision to allocate exclusive territories to the members have to be assessed first as a horizontal agreement. Only if this assessment is positive does it become relevant to assess the vertical agreements between the association and individual members or between the association and suppliers.

3

TERRITORIAL SCOPE OF APPLICATION OF REGULATION 2790/99

The territorial scope of application is comprised of two dimensions. Formally **3.01**. speaking, it refers to the addressees of Regulation 2790/99[1] and the Guidelines;[2] materially speaking it refers to the territorial application of the prohibition laid down in Article 81(1) EC and, correspondingly, the block exemption contained in Regulation 2790/99.

A. Addressees of Regulation 2790/99

From the formal point of view, the addressees of Regulation 2790/99 are the **3.02**. EC Member States. In addition, this Regulation also applies to the EFTA States which are the participating countries in the Agreement on the European Economic Area ('the EEA Agreement'), ie Iceland, Liechtenstein, and Norway. This follows from the Decision of the EEA Joint Committee No 18/2000 of 28 January 2000 amending Annex XIV (Competition) to the EEA Agreement.[3]

Following the incorporation of Regulation 2790/99 into the EEA Agreement, **3.03**. the EFTA Surveillance Authority also incorporated the Guidelines[4] so as to assist companies in the self-assessment of their vertical agreements in light of EEA competition rules. Both Regulation 2790/99 and the Guidelines are therefore applied by the EEA Surveillance Authority as well as the Commission. However, in accordance with the division of tasks pursuant to Article 56 of the EEA Agreement, individual cases will only be dealt with by one surveillance

---

[1] Commission Regulation (EC) No 2790/99 of 22 December 1999 on the application of Article 81(3) of the Treaty to categories of vertical agreements and concerted practices [1999] OJ L336/25 (hereafter the 'Regulation').
[2] Commission Notice—Guidelines on Vertical Restraints [2000] OJ C291/1.
[3] [2001] OJ L103/36.
[4] Commission Notice—Guidelines on Vertical Restraints [2002] OJ C122/1. The same goes for the 'Horizontal Guidelines': see Guidelines on the applicability of Article 53 of the EEA Agreement to horizontal cooperation agreements [2002] OJ C266/1.

authority. Following the provisions of Article 56 EEA Agreement, the Commission, for instance, decides on cases where trade between the EC Member States is affected. The EFTA Surveillance Authority decides if it is only trade between EFTA States that is affected or in cases where the turnover of the undertakings concerned in the territory of the EFTA State equals 33% or more of their turnover in the territory covered by the EEA Agreement.

3.04. Practically speaking, the foregoing implies that the words 'EC' or '(EC) Member States' in Regulation 2790/99 and the Guidelines can in fact be read as meaning 'EEA States'.

B. Territorial Application of the Prohibition of Article 81(1) EC and Regulation 2790/99

(1) Vertical agreements which restrict competition in the EEA

3.05. Materially speaking, the territorial scope of application of the prohibition of Article 81(1) EC (and, correspondingly, the possibility for block exemption under Regulation 2790/99) applies to all agreements which have as their object or effect the prevention, restriction, or distortion of competition within the EEA, provided that they appreciably affect trade between the EEA States. In other words, the prohibition of Article 81(1) EC does not only apply to vertical agreements between companies established in the EEA concerning their intra-EEA activities. Vertical agreements between companies not established in the EEA, or between companies both inside and outside the EEA, can also restrict competition in the EEA. It may concern, for instance, agreements on imports (eg an agreement between a Chinese company and its European distributors, pursuant to which the latter have imposed upon them restrictions on the setting of their minimum price)[5] or agreements on exports outside or re-importation from outside the EEA.

(2) Vertical agreements on exports outside or re-importation from outside the EEA

3.06. In principle, agreements on exports outside or re-importation from outside the EEA are not covered by the prohibition of Article 81(1) EC. In *Bulk Oil*, the Court indeed ruled that 'a measure . . . which is specifically directed at exports of oil to a non-member country is not in itself likely to restrict or distort

---

[5] Paras 5.1 *et seq* discuss the prohibition of vertical price-fixing. Examples of the application of Art 81(1) EC to import agreements: eg Case 22/71 *Béguelin Import v S.A.G.L. Import Export* [1971] ECR 949; Case 71/74 *FRUBO v Commission* [1975] ECR 563; and Case 28/77 *Tepea BV v Commission* [1978] ECR 1398.

competition within the common market. It cannot therefore affect trade within the Community and infringe [Article 81 EC]'.[6]

Notwithstanding this, an agreement does not as a matter of course, fall outside **3.07**. the scope of Article 81(1) EC because it concerns trade outside the EEA. The agreement can infringe Article 81(1) EC if its objective is to limit or exclude re-imports of the products concerned in the EEA. In this respect, reference can be made to the Court's judgment in the *Javico* case.[7] In this case, which is expressly mentioned in the Guidelines (paragraph 46), the Court was asked, amongst other things, the following question:

> Where an undertaking (the supplier) situated in a Member State of the European Union [Yves Saint Laurent] by contract entrusts another undertaking (the distributor) situated in another Member State [Javico] with the distribution of its products in a territory outside the Union, must Article [81(1) EC] be interpreted as prohibiting provisions in that contract which preclude the distributor from effecting any sales in a territory other than the contractual territory, and hence any sale in the Union, either by direct marketing or by re-exportation from the contractual territory?

The facts of the case were that the distribution agreement which Javico had **3.08**. concluded with Yves Saint Laurent (for Russia and Ukraine) contained the following clause:

1. Our products are intended for sale solely in the territory of the Republics of Russia and Ukraine. In no circumstances may they leave the territory of the Republics of Russia and Ukraine.
2. Your company promises and guarantees that the final destination of the products will be in the territory of the Republics of Russia and Ukraine, and that it will sell the products only to traders situated in the territory of the Republics of Russia and Ukraine. Consequently, your company will provide the addresses of the distribution points of the products in the territory of the Republics of Russia and Ukraine and details of the products by distribution point.

A second distribution agreement, for Slovenia, contained the following clause: **3.09**. 'In order to protect the high quality of the distribution of the products in other countries of the world, the distributor agrees not to sell the products outside the territory or to unauthorised dealers in the territory'.

Shortly after the conclusion of the contracts, Yves Saint Laurent discovered that **3.10**. products covered by the agreements with Javico were being sold in the EC. Yves Saint Laurent terminated the contracts and obtained contractual compensation and damages before the competent court. Javico appealed against this decision and the appeal court referred the question cited above to the Court. With

---

[6] Case 174/84 *Bulk Oil v Sun International* [1986] ECR 559, para 44.
[7] Case C–306/96 *Javico International and Javico AG v Yves Saint Laurent Parfums* [1998] ECR I–1983.

reference to earlier case law,[8] the Court, in a first stage, ruled that an agreement which requires a reseller not to resell contractual products outside the contractual territory has as its object the exclusion of parallel imports within the EC and consequently the restriction of competition in the common market. Such provisions, in contracts for the distribution of products within the Community, therefore constitute by their very nature a restriction of competition. However, such anti-competitive conduct may not be struck down under Article 81(1) EC, unless it is capable of affecting trade between Member States.[9]

3.11. In a second stage, the Court transposed these principles to contracts, like those at issue in *Javico*, which are intended to apply in a territory outside the EC. In the case of agreements of this kind, the Court ruled that stipulations of the type mentioned in the question must be construed not as being intended to exclude parallel imports and marketing of the contractual product within the EC, but as being designed to enable the producer to penetrate a market outside the EC by supplying a sufficient quantity of contractual products to that market. It therefore follows, according to the Court, that an agreement in which the reseller (Javico) gives an undertaking to the producer (Yves Saint Laurent) that he will sell the contractual products on a market outside the EC cannot be regarded as having the object of appreciably restricting competition within the common market or as being capable of affecting, as such, trade between Member States.[10]

3.12. Notwithstanding this, the Court did not exclude that such provisions, whilst not being, by their very nature, contrary to Article 81(1) EC, may have *an effect which is contrary to Article 81(1) EC*. Whether this is the case or not must be examined by the national court. In order to undertake that examination, the national court will have to determine the structure of the EC market for the relevant products: eg whether the market is oligopolistic, allowing only limited competition within the EC, whether there are appreciable price differences inside and outside the EC (and whether these price differences are eroded by the level of customs duties and transport costs).[11]

3.13. If that examination shows that the effect of the provisions is to undermine competition in the sense of Article 81(1) EC, the national court must then subsequently examine whether there is any risk of *an appreciable effect on the pattern of trade between the Member States* which may undermine the attainment of the objectives of the common market. According to the Court, this will not be the case if the products intended for markets outside the EC account for only a very small percentage of the total market for those products in the territory of the common market.[12]

---

[8] Case C–297/87 *Tipp-Ex v Commission* [1990] ECR I–261.
[9] Case C–306/96 *Javico International and Javico AG v Yves Saint Laurent Parfums* [1998] ECR I–1983, paras 14–15. [10] ibid, paras 18–21.
[11] ibid, paras 22–4. [12] ibid, paras 25–6.

In conclusion, the answer to the question of the applicability of Article 81(1) EC, **3.14**. namely through Regulation 2790/99, to a *Javico*-like situation cannot be given in the abstract, but must be examined on a case-by-case basis using the criteria laid down by the Court. As regards the effect on inter-State trade, this is now summarized in the Commission's Notice on the effect on trade concept.[13] In the Notice (paragraph 108), the Commission summarizes *Javico* as follows:

> Trade may also be capable of being affected when the agreement prevents re-imports into the Community. This may, for example, be the case with vertical agreements between Community suppliers and third country distributors, imposing restrictions on resale outside an allocated territory, including the Community. If in the absence of the agreement resale to the Community would be possible and likely, such imports may be capable of affecting patterns of trade inside the Community.

(3) Vertical agreements with hardcore restrictions

If a vertical agreement, in accordance with the principles set out above, falls **3.15**. under the prohibition of Article 81(1) EC, it will automatically be block exempted under Regulation 2790/99 to the extent, of course, that it complies with the conditions thereof. This will not be the case if it contains one or several hardcore restrictions as stated in Article 4 of Regulation 2790/99. These restrictions are further discussed in Chapter 5. Notwithstanding this, it is useful in the context of the present discussion on the territorial application of the prohibition of Article 81(1) EC (and the related question of the application of the block exemption of Regulation 2790/99) to clarify the territorial application of hardcore restrictions. This clarification concerns questions such as: Can an agreement between a UK company and its distributor in Mexico contain a provision according to which the distributor agrees not to sell below a minimum sale price (while fixing such a minimum sale price is a hardcore restriction in the sense of Article 4(a) of Regulation 2790/99)? Or, can a UK company require its distributors located in the EEA not to export products to Hong Kong (while such territorial restrictions are, save a number of limited exceptions, a hardcore restriction in the sense of Article 4(b) of Regulation 2790/99)?

The starting point of the analysis is the Guidelines, which (in paragraph 46) state **3.16**. that the 'list of hardcore restrictions applies to vertical agreements concerning trade within the Community'. It is sufficiently well known that intra-EEA export bans and restrictions are contrary to the EC rules on competition.[14] *A contrario*,

---

[13] Commission Notice—Guidelines on the effect on trade concept contained in Articles 81 and 82 of the Treaty [2004] OJ C101/81 (discussed in paras 2.31–2.59 above).

[14] eg Case 19/77 *Miller* [1978] ECR 131; Case T–175/95 *BASF Lacke + Farben AG v Commission* [1999] ECR II–1581, para 133; and Case T–176/96 *Accinauto SA v Commission* [1999] ECR II–1635, para 104.

the application of Regulation 2790/99 is not, in the Commission's opinion, endangered by hardcore restrictions which solely concern trade outside the Community. Accordingly, a UK company can impose on its distributor in Mexico not to sell below a minimum sale price without incurring the risk of losing the benefit of the block exemption of Regulation 2790/99 for the distribution agreement concerned. Needless to say, the antitrust legislation enacted in jurisdictions other than the EEA will be applicable and may rule out such restrictions.

3.17. This rule takes on an extra dimension when it is considered against the background of the prohibition on territorial restrictions contained in Article 4(b) of Regulation 2790/99. Save a limited number of exceptions,[15] Article 4(b) states that the block exemption shall not apply to vertical agreements which have as their object 'the restriction of the territory into which, or of the customers to whom, the buyer may sell the contract goods or services'. Nowhere in Regulation 2790/99 is the territorial scope of application of Article 4(b) limited. Specifically, it is not stated what must be understood by the 'territory'. In other words, on the basis of the wording of Regulation 2790/99, it cannot be excluded that a condition imposed by a UK company on its distributors located in the EEA not to export products to Hong Kong is a territorial restriction in the sense of Article 4(b) which does not qualify for exemption. What is more, on a literal reading, every territorial restriction could in fact be subject to the prohibition of Article 4(b).

3.18. In this respect, the Guidelines do not really offer any solution. They state (at paragraph 46): 'In so far as vertical agreements concern exports outside the Community or imports/re-imports from outside the Community see the judgement in *Javico v Yves Saint Laurent*'. Accordingly, in agreement with the judgment of the Court in *Javico*, the Commission considers that agreements which concern exports outside or re-imports from outside the Community cannot by definition be excluded from the scope of the prohibition of Article 81(1) EC. It should be clear that this does not answer the question of whether or not it is possible to impose an export ban in an agreement on exports outside the EEA without losing the benefit of the block exemption. *Javico* does not address this issue. It only teaches us that such an agreement can come within the scope of the prohibition of Article 81(1) EC.

3.19. In our opinion, it should be possible to rely on the Guidelines and on the fact that paragraph 46, as cited above, also states that the 'list of hardcore restrictions applies to vertical agreements concerning trade within the Community' to conclude that an export ban to a country outside the EEA in an agreement which according to *Javico* may be caught by Article 81(1) EC, does not lead to

---

[15] These are discussed in detail in paras 5.43–5.110 below.

the loss of the block exemption under Regulation 2790/99. In the meanwhile, the Commission's services have confirmed this view informally. The position of the Commission's services is that the territorial scope of Article 4 is limited to the Community and does not include extra-Community trade. As a consequence, a territorial restriction which is caught by the list of hardcore restrictions in Article 4(b) of Regulation 2790/99, but concerns countries outside the EEA, is permissible without individual exemption. The distinction between active and passive sales is irrelevant. The informal advice which we have received has confirmed that even an absolute territorial restriction aimed at territories outside the EEA will benefit from the block exemption (of course on the assumption that the agreement concerned is caught by Article 81(1) EC on the basis of *Javico*).

4

APPLICATION IN TIME OF REGULATION 2790/99

The application in time is governed by Articles 12 and 13 of Regulation **4.01**. 2790/99.[1] According to these provisions, from 1 January 2001 onwards, all vertical agreements must comply with the conditions of Regulation 2790/99 in order to benefit from block exemption under the said regulation. The block exemption expires on 31 May 2010.

This application in time also applies to the non-EC Member States of the EEA **4.02**. Agreement.[2]

---

[1] Commission Regulation (EC) No 2790/99 of 22 December 1999 on the application of Article 81(3) of the Treaty to categories of vertical agreements and concerted practices [1999] OJ L336/25.
[2] Decision of the EEA Joint Committee No 18/2000 of 28 January 2000 amending Annex XIV (Competition) to the EEA Agreement [2001] OJ L103/36.

5

HARDCORE RESTRICTIONS

A. Hardcore Restrictions as 'Object'

Hardcore restrictions, which are listed in Article 4 of Regulation 2790/99,[1] play a **5.01**.
central role in the block exemption. A vertical agreement containing a hardcore
restriction (also referred to as a blacklisted provision) will lose the benefit of the
block exemption. Hence, as a result of the presence of a hardcore restriction it will
no longer be possible to rely on the block exemption for any aspect of the vertical
agreement. The Guidelines[2] summarize the legal position as follows:

> The Block Exemption Regulation exempts vertical agreements on condition that
> no hardcore restriction, as set out in Article 4, is contained in or practised with the
> vertical agreement. If there are one or more hardcore restrictions, the benefit of the
> Block Exemption Regulation is lost for the entire vertical agreement. There is no
> severability for hardcore restrictions.

Before outlining the specific restrictions that are included in the blacklist of **5.02**.
Article 4, the introductory sentence of that provision requires careful consideration. The introductory sentence reads as follows:

> The exemption provided for in Article 2 shall not apply to vertical agreements
> which, directly or indirectly, in isolation or in combination with other factors
> under the control of the parties, have as their object...

Three important principles for the application of Article 4 can be derived **5.03**.
from this:

— It is irrelevant to the application of Article 4 whether the restriction concerned is imposed directly (eg by means of a contractual provision expressly
  imposing the restriction) or whether it is achieved indirectly (eg by making

---

[1] Commission Regulation (EC) No 2790/99 of 22 December 1999 on the application of
Article 81(3) of the Treaty to categories of vertical agreements and concerted practices [1999]
OJ L336/25 (hereafter the 'Regulation').
[2] Commission Notice—Guidelines on Vertical Restraints [2000] OJ C291/1, para 66
(hereafter 'Guidelines').

certain benefits, such as bonuses or discounts, dependent upon a party's compliance with a given restriction).

— It is also irrelevant whether the restriction is imposed in isolation or whether it follows from a combination of factors that are under the control of the parties. However, factors over which the parties do not exercise control may not be taken into account in order to determine whether the blacklist of Article 4 is infringed.

— Finally, Article 4 only applies to vertical agreements that have a blacklisted restriction as their object.[3] The effect of a vertical agreement is not immediately relevant in this context: the wording of Article 4 (which refers only to object and not to effect) is markedly different from that of Article 81(1) EC (which refers in the alternative to object or effect). As the practical implications of this difference in approach are unclear, it is useful to analyse this point in somewhat greater detail.

(1) Different views on the 'object' concept

5.04. The legal test underlying the 'object' concept has been a topic of considerable debate.[4] Some commentators suggest that object has to be understood as 'necessary effect'[5] or 'likely effect'.[6] This approach has been characterized as problematic as the reduction of 'the object category to presumptions of effect does not explain why the presumption is not rebuttable by even the strongest evidence that the agreement does not have such an effect'.[7] Another approach (advocated by those rejecting the necessary effects theory) is to emphasize the subjective intention of the parties as a sufficient criterion for establishing the object of an agreement.[8]

5.05. Recently, the Commission has taken a fairly explicit stance on this issue. While prior case law of the Court and the Commission contained some useful (but still fairly cryptic) hints, the Guidelines on the application of Article 81(3) EC[9] (paragraphs 20–3) addresses the relevant question quite openly:

> (21) Restrictions of competition by object are those that by their very nature have the potential of restricting competition. These are restrictions which in light of the

---

[3] On the lack of consistency in this respect between the introductory language of Art 4 and the final sentence of Art 2(3), see para 2.283 above.
[4] O Odudu, 'Interpreting Article 81(1): Object as Subjective Intention' [2001] ELR 60; O Odudu, 'Interpreting Article 81(1): The Object Requirement Revisited' [2001] ELR 379.
[5] J Faull and A Nikpay, *The EC Law of Competition* (OUP, 1999) 82, para 2.61; V Korah, *An Introductory Guide to EC Competition Law and Practice* (7th edn, Hart Publishing, 2000) 59.
[6] V Korah and D O'Sullivan, *Distribution Agreements under the EC Competition Rules* (Hart Publishing, 2002) 169.   [7] Odudu (n 4 above) 382 and footnote 18.
[8] ibid, 385, footnote 31, where commentators are listed that proceed on the basis that the object requirement is satisfied by subjective intention.
[9] Guidelines on the application of Article 81(3) of the Treaty [2004] OJ C101/97, paras 20–23 (hereafter 'Guidelines on the application of Art 81(3) EC').

objectives pursued by the Community competition rules have such a high potential of negative effects on competition that it is unnecessary for the purposes of applying Article 81(1) to demonstrate any actual effects on the market. This presumption is based on the serious nature of the restriction and on experience showing that restrictions of competition by object are likely to produce negative effects on the market and to jeopardise the objectives pursued by the Community competition rules. Restrictions by object such as price fixing and market sharing reduce output and raise prices, leading to a misallocation of resources, because goods and services demanded by customers are not produced. They also lead to a reduction in consumer welfare, because consumers have to pay higher prices for the goods and services in question.

(22) The assessment of whether or not an agreement has as its object the restriction of competition is based on a number of factors. These factors include, in particular, the content of the agreement and the objective aims pursued by it. It may also be necessary to consider the context in which it is (to be) applied and the actual conduct and behaviour of the parties on the market. In other words, an examination of the facts underlying the agreement and the specific circumstances in which it operates may be required before it can be concluded whether a particular restriction constitutes a restriction of competition by object. The way in which an agreement is actually implemented may reveal a restriction by object even where the formal agreement does not contain an express provision to that effect. Evidence of subjective intent on the part of the parties to restrict competition is a relevant factor but not a necessary condition.

(23) Non-exhaustive guidance on what constitutes restrictions by object can be found in Commission block exemption regulations, guidelines and notices. Restrictions that are blacklisted in block exemptions or identified as hardcore restrictions in guidelines and notices are generally considered by the Commission to constitute restrictions by object. In the case of horizontal agreements restrictions of competition by object include price fixing, output limitation and sharing of markets and customers. As regards vertical agreements the category of restrictions by object includes, in particular, fixed and minimum resale price maintenance and restrictions providing absolute territorial protection, including restrictions on passive sales.

This approach is confirmed in recent decisions of the Commission.[10]

(2) Direct imposition of hardcore restrictions

In the context of Article 4 of the Regulation, the 'object' concept does not pose **5.06**. problems in a case of the direct imposition of blacklisted restrictions. Any such direct imposition may be deemed to meet the 'object' test. For instance, a contract clause imposing retail prices on a dealer, by definition, has a hardcore

---

[10] See *Belgian Architects' Association* [2005] OJ L4/10, para 80: 'The question whether a decision has the object of restricting competition depends on a number of factors. Its object may be deduced from the terms of the decision, its objective aims, the legal and economic context and the conduct of the parties'.

restriction as its object. In other words, in a direct imposition scenario, it suffices to consider the catalogue of practices listed in Article 4 to determine whether a vertical agreement has a hardcore restriction as its object.[11]

(3) Indirect imposition of hardcore restrictions

5.07. Substantially more complex is the situation where a vertical agreement indirectly has a hardcore restriction as its object. The recent judgment of the Court of First Instance in *JCB*[12] provides an excellent basis to show this. In *JCB*, the Commission concluded that the imposition of service support fees on sales effected by authorized distributors outside their territories rendered the distributors' remuneration dependent on the territorial destination of the sale.[13] This practice was regarded by the Commission as restricting cross-border trade.[14] The Court of First Instance did not share the Commission's viewpoint and its assessment proves to be of interest to the issue at hand. JCB argued that the service support fees on out-of-territory sales amounted to no more than a reasonable estimate of actual service costs incurred by the distributor in the receiving territory. Relying on this explanation, the Court of First Instance stated that 'it is important to know whether the fee fixed on the basis of those prior calculations [of the service support fees] reflects a realistic assessment of the cost of after-sales service increased by a reasonable profit margin . . . or whether it was set at an unreasonable level and therefore could have had the object or effect of deterring exports' (paragraph 142). The Court of First Instance concluded that the Commission had proven unable to challenge the method of calculation or to establish that the service support fees had the object (or effect) of preventing out-of-territory sales (paragraph 144). A somewhat similar approach was adopted by the Court of First Instance in respect of JCB's multiple deal trading support (paragraphs 146 *et seq*).

5.08. The *JCB* decision is interesting because it addresses practices directly related to out-of-territory sales. It is undeniable that the service support fees to some extent rendered out-of-territory sales less attractive as the selling distributor had to share part of his margin with the 'receiving' distributor. The Court of First Instance's judgment must be understood as meaning that such simple logic is insufficient to meet the object test.

5.09. At present authoritative guidance on the interpretation of the object test in an 'indirect imposition' context is lacking. Pending further clarification

---

[11] This is confirmed in the Guidelines on the application of Article 81(3) EC, para 23, n 29.
[12] Case T–67/01 *JCB Service v Commission* [2004] OJ C85/23, appeal pending Case C–167/04P [2004] OJ C156/3.   [13] *JCB* [2002] OJ L69/1, para 261.
[14] ibid, para 160.

by the competent authorities, our proposal is to consider the object test as met where:

— the subjective intent to impose a hardcore restriction is proven; or
— in case such subjective intent is difficult or impossible to prove and the practice may have a hardcore restriction as its effect,[15] the parties are unable to demonstrate that their intention is to achieve a (legitimate) aim other than the imposition of a hardcore restriction.

Applying this test to the service support fee in the *JCB* decision, the object test would be met if it can be proven that JCB intended to restrict cross-border selling by means of this practice. In that situation, JCB's subjective intent to implement a hardcore restriction would be proven. The fact that evidence of such subjective intent cannot be found, would not, however, be sufficient to escape the object test. As the service support fee may reasonably be deemed to have a potential negative effect on cross-border selling,[16] it would seem reasonable to suggest that the object test will not be met if JCB is able to advance a legitimate aim other than the illegitimate impediment of cross-border sales. If such an aim can be proven, then the object test is not met. If no such other aim can be proven (or if the stated aim lacks credibility),[17] it would seem reasonable to suggest that the object test is met.[18]

B. Territorial Scope of Application

Regarding the application *ratione loci*, the Guidelines (paragraph 46) provide **5.10.** that the 'list of hardcore restrictions applies to vertical agreements concerning trade within the Community'. This implies that the blacklist does not concern

---

[15] The reference to 'effect' in this context is not intended to mix the object-standard with the effect-standard. The sole purpose of this reference is to define, in the absence of proven subjective intent, a category of practices for which it may reasonably be deemed useful to investigate whether they meet the 'object' standard in an 'indirect imposition' context.

[16] To put it in plain terms, no distributor is attracted by the thought of having to share part of his margin with other distributors in the network and the service support fee may therefore hamper cross-border trade. The observation of the Court of First Instance (para 144) that the JCB system might facilitate cross-border trade is not inconsistent with this statement. The Court of First Instance's observation related to the existence of clear guidelines on the level of the service support fee and not to the existence of a mandatory service support fee payment as such.

[17] The check conducted by the Court of First Instance whether the level of the service support fee was reasonably related to the extra after-sales service costs incurred by the 'receiving' distributor can serve as an example of such a credibility assessment.

[18] It is useful to add that the Commission did not challenge the service support fee on the basis of the object test, but relied on its alleged restrictive effect (see paras 159 *et seq*). This factor does not undermine our analysis; rather to the contrary, it demonstrates that, even for practices that may have a direct impact on cross-border trade, automatic conclusions that the object test is (also) met are to be avoided.

restrictions that apply to extra-Community trade. This territorial limitation is not mentioned *expressis verbis* in Article 4 itself. However, in addition to the Guidelines, informal contacts with DG COMP taught us that this limitation was intended by the drafters of the Regulation. The territorial scope of application of the Regulation is discussed in greater detail in Chapter 3 above.

C. Article 4(a)—Vertical Price Fixing

(1) The principle of the prohibition of vertical price fixing

5.11. Article 4(a) of the Regulation states:

> The exemption provided for in Article 2 shall not apply to vertical agreements which, directly or indirectly, in isolation or in combination with other factors under the control of the parties, have as their object:
>
> (a) the restriction of the buyer's ability to determine its sale price, without prejudice to the possibility of the supplier's imposing a maximum sale price or recommending a sale price, provided that they do not amount to a fixed or minimum sale price as a result of pressure from, or incentives offered by, any of the parties; . . .

5.12. The first restriction that is mentioned in the blacklist consists of vertical price fixing (also called 'resale price maintenance' or 'RPM').[19] Vertical price fixing will be involved where the buyer is required to observe a fixed or minimum resale price. This restriction limits the buyer's ability to apply prices below a given level or to adjust its prices below such a level.

5.13. The Commission is of the opinion that vertical price fixing may have a negative impact on competition in at least two respects:[20]

— First, it results in a reduction in intra-brand competition—that is, competition between distributors of the same brand. Distributors of a given brand will not, or at least not to the same extent, compete on price in respect of the products or services of the brand so that intra-brand price competition is eliminated or substantially reduced.

— Second, vertical price fixing may result in increased transparency on prices. The Commission fears that, particularly in concentrated markets, such transparency will facilitate horizontal collusion between manufacturers or distributors.[21] In this manner, the reduction of intra-brand competition can

---

[19] A general discussion on the US approach to RPM can be found in E Th Sullivan and JL Harrison, *Understanding Antitrust and Its Economic Implications* (LexisNexis 2003) 215–31.
[20] Guidelines, para 112.
[21] This issue is addressed in Case 27/87 *SPRL Louis Erauw-Jacquery v SC la Hesbignonne* [1988] ECR 1919. In para 15 of this judgment the Court of Justice suggests the existence of a clear link between the system of vertical price fixing provided for in the agreement and the

trigger a reduction in inter-brand price competition—that is, competition between suppliers of competing brands.

Elimination or reduction of intra-brand competition

With regard to the first negative effect referred to above, it is difficult to contradict the Commission's opinion. Indeed, vertical price fixing does eliminate or reduce intra-brand price competition. However, it does not eliminate intra-brand competition completely. In addition to price, there are many other factors on which distributors of a given brand can compete[22] (such as the quality of the service). However, given the importance of price as a competitive factor,[23] the Commission is not prepared to accept a reduction of intra-brand competition to factors other than price and excludes, therefore, the benefit of the block exemption for vertical agreements that have vertical price fixing as their object.

5.14.

Price transparency—horizontal collusion

As to the second negative effect, there is slightly more room for debate. The risk that increased price transparency will lead to horizontal collusion between manufacturers or distributors of competing goods or services seems to exist only if vertical price fixing is engaged in by a company with a sufficient degree of market power. It is not self-evident that the same risk applies if vertical price fixing is applied by a smaller market participant. For a smaller player the application of a fixed price could even be a promotional feature to differentiate its position from that of other market participants. To pass such a negative judgment on vertical price fixing applied by smaller market players on account of possible horizontal collusive implications is not necessarily justified. However, the Commission has little sympathy for this position and will, in principle, refuse to accept vertical price fixing, even if applied by the smallest possible market players.[24]

5.15.

---

existence of horizontal price fixing agreements. A striking example of a clear link between horizontal and vertical price fixing is reported in European Commission, *Fifteenth Report on Competition Policy* (OOPEC, 1986) paras 66–7 (*Italian Spectacles sector*).

[22] Case C–198/01 *Consorzio Industrie Fiammiferi (CIF) v Autorità Garante della Concorrenza e del Mercato* [2003] ECR I–8055.

[23] *Mercedes-Benz* [2002] OJ L257/1, para 181; and *Volkswagen AG* [2001] OJ L262/14, para 76. In Commission Decision of 16 July 2003 in *Yamaha* (COMP/37.975/PO) (not yet published), para 151, the Commission observed: 'Provisions restricting the freedom of dealers to fix prices have deprived retailers of an important means of competition. Price competition holds prices to the lowest possible level and encourages trade in goods between Member States, thereby making possible an optimal allocation of resources based on the adaptability of retailers and giving benefit to consumers.'

[24] This is illustrated by the fact that vertical price fixing will not be able to benefit from *de minimis* treatment. See Commission Notice on agreements of minor importance which do not

5.16. The Court and the Commission systematically characterize vertical price fixing as an infringement of Article 81(1) EC[25] that will in principle not be eligible for an exemption pursuant to Article 81(3) EC.[26] The Court has discussed this point at length in *AEG–Telefunken*.[27] In its *Hennessy-Henkel* decision,[28] the Commission also made it very clear that parties should not be optimistic about their chances of obtaining an exemption pursuant to Article 81(3) EC for vertical price-fixing practices.[29]

5.17. In a number of decisions the Commission finds a link between vertical price fixing and the imposition of territorial restrictions.[30] The territorial restrictions aim to avoid the situation that fixed price levels are undercut by cheaper prices offered from other territories. A striking example is the *Yamaha* case[31] where resale price maintenance practices and territorial restrictions were found to go hand in hand.[32]

5.18. Whether vertical price fixing is effectively enforced is immaterial for the application of the prohibition contained in Article 81(1) EC. The Commission assumes that the mere presence of a vertical price-fixing provision in an

---

appreciably restrict competition under Art 81(1) EC establishing the European Community [2001] OJ C368/13, para 11(2)(a) (hereafter '*De Minimis* Notice'). See also Commission Decision of 16 July 2003 in *Yamaha* (COMP/37.975/PO), not yet published, para 153.

[25] In *Yamaha*, para 137, the Commission labelled the obligation of a purchaser to resell at a particular price as 'an obvious restriction of competition that is expressly prohibited by Art 81(1) EC'.

[26] In *Yamaha*, para 178, the Commission stated quite categorically that 'resale price maintenance prevent[s] consumers from taking advantage of the Single Market . . .'; also *Volkswagen AG* [2001] OJ L262/14, paras 95 and 123 (dealer profitability is not a valid justification for exempting vertical price fixing).

[27] Case 107/82 *AEG-Telefunken v Commission* [1983] ECR 3151.

[28] *Hennessy/Henkel* [1980] OJ L383/11.

[29] In exceptional cases, such as the distribution of newspapers and magazines, there seems to be scope for considering an exemption pursuant to Art 81(3) EC: Case 243/83 *Binon* [1985] ECR 2015, para 46, where the Court stated: 'If . . . the fixing of the retail price by publishers constitutes the sole means of supporting the financial burden resulting from the taking back of unsold copies and . . . constitutes the sole method by which a wide selection of newspapers and periodicals can be made available to readers, the Commission must take account of those factors when examining an agreement for the purposes of Article [81(3)]'.

[30] eg *Polistil/Arbois* [1984] OJ L136/9; *Nathan-Bricolux* [2001] OJ L54/1; and Case T–67/01 *JCB Service v Commission* [2004] OJ C85/23, appeal pending Case C–167/04P [2004] OJ C156/3.

[31] The Commission summarized as follows: 'The agreements and/or concerted practices, by restricting sales outside the territories and limiting the dealer's ability to determine its resale prices, were complementary and pursued the same object of artificially maintaining different price levels in different countries. The territorial and price restrictions had the common denominator of ensuring different price levels within the Community.' (*Yamaha*, para 186).

[32] Given that vertical price fixing was the main issue under review, the *Yamaha* decision constitutes one of the leading and most specific cases dealing with this type of antitrust infringement. The decision serves therefore as a useful guide for a better understanding of the precise scope of Art 4(a) Reg 2790/99.

agreement will exert pressure on the pricing behaviour of the party concerned. Hence, even in the absence of enforcement, vertical price fixing will be deemed to have anti-competitive consequences and be caught by Article 81(1) EC.[33]

(2) *Different types of vertical price fixing*

Direct price fixing

The most straightforward application of Article 4(a) of the Regulation is the **5.19**. direct imposition of (vertical) prices by means of a contractual provision or a concerted practice. As the Guidelines (paragraph 17) state, 'in the case of contractual provisions or concerted practices that directly establish the resale price, the restriction is clear cut'.

The application of this principle to agency agreements is somewhat specific. In **5.20**. such agreements, as the principal remains the owner of the goods (and hence acts as the party selling the goods), it is generally accepted that he establishes the sales price. However, for agency agreements that fall within the prohibition contained in Article 81(1) EC, an obligation preventing the agent from sharing his commission (fixed or variable) with the customer amounts to a hardcore restriction within the meaning of Article 4(a) of the Regulation. In practice, this means that the agent must be entitled to lower the effective sales price by reducing his own margin and without affecting the level of income from the principal (Guidelines, paragraph 48).[34]

Indirect price fixing

The Commission emphasizes that vertical price fixing can also be imposed **5.21**. indirectly and offers a number of examples in the Guidelines:

— *Fixing the distribution margin.* This practice may consist of an obligation on the buyer to add a specified amount or percentage on top of its own purchase price for the purposes of establishing its resale price. Conversely, the supplier may require the buyer to take a specified margin (expressed as a fixed amount or a percentage) of a given reference price. In *Yamaha*[35] the Commission discovered an example of such practice:

> The distribution contract for oboes and bassoons stated that the sale price to other dealers will be calculated as follows: your purchasing price × 1.0877 = net

---

[33] eg *Novalliance/Systemform GmbH* [1997] OJ L47/11, para 61. In the past, the Commission has followed the same reasoning for contractually determined territorial restrictions (see *John Deere* [1985] OJ L35/38, paras 29–30). [34] For more details, see paras 7.84–7.87 below.

[35] *Yamaha*, not yet published, paras 81–2 and 144 (n 23 above). Conversely, an isolated case of co-ordination on prices between a supplier and its distributor may be insufficient to establish a vertical price-fixing infringement (Case T–67/01 *JCB Service v Commission* [2004] OJ C85/23, para 129, appeal pending Case C–167/04P [2004] OJ C156/3).

purchasing price distributor...This clause has the object of directly fixing resale prices when selling to other dealers and of artificially harmonising selling prices and discounts between territories, thereby restricting or distorting price competition.

— *Maximum discount levels.* Vertical price fixing can also be implemented by requiring that the buyer complies with maximum discount levels.[36] For instance, the buyer can be requested not to apply discounts that are in excess of a given percentage, calculated by reference to published recommended prices.

In *Mercedes*[37] the Commission condemned a scheme whereby Belgian dealers were prevented from granting discounts in excess of 3%. Mercedes allegedly agreed with a number of its dealers to involve an external agency to conduct test purchases (so-called 'ghost shopping') and to sanction dealers granting 'excessive' discounts with a reduction of their vehicle allocation.

In *Yamaha*[38] the Commission observed as follows:

The Commission has recognised that resale price maintenance can also be achieved through indirect means, such as fixing the maximum level of discount the distributor can grant from a prescribed price level. If Yamaha prohibits rebates of more than 15%, then in reality there is an obligation to respect a minimum price: the recommended prices minus 15%.

— *Financial benefits conditional upon compliance with fixed price levels.* Vertical price fixing can also take the form of granting certain financial benefits (such as discounts or the reimbursement of certain promotional costs) on condition that a given minimum price level is respected. For the purposes of Article 4(a), rewarding compliance with a fixed price level will be treated in the same manner as the direct imposition of vertical prices.[39]

— *Indirect means of fixing resale prices.* The fact that a supplier itself does not fix the resale prices to be applied by its buyers, but requires the buyers to link their resale prices to those applied by third parties, will also be regarded as vertical price fixing within the meaning of Article 4(a).[40] The Commission provides the example of resale prices being linked to the prices of competitors.[41] For instance, if the buyer is expected never to go below the prices of competitors or to increase his prices if the prices of the competition are

---

[36] eg European Commission, *Twenty-Third Report on Competition Policy 1993* (OOPEC, 1994) footnote 228, mentioning the practice of the Rover group to limit the discount which a dealer was allowed to grant to a customer. Dealers granting higher rebates were sanctioned by the deduction of a part of their margin (2%).

[37] *Mercedes-Benz* [2002] OJ L257/1, para 113.   [38] *Yamaha*, para 126 (n 23 above).

[39] eg Case 107/82 *AEG-Telefunken v Commission* [1983] ECR 3151, paras 124–8; and European Commission, *Twenty-Third Report on Competition Policy 1993* (OOPEC, 1994) footnote 228.

[40] Guidelines, para 47; also, Case 107/82 *AEG-Telefunken v Commission* [1983] ECR 3151, paras 87–91.   [41] Guidelines, para 47.

increased, the parties will be deemed to engage in vertical price fixing. While this principle may seem relatively straightforward, its application in practice may present some difficulties. It will indeed be necessary that the alignment of a buyer's prices to those of its competitors occurs at the initiative of the supplier and is not merely the result of the buyer adapting his position voluntarily to pricing initiatives undertaken by his competitors.

—*Sanctions.* The imposition of sanctions in cases of non-compliance with a given resale price level will be regarded as vertical price fixing. The Commission refers to 'threats, intimidation, warnings, penalties, delay or suspension of deliveries or contract terminations'.[42] However, it will always be necessary to demonstrate the link between these sanctions and the requirement to comply with a given resale price level.

Price monitoring

Direct or indirect means of fixing resale prices can be made more effective when **5.22**. combined with measures to identify price-cutters. In this respect, the Commission refers to the implementation of a price monitoring system and the obligation on retailers to report fellow retailers that deviate from the fixed price levels. It is important to note that the presence of price monitoring mechanisms does not, in and of itself, prove the existence of vertical price fixing. The Guidelines (paragraph 47) state that such mechanisms may render vertical price fixing more effective, but no more than that. The underlying vertical price-fixing scheme must, in any event, be proven in order to bring Article 4(a) of the Regulation into play. This is all the more the case since suppliers may have legitimate reasons to follow the pricing applied by their distribution networks. Pricing (being the prime competitive factor) is an obvious point of interest to any supplier. Hence, the fact that suppliers monitor the pricing applied at the distribution level may not be taken as conclusive evidence of vertical price fixing. In the absence of evidence that a buyer is invited (directly or indirectly) to comply with certain agreed minimum price levels, the existence of price monitoring cannot be challenged on the basis of Article 4(a) of the Regulation.

Other practices that may render vertical price fixing more effective include **5.23**. printing recommended resale prices on the products themselves or the supplier obliging the buyer to apply a most-favoured customer clause (Guidelines, paragraph 47). As to the latter concept, we assume that the Commission refers to the obligation of the buyer to apply any price reduction given to a particular customer to all of its other customers. This concept rules out the possibility of

---

[42] ibid. In *Volkswagen AG* [2001] OJ L262/14, para 66, reference is made to threats of termination of the dealer agreement and the commencement of legal proceedings. See also *Hasselblad* [1982] OJ L161/18, paras 36 *et seq* and Case 107/82 *AEG-Telefunken v Commission* [1983] ECR 3151, paras 129–30.

selective price cuts and implies that any price reduction has immediate implications for the overall margin of the reseller with all of its customers. While we have encountered most-favoured customer clauses in contracts involving major customers of a given supplier, we have in our practice never seen the clause operate in the manner suggested here.[43]

5.24. All of these examples must be handled with care. The Guidelines do not list them as evidence of vertical price fixing. They merely state that such measures may render a vertical price-fixing scheme more effective. In other words, such measures may support the implementation of vertical price fixing, but they do not amount to vertical price fixing in themselves.

(3) Recommended and maximum prices

5.25. Article 4(a) distinguishes expressly between the imposition of fixed or minimum resale prices and the practice of imposing maximum resale prices or of recommending resale prices. The latter practices (maximum and recommended resale prices) are not blacklisted and hence do not endanger the applicability of the block exemption.

5.26. The favourable treatment of recommended prices is not a novelty. The fact that, in vertical agreements, recommended prices may not be assimilated to fixed prices has been endorsed by both the Court and the Commission.[44] The fact that the supplier relies on these recommended prices to establish his own sales prices does not alter this conclusion.[45]

5.27. There has been more uncertainty in relation to the EC competition law treatment of maximum resale prices. A favourable hint could be found in Article 6(2) of Regulation 123/85, but its successor (ie Regulation 1475/95) was again less clear.[46] At least in the motor vehicle sector, the Commission seemed prepared not to blacklist the imposition of maximum resale prices. However, for a more general reassuring statement, Regulation 2790/99 and the outcome of

---

[43] For a general discussion on the position of most-favoured treatment clauses in the context of the block exemption, see JS Kurth, 'Meistbegünstigungsklauseln im Licht der Vertikal-GVO' [2003] WuW 28.

[44] Case 191/84 *Pronuptia de Paris GmbH v Pronuptia de Paris Irmgard Schillgallis* [1986] ECR 353, para 25. The Commission has immediately taken up this case law and has applied it particularly in its decision-making on franchising (eg *Pronuptia* [1987] OJ L13/39, para 39; *Yves Rocher* [1987] OJ L8/49, para 49; *Computerland* [1987] OJ L222/12, para 12; *ServiceMaster* [1988] OJ L332/38, para 20; and the (in the meanwhile withdrawn) Commission Regulation (EEC) No 4087/88 of 30 November 1988 on the application of Article 85(3) [now Art 81(3)] EC to certain categories of franchise agreements [1988] OJ L359/46, para 13).

[45] Case T–67/01 *JCB Service v Commission* OJ C85/23, para 130, appeal pending Case C–167/04P [2004] OJ C156/3.

[46] Regulation (EEC) No 123/85 of 12 December 1984 on the application of Article 85(3) [now Art 81(3)] EC to certain categories of motor vehicle distribution and servicing agreements [1985]

the 2000 *Nathan-Bricolux* case[47] had to be awaited. In the latter case, the Commission (at paragraph 87) stated that:

> the Commission no longer believes that an obligation not to exceed a maximum resale price, in this case a multiplier of the price charged in France by Nathan for the same products . . . , in itself necessarily restricts competition . . . However, the maximum price imposed here serves as a ceiling for a range of resale prices, at the bottom end of which is the ban on promotional discounts. As a result, the agreements fix effectively a resale price level (after discounts and rebates), although the range is fairly broad.

This paragraph suggests that, at least until the end of the 1990s, there has been discussion within the Commission as to whether the imposition of maximum resale prices was inside or outside the scope of Article 81(1) EC. With the adoption of Regulation 2790/99, the Commission has confirmed in general terms that maximum resale price fixing can benefit from a favourable competition law regime and is not blacklisted.[48]

The favourable treatment under Regulation 2790/99 will only be awarded to **5.28**. maximum and recommended resale prices 'provided that they do not amount to a fixed or minimum sale price as a result of pressure from, or incentives offered by, any of the parties'.[49] Hence, labelling a price as a maximum or recommended price is not sufficient.[50] The reseller must effectively be entitled to apply these prices as maximum or recommended prices, which means that it must be at liberty to apply prices lower than those communicated as maximum or recommended resale prices.[51] The Guidelines add that the provision of a list of recommended or maximum prices by the supplier to the buyer will not in and of itself be considered to lead to vertical price fixing.

OJ L15/16, Art 6(2): '6. Articles 1, 2 and 3 and Article 4(2) shall not apply where: (2) the manufacturer, the supplier or another undertaking within the distribution system obliges the dealer not to resell contract goods or corresponding goods below stated prices or not to exceed stated rates of trade discount' and Commission Regulation (EC) No 1475/95 of 28 June 1995 on the application of Article 85(3) [now 81(3)] EC to certain categories of motor vehicle distribution and servicing agreements [1995] OJ L145/25, Art 6(1)(6): '1. The exemption shall not apply where: (6) the manufacturer, the supplier or another undertaking directly or indirectly restricts the dealer's freedom to determine prices and discounts in reselling contract goods or corresponding goods'.

[47] *Nathan-Bricolux* [2001] OJ L54/1.

[48] For a recent confirmation, see Notice pursuant to Article 27(4) of Council Regulation (EC) No 1/2003 concerning *Repsol CPP SA* (COMP/B-1/38348) [2004] OJ C258/7.

[49] *Nathan-Bricolux* [2001] OJ L54/1 confirms that this danger may present itself very easily (see more specifically paras 86 *et seq* and 110–11). In this case, the imposed maximum prices were linked to a general ban on special price offers that would be liable to harm the image of the brand. The Commission considered this as an infringement of Art 81(1) EC which could not benefit from an exemption by virtue of Art 81(3) EC.

[50] *Volkswagen AG* [2001] OJ L262/14, para 57.

[51] In *Yamaha*, para 125, the Commission emphasizes that this includes the right to publish prices that are different from the recommended prices: 'It is true that the contracts and their guidelines refer to "recommended prices". However, the guidelines for shops clearly prevented the dealer from announcing either within or outside the shop a price other than the one established in

5.29. While maximum and recommended resale prices are not on the blacklist, this does not mean that they fall automatically outside the scope of Article 81(1) EC. Indeed 'a maximum or recommended price may work as a focal point for resellers, leading to a more or less uniform application of that price level'.[52] Hence, even though the supplier does not impose a particular resale price, the application of maximum or recommended prices may render price levels more uniform than would otherwise have been the case and therefore attract the prohibition of Article 81(1) EC.[53]

5.30. Even if the application of maximum or recommended prices exceptionally runs counter to the prohibition of Article 81(1) EC, this will not pose a problem in the context of the block exemption. Given that genuine maximum or recommended resale prices do not appear on the blacklist, the block exemption will apply to maximum or recommended pricing that is caught by the prohibition of Article 81(1) EC.

D. Article 4(b)—Territorial and Customer Restrictions

5.31. Without any doubt, Article 4(b) is one of the most complex provisions of Regulation 2790/99. This provision prohibits, in broad terms, the imposition of customer and territorial restrictions on buyers or resellers. There are only four specific exceptions to this general prohibition.

5.32. The economic justification for the harsh treatment of both customer restrictions and territorial restrictions is identical. With regard to both types of restriction the Commission is concerned that they may reduce intra-brand price competition and favour market partitioning (and hence price discrimination).[54] These are not new themes. The Commission's decision-making practice over the past decades has also relied on these concerns. In addition, the Commission expresses its concern that there may be a risk of collusion if several suppliers apply customer or territorial restrictions in parallel. This risk may be further increased in a situation of multiple exclusive dealerships, that is, when different suppliers designate the same exclusive dealers within a given territory.[55]

---

the price list. Even if discounts may have been possible, it is clear that the dealer was severely restricted in its freedom to communicate to the customer the price it fixed, and that such discounts, if the dealer was still willing to offer them, could not be communicated in a way contrary to the guidelines.' The fact that in practice dealers occasionally advertise below the recommended prices will not solve the problem: *Yamaha*, not yet published, para 141 (n 23 above).

[52] Guidelines, para 112. Also *Yamaha*, para 141.

[53] The favourable treatment of recommended prices in vertical agreements is in marked contrast with the negative assessment of the use of recommended prices in a horizontal context: *Belgian Architects' Association* [2005] OJ L4/10, paras 60 *et seq.*

[54] Guidelines, paras 161 and 178.   [55] Guidelines, para 164.

It is striking that the approach adopted in Article 4(b) turns the Commission's **5.33.** standard approach to hardcore restrictions upside down. The standard approach relies on a list of precisely defined practices that qualify as hardcore restrictions. A restriction that is not mentioned expressly in the list is not a hardcore restriction and therefore does not endanger the applicability of the block exemption. This approach offers the parties considerable freedom in drafting their agreements. It is sufficient for them to steer away from the precise practices that are specified in the blacklist. On customer and territorial restrictions the Commission has adopted a radically different approach, with a blacklist containing a very general prohibition of these types of restrictions and only four narrowly defined exceptions. As a consequence, in the field of customer and territorial restrictions, the more flexible or more economic philosophy underpinning the Regulation has been abandoned in favour of the straitjacket approach of the past. Contracting parties have no choice but to stick scrupulously to the four exceptions. Any deviation from these exceptions will automatically qualify as a hardcore restriction and result in the benefit of the block exemption being lost for the entire vertical agreement.

In the authors' opinion, the choice of this particular approach for customer and **5.34.** territorial restrictions is regrettable. One would have expected that the drafters of the Regulation would have given economic operators some more leeway, since the straitjacket approach of the previous block exemptions had curtailed the contractual freedom and creativity of the parties specifically in these areas. A striking example is the restriction on active sales outside a distributor's territory. For fear of losing the benefit of the block exemption, most practitioners cautiously copied the relevant provision of Regulation 1983/83[56] when drafting distribution agreements. Under the same regime of the previous block exemption, practitioners were equally reluctant to insert customer restrictions into their distribution agreements. The Regulation has not remedied this situation. Although customer restrictions may assist in organizing the distribution of products or services more efficiently, the Regulation allows a particular type of customer restriction only as a limited exception to the rule of the prohibition of customer restrictions. This exception is subject to such strict conditions and limitations that its practical relevance is doubtful.

(1) The rule of the prohibition of customer and territorial restrictions

Before addressing the four exceptions listed in Article 4(b), it is useful to clarify **5.35.** the rule that the Regulation prohibits customer and territorial restrictions.

---

[56] Commission Regulation (EEC) No 1983/83 of 22 June 1983 on the application of Article 85(3) EC to categories of exclusive distribution agreements [1983] OJ L173/1.

Restrictions imposed on buyers and resellers

5.36. First, it is worth noting that the prohibition of Article 4(b) only concerns customer and territorial restrictions imposed on buyers and resellers. The blacklist does not contain any reference to such restrictions being accepted by the supplier. Hence, if a supplier takes on the obligation vis-à-vis one or more of his distributors not to sell in certain territories or not to approach certain customers or categories of customers, there will be no blacklist problem. The distinction between active and passive sales is not relevant in this context. As customer or territorial restrictions imposed on the supplier are not mentioned on the blacklist, contracting parties are free to agree that the supplier will not sell at all (also not passively) to particular customers or in a given territory.

Restrictions applying in the EEA

5.37. Second, the blacklist only concerns customer and territorial restrictions that apply within the EEA. Reference is made in this context to the discussion in Chapter 3 on the territorial scope of application of the Regulation. If a customer or territorial restriction concerns a non-EEA territory, the restriction does not qualify as a hardcore restriction and therefore will not cause the loss of the benefit of the block exemption. Even if the restriction is deemed to restrict competition within the meaning of Article 81(1) EC in accordance with the *Javico* case law,[57] it can benefit from an automatic exemption by virtue of the Regulation.

Direct customer restrictions

5.38. Third, the Guidelines (paragraph 49) clarify that both direct and indirect customer and territorial restrictions are covered by the prohibition of Article 4(b). A direct restriction will typically consist of a contractual prohibition or limitation to the territories in which, or to the customers to whom, the buyer is entitled to sell. Also the obligation to refer orders of certain customers or of customers located in particular territories to the supplier or to another reseller can be characterized as a direct restriction.[58] The problematic nature of such direct restrictions is well known and it is unlikely that they will be found in distribution agreements that have been prepared with care.

Indirect customer restrictions

5.39. It should therefore not come as a surprise that the Guidelines pay particular attention to indirect restrictions, that is, indirect mechanisms to cause buyers and resellers to comply with a territorial or customer restriction. The following

---

[57] Paras 3.07–3.14 above. [58] Guidelines, para 49.

examples are cited:[59]

— refusal or reduction of bonuses or discounts;
— refusal to supply;
— reduction of supplied volumes or limitation of supplied volumes to the demand within the allocated territory or customer group;
— threat of contract termination;
— profit pass-over obligations; and
— refusal to grant a Community-wide guarantee.

According to the Guidelines, these practices are even more likely to be viewed as restrictive when they are used in conjunction with a monitoring system aimed at verifying the effective destination of the goods. Reference is made in this respect to the use of differentiated labels or serial numbers.[60]   **5.40**.

As discussed above,[61] it is not sufficient for the purposes of Article 4(b) of the Regulation that a vertical agreement has the effect of restricting sales to certain customers or into certain territories. The introductory phrase of Article 4 requires that such a restriction must be the object of the vertical agreement. By the same token, it will not be necessary to measure the effects of a restriction. The blacklist applies as soon as the vertical agreement has a customer or territorial restriction as its object, irrespective of its actual effects.   **5.41**.

Objective justification for customer restrictions

Finally, the Commission accepts that hardcore restraints on intra-brand competition (eg a general prohibition to sell to certain categories of customers) can sometimes escape the blacklist. This will be the case where there is an objective justification related to the product.[62] For instance, a general ban on selling dangerous substances to certain customers for safety or health reasons will be accepted. However, the justification will only withstand scrutiny if the supplier also accepts to refrain from selling the products concerned to the relevant categories of customers.[63]   **5.42**.

(2) First exception: restrictions on active sales

General

Article 4(b), first indent, provides: **5.43**.

> The exemption provided for in Article 2 shall not apply to vertical agreements which, directly or indirectly, in isolation or in combination with other factors

---

[59] ibid; also *Nintendo* [2003] OJ L255/33, para 275.
[60] Monitoring mechanisms are discussed at length in *Nintendo* [2003] OJ L255/33, paras 149, 166, 232, and 274.   [61] Paras 5.01–5.09.
[62] On the 'objective justification' theory, see paras 2.161–2.172.   [63] Guidelines, para 49.

under the control of the parties, have as their object: . . .

(b) the restriction of the territory into which, or of the customers to whom, the buyer may sell the contract goods or services, except:

— the restriction of active sales into the exclusive territory or to an exclusive customer group reserved to the supplier or allocated by the supplier to another buyer, where such a restriction does not limit sales by the customers of the buyer.

5.44. The first exception to the general prohibition of customer or territorial restrictions concerns restrictions on active sales. This exception is, without any doubt, the most complex provision of the Regulation.[64] From the outset, it should be noted that it does not apply to selective distribution agreements, which are the subject of a much more stringent regime on active sales restrictions. This regime is addressed separately below (see paragraphs 5.111 *et seq*).

5.45. The exception dealing with restrictions on active sales requires discussion of the following aspects:

— definition of 'active sales' and 'passive sales' (paragraphs 5.46–5.53);
— relevant principles governing restrictions on active sales prior to Regulation 2790/99 (paragraphs 5.54–5.60);
— restrictions on active sales according to Regulation 2790/99 (paragraphs 5.61–5.85);
— restrictions on active sales to exclusive customer groups within the framework of Regulation 2790/99 (paragraphs 5.86–5.88);
— direct sales rights of the supplier (paragraphs 5.89–5.94);
— the regime governing location clauses (paragraph 5.95).

Definition of active and passive sales

Active sales

5.46. 'Active sales' is a familiar concept to any EC competition lawyer. It dates back to the very first block exemption regulation applicable to distribution agreements, Regulation 67/67.[65] 'Active sales' are to be distinguished from 'passive sales'. The Guidelines address both concepts quite extensively.

5.47. The notion of 'active sales' is defined in the Guidelines (paragraph 50) as:

actively approaching individual customers inside another distributor's exclusive territory or exclusive customer group or customers in a specific territory allocated

---

[64] F Wijckmans and F Tuytschaever, 'Active Sales Restrictions Revisited' [2004] ECLR 107–13.

[65] Regulation No 67/67/EEC of the Commission of 22 March 1967 on the application of Article 85(3) EC to certain categories of exclusive dealing agreements [1967] OJ L57/849; [1967] OJ Spec Ed 10.

exclusively to another distributor through advertisement in media or other promotions specifically targeted at those customer groups or targeted at customers in that territory; or establishing a warehouse or distribution outlet in another distributor's exclusive territory.

Hence, sales efforts initiated by a distributor towards specific customers or specific customer groups will typically qualify as active sales.

Passive sales

As opposed to active sales, passive sales involve 'responding to unsolicited requests from individual customers including delivery of goods or services to such customers'. Nevertheless, the notion of passive sales does not exclude all advertising:

5.48.

> General advertising or promotion in media or on the Internet that reaches customers in other distributors' exclusive territories or customer groups but which is a reasonable way to reach customers outside those territories or customer groups, for instance to reach customers in non-exclusive territories or in one's own territory, are passive sales.[66]

Active v passive sales

The definition of active sales obviously encompasses the establishment of a distribution outlet or the appointment of a sub-dealer. In all other hypotheses, the distinction between active and passive sales is much more delicate and in any event does not depend on whether a sale is concluded with a customer. What is essential is whether there has been a targeted sales effort. For instance, sales following unsolicited e-mails sent to individual customers or specific customer groups (or sales following the unsolicited sending of catalogues) are considered to be active sales. Conversely, correspondence via e-mail or the sending of a catalogue at the initiative of a customer leads to passive sales only.

5.49.

A few examples can illustrate the different scenarios. Consider a given supplier of consumer products who appointed a dealer in the Paris region and a dealer in the Bordeaux region. If the Paris-based dealer undertakes a mailing campaign to potential customers located in the Bordeaux region, he engages in active sales in that region. If the Paris-based dealer advertises in a nationwide French newspaper and as a result of such advertising attracts customers located in the Bordeaux region, he has not engaged in active sales. In this scenario, given the nationwide character of the medium, it is assumed that he has not specifically targeted the Bordeaux customers. The most blatant example of active sales is the opening of a sales outlet: if the Paris dealer opens a shop in the Bordeaux region, he is engaging in active sales in the Bordeaux region.

5.50.

---

[66] Guidelines, para 50.

Sales via the Internet

5.51. As a rule, promotions or sales via the Internet are not regarded as active sales.[67] An exception to this rule is when a website uses banners or links in pages of providers which are specifically available to customers outside the contract territory or to customer groups exclusively allocated to another distributor.[68] The language used on the website is normally not considered a factor of importance in this debate. The Guidelines summarize the Commission's favourable attitude towards the unrestricted use of the Internet as follows:

> Every distributor must be free to use the Internet to advertise or to sell products. A restriction on the use of the Internet by distributors could only be compatible with the Block Exemption Regulation to the extent that the promotion on the Internet or sales over the Internet would lead to active selling into other distributors' exclusive territories or customer groups. In general, the use of the Internet is not considered a form of active sales into such territories or customer groups, since it is a reasonable way to reach every customer. The fact that it may have effects outside one's own territory or customer group results from the technology, i.e. the easy access from everywhere.[69]

The supplier is not entitled to reserve to itself sales or advertising over the Internet. An outright ban on using the Internet as a promotional or transactional tool is therefore not possible, unless there is an objective justification.[70]

5.52. The fact that a dealer makes a sale to a particular customer does not prove in and of itself that he has engaged in active sales towards that customer. Further, the fact that a customer purchases from the dealer as a result of advertising by the dealer is also not decisive. The relevant criterion is whether the dealer has made a sales effort targeted specifically towards particular customers or territories.

---

[67] For a more general discussion of the relationship between Internet selling and the Regulation, see R Fabre, 'Les contrats de distribution et Internet à la lumière du nouveau règlement communautaire, Concurrence & Distribution', Recueil Dalloz, 1 February 2001 (n° 5) chron 437; and S Pautke and JM Schultze, 'Internet und Vertriebskartellrecht: Hausaufgaben für die Europäische Kommission' (2001) 7 Betriebs-Berater 317–23.   [68] Guidelines, para 51.
[69] For a critique that the Commission does not go far enough to embrace the enormous procompetitive potential of new trading models: PM Taylor, 'The Vertical Agreements Regulation—A Critical Appraisal' in A Dashwood *et al* (eds), *Cambridge Yearbook of European Legal Studies 2000* (Hart Publishing, 2002) 525, 539.
[70] A judgment of the Belgian Supreme Court dated 10 October 2002 (*Makro v Beauté Prestige International*) addresses this specific issue. The underlying judgment of the Court of Appeal of Liège had held that, in the context of selective distribution of perfumes, the need to give personal advice served as an objective justification to block Internet sales and promotion. Referring to the Guidelines, the Belgian Supreme Court accepted that the block exemption does not exclude that a vertical agreement may contain a hardcore restriction (such as a ban on Internet selling) provided that the restriction is objectively justified. This case law is remarkable at least in two respects. First, it is surprising that the Supreme Court accepted the relevance of the Guidelines in support of an interpretation that is not necessarily borne out by the Regulation itself. Second, the concept of objective justification is given a broad interpretation in the judgment of the Court of Appeal of Liège (cf Guidelines, para 49). It is not clear whether the Commission had this type of justification (in relation to this type of product) under consideration when providing this exception in the Guidelines.

While the distinction between active and passive sales does not pose any specific **5.53** problems in theory, the contrary is true in practice. It is of course generally not difficult to show that there have been sales in a given territory or to a given customer group, but it is often very difficult to prove that those sales were due to an active sales effort by the dealer concerned. Only in obvious cases (eg advertising included in a magazine that is only sold in another territory or a direct mailing campaign) may it prove feasible to provide compelling evidence. In the absence of such evidence it is, in our experience, difficult to prove the existence of active sales. In that case, the threshold question will typically become whether it was the dealer or the customer that initiated the contact.

Restrictions on active sales prior to Regulation 2790/99

Regulation 2790/99 does not permit any limitation on passive sales by a dealer **5.54** outside his territory. Any restriction on sales outside his territory must therefore, by definition, be limited to active sales.

In respect of active sales, the Commission's approach in the Regulation is **5.55** radically different from that of the previous regime. Apart from the fact that they both exempt active sales restrictions under certain conditions, the previous block exemptions and the Regulation have nothing in common in this area. The essential condition under the previous block exemptions was that the restriction had to be imposed on an exclusive distributor. Regulation 2790/99 drops this condition.

Regulation 67/67 permitted that the exclusive dealer had 'to refrain, outside the **5.56** contract territory and in relation to the contract goods, from seeking customers, from establishing any branch and from maintaining any distribution depot' (Article 2(1)(b)). Similarly, Regulation 1983/83 allowed that the exclusive distributor had 'to refrain, outside the contract territory and in relation to the contract goods, from seeking customers, from establishing any branch and from maintaining any distribution depot' (Article 2(2)(c)). For motor vehicle distribution, the same approach was adopted in Regulation 123/85 (Article 3(8)) and Regulation 1475/95 (Article 3(8)), which allowed exclusive distribution as well as shared exclusivity.[71] Finally, Regulation 4087/88 concerning franchising agreements contained an unlimited possibility to impose active sales restrictions (Article 2(d)).

Block exemption regulations not covering a form of exclusive distribution **5.57** (whether exclusive distribution or shared exclusivity) generally did not permit a restriction on active sales. This resulted implicitly from Regulation 67/67 and

---

[71] Exclusive distribution means that the supplier has committed itself to appointing only one reseller in a particular territory. In the event of shared exclusivity, the supplier commits itself to appoint a restricted number of resellers (two or more) in the contract territory.

expressly from Regulation 1984/83. The latter block exemption, dealing with non-exclusive distribution linked to exclusive purchasing, contained no reference to active sales restrictions. Pursuant to the straitjacket approach, the imposition of such a restriction therefore led to the non-applicability of Regulation 1984/83.

5.58. Prior to Regulation 2790/99, the rationale for block exempting active sales restrictions therefore seemed to be linked to the territorial exclusivity enjoyed by the dealer concerned: the underlying idea must have been that a supplier could expect his exclusive dealers to concentrate their sales efforts on their own contract territory and not seek to sell actively outside their territories. The suggestion that the exemption of active sales restrictions under the old regime found its justification in the necessary protection of the territorial exclusivity enjoyed by the exclusive dealers is incorrect. First, there was no obligation under the previous block exemptions to impose an active sales restriction. Hence, the supplier was free not to impose such a restriction or to limit the territorial scope of the restriction. Second, and more importantly, these block exemptions allowed active sales restrictions directed at territories in which no exclusive distributors had been appointed, but for instance, where several non-exclusive distributors were active.

5.59. For customer restrictions which restrict the dealer in respect of the customers or the customer group he may approach, the Commission Notice concerning Regulation 1983/83 and Regulation 1984/83[72] explicitly stated: 'In principle inadmissible, pursuant to these prescriptions, are the contractual clauses which limit the reseller in his free customer choice' (paragraph 17) or, even more to the point (paragraph 29):

> Incompatible with the regulation would also be the imposed obligation on the exclusive distributor to supply only certain groups of buyers within his defined territory (eg retailers in a certain branch) and to leave the supply of other groups of buyers (eg warehouses) to other resellers, who were appointed by the supplier.

5.60. Regulation 2790/99 embraces a totally different approach. The situation in the territory of the dealer on whom the restriction is imposed has become irrelevant. In addition, the impossibility of enjoying a block exemption for customer restrictions included in a distribution agreement is abandoned.

Restrictions on active sales according to Regulation 2790/99

5.61. An active sales restriction on sales outside the buyer's territory is block exempted under Regulation 2790/99 if certain conditions are fulfilled. These conditions

---

[72] Commission Notice concerning Commission Regulations (EEC) No 1983/83 and (EEC) No 1984/83 of 22 June 1983 on the application of Article 85(3) EC to categories of exclusive distribution and exclusive purchasing agreements [1984] OJ C101/2.

do not stem only from Regulation 2790/99 itself, but also from the Guidelines. Three conditions have to be met:

— the condition of exclusivity;
— the condition of parallel imposition; and
— the condition of the limitation of sales by the buyer's customers.

As the first two conditions are related, they will be analysed together (paragraphs 5.62–5.74 below). The third condition is dealt with separately (paragraphs 5.75–5.85 below).

First and second conditions: exclusivity and the parallel imposition of an active sales restriction

The condition of exclusivity. The first condition flows directly from the **5.62.** wording of Article 4(b), first indent, namely that the restriction must be directed at a territory reserved exclusively to the supplier or allocated exclusively to another buyer. It would appear from the Guidelines (paragraph 50) that a supplier can reserve a territory for itself even if the supplier is not commercially active in that territory (eg because he is still seeking a suitable dealer).[73] For a territory to be allocated exclusively to another buyer, the Guidelines (paragraph 50) clarify the position that the supplier must agree to sell his products to only one distributor. The exception of Article 4(b), first indent, therefore does not apply to shared exclusivity, nor to situations where the supplier has appointed only one distributor, but retains the freedom to appoint additional dealers at a later point in time.

The condition of the parallel imposition. The second condition does not **5.63.** flow from Article 4 of Regulation 2790/99 itself. It is added by the Commission in its Guidelines (paragraph 50), where it states that a territory will be considered exclusively allocated only 'if the exclusive distributor is protected against active selling into his territory . . . by the supplier and all the other buyers of the supplier inside the Community'. The practical consequence of this is that an active sales restriction imposed on a buyer can only be exempted under Regulation 2790/99 where a similar restriction is imposed on all other buyers of the supplier in the EEA and on the supplier itself. Put differently, an active sales restriction will escape the blacklist only if the supplier, as well as all other buyers of the supplier in the EEA, commit to abstain from actively selling into the exclusive territory concerned. Hereafter this second condition is referred to as the 'parallel imposition of an active sales restriction'.

---

[73] The question has been raised whether such a reservation must meet certain requirements: FJ Semler and M Bauer, 'Die neue EU-Gruppenfreistellungsverordnung für vertikale Wettbewerbsbeschränkungen—Folgen für die Rechtspraxis' [2000] Der Betrieb, 193, 198. It would seem to be sufficient, however, to make such a reservation and to bring it in an appropriate form to the attention of the distribution network.

5.64. According to the wording of the Guidelines (paragraph 50), the condition of the parallel imposition of an active sales restriction only applies to restrictions aimed at territories where a dealer has been appointed. Although it is not very logical, the Guidelines contain no reference to the necessity of the parallel imposition of an active sales restriction aimed at territories which the supplier has reserved for itself. The Guidelines do not indicate whether this difference in treatment is intended. It may therefore be safer to extend the active sales restriction to territories reserved by the supplier. However, given the language used in the Guidelines, it would seem inappropriate to contest the legality of an active sales restriction on this point.

5.65. Furthermore, the condition of the parallel imposition of an active sales restriction refers to 'the supplier and all the other buyers of the supplier inside the Community'. This language has specific implications in the context of multi-layered distribution networks. If a multinational producer of certain products has designated an independent exclusive importer in each Member State, the producer will qualify as the 'supplier' and the designated exclusive importers will qualify as 'buyers'. Hence, in order to comply with the condition of the parallel imposition of an active sales restriction, the restriction will have to be assumed by the producer and by each of the exclusive importers. If the exclusive importers, in their turn, set up a network of independent dealers within their respective territories, it should be immaterial whether these dealers are subject to an active sales restriction as they are not buyers of the producer, but buyers of the importers. Hence, for the purposes of checking the validity of the active sales restriction imposed on the exclusive importers, the position of the local dealers (at least according to the language of the Guidelines) is irrelevant.

5.66. Given Article 11(1) of Regulation 2790/99, the situation may become more complex. Article 11(1) provides that the concepts of 'supplier' and 'buyer' include their respective connected undertakings. Hence, in the example given above, an exclusive importer connected to the producer will be deemed to be covered by the concept of 'supplier'. This means that the independent dealers of that importer will also be 'buyers' for the purposes of the condition of the parallel imposition of an active sales restriction on the exclusive importers. The logical consequence is that the (connected) exclusive importer will have to ensure that his dealers are also subject to an active sales restriction directed at the territories of the other exclusive importers. However, Article 11(1) does not affect the position of the dealers of independent exclusive importers. These dealers do not qualify as buyers of the producer or of the connected exclusive importer. The validity of the active sales restriction imposed on the exclusive importers therefore remains unaffected by the decision of the independent importers to impose or not to impose an active sales restriction on their dealers.

It is unclear whether such additional complexities are intentional. Be that as it **5.67**. may, if it is accepted that the validity of an active sales restriction depends on compliance with the condition of the parallel imposition of an active sales restriction and that Article 11 of Regulation 2790/99 applies to this condition,[74] the parties will have no choice but to take these complexities into account. The failure to comply with the condition of the parallel imposition indeed blacklists the active sales restriction and endangers the applicability of the block exemption to the vertical agreement in its entirety.

In summary, the new active sales approach of Regulation 2790/99 is as follows: **5.68**.

(1) Whether or not a dealer has been appointed exclusively within his contract territory has become irrelevant to the decision of whether it is lawful to impose an active sales restriction on it. The conditions of Regulation 2790/99 and the Guidelines exclusively concern the target territory, that is, the territory at which the restriction is aimed.

(2) An active sales restriction may be imposed only if it concerns a territory which the supplier has reserved for itself or where it has agreed to appoint only one distributor. As a result, an active sales restriction is blacklisted where it concerns:
   — a territory which the supplier did not allocate to a dealer, nor reserve for itself;
   — a territory which the supplier allocated to one dealer, but where he reserves the right to appoint additional dealers; or
   — a territory which the supplier has already allocated to several dealers.

(3) An active sales restriction must be accompanied by the imposition of the same restriction on the supplier and on all his other buyers in the EEA.

Example. Suppose that an importer of hi-fi sets has put in place a distribution **5.69**. network in six Member States: the United Kingdom, Ireland, France, and the Benelux. The importer reserved the Netherlands and Luxembourg for itself. In Belgium, two dealers are appointed on the basis of shared exclusivity. In France, the importer currently only has one dealer but has the right to appoint others. In Ireland, his network consists of one dealer and a number of own distribution outlets. Finally, in the United Kingdom he appointed only one dealer. The UK distribution agreement moreover provides that the importer will not appoint other dealers in the country, nor engage in active sales in this area itself.

In this example, an active sales restriction will only be covered by Regulation **5.70**. 2790/99 if it concerns the Netherlands and Luxembourg (reserved to the importer) and the United Kingdom (contractual commitment not to appoint

---

[74] This seems difficult to dispute. Art 11(1) states 'For the purposes of this Regulation, . . .' and therefore claims to be of general application.

other dealers, nor to engage in active sales). An active sales restriction will not be permissible for Belgium (more than one dealer), France (the importer has the right to appoint additional dealers), or Ireland (active sales by the importer through his own outlets).

5.71. If the importer wishes to prohibit active sales in the United Kingdom by dealers appointed elsewhere, the importer must impose a restriction to that effect on itself and on all his other dealers in the EEA. In other words, assuming the importer limits his activities to the above Member States, he must assume the restriction on himself, as well as impose it on his dealers in Belgium, France, and Ireland.

5.72. If the importer were to expand his activities to Spain, he must impose the restriction on his Spanish distribution network as well. If the importer were to appoint a dealer, say, in Alicante, without imposing an active sales restriction to the United Kingdom on this dealer, the condition of parallel imposition is no longer met. As a result, not only the dealer in Alicante, but also the dealers in Belgium, France, and Ireland would be entitled to engage in active sales in the United Kingdom, as the active sales restriction imposed on them would no longer be enforceable.

5.73. What is more, because territorial restrictions are blacklisted, any oversight regarding the parallel imposition of the active sales restriction on all EEA dealers leads to the inapplicability of Regulation 2790/99 to the distribution agreements in their entirety. As a result, the importer would no longer be able to rely on the block exemption to enforce any restriction of competition coming within the scope of Article 81(1) EC (eg location clauses or non-compete clauses meeting the conditions of Article 81(1) EC). The consequences of the failure to impose an active sales restriction towards the United Kingdom on the Alicante dealer are therefore potentially far-reaching.

5.74. It follows from the above that a dealer whose contract is terminated for the alleged infringement of a non-compete obligation has every interest to examine closely the enforceability of the active sales restriction contained in his agreement. If there is no such enforceability, either because the first (characteristics of the target area) or the second (parallel imposition) conditions are not met, the distribution agreement infringes the blacklist of Article 4 of Regulation 2790/99 and therefore the importer can no longer rely on Article 5 of Regulation 2790/99 to safeguard the enforceability of the non-compete clause.

Third condition: no limitation of sales by the customers of the buyer

5.75. Article 4(b), first indent, contains a third condition, namely that the active sales restriction may 'not limit sales by the customers of the buyer'. Regrettably, the Guidelines do not offer any clarification of this condition.

It may be assumed that this condition is not met in cases where, as part of the **5.76**. active sales restriction, the supplier requires his buyer to impose limits on the sales possibilities of his buyer's customers. It would, for example, seem difficult to contest that an obligation for the buyer to impose a territorial sales restriction on its customers qualifies as a limitation of the sales possibilities of these customers. This would also be the case where the buyer is required by the supplier to prevent his customers from actively selling to particular categories of customers. In other words, an obligation of the buyer to pass on his own active sales restriction to the next level seems incompatible with the third condition.

Analysing this third condition in further detail, one discovers some surprising **5.77**. practical consequences. In this respect, it is useful to distinguish three possible scenarios.

Sub-dealers.   The first scenario concerns distribution systems where the sup- **5.78**. plier appoints a dealer and the dealer in turn is allowed to designate sub-dealers. The sub-dealers purchase the relevant products from the dealer and, as a result, are the customers of the dealer. The stringent application of the third condition would imply that the supplier is not entitled to request that his dealers impose the same active sales restriction on the sub-dealers as the dealer himself assumes. On any reasonable view, this cannot have been the intention of the drafters of the Regulation.

The imposition of any active sales restriction on a dealer network becomes **5.79**. meaningless if the restriction can be circumvented via the appointment of sub-dealers. The fact that a supplier allows its dealers to appoint sub-dealers would imply that the supplier has to accept that the active sales restriction imposed on the dealers can be undermined via the sub-dealers. Such an interpretation is not very logical and is inconsistent with the second condition. The condition of the parallel imposition of the active sales restriction essentially aims to secure that the restriction is applied across the entire network in the EEA. The Commission's insistence on the second condition in the Guidelines is difficult to reconcile with a scenario where the supplier is forced to accept (as a result of the third condition discussed here) that he cannot require the sub-dealers to comply with the same active sales restriction. This interpretation of Article 4(b), first indent, lacks coherence.

A more sensible reading of the third condition would be that the concept **5.80**. of 'customers of the buyer' is not intended to encompass sub-dealers. This interpretation ensures that the imposition of active sales restrictions in a multi-layer distribution network remains meaningful.

Independent resellers.   The second scenario concerns sales by a dealer **5.81**. to independent resellers. The difference between this and the first scenario is that independent resellers do not qualify as sub-dealers and therefore are not part of the distribution network. The third condition implies that the dealer cannot be forced by his supplier to impose limitations on the sales possibilities of the independent resellers. The application of the third condition in this context seems workable and meaningful. However, there is room for possible abuse. It would seem difficult to defend the position that a dealer may deliberately rely on independent resellers to circumvent his own active sales restriction. A good faith implementation of the active sales restriction by the dealer implies that he does not rely on third parties to conclude transactions which he is not himself authorized to conclude. Hence, a meaningful interpretation of the third condition in the context of independent resellers is that:

—a supplier may not require from his dealers that they limit the sales possibilities of such resellers;

—a supplier may object to the deliberate involvement by his dealers of independent resellers with the purpose of circumventing the dealers' own active sales restrictions.

5.82. The fact that a supplier is not entitled to require his dealers to impose sales limitations on their customers does not mean that the dealers themselves (without being prompted by the supplier) may not impose such limitations. Provided that the limitations are compatible with the block exemption, the dealers are at liberty to prescribe contractual limitations for their customers. Such limitations are independent of the active sales restrictions imposed by the supplier on the dealers and are therefore compatible with the third condition.

5.83. **Final customers.** The third scenario concerns situations where the customer of the dealer purchases the relevant products for his own purposes. In other words, the customer is not a reseller or trader. While the relevance for competition is much more limited than in the second scenario, we assume in this context that the third condition also means that the supplier cannot limit the sale (possibly second-hand) by the customer.

Practical solutions

5.84. The conditions on which the validity and enforceability of an active sales restriction are dependent are very complex and, as a result, there is a genuine risk of mistakes. Any uncertainty in relation to this matter can be solved or eliminated essentially in two ways:

The first solution is to include a clause which reads as follows:

> The [distributor] will exercise his activities within [the territory]. The [distributor] shall not engage in active sales in territories which are exclusively reserved for the [supplier] or exclusively allocated to other distributors appointed by the supplier.

This type of clause ensures compliance with the Commission's conditions even where there are changes within the distribution network (eg an additional dealer is appointed in a territory which used to be exclusive; an exclusive dealer is terminated without there being an immediate replacement). However, since dealers are often unaware of the characteristics of the entire distribution network, this type of clause may have undesirable consequences from a competition law perspective. It may indeed cause dealers to become reluctant to engage in any active sales outside their territory in order to avoid any possible breach of contract. As a result, the position on active sales restrictions runs the risk, *de facto*, of remaining the same as that existing at the time of Regulation 67/67 and Regulation 1983/83.

A second, more radical, but at the same time more careful and possibly more **5.85.** dealer-friendly, solution is to simply avoid the non-enforceability risks attached to active sales restrictions by removing them from the distribution agreements. It goes without saying that the choice in favour of this option will depend on the circumstances, such as: the bargaining power of the dealers, the complexity of the distribution network (simple distribution networks being less prone to being confronted with problems of non-enforceability), the importance of other restrictions of competition (such as location clauses or non-competes) and the need to secure their enforceability. Generally speaking, however, there are many instances in which there is much to say in favour of this radical solution, in particular if the supplier has a complex distribution network consisting of many dealers and if (given the nature of the sales efforts in the market concerned) the supplier may face evidentiary problems in establishing active sales on the part of its dealers.

Restrictions on active sales to an exclusive customer group according to Regulation 2790/99

Regulation 2790/99 permits the exclusive allocation of a group of customers to **5.86.** a given dealer or to the supplier itself. Such an allocation cannot be phrased in absolute terms. If the supplier decides to make use of this possibility, it is entitled to do so only under the same conditions as those discussed above for the protection of a dealer territory. Passive sales towards such customer groups must remain permitted at all times. A restriction on active sales towards a particular customer group will be compatible with the block exemption if it meets the following (cumulative) conditions:

— the customer group is reserved by the supplier or is allocated on an exclusive basis to a single distributor; and
— if the customer group is allocated to a single distributor, the supplier and all of the buyers of the supplier are subject to an active sales prohibition with regard to the customer group concerned; and
— the active sales prohibition does not limit the sales by the buyers of the distributor.

5.87. A standard clause that ensures compliance (at least formally) with these conditions can be drafted as follows:

> The [distributor] shall not engage in active sales in relation to the customer groups described in Attachment X, which are exclusively reserved for the [supplier] or exclusively allocated to another distributor appointed by the supplier.

5.88. While this is not expressly set forth in the Regulation, the Guidelines (paragraph 50) provide that 'the supplier is allowed to combine the allocation of an exclusive territory and an exclusive customer group by for instance appointing an exclusive distributor for a particular customer group in a certain territory'. In the case of such a combination, the conditions of Article 4(b) will have to be fulfilled both in respect of the customer group and the relevant territories. This implies that the exclusivity granted to the distributor must be confined to a given customer group within a given territory. In particular, the condition of the parallel imposition of the active sales restriction will have to be drafted very carefully in order to ensure that the supplier and all of the buyers of the supplier are subject to an active sales prohibition that is limited to the customer group concerned within the territory concerned. Hence, the condition that the parallel imposition may not extend to customers within the territory other than those exclusively reserved to the distributor, nor may it cover the same customer group, but in other territories than that to which the exclusivity of the distributor applies.

Direct sales by the supplier

5.89. Prior to the entry into force of Regulation 2790/99, the supplier could freely stipulate the right to supply certain customers itself. Suppliers traditionally made use of this possibility for important customers (eg governments, supermarket chains). Since the entry into force of Regulation 2790/99, the combination of such direct sales with an active sales restriction raises some difficulties. The Guidelines remain silent on this issue.

5.90. If a supplier reserves the right to sell to certain customer groups in a given territory, he does not, in relation to those customer groups, respect the exclusivity of the dealer appointed in that territory. As a result of his sales initiatives in the exclusive territory concerned, the supplier does not comply with the condition of the parallel imposition of the restriction on active sales as laid down in the Guidelines (paragraph 50). This condition requires that the supplier undertakes not to engage in active sales in the territory concerned. By reserving the right to approach certain customer groups, the condition is not met.

5.91. Careful drafting continues to make it possible to combine direct sales in an exclusive dealer territory with an enforceable active sales restriction. This can be done by defining the dealer's exclusivity on the basis of two parameters—territory and customer groups—and to grant territorial exclusivity only for those customer groups which the supplier has no intention of supplying itself.

Assume that an importer of office supplies wishes to appoint an exclusive dealer in **5.92**. Scotland, but wants to retain a direct sales right to companies with more than 150 employees. Under those circumstances, the best solution is to grant the dealer exclusivity for all customers in Scotland, save for companies with more than 150 employees. As a result, the dealer's exclusivity is not only confined territorially (Scotland), but also by reference to a specific customer group (all customers having less than 150 employees). An active sales restriction imposed on dealers outside Scotland must then, in turn, be restricted to the exclusive customers of the Scottish dealer (ie all customers except for companies with more than 150 employees). The Guidelines (paragraph 50) expressly allow such a combination of the allocation of an exclusive territory with an exclusive customer group.

In practice, this type of active sales restriction will not be very workable. As the **5.93**. Scottish dealer does not have exclusive rights with respect to companies with more than 150 employees, it will have to tolerate the fact that other dealers may actively seek customers in his territory. Whilst these sales efforts must in theory be limited to companies with more than 150 customers, there is a clear potential for abuse.

In our view, a more practicable solution for the importer is to reserve the **5.94**. companies with more than 150 employees exclusively for itself. In so doing, it is entitled to impose an active sales restriction on all dealers inasmuch as those customers are concerned. The Scottish dealer's exclusivity would remain the same, namely all customers in Scotland, save companies with more than 150 employees. In so doing, the customers that are exclusively reserved, either to the importer or to the dealer, make up the entirety of customers in Scotland. This, in turn, makes it possible to impose a flat prohibition on active sales in Scotland on all dealers outside Scotland.

Location clauses

Location clauses impose restrictions on a distributor's ability to determine the **5.95**. location of his business premises or to open additional outlets.[75] Article 4(c) of the Regulation, which is discussed below,[76] contains an explicit reference to location clauses in the context of selective distribution agreements. However, location clauses are not addressed in the Regulation or in the Guidelines with regard to non-selective distribution systems. The analysis for such systems, which has been confirmed to us informally by officials of DG COMP, can be summarized as follows:

— If a distributor is given a specific exclusive territory, it will be possible to impose a location restriction within that territory. This restriction may entail

---

[75] Guidelines, para 54.   [76] Paras 5.116–5.119.

that the distributor is prevented, within his exclusive territory, from changing premises or locations or from opening additional premises without the supplier's prior consent. This approach is logical. The allocation of an exclusive territory to a given distributor implies that the distributor is expected to develop sales in that territory. In view of this, it is reasonable to suggest that the location clause should not be deemed to have as its object the limitation of the distributor's sales efforts within that territory. In the absence of such an 'object', Article 4(b) does not enter into play.

— If a location clause is imposed with regard to territories outside the distributor's exclusive territory, the conditions of Article 4(b), first indent, of the Regulation will have to be complied with. A limitation on the ability to change locations or to open additional outlets qualifies as an active sales restriction. Hence, the conditions for the compatibility of active sales restrictions with the block exemption must be complied with for the enforceable imposition of a location clause.

(3) *Second exception: customer restrictions imposed on wholesalers*

5.96. Article 4(b), second indent, provides:

> The exemption provided for in Article 2 shall not apply to vertical agreements which, directly or indirectly, in isolation or in combination with other factors under the control of the parties, have as their object: . . .
>
> (b) the restriction of the territory into which, or of the customers to whom, the buyer may sell the contract goods or services, except:
> — the restriction of sales to end users by a buyer operating at the wholesale level of trade.

5.97. The second exception is substantially less complex and requires less comment than the first. According to the exception, wholesalers may be expected to confine their business to the wholesale level of trade and not to become active as a retailer. The prohibition may be absolute and concern both active and passive sales.

5.98. Both the Court[77] and the Commission[78] established this principle some time ago. In its recent *Yamaha*[79] decision the Commission relied on this case law to summarize the rationale for this approach as follows:

> . . . competition would be distorted if wholesalers, whose costs are in general proportionally lower precisely because of the marketing stage at which they operate, would compete with retailers at the retail stage, in particular on supplies to private customers . . .

---

[77] Case 26/76 *Metro I* [1977] ECR 1875, para 29.
[78] *Villeroy & Boch* [1985] OJ L376/15, para 36.   [79] Para 93 (n 23 above).

The text of the Regulation does not stipulate whether the second indent of Article 4(b) contains an all-or-nothing exception. In other words, it is not clear whether or not this exception is compatible with a scenario whereby a wholesaler is allowed to sell to particular categories of end-users (eg multinational companies), but must refrain from selling to other end-users (eg private persons and local companies). It could be argued that by allowing sales to a particular group of customers, the wholesaler can only be prevented from selling to all other customer groups on the basis of the first indent of Article 4(b), but no longer on the basis of the second indent. In practice, this would mean that for these other customer groups only an active sales restriction (complying with the conditions discussed at paragraphs 5.61–5.85 above) could be imposed rather than an outright prohibition.

We believe that this reading is too stringent and hampers a flexible organization of a supplier's distribution system. Hence, we favour the interpretation that allowing a wholesaler to deal directly with certain categories of end-users does not deprive the supplier of the right to require the wholesaler to abstain from dealing with any other categories of end-users ('*qui peut le plus, peut le moins*').

(4) Third exception: restriction of sales to unauthorized distributors in the context of a selective distribution system

Article 4(b), third indent, provides: **5.99**.

> The exemption provided for in Article 2 shall not apply to vertical agreements which, directly or indirectly, in isolation or in combination with other factors under the control of the parties, have as their object: . . .
>
> (b) the restriction of the territory into which, or of the customers to whom, the buyer may sell the contract goods or services, except:
> — the restriction of sales to unauthorised distributors by the members of a selective distribution system . . .

The third exception does not add very much. The definition of a selective **5.100**. distribution system included in Article 1(d) of Regulation 2790/99 provides expressly that the authorized distributors 'undertake not to sell [the] goods or services to unauthorised distributors'. Accordingly, this exception reflects no more than one of the essential features of selective distribution.[80]

---

[80] More guidance on this type of distribution can be found at paras 7.25 *et seq* below. Relevant Commission Decisions with respect to selective distribution include *Yves Saint Laurent* [1992] OJ L12/24; *Givenchy* [1992] OJ L236/11; and *Grundig's EC Distribution System* [1994] OJ L20/15. Relevant case law of the Court of Justice and the Court of First Instance includes Case T–19/91 *Vichy v Commission* [1992] ECR II–415; Case T–19/92 *Leclerc v Commission* [1996] ECR II–1851; Case T–88/92 *Leclerc v Commission* [1996] ECR II–1961; Case 26/76 *Metro I* [1977] ECR 1875; Joined Cases 209 to 215 and 218/78 *FEDETAB* [1980] ECR 3125; Case 75/84 *Metro II* [1986] ECR 3021; Case C–376/92 *Metro v Cartier* [1994] ECR I–15; Case C–230/96 *Cabour v Arnor* [1998] ECR I–2055; and Case C–70/97P *Kruidvat v Commission* [1998] ECR I–7183.

5.101. A combined reading of Articles 1(d) and 4(b), third indent, of Regulation 2790/99 demonstrates that the exception included in the latter provision is not phrased very precisely. The general definition of selective distribution (in Article 1(d)) requires that there is a complete prohibition on sales to unauthorized resellers. A mere restriction of such sales is short of an outright ban and hence inconsistent with the definition. In order to achieve consistency, the exception contained in Article 4(b), third indent, must be read as a complete prohibition on sales to unauthorized distributors. The imposition of such a prohibition is not within the discretion of the supplier. If the supplier intends to set up a selective distribution system, he must provide for such a prohibition. The failure to do so will result in his distribution system no longer qualifying as a selective system.

(5) Fourth exception: restrictions on the resale of components

5.102. Article 4(b), fourth indent of the Regulation provides:

> The exemption provided for in Article 2 shall not apply to vertical agreements which, directly or indirectly, in isolation or in combination with other factors under the control of the parties, have as their object: ...
>
> (b) the restriction of the territory into which, or of the customers to whom, the buyer may sell the contract goods or services, except:
> — the restriction of the buyer's ability to sell components, supplied for the purposes of incorporation, to customers who would use them to manufacture the same type of goods as those produced by the supplier ...

5.103. The final exception to the prohibition of customer and territorial restrictions concerns the resale of components. If components are supplied for the purposes of incorporation, the supplier is entitled to prevent his buyer from reselling the relevant components to customers who would use them to manufacture the same type of goods as those manufactured by the supplier. According to the Guidelines (paragraph 52), the concept of 'component' includes any intermediate goods and 'incorporation' covers the use of any input to produce goods.

5.104. Practically speaking, this exception is intended to cover situations such as the following: A producer of photocopiers supplies a component to a producer of printers. The objective of the transaction is that the second producer incorporates this component into his own printers. The first producer is then entitled to require that the second producer does not sell the component to another producer of photocopiers for purposes of incorporation.

5.105. The terms of this fourth exception are quite narrow. It applies only to components 'supplied for the purposes of incorporation' and hence not to components delivered for repair and maintenance purposes. Strictly speaking, the customer restriction could not be imposed in the latter case. This interpretation would not seem to be correct to us. The validity of the customer restriction should not be dependent on the purpose for which the components are delivered. Irrespective of the purpose for which the components are supplied to the (initial) buyer (ie for incorporation purposes or for repair and maintenance purposes), it should be possible to prevent that these components are resold by the buyer to a third party who will incorporate them in the context of his own production.

It is furthermore noteworthy that this exception does not refer to competing **5.106.** products, but to goods of the same type. This means that in the context of our example there will be no need to establish that the various photocopiers are competing products. The mere fact that photocopiers are involved is sufficient.

Finally, the Regulation suggests that the exception applies only if the third party **5.107.** customer uses the components for production purposes. A fair reading of the Regulation would require that it cannot be sufficient to involve another party (that is not engaged in production activities) to purchase the components in order to render the exception inapplicable and to then have that party sell the components to another producer.

Given the severe consequences of a possible misreading of this exception **5.108.** (ie infringement of the blacklist and loss of the block exemption for the entire vertical agreement), it is regrettable that the Guidelines do not offer any clarification as to the precise objective and meaning of this provision. Until such time as the precise scope of the exception becomes clarified, caution is warranted when relying on this exception.

The blacklist contains another provision dealing with the resale of components. **5.109.** This provision is contained in Article 4(e) and is discussed at paragraphs 5.124–5.129 below.

(6) Final comments on the exceptions regarding the prohibition of territorial and customer restrictions

Adopting a bird's eye view on the four exceptions to the prohibition of customer **5.110.** and territorial restrictions included in Article 4(b), it should now be clear that the Commission has not given the market players much room for creative solutions in this field. The first exception allows restrictions on active sales, but under considerably stricter conditions than before (eg the regime of Regulation 1983/83). Furthermore, the conditions that must be met in order to block exempt an active sales restriction, are so strict that mistakes are almost certainly bound to be made. The second and third exceptions do little more than to confirm two self-evident aspects of a particular distribution regime (ie no sales to end-users by wholesalers and no sales to unauthorized distributors in the context of selective distribution). Finally, the scope of the fourth exception is also very limited by allowing, in a limited number of cases, the prohibition of sales of components to customers that would use them for certain manufacturing purposes. The general conclusion is therefore that, in practical terms, the Regulation offers hardly any room for the imposition of customer or territorial restrictions. At least in this area, the straitjacket approach still prevails.

E. Territorial and Customer Restrictions in the Context of a Selective Distribution System

(1) General

5.111. Article 4(c) and (d) of the Regulation provide:

> The exemption provided for in Article 2 shall not apply to vertical agreements which, directly or indirectly, in isolation or in combination with other factors under the control of the parties, have as their object: . . .
>
> (c) the restriction of active or passive sales to end users by members of a selective distribution system operating at the retail level of trade, without prejudice to the possibility of prohibiting a member of the system from operating out of an unauthorised place of establishment;
> (d) the restriction of cross-supplies between distributors within a selective distribution system, including between distributors operating at different level of trade.

5.112. Article 4(c) contains a specific regime regarding customer and territorial restrictions in the context of selective distribution.[81] This provision blacklists the restriction of active and passive sales to end-users by selective distributors operating at the retail level of trade.[82]

5.113. From the viewpoint of legal drafting, the inclusion of this separate provision is slightly surprising. The general principle that no territorial or customer restrictions may be imposed on the members of a selective distribution network already follows from Article 4(b). It would have been sufficient for the Commission to mention in the first indent of Article 4(b) that the exception regarding active sales restrictions applies only in the context of systems other than selective distribution systems operating at the retail level of trade.

5.114. Article 4(c) should be read in conjunction with Article 4(d). The latter provision deals with sales in the context of a selective distribution system to parties that

---

[81] The concept of 'selective distribution' is explained in paras 7.25–7.27 below. The possible competition risks associated with the application of such restrictions in a selective distribution context are a reduction in intra-brand competition and, especially in the case of cumulative effect, foreclosure of certain type(s) of distributors and facilitation of collusion between suppliers or buyers (Guidelines, para 185).

[82] Including when purchasing agents act on behalf of end-users, dealers in a selective distribution system cannot be restricted (Guidelines, para 53).

are not end-users. Article 4(d) blacklists restrictions of cross-supplies between distributors that are part of a selective distribution system. It is irrelevant whether the distributors are acting at the same or at a different level of trade. Hence, members of a selective distribution system must be at liberty to actively approach their fellow members with the aim of exploring cross-supply opportunities. This also means that a selective distributor active at the retail level should be free to source from a selective distributor active at the wholesale level in another Member State. Cross-supplies of this nature are favoured by the Commission because they help in reducing price differences throughout the Community.

Given that Article 4(b) contains a general prohibition on customer and terri- **5.115**. torial restrictions, Article 4(d) is therefore superfluous. The third indent of Article 4(b) accepts, as an exception, the prohibition of sales to unauthorized distributors. The logical consequence of the drafting of Article 4(b) is that restrictions on cross-supplies between selective distributors are not covered by any exception and hence are blacklisted. So Article 4(d) blacklists a practice that is already blacklisted in Article 4(b).

(2) Location clauses

Article 4(c), *in fine*, allows 'prohibiting a member of the system from operating **5.116**. out of an unauthorised place of establishment'. This is of practical relevance. The language of this part of the provision suggests that it is not limited to selective distributors that are active at the retail level. Article 4(c) is phrased in general terms and so the favourable treatment of location clauses applies irrespective of the level of trade involved.

The location clause regime of Article 4(c) entails no obligation for the supplier **5.117**. to approve or accept new or additional locations that meet the objective quality standards applied within the selective distribution system. The Guidelines (paragraph 54) specify in this respect that 'selected dealers may be prevented from running their business from different premises or from opening a new outlet in a different location'.[83] Hence, a complete prohibition on opening new or additional outlets is compatible with the block exemption. Accordingly, the treatment of location clauses in Regulation 2790/99 is much more liberal than it is in Regulation 1400/2002.[84]

The favourable treatment of location clauses in selective distribution has signi- **5.118**. ficant consequences. Location clauses will in many sectors reduce the territorial scope of activity of the distributor concerned. In any event, it eliminates one form

---

[83] With respect to mobile outlets ('shop on wheels'), the Guidelines (para 54) even state that 'an area may be defined outside which the mobile outlet cannot be operated'.
[84] Paras 11.204–11.211 below.

of active sales, namely the establishment of outlets. In the absence of the final part of Article 4(c), such a restriction, being an active sales restriction, would have been blacklisted.

5.119. As discussed above, location clauses outside a distributor's territory are only valid for non-selective systems if they comply with the three conditions underlying Article 4(b), first indent, of the Regulation. In a selective distribution context, the final part of Article 4(c) renders location restrictions valid without conditions. In this case the three conditions applicable to Article 4(b), first indent, are irrelevant. This results in a marked difference in the treatment of location clauses depending on the distribution formula that is chosen. The quasi-unconditional and unlimited validity of location clauses in the selective distribution context sharply contrasts with the strict conditions that apply to such clauses in a non-selective system. The Guidelines do not explain this difference in treatment.

(3) Combining exclusive and selective distribution

5.120. The combination of exclusivity and selectivity within a given distribution system may complicate matters. Two scenarios can be distinguished. The first scenario consists of the supplier combining exclusivity and selectivity for all dealers. This implies that the dealers must meet certain selection criteria (eg quality standards, the obligation not to resell to unauthorized dealers) and that at the same time, they enjoy territorial exclusivity. In the second scenario, the supplier wishes to combine exclusive distribution (without selectivity) in one territory (eg Poland) with selectivity (without exclusivity) in another (eg Germany).

5.121. Art 4(c) of Regulation 2790/99 allows the combination contained in the first scenario provided that no restriction on active or passive sales is imposed. The Guidelines (paragraph 53) state expressly: 'Selective distribution may be combined with exclusive distribution provided that active and passive selling is not restricted anywhere'. Dealers may nevertheless be held to a location clause, meaning that the most aggressive form of active sales (ie the establishment of a sales outlet), may be prohibited by the supplier. In essence, the combination reflected in this first scenario consists of a system of quantitative selective distribution.

5.122. As to the second scenario (consisting of selective distribution in, for example Germany and exclusive distribution in, for example Poland), Article 4(c) read in conjunction with Article 4(b), first indent, seems to prevent the imposition of any restrictions on active sales:

— Article 4(c) prevents outright (with the limited exception of a location restriction) the imposition of an active sales restriction on the selective distributors in Germany.

—Article 4(b), first indent, on the other hand, renders the validity of an active sales restriction subject to the imposition of the same restriction on all other buyers of the supplier within the EEA. This is the so-called condition of the parallel imposition of an active sales restriction.[85]

The fact that no active sales restriction can be imposed on the members of the selective distribution system (as a result of Article 4(c)) makes it impossible to meet the condition of the parallel imposition.

Informal contacts have nonetheless shown that DG COMP has a different view, and that in this second scenario, it allows an active sales restriction on the dealers in Germany for their sales in Poland. While this is difficult to reconcile with the wording of the Regulation, DG COMP is of the opinion that a different interpretation would prevent companies from setting up a system of exclusive distribution in a given territory (eg a territory where the network has not been developed to an extent that permits selective distribution), while reserving selective distribution to territories where the distribution network already meets higher standards. This interpretation by DG COMP can only be applauded as it enables producers to develop their distribution networks in line with commercial reality. The problem of course remains that neither the Community courts, nor the national courts are bound by the Commission's views and may at any time adopt a more narrow reading of Regulation 2790/99.[86] **5.123.**

F. Restrictions on the Sale of Spare Parts

Article 4(e) of the Regulation provides: **5.124.**

> The exemption provided for in Article 2 shall not apply to vertical agreements which, directly or indirectly, in isolation or in combination with other factors under the control of the parties, have as their object: . . .
>
> (e) the restriction agreed between a supplier of components and a buyer who incorporates those components, which limits the supplier to selling the components as spare parts to end-users or to repairers or other service providers not entrusted by the buyer with the repair or servicing of its goods.

The final provision on the blacklist is very specific and concerns restrictions on the sale of components or spare parts. These restrictions are particularly relevant in the context of subcontracting agreements, which are discussed in more detail in Chapter 8 below. **5.125.**

---

[85] Para 5.63 above.
[86] Note that Reg 1400/2002 (recital 13 and Art 4(1)(d)) lends support to DG COMP's interpretation.

5.126. The starting point of Article 4(e) is the relationship between a supplier of components and a buyer that uses such components for the purposes of incorporation. For instance, an OEM[87] of photocopiers purchases a particular component from a component producer and uses the relevant component to produce photocopiers. The issue addressed in Article 4(e) is the type of restrictions that can be imposed on the component supplier within the framework of the Regulation with regard to the supply of the components as spare parts.

5.127. Depending on the type of customer to which the component supplier intends to sell the spare parts, three different hypotheses can be distinguished:

— Under the regime of Regulation 2790/99, the supplier cannot be prevented from supplying the spare parts to end-users. This means that the supplier must be entitled to sell spare parts to purchasers that intend to use these parts for their own purposes.

— The supplier may be prevented from supplying the components as spare parts to repairers or other service providers that have been entrusted by the OEM with the repair or servicing of his goods. As stated in the Guidelines (paragraph 56), 'the original equipment manufacturer may require his own repair and service network to buy the spare parts from it'.

— The supplier may not be restricted from supplying the spare parts to independent repairers and service providers.

5.128. The prohibition of restrictions on sales to end-users or independent repairers and service providers applies to direct and indirect restrictions alike. The Guidelines (paragraph 56) provide that 'indirect restrictions may arise in particular when the supplier of the spare parts is restricted in supplying technical information and special equipment which are necessary for the use of the spare parts'. This example is certainly not new and most likely stems from the Commission's experience within the motor vehicle sector.[88]

5.129. The objectives pursued by Article 4(e) are relatively straightforward. First, the Commission seeks to ensure that the independent aftermarket has efficient access to spare parts. Furthermore, the Commission most likely intends to exert pressure on the price level of the parts. The OEM and its repair and maintenance network will experience price pressure from the component supplier and the independent repairers and service providers as a result of the direct supply relationship between the latter. This pressure will limit the ability of the OEM and its network to impose high prices for spare parts.

---

[87] OEM stands for 'original equipment manufacturer'.
[88] Reg 1475/95, Art 6(1)(12); Reg 1400/2002, Art 4(2).

6

THE NON-COMPETE OBLIGATION

A. Definition

(1) The non-compete obligation—a broad definition

Article 5 of Regulation 2790/99[1] contains special provisions relating to non-compete obligations. Before discussing these provisions, it is necessary to clarify that the definition of the term 'non-compete obligation' given in Article 1(b) of the Regulation covers two different types of restriction: **6.01**.

(1) Any direct or indirect obligation causing the buyer not to manufacture, purchase, sell or resell goods or services which compete with the contract goods or services.

(2) Any direct or indirect obligation on the buyer to purchase from the supplier or from another undertaking designated by the supplier more than 80% of the buyer's total purchases of contract goods or services and their substitutes on the relevant market, calculated on the basis of the value of its purchases in the preceding calendar year.

Given this dual definition, it is remarkable that the Guidelines do not refer at all to the first type of non-compete obligation. Only the second type of restriction is dealt with and it is even presented as the typical example of a non-compete obligation.[2] This approach lacks nuance, as may be illustrated by the following differences between the two types of restriction. A buyer of product A having accepted a restriction of the first type is not allowed to manufacture, purchase, sell, or resell any products, to the extent such products would compete with product A. If the buyer accepts a restriction of the second type, even when undertaking to purchase 100% of its total purchases of product A and its **6.02**.

---

[1] Commission Regulation (EC) No 2790/99 of 22 December 1999 on the application of Article 81(3) of the Treaty to categories of vertical agreements and concerted practices [1999] OJ L336/25 (hereafter the 'Regulation').

[2] Commission Notice—Guidelines on Vertical Restraints [2000] OJ C291/1, para 58 (hereafter 'Guidelines').

substitutes from the supplier, there will be room left for the buyer to manufacture and sell products which compete with product A. The buyer has indeed
committed itself only to buying 100% of its total purchases (not requirements)
of a certain type of product from the supplier calculated on the basis of the value
of its purchases in the preceding calendar year. In this respect, a non-compete
obligation of the second type is less restrictive than a non-compete obligation of
the first type. By contrast, in the first scenario the buyer is not obligated to
purchase Product A from the supplier, but may obtain them from any other
seller (eg a distributor of product A established in another Member State). This
would not be possible with a non-compete obligation of the second type, where
it is essential that the buyer obtains the contract products from the supplier or
from an undertaking designated by the supplier.

6.03. The distinction between the two types of non-compete provision is not without
importance, especially where there are substantial regional or national price
differences. By using a restriction of the second type, a supplier is able to prevent
its buyer from exploiting differences in regional or national price levels. With a
restriction of the first type, that would not be possible since a buyer in that
situation remains free to obtain the contract products from a supplier of its
choice.

6.04. The Commission's concerns with non-compete obligations focus almost
exclusively on problems of potential market foreclosure[3] and appear to lose sight
of the fact that non-compete obligations of the second type may be used as an
instrument to prevent cross-supplies and therefore restrict parallel trade. This
approach is all the more surprising given the Commission's emphasis on the
need to preserve the possibility of cross-supplies elsewhere in the Regulation[4]
and indeed in its decision-making practice.[5] In view of these differences, it
would seem more accurate to refer to restrictions of the first type as non-
compete obligations and to restrictions of the second type as exclusive purchase
obligations.[6]

(2) The non-compete obligation—a narrow definition

6.05. The definition of a non-compete obligation of the first type given in Article 1(b)
of the Regulation does not require much explanation, except perhaps to clarify
that it covers both direct and indirect obligations not to manufacture or trade in

---

[3] Reg 2790/99, recital 11.
[4] Reg 2790/99, Art 4(d) dealing with selective distribution (para 5.114 above), is clearly inspired
by this concern.
[5] *JCB* [2002] OJ L69/1, confirmed by the Court of First Instance in Case T–67/01 *JCB
Service v Commission* [2004] OJ C85/23, paras 111–18, appeal pending Case C–167/04P [2004]
OJ C156/3.   [6] In practice, vertical agreements often combine both types of restriction.

products that compete with the contract products. Although not stated explicitly by the Commission, it may be assumed that an indirect obligation is any obligation that indirectly causes the buyer not to manufacture, purchase or sell contract products. For example, contract provisions that allow the supplier to reduce or cancel bonuses or rebates, terminate the agreement, change the contract territory, or cancel the exclusivity from which the buyer benefits in the event that the buyer manufactures, purchases, or sells competing products, must probably be regarded as indirect non-compete obligations.[7]

It is also necessary to clarify the meaning of the term 'goods or services that compete with the contract goods or services'. Neither the Regulation, nor the Guidelines define the meaning of these words used in Article 1(b) of the Regulation. In this particular context, it seems appropriate to define competing products or services as products or services that are considered substitutable by buyers. Supply-side substitutability would not seem relevant, since this would not permit the identification of competing products, but merely of producers that are capable of putting competing goods or products on to the market in the short term. Likewise, it seems appropriate not to take into account geographic considerations. The question of whether a particular product or service is already sold on the relevant geographic market is not helpful for the analysis since the effect (and sometimes perhaps even the objective) of a non-compete obligation may be to prevent such sales from taking place.   **6.06**.

A clause that prohibits a buyer from manufacturing or selling certain products that do not compete with the contract products is, by its very nature, not a non-compete obligation (eg a manufacturer of motorcycles of brand A prohibits its motorcycle dealers to sell lawn mowers of brand A). Such a clause is not subject to Articles 4 or 5 of the Regulation and hence may be block exempted. Indeed, the Regulation automatically exempts all restrictions of competition contained in vertical agreements, except where the agreement contains hardcore restrictions or, for any other reason, falls outside the scope of application of the Regulation (eg a market share in excess of 30%). Within these limits, a clause of this type is exempted automatically.   **6.07**.

(3) The exclusive purchase obligation

As indicated in paragraphs 6.01–6.04 above, the Regulation treats an exclusive purchase obligation as a sub-species of a non-compete obligation. In order to prevent avoidance, Article 5 covers not only situations where the purchaser must buy 100% of its purchases from the supplier. Article 5 comes into play as of the moment the purchaser, directly or indirectly, commits itself to buy more than   **6.08**

---

[7] By analogy with the approach taken by the Commission in relation to indirect obligations not to export: Guidelines, para 49.

80% of its total purchases of the contract goods or services and their substitutes on the relevant market from the supplier or another undertaking designated by the supplier. In view of this, parties that wish to include minimum purchase quotas in their agreements—even if they have no intention of imposing a *de facto* exclusive purchase obligation—are well-advised to verify whether the agreed purchase quotas comply with the 80% rule. This is not to say that the mere fact that the buyer obtains more than 80% (or even 100%) of its total purchases of contract products and their substitutes from the supplier means that it must be considered as evidence of the existence of a non-compete obligation. This will only be the case if the buyer is, directly or indirectly, obligated to do so.

6.09. It deserves mentioning that the 80% rule relates to the total purchases by the buyer of the contract products (or services) and their substitutes. Thus, when a buyer commits itself to purchase 100% of the contract products (products A) from the supplier, but remains free to purchase substitutable products B, the buyer's obligation to purchase 100% of products A from the supplier is not a non-compete obligation, provided its purchases of products B amount to at least 20% of its total purchases of products A and B together. Somewhat surprisingly, since the 80% rule is based on the purchases made by the buyer, the situation where the buyer must purchase 100% of products A from the supplier, but manufactures products B itself (instead of purchasing them), will be covered by the definition of a non-compete obligation. From a conceptual point of view, it appears difficult to justify this difference in treatment

6.10. The 80% rule is calculated on the basis of the value of the buyer's purchases in the preceding calendar year.[8] The calculation must therefore be made on the basis of value figures (not volume figures), using data from the preceding calendar year (not the preceding fiscal year). The Guidelines (paragraph 58) add that where no purchasing data are available for the preceding calendar year, the parties may use the buyer's (ie not the parties' or the supplier's) best estimate of its total annual requirements. An example may serve to illustrate this: If in the calendar year preceding the execution of a supply agreement relating to products A, the buyer purchased €1 million of competing products B, the calculation basis for the 80% rule is not necessarily limited to €1 million, but may be the buyer's best estimate of its total requirements of products A and B combined, which may exceed € 1 million. Similar principles apply where the buyer has not purchased competing products in the preceding calendar year. Also in such a case, the parties may, during the first contract year, proceed on the basis of the buyer's best estimates of its total annual purchases.

6.11. An important practical question is whether, and if so under what circumstances, an obligation for the buyer to achieve a certain minimum sales quota may

---

[8] Reg 2790/99, Art 1(b), *in fine.*

amount to a non-compete obligation that is subject to Article 5 of the Regulation. The answer to this question is not self-evident. It is an essential characteristic of the non-compete obligation (narrow definition) that the buyer is under a, direct or indirect, obligation not to manufacture, purchase, or sell any products that compete with the contract products. It seems difficult to sustain that an obligation to achieve minimum sales quotas directly causes the buyer not to manufacture, purchase, or sell competing products. Indeed, the buyer's contractual freedom to trade in competing products remains unaffected by an obligation to achieve a minimum sales quota. Must such an obligation then be regarded as an indirect obligation not to trade in competing products? *Prima facie*, this would not appear to be the case. In most instances, an obligation to achieve certain minimum sales quota cannot be considered as an indirect means of forcing the buyer not to trade in *any* competing products at all (which is what the definition in Article 1(b) of the Regulation requires). Depending upon the height of the sales quota, it could be that in certain instances sales quota may constitute an indirect means of forcing the buyer to limit most of its sales to sales of contract products, but such a situation would not be covered by the narrow definition of a non-compete obligation contained in Article 1(b) of the Regulation (since that definition is limited to an obligation *not* to sell competing products).

The economic effects of such an obligation are therefore rather similar to those **6.12**. flowing from an exclusive purchase obligation, which is the second type of restriction covered by the definition contained in Article 1(b) of the Regulation. However, it is also difficult to defend the position that an obligation to realize a certain minimum sales quota must always be considered as being tantamount to an exclusive purchase obligation (ie the second type of restriction covered by Article 1(b) of the Regulation). It is indeed an essential element of that definition that the buyer is, directly or indirectly, obligated to obtain more than 80% of its total purchases of contract products and competing products from the supplier or a third party designated by the supplier. This latter aspect will normally not be present when the buyer is merely obliged to achieve a minimum sales quota, since in such a situation the buyer would retain its freedom to choose its source of supply. We would therefore conclude that obligations to achieve a minimum sales quota are normally not to be considered as non-compete obligations within the meaning of Article 1(b) of the Regulation. This may however exceptionally be otherwise, namely where the sales quota are so high that there is little or no room left for the buyer to purchase other products than contract products and still meet its minimum sales quota and the buyer cannot turn to other sources of supply than the supplier or third parties designated by the supplier.

B. Conditions Applicable to Non-Compete Obligations

(1) Non-compete obligations during the term of the agreement

6.13. Article 5 of the Regulation defines three restrictions that are not exempted by the Regulation. The first of these restrictions, covered in paragraph (a) of Article 5, relates to non-compete obligations applicable during the term of the agreement:

> The exemption provided for in Article 2 shall not apply to any of the following obligations contained in vertical agreements:
>
> (a) any direct or indirect[9] non-compete obligation, the duration of which is indefinite or exceeds five years. A non-compete obligation which is tacitly renewable beyond a period of five years is to be deemed concluded for an indefinite duration.

Indefinite duration

6.14. A first category of non-compete obligations (a term which includes both non-compete obligations in the narrow sense of the word and the exclusive purchase obligations defined in Article 1(b) of the Regulation) that are excluded from exemption, are non-compete obligations entered into for an indefinite period of time. It should be stressed from the outset that the exclusion from the automatic exemption granted by the Regulation applies *ab initio* and not just after five years. The Guidelines do not explain why non-compete obligations entered into for an indefinite duration are excluded from the group exemption, presumably because the reasons for the exclusion are well-known. The condition that non-compete obligations may not be entered into for an indefinite period of time seeks to avoid situations where, due to the buyer's passiveness, the non-compete obligation extends beyond the maximum period of five years allowed under the Regulation. One could of course reply that the buyer is an undertaking and, being a professional buyer, may be expected to know when it is in its interest to terminate the non-compete obligation. However, such an argument overlooks the fact that in most instances it will not be possible for the buyer to terminate the non-compete obligation, without at the same time terminating the agreement itself. Since most buyers would refrain from such a radical solution, it is indeed likely that in many cases non-compete obligations entered into for an indefinite duration would last longer than the maximum permitted duration of five years.

Tacit renewal

6.15. The Regulation expressly provides that a non-compete obligation which is tacitly renewable beyond a period of five years must be deemed to have been

---

[9] The words 'direct or indirect' are redundant since they are already included in the definition of the term non-compete obligation in Reg 2790/99, Art 1(b).

concluded for an indefinite duration.[10] In doing so, the Regulation confirms the approach taken by the Commission in its 1984 Notice on exclusive distribution and exclusive purchasing agreements,[11] which was endorsed by the Court of First Instance in *Langnese-Iglo GmbH & Co KG v Commission*.[12] To avoid misunderstanding, the mere fact that a non-compete obligation is tacitly renewable does not prevent the exemption from applying. This will only be so if the non-compete obligation is tacitly renewable in such a manner that its total duration would exceed five years. For example, a non-compete obligation with an initial duration of three years, which provides for tacit renewal for a single period of two years, does not cause problems under the Regulation.[13] By contrast, a non-compete obligation which is tacitly renewable beyond a period of five years, but which during the life of the agreement is expressly terminated by the parties before the expiry of the five-year period, does not benefit from exemption.[14]

Neither the Regulation nor the Guidelines specifically address the situation **6.16**. where the tacit renewal of the non-compete obligation is the consequence of a statutory instead of a contractual provision. Under Belgian law, for example, certain types of distributorship agreements are tacitly renewable pursuant to a mandatory legal provision. If such agreements contain a non-compete obligation, the non-compete obligation is tacitly renewable as well, beyond a period of five years. Parties to such agreements are therefore well-advised to dissociate the duration of the non-compete obligation from the duration of the distributorship agreement itself.

Express renewal

Article 5(a) of the Regulation exempts non-compete obligations only if their **6.17**. duration is fixed and does not exceed five years. As indicated earlier, the group exemption does not apply to non-compete obligations which are tacitly renewable in such a manner that their total duration would exceed five years. However, there is no rule which prevents the parties from expressly renewing the non-compete obligation after five years (or before the expiry of five years, but where the combined duration of the initial non-compete obligation and its renewal exceed five years). The Guidelines (paragraph 58) stress that such a

---

[10] Reg 2790/99, Art 5(a).

[11] Commission Notice concerning Commission Regulations (EEC) No 1983/83 and (EEC) No 1984/83 of 22 June 1983 on the application of Article 85(3) of the Treaty to categories of exclusive distribution and exclusive purchasing agreements [1984] OJ C101/2.

[12] Case T–7/93 *Langnese-Iglo* [1995] ECR II–1533, para 138.

[13] JM Schulze, S Pautke, and DS Wagener, *Vertikal-GVO Praxiskommentar* (Verlag Recht und Wirtschaft GmbH, 2001) para 660.

[14] C Liebscher, E Flohr, and A Petsche, *Handbuch der EU-Gruppenfreistellungsverordnungen* (CH Beck, 2003) para 161.

renewal requires the explicit consent of both parties. The purpose of this condition is to make sure that, at the expiry of the non-compete obligation, the buyer recovers its freedom to negotiate with competing suppliers and to enter into an agreement with one or more of them, or to continue its contractual relationship with the supplier on the same terms and conditions or other terms and conditions. For this reason, a five-year agreement which contains a non-compete obligation and which may be unilaterally renewed by the supplier, does not meet the conditions of Article 5(a) of the Regulation. In our view, even though the Guidelines stress the fact that both parties must explicitly consent to the renewal of the non-compete obligation beyond five years, it would not be a problem under the Regulation if the option to renew the agreement (and the non-compete obligation contained therein) were solely granted to the buyer.[15]

6.18. The freedom of the buyer to consent to the renewal of the non-compete obligation (in practice often the supply or distribution agreement which contains the non-compete obligation) must be effective and not merely theoretical. If there are practical obstacles that hinder the buyer from effectively terminating the non-compete obligation after five years, the block exemption will not apply to the non-compete obligation.[16] The Guidelines give some examples of situations in which the buyer's freedom to effectively terminate the non-compete obligation would be hindered. These examples deal with loans and equipment provided by the supplier. It would be erroneous to regard the examples given in the Guidelines as general rules that apply in any situation. The correct approach should rather be to evaluate each individual case on its own merits and to examine in light of the circumstances of each case whether the buyer is economically tied to the supplier or whether it may exercise its freedom to contract with competing suppliers without suffering economic harm.

6.19. Non-compete obligations that were in force on 31 May 2000 and satisfied the conditions of Regulations No 1983/83,[17] No 1984/83,[18] or No 4087/88,[19] without satisfying the conditions of the Vertical Restraints block exemption regulation, benefited from a transitional period. If they were made compatible with the requirements of the Regulation before 31 December 2001, they continue to benefit from exemption under the Regulation.[20] With respect to non-compete obligations, the Guidelines (paragraph 70) clarify that it is sufficient to amend existing non-compete obligations at the latest on 31 December

---

[15] Schulze, Pautke, and Wagener (n 13 above) para 665.   [16] Guidelines, para 58.
[17] Commission Regulation (EEC) No 1983/83 of 22 June 1983 on the application of Article 85(3) of the Treaty to categories of exclusive distribution agreements [1983] OJ L173/1.
[18] Commission Regulation (EEC) No 1984/83 of 22 June 1983 on the application of Article 85(3) of the Treaty to categories of exclusive purchasing agreements [1983] OJ L173/5.
[19] Commission Regulation (EEC) No 4087/88 of 30 November 1988 on the application of Article 85(3) of the Treaty to categories of franchising agreements [1988] OJ L359/46.
[20] Reg 2790/99, Art 12(2).

2001 in such a manner that their remaining duration as of 1 January 2002 does not exceed five years. For example, a ten-year non-compete obligation entered into on 1 January 1998 benefits from the group exemption if it was amended before 31 December 2001 in such a manner that it expires at the latest on 31 December 2006 (instead of 31 December 2007). The fact that at that point in time, the non-compete obligation will have been in existence for nine years does not pose a problem under the Regulation. The reduction of the duration of the non-compete obligation may be achieved by mutual agreement between supplier and buyer, but it is also possible that the supplier may unilaterally exempt the buyer from compliance with the non-compete obligation to the extent that it would run beyond 31 December 2006.

Exception

The rule that non-compete obligations must have a fixed duration (not to **6.20**. exceed five years) suffers from an exception when the buyer sells the contract products or services from premises and land owned by the supplier or leased by the supplier from third parties not connected to the supplier.[21] In such a situation the duration of the non-compete obligation may extend to the entire period during which the buyer occupies the premises and land owned or leased by the supplier.[22] According to the Guidelines (paragraph 59) it would not be reasonable to expect a supplier to allow competing products to be sold from premises and land owned by the supplier without its permission. Although not expressly mentioned in the Guidelines, it is clear from the text of the Regulation that the same rule will apply where the supplier does not own the land and premises but leases them from a third party. Since ownership and leasehold rights are treated alike, it seems reasonable to interpret the Regulation in such a manner that the exception applies as of the moment the supplier has rights to the land and premises from which the contract goods or services are to be sold by the buyer and may use these rights to grant to the buyer the right to do so. The precise legal structure used to achieve that purpose would not seem relevant for the purposes of the Regulation. Rights that are similar to ownership rights or leasehold rights (eg *usufruct* rights) should therefore also be able to benefit from the exception.

The Regulation does not stipulate anything with respect to the manner in which **6.21**. the supplier must put the land and premises at the disposal of the buyer. One may therefore assume that the parties may freely determine this[23] and that it is also irrelevant whether the buyer must pay for the right to use the land and

---

[21] For an application of these principles by a national competition authority, see *Royalty v Heineken*, decision 2036–121 of 1 April 2003 by the Director-General of the Dutch Competition Authority available at www.nmanet.nl (in Dutch only).   [22] Reg 2790/99, Art 5(a).
[23] Schulze, Pautke, and Wagener (n 13 above) para 674.

premises owned or leased by the supplier. In our view, formulas whereby the buyer must pay for the right to use the land and premises owned or leased by the supplier may benefit from the exception, provided that the conditions at which the buyer may use the land and premises are not such that the buyer must be deemed to be the economic owner of the land and premises.[24]

6.22. The Guidelines (paragraph 59) state in general terms that artificial ownership constructions intended to avoid the five-year limit will not benefit from the exception. The requirement that, if the supplier leases the land and premises from a third party, such party may not be connected with the buyer, is motivated by similar considerations.[25] Constructions through which the supplier leases the land and premises from the buyer, or a third party connected to the buyer (eg a company controlled by the buyer) will therefore not benefit from the exception. This does not imply that such constructions—which are commonly used in certain markets (eg distribution of petrol in gas stations, distribution of beer through pubs)—are henceforth illegal. Rather, the block exemption granted by the Regulation will not apply to the non-compete obligations contained in these agreements if they are of indefinite duration or exceed a fixed duration of five years.

(2) The non-compete obligation after termination of the agreement

6.23. Article 5(b) of the Regulation provides under which circumstances it is possible to impose a non-compete obligation after the termination of the agreement:

> The exemption provided for in Article 2 shall not apply to any of the following obligations contained in vertical agreements: . . .
>
> b. any direct or indirect obligation causing the buyer, after termination of the agreement, not to manufacture, purchase, sell or resell goods or services, unless such obligation:
> — relates to goods or services which compete with the contract goods or service, and
> — is limited to the premises and land from which the buyer has operated during the contract period, and
> — is indispensable to protect know-how transferred by the supplier to the buyer,
>
> and provided that the duration of such non-compete obligations is limited to a period of one year after termination of the agreement; this obligation is without prejudice to the possibility of imposing a restriction which is unlimited in time on the use and disclosure of know-how which has not entered the public domain.

---

[24] By analogy reference can be made to the arguments developed by the European Commission in its decision in *Tetra Pak II* [1992] OJ L72/1, para 59.

[25] Reg 2790/99, Art 5(a), *in fine*.

It is clear from the wording of Article 5(b) of the Regulation that the restriction **6.24.** which is the subject of this provision is not a non-compete obligation as defined in Article 1(b) of the Regulation.[26] Article 5(b) provides in general terms that any direct or indirect obligation causing the buyer, after termination of the agreement, not to manufacture, purchase, sell, or resell goods or services does not qualify for exemption under the Regulation, unless certain conditions are met. This provision also applies therefore to goods and services which do not compete with the contract goods or services.[27] As indicated earlier, it would be possible under the Regulation to impose such a restriction during the term of the agreement.[28]

After termination of the agreement, obligations not to trade in or produce **6.25.** goods or services which compete with the contract goods or services qualify for exemption under the Regulation only if four conditions are met. These four conditions apply cumulatively. It may be noted that the Regulation does not distinguish between different forms of contract termination. Whether the agreement terminates following the expiry of its term or is terminated for convenience, for cause, or on any other ground, does not make any difference under the Regulation. The rule as set out in Article 5(b) remains the same.

The first of the conditions mentioned in Article 5(b) is that the restriction must **6.26.** relate to goods or services which compete with the contract goods or services. Failing the provision of a definition in the Regulation of what constitutes competing goods, it is proposed to use the same concept as for the interpretation of a non-compete obligation which applies during the term of the agreement. In other words, reference is made to goods or services that are regarded as being substitutable by buyers.[29]

The second condition is that the scope of the restriction must be limited to the **6.27.** land and premises from which the buyer has operated during the contract period. Therefore, if the buyer moves premises after termination of the agreement, for example because these premises were let to the buyer by the supplier, it would not be possible to impose a post-term non-compete obligation. If taken literally, this would mean that fairly common provisions which prevent the buyer from developing competing activities in the immediate vicinity of the contract premises after contract termination would no longer be possible. This would be regrettable as this would leave room for buyers to circumvent the legitimate concerns of the supplier. The former block exemption regulation applying to certain categories of franchise agreements (Regulation 4087/88) was more liberal in this respect. That regulation offered an exemption for obligations of the franchisee not to engage, directly or indirectly, in any similar

---

[26] Para 6.01 above.   [27] Schulze, Pautke, and Wagener (n 13 above) para 678.
[28] Para 6.07 above.   [29] Para 6.06 above.

business in the territory where it has exploited the franchise for a maximum period of one year after termination of the agreement, provided that this obligation is necessary to protect the franchisor's industrial or intellectual property rights or to maintain the common identity and reputation of the franchised network.[30]

6.28.   As a third condition, the Regulation imposes that the obligation must be indispensable to protect know-how transferred by the supplier to the buyer. Article 1(f) of the Regulation defines the term 'know-how' as 'a package of non-patented practical information resulting from experience and testing by the supplier, which is secret, substantial and identified'. Each of these last three terms (secret, substantial, and identified) is also defined in the Regulation. 'Secret' means that the know-how is not generally known or easily accessible. 'Substantial' means that the know-how includes information which is indispensable to the buyer for the use, sale or resale of the contract goods or services and 'identified' means that the know-how must be described in a sufficiently comprehensive manner so as to make it possible to verify that it fulfils the criteria of secrecy and substantiality.

6.29.   The fourth and last condition is that the duration of the non-compete obligation may not exceed one year after termination of the agreement, without prejudice to the possibility of imposing a restriction which is unlimited in time on the use and disclosure of know-how which has not entered the public domain. In other words, the buyer must have the right to engage in competing activities after one year following termination of the agreement, but in doing so may not make use of know-how transferred by the supplier. In practice it may be difficult for the supplier to prove that its former buyer makes use of know-how previously transferred by the supplier. The possibility left by the Regulation for the supplier to prohibit such use may therefore have little practical impact.

(3) Non-compete obligations imposed on members of selective distribution systems

6.30.   It is permitted under the Regulation to impose non-compete obligations on members of a selective distribution system within the limits set by Article 5(a) and (b) of the Regulation. Such obligations must however apply to the sale of competing brands in general.[31] Article 5(c) of the Regulation indeed provides that the Regulation does not apply to 'any direct or indirect obligation causing the members of a selective distribution system not to sell the brands of particular competing suppliers'.

---

[30]   Reg 4087/88, Art 3(1)(c); also, para 2.288 above.
[31]   Guidelines, para 61. Schulze, Pautke, and Wagener (n 13 above) para 697.

This requirement is somewhat surprising. According to the Guidelines the aim **6.31.** of the provision is to avoid a situation whereby a number of suppliers using the same selective distribution outlets prevent one specific competitor or certain specific competitors from using these outlets to distribute their products.[32] These reasons are not necessarily convincing. First, as expressly admitted in the Guidelines, the exclusion is aimed at preventing a form of collective boycott, that is, a horizontal agreement to which the Regulation does not apply anyway. Second, it is hard to see why this is a specific concern for selective distribution systems and not for other distribution formulas.

Since the Guidelines state that the objective of Article 5(c) is to avoid a specific **6.32.** competitor or certain specific competitors from being excluded from using distribution outlets, it remains possible in our opinion for a supplier to provide that its selective distributor may not sell competing products in general, but to allow certain exceptions to this general prohibition (provided this is not an indirect attempt to exclude one specific or certain specific competitors).

C. Consequences if the Conditions Are Not Met

(1) The severability principle

Contrary to what is the case for the hardcore restrictions listed in Article 4 of the **6.33.** Regulation, the failure to comply with the conditions defined in Article 5 only results in the non-applicability of the block exemption to the non-compete obligation. All other restrictions contained in the agreement may still benefit from the exemption granted pursuant to Article 2 of the Regulation. The Guidelines refer in this respect to the so-called severability principle.[33]

(2) Consequences for the relevant provision

The severability principle gives rise to a number of questions, which may also be **6.34.** interesting from a practitioner's point of view. A first question deals with the consequences under Article 81(1) EC of the failure to comply with the conditions imposed by Article 5 of the Regulation. In other words, is it possible to deduce from the non-applicability of the group exemption to a non-compete obligation that this provision is necessarily contrary to Article 81(1) EC? The answer to this question is negative. According to well-established case law of the Court of Justice, group exemptions merely offer certain possibilities enabling undertakings to remove their agreements from the scope of the prohibition contained in Article 81(1) EC. An undertaking is not however compelled to make use of these possibilities. Nor do group exemptions have the effect of

---

[32] Guidelines, para 61.   [33] ibid, para 67.

amending the content of agreements or of rendering them void when all of the conditions laid down in the group exemption regulation are not satisfied.[34] When these conditions are not met, the agreement at issue will only fall within the scope of the prohibition contained in Article 81(1) EC if its object or effect is to appreciably restrict competition within the common market and it is capable of affecting trade between Member States.[35] There is, in other words, no automatic conclusion that agreements which do not satisfy the conditions laid down in group exemption regulations fall within the scope of Article 81(1) EC. This conclusion may only be reached if an evaluation of the agreement in its legal and economic context reveals that it meets the conditions of Article 81(1) EC and does not qualify for an exemption under Article 81(3) EC.

(3) The Delimitis *test*

6.35. The case law of the Court of Justice formulates certain criteria to determine whether a non-compete obligation must be deemed to fall within the scope of application of Article 81(1) EC. *Stergios Delimitis v Henninger Braü*[36] is one of the leading cases in this respect. It deals with the compatibility with Article 81(1) EC of an exclusive purchase obligation imposed by a brewery on a publican in the context of a beer supply agreement. However, the wording and rationale used by the Court suggests that the principles developed in *Delimitis* apply in general to non-compete obligations in the broad sense of the term.[37]

6.36. The *Delimitis* test can be summarized as follows. First of all, the Court indicates that although beer supply agreements which contain an exclusive purchase obligation do not have the object of restricting competition within the meaning of Article 81(1) EC, it is nevertheless necessary to ascertain whether they have the effect of preventing, restricting, or distorting competition.[38] This requires an analysis to be made in two stages. In the first stage, the effects of the agreement, taken together with other contracts of the same type, on the opportunities of national competitors and those of other Member States to gain access to the relevant market or to increase their market share on that market, must be assessed. If an examination of the effects of the agreement and of all similar agreements entered into on the relevant market and of all other relevant legal and economic circumstances shows that these agreements do not have the cumulative effect of denying access to the relevant market to new national and foreign competitors, the individual agreements comprising the bundle of agreements cannot be held to restrict competition within the meaning of Article

---

[34] Case 10/86 *VAG France* [1986] ECR 4071, para 12; and Joined Cases T–185/96, T–189/96, and T–190/96 *Riviera Auto Service Etablissements Dalmasso* [1999] ECR II–93, para 30.
[35] Case C–230/96 *Cabour* [1998] ECR I–2055, para 48.
[36] Case C–234/89 [1991] ECR I–935.   [37] ibid, para 10, *in fine*.
[38] ibid, para 13.

81(1) EC.[39] If the examination reveals that it is difficult to gain access to the relevant market, it is necessary—as the second stage of the test—to assess whether the agreements entered into by the brewery in question contribute significantly to the cumulative effect produced by the totality of the similar contracts found on the market. If that is the case, these agreements are caught by the prohibition contained in Article 81(1) EC. However, if the contribution to the cumulative effect is insignificant, the agreements are not caught by Article 81(1) EC.[40]

The two-stage test developed by the Court can be described further as follows. The first stage—during which it is assessed whether it is difficult to gain access to the relevant market—examines, *inter alia*, the existence of a bundle of similar agreements that restrict market access. Factors that play a role in this respect are the number of tied sales outlets compared to the number of outlets not tied to suppliers, the duration of the commitments entered into, the quantities of product to which the commitments relate, as well as the proportion between those quantities and the quantities of product sold by resellers which are not tied to suppliers.[41] The Court indicates however that the existence of such a bundle of similar agreements, even if it has a considerable effect on the opportunities for gaining access to the markets, is not sufficient in itself to support a finding that the relevant market is inaccessible, since it is only one element, *inter alia,* to be taken into consideration. In that connection, it is necessary to examine whether there are concrete possibilities for new competitors to enter the market (eg by acquiring a brewery already established on the market together with its network of sales outlets or by opening new sales outlets). The presence of wholesalers not tied to producers is also a factor capable of facilitating market access.[42] **6.37**.

Apart from the existence of bundles of similar agreements, account must be taken of the competitive conditions prevailing on the relevant market. In this respect, the Court points to factors such as the number and size of the producers present on the market, the degree of market saturation, and the loyalty of consumers to existing brands. A saturated market which is characterized by consumer loyalty to a limited number of brands is, generally speaking, more difficult to penetrate than a market which is in full expansion in which a large number of small producers are operating without strong brand names.[43] **6.38**.

If the first stage of the test reveals that it is difficult for newcomers to gain access to the relevant market, the second stage of the *Delimitis* test examines whether the agreement at issue contributes significantly to the cumulative effect produced by the totality of similar contracts found on the market. According to the Court, under Community rules of competition, the responsibility for such an **6.39**.

---

[39] ibid, para 23. [40] ibid, para 24. [41] ibid, para 19. [42] ibid, para 21.
[43] ibid, para 22.

effect of closing off the market must be attributed to the breweries which make a substantial contribution thereto.[44] The extent to which the individual agreement contributes to the cumulative market foreclosure effect is determined mainly by the market position of the contracting parties and by the duration of the agreement. The market position is to be evaluated not only from the point of view of market share, but also by taking into account the number of sales outlets tied to the supplier or to the supplier's group, in relation to the total number of sales outlets in the relevant market. As regards duration, a supplier with a relatively small market position, which ties its outlets for a duration which is manifestly excessive in relation to the average duration of similar agreements on the market may contribute as significantly to the sealing-off of the market as a supplier in a strong market position.[45]

6.40.   The *Delimitis* test has become a standard test in Community competition law. Since 1991, the Court of Justice and Court of First Instance have had numerous occasions to confirm and refine the *Delimitis* test.[46]

(4) Consequences for the remaining provisions

6.41.   As stated in paragraph 6.33 above, the severability principle implies that non-compete obligations which do not satisfy the conditions of Article 5 of the Regulation are excluded from exemption under the Regulation, without affecting the applicability of the Regulation to the remaining provisions of the agreement. The inapplicability of the exemption to the non-compete obligation triggers the necessity of having to conduct an individual assessment of the non-compete obligation under Article 81(1) EC.[47] If this assessment reveals that the non-compete obligation is prohibited under Article 81(1) EC and is not exempted under Article 81(3) EC, it will be considered as null and void pursuant to Article 81(2) EC.

6.42.   At this point the question arises of the consequences of the nullity of the non-compete obligation for the remaining provisions of the agreement.[48] In *Kerpen & Kerpen*, the Court of Justice held that the consequences of the automatic nullity decreed by Article 81(2) EC for other parts of the agreement, as well as for any orders and deliveries made on the basis of such an agreement, are not a matter for Community law, but must be decided under applicable national

---

[44] ibid, para 24.   [45] ibid, para 26.

[46] Case T–7/93 *Langnese-Iglo v Commission* [1995] ECR II–1533; Case T–9/93 *Schöller Lebensmittel v Commission* [1995] ECR II–1611; Case C–214/99 *Neste* [2000] ECR I–11121; and Case T–25/99 *Roberts & Roberts v Commission* [2001] ECR II–1881. For interesting applications by the European Commission, see *Interbrew* [2002] OJ C283/14 and *Repsol CPP SA* [2004] OJ C258/7.   [47] Para 6.34 above.

[48] Also, paras 1.71–1.77 above.

law.[49] Under certain national laws, for example Belgian law, the nullity of a contractual provision only leads to the nullity of the agreement as a whole, if the null and void provision is inextricably linked to the remainder of the agreement, in view of the will expressed by both parties or as a result of the structure of the agreement.[50]

It is at least questionable whether the severability principle embedded in the Regulation is compatible with the consequences of *Kerpen & Kerpen*. In other words, is there still room for national law to declare the entire agreement null and void (because the non-compete obligation contained therein is null and void and is inextricably linked to the remainder of the agreement), or does the severability principle (and therefore the applicability in principle of the group exemption to the remaining contractual provisions) entail that the nullity sanction, if any, decreed under national law may not extend to the entire agreement? In order to resolve this question, it seems appropriate to distinguish between situations where the remaining contract provisions benefit from exemption under the Regulation and situations where that is not the case (eg because they are not restrictive of competition). If the block exemption does not apply to the remaining contract provisions, then there is no reason to deviate from the consequences of *Kerpen & Kerpen*.

6.43.

However, if (some) of the remaining contract provisions are restrictive of competition and qualify for an exemption under the Regulation, it might perhaps be argued that the full effectiveness of the Regulation is undermined if the remaining contract provisions are declared as null and void, even though they qualify for an exemption. In our view, it would be wrong to answer this question on the basis that Community law must take precedence over national law and that, therefore, the nullity sanction decreed under national law may not extend to contract provisions that would otherwise have benefited from exemption under the Regulation. It follows indeed from Article 81(2) EC, as interpreted by the Court of Justice, that the consequences of the nullity under Article 81(2) EC of one contractual provision for the remaining contract provisions are a matter of national law. This issue should therefore not be resolved differently than where a contract provision is null and void under national law, for example, for lack of consent. In such a case, it would be pointless to apply the block exemption to provisions that are null and void under national law. If national law leads to the nullity of the entire agreement there is, severability notwithstanding, no agreement left to which the group exemption might be applied.[51]

6.44.

---

[49] Case 319/82 *Kerpen & Kerpen* [1983] ECR 4173, para 12.

[50] Court of Appeal, Brussels, 28 June 1995, in H de Bauw and E Gybels (eds), *Jaarboek Handelspraktijken & Mededinging 1995* (Kluwer Rechtswetenschappen, 1996) 576.

[51] V Korah and D O'Sullivan, *Distribution Agreements under the EC Competition Rules* (Hart Publishing, 2002) 208.

6.45. The solution as defended here is not contrary to Article 3(2) of Regulation 1/2003 on the implementation of the rules on competition laid down in Articles 81 and 82 of the Treaty,[52] which provides that national rules of competition may not lead to the prohibition of agreements which may affect trade between Member States, but which are covered by a regulation applying Article 81(3) EC. Indeed, Article 3(3) of the same regulation clarifies that the prohibition contained in Article 3(2) does not prevent the application of provisions of national law that predominantly pursue an objective different from that pursued by Articles 81 and 82 EC. Principles of national contract law must presumably be regarded as pursuing predominantly other objectives than those pursued by Articles 81 and 82 EC.

---

[52] [2003] OJ L1/1.

7

FREQUENTLY USED DISTRIBUTION FORMULAS

A. Introduction

Prior to the entry into force of Regulation 2790/99, different legal instruments **7.01**. applied to the EC competition law analysis of a number of frequently used distribution formulas:

—**Exclusive and non-exclusive distribution**: Separate block exemption regulations applied to each of these distribution formulas, as follows:
  • Commission Regulation (EEC) No 1983/83 of 22 June 1983 on the application of Article 85(3) of the Treaty to categories of exclusive distribution agreements:[1] this block exemption applied only to cases where the supplier had appointed a single distributor within a given contract territory;
  • Commission Regulation (EEC) No 1984/83 of 22 June 1983 on the application of Article 85(3) of the Treaty to categories of exclusive purchasing agreement:[2] this block exemption applied only to cases where the non-exclusive distributor was subject to an exclusive purchase requirement.
—**Selective distribution**: No block exemption regulation was applicable to selective distribution. However, guidance on the EC competition law analysis of selective distribution could be found in a series of Court judgments and Commission decisions on selective distribution.[3]
—**Franchising**: Following the Court's judgment in *Pronuptia*,[4] franchising too was the subject of a number of Commission decisions.[5] In a subsequent

---

[1] [1983] OJ L173/1.   [2] [1983] OJ L173/5.
[3] For a review, see A Jones and B Sufrin, *EC Competition Law: Text, Cases and Materials* (OUP, 2001) 509–15.   [4] Case 191/84 *Pronuptia* [1986] ECR 353.
[5] *Pronuptia* (Case IV/30937) [1987] OJ L13/39; *Yves Rocher* (Cases IV/M31428–IV/M31432) [1987] OJ L8/49; *Computerland* (Case IV/M32034) [1987] OJ L222/12; and *ServiceMaster* (Case IV/M32358) [1988] OJ L332/38.

stage, the Commission decided to consolidate this decision-making practice and adopt a specific block exemption on franchise agreements: Commission Regulation (EEC) No 4087/88 of 30 November 1988 on the application of Article 85(3) of the Treaty to categories of franchise agreements.[6]

—**Agency**: There was no block exemption regulation applicable to agency. However, guidance on the EC competition analysis of agency agreements could be found in the case law of the Court of Justice and in a notice issued by the Commission.

7.02. At present, the EC competition law analysis of these different types of distribution formula is governed by a single legal instrument, ie Regulation 2790/99, as well as the accompanying Guidelines.[7] This Chapter analyses how these types of distribution formula are dealt with under Regulation 2790/99. Specific attention is given to the restrictions of competition which the different distribution formulas typically impose, namely:

— territorial protection of the distributor (against the supplier as well as against other distributors);
— territorial restrictions imposed on the distributor;
— customer restrictions imposed on the distributor;
— non-compete obligations; and
— exclusive purchasing requirements.

7.03. The purpose of this Chapter is not to provide an in-depth analysis of the various provisions of Regulation 2790/99. That is done elsewhere in this publication. The objective is rather to provide a succinct overview of the manner in which the typical restrictions listed above can be used in the context of the standard distribution formulas. It must be borne in mind that this overview is confined to the situations where Regulation 2790/99 is applicable. The position outside the context of Regulation 2790/99, which is addressed in Chapter 10 below, is less predictable.

B. Exclusive Distribution

7.04. Under Regulation 2790/99, exclusive distribution means that the supplier agrees to sell his products only to one distributor for resale in a particular territory.[8] It is

---

[6] [1988] OJ L359/46.

[7] Commission Notice—Guidelines on Vertical Restraints [2000] OJ C291/1 (hereafter 'Guidelines'). Provided, of course, that the market share threshold of 30%, as well as the other conditions for the application of Commission Regulation (EC) No 2790/1999 of 22 December 1999 on the application of Article 81(3) of the Treaty to categories of vertical agreements and concerted practices [1999] OJ L336/21, as discussed in Chapter 2, are fulfilled. If not, an individual assessment under Art 81 EC is required.   [8] Guidelines, para 161.

also referred to as 'sole exclusivity'. Prior to Regulation 2790/99, exclusive distribution could be block exempted under Regulation 67/67[9] and subsequently under Regulation 1983/83.[10] These block exemption regulations did not apply to shared exclusivity, pursuant to which the supplier agrees to supply a specified number of undertakings for resale only within a defined territory of the common market. As opposed to this, for motor vehicle distribution, the sector-specific block exemption at the time, Regulation 123/85,[11] did allow shared exclusivity. In this section, both sole and shared exclusivity are discussed.

(1) Territorial protection

Territorial protection against the supplier

7.05. The territorial protection which exclusive distributors may enjoy against their suppliers is a relatively straightforward matter. Nothing prevents the supplier from agreeing to certain limits on his supply policy to give territorial protection to his distributors (both in the case of sole and of shared exclusivity). Regulation 2790/99, for instance, allows for a supplier to agree only to supply his products to the exclusive distributor(s) in a given territory of the common market. The supplier can also agree not to make any direct sales to customers located in the distributor's contract territory.

7.06. In short, Regulation 2790/99 does not impose any limits on the supplier's freedom to accept restrictions on his ability to compete with his exclusive (sole or shared) distributors. Even a commitment to refrain, in the most absolute terms, from competing with the distribution network is compatible with the block exemption.

Territorial protection against other distributors

7.07. The territorial protection which an exclusive distributor may enjoy against distributors appointed by the supplier in other territories of the common

---

[9] Regulation (EEC) No 67/67 of the Commission of 22 March 1967 on the application of Article 85(3) of the Treaty to certain categories of exclusive dealing agreements [1967] OJ 57/849.

[10] Commission Regulation (EEC) No 1983/83 of 22 June 1983 on the application of Article 85(3) of the Treaty to categories of exclusive distribution agreements [1983] OJ L173/1.

[11] Commission Regulation (EEC) No 123/85 of 12 December 1984 on the application of Article 85(3) of the Treaty to certain categories of motor vehicle distribution and servicing agreements [1985] OJ L15/16, Art 1, which reads: 'Pursuant to Article 85(3) of the Treaty it is hereby declared that subject to the conditions laid down in this Regulation Article 85(1) shall not apply to agreements to which only two undertakings are party and in which one contracting party agrees to supply within a defined territory of the common market: *only to the other party, or only to the other party and to a specified number of other undertakings within the distribution system*, for the purpose of resale certain motor vehicles intended for use on public roads and having three or more road wheels, together with spare parts therefore' (emphasis added).

market is somewhat more complex. The question which arises is whether the supplier can impose restrictions on the latter distributors in order to grant territorial protection to his exclusive distributor. The answer to this question is different depending on whether sole or shared exclusivity is involved:

— **Sole exclusivity**. In a system of sole exclusivity, an exclusive distributor may be protected, to a certain degree, against competition from distributors appointed in other territories.

Passive sales[12] must at all times be allowed. Hence, an exclusive distributor cannot object to the fact that other distributors sell to customers located in his territory, in cases where such sales have not been solicited by those other distributors (passive sales).

However, the supplier will be able to impose active sales restrictions on the other distributors in order to protect his exclusive distributors. The compatibility of such active sales restrictions with the block exemption will depend on whether the conditions of Article 4(b), first indent, of Regulation 2790/99 and the Guidelines (paragraph 50) are met. These conditions, which are discussed in detail in paragraphs 5.61–5.85 above, include the exclusivity condition, the condition of the parallel imposition of the active sales restriction, and the prohibition to limit sales by the distributor's customers. If the conditions are fulfilled, the supplier is entitled to prohibit his exclusive distributors from actively selling in each other's territories, ie from actively approaching customers in the other distributors' territory and from establishing a warehouse or distribution outlet in such a territory.

— **Shared exclusivity**. Shared exclusivity does not qualify as exclusive distribution under Regulation 2790/99. Given that shared exclusivity implies that several distributors have been appointed in a territory, the conditions for exclusivity under Regulation 2790/99 are not fulfilled. Accordingly, it will not be possible to grant territorial protection to the distributors who have been given the shared exclusivity of a given territory. This means that distributors appointed outside the territory must be entitled to actively approach customers within the territory of the distributors with shared exclusivity and must even be free to establish a warehouse or distribution outlet there. So, shared exclusivity does not provide any territorial protection against active sales from distributors appointed outside the territory.

Given the fact that, in a system of sole exclusivity, a supplier is entitled to impose active sales restrictions on his distributors (subject to the conditions referred to above), it will in many cases make sense not to have large contract territories within which a system of shared exclusively is set up, but instead

---

[12] The concepts of 'active sales' and 'passive sales' are discussed in more detail in paras 5.46–5.53 above.

to divide that large territory into several smaller areas and to apply sole exclusivity within each of those smaller areas.

(2) *Territorial restrictions*

In the case of both sole and shared exclusivity, it is possible to impose restrictions on the activities of the exclusive distributors outside their territory. These restrictions can be summarized as follows: **7.08.**

— passive sales outside the territory must at all times be allowed. Hence, it is not possible to prevent an exclusive (sole or shared) distributor from engaging in passive sales outside his contract territory;
— active sales outside the territory (including the establishment of a distribution outlet) must also be allowed if they concern sales to territories which the supplier has not reserved for himself or has not allocated to a sole exclusive distributor;
— active sales outside the territory may be prohibited if they concern sales to territories which the supplier has reserved for himself or which he has allocated to a (sole) exclusive distributor, provided the three cumulative conditions contained in Article 4(b), first indent, of Regulation 2790/99, *juncto* the Guidelines (paragraph 50) are complied with.[13] It is important to note that these conditions need only be fulfilled in respect of the target territory (ie the territory in which the distributor is not expected to engage in active sales).

It follows from this that the territorial restrictions which a supplier is entitled to impose on an exclusive distributor are identical in cases of sole or shared exclusivity. In other words, the type of exclusivity a distributor enjoys is irrelevant in determining the territorial restrictions which the supplier may decide to impose on him under Regulation 2790/99. **7.09.**

(3) *Customer restrictions*

The customer restrictions which are allowed under Regulation 2790/99 are identical for all exclusive distributors. Therefore, the distinction between sole and shared exclusivity is irrelevant in this respect as well. The same goes for the distinction between sales to other resellers (whether members or not of the supplier's distribution network) and final consumers. In other words, the customer's profile is also irrelevant.[14] **7.10.**

No restrictions may be imposed on passive sales. Hence, it will not be possible to reserve certain customers completely for specified distributors. If an exclusive **7.11.**

---

[13] These conditions are discussed in detail in paras 5.61–5.85 above.
[14] Note that this section does not deal with exclusive distribution which takes the form of quantitative selective distribution. This distribution formula is discussed in paras 7.25–7.37 below.

distributor is approached by a given customer (passive sales scenario), he cannot be prevented from selling to that customer.

7.12. Any customer restriction must therefore by definition be limited to active sales. A supplier may prohibit his exclusive distributors (sole or shared exclusivity) from making active sales to certain customers or customer groups provided that the three cumulative conditions contained in Article 4(b), first indent, of Regulation 2790/99, *juncto* the Guidelines (paragraph 50) are complied with.[15] If one or more of these conditions are not complied with, then the exclusive distributor must be entitled to actively approach the customers or customer groups concerned.

(4) Non-compete obligation

7.13. A supplier can impose a non-compete obligation on his distributors both in the case of sole and of shared exclusivity. Hence, the nature of the exclusivity is immaterial to the treatment of non-compete obligations under Regulation 2790/99. Such obligations will benefit from the block exemption if they are imposed for a fixed term of no more than five years. The details of this condition (limitation in time) are discussed in paragraphs 6.13–6.23 above.

(5) Exclusive purchasing

7.14. Prior to Regulation 2790/99, a supplier could require his exclusive distributor to purchase the contract products exclusively from him without any limitation in time. The position is different under Regulation 2790/99. The block exemption assimilates certain exclusive and quasi-exclusive purchase requirements to non-compete obligations. The assimilation applies where the distributor is required to purchase more than 80% of his requirements of the contract goods (including all substitutes) from the supplier or from an undertaking designated by the supplier. In that case, the purchase requirement must be entered into for a fixed term of no more than five years in order to be exempted on the basis of Regulation 2790/99.

7.15. In practical terms, if the exclusive distributor is entitled to do business in competing products and systematically purchases 20% or more of his needs from competing suppliers, he may be obliged to purchase the contract products exclusively from the supplier without any limitation in time. This implies, *inter alia*, that the exclusive distributor is not entitled to purchase the contract products from other distributors of the supplier. As soon as the distributor is required to purchase more than 80% of his total requirements from the

---

[15] These conditions are discussed in detail in paras 5.86–5.88 above.

supplier, the obligation must be limited in time to a fixed term of five years. For more details, reference is made to paragraphs 6.08–6.12 above.

C. Non-Exclusive Distribution

(1) Territorial protection

Territorial protection against the supplier

Non-exclusive distribution, by definition, implies that the supplier is entitled to **7.16**. appoint additional distributors, even in the immediate vicinity of the non-exclusive distributor. In such a setting, the question concerning the territorial protection against the appointment of other distributors does not arise. As soon as the supplier accepts certain restrictions as to his ability to appoint additional distributors, a situation of sole or shared exclusivity (of some form) enters into play and the principles set forth in paragraph 7.07 above can be relied upon.

As regards direct sales to customers—ie sales competing with the non-exclusive **7.17**. distributor—the supplier is entitled to voluntarily assume certain restrictions or even an outright prohibition. Hence, it is compatible with the block exemption that the supplier accepts not to compete with his non-exclusive distributors. In this regard, the non-exclusive distributor can enjoy the same protection as an exclusive distributor.

Territorial protection against other distributors

Given that non-exclusive distribution does not comply with the exclusivity **7.18**. condition of Article 4(b), first indent, of Regulation 2790/99 and the Guidelines (paragraph 50), the non-exclusive distributor does not qualify for any protection against active and passive sales by other distributors belonging to the supplier's distribution network. Accordingly, these other distributors may not have any restrictions imposed on their activities of competing with the non-exclusive distributor in the latter's territory. Such competing activities may include not only active marketing, but also the establishment of a warehouse or an outlet.

(2) Territorial restrictions

No distributor can be prevented from engaging in passive sales. Accordingly, **7.19**. non-exclusive distributors must also be allowed to handle unsolicited requests from a customer, irrespective of where the customer is located within the EEA.

Non-exclusive distributors may be subjected to territorial restrictions con- **7.20**. cerning their active sales policy outside their territory, on the condition that the three cumulative conditions of Article 4(b), first indent of Regulation 2790/99 and the Guidelines (paragraph 50) are fulfilled. This means that the restrictions on active sales imposed on the non-exclusive distributor may only concern territories which the supplier reserved to himself or allocated on an exclusive basis (sole exclusivity) to another distributor. For more details on this condition and the two other conditions, reference is made to the previous discussion at paragraphs 5.61–5.85 above.

(3) Customer restrictions

7.21. A non-exclusive distributor may be subjected to the same customer restrictions as an exclusive distributor (paragraph 7.17 above).

7.22. A non-exclusive distributor may be given certain exclusive rights with respect to certain customer groups. In this respect, it is irrelevant that a non-exclusive distributor does not have an exclusive territory. However, under no circumstances may the exclusivity rights which a non-exclusive distributor can claim, protect him against passive sales by the supplier's other distributors. Passive sales are possible at all times. Therefore, the maximum protection that is provided is against active sales only, and always on the condition that the three cumulative conditions of Article 4(b), first indent, of Regulation 2790/99 and the Guidelines (paragraph 50), as discussed at paragraphs 5.86–5.88 above, are complied with.

(4) Non-compete obligation

7.23. Regulation 2790/99 does not distinguish between exclusive and non-exclusive distribution in terms of non-compete obligations. Accordingly, reference can be made to what was said above in respect of non-compete obligations imposed on exclusive distributors (paragraph 7.13 above).

(5) Exclusive purchasing

7.24. Prior to Regulation 2790/99, a non-exclusive distribution agreement could be block exempted under Regulation 1984/83 (exclusive purchasing) on condition that it contained an exclusive purchasing requirement.[16] This is no longer the case. Regulation 2790/99 applies to non-exclusive distribution agreements irrespective of whether or not these contain an exclusive purchasing requirement. The conditions under which such a requirement may be imposed are the same as those discussed in respect of exclusive distribution agreements (paragraphs 7.14 and 7.15 above).

---

[16] Reg 1984/83, Art 1 (n 2 above).

D. Selective Distribution

Before Regulation 2790/99, selective distribution agreements were not the **7.25**.
subject of a specific block exemption regulation, even though a number of block
exemption regulations addressed certain essential features of selective distribution (in particular the prohibition of sales to non-authorized distributors).[17]
Instead, selective distribution was the subject of an extensive decision-making
practice of the Commission.[18] These decisions made a distinction between
purely qualitative selective distribution and quantitative selective distribution.
According to the Guidelines (paragraph 185), the difference is as follows:

> Purely qualitative selective distribution selects dealers only on the basis of objective
> criteria required by the nature of the product such as training of sales personnel,
> the service provided at the point of sale, a certain range of the products being sold
> etc. The application of such criteria does not put a direct limit on the number of
> dealers. Purely qualitative selective distribution is in general considered to fall
> outside Article 81(1) for lack of anti-competitive effects ... Quantitative selective
> distribution adds further criteria for selection that more directly limit the potential
> number of dealers by, for instance, requiring minimum or maximum sales, by
> fixing the number of dealers, etc.

For the purposes of Regulation 2790/99, the distinction between purely qua- **7.26**.
litative and quantitative selective distribution is not essential: both types of
selective distribution qualify for block exemption under the same conditions.
This may help to explain why Regulation 2790/99 (Article 1(d)) adopts a very
broad definition of selective distribution. It defines it as:

> a distribution system where the supplier undertakes to sell the contract goods or
> services, either directly or indirectly, only to distributors selected on the basis of
> specified criteria and where these distributors undertake not to sell such goods or
> services to unauthorised distributors.

This definition not only makes no distinction between purely qualitative and **7.27**.
quantitative selective distribution, but also does not mention the nature of the
product. Indeed, although the Commission's decision-making practice normally requires that selective distribution must be required by the nature of the
product,[19] the Guidelines confirm that Regulation 2790/99 'exempts selective
distribution regardless of the nature of the product concerned'.[20] However, it
does add to this that, where the nature of the product does not require selective

---

[17] Reg 123/85 and Reg 1475/95 (motor vehicle distribution), Art 4(1)(1) which permits the
supplier to impose on his dealer the obligation to observe, for distribution and servicing, certain
minimum standards; a similar obligation can be found in the former block exemption regulation
for franchising, Reg 4087/88, Art 3(1). Also the prohibition to sell to unauthorized traders (which
is a typical feature of any selective distribution system) benefited from an automatic exemption in
these two block exemption regulations.   [18] For a list of cases, see para 5.100 above.
[19] PM Roth (ed), *Bellamy and Child. European Community Law of Competition* (5th edn,
Sweet & Maxwell, 2001) paras 7.093–7.095.   [20] Guidelines, para 186.

distribution, this may lead to appreciable anti-competitive effects and to the withdrawal of the benefit of the block exemption regulation.[21]

(1) Territorial protection

Territorial protection against the supplier

7.28. Given that Regulation 2790/99 allows quantitative selective distribution, the supplier is entitled to commit himself to appointing only one or a limited number of dealers in a given territory.[22] Also, Regulation 2790/99 does not prevent the supplier from deciding not to enter into direct competition with his selective dealers (via direct sales). Such a commitment on the part of the supplier not to compete with its selective distributors may be phrased in absolute terms.

Territorial protection against other members of the selective distribution system

7.29. Territorial protection against competition from the other members of a selective distribution system is not possible. Even in cases of quantitative selective distribution, Article 4(c) of Regulation 2790/99 does not allow restrictions on active and passive sales to end-users by the other members of the selective distribution system. Hence, no restriction can be imposed on a selective distributor in respect of the territorial scope of its marketing activities. Accordingly, members of a selective distribution system cannot be restricted in relation to the users or the purchasing agents (acting on behalf of those users) to whom they may sell.[23]

7.30. The only exception[24] to this rule is that the supplier may prohibit a member of the system from operating out of an unauthorized place of establishment:

> Selected dealers may be prevented from running their business from different premises or from opening a new outlet in a different location. If the dealer's outlet is mobile ('shop on wheels'), an area may be defined outside which the mobile outlet cannot be operated.[25]

On the basis of this exception, a limited degree of territorial protection can be organized by the supplier: the supplier can prevent its selective distributors from setting up outlets in each other's distribution territories.

(2) Territorial restrictions

7.31. If a supplier operates an EEA-wide selective distribution system, no territorial restrictions, other than a location clause, may be imposed. It follows directly

---

[21] ibid.   [22] Guidelines, para 53.   [23] ibid.
[24] Reg 2790/99, Art 4(c), *in fine*.   [25] Guidelines, para 54.

from Article 4(c) of Regulation 2790/99 that the members of the system may not be restricted in any other way in either their active or passive sales.

If a supplier does not operate an EEA-wide selective distribution system, but **7.32**. combines selective distribution in some territories with exclusive distribution in others, the Commission allows additional territorial restrictions on the appointed distributors. In particular, the Commission allows an active sales restriction to the extent that this restriction is confined to territories in which an exclusive distributor has been appointed. The conditions for the validity of the restriction under Regulation 2790/99 are the same as those discussed in paragraphs 5.61–5.85. It has previously been pointed out that this position, albeit difficult to reconcile with the wording of the Regulation, should be applauded (see paragraph 5.123 above).

(3) Customer restrictions

End-users

A supplier may not impose end-user restrictions on the members of his selective **7.33**. distribution system. Article 4(c) Regulation 2790/99 identifies the restriction of active or passive sales to end-users by members of a selective distribution system operating at the retail level of trade as a hardcore restriction. To cite the Guidelines (paragraph 179), '[a] combination of exclusive customer allocation and selective distribution is normally hardcore, as active selling to end-users by the appointed distributors is usually not left free'.

Resellers

The situation is different at the level of the resellers. That members of a selective **7.34**. distribution system are not entitled to sell to unauthorized distributors is an essential feature of selective distribution. Put differently, selective distribution in the sense of Regulation 2790/99 requires that the appointed distributors are prohibited from selling to resellers who are not part of the system. The prohibition must concern both active and passive sales. Inversely, appointed distributors must be free to sell to other appointed distributors. Indeed, according to Article 4(d) Regulation 2790/99, the restriction of cross-supplies between appointed distributors is a hardcore infringement. This principle applies irrespective of the level of trade at which the distributors are operating: as soon as a distributor is admitted to a selective distribution system, he must be free to supply to (and to be supplied by) other distributors who are part of that system.

(4) Non-compete obligation

The same principles as those explained in the context of exclusive distribution **7.35**. (paragraph 7.13 above) also apply here. Accordingly, a member of a selective distribution system may be subject to a non-compete obligation imposed upon it in accordance with Article 5 of Regulation 2790/99.

7.36. Article 5(c) of Regulation 2790/99 contains a specific condition for selective distribution, namely that the block exemption does not cover 'any direct or indirect obligation causing the members of a selective distribution system not to sell the brands of particular competing suppliers'. This condition is addressed in more detail in paragraphs 6.30–6.32 above.

(5) Exclusive purchasing

7.37. An exclusive purchasing requirement is not allowed within the framework of a selective distribution system: cross-supplies between the system's members, even if they are operating at different levels of trade, must be allowed. An exclusive purchasing requirement is therefore a hardcore restriction pursuant to Article 4(d) Regulation 2790/99.

E. Franchising

(1) General

7.38. Prior to Regulation 2790/99, franchising was the subject of a specific block exemption regulation, that is, Regulation 4087/88:

— Article 1(3)(b) Regulation 4087/88 defined a 'franchise agreement' as 'an agreement whereby one undertaking, the franchisor, grants the other, the franchisee, in exchange for direct or indirect financial consideration, the right to exploit a franchise for the purposes of marketing specified types of goods and/or services';

— Article 1(3)(a) defined a 'franchise' as 'a package of industrial or intellectual property rights relating to trade marks, trade names, shop signs, utility models, designs, copyrights, know-how or patents, to be exploited for the resale of goods or the provision of services to end users'.

7.39. Regulation 2790/99 ended this separate treatment. Franchising now qualifies for block exemption under Regulation 2790/99, although it can be held that the above definitions, in and of themselves, have not lost their practical value.

Importance of Article 2(3) of Regulation 2790/99

7.40. Fundamental to the applicability of the block exemption regulation to franchising agreements is Article 2(3) of Regulation 2790/99. This concerns IPRs and provides that five conditions must be fulfilled before the block exemption regulation can apply to vertical agreements containing IPR provisions (see paragraphs 2.267–2.283 above). An essential feature of any franchising agreement is that the franchisor communicates the IPRs to his franchisees. So the question is, at what point do IPRs constitute the primary object of a franchising agreement and thereby exclude the application of Regulation 2790/99?

Commercial franchising

As far as commercial franchising is concerned, the Guidelines (paragraphs **7.41**. 42 and 43) advocate a flexible approach to Article 2(3) of Regulation 2790/99 to include commercial franchising in the scope of application of Regulation 2790/99:

> Franchise agreements contain licences of intellectual property rights relating to trade or signs and know-how for the use and distribution of goods or the provision of services. In addition to the licence of IPR, the franchisor usually provides the franchisee during the life of the agreement with commercial or technical assistance, such as procurement services, training, advice on real estate, financial planning etc. The licence and the assistance are integral components of the business method being franchised.

> Licensing contained in franchise agreements is covered by the Block Exemption Regulation if all five conditions listed in point 30 are fulfilled. This is usually the case, as under most franchise agreements, including master franchise agreements, the franchisor provides goods and/or services, in particular commercial or technical assistance services, to the franchisee. The IPRs help the franchisee to resell the products supplied by the franchisor or by a supplier designated by the franchisor or to use those products and sell the resulting goods or services.

Industrial franchising

The applicability of Regulation 2790/99 to industrial franchising is much less **7.42**. obvious. Given that the communication of know-how in the context of industrial franchising is not, in principle, aimed at commercialization, the chances that industrial franchising can be block exempted under Regulation 2790/99 are slim.[26] This is illustrated by the Guidelines (paragraph 42), where it states that franchise agreements, '*with the exception of industrial franchise agreements*, are the most obvious example where know-how for marketing purposes is communicated to the buyer' (emphasis added).

Once it has been determined that a (commercial) franchising agreement is **7.43**. within the scope of Regulation 2790/99, the most common restrictions included in such an agreement can be assessed from the perspective of the block exemption as follows.

---

[26] For a critique on the fact that Reg 2790/99, in principle, does not cover industrial franchising, see R Subiotto and F Amato, 'Preliminary Analysis of the Commission's Reform Concerning Vertical Restraints' (2000) 2 World Competition 20–1.

(2) *Territorial protection*

Territorial protection against the supplier

7.44. The franchisor is entitled to impose upon itself the obligation not to enter into competition with its franchisees, ie to abstain from direct sales. In addition, the franchisor can contractually agree not to appoint additional franchisees within a given territory.

Territorial protection against other franchisees

7.45. Franchise systems are usually based on the principle of selectivity, implying that franchisees are forbidden to sell to unauthorized distributors. In such cases, Regulation 2790/99 does not permit the franchisor to grant extensive territorial protection to his franchisees. Such protection against other franchisees will essentially be limited to a location clause (paragraph 7.31 above). Surprisingly, Regulation 2790/99 does not require that a franchise system must be based on selectivity. In order to qualify for the block exemption regulation, a franchise system without selectivity will have to comply either with the rules set out above on exclusive distribution (paragraphs 7.07–7.09) or with those on non-exclusive distribution (paragraph 7.18).

(3) *Territorial restrictions*

7.46. To what extent a franchisor may impose territorial restrictions on his franchisees depends on whether or not the franchise system in question is of a selective nature:

— If it is, the rules set out above on selective distribution (paragraphs 7.31–7.32) will apply.
— If it is not, the rules set out above on exclusive (paragraphs 7.08 and 7.09) or non-exclusive distribution (paragraphs 7.19 and 7.20) will apply.

(4) *Customer restrictions*

7.47. The customer restrictions which a franchisor may impose upon his franchisees also depend on the selective nature of the franchise system:

— If the franchise system is selective, the rules on selective distribution must be complied with (paragraphs 7.33 and 7.34 above).
— If it is not, then the rules set out above on exclusive (paragraphs 7.10–7.12) or non-exclusive (paragraphs 7.21 and 7.22) distribution will apply.

(5) Non-compete obligation

The Guidelines accept that a non-compete obligation on the goods or services **7.48.** purchased by the franchisees may be outside the scope of Article 81(1) EC. This will be the case if the non-compete obligation is necessary to maintain the common identity and reputation of the franchised network.[27] Similarly, given that they are generally considered to be necessary to protect the franchisor's IPR, an obligation on the franchisee not to engage, directly or indirectly, in any similar business, as well as an obligation on the franchisee not to use know-how licensed by the franchisor for purposes other than the exploitation of the franchise, may also escape Article 81(1) EC.[28] In such cases, the duration of the non-compete obligation is irrelevant under Article 81(1), as long as it does not exceed the duration of the franchise agreement.[29]

If the non-compete obligation falls under Article 81(1) EC, it will be block **7.49.** exempted under the conditions of Article 5 of Regulation 2790/99. In the case of a franchise system that is selective, specific attention must be paid to the conditions of Article 5(c) of Regulation 2790/99. Finally, the conditions which Article 5(b) imposes on post-termination non-compete obligations are also particularly relevant in the context of franchising. Franchising seems to be the obvious distribution formula that qualifies for a post-termination non-compete obligation.

(6) Exclusive purchasing

Given the specific nature of franchising, the possibility is not excluded that an **7.50.** exclusive purchase obligation will escape the prohibition of Article 81(1) EC. The obligation will need to meet the test of an ancillary restraint, which may prove to be difficult.[30]

Whether or not a franchisor is entitled to impose an exclusive purchasing **7.51.** requirement on his franchisees (in the case that it is covered by Article 81(1) EC) depends upon the selective nature of its franchise system:

— If the franchise system takes the form of a selective distribution system, this will not be possible, given that cross-supplies between appointed franchisees must be allowed at all times, in accordance with Article 4(d) of Regulation 2790/99.

— In the absence of a selective distribution system, nothing prevents the supplier from imposing an exclusive purchasing obligation in accordance with

---

[27] Guidelines, para 200.   [28] ibid, para 44.   [29] ibid, para 200.
[30] On ancillary restraints in the context of franchising, see paras 2.159 and 2.160 above. See the treatment of purchase requirements in the previous block exemption (Reg 4087/88), Arts 3(1)(a) and (b), and 4(a).

the rules set out above on exclusive (paragraphs 7.14 and 7.15) or non-exclusive (paragraph 7.24) distribution.

F. Agency

(1) Introduction

7.52. Before addressing the restrictions in the context of agency, it is essential to describe in somewhat greater detail the way in which agency fits into the overall EC competition law framework of vertical agreements. In the past, agency has never been covered by any block exemption and even now not all types of agency agreement are covered by Regulation 2790/99. This is the reason why a more detailed description of the relevant background is called for.

Agency under the Regulation

7.53. Article 1 of Regulation 2790/99, which defines certain essential terms, clarifies in paragraph (g) the meaning of the term 'buyer' as follows: 'buyer' includes an undertaking which, under an agreement falling within Article 81(1) of the Treaty, sells goods or services on behalf of another undertaking'.

7.54. This provision extends the benefit of the block exemption to agency agreements, in so far as they fall within the scope of application of Article 81(1) EC and satisfy all of the conditions for exemption defined in the Regulation. The Regulation contains no other provisions on agency. The reason being that the Regulation treats agency agreements falling within the scope of application of Article 81(1) EC in the same manner as other vertical agreements.[31]

Agency under the Guidelines

7.55. The Guidelines, unlike the Regulation, deal with agency agreements in some detail. Paragraphs 12 to 20 in particular deal extensively with the questions of under what circumstances and to what extent provisions in an agency agreement may be covered by Article 81(1) EC. This section of the Guidelines replaces the Commission Notice of 1962,[32] on exclusive dealing contracts with commercial agents. Before commenting on the analysis made in the Guidelines (paragraphs 7.63–7.83), the case law of the Court of Justice on the application of the EC competition rules to agency agreements will be considered briefly (paragraphs 7.59–7.62). For clarity's sake, it should be borne in mind that the term 'agent' covers any undertaking that negotiates and/or concludes contracts for the sale of

---

[31] Guidelines, para 13, *in fine*.   [32] [1962] OJ 139/2921.

goods or services by the principal, whether or not the agent acts in its own name or in the name of the principal.[33]

Commercial Agency Directive

Paragraph 12 of the Guidelines state that the section in the Guidelines dealing **7.56.** with agency agreements should be read in conjunction with Council Directive (EEC) No 86/653 on the co-ordination of the laws of the Member States relating to self-employed commercial agents.[34] While this is certainly correct, the respective scope of the Guidelines and that of the Commercial Agency Directive should, nevertheless, be clearly distinguished. The Guidelines only deal with the application of Articles 81 and 82 EC to agency agreements, whereas the Commercial Agency Directive harmonizes certain aspects of the contractual relationship between agent and principal.

The fact that a particular agency agreement complies with the Commercial **7.57.** Agency Directive (as implemented in national law) does not mean that it benefits from any safe-harbour treatment under Article 81 and/or Article 82 EC. In particular, the rule contained in Article 20(3) of the Commercial Agency Directive, which states that restraints of trade clauses are valid for not more than two years after contract termination, may not be interpreted as meaning that such clauses necessarily comply with Articles 81 and 82 EC. This should be verified separately for each individual case, in accordance with the Guidelines issued by the Commission and subject to the case law of the Court of Justice.

In addition, it is now clearly established that, whilst under the Guidelines the **7.58.** term 'agent' includes undertakings that act in their own name, but on behalf of a principal (so-called '*commissionnaires*'), the Commercial Agency Directive does not apply to these *commissionnaire* agreements.[35]

(2) Agency agreements in the case law of the Court of Justice

There are relatively few judgments by the Court of Justice on the application of **7.59.** Articles 81 and 82 EC to agency agreements. Moreover, it is not easy to distil clear and simple guidelines from the limited number of judgments that exist on the subject. *Suiker Unie*,[36] one of the first cases in which the Court was confronted with the application of the competition rules to agency agreements, illustrates this particularly well. This case deals, amongst many other matters, with the question of whether a provision in an agency agreement, pursuant to which the agent may not trade in products that compete with the principal's products

---

[33] The term 'agent' as used in the Guidelines therefore includes so-called '*commissionnaires*'.
[34] [1986] OJ L382/17.   [35] Case C–85/03 *Mavrona v Delta* [2004] ECR I–1573.
[36] Joined Cases 40–48, 50, 54–56, 111, 113, and 114/73 *Suiker Unie v EC Commission* [1975] ECR 1663.

without the latter's consent, is compatible with Articles 81 and 82 EC. The Court took the position that provided that the agent is a genuine agent then a prohibition against trading in competing products is not in itself contrary to Article 81 or 82 EC.[37] For both articles, the rationale followed by the Court is similar: agents must carry out the principal's instructions and work for his benefit. Therefore, they may in principle be treated as auxiliary organs forming an integral part of their principal's undertaking and, like a commercial employee, must be considered as forming an economic unit with the undertaking of the principal.[38]

7.60. The reasoning followed by the Court is fairly clear and to a large extent, though not entirely, convincing. Agents do act on behalf of their principal and therefore must follow the latter's instructions in relation to transactions negotiated or concluded on its behalf. For that reason, agents do not appear on the market as independent sources of supply of the relevant products or services. The Court could have stopped its analysis at this stage of the argument: indeed, Article 81 EC should not apply to undertakings that do not act on the relevant market as independent suppliers of products or services. However, the Court takes the argument one step further and opines that an agent—as an auxiliary organ of the principal—must be deemed to form an economic unit with the principal's undertaking (like a commercial employee). In doing so, the Court probably attempted to find support from two previous judgments given in response to references for preliminary rulings. Both in *Consten and Grundig v EC Commission* and in *Italy v EC Commission*, the Court had held in *dicta* that Article 81 EC only applies to agreements between several undertakings and therefore not to a producer who integrates the distribution of his own products within his undertaking, for example by means of commercial representatives.[39] In our view, the final step in the Court's reasoning is unnecessary and has significantly hindered the development of a coherent framework of analysis within which agency agreements should be examined under Articles 81 and 82 EC. The analogy between agents and commercial employees of the principal—which is used to justify the position that a (genuine) agent forms an economic unit with the principal—leads to an unnecessarily narrow definition of agency agreements falling outside the scope of Article 81 EC. This is made clear by the next landmark case on agency in the Court's case law, namely *Vereniging van Vlaamse Reisbureaus*.[40]

7.61. *Vereniging van Vlaamse Reisbureaus* deals with a reference for a preliminary ruling, questioning the legality, under Article 81(1) EC, of a contractual ban

---

[37] *Suiker Unie v EC Commission* [1975] ECR 1663; for Art 81 EC, para 540; and for Art 82 EC, para 481.   [38] *Suiker Unie v EC Commission* [1975] ECR 1663, paras 480 and 539.
[39] Cases 56 and 58/64 *Consten and Grundig v EC Commission* [1966] ECR 340; and Case 32/65 *Italy v EC Commission* [1966] ECR 407.
[40] Case 311/85 *Vereniging van Vlaamse reisbureaus* [1987] ECR 3801.

imposed by a tour operator on a travel agent to share its commission or to grant a rebate to a customer. Before answering this question, the Court first had to rule on the question of whether the agreement between the tour operator and the travel agent could fall within the scope of application of Article 81 EC. The Belgian Government argued that such an agreement was not covered by Article 81(1) EC because the travel agent did not conclude the agreements with its customers in its own name, but did so in the name of and on behalf of the tour operator organizing the trip. Therefore, the agent was to be considered as an auxiliary organ of the tour operator, which meant that Article 81 EC could not apply to the contractual relationship between these two parties.[41] The Court disagreed. It referred to the fact that, on the one hand, the travel agent sold package tours on behalf of a great number of tour operators and that, on the other hand, tour operators sold package tours through a great number of travel agents. For those reasons, the travel agent could not be considered as an auxiliary organ of the tour operator that was integrated in the latter's undertaking.[42] In doing so the Court, in our opinion, erroneously stressed the criterion that the agent should form an economic unit with the principal, instead of focusing on whether (in reality) the agent acts on behalf of the principal, who bears the risks associated with the transactions negotiated or concluded by its agent. Thus, the Court limited the exception to the application of Article 81 EC to the relatively obvious situation of a commercial representative,[43] but appears to overlook the fact that undertakings that are not integrated in the undertaking of their principal also often appear on the market merely to carry out the instructions of a principal, and therefore not as independent sources of supply of the relevant products or services.

The integration criterion has continued to play a role in later case law of the Court of Justice. Consequently, in *VAG Leasing*[44] the Court of Justice held that representatives lose their character as independent traders only if they do not **7.62.**

---

[41] ibid, para 19.

[42] ibid, para 20. In his opinion in *Binon*, Advocate-General Slynn used a similar argument to support the view that AMP was not a genuine agent. AMP had concluded agency agreements with 471 publishers and the Advocate-General failed to see how AMP could form one economic unit with 471 different principals: Case 243/83 *Binon v AMP* [1985] ECR 2015.

[43] In its written observations before the Court, the Commission defended the position that the exception referred to in *Suiker Unie* was limited to situations where the agent acts in the same manner as a commercial representative employed by the principal. While the Commission accepted that the travel agent did not bear any financial risks flowing from the travel contracts and that the tour operator determined the terms and conditions of these contracts, the Commission observed that the travel agent was an independent service provider who acted for several principals, which meant that the contract between the travel agent and the tour operator fell within the scope of application of Art 81 EC (at p 3808). In its Guidelines, the Commission abandoned this view (Guidelines, para 13).

[44] Case C–266/93 *Bundeskartellamt v Volkswagen AG and VAG Leasing GmbH* [1995] ECR I–3477.

bear any of the risks resulting from the contracts negotiated on behalf of the principal and operate as auxiliary organs forming an integral part of the principal's undertaking.[45] The Court therefore maintains the integration criterion, but also mentions a second criterion, namely the absence of risks resulting from the contracts negotiated on behalf of the principal. In other words, the Court uses a double criterion.[46] As will be shown later, the Commission adopts a different position to this in the Guidelines.[47]

(3) Agency agreements under the Guidelines

Introduction

7.63. The provisions on agency agreements in the Guidelines are the result of a long period of reflection. As long ago as 1990, the Commission indicated that, in its view, some of the principles contained in the 1962 Notice were no longer accurate. Over the following years, the Commission prepared various drafts of a new notice on agency agreements and even discussed some of them with representatives of the Member States. However, the Commission never managed to produce a final version of a new notice on the application of Article 81 EC to agency agreements.[48] The Commission's efforts in this area were only finalized within the broader context of the revision of EC competition rules applicable to vertical restraints. As a result, paragraphs 12 to 20 of the Guidelines on Vertical Restraints replace the 1962 Notice on exclusive dealing contracts with commercial agents.

7.64. The Guidelines contain several principles that depart significantly from the case law of the Court of Justice and also, sometimes, from the positions defended by the Commission itself in the past. This section presents, in a systematic manner, the framework of analysis applicable to agency agreements as proposed by the Commission in the Guidelines and will show, where applicable, how this differs from the case law of the Court of Justice.

---

[45] ibid, para 19.

[46] The Court of First Instance also uses a double criterion: Case T–66/99 *Minoan Lines v Commission* [2003] ECR II–5515, paras 126–8, appeal pending, Case C–121/04P and Case T–325/01 *DaimlerChrysler v EC Commission*, judgment of 15 September 2005, not yet published, at paras 87 and 88.

[47] The Commission's insistence in *Mercedes-Benz*, that the Court of Justice does not treat the integration criterion as a separate criterion from the allocation of risks between agent and principal, is difficult to reconcile with the clear language used in *VAG Leasing*. *Mercedes-Benz* [2002] OJ L257/1, para 163. On appeal, the Commission confirmed before the Court of First Instance that, in the Commission's view, the integration criterion is not a separate criterion. Case T–325/01 *DaimlerChrysler v EC Commission*, judgment of 15 September 2005, para 65.

[48] It is also striking to see that the Commission, in its case law preceding the adoption of the Guidelines, did not systematically use a uniform criterion. For example, in *Distribution of railway tickets by travel agents* [1992] OJ L366/47, paras 43–6 it used the same (double) criterion as the Court of Justice. By contrast, in *ARG/Unipart* [1988] OJ L45/34, para 26, absence of risk appears to have been the sole criterion used by the Commission.

The Guidelines start with the proposition that it is necessary to distinguish **7.65**. between genuine and non-genuine agency agreements.[49] This sounds familiar and appears to be in keeping with the classic approach adopted under EC competition law. However, the Guidelines are innovative in two important respects: first, in the definition of the criterion for distinguishing genuine agency agreements from non-genuine agency agreements; and second, with respect to the consequences under Article 81 EC of the finding in any particular case, that the agency agreement at issue is a genuine agency agreement. Both these issues are dealt with separately below.

The distinction between genuine and non-genuine agency agreements

The Commission defines the criterion for distinguishing between genuine and **7.66**. non-genuine agency agreements as follows:

> The determining factor in assessing whether Article 81(1) is applicable is the financial or commercial risk borne by the agent in relation to the activities for which he has been appointed as an agent by the principal. In this respect it is not material for the assessment whether the agent acts for one or more principals.[50]

The Guidelines, therefore, no longer mention the integration criterion, not- **7.67**. withstanding the express reference thereto in the case law of the Court of Justice, notably in *VAG Leasing*.[51] The elimination of the integration criterion also implies, correctly in our opinion, that agents acting on behalf of several prin- cipals can no longer be disqualified as genuine agents solely for that reason. Only the question of whether the agent bears financial or commercial risks in relation to the activities for which it has been appointed as agent is henceforth decisive. And rightly so: when an agent bears no risks in relation to the contracts negotiated or concluded on behalf of the principal, the agent does not act as an independent market participant in relation to the relevant products or services. The agent's market behaviour must therefore be attributed to the principal. For that reason Article 81 EC is not applicable, even if the agent's undertaking is separate from that of the principal.[52]

Since the absence of risk is now the decisive criterion, the question arises as to **7.68**. what types of risks should be taken into consideration in assessing whether a particular agent is genuine or not. First of all, since the Guidelines accept that a genuine agent may be an undertaking separate from the principal, it is clear that general business risks borne by the agent (general investments in business premises, telecommunication and office equipment, personnel, etc) are immaterial to the assessment.[53] Furthermore, the Guidelines repeatedly stress

---

[49] Guidelines, para 13.   [50] ibid.
[51] Case C–266/93 *Bundeskartellamt v Volkswagen AG and VAG Leasing GmbH* [1995] ECR I–3477, para 19.   [52] Guidelines, para 15.
[53] ibid.

that the determining factor is the (absence of) financial or commercial risk borne by the agent in relation to the activities for which it was appointed as an agent by the principal. It follows therefore that specific risks, borne by the agent in relation to activities other than those for which it was appointed as agent, should likewise be immaterial to the assessment.[54]

7.69. The risks to be considered are, according to the Guidelines, twofold. First, there are those risks that are directly related to the activities undertaken pursuant to the agency agreement. This means at the very least that for genuine agency agreements for the supply or purchase of goods, property in the contract goods should not vest in the agent.[55] For agency contracts for the supply of services, genuine agents should not supply the contract services themselves.[56] A second category of risks to be considered are risks related to market-specific investments, that is, investments made by an agent in order to carry out the type of activities for which it was appointed as agent, and which can no longer be used by the agent when leaving that field of activity. If the agent bears such risks, it will not be considered a genuine agent and will be treated as an independent reseller.[57]

7.70. While stressing that each case should be tested on its individual merits, and that economic reality takes precedence over legal form, the Guidelines illustrate these principles as follows.[58]

Costs of supply (or purchase), including transportation

7.71. The Guidelines state that agents, in order to be considered as genuine agents, may not contribute to the costs of supply or of purchase of the contract goods, including transportation costs. This does not preclude the agent from carrying out the transport service, provided that the principal covers the costs involved. In *Mercedes-Benz*, the fact that the Mercedes-Benz agents had to bear the transport costs and risks in respect of new vehicles was one element, *inter alia*, upon which the Commission relied to hold that Article 81 EC was applicable to the restrictions agreed between Mercedes-Benz and its agents.[59]

---

[54] This position conflicts with the stance taken by the Court of Justice in *VAG Leasing*. In that case, the Court of Justice decided that the German VAG dealers carried on their main business of sales and after-sales service in their own name and for their own account. This was one reason, *inter alia*, why the VAG dealers had to be considered as independent traders, rather than as agents of VAG Leasing (Case C–266/93 *Bundeskartellamt v Volkswagen AG and VAG Leasing Gmbh* [1995] ECR I–3477, para 19).

[55] Guidelines, para 16. The Guidelines limit themselves to transfer of title, but it appears self-evident that a similar comment applies to transfer of risk.   [56] ibid.

[57] ibid, para 15.   [58] ibid, para 16.

[59] *Mercedes-Benz* [2002] OJ L257/1, para 157. On appeal, the Court of First Instance ruled on factual grounds that the Commission had exaggerated the transport risks borne by the Mercedes-Benz agents. Case T–325/01 *DaimlerChrysler v EC Commission*, judgment of 15 September 2005, paras 104 to 106.

Sales promotion

In order to be considered as genuine agents, agents may not directly or indir- **7.72**.
ectly be obliged to invest in sales promotions of the contract products, for
example by having to contribute to the advertising budget of the principal[60] or
by having to acquire demonstration vehicles on their own account and at their
own risk.[61] However, in our opinion, a general obligation on the agent to use
his best efforts to promote the sale of the contract goods or services should not
prevent the agent from qualifying as a genuine agent.[62]

Stocks

If an agent maintains stocks of the contract goods at his own cost or risk, **7.73**.
including the cost of financing the stocks and the cost of loss of stocks, he will
not be considered as a genuine agent.[63] The Guidelines state that a genuine
agent must have the possibility to return unsold stocks to the principal without
charge and that the risk of loss of the stocks should be borne by the principal.
This is without prejudice to the agent's liability if stocks are lost or damaged due
to the agent's fault. It is therefore possible under the Guidelines to have a
situation where the genuine agent carries a consignment stock of contract goods,
provided that title and risk remain with the principal and that the principal also
bears all costs of financing or maintaining the stocks.

Service

The Guidelines state that a genuine agent may not provide after-sales service, **7.74**.
repair service, or warranty service, without being fully reimbursed by the
principal. In *Mercedes-Benz*, the Commission pointed out that agents still bear a
risk in relation to warranty work if they are reimbursed on the basis of standard
rates determined by the manufacturer, which do not necessarily correspond to
the costs effectively incurred by the agent.[64] This type of risk was one of the
elements which led the Commission to hold that the *Mercedes-Benz* agents were
not genuine agents.[65]

---

[60] Guidelines, para 16.   [61] *Mercedes-Benz* [2002] OJ L257/1, para 158.
[62] In this respect, the European Parliament stated that 'attention should be paid to the actual
current economic situation, which is that an agent, in order to implement the agreement
properly, does have to bear a certain financial or economic risk, such as a contribution to publicity
costs; [. . .] paragraph 17 of the Guidelines should at least stipulate that a small contribution to
publicity costs, by an agent, should have no bearing on the fact that the agreement lies outside the
scope of Article 81(1)', Minutes of 3 May 2000, A5–0077/2000.
[63] In *DaimlerChrysler v. Commission*, the Court of First Instance stresses that absence of risk in
relation to stockholding of vehicles is a crucial criterion to determine whether an agent is genuine
or must be assimilated to an independent trader. Case T–325/01 *DaimlerChrysler v EC Commission*, judgment of 15 September 2005, paras 96 to 99.
[64] *Mercedes-Benz* [2002] OJ L257/1, para 159(a).
[65] On appeal, the Court of Justice disagreed with the Commission on factual grounds and
held that the Commission had failed to show that the provision of warranty services by the

Investments

7.75. Investments made by the agent in its undertaking which enable it to carry out its sales activities as an agent in general are immaterial to the assessment of whether the agent is genuine or not. The Guidelines clarify, however, that when an agent makes market-specific investments it can no longer be considered as a genuine agent. Market-specific investments are investments in equipment, premises, or training of personnel that are specific to the type of activities for which the agent is appointed by its principal and which cannot be used for other activities. Investments in petrol storage tanks in the case of petrol retailing and specific software to sell insurance policies in the case of insurance agents are examples of market-specific investments given in the Guidelines.[66]

Product liability

7.76. According to the Guidelines, it is not possible for a genuine agent to accept liability towards third parties for damage caused by the products sold. This is without prejudice to the possibility of holding the (genuine) agent liable for its own fault (eg in relation to damage caused by erroneous product information supplied by the agent to the principal's customer).

Liability for non-performance by the customer

7.77. Genuine agents may not accept liability for a customer's non-performance of the contract. This does not prevent clauses pursuant to which the agent's right to commission is extinguished in the event of non-performance by the customer.[67] Likewise, the principal may claim damages from the (genuine) agent if the latter is at fault (eg a failure by the agent to communicate information on the customer's financial reliability to the principal).

7.78. Even when an agent acts on behalf of a principal and follows the latter's instructions, the Guidelines will treat the agent as a non-genuine agent if it bears one or more of the above risks. As a result, Article 81 EC may apply to the agency agreement in the same manner as to any other vertical agreement.[68]

7.79. To summarize, by no longer using the integration criterion, the Guidelines allow greater scope for agency agreements to be considered as genuine agency agreements. At the same time, the Guidelines adopt a very strict approach to the requirement that genuine agents may not bear risks that are directly related to

---

Mercedes-Benz agents entailed 'exceptional risks'. Case T–325/01 *DaimlerChrysler v EC Commission*, judgment of 15 September 2005, para 111.

[66] Or investments in special equipment necessary to carry out customer and guarantee service: *Mercedes-Benz* [2002] OJ L257/1, para 159(b).

[67] The extinction of the agent's right to commission is governed by Council Directive (EEC) No 86/653 on the co-ordination of the laws of the Member States relating to self-employed commercial agents [1986] OJ L382/17, Art 11.   [68] Guidelines, para 17.

the activities for which the agent has been appointed by the principal. In *Mercedes-Benz*, the Commission confirmed the strict approach defended in the Guidelines. While the Commission's efforts to distinguish genuine agents from non-genuine agents on the basis of economic criteria should be approved, it would appear that the Commission's position on the degree of risk that genuine agents may bear is, in some respects, overly strict. The Court of First Instance's approach in *DaimlerChrysler v EC Commission*, where the Court uses as criterion that the agent must bear 'substantial economic risks' in order to be considered as a non-genuine agent, must therefore be approved.[69]

Consequences of the distinction between genuine and non-genuine agency agreements

Under a classic competition analysis, genuine agency agreements fall outside the scope of application of Article 81 EC.[70] Without any further explanation, the Guidelines qualify this principle significantly. Henceforth, the Commission's position on the subject is as follows: **7.80**.

> If an agency agreement does not fall within the scope of application of Article 81(1), then all obligations imposed on the agent in relation to the contracts concluded and/or negotiated on behalf of the principal fall outside Article 81(1).[71]

It follows that the Guidelines limit the non-applicability of Article 81(1) EC only to certain clauses in the (genuine) agency agreement, namely those clauses that relate to the contracts which the agent concludes or negotiates on behalf of the principal. The Guidelines clarify that this wording refers to two categories of clauses in (genuine) agency agreements. First, clauses which define the terms and conditions of sale or purchase (including price) of the contracts that the agent concludes or negotiates on behalf of the principal. Second, clauses that fix the scope of activity of the agent in relation to the goods or services covered by the agency agreement; in other words, clauses that limit the territory in which, or the customers to whom, the agent may sell the contract goods or services.[72] For both categories of clause, the Guidelines accept that if the principal is to bear the risk flowing from the contracts concluded or negotiated by the agent on behalf of the principal, it is essential that the latter is able to determine the commercial strategy. For that reason, such clauses, provided that they are contained in a genuine agency agreement, do not fall within the scope of Article 81(1) EC. **7.81**.

Other clauses in a (genuine) agency agreement may still be covered by Article 81(1) EC. Specifically, the Guidelines identify two types of clause that must be **7.82**.

---

[69] Case T–325/01 *DaimlerChrysler v EC Commission*, judgment of 15 September 2005, paras 111 and 112.

[70] Commission Notice on exclusive dealing contracts with commercial agents [1962] OJ 139/2921. [71] Guidelines, para 18.

[72] ibid.

evaluated in light of the provisions of Article 81(1) EC, even if they form part of genuine agency agreements. In this respect, the Guidelines refer to 'provisions which concern the relationship between the agent and the principal'.[73] The language used here is somewhat unfortunate, since it does not describe in a sufficiently precise manner the types of provision that the Commission has in mind. Clauses dealing with the calculation and the payment of commission also concern the relationship between the agent and the principal, but these are obviously not what the Guidelines have in mind. Rather, the Guidelines refer to provisions that prevent the principal from appointing other agents in respect of a given type of transaction, customer or territory (ie exclusive agency provisions) and provisions that prevent the agent from acting as an agent or distributor for undertakings which compete with the principal (non-compete provisions).

7.83. Bearing in mind these specificities of the treatment of agency agreements in EC competition law, each of the restrictions of competition which have so far been discussed in respect of the other frequently used distribution formulas are discussed hereafter, except one; namely exclusive purchasing requirements. Given that the (genuine) agent, in exercising its function, does not purchase the relevant contract goods,[74] questions as to the exclusive nature of the co-operation between the principal and the agent are addressed solely in the section on non-compete obligations. Instead, attention is now given to the EC competition law treatment of clauses in agency agreements defining the price and other terms and conditions of sale of the contract goods. The position in respect of this issue differs from that which is applicable to the other distribution formulas discussed above. For the sake of completeness, it may be added that the Guidelines warn against the potential horizontal effects of agency agreements.[75]

(4) Clauses defining the price and other conditions of sale

7.84. Clauses that relate to the contracts which the agent concludes or negotiates on behalf of the principal are, in the first place, clauses defining the price and other terms and conditions of sale (or purchase) at which the agent must sell (or purchase) the contract goods on behalf of the principal. That these clauses must

---

[73] Guidelines, para 19.   [74] Para 7.69 above.

[75] The Guidelines, para 20, point out that agency agreements may fall foul of Art 81(1) EC, even if the agent is a genuine agent, when they facilitate collusion. The examples discussed in the Guidelines all deal with collusion between principals and must therefore be regarded as examples of horizontal conduct that, strictly speaking, fall outside the scope of the Guidelines. A first example mentioned in the Guidelines is a case where a number of principals use the same agents, while collectively excluding others from using these agents. This is, in other words, a collective boycott. Reg 2790/99, Art 5(c) deals with a similar set of facts, but focuses on selective distribution (para 6.30 above). The second example referred to in the Guidelines is one where principals use their agents to collude on marketing strategy or to exchange sensitive market information. This is once again an example that has nothing to do with the vertical effects on competition caused by agency agreements.

be deemed as falling outside the scope of application of Article 81(1) EC is not at all surprising. Since the agent acts on behalf of the principal, who bears the risks attached to the contracts concluded or negotiated by the agent, the agent must follow the instructions of the principal as regards price, rebates, payment terms, conditions of delivery, customer guarantees, etc. In this respect, the agent's conduct on the market is not independent, but should rather be attributed to the principal. Therefore, Article 81(1) EC does not apply.

In our opinion, this does not mean that a principal would act in breach of **7.85**. Article 81(1) EC if it were to impose the sales price and other terms and conditions of sale upon a non-genuine agent. As long as the agent, genuine or non-genuine, truly acts on behalf of the principal (ie negotiates and/or concludes sale or purchase contracts on behalf of the principal), the latter must have the right to determine the price and other commercial terms and conditions of the contract concluded with the customer, since it is the principal that will be bound by that contract.

As regards the sales price, it must be added that a non-genuine agent, even **7.86**. though it remains bound by the instructions given by the principal in this respect, must have the right to share its commission with the customer. If the non-genuine agent makes use of this right, the principal's income remains undiminished (the principal receives the full sales price), but the price effectively paid by the customer, after taking into account the benefit of the shared commission, is lower than the sales price imposed by the principal.[76] In this respect, the Guidelines concur with the case law of the Court of Justice in *Vereniging van Vlaamse Reisbureaus*.[77]

Finally, if the non-genuine agent acts on its own behalf—and is therefore in fact **7.87**. a reseller—the principal does not have the right to impose the sales price or other terms and conditions of sale. Doing so would amount to vertical price fixing, which is a hardcore infringement.

(5) *Territorial protection*

Territorial protection against the principal

Whilst this is not expressly stated in the Guidelines, it must be assumed that **7.88**. an obligation for the principal not to make direct sales in the territory allocated to the (genuine) agent is not restrictive of competition within the

---

[76] Guidelines, para 48. The possibility for the (non-genuine) agent to share its commission with the customers of the principal or to grant rebates to them leaves room for price competition between agents acting on behalf of the same principal; *Eirpage* [1991] OJ L306/22, para 6; *Repsol CPP SA* [2004] OJ C258/7, paras 18–20. [77] Para 7.61 above.

meaning of Article 81(1) EC. The same solution applies to contract provisions with a similar effect; for example, clauses pursuant to which the principal may not make active direct sales in the agent's territory, or clauses under which the principal may make such sales, but must pay a commission to the agent, even though the latter has not intervened in the sale. Given that there is no inter-brand competition between the principal and his agents, such obligations cannot, in general, be taken to limit competition in the sense of Article 81(1) EC.

7.89. Even if territorial protection granted against the principal were to restrict competition, it can benefit from the block exemption contained in Regulation 2790/99 if the conditions for exemption are all met.

Territorial protection against the principal's other agents

7.90. As stated above (paragraph 7.83), a first category of clauses in agency agreements which, according to the Guidelines (paragraph 19), may come within the scope of Article 81(1) EC, even if the agent is a genuine agent, is a clause that prevents the principal from appointing other agents in respect of a given type of transaction, territory, or customer group (exclusive agency provisions). Notwithstanding this, the Commission is of the opinion that exclusive agency provisions will not, in general, result in anti-competitive effects, since they concern only intra-brand competition. Furthermore, if such exclusivity provisions are covered by the prohibition contained in Article 81(1) EC, they can benefit from the block exemption. In such a situation, since the agent will then be assimilated to a reseller,[78] the degree of protection that the exclusive agent may enjoy will be largely influenced by the territorial restrictions imposed on the other agents appointed by the principal (eg the exclusive agents appointed in other territories).[79]

(6) *Territorial restrictions*

7.91. In respect of territorial restrictions, as with most restrictions contained in agency agreements, it is essential to make a distinction between genuine and non-genuine agencies.

7.92. The Guidelines (paragraph 18) exclude from the scope of application of Article 81(1) EC not only the principal's instructions regarding the sales price and other terms and conditions of sale (paragraphs 7.82 and 7.85 above), but also the contractual provisions that fix the permitted scope of activity of the genuine agent in relation to the contract goods or services. In this respect, they state that the ability of the principal to fix the scope of activity of the genuine agent is essential since it is the principal who bears the risks attached to the contracts

---

[78] Guidelines, para 15.   [79] Paras 5.62 *et seq* above.

concluded or negotiated by the agent and must therefore be able to determine the commercial strategy to be followed by the agent. On this basis, the Guidelines accept that a principal, without infringing Article 81(1) EC, may impose territorial limitations on the right of his genuine agent to sell contract products or services. In our opinion, the right of the principal to impose such limitations may even take the form of an absolute prohibition to sell contract products or services on behalf of the principal within a certain territory.[80]

That being said, the parties would be well-advised to take into consideration the risk that their agency agreement—perhaps contrary to their expectations—could be regarded as a non-genuine agency agreement. Indeed, in such cases, absolute territorial limitations will be regarded as hardcore restrictions, with all of the resulting negative consequences.[81] In fact, the regime applicable to territorial restrictions will, in that case, be no different from that of the corresponding distribution formula (ie exclusive distribution, non-exclusive distribution, or selective distribution). Reference can be made to the discussion of territorial restrictions in respect of these formulas. **7.93**.

(7) Customer restrictions

The Guidelines (paragraph 18) put customer restrictions on the same footing as territorial restrictions. Accordingly, what was said in the previous paragraph on territorial restrictions applies to customer restrictions as well. Without infringing Article 81(1) EC, the principal may impose limitations on the customers to whom the genuine agent may or may not sell the contract products or services. In our opinion, the right of the principal to impose such limitations may take the form of an absolute prohibition to sell contract products or services on behalf of the principal to certain customers. Also in this respect, the caveat applies that the parties must take into consideration the risk that their agency agreement may be regarded as a non-genuine agency agreement. In the case of non-genuine agencies, the block exemption regime applicable to the corresponding distribution formula can be relied upon. **7.94**.

(8) Non-compete obligation

The second category of provisions which concern the relationship between the agent and the principal and which, according to the Guidelines (paragraph 19), must be tested under Article 81(1) EC, even if the agent is a genuine agent, are non-compete provisions; that is, provisions that prevent the agent from acting as an agent or distributor for undertakings which compete with the principal. **7.95**.

---

[80] This point of view is confirmed by the Court of First Instance in Case T–325/01 *DaimlerChrysler v EC Commission*, judgment of 15 September 2005, not yet published, para 122.
[81] These consequences are discussed in Ch 5 above.

7.96. Non-compete provisions, including post-term non-compete provisions, concern inter-brand competition and may infringe Article 81(1) EC if they lead to foreclosure on the relevant market where the contract products or services are sold or purchased.[82] The question of whether non-compete provisions will in fact lead to market foreclosure must be resolved in each individual case in accordance with the criteria developed by the Court of Justice in *Delimitis*.[83]

7.97. If a particular non-compete provision is found to lead to or to contribute significantly to market foreclosure, and therefore infringes Article 81(1) EC, it may still qualify for an automatic exemption pursuant to Article 5 of the Regulation, provided that the conditions for exemption listed within that article are met. By assessing non-compete provisions in genuine agency agreements under Article 81(1) EC, the Guidelines arguably depart from the case law of the Court of Justice in *Suiker Unie*.[84]

---

[82] Guidelines, para 19. The Commission examined this question in some detail in *Repsol CPP SA* [2004] OJ C258/7, para 17: a case dealing with the distribution of fuel for motor vehicles through service stations in Spain. In that case, the Commission adopted the position that the question of whether the operators of Repsol's service stations were genuine agents was irrelevant as far as the non-compete clauses were concerned, owing to their effects on inter-brand competition: [2004] OJ C258/7, para 17.   [83] Paras 6.35 *et seq* above.

[84] Para 7.59 above.

8

SUBCONTRACTING AGREEMENTS

A. Introduction

Subcontracting agreements are agreements in which a firm (the contractor) **8.01**. entrusts to another firm (the subcontractor) the manufacture of certain goods or the supply of certain services. In the context of this type of agreement, a contractor often puts technology (IPRs or know-how) or equipment ('tooling') at the disposal of its subcontractor. In return for this, it frequently does not want the subcontractor to use the technology or tooling for any other purposes than the implementation of the agreement. In other words, it does not want the subcontractor to enter the market independently with the products or services manufactured by using the contractor's technology or tooling. Therefore, it frequently wishes to impose an exclusive supply-back obligation on its subcontractors.

Guidance on the competition law assessment of this type of production **8.02**. agreement can be found in the Commission's Notice of 18 December 1978 concerning the assessment of certain subcontracting agreements in relation to Article 85(1) of the EEC Treaty ('the Subcontracting Notice').[1] In the Subcontracting Notice, which continues to apply to the present day, the Commission sets out which restrictions imposed on subcontractors do not infringe Article 81(1) EC.

Since the Subcontracting Notice, however, various other legal instruments have **8.03**. also come to have a bearing on subcontracting agreements. Whether or not a given subcontracting relationship comes within the scope of Article 81(1) EC and, if so, whether or not the restrictions which they contain qualify for the application of Article 81(3) EC, is therefore no longer a matter of a mere check on whether the conditions of the Subcontracting Notice are fulfilled, but instead requires a more complex legal analysis.

---

[1] [1979] OJ C1/2.

8.04. It goes without saying that a correct EC competition law analysis of many subcontracting relationships will require a relatively complex economic assessment.[2] The purpose of this Chapter is not to provide such a fully-fledged assessment, but to present in a systematic way, the legal parameters which demarcate the EC competition law analysis of the different categories of subcontracting agreements. It incorporates informal views obtained from DG COMP on a number of issues which are not expressly dealt with in the applicable legal instruments. It is only in a second stage, once it has been established where a given subcontracting relationship fits within the legal framework, that a more detailed economic analysis may be warranted. In this respect, this Chapter provides some key guidelines. Throughout the Chapter, the emphasis lies on the question which most concerns the marketplace, namely the enforceability of exclusive supply-back obligations and the corresponding impossibility for subcontractors to enter the market independently with the contract products or to make them available to third parties.

B. Legal Framework

8.05. The Commission's overall line of thinking on subcontracting is summarized in the Horizontal Guidelines.[3] These guidelines distinguish between three categories of production agreements, one of which being subcontracting.[4] Specifically on subcontracting, the Guidelines (paragraph 80) read as follows:

> Subcontracting agreements are vertical agreements. They are therefore, to the extent that they contain restrictions of competition, covered by the Block Exemption Regulation [ie Regulation 2790/99] and the Guidelines on Vertical Restraints. There are however two exceptions to this rule: Subcontracting agreements between competitors, and subcontracting agreements between non-competitors involving the transfer of know-how to the subcontractor.

8.06. The Horizontal Guidelines add two footnotes to this:

— First, as regards subcontracting agreements between competitors, reference is made to Article 2(4) of Regulation 2790/99, which includes certain vertical agreements between competing undertakings in the scope of Regulation 2790/99.

— Second, as regards subcontracting agreements between non-competitors involving the transfer of IPRs or know-how to the subcontractor, reference

---

[2] T Pick, 'Sub-contracting Agreements under E.U. Competition Law—Applicability of Article 81 E.C.' [2002] ECLR 154, 154–5.

[3] Commission Notice—Guidelines on the applicability of Article 81 of the EC Treaty to horizontal cooperation agreements [2001] OJ C3/2 (hereafter 'Horizontal Guidelines').

[4] The other categories are joint production agreements and (unilateral or reciprocal) specialization agreements: Horizontal Guidelines, para 79.

is made to Article 2(3) of Regulation 2790/99 and to the Guidelines, so as to remind the reader that subcontracting arrangements between non-competitors under which the contractor only provides specifications which describe the goods or services to be supplied by the subcontractor (hence, no IPRs or know-how) may fall within the scope of application of Regulation 2790/99.

The Horizontal Guidelines (paragraph 81) continue as follows: **8.07**.

> Subcontracting agreements between competitors are covered by these guidelines. Guidance for the assessment of subcontracting agreements between non-competitors involving the transfer of know-how to the subcontractor is given in a separate Notice.

Two footnotes are added to this paragraph as well: **8.08**.

— First, as regards subcontracting agreements between competitors, the Horizontal Guidelines mention:

> If a subcontracting agreement between competitors stipulates that the contractor will cease production of the product to which the agreement relates, the agreement constitutes a unilateral specialisation agreement which is covered, subject to certain conditions, by the Specialisation Block Exemption Regulation.[5]

— Second, there is a reference to the Subcontracting Notice inasmuch as the assessment of subcontracting agreements between non-competitors involving the transfer of know-how is concerned.

In summary, the Horizontal Guidelines identify five legal instruments relevant **8.09**. to the EC competition law assessment of subcontracting agreements: Regulation 2790/99,[6] Regulation 2658/2000[7] (specialization agreements), the Subcontracting Notice, the (Vertical) Guidelines[8] as well as the Horizontal Guidelines.

The Horizontal Guidelines do not refer to the technology transfer block **8.10**. exemption regulation (the 'TTBER' or Regulation 772/2004)[9] as a sixth

---

[5] Commission Regulation (EC) No 2658/2000 of 29 November 2000 on the application of Article 81(3) of the Treaty to categories of specialisation agreements [2000] OJ L304/3.

[6] Commission Regulation (EC) No 2790/1999 of 22 December 1999 on the application of Article 81(3) of the Treaty to categories of vertical agreements and concerted practices [1999] OJ L336/21.

[7] Commission Regulation (EC) No 2658/2000 of 29 November 2000 on the application of Article 81(3) of the Treaty to categories of specialisation agreements [2000] OJ L304/3.

[8] Commission Notice—Guidelines on Vertical Restraints [2000] OJ C291/1 (hereafter 'Guidelines').

[9] Commission Regulation (EC) No 772/2004 on the application of Article 81(3) of the Treaty to categories of technology transfer agreements [2004] OJ L123/11.

candidate for the analysis of subcontracting agreements. To this end, one must consult the TTBER Guidelines[10] (paragraph 44), which read:

> The TTBER covers 'subcontracting' whereby the licensor licenses technology to the licensee who undertakes to produce certain products on the basis thereof exclusively for the licensor. Subcontracting may also involve the supply of equipment by the licensor to be used in the production of goods and services covered by the agreement. For the latter type of subcontracting to be covered by the TTBER, the licensed technology and not the supplied equipment must constitute the primary object of the agreement. Subcontracting is also covered by the Commission's Notice concerning the assessment of certain subcontracting agreements in relation to Article 81(1) of the Treaty. According to this notice, which remains applicable, subcontracting agreements whereby the subcontractor undertakes to produce certain products exclusively for the contractor generally fall outside Article 81(1). However, other restrictions imposed on the subcontractor such as the obligation not to conduct or exploit his own research and development may be caught by Article 81.

8.11. It follows from the above that there are essentially three factors in identifying the appropriate legal framework for the assessment of a given subcontracting relationship:

— the agreement is between competitors or between non-competitors;
— the contractor ceases the production of the products to which the sub-contracting agreement relates or not; and
— the agreement involves the transfer of IPR, know-how, or tooling or not.

Beginning with the overall distinction between subcontracting between competitors and subcontracting between non-competitors, the applicability of each of the legal instruments is discussed below.

C. Subcontracting Between Competitors

(1) Methodology: six questions

8.12. The EC competition law analysis of subcontracting between competitors can be completed by means of the following checklist of questions:

1. Does the subcontracting agreement come within the scope of Article 81(1) EC (paragraph 8.13)?
2. If so, does the subcontracting agreement appreciably restrict competition in the sense of Article 81(1) EC (paragraphs 8.14–8.15)?
3. If so, is the subcontracting agreement a technology transfer agreement covered by the TTBER (paragraphs 8.16–8.19)?

---

[10] Commission Notice—Guidelines on the application of Article 81 of the EC Treaty to technology transfer agreements [2004] OJ C101/02.

4. If not, is the subcontracting agreement a unilateral specialization agreement covered by Regulation 2658/2000 (paragraphs 8.20–8.21)?
5. If not, is the subcontracting agreement covered by Regulation 1400/2002 or by Regulation 2790/99 (paragraphs 8.22–8.24)?
6. Finally, are the restrictions of competition which the agreement contains enforceable according to the Horizontal Guidelines (paragraphs 8.25–8.31)?

(2) First question: does the subcontracting agreement come within the scope of Article 81(1) EC?

The answer to the first question will be positive and the subcontracting **8.13.** agreement will be within the scope of Article 81(1) EC if it is an agreement in the sense of Article 81(1) EC and it appreciably affects inter-State trade. Both requirements have been discussed above, respectively at paragraphs 2.66–2.85 for the concept 'agreement' (which should pose little, if any, problems as an agreement will typically be available) and at paragraphs 2.27–2.60 for the concept of the appreciable effect on inter-State trade.

(3) Second question: does the subcontracting agreement appreciably restrict competition in the sense of Article 81(1) EC?

Subcontracting agreements between competitors do not necessarily come within **8.14.** the scope of application of Article 81(1) EC. According to the Horizontal Guidelines (paragraph 89), subcontracting agreements between competitors do not fall under Article 81(1) EC if they are limited to individual sales and purchases on the merchant market without any further obligations and without forming part of a wider commercial relationship between the parties. Notwithstanding this, such an agreement can fall under Article 81(1) EC (eg on account of restrictions on passive sales, resale price maintenance).

There are other circumstances in which subcontracting between competitors **8.15.** may be outside the scope of Article 81(1) EC. Reference can be made, for example, to the *De Minimis* Notice.[11] Subcontracting agreements between competitors will not be covered by the prohibition of Article 81(1) EC if they comply with the *De Minimis* Notice. To this end, attention must be given in particular to the parties' market share and to the absence of certain hardcore restrictions. As discussed above (paragraphs 2.125–2.136), the *De Minimis*

---

[11] Commission Notice on agreements of minor importance which do not appreciably restrict competition under Article 81(1) of the Treaty establishing the European Community [2001] OJ C368/13 ('*De Minimis* Notice').

Notice does not apply to certain hardcore restrictions. It is relevant for sub-contracting agreements that it does not apply to the restriction agreed between a supplier of components (subcontractor) and a buyer (contractor) who incorporates those components into its final products, if that restriction prohibits the supplier/subcontractor from selling the components as spare parts to end-users, independent repairers, or other service providers (point 11(2)(e)).[12] To the extent that a subcontracting agreement contains this type of exclusive supply-back obligation, the *De Minimis* Notice will in any event not apply and the third question will have to be addressed. In the absence of this or any other hardcore restriction, the subcontracting agreement may be covered by the *De Minimis* Notice if the aggregate market share held by the competitors does not exceed 10% on any of the relevant markets affected by the agreement (point 7(a)). In the case of subcontracting agreements, the relevant market may be both the market for the intermediate products (ie the contract products) and the market for the final products.

(4) Third question: is the subcontracting agreement a technology transfer agreement covered by the TTBER?

8.16. If the subcontracting agreement is a technology transfer agreement[13] in the sense of the TTBER (ie permitting the production of contract products) the agreement may enjoy the safe harbour under the TTBER provided that it complies with certain conditions. These conditions are essentially that:

— the agreement must not have a hardcore restriction as stated in Article 4(1) of the TTBER as its object; and
— the combined market share of the two competitors must not exceed 20% on the affected relevant technology and product market (Article 3(1) TTBER). Guidance on the concept of 'technology market' can be found in the TTBER Guidelines (paragraph 22). The concept of 'product market' has been discussed in paragraphs 2.220–2.222 above. Guidance on the market share calculation can also be found in the TTBER Guidelines (paragraphs 23 and 77 *et seq*).

8.17. If a subcontracting agreement is a technology transfer agreement which is in line with the conditions of the TTBER, informal guidance from DG COMP has taught us that the contractor (licensor) is entitled to impose an exclusive supply-back obligation on its subcontractor (licensee). In DG COMP's view, Article 4(1)(c) of the TTBER, which, with limited exceptions, classifies customer and territorial restrictions as hardcore restrictions, does not apply to

---

[12] Compare with Art 4(e) of Reg 2790/99: see paras 8.24 and 8.51–8.53 below.
[13] On this concept, see TTBER, Art 1 (1)(b) as discussed in paras 2.197 *et seq* above.

an exclusive supply-back obligation in the context of a subcontracting agreement. The reason is that Article 4(1)(c) is deemed only to cover restrictions on the supply to third parties and that a contractor (licensor) should not be considered a 'customer' for the purposes of Article 4(1)(c) when he sub-contracts the production of a certain component. Accordingly, an exclusive supply-back obligation in a subcontracting agreement is deemed not to constitute a 'customer' restriction and hence is also deemed not to raise the risks that Article 4(1)(c) seeks to address, even if the obligation is between competitors.

We take note of this position. It implies that an exclusive supply-back obliga-   **8.18**. tion between a competing contractor and subcontractor is not a hardcore restriction under the TTBER, and that it will have to be checked on a case-by-case basis whether or not the obligation restricts competition in the sense of Article 81(1) EC. If so, it must be assessed whether the supply-back obligation, as well as the other restrictions of competition which the subcontracting agreement contains, qualify for exemption under Article 81(3) EC. For agreements between competitors, that assessment will be performed on the basis of the TTBER Guidelines (in particular Part IV thereof)[14] and also on the basis of the Horizontal Guidelines.[15] The guidelines on subcontracting which are contained in the latter are discussed in paragraphs 8.25 *et seq* below.

Theoretically speaking, the situation may arise where an exclusive supply-back   **8.19**. obligation itself may comply with the conditions of Article 81(3) EC, but is nevertheless unenforceable because the subcontracting agreement of which it forms a part contains one or several hardcore restrictions, which render all restrictions of competition of the subcontracting agreement unenforceable. Bearing this in mind, it may be relevant to refine DG COMP's view with respect to subcontracting agreements between competing undertakings who are not independent suppliers in the market for the contract products. If they are not, it would appear that the exclusive supply-back obligation may be covered by the Subcontracting Notice and therefore be outside the scope of Article 81(1) EC.[16] In accordance with the wording of the TTBER Guidelines, the TTBER would then only apply to the other restrictions of competition in the

---

[14] Part IV of the TTBER Guidelines deals with the application of Art 81(1) and (3) outside the scope of the TTBER.

[15] Horizontal Guidelines, para 11: 'to the extent that vertical agreements . . . are concluded between competitors, the effects of the agreement on the market and the possible competition problems can be similar to horizontal agreements. Therefore, these agreements have to be assessed according to the principles described in the present guidelines.'

[16] PM Roth (ed), *Bellamy & Child. European Community Law of Competition* (5th edn, Sweet & Maxwell, 2001) para 7–186 also understands the Commission's statement in the Horizontal Guidelines as that the Subcontracting Notice does not apply to agreements between competitors in this way.

subcontracting agreement.[17] If those other restrictions would not qualify for block exemption (eg because the agreement contains one or several hardcore restrictions) the exclusive supply-back obligation would not be endangered, given that it is outside the scope of Article 81(1) EC.

(5) Fourth question: is the subcontracting agreement a unilateral specialization agreement covered by Regulation 2658/2000?

8.20. If a subcontracting agreement concluded between competitors is not covered by the TTBER, it may constitute a unilateral specialization agreement, provided that the contractor will cease[18] the production of the product to which the agreement relates. If so, it may be covered by Regulation 2658/2000 (ie the block exemption regulation on specialization agreements) if it complies with certain conditions. These conditions are essentially that:

— the agreement must not have any of the hardcore restrictions as stated in Article 5 of Regulation 2658/2000 as its object: the hardcore restrictions concern price fixing, output limitation, or market or customer allocation; and

— the combined market share of the parties on the relevant market must not exceed 20%. The market share of the parties is calculated in accordance with Article 6 of Regulation 2658/2000.

8.21. If a subcontracting agreement is a unilateral specialization agreement which is covered by, and complies with the conditions of, Regulation 2658/2000, the contractor is entitled to impose an exclusive supply-back obligation on its subcontractor. Article 3(1) of Regulation 2658/2000 indeed provides that the block exemption shall apply where '(a) the parties accept an exclusive purchase and/or exclusive supply obligation in the context of a unilateral . . . specialisation agreement . . .' Article 2(8) of Regulation 2658/2000 defines an 'exclusive supply obligation' as 'an obligation not to supply a competing undertaking other than a party to the agreement with the product to which the specialisation agreement relates'. According to Art 2(9), an 'exclusive purchase obligation' is 'an obligation to purchase the product to which the specialisation agreement relates only from the party which agrees to supply it'. Both are covered by the block exemption. In addition, it should be noted that the contractor may impose such an exclusive purchase or supply obligation irrespective of whether it supplies the subcontractor with IPRs, know-how, or tooling. This is logical. Although one of the parties will cease the production of the contract products,

---

[17] Para 8.10 above.

[18] The Horizontal Guidelines (para 37) indeed mention 'will cease', which seems to imply that the contractor must not cease production immediately after the start of the subcontracting relationship.

the parties are actual competitors and hence may be deemed to have the IPRs, know-how, and tooling necessary to produce the contract products at their disposal.

(6) Fifth question: is the subcontracting agreement covered by Regulation 1400/2002 or Regulation 2790/99?

Subcontracting agreements are vertical agreements. If a subcontracting agreement which appreciably affects competition in the sense of Article 81(1) EC is concluded between competitors, and is not within the scope of application of the TTBER or Regulation 2658/2000, it may be covered by Article 2(3) of Regulation 1400/2002 (in the case of motor vehicle distribution) or, as a residual category, by Article 2(4) of Regulation 2790/99.[19] **8.22.**

The conditions which Article 2(3) of Regulation 1400/2002 contains for the application of Regulation 1400/2002 to an agreement between competitors are stated in paragraph 11.34 below. Those which Article 2(4) contains for the application of Regulation 2790/99 to an agreement between competitors are discussed in paragraphs 2.296–2.301 above. If a subcontracting agreement between competitors is covered either by Regulation 1400/2002 or Regulation 2790/99, it will need to be checked whether the restrictions of competition which it contains qualify for block exemption. If this is not the case, an individual Article 81(3) EC assessment is required. While there is no presumption of illegality outside the block exemption regulation,[20] it will be recalled that hardcore restrictions are unlikely to fulfil the conditions of Article 81(3) EC.[21] **8.23.**

In this respect, reference is made to both Article 4(1)(j) of Regulation 1400/2002 and Article 4(e) of Regulation 2790/99, which, in varying degrees (the regime of Regulation 1400/2002 being more restrictive than that of Regulation 2790/99), blacklist an exclusive supply-back obligation imposed on **8.24.**

---

[19] According to Reg 2790/99, Art 2(5), as discussed in paras 2.173 *et seq* above, Reg 2790/99 does not apply to vertical agreements (including subcontracting agreements between non-competitors) the subject matter of which fall within the scope of any other block exemption regulation. Thus, it applies by default only and does not cover subcontracting agreements 'where they relate to the conditions under which the parties may purchase, sell or resell new motor vehicles, spare parts for motor vehicles or repair and maintenance services for motor vehicles' (Commission Regulation (EC) No 1400/2002 of 31 July 2002 on the application of Article 81(3) of the Treaty to categories of vertical agreements and concerted practices in the motor vehicle sector [2002] OJ L203/30, Art 2(1)). A 'motor vehicle' is 'a self-propelled vehicle intended for use on public roads and have three or more road wheels' (Art 1(1)(n)), and hence does not include motor bikes, tractors, or construction equipment (bulldozers, excavators, etc). For the latter, the general regime of Reg 2790/99 continues to be relevant. Reg 1400/2002 is discussed in detail in Ch 11 below. [20] Guidelines, para 62.

[21] Guidelines on the application of Article 81(3) of the Treaty [2004] OJ C101/97, para 46 (hereafter 'Guidelines on the application of Art 81(3) EC').

a subcontractor (supplier of components) by a contractor who incorporates those components in its final products. Neither under the regime of Regulation 1400/2002 nor under Regulation 2790/99, is the contractor therefore able to impose an absolute exclusive supply-back obligation on its subcontractor.[22]

(7) Sixth question: are the restrictions of competition which the subcontracting agreement contains enforceable according to the Horizontal Guidelines?

8.25. Finally, if a subcontracting agreement concluded between competitors restricts competition in the sense of Article 81(1) EC and is not covered by, or does not comply with the conditions of, any block exemption regulation, then the Horizontal Guidelines will be the appropriate framework to determine whether it meets the criteria for exemption under Article 81(3) EC. The Horizontal Guidelines (paragraph 100) specifically address the competition issues which may arise from subcontracting agreements between competitors: they may lead to foreclosure problems (discussed at paragraphs 8.26 and 8.27 below) and may have spill-over effects (discussed at paragraphs 8.28–8.31 below).

Foreclosure problems

8.26. Two types of foreclosure problem are identified in the Horizontal Guidelines:

— First, an exclusive supply-back obligation may take the form of an exclusive supply obligation pursuant to which the subcontractor may only supply the contract products to the contractor.
— Second, an exclusive supply-back obligation may also take the form of an exclusive purchase obligation, according to which the contractor will exclusively purchase the contract products from the subcontractor.

8.27. As regards these exclusivity obligations, the Horizontal Guidelines point at possible foreclosure problems if the parties have a strong position as either suppliers or buyers on the relevant input market. The reason for this is that subcontracting could then either lead to other competitors not being able to obtain this input at a competitive price or to other suppliers not being able to supply the input competitively if they will be losing a large part of their demand.

Spill-over effects

8.28. Spill-over effects, ie the effects of a given subcontracting relationship on the parties' competitive behaviour as market suppliers, may occur if the input which the contractor purchases from the subcontractor (a competing manufacturer of

---

[22] More details are given below in para 8.50 *et seq.*

248

final products) is an important component in terms of costs and the parties have a strong position in the downstream market for the final product.[23] Conversely, given that an effect on the parties' competitive behaviour as market suppliers is unlikely if they only have a small proportion of their total costs in common, subcontracting agreements are unlikely to lead to spill-over effects where the input which the contractor purchases from his subcontractor only accounts for a small proportion of the production costs of the final product.[24]

A contrario, it follows from the above considerations that the less important the position of the parties on either the input market or the downstream market for the final product (read: the less this market share exceeds 20%) and the less important the commonality of costs, the greater the likelihood that the sub-contracting agreement will qualify for the application of Article 81(3) EC (eg on account of efficiency gains). Subcontracting agreements between competitors whose combined market share is above 20% need not necessarily comply with additional requirements compared to those between competitors whose combined market share is below 20% in order to qualify for exemption. In this respect, the Horizontal Guidelines (paragraph 96) essentially confirm that much will depend on the facts of the case:

> a moderately higher market share than allowed for in the block exemption does not necessarily imply a high concentration ratio. For instance, a combined market share of the parties of slightly more than 20% may occur in a market with a moderate concentration (HHI below 1800).[25] In such a scenario a restrictive effect is unlikely. In a more concentrated market, however, a market share of more than 20% may, alongside other elements, lead to a restriction of competition . . . The picture may nevertheless change, if the market is very dynamic with new participants entering the market and market positions changing frequently.

By way of conclusion, we provide the example of the Commission's competition analysis of a subcontracting agreement between competitors (Horizontal Guidelines, paragraph 114). It concerns an agreement concluded between two competitors, whereby company A will:

— purchase 60% of its requirements for an intermediate product Y (which A so far has produced only for internal consumption) from its competitor company B (which is also selling the intermediate product Y to third-party customers and has a market share of 10% for Y), and
— continue to produce 40% of Y in-house in order not to lose the know-how related to such production.

8.29.

8.30.

---

[23] Horizontal Guidelines, para 100.   [24] ibid, para 88.
[25] 'HHI' stands for 'Herfindahl-Hirshmann Index', which sums up the squares of the individual market shares of all competitors. With an HHI below 1,000 the market concentration can be characterized as low, between 1,000 and 1,800 as moderate and above 1,800 as high: Horizontal Guidelines, para 29.

The intermediate product Y is an input into the production of the final product X (accounting for 10% of the cost for X), and it is for the final product X that companies A and B are competitors. Company A has a market share of 15%, and company B of 20% for final product X.

8.31. In its example, the Commission considers as a first step whether or not company A is a realistic potential entrant into the merchant market for sales of the intermediate product Y to third parties. If this is not the case, the agreement on the intermediate product Y does not restrict competition with respect to Y. In addition, given the low commonality of costs (the intermediate product Y represents a mere 10% of the cost of the final product X), the Commission considers that spill-over effects into the market for the final product X are unlikely. Conversely, if company A were to be a realistic potential entrant into the merchant market for sales of the intermediate product Y to third parties, one must consider the market position of company B for intermediate product Y. Since that share is only 10%, the agreement on Y is unlikely to restrict competition to an extent that would be contrary to Article 81(3) EC. What is more, given that the parties' combined market share for Y would not exceed 10%, they could claim that their agreement is covered by the *De Minimis* Notice and hence is outside the scope of Article 81(1) EC.

D. Subcontracting Between Non-Competitors

(1) Methodology

8.32. The EC competition law analysis of subcontracting between non-competitors can be done on the basis of the following checklist of questions:

1. Does the subcontracting agreement come within the scope of Article 81(1) EC (paragraph 8.33)?
2. If so, does the subcontracting agreement appreciably affect competition in the sense of Article 81(1) EC (paragraphs 8.34–8.46)?
3. If so, is the subcontracting agreement a technology transfer agreement covered by the TTBER (paragraphs 8.47–8.49)?
4. If not, is the subcontracting agreement covered by Regulation 1400/2002 (motor vehicle distribution) or Regulation 2790/99 (paragraphs 8.50–8.56)?
5. Finally, if not, are the restrictions of competition which the subcontracting agreement contains enforceable pursuant to the (Vertical) Guidelines (paragraph 8.57)?

(2) First question: does the subcontracting agreement come within the scope of Article 81(1) EC?

The answer to the first question will be positive and the subcontracting **8.33.** agreement will be within the scope of Article 81(1) EC if it is an agreement in the sense of Article 81(1) EC and appreciably affects inter-State trade. Both requirements have been discussed above, respectively at paragraphs 2.66–2.85 for the concept 'agreement' (which should pose little, if any, problems as an agreement will typically be available) and at paragraphs 2.27–2.60 for the concept of the appreciable effect on inter-State trade.

(3) Second question: does the subcontracting agreement appreciably affect competition in the sense of Article 81(1) EC?

General

The question of whether a subcontracting agreement between non-competitors **8.34.** appreciably restricts competition in the sense of Article 81(1) EC can be ana-lysed from at least three different angles:

— the Horizontal Guidelines;
— the Subcontracting Notice; and
— the *De Minimis* Notice.

Subcontracting between non-competitors according to the Horizontal Guidelines

The Horizontal Guidelines (paragraph 86) posit the rule that subcontracting **8.35.** agreements between non-competitors do not in principle fall within the scope of Article 81(1) EC:

> Unless foreclosure problems arise, production agreements between non-competitors are not normally caught by Article 81(1). This is also true for agreements whereby inputs or components which have so far been manufactured for own consumption (captive production) are purchased from a third party by way of subcontracting . . . , unless there are indications that the company which so far has only produced for own consumption could have entered the merchant market for sales to third parties without incurring significant additional costs or risks in response to small, permanent changes in relative market prices.

In this respect, the Horizontal Guidelines confirm, specifically with respect to **8.36.** subcontracting agreements, the general rule that co-operation between non-competitors does not fall under Article 81(1) EC.[26] They also recall the excep-tion to this rule, namely that if the parties to the agreement have significant

---

[26] Horizontal Guidelines, para 24.

market power and hence are important purchasers or suppliers, their co-operation may create foreclosure problems.[27] Further, they also claim that Article 81(1) EC will apply if the co-operation is in reality a co-operation between potential competitors. The addition of this exception is potentially far-reaching, given that most in-house producers with spare capacity can be assumed to have the potential to enter the market.

Subcontracting between non-competitors according to the Subcontracting Notice

8.37. Certain clauses of subcontracting agreements between non-competitors may be covered by the Subcontracting Notice and for that reason fall outside Article 81(1) EC.

8.38. This follows from the Horizontal Guidelines (paragraph 81) which, as cited above, state:

> Guidance for the assessment of subcontracting agreements between non-competitors involving the transfer of know-how to the subcontractor is given in a separate Notice [ie the Subcontracting Notice].

It also follows from Article 2(3) of Regulation 2790/99, as explained by the Guidelines (paragraph 33), which state the following:

> [Regulation 2790/99] does not apply when the IPRs are provided by the buyer to the supplier, no matter whether the IPRs concern the manner of manufacture or of distribution. An agreement relating to the transfer of IPRs to the supplier and containing possible restrictions on the sales made by the supplier is not covered by [Regulation 2790/99]. This means in particular that subcontracting involving the transfer of know-how to a subcontractor does not fall within the scope of application of [Regulation 2790/99].

8.39. Accordingly, the Subcontracting Notice subtracts certain restrictions of competition from Article 81(1) EC on condition that the contractor provides the subcontractor with technology (IPRs, know-how) or tooling. These must be such that if the subcontractor would not have access to them, he would not be capable of being an independent supplier in the market for the contract products. To this end, the IPRs, know-how, or tooling must comply with the following two cumulative conditions:

— it must be necessary for the subcontractor to manufacture goods which differ in form, function, or composition from other goods manufactured or supplied on the market, and

---

[27] ibid. For the same exception regarding subcontracting agreements between competitors, see paras 8.26 and 8.27.

— it must not already be at the disposal of the subcontractor or not be accessible under reasonable conditions.[28]

The Subcontracting Notice does not clarify what must be understood by these conditions. Particularly for the second condition, the absence of guidance is regrettable as this may lead to contrary views on the notion 'reasonable conditions'. **8.40**.

However, on the assumption that these conditions are complied with, the contractor is entitled to oblige the subcontractor to use the IPRs, know-how, or tooling exclusively for the purposes of the subcontracting agreement and not to make them available to third parties, as well as to oblige the subcontractor to supply the goods, services, or work resulting from the use of the IPRs, know-how, or tooling only to the contractor.[29] **8.41**.

In respect of the provision of technology by the contractor, the following restrictions will also fall outside Article 81(1) EC:[30] **8.42**.

— an undertaking by either of the parties not to reveal manufacturing processes or other know-how of a secret character, or confidential information given by the other party during the negotiation and performance of the agreement, as long as the know-how or information in question has not become public knowledge,
— an undertaking by the subcontractor not to make use, even after expiry of the agreement, of manufacturing processes or other know-how of a secret character received by him during the currency of the agreement, as long as they have not become public knowledge,
— an undertaking by the subcontractor to pass on to the contractor on a non-exclusive basis any technical improvements which he has made during the term of the agreement, or, where a patentable invention has been discovered by the subcontractor, to grant non-exclusive licences in respect of inventions relating to improvements and new applications of the original invention to the contractor for the term of the patent held by the latter.

This undertaking by the subcontractor may be exclusive in favour of the contractor in so far as improvements and inventions made by the sub-contractor during the term of the agreement are incapable of being used independently of the contractor's secret know-how or patent, since this does not constitute an appreciable restriction of competition.

---

[28] Subcontracting Notice, para 2. The Notice (para 2, *in fine*) specifies that the latter condition is not fulfilled 'when the contractor provides no more than general information which merely describes the work to be done. In such circumstances the restriction could deprive the subcontractor of the possibility of developing his own business in the fields covered by the agreement'. [29] Subcontracting Notice, para 2.
[30] ibid, para 3.

8.43. In addition to the above restrictions, where the subcontractor is authorized by a subcontracting agreement to use a specified trademark, trade name, or 'get up', the contractor may at the same time forbid such use by the subcontractor in the case of goods, services, or work which are not to be supplied to the contractor.[31]

Subcontracting agreements between non-competitors according to the *De Minimis* Notice

8.44. A third category of subcontracting agreements which do not fall under Article 81(1) EC are those agreements which are covered by the *De Minimis* Notice. In this respect, attention must be given in particular to the parties' market share and to the absence of certain hardcore restrictions.

8.45. As regards the parties' market share, a subcontracting agreement between non-competitors is deemed not to restrict competition in an appreciable way if the market share held by each of the parties to the agreement does not exceed 15% on any of the relevant markets affected by the agreement, which in the case of subcontracting agreements may be the market for the intermediate products (ie the contract products) and for the final product(s).

8.46. As regards the absence of certain hardcore restrictions, reference can be made to what was said in paragraph 8.15 above. The *De Minimis* Notice (point 11(2)(e)) excludes from its application an exclusive supply-back obligation agreed between a supplier of components and a buyer who incorporates those components in its final products which limits the supplier/subcontractor from selling the components as spare parts to end-users, independent repairers, or other service providers. Clearly, the fact that this type of hardcore restriction is not covered by the *De Minimis* Notice is of little practical relevance in the case where the conditions for the application of the Subcontracting Notice are fulfilled. On application of the latter, the exclusive supply-back obligation will fall outside Article 81(1) EC.

(4) Third question: is the subcontracting agreement a technology transfer agreement covered by the TTBER?

8.47. For the sake of completeness, restrictions of competition other than an exclusive supply-back obligation will have to be analysed under the TTBER and the accompanying TTBER Guidelines if the subcontracting agreement is a technology transfer agreement. In this respect, it will be recalled that the TTBER Guidelines (paragraph 44), as cited above, state:

> According to this notice [ie the Subcontracting Notice], which remains applicable, subcontracting agreements whereby the subcontractor undertakes to produce certain products exclusively for the contractor generally fall outside Article 81(1).

[31] ibid, para 4.

However, other restrictions imposed on the subcontractor such as the obligation not to conduct or exploit his own research and development may be caught by Article 81.

As regards the other restrictions entered into between two—in the present case: **8.48**. non-competing—undertakings, they will be able to enjoy the safe harbour of the TTBER if:

— the agreement does not have any of the hardcore restrictions stated in Article 4(2) of the TTBER as its object; and
— the individual market share of the parties concerned does not exceed 30% on the affected relevant technology and product market (Article 3(2) TTBER). Guidance on the concept of 'technology market' can be found in the TTBER Guidelines (paragraph 22). The concept of the 'product market' has been discussed in paragraphs 2.220–2.222 above. Guidance on the market share calculation can be found in the TTBER Guidelines (paragraphs 23 and 77 *et seq*).

If the subcontracting agreement is a technology transfer agreement which is **8.49**. covered by, but does not comply with the conditions of the TTBER, guidance on whether or not the agreement meets the criteria for exemption under Article 81(3) EC can be found in the TTBER Guidelines. An exemption under Article 81(3) EC is unlikely if the subcontracting agreement has one or several hardcore restrictions in the sense of Article 4(2) of the TTBER as its object. The situation is different if the subcontracting/technology transfer agreement falls outside the TTBER for the sole reason that the parties exceed the market share safe harbour of the TTBER. In that case, the Article 81(3) EC assessment of the different restraints will need to be performed on the basis of Part IV of the TTBER Guidelines and in particular paragraphs 152–203 thereof, concerning the application of Article 81 EC to various types of licensing restraints.

(5) Fourth question: is the subcontracting agreement covered by Regulation 1400/2002 or Regulation 2790/99?

If the answer to the second question is positive and the agreement is not a **8.50**. technology transfer agreement covered by the TTBER, the applicable legal framework for the EC competition analysis of the subcontracting agreement between non-competitors will be Regulation 1400/2002 in the case of motor vehicle distribution or, as a residual category, Regulation 2790/99. Because the contractor does not provide the subcontractor with IPRs, know-how, or tooling in the sense of the Subcontracting Notice,[32] Regulation 1400/2002 and

---

[32] In the hypothesis where the contractor provides IPRs to the subcontractor, the applicability of Reg 1400/2002 is excluded on the basis of Art 2(2)(b) thereof and that of Reg 2790/99 on the basis of its Art 2(3).

Regulation 2790/99 adopt a more stringent position on certain restrictions of competition. Specifically, both of them blacklist the imposition of certain exclusive supply-back obligations.

The regime of Regulation 2790/99

8.51. Article 4(e) of Regulation 2790/99 blacklists vertical agreements which have as their object:[33]

> the restriction agreed between a supplier of components [ie the subcontractor] and a buyer who incorporates those components [ie the contractor], which limits the supplier to selling the components as spare parts to end-users or to repairers or other service providers not entrusted by the buyer with the repair or servicing of its goods.

8.52. Pursuant to Regulation 2790/99 only a contractors authorized service and repair network may be required to buy spare parts from it. End-users, independent repairers, or other service providers must be able to obtain the spare parts, as well as relevant technical information and special equipment necessary for the use of spare parts, directly from the subcontractor. In so doing, the Commission guarantees these parties' access to spare parts and creates pressure on the price level of spare parts by putting the OEMs and their service and repair networks in direct competition with independent repairers and service providers.

8.53. Conversely, Article 4(e) of Regulation 2790/99 distinguishes between (i) components used as spare parts, and (ii) components used for the incorporation in a final product. The hardcore restriction contained in Article 4(e) only covers the former. This means that an OEM is entitled to impose an exclusive supply-back obligation on its subcontractor for those components that are meant to be incorporated in the OEM's final products.

The regime of Regulation 1400/2002

8.54. The counterpart of Article 4(e) of Regulation 2790/99 in Regulation 1400/ 2002 is Article 4(1)(j) which, in its turn, blacklists vertical agreements which have as their object:

> the restriction agreed between a supplier of original spare parts [ie the subcontractor] or spare parts of matching quality, repair tools or diagnostic or other equipment and a manufacturer of motor vehicles [ie the contractor], which limits the supplier's ability to sell these goods or services to authorised or independent distributors or to authorised or independent repairers or end users.

8.55. Article 4(1)(j) expresses the Commission's desire to ensure effective competition on the repair and maintenance markets and to allow repairers to offer end-users

---

[33] The fact that vertical agreements have a restrictive effect is insufficient to bring the hardcore restriction into play. More details on 'restrictive object' and 'restrictive effect' are given in paras 5.01–5.09 above.

competing spare parts such as original spare parts and spare parts of matching quality.[34] As a consequence, like Regulation 2790/99, Regulation 1400/2002 does not entitle a manufacturer to carve out the after-market for itself and its authorized distribution and service network. Moreover, the leverage of an OEM under the specific regime of Regulation 1400/2002 is even more restricted than under the general regime of Regulation 2790/99: the OEM is indeed not even entitled to oblige its own dealer and service network to buy original spare parts or spare parts of matching quality exclusively from it.

Notwithstanding this, the distinction between components used for the assembly **8.56**. of a new motor vehicle and original spare parts and spare parts of matching quality also applies in the context of Regulation 1400/2002. This transpires from the Explanatory Brochure on Regulation 1400/2002, in which the Commission expressly distinguishes between both. In Section 7 (*'Distribution of and access to spare parts'*), express reference is made to the fact that 'in some specific cases manufacturers have supply agreements with part manufacturers that only manufacture and supply spare parts for a vehicle and do not manufacture its components'. The hardcore restriction listed in Article 4(1)(j) thus only applies to original spare parts or spare parts of matching quality. It does not apply to components used for the assembly of new motor vehicles. Provided the other conditions of Regulation 1400/2002 are fulfilled, the OEM may therefore impose an exclusive supply-back obligation on its component manufacturer.

(6) Fifth question: are the restrictions of competition which the subcontracting agreement contains enforceable pursuant to the (Vertical) Guidelines?

Subcontracting agreements between non-competitors, which do not come **8.57**. within the scope of the Subcontracting Notice (because they contain restrictions in the sense of Article 81(1) EC) and are not covered by any block exemption regulation (eg because they exceed the market share thresholds), must be assessed in accordance with the (Vertical) Guidelines. In this respect, reference can be made to the analysis of the competitive concerns raised by exclusive supply (especially the risk of foreclosure) in Chapter 10 (paragraphs 10.99 *et seq*). By way of conclusion, we would like to indicate that the (Vertical) Guidelines, as opposed to the Horizontal Guidelines, do not contain a separate discussion on subcontracting agreements, but that they do give an example which includes exclusive supply in a subcontracting context. The example (at paragraph 213 of the Guidelines) is as follows:

> On a market for a certain type of components (intermediate product market) supplier A agrees with buyer B to develop, with his own know-how and

---

[34] Reg 1400/2002, recital 23.

considerable investment in new machines and with the help of specifications supplied by buyer B, a different version of the component. B will have to make considerable investments to incorporate the new component. It is agreed that A will supply the new product only to buyer B for a period of five years from the date of first entry on the market. B is obliged to buy the new product only from A for the same period of five years. Both A and B can continue to sell and buy respectively other versions of the component elsewhere. The market share of buyer B on the upstream component market and on the downstream final goods market is 40%. The market share of the component supplier is 35%. There are two other component suppliers with around 20–25% market share and a number of small suppliers.

Given the considerable investments, the agreement is likely to fulfil the conditions for exemption in view of the efficiencies and the limited foreclosure effect. Other buyers are foreclosed from a particular version of a product of a supplier with 35% market share and there are other component suppliers that could develop similar new products. The foreclosure of part of buyer B's demand to other suppliers is limited to maximum 40% of the market.

(7) Concluding remarks

8.58. We would like to make three concluding remarks on the legal regime applying to subcontracting agreements between non-competitors. First, given that an OEM is not entitled to 'carve out' the spare part market for itself and its authorized dealer and service network, it is likely to think twice before it provides IPRs, know-how, or tooling to its subcontractors. Indeed, as stated above (paragraph 8.39), if an OEM obliges its subcontractor to use the IPRs, know-how, or tooling exclusively in the framework of their agreement, such an obligation will fall outside Article 81(1) EC only if the subcontractor cannot be expected to acquire the IPRs, know-how, or tooling itself under reasonable conditions. Since it may not always be clear when a subcontractor can reasonably be expected to acquire the tooling himself (let alone what the opinion of the investigating competition authority on this matter might be), an OEM may find itself confronted with the situation where it cannot legally prevent a subcontractor from becoming its competitor in the after-market, and this by means of technology or equipment belonging to the OEM.

8.59. Second, even if an exclusive supply-back obligation is blacklisted pursuant to Regulations 2790/99 and 1400/2002, this does not, according to us, mean that the contractor is entirely powerless vis-à-vis the subcontractor's use of the contractor's IPRs, know-how, or tooling. Often, a contractor will make IPRs, know-how, or tooling available to the subcontractor free of charge or against a fee which does not fully reflect the manufacturer's investment. The reason for this is that any fee which the contractor charges to the subcontractor for the use of such IPRs, know-how, or tooling is likely to be reflected in the price which the subcontractor, in its turn, charges to the contractor. If the subcontractor wishes to start production on its own account or for that of a third party by means of the contractor's IPRs, know-how, or tooling, Article 4(1)(j) of Regulation 1400/2002, or Article 4(e) of Regulation 2790/99, do not appear to stand in the way of the contractor's right to receive financial compensation from the subcontractor. Such financial compensation could take at least two different forms:

— First, in the form of a license fee construction. According to such a construction, the subcontractor would be entitled to use the subcontractor's technology (IPRs, know-how) or tooling for his proper account only if the parties have agreed on a license fee. The same could apply if the contractor has provided the subcontractor with IPRs, know-how, or tooling which the contractor himself has licensed from a third party or also in cases where the contractor has put R & D efforts in the development of a given production method.

— Second, as regards the tooling, the subcontractor could also, instead of paying a licence fee, be given the choice to purchase the tooling, at market conditions, taking into account any IPRs and/or know-how pertaining to the tooling or the products manufactured by means of the tooling, as well as its wear and tear.

In both cases, we are of the opinion that the object of the financial compensation is not to restrict the subcontractor's sales to third parties but is instead to grant the contractor a reasonable and fair compensation for his investment efforts.

Finally, the freedom which a subcontractor has to enter the market independ- **8.60**. ently cannot be taken to mean that he is entitled to infringe the contractor's trademark. In this respect, the Commission is difficult to understand where, in its Explanatory Brochure on Regulation 1400/2002 (Question 104), it addresses the issue of IPRs in the context of Regulation 1400/2002 as follows:

> IPRs or know how may not be used by the supplier . . . to restrict the spare part manufacturer's right to sell the spare parts in question to authorised and independent repairers. If the supplier were to use IPRs or know how in this way, [Regulation 1400/2002] would not apply to the its [sic] distribution system.

On any reasonable view, this sweeping statement cannot apply to trademarks, which must constitute a general exception to the principle of the supplier's right to independent market access. It would appear that it is only in exceptional cases that it would be possible for a competition authority to correctly invoke Article 4(1)(j) of Regulation 1400/2002 against a given use of a trademark (eg if an OEM would require its subcontractors to purchase tooling that can only be used to produce parts which are trademark-tagged and it would do so with the aim of making sure that the subcontractor does not enter the market independently).

9

DISAPPLICATION AND WITHDRAWAL

A. Introduction

(1) Block exemption

Agreements that fall within the scope of application of Regulation 2790/99 and **9.01**. meet all of the conditions imposed by it, benefit from an automatic exemption pursuant to Article 81(3) EC. This is an essential characteristic of block exemption regulations. Based on its experience, the Commission defines a category of agreements which, if all of the conditions listed in the block exemption regulation are met, can be regarded as normally satisfying the conditions laid down in Article 81(3) EC without it being necessary to examine each agreement on its own individual merits.[1] It follows, therefore, that when a restrictive agreement is covered by a block exemption regulation, parties are relieved of the burden of showing that their individual agreement satisfies each of the four conditions laid down in Article 81(3) EC. With little sense of nuance, the Guidelines (paragraph 71) refer in this respect to a presumption of legality.[2] Notwithstanding this presumption of legality, even if the conditions of a block exemption regulation are met, it may be that in reality a particular agreement, on its own or together with other similar agreements, produces effects that are incompatible with the exemption conditions laid down in Article 81(3) EC.

---

[1] Case T–7/93 *Langnese Iglo v EC Commission* [1995] ECR II–1533, para 174 : 'A block exemption is not, by definition, subject to case by case verification that the exemption conditions laid down by the Treaty are actually fulfilled'.

[2] If the presumption applies, it must be respected (ie it is not refutable) unless and until the benefit of the block exemption is withdrawn (Reg 2790/99, Arts 6 and 7) or the Commission issues a regulation excluding a series of agreements from the scope of application of the Regulation (Reg 2790/99, Art 8).

(2) Corrective measures

9.02. It is for that reason that Council Regulation 19/65,[3] which forms the legal basis of the Regulation,[4] contains two types of corrective measures. First, it provides, in Article 1(a), that block exemption regulations may stipulate the conditions that may lead to the exclusion from their scope of application of certain parallel networks of similar agreements or concerted practices operating on a particular market. The Regulation has made use of this possibility in Article 8. Second, Article 7 of Regulation 19/65 provided that the Commission, and under certain circumstances the competent authorities of the Member States, may withdraw the benefit of the application of a block exemption regulation if, in a particular case, agreements or concerted practices have effects that are incompatible with Article 81(3) EC. Article 7 of Regulation 19/65 was repealed by Regulation 1/2003 and replaced by a similarly worded Article 29. This second type of corrective measure can be found in Articles 6 and 7 of the Regulation. The disapplication procedure (Article 8) and the withdrawal procedure (Articles 6 and 7) are discussed separately in the following sections.

B. Disapplication

(1) Parallel networks

9.03. Pursuant to Article 8(1) of the Regulation, where parallel networks of similar vertical restraints cover more than 50% of a relevant market, the Commission may, by regulation, declare that the Regulation does not apply to vertical agreements or concerted practices containing specific restraints relating to that particular market. The disapplication procedure therefore specifically targets parallel networks of vertical agreements having similar effects on competition within a particular market. Because of the cumulative effect of parallel networks, it is possible that access to the relevant market or competition therein is restricted to a degree that is incompatible with Article 81 EC, even though all of the individual agreements concerned might satisfy the conditions for exemption listed in the Regulation. Merely by way of example, the Guidelines refer to two possible situations where disapplying the Regulation might be an appropriate remedy. The first example given is where parallel networks of selective distribution cover more than 50% of a market and make use of selection criteria that are not required by the nature of the contract goods or that discriminate

---

[3] Council Regulation (EEC) No 19/65 on the application of Article 85(3) of the Treaty to certain categories of agreements and concerted practices [1965] OJ Spec Ed 36/533, as amended by Council Regulation 1215/1999 [1999] OJ L148/1.   [4] Reg 2790/99, recital 1.

against certain forms of distribution capable of selling these goods.[5] A second example mentioned in the Guidelines relates to parallel networks of single-branding arrangements.[6] In both cases, market access might be restricted.

(2) *The 50% rule*

The Commission may only issue a regulation to disapply the Regulation where **9.04**. parallel networks of similar vertical restraints cover more than 50% of the relevant market(s). As a result, any such regulation will at least have to define the relevant product and the geographic market(s) covered by the disapplication measure, identify the type of restraint that is present in the parallel networks of vertical agreements, and quantify the percentage of the relevant market(s) that is covered by the restraint. The disapplication measure will only relate to one or more types of vertical restraint in one or more relevant markets as described in the disapplication regulation and only to the extent specified therein. It is clear from the Guidelines that, both as regards the decision to disapply the block exemption contained in the Regulation and the extent of the disapplication measure, the Commission seeks to reserve for itself a wide margin of discretion.[7]

(3) *Transition period*

Importantly, the period of time between the adoption of the regulation dis- **9.05**. applying the block exemption and its application must be at least six months.[8] The purpose of this six-month transition period is to allow the undertakings concerned to adapt their agreements so as to take account of the provisions of the regulation disapplying the block exemption.[9] For reasons of legal certainty, it would have been better to have this six-month period starting on the date of publication of the regulation, rather than on its date of adoption.

(4) *No retroactive effect*

Regulations adopted by the Commission pursuant to Article 8 of Regulation **9.06**. 2790/99 have no retroactive effect. Vertical agreements that are covered by a disapplication regulation, but satisfy the exemption conditions as stipulated under Regulation 2790/99, will continue to be block exempted until the date of entry into effect of the disapplication regulation. After that date, the block exemption will lapse to the extent indicated in the disapplication regulation and, unless they are adapted so as to meet the conditions imposed by the

---

[5] Guidelines, para 83.   [6] ibid, para 85.   [7] ibid, para 85.   [8] Reg 2790/99, Art 8(2).
[9] Guidelines, para 86. Reg 19/65, Art 1(a) provides that the transition period may not be shorter than six months.

disapplication regulation in question, vertical agreements covered by such a regulation will have to be reviewed on their individual merits under Article 81(1) and (3) EC.

(5) Disapplication by Commission regulation

9.07. Declarations of inapplicability pursuant to Article 8 of the Regulation must take the form of a Commission regulation. When adopting such a regulation the Commission, if so requested by a Member State, will have to consult the Advisory Committee.[10] The Guidelines add that such a measure is not addressed to individual undertakings but concerns all undertakings whose agreements are defined in the regulation disapplying the block exemption.[11] Presumably, the Commission thereby seeks to lay the foundations of the argument that individual undertakings do not have legal standing to challenge the validity of a regulation adopted under Article 8 of the Regulation.[12] It remains to be seen whether the Community courts share this approach.

C. Withdrawal

(1) Individual agreements

9.08. The withdrawal of the block exemption, like a declaration of inapplicability, is a corrective measure that may be used when agreements satisfy the conditions for a block exemption but nevertheless produce effects on competition that are incompatible with Article 81 EC. Disapplication always requires the existence of parallel networks of similar vertical restraints that cover more than 50% of the relevant market.[13] In the case of a withdrawal of the block exemption, this condition may, but does not have to be fulfilled. Withdrawal decisions may deal with an individual agreement, provided that it can be shown that the agreement in question falls within the scope of Article 81(1) EC and does not satisfy the conditions for exemption laid down in Article 81(3) EC. The Guidelines give as an example the case where an exclusive distributor has significant market power in the downstream market, where he resells the contract products or services.[14] The withdrawal procedure may also be applied to situations where competition is restricted to a degree incompatible with Article 81 EC as a result of the

---

[10] Reg 19/65, Art 6(1)(b).   [11] Guidelines, para 80.
[12] Pursuant to Art 230(4) of the Treaty, any natural or legal person may institute annulment proceedings before the Court of First Instance against a decision addressed to that person or against a decision which, although in the form of a regulation or a decision addressed to another person, is of direct and individual concern to the former.   [13] Para 9.04 above.
[14] Guidelines, para 73.

cumulative effects of parallel networks of similar vertical agreements. In such a case, a withdrawal is similar to a disapplication. However, it must always be borne in mind that a withdrawal is addressed to one or more individual undertakings, whereas a disapplication measure defines a category of vertical agreements in a specific relevant market that, after the expiry of a transition period, are excluded from the scope of application of the Regulation. The burden of proof that the agreement falls within the scope of Article 81(1) EC and does not fulfil the conditions of Article 81(3) EC lies with the authority that adopts the withdrawal decision.[15]

(2) *Withdrawal by Commission decision*

Withdrawal measures take the form of a Commission decision. The Commission has the power to withdraw the benefit of the block exemption and has the exclusive power to do so unless the agreements concerned have effects that are incompatible with Article 81 EC in the territory of a Member State, or in a part thereof, which has all of the characteristics of a distinct geographic market. In this latter case, the competent authority of that Member State[16] also has the power to withdraw the benefit of the Regulation, concurrently with the Commission.[17] Whilst reserving the right to take on certain cases displaying a particular Community interest, the Commission has indicated that cases of concurrent competence often lend themselves to decentralized enforcement by the NCAs.[18] The effects of decisions by NCAs to withdraw the benefit of the Regulation are limited to the territory of that Member State (or that part of their territory to which the withdrawal relates).[19] **9.09**.

(3) *No retroactive effect*

Withdrawal decisions only produce effects for the future.[20] It is only as of the effective date of the withdrawal that the agreement concerned will lose the benefit of automatic exemption under the Regulation. Undertakings that are party to the agreement may not be held liable for the incompatibility of their agreement with the provisions of Article 81 EC in the period preceding the effective date of withdrawal. The statement in the Guidelines that the Commission may withdraw the benefit of the block exemption and establish an infringement of Article 81(1) EC may not be interpreted otherwise.[21] Article 81 **9.10**.

---

[15] ibid, para 72.
[16] Only the NCAs have the power to withdraw the benefit of block exemption and not the national courts of the Member States (unless the national court has been designated as a competition authority of a Member State pursuant to Reg 1/2003, Art 35(1) and acts in that capacity). [17] Guidelines, para 77.
[18] ibid, para 77. [19] Reg 2790/99, Art 7. [20] Guidelines, para 75.
[21] ibid, para 71.

EC will be infringed only if the undertakings concerned do not amend their agreement after the effective date of withdrawal.

(4) Inapplicability to future agreements

9.11. The Court of First Instance has clarified that the Commission is not empowered, by means of an individual decision, to restrict or limit the legal effects of a legislative measure, such as a block exemption regulation, unless such a legislative measure provides a legal basis for doing so. For that reason and in the absence of a provision in the Regulation stating otherwise, the Commission has no power to withdraw the benefit of the block exemption from future agreements.[22] This issue does not arise in respect of the disapplication of the block exemption contained in the Regulation.[23] A disapplication regulation is general in nature and applies to all agreements, whether existing or future, in the relevant market(s) identified in the disapplication regulation.

(5) Withdrawal procedure

9.12. When a national competition authority intends to pursue the withdrawal of the block exemption in relation to one or more specific agreements, it will apply its own procedural rules. The Commission states in the Guidelines that when it withdraws the benefit of the block exemption under Article 6 of the Regulation, it establishes an infringement of Article 81(1) EC. It therefore follows that the procedure to be followed is similar to that in infringement cases.[24] This may explain why in the past the Commission has applied the withdrawal procedure in only a limited number of cases.[25]

---

[22] Case T–7/93 *Langnese-Iglo v EC Commission* [1995] ECR II–1533, para 208; and Case T–9/93 *Schöller Lebensmittel v EC Commission* [1995] ECR II–1611, para 162. Both these cases related to the powers of withdrawal of the Commission under Regulation (EEC) No 1984/83 of 22 June 1983 on the application of Article 85(3) of the Treaty to categories of exclusive purchasing agreement [1983] L173/5, in particular Art 14 thereof, but the Court's holding remains valid for the Regulation. [23] Paras 9.03–9.07 above.

[24] L Ortiz Blanco, *EC Competition Procedure* (1st edn, OUP, 1996) 310–11.

[25] Examples under Reg 1984/83 are *Langnese-Iglo* [1993] OJ L183/19 and *Schöller Lebensmittel* [1993] OJ L183/1. An example under Commission Regulation (EEC) No 123/85 of 12 December 1984 on the application of Article 85(3) of the Treaty to certain categories of motor vehicle distribution and servicing agreements [1985] OJ L15/16 is *Eco System/Peugeot* [1992] OJ L66/1.

PART III

VERTICAL AGREEMENTS OUTSIDE THE SCOPE OF REGULATION 2790/99

10

VERTICAL AGREEMENTS FOR COMPANIES WITH A LARGE MARKET SHARE

A. Introduction

A distribution agreement may fall outside the scope of Regulation 2790/99 for **10.01**. a variety of reasons. It may have one or more hardcore restrictions as its object,[1] it may include IPRs in a manner that is incompatible with the requirements of the block exemption,[2] or it may involve competitors.[3] Among the most important categories of distribution agreements that cannot benefit from the block exemption are those that exceed the market share limit. The application of the block exemption is indeed subject to the condition that the supplier's market share does not exceed 30%.[4] In one hypothesis (ie where an exclusive supply obligation is imposed on the supplier)[5] it is not the supplier's but the buyer's market share that will be relevant for calculating the market share that must remain within the 30% limit. A temporary increase of the market share beyond the 30% level does not immediately rule out the applicability of the block exemption as the Regulation contains a transitory regime covering such situations.[6]

---

[1] Ch 5 discusses how the inclusion of a hardcore restriction in a distribution agreement renders the block exemption inapplicable to the agreement as a whole.

[2] For the details on these requirements, see Regulation (EC) No 2790/1999 of 22 December 1999 on the application of Article 81(3) of the Treaty to categories of vertical agreements and concerted practices (hereafter 'Reg 2790/99') [1999] OJ L336/21, Art 2(3) and paras 2.267–2.290 above.

[3] Only in exceptional cases will distribution agreements between competitors fall within the scope of application of Reg 2790/99, see paras 2.292–2.301 above.

[4] For details on the market share calculation, see paras 2.248–2.266 above.

[5] With regard to the exclusive supply concept that is relevant in this context, see Reg 2790/99, Art 3(2) and paras 2.209 *et seq* above.

[6] For details on the transitory regime, see paras 2.212–2.266 above and, for practical examples, see paras 2.261–2.266 above.

10.02. This chapter addresses the EC competition law assessment that is called for in respect of distribution agreements that exceed the market share limit and for that reason cannot benefit from the block exemption.[7] The Guidelines (paragraph 62) emphasize that such agreements may 'not be presumed to be illegal but may need individual examination' and offers guidance as to the manner in which companies can make their own assessment.

10.03. In contrast with the considerable degree of legal certainty that is offered to distribution agreements that are covered by the block exemption, the individual examination of distribution agreements that exceed the 30% limit lacks predictability.[8] Such an individual examination is almost by definition case-specific.[9] The Commission warns against a mechanical application of the Guidelines and insists that 'each case must be evaluated in the light of its own facts'.[10] Furthermore, any individual assessment is sensitive to material changes of the facts.[11] Hence, a favourable outcome to an individual examination at a given point in time does not guarantee that such an outcome will remain valid over time.

10.04. This chapter strives to provide a systematic overview of the relevant principles and hence to increase the predictability of the outcome of the individual assessment of distribution agreements exceeding the 30% limit. The aim is to offer as much concrete guidance as possible. So where it seems safe to do so, the Guidelines are translated into black and white rules. In this respect, a conservative approach is adopted, meaning that concrete and case-specific evidence may justify vertical restraints which are more restrictive than those suggested in this chapter. In exceptional cases (eg in markets that are particularly susceptible to collusion or display an unusually weakened competitive structure) a more stringent analysis may be called for. In the vast majority of cases, however, the approach suggested in this chapter would appear to offer a defensible and predictable way forward.

10.05. The Chapter has been organized so as to achieve a degree of consistency with Chapter 7 which summarizes the block exemption regime applicable to the

---

[7] Guidance can also be found in V Korah and D O'Sullivan, *Distribution Agreements under the EC Competition Rules* (Hart Publishing, 2002) 227 *et seq*.

[8] We are not aware of any study of the welfare cost due the lack of predictability of the antitrust principles. Confronted with insufficient predictability or legal certainty, companies often tend, in our experience, to opt for suboptimal (but easy to understand) solutions. For instance, the complex regime of Reg 2790/99 regarding restrictions on active sales is very sensitive to network changes and hence triggers legal uncertainty. As a result, many companies have steered away from the imposition of active sales restrictions, even in cases where such restrictions were fully justified.

[9] Commission Notice—Guidelines on Vertical Restraints [2000] OJ C291/1, para 71 (hereafter 'Guidelines'), para 3; Commission Notice—Guidelines on the application of Article 81(3) of the Treaty (hereafter 'Guidelines on the application of Art 81(3) EC'), para 6.

[10] ibid. [11] Guidelines on the application of Art 81(3) EC, para 44.

most frequently used distribution formulas. We first assess whether the use of a distribution formula, as such, poses a problem in cases where the market share of the supplier (or, as the case may be, that of the buyer) exceeds the 30% limit (paragraphs 10.06–10.21). Subsequently, we review the EC competition law principles applying to individual vertical restraints. First, some general remarks regarding the assessment of these individual restraints (paragraphs 10.22–10.35), as well as the methodology that will be used for conducting an individual assessment of the vertical restraints (paragraphs 10.36–10.37), are given. Each restraint is then analysed individually (paragraphs 10.38–10.121). The chapter concludes by offering guidance on the antitrust implications of the inclusion of certain combinations of vertical restraints in distribution agreements falling outside the block exemption (paragraphs 10.122–10.133).

B. Frequently Used Distribution Formulas

Chapter 7 discusses a number of frequently used distribution formulas from the perspective of Regulation 2790/99. The formulas are exclusive distribution, non-exclusive distribution, selective distribution (qualitative and quantitative), franchising, and agency. All of these formulas can benefit from an automatic exemption if the 30% limit is not exceeded and as long as they do not have certain hardcore restrictions as their object. **10.06**.

This section reviews whether a supplier with a market share in excess of 30% is confronted with obstacles to the use of any of these distribution formulas. In other words, the issue addressed here is whether any of the above-mentioned distribution formulas must, as a matter of principle, be ruled out on account of the fact that the supplier's market share exceeds the 30% limit. For this purpose, stripped-down versions of these formulas are considered, ie the distribution formula in its basic form including only such restraints as are inherent in the formula and without any specific vertical restraints that may often be used in combination with the formula, but which are not strictly necessary for the application of the formula.[12] **10.07**.

In order to arrive at meaningful guidance in this context, the issue is approached from two angles: **10.08**.

— The Guidelines offer some insight as to whether the Commission automatically accepts the use of a given distribution formula, requires a further individual assessment before a particular distribution formula will be

---

[12] For instance, exclusive distribution will often be combined with a non-compete obligation. In this section, exclusive distribution is considered as such, it being assumed that no restrictions other than those inherently necessary for the formula are provided for. This means that, for the purposes of this section, it is assumed that no non-compete obligation is included and that the only specific restraint that is provided for is the territorial exclusivity guaranteed to the distributor.

available to a +30% supplier or rules out the application of the formula by
such a supplier;

— Regulation 1400/2002[13] may serve as a yardstick for present purposes. The
Commission has made it clear that the approach adopted in Regulation
1400/2002 is stricter and more conservative than the regime applicable in
the context of Regulation 2790/99.[14] Hence, to the extent that Regulation
1400/2002 deals with distribution formulas in cases where the supplier has a
market share in excess of 30%, this can be a useful second indicator.

(1) Exclusive distribution

10.09. Both the Guidelines and Regulation 1400/2002 suggest that a +30% supplier
cannot automatically avail itself of exclusive distribution. The Guidelines
(paragraph 163) state expressly that 'above the 30% market share threshold
there may be a risk of a significant reduction of intra-brand competition' and
that 'in order to be exemptable, the loss of intra-brand competition needs to be
balanced with real efficiencies'. Regulation 1400/2002 limits its automatic
exemption of exclusive distribution to a maximum market share of 30% and
hence contains no explicit support for the use of exclusive distribution beyond
that limit.

10.10. The conclusion is therefore that a +30% supplier will have to conduct an
individual examination of the exclusivity offered to its distributors and should
not automatically assume that its reliance on exclusive distribution will comply
with Article 81 EC. Practically speaking, the territorial protection offered by
the +30% supplier to its distributor(s) requires a case-specific examination.
Guidance for this individual assessment is provided in paragraphs 10.38–10.54
below. This conclusion is valid for all types of exclusive distribution, including
cases of shared exclusivity.[15]

(2) Non-exclusive distribution

10.11. Non-exclusive distribution in its purest form does not, in principle, result in an
appreciable restriction of competition. This formula can be compared with

---

[13] Commission Regulation (EC) No 1400/2002 of 31 July 2002 on the application of Article
81(3) of the Treaty to categories of vertical agreements and concerted practices in the motor
vehicle sector [2002] OJ L203/30 (hereafter 'Reg 1400/2002'). This is the sector-specific block
exemption applicable to the distribution and repair and maintenance of motor vehicles, discussed
in Ch 11 below.

[14] Reg 1400/2002, recitals 2 and 7; and European Commission, *Explanatory brochure for
Commission Regulation (EC) No 1400/2002 of 31 July 2002 on the application of Article 81(3)
of the Treaty to categories of vertical agreements and concerted practices in the motor vehicle
sector*, 11; available at http://europa.eu.int/comm/competition/car_sector/explanatory_
brochure_en.pdf (hereafter the 'Explanatory Brochure').

[15] For a description of such different types, see para 7.04 above.

qualitative selective distribution,[16] with the additional pro-competitive feature that the non-exclusive distributors are entitled to resell the contract products or services to the customers of their choice (including traders that are not part of the distribution network).[17] Hence, non-exclusive distribution is, in principle, available to any +30% supplier, without further examination. Such examination will only be called for as soon as the non-exclusive distribution formula is combined with certain specific vertical restraints (such as some form of territorial protection or restriction, a customer restriction, or a non-compete obligation).

To be on the safe side, it is better to check the practical effects of the non-   **10**.12.
exclusive distribution formula. For instance, it is possible that the supplier *de facto* limits the number of distributors and thus creates a scenario which raises the same competition law concerns as those that may be triggered by exclusive distribution. If the practical implementation of a non-exclusive distribution regime triggers restrictions of competition (intra-brand, inter-brand, or both), a review of the relevant restrictions as set forth below is advisable.[18] It can be assumed that a +30% supplier will normally be aware of the fact that he is no longer operating non-exclusive distribution in its pure form, either because his objective was to restrict competition or because he perceives the restrictive effects on the market.[19]

(3) Quantitative selective distribution

Both the Guidelines and Regulation 1400/2002 contain favourable indications   **10**.13.
for quantitative selective distribution in +30% situations.

Subject to three conditions, the Commission accepts in its Guidelines that   **10**.14.
quantitative selective distribution will normally not create net negative effects.[20]
The conditions are the following:

(1) the supplier is the only one using quantitative selective distribution on the market or the share of the market covered by selective distribution is below 50%;[21]

---

[16] Paras 10.17–10.18 below.   [17] Guidelines, para 188.
[18] Neither the Guidelines, nor Reg 1400/2002 offer any additional comfort in respect of restrictive non-exclusive distribution systems. Hence, the standard review of the vertical restraints will have to be conducted.
[19] For instance, a *de facto* limitation of the number of non-exclusive distributors may facilitate collusion between the distributors and result in a systematic alignment of their prices on the prices recommended by the supplier.   [20] Guidelines, para 187.
[21] The Guidelines (ibid) also state that no problem is likely to arise where the market coverage ratio exceeds 50%, but the aggregate market share of the five largest suppliers is below 50%. In situations, such as those contemplated here (involving a +30% supplier using selective distribution), such a scenario seems exceptional.

(2) the supplier does not occupy a position of dominance; and

(3) the nature of the contract goods requires the use of selective distribution and the selection criteria are necessary to ensure the efficient distribution of the relevant goods.

10.15. Regulation 1400/2002 grants an automatic exemption for quantitative selective distribution of new motor vehicles up to a market share limit of 40%.[22] The same favourable treatment is not awarded to the distribution of spare parts and repair and maintenance services, which remain subject to the 30% limit. All in all, the higher market share limit of 40% for new motor vehicles can, given the competition law problems identified in the past by the Commission on the markets concerned, be relied upon as a positive sign.

10.16. In practical terms, if the conditions outlined in the Guidelines are not met or if the supplier has a market share exceeding 40%, it is advisable to conduct an individual examination of the competitive implications due to the limitation of the number of authorized distributors. Guidance on such examination is provided below.

(4) Qualitative selective distribution

10.17. The Guidelines confirm that 'purely qualitative selective distribution is in general considered to fall outside Article 81(1) EC for lack of anti-competitive effects'.[23] Three conditions must however be met in order to justify such favourable treatment:

(1) the nature of the product must necessitate the use of selective distribution;

(2) the resellers must be chosen on the basis of objective criteria of a qualitative nature[24] that are laid down uniformly for all potential resellers and that may not be applied in a discriminatory manner; and

(3) the criteria may not go beyond what is necessary.[25]

The same positive treatment of qualitative selective distribution is reflected in Regulation 1400/2002 which grants an automatic exemption without any market share limit.[26]

10.18. In view of this, purely qualitative selective distribution can be characterized as a safe option for a +30% supplier.

---

[22] Reg 1400/2002, Art 3(1), para 2.   [23] Para 185.

[24] Certain criteria may *prima facie* seem qualitative in nature, but nevertheless indirectly limit the number of authorized distributors. The Guidelines (para 189) give the example of the requirement to achieve a minimum amount of annual purchases. A selective distribution system that contains such an indirect limitation of the number of authorized distributors will not qualify as a purely qualitative selective distribution system.   [25] ibid.

[26] Reg 1400/2002, Art 3(1), para 3.

(5) Franchising

Franchising, including no vertical restraints, presents a viable option for suppliers with a market share exceeding 30%. This distribution formula (in its most basic form) can indeed be assimilated with a non-exclusive distribution formula; the sole difference being that, in the case of franchising, a package consisting of IPRs, commercial and technical assistance, a business method, etc is offered to the franchisees.[27]   **10.19.**

Most franchising systems nevertheless impose some restrictions on the franchisor, the franchisee, or both.[28] Accordingly, the analysis will have to focus on the individual restraints, rather than on the distribution formula as such. With very limited exceptions, these restraints will have to be analysed in exactly the same manner as if no franchising were applied.[29] Hence, unless specific reference is made to franchising in the discussion of the individual vertical restraints below, it can be assumed that the analysis applies to franchising.   **10.20.**

(6) Agency

The same approach as for franchising can be suggested in respect of agency. In the absence of individual vertical restraints, the agency formula as such should be available to any +30% supplier. The real issue will be whether the restrictions imposed on the principal, the agent or both meet the test of Article 81 EC. The analysis presented below in respect of individual restraints can, in principle, be applied to all cases of non-genuine agency.[30]   **10.21.**

C. Assessment of Individual Vertical Restraints

(1) Structure

This section addresses the assessment of individual vertical restraints imposed by a supplier with a market share exceeding 30%. It is organized as follows. First, a number of general principles that are relevant to the assessment of any type of vertical restraint are described (paragraphs 10.23–10.35). Second, the methodology proposed to conduct an individual assessment is presented (paragraphs 10.36 and 10.37). Third, the vertical restraints that have been discussed in Chapter 7 are addressed from the perspective of a +30% supplier   **10.22.**

---

[27] Guidelines, para 199.
[28] ibid. Reference is made to selectivity, non-compete obligations and/or exclusivity.
[29] Guidelines, para 200.
[30] On the distinction between genuine and non-genuine agency, see paras 7.66 *et seq.*

(paragraphs 10.38–10.121). Given their specific treatment in the context of Regulation 2790/99, exclusive supply obligations imposed by +30% buyers are also dealt with.

(2) General principles

10.23. The Guidelines contain a number of general principles that are useful for the assessment of any vertical restraint. These principles are as follows.

No individual exemption for hardcore restraints

10.24. Vertical restraints that are blacklisted under Regulation 2790/99 will normally not be eligible for an individual exemption.[31] Although it is in theory not excluded that such restraints may meet the test of Article 81(3) EC, a +30% supplier should proceed on the assumption that it is unlikely that this will be the case. Given the conservative approach adopted in this chapter, the recommended approach is not to include hardcore vertical restraints in distribution agreements of +30% suppliers.

10.25. It goes without saying that this position is confined to the hypothesis where the hardcore restriction qualifies as an appreciable restriction of competition in the sense of Article 81(1) EC and hence is in need of an individual exemption. There are cases where such a restriction will not be deemed to fall within the prohibition of Article 81(1) EC. This is notably so when the restriction 'is objectively necessary for the existence of an agreement of that type or of that nature'.[32] The typical example concerns the imposition of territorial restraints in order to motivate the distributor to penetrate new markets. The Guidelines (paragraph 119(10)) point out that, in the case of a new geographic market and irrespective of the market share of the supplier, it will be possible to impose both active and passive sales restrictions on the supplier's distributors outside the new market, in order to protect the efforts of the distributor appointed in that new market. Such active and passive sales restrictions are deemed to stay outside the prohibition of Article 81(1) EC for a period of two years after the introduction of the product on the new market.

10.26. In summary, if due to particular circumstances (such as the entry of new geographic markets) a hardcore restriction does not qualify as an appreciable restriction of competition, it will be possible for a +30% supplier to implement such a hardcore restriction. Aside from these exceptional circumstances, hardcore

---

[31] Guidelines, para 46; and Guidelines on the application of Art 81(3) EC, para 79.
[32] Guidelines on the application of Art 81(3) EC, para 18(2). See also, paras 2.161 *et seq* above.

restrictions will qualify as an appreciable restriction of competition and, as stated above, are very unlikely to qualify for an individual exemption.

Abuses of dominance not eligible for an individual exemption

The Guidelines have created some confusion as to the possibility for a dominant player to rely on Article 81(3) EC by stating that 'where an undertaking is dominant or becoming dominant as a consequence of the vertical agreement, a vertical restraint that has appreciable anti-competitive effects can in principle not be exempted'.[33] This statement suggests that a dominant company will in principle never be able to meet the fourth condition of Article 81(3) EC.[34] Subsequently the Commission has put forward a much more nuanced position:[35]   **10.27.**

> since Articles 81 and 82 both pursue the aim of maintaining effective competition on the market, consistency requires that Article 81(3) be interpreted as precluding any application of this provision to restrictive agreements that constitute an abuse of a dominant position. However, not all restrictive agreements concluded by a dominant undertaking constitute an abuse of a dominant position.

The general principle to be retained for present purposes is therefore that a dominant company's vertical restraints are not by definition excluded from an exemption on the basis of Article 81(3) EC, but that the conditions of Article 81(3) EC will never be fulfilled if the vertical restraint qualifies as an abuse within the meaning of Article 82 EC.[36] Tying and non-compete obligations are typical examples of infringements of Article 82 EC that cannot be saved via Article 81(3) EC.   **10.28.**

Market power as central concept

The Commission accepts that most vertical restraints will normally not pose a problem as long as there is enough inter-brand competition.[37] Inter-brand competition will be deemed insufficient if there is some degree of market power at the level of the supplier, the buyer, or at both levels.[38] More specifically, it is suggested that vertical restraints can only have negative consequences for competition if an undertaking has significant market power.[39] Where   **10.29.**

---

[33] Guidelines, para 135. For a critique, S Bishop and D Ridyard, 'E.C. Vertical Restraints Guidelines: Effects-based or Per Se Policy?' [2002] ECLR 35, 36.
[34] This position seems to have been the Commission's view for some time following the adoption of the Guidelines: see paras 2.168–2.172 above.
[35] Guidelines on the application of Art 81(3) EC, para 106 and accompanying n 92. For the reason behind this change in approach, see para 2.168 above.   [36] Para 1.15 above.
[37] Guidelines, paras 6 and 119.   [38] ibid, paras 6, 102, and 119.
[39] Bishop and Ridyard (n 33 above): 'Economic theory shows that unless a firm has significant market power, vertical restraints cannot have adverse consequences for competition'.

there is market power, the Commission states that the protection of inter- and intra-brand competition becomes important.[40]

10.30. The (Vertical) Guidelines and the Guidelines on the application of Art 81(3) EC use slightly different wording to define the concept of market power. The Guidelines (paragraph 119) provide that 'market power is the power to raise price above the competitive level and, at least in the short term, to obtain supra-normal profits'. The Guidelines on the application of Art 81(3) EC (paragraph 25) state that market power 'is the ability to maintain prices above competitive levels for a significant period of time or to maintain output in terms of product quantities, product quality and variety or innovation below competitive levels for a significant period of time'. Both the Guidelines (paragraph 119) and the Guidelines on the application of Art 81(3) EC (paragraph 26) clarify that the level of market power that is required to trigger the application of Article 81(1) EC is lower than that needed to establish dominance within the meaning of Article 82 EC.

10.31. High market shares are considered to be a good indicator of market power.[41] They are however not decisive. For instance, low entry barriers may render access to the market easy so that a high market share can easily be eroded due to new entry. It is not specified which level of market share is likely to trigger a finding of market power.[42] The Guidelines (paragraph 119) state that a market is unconcentrated and hence normally displays enough inter-brand competition if the HHI[43] is below 1,000. This clarification does not assist in defining the market share level that is relevant for a finding of market power. Indeed, as soon as there is one +30% supplier in a given market, the HHI will always exceed the level of 1,000.

10.32. Given the conservative approach of this chapter, we proceed on the assumption that a +30% supplier who cannot benefit from the block exemption, including the regime covering temporary increases above the 30% level, needs to assess the vertical restraints addressed in this chapter assuming that he has the requisite market power to bring Article 81(1) EC into play.[44] This does not mean that all

---

[40] Guidelines, para 6.   [41] ibid, para 122.

[42] The number of markets that may have to be taken into consideration in the case of an individual assessment may be greater than those considered for the purposes of assessing whether the 30% limit of Reg 2790/99 is complied with. For instance, the competitive impact on downstream markets may be relevant to the individual assessment (Guidelines, para 96).

[43] The HHI (which stands for 'Herfindahl-Hirschmann Index') sums up the squares of the individual market shares of all competitors.

[44] For instance, while maximum or recommended resale prices in principle do not infringe Art 81(1) EC, the Guidelines (paras 225–8) suggest that the position may be different in the case of a supplier with market power. In such a case, the distributors may find it difficult to go against the will of the supplier and may be inclined to apply the preferred sale price of the supplier. A second risk is that, in a narrow oligopoly, these prices may facilitate collusion.

+30% suppliers must be deemed to possess market power. Additional factors such as low entry barriers or countervailing buying power may disprove a finding of market power.

Distinction between the reduction of inter-brand competition v intra-brand competition

While there are many ways to group vertical restraints, the most important one **10.33.** is based on the distinction between restraints reducing inter-brand competition (ie competition between suppliers of competing brands) as opposed to those reducing intra-brand competition (ie competition between distributors of the same brand). Given the central role played by inter-brand competition in the application of the antitrust rules, it should come as no surprise that the reduction of inter-brand competition is considered to be more harmful than the reduction of intra-brand competition. Hence, as a general rule, it should be easier to make an Article 81(3) EC case for vertical restraints leading to the reduction of the latter.

Summary

Based on the foregoing, the supplier's market position leads us to distinguish **10.34.** between three scenarios:

(1) The supplier is dominant in the sense of Article 82 EC. Hardcore restrictions and vertical restraints amounting to an abuse will not be eligible for an individual exemption pursuant to Article 81(3) EC.

(2) The supplier has market power, but is not dominant in the sense of Article 82 EC. As a rule, hardcore restrictions will not be eligible for an exemption pursuant to Article 81(3) EC, but the supplier may nonetheless be able to prove that vertical restraints that qualify as an abuse within the meaning of Article 82 EC meet the conditions of Article 81(3) EC.

(3) The supplier has no market power, but nevertheless cannot benefit from the block exemption on account of his market share. As a rule, hardcore restrictions will not be eligible for an exemption pursuant to Article 81(3) EC. For all other vertical restraints, it should be relatively easy for the supplier to demonstrate that an individual exemption on the basis of Article 81(3) EC is justified as its lack of market power serves to indicate that there is sufficient inter-brand competition. It is submitted that such a supplier is entitled to an individual exemption, provided that it applies the block exemption by analogy.

In all of the aforesaid scenarios, it remains possible to argue that a vertical **10.35.** restraint does not appreciably restrict competition in the sense of Article 81(1)

EC and hence does not need an individual exemption. Reference can be made to the example of territorial restraints related to the opening up of new geographic markets.[45] There are other possibilities. For instance, there is support[46] for the proposition that a non-compete obligation containing an easy, flexible, and rapid exit possibility for the party that is subject to the restriction does not appreciably restrict competition, even if it is imposed by a supplier with a market share of well in excess of 30%.

(3) Methodology for assessment

10.36. The vertical restraints that are analysed below are the following:

— territorial protection awarded to distributors;
— territorial restrictions imposed on distributors;
— exclusive customer allocation;
— customer restrictions imposed on distributors;
— non-compete obligations and quantity forcing on distributors;
— exclusive supply and quantity forcing on the supplier; and
— exclusive purchasing.

10.37. For each of these restraints the following methodology is applied :

— First, the competitive concerns which the vertical restraint may entail are identified.
— Second, the intensity of the restriction is assessed by considering the characteristics of the market[47] and the features of the restriction. A clear understanding of how the restraint is measured in terms of its intensity is crucial. As stated in the Guidelines on the application of Art 81(3) EC (paragraph 79) 'the more restrictive the restraint the stricter the test under the third condition'. It is recalled that the third condition of Article 81(3) EC consists of the indispensability standard. Hence, the higher the restrictive intensity of a vertical restraint, the higher the burden of proving that the conditions of Article 81(3) EC are met.
— Third, the efficiencies accepted by the Commission as a justification for a given vertical restraint are identified.

---

[45] Para 10.25 above.

[46] cf the Dutch Competition Authority's investigation of Heineken's supply agreements, paras 2.151–2.154 above.

[47] As part of the methodology it will be assumed that, on account of his market share, the supplier has market power or occupies a dominant position. Hence, absent specific circumstances, the application of Art 81(1) EC to the vertical restraints under consideration is likely to be triggered due to such market power. Put differently, in order to escape a finding that the vertical restraint amounts to an appreciable restriction of competition, a specific justification (based, for instance, on the characteristics of the market or the features of the restraint) will be needed.

— Finally, any concrete guidance given by the Commission regarding the conditions under which it is likely to accept that the vertical restraint is eligible for an individual exemption is stated.

(4) Territorial protection

A common feature of distribution agreements is the granting of territorial **10.38**. protection to the distributor. Such protection can be given in different ways. The distributor can be given some form of territorial exclusivity (sole or shared exclusivity). Such territorial exclusivity can be combined with territorial restrictions imposed on the distributors located in other territories. The supplier may also undertake not to compete directly with the distributor within its territory.

Competitive concerns

The Guidelines (paragraph 109) place territorial protection awarded to the **10.39**. distributor under the heading of the 'limited distribution group' (ie agreements limiting the number of buyers to which the supplier is selling). The main negative effects on competition of the limited distribution group in general and territorial protection in particular are the following.[48]

Reduction of intra-brand competition

This is relatively straightforward. If the number of distributors marketing a **10.40**. given brand is reduced or limited, there is a risk that intra-brand competition may be reduced. However, there is no automatic link between territorial protection and reduced intra-brand competition. For instance, if the territories are not too extensive and the distributors are allowed to resell to traders that are not part of the network, it may well be that the territorial protection does not result in a reduction of intra-brand competition and may even foster such competition.

Foreclosure of the purchase market

Certain buyers may no longer be able to purchase the relevant products from **10.41**. the supplier. While this risk may be real in cases where the territorial protection is combined with an exclusive supply obligation, it seems highly exceptional that territorial protection as such would trigger this type of foreclosure problem. As restrictions on passive sales are a hardcore restriction and will not be eligible for individual exemption, the territorial protection will normally not prevent buyers (even those situated outside the network) from buying the products.

---

[48] Guidelines, para 110.

Hence, the risk of foreclosure of the purchase market triggered by territorial protection must not be overestimated and, absent specific circumstances,[49] is not a major competitive concern.[50]

Facilitating collusion

10.42. The risk that collusion across brands may be facilitated requires that several suppliers limit the number of distributors. Such reduced numbers of distributors would make it easier to collude either at the supplier's level, the distributor's level or both. There is no automatic link between territorial protection and the facilitation of collusion. Such risk would require that fairly large territories are extended to the distributors (so that their number is sufficiently reduced) and that most or all of the competing suppliers do the same. Absent these circumstances, it seems speculative to suggest that territorial protection facilitates inter-brand collusion.

Market partitioning[51]

10.43. The risk of market partitioning is listed separately and is linked to the possibility of engaging in price discrimination. It is relevant that the Guidelines (paragraph 172) mention this risk only in cases where exclusive distribution is combined with exclusive purchasing. As a consequence, the risk of market partitioning will normally not be of concern in cases which only involve territorial protection. Sufficient arbitrage will remain possible.

Measurement of restrictive intensity

10.44. The characteristics of the market and the features of the vertical restraint at issue that influence the restrictive impact can be summarized as follows:

Market characteristics

10.45. The market characteristics that may induce the competitive concerns outlined above are the following :

— **The market position of the supplier and its competitors** plays a central role. The Guidelines (paragraph 163) take the view that the presence of a supplier with a +30% market share implies that inter-brand competition may be limited and that the application of territorial protection by such a supplier entails 'a risk of significant reduction of intra-brand competition'. This risk can be counter-balanced by demonstrating that, notwithstanding the +30% market share of the supplier, there is keen inter-brand competition. In the

---

[49] The fact that the supplier appoints only one or a very limited number of distributors for the whole Community may be pertinent in this context.
[50] The Guidelines (para 166) seem to endorse this.　　[51] Guidelines, para 161.

absence of evidence of such keen inter-brand competition, considerable importance will be attached to the restrictive impact of territorial protection on intra-brand competition.

— **The profile of the supplier's competitors** is not only important to measure inter-brand competition, but also to assess the risk of (horizontal) collusion.[52] If the number of competitors is rather small and their market position is fairly similar (market share, capacity, distribution network), territorial protection offered to distributors may create a risk of collusion. The risk of collusion may be enhanced if several suppliers operate through the same exclusive distributors. The higher the cumulative market share of the brands distributed by the same exclusive distributor, the higher the risk of collusion.

— The Guidelines (paragraph 165) acknowledge that **entry barriers** are less important in the assessment of the restrictive impact of territorial protection. They seem to accept that the restrictive impact of territorial protection does not materially increase due to the presence of entry barriers for the suppliers. However, it is worth recalling that low entry barriers at the supplier level may be a factor of importance to counter-balance the presumption that inter-brand competition is reduced due to the presence of a +30% supplier.[53]

— **Buying power** is cited in the Guidelines (paragraph 122) as a factor that may create a risk of foreclosure on the purchase market and collusion on the side of the buyers. This will only be the case if the buying power results in large exclusive territories being awarded to a limited number of distributors across different brands. In the absence of such a scenario, buying power should normally rate as a factor that may counteract the exercise of market power and trigger increased inter brand and intra-brand competition.

— The **maturity of the market** is a negative factor for the measurement of the impact of territorial protection on intra-brand competition. The Guidelines (paragraph 168) suggest that the loss of intra-brand competition is less of a concern if the market is characterized by growing demand, changing technologies, and changing market positions. The underlying assumption is probably that in such markets the level of inter-brand competition is sufficient to outweigh the impact of territorial protection on intra-brand competition.

— As to the **level of trade**, the position is different depending on whether the territorial protection is applied at the retail level as opposed to the wholesale level. The risk of loss of intra-brand competition is greater at the retail level (particularly in the case of large exclusive territories) than it is at the wholesale level. At the wholesale level the Guidelines (paragraph 170) are essentially concerned with a possible risk of collusion if several suppliers operate through the same exclusive wholesalers.

---

[52] ibid, para 164.   [53] ibid, para 122.

— The **nature of the product** is not listed as a relevant factor for the assessment of the restrictive impact of territorial protection.[54]

Features of the vertical restraint

10.46. The correct assessment of territorial protection is not only governed by the market characteristics, but must also take due account of the specific features of the protection that is offered. The restrictive intensity of the territorial protection may indeed differ substantially depending on its features.

— The key features in the present context are the **size of the territories** allocated to the distributors and the **number of distributors** that are appointed by the supplier. The competitive risks outlined above are sensitive to these factors. Whether the supplier operates with sole exclusivity or shared exclusivity seems less relevant. The risks are indeed greater if two distributors share a large exclusive territory (eg a given country) as opposed to a situation where the supplier appoints a sole distributor in each of the provinces or similar administrative regions of that country.

— Another important factor is whether the distributors benefit from **protection against active sales** into their territories. If no such protection is granted or if such protection is limited to a prohibition to set up outlets (location clause), the impact on intra-brand competition is likely to be less important compared to the situation where only passive sales must be accepted by the exclusive distributor in his territory.

— The **protection against the supplier** which the exclusive distributor enjoys can be considered. The fact that the supplier undertakes not to compete with its exclusive distributors seems in most cases not to materially alter the outcome of the assessment.

— Specific mention must be made of **territorial protection in a selective distribution system**. By definition, selective distribution encompasses a customer restriction (ie the authorized distributor is not entitled to sell to unauthorized resellers). Hence, in order to assess the restrictive intensity of the territorial protection, it will be necessary to consider such protection in combination with the possible reduction of intra-brand competition resulting from the prohibition on sales to unauthorized resellers. Concrete guidance on the possibilities for a +30% supplier to award territorial protection to its selective distributors is given in paragraph 10.54 below.

Efficiencies

10.47. The Guidelines suggest which efficiencies can usefully be invoked to justify the restrictive impact of territorial protection. This list is not exhaustive[55] and

---

[54] Guidelines, para 173.   [55] ibid, para 116.

companies should feel free to present other efficiencies than those listed in the Guidelines. Evidence of such efficiencies is essential in order to meet the first condition of Article 81(3) EC (ie the contribution to improving the production or distribution of goods).[56] The efficiencies listed in the Guidelines with regard to territorial protection are the following.

Free-rider problem

Territorial protection may assist in avoiding the possibility that one distributor free-rides on the promotion efforts of another distributor. **10.48**.

A typical free-rider problem exists where customers approach one distributor for information or are attracted to the product as a result of that distributor's promotional efforts and go to a different distributor (who has not made these efforts and therefore not incurred the related costs) to effect the purchase. The Guidelines (paragraph 116(1)) provide that free-riding can only occur on pre-sales services and not on after-sales services[57] and that the product will need to be relatively new or technically complex and of a reasonably high value.[58] It will be more difficult to claim this efficiency if effective pre-sales service requirements can be imposed by contract on all distributors. **10.49**.

A special case of the free-rider problem may exist in the context of the opening up or entry of new geographic markets.[59] Territorial protection of the distributor may in such instances be called for in order to motivate the distributor to make the 'first time investments' to establish the brand in the market. This free-rider problem may even justify the imposition of a temporary restriction on passive sales into the new geographic market. **10.50**.

Certification free-rider issue

In order to introduce a new product, it may be necessary to place it first with premium stores, ie retailers that have a reputation of stocking only quality products. This may in practice only be possible if such retailers receive (at least for a limited period of time) territorial protection. The Guidelines (paragraph 116(3)) provide that the certification free-rider issue is most likely to occur with 'experience goods'[60] or complex goods having a certain purchase value. **10.51**.

---

[56] Guidelines on the application of Art 81(3) EC, paras 48 *et seq*.
[57] This may be true in cases where the after-sales services are directly linked to the sale of the product. However, if there is an independent market for after-sales services (eg in the motor vehicle business), it is conceivable that a free-rider problem may occur in such a market.
[58] Guidelines, para 174.
[59] ibid, para 116 (2). Also, L Peeperkorn, 'E.C. Vertical Restraints Guidelines: Effects-based or Per Se Policy?—A Reply' [2002] ECLR 38, 38–9.
[60] ie goods whose qualities are difficult to judge prior to consumption (Guidelines, para 174).

Hold-up problem

10.52. This problem occurs if the distributor must make relationship-specific invest-ments of a long-term and asymmetric nature.[61] An investment is relationship-specific when, after termination of the distribution agreement, it cannot be used by the distributor to purchase or use products of competing suppliers and can only be sold at a significant loss. The condition of the long-term nature of the investment is met if the distributor cannot recoup the investment in the short term. The investment will be deemed asymmetric if one party invests more than the other party. It is reasonable to suggest that only relationship-specific investments that cannot be recouped in the short term are to be taken into account for the purposes of assessing that the condition of asymmetry is met.

Economies of scale

10.53. Territorial protection may be a manner to concentrate sales and hence to exploit economies of scale.[62] Such economies of scale reduce costs and hence make it possible to charge a lower price for the product.

Concrete guidance

10.54. Based on the position adopted by the Commission, most importantly in the Guidelines, the following concrete guidance can be offered with regard to the compatibility with Article 81 EC of territorial protection (ie restriction of active and passive sales) offered by a +30% supplier:

— With one limited exception, it will not be possible to protect a distributor against passive sales. The exception concerns the opening up or entry of new markets. Passive sales may be prevented for a period of up to two years fol-lowing the introduction of the product on to such markets.[63] The restriction of passive sales in that context will be deemed not to amount to an appre-ciable restriction of competition and hence will fall outside the prohibition of Article 81(1) EC.

— Protection of a distributor against active and passive sales will normally not be possible in the case of selective distribution. Active and passive sales restrictions are blacklisted by Regulation 2790/99 in the case of selective distribution agreements. Hence, it is highly unlikely that an individual exemption will be available for such restrictions in a scenario where the supplier holds a market share of more than 30%.

— Regulation 2790/99 does not blacklist clauses in a selective distribution context preventing distributors from setting up new or additional outlets. The possibility to grant territorial protection via the imposition of a location

---

[61] Guidelines, para 116(4).   [62] ibid, para 116 (6).
[63] Guidelines on the application of Art 81(3) EC, para 18; and Guidelines, para 119(10).

clause on other distributors therefore requires, in any event, an individual examination.

— No concrete guidance can be offered on the grant of exclusivity (sole or shared). An individual examination will be needed in all +30% scenarios. The intensity of the restraint will have to be measured against the efficiencies invoked.

— The same is true for the protection against active sales outside the context of selective distribution. There seem to be no reasons to limit the individual examination of active sales restrictions to cases where the strict conditions of Regulation 2790/99 are met.[64] For instance, the fact that a restriction on active sales benefits territories characterized by shared exclusivity should not as a matter of course exclude a positive Article 81(3) EC finding.

— An undertaking on the part of the supplier not to enter into direct competition with its distributors should, disregarding specific circumstances, not present major problems in a +30% scenario. The intensity of such a restriction seems limited.

(5) Territorial restrictions

Closely related to the issue of territorial protection is the issue of the imposition of territorial restrictions on the distributor. In essence, territorial restrictions are a means to organize and implement the territorial protection of other distributors.[65] Hence, no elaborate discussion of this type of restraint is called for. It mirrors the discussion on territorial protection.   **10.55**.

Competitive concerns

The Guidelines (paragraph 113) place territorial restrictions under the heading of the 'market partitioning' restraints. These restraints limit the distributor in where he resells a particular product. The competitive concerns identified in the Guidelines (paragraph 114) are the same as those listed for territorial protection (reduction of intra-brand competition, market partitioning, risk of collusion). Foreclosure of the purchase market, which is mentioned in respect of territorial protection, is not listed for territorial restrictions.   **10.56**.

Measurement of restrictive intensity

The Guidelines do not contain specific guidance on the factors that may be relevant in measuring the intensity of territorial restrictions.   **10.57**.

---

[64] Ch 5 above.

[65] Guidelines, para 161, where territorial protection (exclusivity) and territorial restrictions are presented as being usually linked.

Market characteristics

10.58. Given the close link between territorial protection and territorial restrictions, it can be assumed that the market characteristics that are mentioned in paragraph 10.45 above (market position of the supplier and its competitors, profile of the supplier's competitors, entry barriers, buying power, maturity of the market, level of trade) are also relevant for the assessment of territorial restrictions.

Features of the vertical restraint

10.59. Territorial restrictions can take many forms. They include the classic restrictions on active and passive sales. Location clauses also qualify as a territorial restriction. There are various types of location clause, whose competitive impact is different: a complete prohibition from changing locations and opening additional outlets; a prohibition to open additional outlets outside a given territory combined with the freedom to move the location or to open additional outlets within that territory; a prohibition from changing the primary location combined with the freedom to open additional outlets, etc. In order to measure the restrictive intensity of a given territorial restraint correctly, it will be important to identify its specific features. Given the variety of location clauses, there may be considerable differences as to their competitive impact.

Efficiencies

10.60. The efficiencies that can justify the imposition of territorial restrictions are necessarily the same as those that justify territorial protection (avoidance of the free-rider problem, certification free-rider issue, hold-up problem, or economics of scale). Territorial restrictions indeed serve to implement the territorial protection required by another distributor. The efficiencies need not be proven for the distributor that is subject to the territorial restriction, but must be for the distributor that benefits from the protection resulting from the imposition of the territorial restriction.

Concrete guidance

10.61. Reference is made to the guidance mentioned in paragraph 10.54 above with regard to active and passive sales.

(6) Exclusive customer allocation

10.62. In addition to territory-based vertical restraints, customer-related restraints are common in distribution agreements. The Guidelines (paragraphs 109 and 178) define exclusive customer allocation as 'an undertaking on the part of the supplier to sell his products only to one distributor for resale to a particular class of customers'. It is not entirely clear why the Guidelines adopt such a narrow definition and do not expand it to cases where a limited number of distributors (as opposed to a single distributor) are given preferential rights with regard to a particular class of customers. Similar to territorial protection, the analysis of sole or shared customer exclusivity is not necessarily very different.

The Guidelines do not specify what exclusive customer allocation stands for in practice, namely the (limited) protection awarded to a given distributor by imposing an active sales restriction towards a particular class of customers on all other distributors of the supplier.[66] **10.63.**

Competitive concerns

Exclusive customer allocation is part of the limited distribution group of vertical restraints and hence presents similar competitive concerns to territorial protection.[67] The Guidelines (paragraphs 110 and 178) refer to the reduction of intra-brand competition, facilitation of collusion and the risk of market partitioning. The observations above (paragraphs 10.38–10.43) in respect of these concerns in the context of territorial protection are also relevant in this context. **10.64.**

The Guidelines (paragraph 180) refer to one specific aspect of exclusive customer allocation that may have a particularly limiting effect on intra-brand competition. The aspect referred to is the reduction or elimination of arbitrage by customers and non-appointed distributors. The Commission's harsh[68] stance in respect of exclusive customer allocation practiced by +30% suppliers is attributable to this concern. **10.65.**

Measurement of restrictive intensity

Market characteristics

The Guidelines (paragraph 179) refer expressly to the description of the market characteristics discussed in the context of territorial protection. Hence, the description of these characteristics (market position of the supplier and its competitors, profile of the supplier's competitors, entry barriers, buying power, maturity of the market, level of trade) in paragraph 10.45 above is also relevant here. **10.66.**

Features of the vertical restraint

As to the nature of the protection that can be offered to distributors with regard to a particular class of customers, the position is relatively straightforward. The supplier may undertake not to sell directly to the class of customers concerned and require the other distributors not to engage in active sales towards the class. Any more far-reaching protection (eg restriction on passive sales) is not eligible **10.67.**

---

[66] Guidelines, para 183.   [67] ibid, para 109.   [68] Para 10.69 below.

for an individual exemption, as it amounts to a hardcore restriction. The only additional feature that is relevant for the competition law assessment is the duration of the protection.[69] In order to be potentially exempt, the exclusive customer allocation must be confined to the depreciation period of the investments made by the distributor in order to meet the specific requirements for the class of customers concerned.[70]

Efficiencies

10.68. The efficiencies that may justify the exclusive customer allocation essentially concern free-rider and hold-up problems.[71] This means that customer-specific investments are needed to bring these efficiencies into play.

Concrete guidance

10.69. The Guidelines (paragraph 180) are relatively pessimistic as to the possibility of the exemption of exclusive customer allocation in a +30% scenario:

> [A]bove the 30% market share threshold of the Block Exemption Regulation exclusive customer allocation is unlikely to be exemptable unless there are clear and substantial efficiency effects.

The allocation of final consumers is deemed unlikely to lead to any efficiencies and is therefore unlikely to be exempted.[72] Also, given that exclusive customer allocation is a hardcore restraint in a selective distribution context, no individual exemption will be possible in a +30% scenario.[73]

10.70. In practice, exclusive customer allocation is therefore conceivable in a +30% scenario only if the following conditions are met:

— the relevant customers are professional buyers with identifiable differentiated needs;
— the sale to these customers requires substantial relationship-specific investments on the part of the distributor;
— the exclusive customer allocation is confined to a commitment of the supplier not to sell directly to the customers concerned and to the prohibition of active sales imposed on all other distributors;
— the term of the exclusive customer allocation is limited to the depreciation period of the relevant investments; and
— the distributor does not operate within a selective distribution system.

10.71. The Guidelines do not offer specific guidance regarding the commitment of the supplier not to engage in direct sales towards a given class of customers (without

---

[69] cf Guidelines, para 183.   [70] ibid, para 182.
[71] ibid, paras 116(1), 116(4), and 182.   [72] ibid, para 182.   [73] ibid, para 179.

the imposition of any active sales restriction on the other distributors). As the competitive concerns (including the elimination or reduction of arbitrage) stated in the Guidelines do not apply to such a scenario, a much more lenient treatment seems appropriate.

(7) Customer restrictions

Two broad categories of customer restrictions can be distinguished: **10.72**.

— the restrictions imposed on a distributor to grant customer protection to another distributor (eg the restriction on active sales imposed in the context of an exclusive customer allocation scenario); and
— the customer restriction that is inherent in any system of selective distribution (ie the prohibition on selling to unauthorized resellers or traders).

The assessment of these two categories is radically different.

Protection of customers allocated to other distributors

Reference can be made to the discussion above regarding exclusive customer   **10.73**. allocation. It is only if and when the restrictive conditions outlined in paragraph 10.70 are fulfilled that an active sales restriction aimed at a particular class of customers will be eligible for an individual exemption in a +30% context. A more elaborate discussion involving a measurement of the restrictive intensity of the restraint is therefore not necessary.

An important exception stated in the Guidelines (paragraph 119(10)) concerns   **10.74**. the genuine testing of a new product with a limited customer group. The distributors appointed to sell the products on the test market may be restricted in their active sales outside the test market for a maximum period of one year. Such a restriction falls outside the prohibition of Article 81(1) EC.

Selective distribution

The prohibition on selling to unauthorized resellers is part of the definition of   **10.75**. selective distribution. Provided that the conditions reflected in paragraph 10.17 above are met, qualitative selective distribution (including the said prohibition) in principle falls outside Article 81(1) EC. Hence this customer restriction does not trigger any specific competition law concerns. As discussed above, it is the combination of the said customer restriction with the limitation of the number of authorized distributors that requires a more careful and complex assessment in a +30% scenario. This combination (ie quantitative selective distribution) is dealt with in paragraphs 10.13–16 above.

(8) *Non-compete obligations and quantity forcing on the distributors*

10.76. A common feature in distribution agreements is an obligation or an incentive scheme which makes the buyer purchase practically all his requirements of a particular market from only one supplier.[74] The type of arrangements that fall within this category include straightforward non-compete obligations, quantity forcing on the distributor (such as minimum purchase requirements), loyalty rebate schemes, and English clauses.[75] A somewhat special type which falls in this category is tying.[76] Contrary to the vertical restraints discussed thus far, non-compete and similar obligations have a direct impact on inter-brand competition.

Competitive concerns

10.77. Non-compete obligations and quantity forcing on the distributors are part of the so-called 'single branding group' of vertical restraints.[77] The competitive concerns to which these restraints can give rise are the following.[78]

Foreclosure of the market

10.78. As a result of the non-compete obligation or quantity forcing, the distributors concerned cannot operate for other suppliers (or can but only to a lesser extent). Depending on the characteristics of the market, this may result in a foreclosure effect. Such a foreclosure effect is however no automatic consequence of the imposition of obligations of this nature.

Facilitating collusion

10.79. In cases where a number of major suppliers enter into non-compete arrangements (cumulative effect), market shares may become more rigid, and collusion may be facilitated. This is again no automatic consequence of the use of non-compete or similar arrangements. Specific market circumstances will be required before it is reasonable to assume that such arrangements facilitate collusion.

Reduction of inter-brand competition

10.80. Due to non-compete or similar arrangements there will be no or reduced in-store competition between brands. Whether this poses a problem depends on whether in-store competition is indeed a driver of competition. It is very possible in certain sectors that inter-brand competition is in fact enhanced as a

---

[74] ibid, para 138.   [75] ibid, para 152.
[76] ibid, para 106. Tying is not further discussed in this section. Guidance in relation to this issue is contained in the Guidelines, paras 215–24.   [77] ibid, para 106.
[78] ibid, paras 107 and 138.

result of the non-compete obligation as the focus of each distributor on a single brand may result in sharper inter-brand competition.

Measurement of restrictive intensity

The characteristics of the market and the features of a non-compete or similar obligation that influence its restrictive impact can be summarized as follows. **10.81**.

Market characteristics

The **market position of the supplier** is of considerable importance.[79] The **10.82**. higher the market share and more particularly the higher its tied market share (ie the part of its market share sold under a single branding obligation),[80] the greater is the risk that there will be foreclosure.

The **market position of the supplier's competitors** is also important in assessing **10.83**. possible foreclosure effects.[81] As long as the competitors are sufficiently numerous and strong, foreclosure is less likely. The likelihood of foreclosure increases when competitors are significantly smaller than the supplier imposing the non-compete or similar obligations. If there is cumulative use of non-compete obligations by a number of important suppliers, including a +30% supplier, the chances that potential entrants may be foreclosed are substantial.[82]

Entry barriers are essential for the assessment.[83] If it is relatively easy for **10.84**. competing suppliers to find alternative distributors, there is no genuine risk of foreclosure.

Countervailing buying power may also have distinct consequences for the **10.85**. assessment. Powerful distributors will be reluctant to accept non-compete arrangements unless there are valid reasons to do so. However, the other side of the coin is that the more powerful or important the distributor is on the market concerned, the greater the foreclosure effect may be if other suppliers cannot operate through that distributor.

Regarding the **level of trade**, the risk of foreclosure is more important at the **10.86**. retail level than at the wholesale level.[84] In addition, the reduction of in-store competition applies in principle only at the retail level.

With regard to the **nature of the products**, competition law problems are more **10.87**. likely in the case of final goods than in the case of intermediate goods.[85]

Having regard to these factors, the Guidelines (paragraph 148) conclude that **10.88**. 'for final products at the retail level, significant anti-competitive effects may start

---

[79] ibid, para 140.   [80] ibid, para 141.   [81] ibid, para 142.
[82] *A contrario* Guidelines, para 143.   [83] ibid, para 144.   [84] ibid, paras 147–8.
[85] ibid, paras 146–8.

to arise, taking into account all relevant factors, if a non-dominant supplier ties 30% or more of the relevant market'.

Features of the vertical restraint

10.89. Two features of non-compete or similar obligations may have a considerable impact on their restrictive intensity.

10.90. **Duration of the non-compete or similar obligation.**   The longer the term of the restriction,[86] the higher the risk that the competitive concerns outlined above may materialize. The impact of the term may be mitigated if there is strong initial competition for obtaining the single branding contracts.[87]

10.91. **Form of the single branding restriction.** A straightforward non-compete obligation is obviously the most restrictive of the single branding restrictions. Quantity forcing on the distributor (eg by means of minimum annual purchase requirements or loyalty-inducing incentive schemes) may leave some room for the distributor to handle competing brands and is likely to have a weaker impact on competition.[88]

Efficiencies

10.92. The efficiencies which may justify single branding obligations include the following.

Free-rider problem

10.93. A supplier may suffer from free-rider problems if the supplier invests for its distributors and such investments attract customers for competing brands.[89] The Guidelines (paragraph 116(1)) state that free-riding between suppliers is restricted to cases of generic (ie not brand-specific) promotion at the premises of the distributor.[90]

Hold-up problem

10.94. A non-compete obligation or quantity forcing on the buyer may be justified if the supplier makes relationship-specific investments.[91] The conditions that must be met in that case are, *mutatis mutandis*, the same as those outlined in paragraph 10.52 above.

Specific hold-up problem

10.95. This problem occurs where the supplier transfers substantial know-how to the distributor that is indispensable to the distributorship.[92] The supplier wishes to

---

[86] This may be a fixed term or the ease with which the non-compete arrangement can be terminated (eg by means of a short notice period).   [87] Guidelines, para 108.
[88] ibid, para 152.   [89] ibid, para 116 (1).   [90] ibid.   [91] ibid, para 116(4).
[92] ibid, para 116(5).

avoid the said know-how being used by the distributor to the benefit of competing suppliers. This will typically be the case in franchising systems.[93]

Economies of scale

Quantity forcing (such as annual minimum purchase requirements) may enable the supplier to exploit economies of scale.[94] It may be assumed that a straightforward non-compete obligation cannot be justified on the basis of alleged economies of scale. **10.96**.

Capital market imperfections

Given its better knowledge of the distributor and via the extra security of an exclusive relationship, the supplier may be in a better position to provide financing than banks and other standard providers of finance.[95] The Guidelines (paragraph 156) state that the instances where the supplier may be better placed are limited. Even if the supplier is a more efficient provider of capital, the Guidelines consider that a loan can only justify a non-compete obligation if the buyer is not prevented from terminating the obligation and repaying the outstanding part of the loan at any point in time and without payment of any penalty.[96] **10.97**.

Concrete guidance

The Guidelines offer concrete guidance on the likely outcome of the individual assessment of non-compete obligations and quantity forcing on the distributor in +30% scenarios: **10.98**.

— Dominant companies will in principle not be allowed to impose non-compete obligations[97] or to apply fidelity rebate schemes or English clauses.[98]
— For non-dominant companies, the Guidelines offer the following guidance.[99] Non-compete obligations of less than one year are likely to receive a favourable assessment. If the non-compete obligation is entered into for a term ranging between one and five years, an individual examination of the pro- and anti-competitive effects is called for. The period of depreciation of the relationship-specific investments may be an important factor in this context.[100] Non-compete obligations exceeding five years are allowed in exceptional circumstances only. This may be the case if substantial know-how is transferred

---

[93] ibid, para 157.   [94] ibid, para 116(6).   [95] ibid, para 116(7).
[96] ibid. In order to render such exit feasible, the loan will have to be structured in a particular manner and repayment of the loan must be allowed at any time and without a penalty.
[97] Guidelines, para 141.   [98] ibid, para 152.   [99] ibid, para 141.
[100] ibid, para 155.

to the distributor[101] or where the non-compete obligation is combined with exclusive distribution.[102]

— A non-compete obligation imposed on franchisees will escape the prohibition of Article 81(1) EC if such obligation is necessary to maintain the common identity and reputation of the franchised network.[103] The obligation may be imposed for the full term of the franchise agreement.

(9) *Exclusive supply and quantity forcing on the supplier*

10.99. The concept of exclusive supply is given a specific and narrow definition in Regulation 2790/99. It means that the supplier undertakes to supply only one purchaser in the whole of the Community.[104] The Guidelines add to this that, for intermediate goods or services, 'exclusive supply' means that there is only one buyer inside the Community or that there is only one buyer in the Community for the purposes of a specific use.[105] This is the concept that is addressed here.

10.100. Cases where the supplier undertakes to supply its final products to more than one distributor within the Community (eg one distributor per Member State or another geographic area) should be analysed in accordance with the principles governing the assessment of exclusive distribution. The market foreclosure concerns discussed in this section are nevertheless relevant: the less distributors appointed in the Community, the greater the purchase market foreclosure concerns.

10.101. Quantity forcing on the supplier may have competitive implications that are similar to an exclusive supply scenario. This will be the case if the volumes that the supplier is required to supply to a single distributor limit the supplier in its ability to supply other distributors or customers.

Competitive concerns

10.102. Exclusive supply is part of the so-called 'limited distribution group' of vertical restraints.[106] The concerns to which this group may give rise include foreclosure of the purchase market, the facilitation of collusion and reduction of intra-brand competition.[107] The most important of these issues in the context of exclusive supply obligations is the foreclosure risk.[108]

---

[101] ibid, para 157. In that case, the non-compete obligation may even fall outside Art 81(1) EC: Guidelines, para 116(5).   [102] Guidelines, para 158.
[103] ibid, para 200.   [104] Reg 2790/99, Art 1(c), as discussed in para 2.232 above.
[105] Guidelines, para 202.   [106] ibid, para 109.   [107] ibid, para 110.
[108] ibid, para 204.

Measurement of restrictive intensity

The characteristics of the market and the features of the vertical restraint at issue   **10.103.**
that influence the restrictive impact of exclusive supply can be summarized as
follows.

Market characteristics

The **market position of the supplier** does not seem to be a major factor   **10.104.**
in the assessment. The Guidelines (paragraph 208) indeed link the position
of the supplier to the circumstances in which an exclusive supply obligation is
likely to be accepted. They note that this will mostly be the case with weak
suppliers, as strong suppliers will not easily accept being cut off from alternative
customers.

The **market position of other suppliers** also does not seem to play a pre-   **10.105.**
ponderant role in the assessment.

The focus of the analysis is on the **position of the buyer** (ie the distributor). In   **10.106.**
this respect regard must be had both to the upstream purchase market and the
downstream market.[109] The market share on the purchase market will influence
its ability to impose an exclusive supply obligation. It is however the market
share on the downstream market that determines whether consumers will experience negative effects. According to the Guidelines (paragraph 92), negative
competitive effects are to be expected if the purchaser has a market share in
excess of 30% on both markets. Even if the buyer's market share on the
upstream market does not exceed 30%, significant foreclosure effects may still
result if the market share of the buyer on his downstream market exceeds 30%.

The **market position of the competing buyers** (ie distribution channels) may   **10.107.**
influence the level of foreclosure. If the other buyers have similar buying power
and can offer the suppliers similar sales possibilities, foreclosure is not very
likely.[110] However, if a number of major buyers all enter into exclusive supply
arrangements with the majority of the suppliers on the market, potential
entrants risk being foreclosed.

The **absence of entry barriers** may exclude or limit the risk of foreclosure. For   **10.108.**
instance, if competing buyers are themselves able to offer the goods or services
efficiently via vertical integration, foreclosure will normally not present a problem.[111] The same is true if alternative suppliers (other than those subject to an
exclusive supply obligation) can readily switch to the products or services

---

[109] ibid, para 204. It is to be noted that, for the purposes of assessing the 30% limit in the
context of Reg 2790/99, only the upstream purchase market is taken into consideration
(Guidelines, para 92).   [110] ibid, para 206.
    [111] ibid, para 207.

concerned to address demand of distribution channels that do not have access to such products or services as a result of the existing exclusive supply obligations.

10.109. The **nature of the product** can also play a role in determining the risk of foreclosure. Such risk is greater for heterogeneous products (with different grades and qualities) and branded final products, than for intermediate (ie input) products or where the product is homogeneous.[112]

Features of the vertical restraint

10.110. Two features of the exclusive supply obligation have a major influence on its foreclosure impact :

— **Duration**. The longer the term of the exclusive supply obligation, the greater its possible foreclosure effect will be.[113]

— **Tied share**. The tied supply share reflects the part of the relevant market share that is coupled with an exclusive supply obligation. The higher such tied share is, the greater the risk of foreclosure.[114]

Efficiencies

10.111. The Guidelines (paragraph 211) are not very optimistic with regard to the efficiencies that can be invoked to compensate for the anti-competitive effects of an exclusive supply obligation. They refer to hold-up problems,[115] as being more likely in respect of intermediate goods than final goods. Economies of scale in distribution[116] are stated as not being a likely justification.[117] The issue of capital market imperfection may present a way out, but only in the case where the loan has been provided by the distributor (which is an uncommon scenario).[118] So if exclusive supply obligations have an appreciable foreclosure effect, it will be difficult to prove the efficiencies that may compensate for such an effect.

Concrete guidance

10.112. If the buyer has a market share exceeding 30%, the following concrete guidance can be distilled from the Guidelines:

— When a buyer is dominant on the downstream market, exclusive supply will easily be deemed to have significant anti-competitive effects.[119] If so, an exemption pursuant to Article 81(3) EC may be ruled out.[120]

---

[112] ibid, paras 209–10.   [113] ibid, para 205.   [114] ibid.
[115] ibid, paras 116(4) and (5). The Guidelines (para 212) add that quantity forcing (such as a minimum supply obligation) could well be a less restrictive alternative.
[116] Guidelines, para 116(6).
[117] ibid, para 211. Also here, quantity forcing on the supplier is referred to as a possible less restrictive alternative.   [118] ibid, para 116(7).
[119] ibid, para 204.   [120] ibid, para 211.

— Exclusive supply arrangements entered into between non-dominant companies for a term of less than five years will usually require an ad hoc assessment of the pro- and anti-competitive effects. If the buyer's market share is in excess of 30% (on both the upstream and the downstream markets), the presumption is that negative effects are to be expected.[121] The presumption is not an absolute one. It may be overcome by argument, such as the absence of entry barriers.[122] If this proves to be impossible, it will be difficult in a distribution context (which typically involves final goods) to present sufficiently compelling efficiencies for the exclusive supply arrangement. The parties will, in that context, have to justify why a lesser restraint (such as quantity forcing) is not sufficient to achieve the relevant efficiencies.
— Exclusive supply arrangements (presenting foreclosure effects) for a term of more than five years are unlikely to be exempted.[123]

(10) Exclusive purchasing

Exclusive purchasing must be distinguished from a non-compete obligation.[124]   **10.113.**
The latter prevents the distributor from becoming active in products that are competing with the contract products that are purchased from the supplier. In the case of exclusive purchasing, the distributor remains free to handle competing products. Exclusive purchasing consists of an obligation or incentive scheme agreed between the supplier and the distributor according to which the latter will purchase its requirements of the contract products exclusively from the supplier or a third party designated by the supplier.[125] This implies that the distributor is not entitled to purchase the contract products from any other sources, including the other distributors appointed by the supplier.

Competitive concerns

Exclusive purchasing is part of the so-called 'market partitioning group' of   **10.114.**
vertical restraints.[126] The competitive concerns which exclusive purchasing may entail are a possible reduction in intra-brand competition (that may help the supplier to partition the market and may facilitate price discrimination) and the facilitation of collusion when most or all competing suppliers apply limitations on sourcing or resale possibilities.[127]

Throughout the Guidelines exclusive purchasing is mostly assessed in combi-   **10.115.**
nation with other vertical restraints.[128] When considered in isolation, exclusive

---

[121] ibid, para 204.   [122] ibid, para 207.   [123] ibid, para 204.
[124] For an example of a possible mix-up of the concepts, Guidelines on the application of Art 81(3) EC, para 82. For more details on the distinction, paras 6.01–6.04 above.
[125] Guidelines, para 113.   [126] ibid.   [127] ibid, para 114.
[128] eg Guidelines, paras 172 and 177.

purchasing affects only a particular aspect of intra-brand competition: it prevents a specific type of arbitrage by eliminating the possibility of cross-supplies between appointed distributors.[129] Many other forms of intra-brand competition are left intact, such as the competition between distributors or via resale channels that have not been designated by the supplier, but purchase the contract products from the official distributors. The risk that exclusive purchasing, considered in isolation, may contribute to collusion (either at the level of the suppliers or the distributors) is equally far from being self-evident and requires quite specific circumstances.

Measurement of restrictive intensity

10.116. The Guidelines do not address the market characteristics or the specific features that may impact the restrictive intensity of exclusive purchasing.

Market characteristics

10.117. In the absence of more specific guidance, it seems prudent to rely on the discussion of other vertical restraints that are part of the market partitioning group (such as territorial and customer restrictions).

10.118. A number of specific comments can be added to these. As stated above, the impact of exclusive purchasing on intra-brand competition essentially consists of the elimination of arbitrage between distributors. In many cases the importance of such arbitrage should not be overestimated. For instance, if the products are bulky and transport costs are high, the possibility for cross-supplies may not really be available[130] and it would be erroneous to suggest that exclusive purchasing reduces intra-brand competition. The same can be said where the supplier applies the same price level throughout the Community when supplying its network. It is obviously possible that distributors in such a scenario engage in cross-supplies by cutting their margins, but beside this, the importance of such cross-supplies must not be overstated. There is normally no real incentive for the distributors to engage in this type of arbitrage. After all, why would they reduce their margins in order to be able to sell to other distributors that may compete with them to sell the products concerned in the market?

Features of the vertical restraint

10.119. The most important feature that may be relevant to the measurement of the intensity of the restriction is its term. In this respect it will be recalled that the former Regulation 1984/83[131] granted an automatic exemption for exclusive purchasing up to a fixed term of five years.

---

[129] ibid, para 172.   [130] Guidelines, para 175.
[131] Regulation (EEC) No 1984/83 of 22 June 1983 on the application of Article 85(3) of the Treaty to categories of exclusive purchasing agreement [1983] L173/5.

Efficiencies

The efficiencies mentioned by the Guidelines in relation to exclusive purchasing **10.120**. are the achievement of economies of scale[132] and the avoidance of a hold-up problem where investments are made by the supplier.[133] The economies of scale argument risks being somewhat problematic as the same efficiency seems to be readily achievable via a lesser vertical restraint, such as quantity forcing on the distributors (obligation to order particular minimum quantities at a time or with certain fixed intervals).

Concrete guidance

The Guidelines do not offer any concrete guidance for exclusive purchasing as **10.121**. such. Given the fact that the restriction of cross-supplies between selective distributors is blacklisted in Article 4(d) of Regulation 2790/99, exclusive purchasing will not be given a favourable individual assessment in the context of a selective distribution system. Outside the context of selective distribution, exclusive purchasing is likely to attract criticism if it is combined with other vertical restraints. However, it must not be readily assumed that exclusive purchasing, in and of itself, is likely to appreciably impact competition.

D. Combinations of Vertical Restraints

The objective of this section is not to present a complete analysis of the **10.122**. assessment to be made of combinations of vertical restraints. Such assessment requires a careful analysis of the market characteristics, the specific features of the vertical restraints concerned and the impact on competition of their interplay. The Guidelines (paragraph 119(6)) state that 'in general, a combination of vertical restraints aggravates their negative effects', but hasten to add that 'certain combinations of vertical restraints are better for competition than their use in isolation from each other'. Hence, a careful and balanced approach to the assessment of combinations of vertical restraints is called for.

This section brings together the statements of the Guidelines on certain com- **10.123**. binations of vertical restraints. These statements provide an indication as to the ramifications of their individual assessment.

(1) Exclusive distribution and territorial restrictions

The Guidelines (paragraph 50) present the grant of territorial exclusivity in **10.124**. combination with the imposition of territorial restrictions (restriction on active sales) on the other distributors towards the exclusive territory as a logical

---

[132] Guidelines, paras 116(6) and 118.   [133] ibid, para 116(4).

combination. Hence, if efficiencies justify territorial exclusivity, they are likely to justify the imposition of territorial restrictions as well.

(2) Exclusive distribution and non-compete obligation

10.125. In respect of the combination of exclusive distribution and a non-compete obligation, the main concern is that of foreclosure.[134] The central issue is whether competing suppliers or potential entrants may face difficulties in appointing distributors to market their products. This may be the case if a leading supplier has set up a dense network of exclusive distributors with small territories that are bound by a non-compete obligation.[135] The same problem may occur in the case of a cumulative effect.[136]

10.126. In the absence of foreclosure problems, the Guidelines consider the combination of exclusive distribution and non-compete obligations favourably as it increases the incentive for the distributor to focus his efforts on the brand concerned.[137] Unless the supplier is dominant, the Guidelines (paragraph 158) suggest that it may be justified to impose the non-compete obligation for the full term of the exclusive distribution agreement. This applies in particular to distribution agreements concluded at the wholesale level.[138]

(3) Exclusive distribution and exclusive purchasing

10.127. The combination of exclusive distribution and exclusive purchasing is viewed much less favourably in the Guidelines.[139] The main concern is that the combination reduces intra-brand competition and facilitates market partitioning. The ultimate concern seems to be that the combination incites price discrimination.

10.128. Exclusive distribution is said to limit arbitrage by customers and exclusive purchasing may further reduce intra-brand competition by eliminating arbitrage between distributors. The combination is therefore 'unlikely to be exempted for suppliers with a market share above 30% unless there are very clear and substantial efficiencies leading to lower prices for all final consumers'.[140]

(4) Selective distribution and non-compete obligation

10.129. This combination may trigger a foreclosure problem for other suppliers. In order to assess this risk, the principles governing the single branding group must be applied.[141]

---

[134] Guidelines, para 165.   [135] ibid, para 171.
[136] ibid. This means that several suppliers apply a distribution system based on territorial exclusivity in combination with single branding.   [137] Guidelines, paras 158 and 171.
[138] ibid, para 171.   [139] ibid, paras 172 and 177.   [140] ibid, para 172.
[141] ibid, para 193.

(5) *Selective distribution and exclusive distribution*

The combination of exclusive and selective distribution (even if active sales **10.130**. between territories remain free) by a supplier having a market share in excess of 30% will only exceptionally be deemed to fulfil the criteria of Article 81(3) EC. This will be the case where the combination is 'indispensable to protect substantial and relationship-specific investments made by the authorised dealers'.[142]

The tough stance on this particular combination is somewhat surprising. A **10.131**. distribution formula consisting of territorial exclusivity, selectivity, and absence of restrictions on active sales is in fact a specific form of quantitative selective distribution. The feature of territorial exclusivity does not radically change the analysis as it will depend *inter alia* on the size of the territory whether the competitive impact is markedly different from quantitative selectivity that is not organized on the basis of territorial exclusivity. It seems that it should be recommended to review the specific features of the combination carefully before arriving at any conclusions.[143]

(6) *Selective distribution and exclusive customer allocation*

A combination of selective distribution and exclusive customer allocation is **10.132**. normally a hardcore restriction.[144] The chances that this combination will survive an individual Article 81(3) EC assessment are thus remote.

(7) *Exclusive supply and non-compete obligation*

The Guidelines (paragraph 208) state that this combination (which in fact **10.133**. amounts to reciprocal exclusivity) may be found in cases where the suppliers are strong. In the case of relationship-specific investments on both sides (hold-up problem), the combination may be justified below the level of dominance. They also suggest that the chances for such a justification are greater in the case of industrial supply agreements (ie exclusive supply for intermediate goods or services).

---

[142] ibid, para 195.
[143] See in particular, the relatively favourable assessment of quantitative selectivity reflected in the Guidelines, para 187.
[144] ibid, para 179.

Part IV

MOTOR VEHICLE DISTRIBUTION UNDER REGULATION 1400/2002

11

THE MOTOR VEHICLE DISTRIBUTION BLOCK EXEMPTION

A. Introduction

(1) Historical background

For an overview of the historical background of Regulation 1400/2002,[1]   **11.01**.
reference is made to Chapter 1 (paragraphs 1.49–1.61).

(2) A more economic and less prescriptive approach

In the process that would finally culminate in the adoption of Regulation 1400/   **11.02**.
2002, one of the recurring themes was that the previous block exemption
regulation applying to the sector, Regulation 1475/95,[2] had a straitjacket effect.
The Commission describes this effect as one 'whereby, by exempting only one
model for distribution, the Regulation encourages all suppliers to use near
identical distribution systems, leading to rigidity'.[3] Tsoraklidis[4] characterizes
the straitjacket effect of Regulation 1475/95 as powerful and concludes that 'all
current motor vehicle distribution systems are modelled on Regulation 1475/
95, thereby impeding the development of innovative distribution systems'.

---

[1] Commission Regulation (EC) No 1400/2002 of 31 July 2002 on the application of Article
81(3) of the Treaty to categories of vertical agreements and concerted practices in the motor
vehicle sector [2002] OJ L203/30.
[2] Commission Regulation (EC) No 1475/95 on the application of Article 85(3) of the Treaty
to certain categories of motor vehicle distribution and servicing agreements [1995] OJ L145/25.
[3] European Commission, *Explanatory brochure for Commission Regulation (EC) No 1400/2002
of 31 July 2002 on the application of Article 81(3) of the Treaty to categories of vertical agreements
and concerted practices in the motor vehicle sector*, footnote 14, available at http://europa.eu.int/
comm/competition/car sector/explanatory_brochure_en.pdf (hereafter 'Explanatory Brochure').
[4] L Tsoraklidis, 'Towards a New Motor Vehicle Block Exemption—Commission Proposal for
Motor Vehicle Distribution, Adopted on 5 February 2002' (2002) 2 EC Competition Policy
Newsletter 31.

With the adoption of Regulation 1400/2002, the Commission intended to 'free . . . the sector from the straitjacket effect associated with the previous rules'[5] and no longer to 'prescribe a single rigid model for car distribution in Europe, but rather [to] leave . . . a wide number of choices open to carmakers, distributors and dealers'.[6]

11.03.   Whether Regulation 1400/2002 is less prescriptive than Regulation 1475/95 is controversial, to say the least.[7] As will become apparent from the discussion of Regulation 1400/2002 below, radically alternative distribution methods are either not encouraged (see the hypothesis of distribution via supermarkets)[8] or not perceived as major solutions to the problems at hand (see the role to be attributed to the Internet in motor vehicle distribution).[9] Where the Commission refers to an increased freedom of choice, it essentially refers to the choice between exclusive distribution and selective distribution.[10]

11.04.   Legal commentators have questioned whether the choice presented by the Commission is genuine.[11] Both business reality and the economics underlying

---

[5] M Martinez Lopez, 'New Explanatory Brochure on Commission Block Exemption Regulation No 1400/2002 on the Motor Vehicle Sector: Bringing Competition Rules Closer to Consumers and Market Operators' (2003) 1 EC Competition Policy Newsletter 59.

[6] Commission Press Release, IP/02/1073, 17 July 2002; E van Ginderachter, 'Concurrence: Les nouvelles règles applicables au secteur automobile' [2002] Journal des Tribunaux Droit Européen 233, 235 and S Vezzoso, 'On the Antitrust Remedies to Promote Retail Innovation in the EU Car Sector' [2004] ECLR 190.

[7] It is inaccurate to suggest that Reg 1475/95 imposed a combination of exclusive and selective distribution as the sole distribution method that could benefit from the block exemption. Reg 1475/95 required the use of exclusive distribution (which could even take the form of shared exclusivity and thereby the dealer territories could be kept very small) and exempted (but did not require) the use of selectivity. The suggestion in (European Commission, *Report on the Evaluation of Regulation (EC) No 1475/95 on the application of Article 85(3) of the Treaty to certain categories of motor vehicle distribution and servicing agreements*, 15 November 2000, COM(2000)743 final, available at http://europa.eu.int/eur-lex/en/com/rpt/2000/com2000_0743en01.pdf (hereafter 'Evaluation Report') (pp 12–14) (n 9 below) that motor vehicles are exceptional in this respect, as the distribution of comparable products occurs through less restrictive distribution methods, is not entirely fair. It will be recalled that the *BMW* decision (*Bayerische Motoren Werke AG* [1975] OJ L29/1) did not only concern motor vehicles, but also motorcycles, and that Honda applied for an individual exemption in respect of a motorcycle distribution system based on Reg 123/85, but this was rejected by the Commission (European Commission, *Twenty-first Report on Competition Policy 1991*, point 91 and Commission Press Release, IP/95/544, 3 July 1992).

[8] Commission Press Releases, MEMO/02/18, 5 February 2002 and IP/02/1073, 17 July 2002.

[9] The Internet seems to be perceived as a significant information tool (eg to facilitate price comparisons) (Evaluation Report, 149, paras 143 and 154 and footnote 191), but not as a sales tool (Commission Press Releases, MEMO/02/18, 5 February 2002 and IP/02/1073, 17 July 2002 and A Hermel, 'La distribution automobile: les problèmes actuels, les réponses à venir' (2002) 59 Petites Affiches, 11).

[10] Commission Press Releases, IP/03/1318, 30 September 2003, IP/02/196, 5 February 2002 and IP/02/1073, 17 July 2002.

[11] Automotive Sector Groups of HB and LWWK, 'Flawed Reform of the Competition Rules for the European Motor Vehicle Distribution Sector' [2003] ECLR 254; J Creutzig, 'Der Automobilvertrieb ab Oktober 2002—Kritische Anmerkungen zur Kfz-GVO 1400/2002' (2002) 10 Wettbewerb in Recht und Praxis 1124, 1126 ('Die programmatische Aussage der

motor vehicle distribution suggest that these commentators may well be right. Motor vehicle producers perceive the imposition of qualitative requirements on their dealer networks as an important feature to attract customers and hence to engage in inter-brand competition. While Regulation 1400/2002 does not seem to prevent the imposition of certain qualitative restrictions on authorized exclusive dealers, it is beyond dispute that the exclusive dealers must be entitled to resell to independent dealers and that such independent players cannot be subjected by the producer to any requirements of a qualitative nature.[12] Motor vehicle producers will inevitably face difficulties to convince their networks to make the necessary investments to meet the set qualitative targets if they are confronted with free-riders that can legally put new vehicles of the same brand on the market without engaging in these types of investment. Hence, any car producer that sets qualitative standards requiring sizeable investments by its network will have no genuine choice between exclusive and selective distribution. Such a producer will be compelled to work with selective distribution.[13]

In the context of after-sales services and parts distribution, Regulation 1400/2002 is clearly intended by DG COMP to have a prescriptive effect. As discussed below,[14] DG COMP takes the view that in both areas producers will have a market share that exceeds 30%. Under those circumstances they can only benefit from the block exemption if they implement a (purely) qualitative selective distribution system. In other words, the alternatives of exclusive distribution or quantitative selective distribution are in practice not open to them. **11.05**.

It is correct that Regulation 1400/2002 is more flexible by no longer requiring that the dealer must engage both in sales of vehicles and in their repair and maintenance.[15] Pure sales agreements and pure servicing agreements can now also benefit from the block exemption. The reorganization of the link between **11.06**.

Kommission, mit der neuen GVO aus dem Zwangsjacken-Effekt herausgeführt und wirkliche Wahlrechte geschaffen zu haben, entpuppt sich nach alledem bedauerlicherweise als eine Illusion') and Y van Couter and G Bogaert, 'De Groepsvrijstelligsverordening nr. 1400/2002: meer dan een "pit-stop" voor de automobielconcessieovereenkomsten...' [2003] Tijdschrift voor Belgisch Handelsrecht 458–96, para 13, 465–6.

[12] Reg 1400/2002, Art 4(1)(b); Vezzoso (n 6 above) 194, and Automotive Sector Groups of HB and LWWK (n 11 above) 257.

[13] This explains why in practice all of the established brands have, in the meantime, opted for selective distribution (Commission Press Release, IP/03/1318, 30 September 2003). Commissioner Monti referred to the exception of Suzuki, that has allegedly chosen exclusive distribution (M Monti, *The New Legal Framework for Car Distribution*, speech 03/59, 6 February 2003; Commission Press Release, IP/04/585, 3 May 2004). Suzuki can probably afford this approach due to the lack of investments required from its dealers and the fact that most of its dealers also distribute one or more other brands. In the latter case Suzuki may well indirectly rely on the qualitative requirements imposed by the main brands sold by the dealer. Given its limited market share, Suzuki is also not a good example of a producer selecting exclusive distribution in the context of Reg 1400/2002. Benefiting in all likelihood from *de minimis* treatment, Suzuki most likely does not need the block exemption. [14] Paras 11.70–11.72.

[15] Paras 11.134 *et seq*.

sales and servicing will not trigger a major change in the market as many car producers already had designated service points (that do not engage in car sales activities) prior to the entry into force of the new Regulation.[16]

11.07. The prescriptive effect of Regulation 1400/2002 (resulting from the fact that producers almost inevitably will end up with quantitative selective distribution for vehicle sales and qualitative selective distribution for after-sales services and parts sales) is further enhanced by the detailed provisions included in Articles 3, 4, and 5 of Regulation 1400/2002 and the extensive interpretation given to these provisions in the Explanatory Brochure and the Frequently Asked Questions.[17] Many examples are given below. Practitioners that have assisted car producers with the implementation of Regulation 1400/2002 can confirm that the impact of a block exemption (including DG COMP's interpretation of the same) on the drafting of the new agreements has rarely been so direct and so detailed.[18]

11.08. Finally, as to the more economic approach underlying Regulation 1400/2002, reference is mostly made to the market share limits that are included in the block exemption.[19] The reliance on market share limits, however, does not in itself imply that more economics have been injected into the Regulation. It simply means that companies with a sizeable market presence cannot avail themselves of the block exemption and will have to conduct an individual assessment in order to determine whether or not their networks are covered by Article 81(3) EC. If more economics are involved, it is also not due to the fact that (as in the case of Regulation 2790/99) operators enjoy considerable freedom in devising their distribution systems, as long as they steer away from a very limited list of hardcore restrictions. The 'more economics' label in the context of Regulation 1400/2002 can only be taken to mean that, based on its own economic assessment of the motor vehicle sector, the Commission has deliberately opted for a very specific distribution model in which it has rigorously defined what it expects

---

[16] H Gambs, 'The First Case of Application of the New Motor Vehicle Block Exemption Regulation: Audi's Authorised Repairers' (2003) 2 EC Competition Policy Newsletter 53, 54; N Giroudet-Demay, 'Incidences du règlement automobile (C.E.) N° 1400/2002 sur l'organisation de l'après-vente de la marque' (29 November 2002) 239 Petites Affiches 13, 14. Also, the references to Volkswagen, Audi, and Ford in Commission Press Releases, IP/02/1073, 17 July 2002 and IP/03/80, 20 January 2003.

[17] The contrast between Commission Regulation (EC) No 2790/1999 of 22 December 1999 on the application of Article 81(3) of the Treaty to categories of vertical agreements and concerted practices [1999] OJ L336/21 and Reg 1400/2002 is sharp in this respect. European Commission—Directorate General Competition, *Frequently Asked Questions*, available at http://europa.eu.int/comm/competition/car_sector/distribution/faq_en.pdf (hereafter 'Frequently Asked Questions').

[18] I Buelens, 'Verruiming van de concurrentie op de Europese markt voor de verkoop en herstelling van motorvoertuigen?' (2002–2003) 3 Het Poelaertplein 18, 19.

[19] Reg 1400/2002, Arts 3(1) and 3(2); Explanatory Brochure, chapter 6 and Y Makhlouf and M Malaurie-Vignal, 'Synthèse du Règlement d'exemption N° 1400/2002 du 31 juillet 2002' (2002) 239 Petites Affiches 6, 11.

from the various actors. In doing so, the Commission has come very close to regulating the sector.

(3) Aims of Regulation 1400/2002: radical promotion of intra-brand competition

The aims underlying the changes to the block exemption regime do not so much concern the promotion of choice between various distribution formulas; Regulation 1400/2002 rather reflects a clear policy choice by the Commission to create conditions that will trigger increased intra-brand competition.   **11.09**.

The aims of Regulation 1400/2002 are directly linked to the Commission's findings in the Evaluation Report: **11.10**.

> The Commission's own evaluation report showed that several of the aims underlying Regulation 1475/95 have clearly not been achieved. European consumers do not derive their fair share of benefits from the system, competition between dealers is not strong enough and dealers remain too dependent on car manufacturers. Consumers have also in practice found it difficult to exercise their Single Market right to take advantage of price differentials between Member States and buy their vehicle wherever the price is lowest.[20]

These findings have pushed the preparation of the new regulation in the direction of both increased market integration and increased dealer independence vis-à-vis the manufacturers.[21] In a sense, these two aims go hand in hand. The philosophy is clearly that the more the dealers are independent (ie the less they have to fear or take account of the reaction of the car manufacturers), the more they will engage in intra-brand competition outside the territories in which they are designated or expected to operate. Measures to strengthen dealer independence are supplemented in Regulation 1400/2002 with provisions aimed specifically at facilitating cross-border trade.[22]

While the unrestricted possibility offered by Regulation 1400/2002 for dealers to engage in multi-branding is one of the striking novelties, the promotion of increased inter-brand competition is not one of the main aims of the new Regulation. The Evaluation Report[23] concluded that 'there is currently reason to believe that effective inter-brand competition exists in the European Union'. Hence, there was no apparent need to implement measures to increase   **11.11**.

---

[20] Commission Press Release, IP/02/1073, 17 July 2002 and Tsoraklidis (n 4 above) 31.
[21] D Gerard, ' "Regulated Competition" in the Automobile Distribution Sector: A Comparative Analysis of the Car Distribution System in the US and the EU' [2003] ECLR 518, 527 and van Ginderachter (n 6 above) 235–6.
[22] The most important of such measures is the abolition of the location clause as of 1 October 2005, Reg 1400/2002, Art 12(2) and Commission Press Release, IP/05/1208, 30 September 2005. Paras 11.204–11.211 below.   [23] Evaluation Report (n 7 above) 73.

inter-brand competition as such. However, the Evaluation Report[24] also identified multi-branding as a factor that may strengthen dealer independence:[25] the less a dealer is dependent on the brand(s) of a single manufacturer, the more the dealer will be inclined to determine its own competitive course of action in respect of a given brand.[26] This explains how the abolition of the restrictions on multi-branding can be reconciled with the findings in the Evaluation Report. In its press releases concerning the new block exemption, the Commission made no reference to increased inter-brand competition and placed the issue of multi-branding systematically in the context of dealer independence.[27]

11.12. In addition to the radical choice in favour of increased intra-brand competition on vehicle sales, Regulation 1400/2002 is intended to foster competition in respect of after-sales services and parts distribution.[28] This trend was already present in Regulation 1475/95, but is taken considerably further in the context of the new regime. A perfect illustration of the radical manner in which the Commission intends to promote competition in those areas is by the mandatory use of qualitative selective distribution. Quantitative limitations on the number of network members are lifted and any candidate that meets the producer's qualitative requirements must be allowed to operate as an authorized service outlet or parts distributor.

(4) Structure of Regulation 1400/2002

11.13. While the structure of Regulation 1400/2002 resembles that of Regulation 2790/99, it does, however, contain a number of significant differences and is substantially more complex.

11.14. As with Regulation 2790/99, Articles 1 and 2 of Regulation 1400/2002 contain a set of definitions and the scope of application of the block exemption, respectively.

---

[24] ibid, para 208.

[25] References to consumer demand for dealers selling more than one brand as a justification for lifting the restrictions on multi-branding are not particularly compelling from a competition law perspective (Commission Press Releases, MEMO/02/18, 5 February 2002 and IP/02/1073, 17 July 2002).

[26] On the link between multi-branding and dealer independence: L Idot, 'Le nouveau règlement d'exemption relatif à la distribution automobile' (2002) 50 JCP—La Semaine Juridique Entreprises et Affaires, 2000, 2002 and P Arhel, 'Vers l'adoption d'un nouveau Règlement "Automobile"' (2002) 64 Petites Affiches 7, 15.

[27] Commission Press Releases, IP/02/196, 5 February 2002 and IP/02/1073, 17 July 2002. DG COMP's justification for the new rules on multi-branding are, however, not always formulated in this sense. Tsoraklidis (n 4 above) 32, for instance, does not mention dealer independence (and hence intra-brand competition) as the driver for the changed regime and refers instead to 'in store multi-branding, which increases inter-brand competition and facilitates consumer choice . . .'.

[28] Commission Press Releases, IP/02/196, 5 February 2002, IP/02/1073, 17 July 2002 and MEMO/02/174, 17 July 2002.

Article 3

Article 3 provides certain general conditions. A failure to meet these conditions **11.15.** implies the loss of the benefit of the block exemption as a whole. From that perspective, a failure to meet the requirements of Article 3 has the same legal implications as an infringement of the list of hardcore restrictions included in Article 4.

The only condition imposed in Article 3 of Regulation 2790/99 is a market **11.16.** share limit of 30%. This market share limit remains applicable irrespective of the distribution formula that is chosen by the parties.[29] The position is substantially more complex under Regulation 1400/2002 in that it contains two sets of general conditions.

The first set of conditions are also market share related. The applicability of **11.17.** the block exemption as such is not rendered dependent on whether a given market share level is exceeded; rather, the market share test is linked to the applicability of the block exemption to a given distribution formula. Qualitative selective distribution is not subject to any market share limit, whilst quantitative selectivity for motor vehicles can be exempted up to a market share of 40% and up to a market share of 30% for parts and after-sales services. All other distribution formulas are subject to a limit of 30%. This matter will be addressed in detail below.[30]

The second set of conditions included in Article 3 of Regulation 1400/2002 has **11.18.** no parallel in Regulation 2790/99. Article 3(3) to (6) lists a number of requirements that must be included in vertical agreements that wish to benefit from the block exemption. These conditions concern a variety of matters, such as the transfer of the rights and obligations of an authorized dealer or repairer, term and termination requirements, and dispute resolution mechanisms.[31]

Article 4

Article 4 lists the hardcore restrictions. As in the case of Regulation 2790/99, **11.19.** infringements of Article 4 will render the block exemption inapplicable as a whole. The list of hardcore restrictions is substantially longer than that of Regulation 2790/99 and can be divided into four parts. The first part (Article 4(1)(a) to (e)) applies to all vertical agreements covered by the block exemption. This list is similar to that included in Regulation 2790/99. The second part (Article 4(1)(f) and (g)) applies only to vertical agreements that concern the sale

---

[29] The only complicating factor being that, if the vertical agreement contains an exclusive supply obligation, the market share limit must be calculated from the perspective of the purchaser as opposed to that of the supplier. [30] Paras 11.50–11.87 below.
[31] Paras 11.88–11.108 below.

of new motor vehicles. The third part (Article 4(1)(h) and (i)) applies only to vertical agreements concerning the sale of repair and maintenance services and of spare parts. The fourth part (Article 4(2)) concerns the obligations of motor vehicle suppliers to make certain technical information and equipment available to independent operators who are directly or indirectly active in the repair and maintenance of motor vehicles.

Article 5

11.20. Article 5 contains a number of so-called 'specific conditions'. The difference from Articles 3 and 4 is that the failure to comply with one or more of these specific conditions does not entail the loss of the block exemption as a whole. It simply implies that the block exemption does not cover the specific obligation that is not in conformity with Article 5. The remainder of the vertical agreement can continue to benefit from the block exemption. The specific conditions of Article 5 concern the imposition of non-compete obligations (Article 5(1)), the ability to sell leasing services (Article 5(2)(a)) and location restrictions (Article 5(2)(b) and 5(3)).

Articles 6 to 12

11.21. Article 6 enables the Commission to withdraw the benefit of the block exemption in particular cases. Article 7 entitles the Commission to declare the block exemption inapplicable, under certain circumstances, to a particular relevant market. Articles 8 and 9 provide guidance on the calculation of market shares and turnover, respectively, for the purposes of the Regulation. Article 10 governs the transitional period (which expired on 30 September 2003). Article 11 imposes a monitoring and evaluation obligation on the Commission and Article 12 governs the application *ratione temporis* of the Regulation.

B. Scope of Application

(1) Type of agreements covered

11.22. Article 2(1) describes the scope of application of Regulation 1400/2002 in general terms as follows:

> Pursuant to Article 81(3) of the Treaty and subject to the provisions of this Regulation, it is hereby declared that the provisions of Article 81(1) shall not apply to vertical agreements where they relate to the conditions under which the parties may purchase, sell or resell new motor vehicles, spare parts for motor vehicles or repair and maintenance services for motor vehicles.

The second subparagraph of Article 2(1) specifies that the block exemption shall apply only 'to the extent that such vertical agreements contain vertical restraints'.[32]   **11.23**.

(2) Applicability of Article 81(1) EC

The block exemption will only be relevant to the extent that the vertical   **11.24**. agreement concerned is covered by the prohibition of Article 81(1) EC. In the absence of a restriction of competition within the sense of Article 81(1) EC, there is no need for the parties to avail themselves of a block exemption (or any exemption whatsoever). In order to fall within the scope of Article 81(1) EC, it will be necessary that the vertical agreement has an appreciable effect on trade between Member States and entails an appreciable restriction of competition.

As to the required effect on inter-State trade, the Commission seems to assume   **11.25**. quite readily that vertical agreements in the motor vehicle distribution sector will meet the test. It refers in this respect to the fact that a network that extends across the whole territory of a Member State will usually have an appreciable effect on trade between Member States.[33] Also, in the Commission decisions or Court judgments concerning motor vehicle distribution adopted by the Commission to date, this condition for the application of Article 81(1) EC has never posed a problem.[34] Hence, in the absence of exceptional circumstances,[35] vertical agreements in the motor vehicle distribution sector will not be able to escape the prohibition of Article 81(1) EC for lack of effect on inter-State trade.

The position is somewhat more complex in respect of the requirement that   **11.26** the vertical agreement must entail an appreciable restriction of competition. The Commission accepts[36] that vertical agreements of the type covered by Regulation 1400/2002 can benefit from the '*De Minimis* Notice'.[37] This Notice quantifies what constitutes an appreciable restriction of competition by means of market share thresholds. Generally speaking, the thresholds are 15% for

---

[32] 'Vertical restraints' are defined as 'restrictions of competition falling within the scope of Article 81(1), when such restrictions are contained in a vertical agreement' (Reg 1400/2002, Art 1(1)(d)).   [33] Explanatory Brochure 7.

[34] *Volkswagen AG v Commission of the European Communities* Case T–62/98 [2000] ECR II–2707–2846, consideration 179 and references made there; *Volkswagen I* [1998] OJ L124/60, paras 149–50; *Opel* [2001] OJ L59/1 paras 140–1; *Volkswagen II* [2001] OJ L262/14, paras 81–91 and *DaimlerChrysler* [2002] OJ L257/1, paras 191–8.

[35] The chances that the 'appreciable effect on trade between Member States' test is not met, are greater in the context of second-tier agreements (eg sub-dealer agreements) than in the case of agreements between producers or their sales companies and (main) dealers or workshops.

[36] Explanatory Brochure 23, question 7.

[37] Commission Notice on agreements of minor importance which do not appreciably restrict competition under Article 81(1) of the Treaty establishing the European Community (*de minimis*) [2001] OJ C368/13 (hereafter '*De Minimis* Notice').

vertical agreements and 10% for horizontal agreements. However, if the market is foreclosed by the application of parallel networks of similar vertical agreements by several companies, the *de minimis* threshold is reduced to 5%.[38]

11.27. As to motor vehicle distribution, the Commission takes the view that the reduced *de minimis* threshold of 5% is relevant. The Evaluation Report[39] refers several times to the existence of parallel networks. Informal guidance obtained from DG COMP by certain producers also suggests that the *de minimis* treatment is only granted up to 5%. The Commission's press release regarding the distribution system of Porsche[40] lends further support to this position.[41]

11.28. The fact that a given producer can benefit from the *de minimis* treatment does not mean that it can simply ignore the block exemption. The producer concerned will be able to set aside the requirements laid down in Articles 3 (general conditions) and 5 (specific conditions).[42] However, the producer still has to comply with the hardcore restrictions included in Article 4. The Commission takes the view that the hardcore restrictions listed in Article 4 are 'severely anti-competitive restraints [. . .] which in general appreciably restrict competition even at low market shares'.[43] Hence, even if the 5% threshold is not exceeded, the hardcore restrictions have to be taken into account.

11.29. Different from vehicle sales, the Commission suggests that the *de minimis* threshold is likely to be exceeded for agreements entered into by a producer with its authorized repair network.[44] As Commissioner Monti adopted a similar position in respect of parts distribution,[45] the same observation may apply there.

11.30. In practical terms, the Commission's position seems to be that the *de minimis* treatment can only apply in respect of vehicle distribution, and not in respect of parts distribution or authorized repair and maintenance services. In the case of vehicle distribution, the *de minimis* threshold is 5% as opposed to the general

---

[38] *De Minimis* Notice, paras 7 and 8.

[39] Evaluation Report (n 7 above) paras 20 and 82.

[40] Commission Press Release, IP/04/585, 3 May 2004 and European Commission, *Report on Competition Policy 2004* (SEC(2005) 805 final), 42.

[41] Certain literature is vigorously opposed to the application of the notice in the context of the motor vehicle distribution sector and considers that its application results in a distortion of competition. L Vogel and J Vogel, 'Quelles améliorations peut-on apporter au projet de règlement sur la distribution automobile?' (2002) 20 JCP—La Semaine Juridique Entreprise et Affaires 794, 795.

[42] The most important features that a *de minimis* producer would be able to include in its agreements are therefore a non-compete obligation and a location clause. Commission Press Release, IP/04/585, 3 May 2004 regarding the distribution network of Porsche.

[43] Reg 1400/2002, recital 12; Explanatory Brochure 23, question 7, footnote 47 and European Commission, *Report on Competition Policy 2004* (n 40 above) 42.

[44] Explanatory Brochure 23, question 7; Commission Press Release, IP/04/585, 3 May 2004 and European Commission, *Report on Competition Policy 2004* (n 40 above) 42.

[45] Monti (n 13 above) and Frequently Asked Questions (n 17 above) 9, question 16.

threshold of 15% and, while Articles 3 and 5 can be ignored, the same is not true for the hardcore restrictions included in Article 4.

(3) Vertical agreements

The concept of 'vertical agreements' is defined as 'agreements or concerted **11.31**. practices entered into by two or more undertakings, each of which operates, for the purposes of the agreement, at a different level of the production or distribution chain'.[46] This definition calls for a number of observations that have direct practical relevance:

— As in the case of Regulation 2790/99, the block exemption applies only if the relevant agreement is entered into between two separate undertakings. This implies that intra-group agreements do not fall within the scope of application of Regulation 1400/2002. This is logical as intra-group agreements will normally not fall within the prohibition of Article 81(1) EC as the two-party requirement is not met.[47] This means, for instance, that agreements between a producer and its subsidiaries who serve as national importers, or agreements between a producer and its wholly-owned dealers are outside the scope of the block exemption and will not have to comply with its requirements.

— At least two of the parties to the vertical agreement must, for the purposes of the agreement, operate at a different level of the production or distribution chain. This means that horizontal agreements are not covered by the block exemption. Furthermore, agreements entered into with end-users are also outside the scope of the block exemption. These end-users (even if they are companies) do not meet the criterion of being active, for the purposes of the agreement, at a different level of the production or distribution chain. They may indeed be active at such a different level, but that will not be for the purposes of the vertical agreement concerned. The practical implications are quite far reaching. For instance, agreements pursuant to which

---

[46] Reg 1400/2002, Art 1(1)(c).

[47] The leading case for determining whether Art 81(1) EC can be applied between a parent company and its subsidiary company is Case T–102/92 *Viho v Commission* [1995] ECR II–17, paras 47–55 (confirmed by the Court of Justice in Case C–73/95P *Viho v Commission* [1996] ECR I–5457), in which it is stated that: 'Where, as in this case, the subsidiary, although having a separate legal personality, does not freely determine its conduct on the market but carries out the instructions given to it directly or indirectly by the parent company by which it is wholly controlled, Article 85(1) does not apply to the relationship between the subsidiary and the parent company with which it forms an economic unit.' The judgment in Case C–73/95P, para 16 adds: 'Parker and its subsidiaries thus form a single economic unit within which the subsidiaries do not enjoy real autonomy in determining their course of action in the market, but carry out the instructions issued to them by the parent company controlling them'. WPJ Wils, 'The Undertaking as Subject of E.C. Competition Law and the Imputation of Infringements to Natural or Legal Persons' [2000] ECLR 99.

a producer, importer, or dealer sells vehicles to fleet customers (including leasing companies) will not be covered by the block exemption.
— The definition of 'vertical agreements' applies to all levels of trade.[48]
— Agency agreements can also be covered by the block exemption, provided that so-called 'non-genuine' agents are involved.[49]

11.32. Article 2(2)(a) expressly provides that the Regulation applies to vertical agreements:

— entered into between an association of undertakings and its members *or* between such an association and its suppliers;
— provided that
  (i) all the members of the association are distributors of motor vehicles or spare parts for motor vehicles or are repairers; *and*
  (ii) no individual member of the association has a total annual turnover exceeding € 50 million (calculated at group level).[50]

11.33. While these vertical agreements may fall within the scope of Regulation 1400/2002, the horizontal agreements concluded in this context (eg the agreements entered into between the members or the decisions adopted by the association) must be assessed separately under Article 81(1) EC.[51]

11.34. As a general rule, the block exemption does not apply to vertical agreements entered into between competitors.[52] The concept of competitors comprises both actual and potential suppliers on the same product market.[53] The Regulation contains, however, three exceptions to this general principle.[54] The block exemption applies to non-reciprocal vertical agreements between competitors whereby:

— the buyer has a total annual turnover (calculated at group level)[55] not exceeding € 100 million; or

---

[48] Examples listed in the Explanatory Brochure 18–19.
[49] Explanatory Brochure 20, question 5; *DaimlerChrysler* [2002] OJ L257/1, paras 153–68 and Case T–325/01, *DaimlerChrysler v Commission*, judgment of 15 September 2005, not yet reported, paras 81–120.
[50] The relevant turnover must be calculated for the previous financial year and include the turnover for the entire group (see the concept of connected undertakings as defined in Reg 1400/2002, Art 1(2)), excluding (i) all taxes and other duties, and (ii) intra-group turnover (Reg 1400/2002, Art 9(1)). The exemption remains applicable where, for any period of two consecutive financial years, the total turnover limit is exceeded by no more than 10% (Reg 1400/2002, Art 9(2)).
[51] Commission Notice—Guidelines on the applicability of Article 81 of the EC Treaty to horizontal co-operation agreements [2001] OJ C3/2 (hereafter 'Horizontal Guidelines').
[52] Reg 1400/2002, Art 2(3), first subparagraph.
[53] ibid, Art 1(1)(a). Note that the provision does not contain a reference to the companies being actual or potential competitors in the same geographic market.
[54] ibid, Art 2(3), second subparagraph.   [55] ibid, Art 9.

— the supplier is a manufacturer and a distributor of goods, while the buyer is a distributor not manufacturing goods competing with the contract goods;[56] or

— the supplier is a provider of services at several levels of trade, while the buyer does not provide competing services at the level of trade where it purchases the contract services.[57]

Finally, Article 2(2)(b) spells out that the block exemption also applies to vertical agreements that provide for the assignment to the buyer, or the use by the buyer, of intellectual property rights.[58] This will however only be so if the provisions dealing with the intellectual property rights: **11.35**.

— do not constitute the primary object of the agreement;

— are directly related to the use, sale or resale of goods or services by the buyer or its customers;[59] *and*

— do not contain restrictions of competition having the same object or effect as vertical restraints that are not exempted under the Regulation.[60]

(4) Purchase, sale or resale

Reference can be made to the observations regarding the corresponding language in Regulation 2790/99.[61] It is clear from the wording of Article 2(1) that the benefit of the block exemption is no longer reserved to resale (ie distribution) agreements. Agreements covering merely the sale and/or purchase of motor vehicles, parts, or repair and maintenance services (without imposing conditions as to their resale) may also be covered. This will for instance be the case where a producer or importer sources parts from a given parts producer. **11.36**.

---

[56] As a consequence of this exception, dual distribution (ie where the producer also distributes through dealers that are part of the same group) does not pose a problem for the application of the block exemption (Explanatory Brochure 19, question 4). This exception also applies to a situation where a group that produces cars that belong to a particular relevant market acts as the importer or distributor of cars belonging to a different relevant market.

[57] The position under this exception of an agreement pursuant to which an authorized repairer subcontracts certain repair and maintenance work to another authorized repairer (eg in order to improve its geographic coverage) is not clear. It may be assumed that, if both repairers remain active in the same type of repair work, they must be considered competing service providers. At the same time, the authorized repairer which subcontracts repair work will typically not be active at different levels of trade.

[58] This implies that, if the intellectual property rights are provided by the buyer to the supplier, the block exemption will not be applicable. This would be the case, for instance, where a producer of motor vehicles subcontracts the production of certain parts and provides the parts producer with certain technical know-how required for the production of those parts.

[59] Examples would be the right to affix trademarks in the showroom or the disclosure of know-how for the provision of repair work in respect of the motor vehicles of a given brand (Explanatory Brochure 19, n 36).

[60] van Couter and Bogaert (n 11 above) para 10, 465.   [61] Paras 2.119–2.122 above.

(5) The relevant goods and services

11.37. The block exemption applies only if the vertical agreement concerns new motor vehicles, spare parts for motor vehicles, or repair and maintenance services for motor vehicles.

New motor vehicles

11.38. The Regulation defines a 'motor vehicle' as a 'self propelled vehicle intended for use on public roads and having three or more road wheels'.[62] Hence, vehicles that are not self-propelled (such as horse-drawn wagons,[63] caravans or bicycles), have less than three wheels (such as motorcycles[64] or bicycles) or are not intended for use on the public roads (tractors or earthmoving equipment)[65] are not covered by the block exemption. The vehicles that do qualify as a motor vehicle include passenger cars, light commercial vehicles, medium and heavy trucks, city and intercity buses, and touring coaches.

11.39. Vertical agreements relating to the second-hand market are excluded from the scope of application of the block exemption.[66] The motor vehicles must be new in order to be covered. In order to determine whether a vehicle is still new, parties will have to rely on trade usage.[67] The Commission takes the view that, for a buyer, a vehicle will no longer be considered new as soon as it has been registered and driven on the road by another consumer, while a vehicle that has been registered for one day without having been used must still be considered new.[68] This description does not necessarily address some of the practical problems that may arise. For instance, a showroom model (that has not been used for test driving purposes) will most likely qualify as a new vehicle. The position of vehicles that have been used to conduct test drives is less clear. Depending on the extent to which they have been used for that purpose, it is conceivable that they may lose the status of a new car.

11.40. A somewhat different way to approach the 'new' car issue is to acknowledge that certain restrictions that can be imposed in respect of new cars are not exempted by Regulation 1400/2002 with regard to non-qualifying vehicles. For instance, the restriction on sales to independent traders in the context of a selective distribution system[69] and the requirement that cross-supplies between members

---

[62] Reg 1400/2002, Art 1(1)(n).   [63] Explanatory Brochure 16, footnote 32.

[64] Explanatory Brochure 16, footnote 32 and European Commission, *Twenty-first Report on Competition Policy 1991*, para 91 (re: non-applicability of Reg 123/85 to motorcycle distribution).

[65] Explanatory Brochure 16, footnote 32; Commission Press Release, IP/90/917, 16 November 1990 and F Wijckmans and A Vanderelst, 'The EC Commission's Draft Regulation on Motor Vehicle Distribution: Alea iacta est?' [1995] ECLR 225, 227. The fact that the vehicle may occasionally circulate on the public roads (such as a tractor) is not sufficient to pass the test. If the vehicle is not intended for use on the public roads, it will not qualify as a motor vehicle for the purposes of the block exemption.   [66] Explanatory Brochure 16, footnote 33.

[67] Explanatory Brochure 46, footnote 103.   [68] ibid.   [69] Art 4(1)(b)(iii).

of a selective system remain free and unrestricted[70] apply only to new motor vehicles. It may be helpful in defining whether a motor vehicle is new also to consider whether there may be an attempt to avoid these restrictions by artificially qualifying a vehicle as no longer being new. In other words, in addition to trade usage, the overall logic underlying the Regulation may contribute to the resolution of the definition issue.

Spare parts for motor vehicles

Spare parts are defined as 'goods which are to be installed in or upon a motor vehicle so as to replace components of that vehicle, including goods such as lubricants which are necessary for the use of a motor vehicle, with the exception of fuel'.[71] With the addition of 'goods which are necessary for the use', the definition in Regulation 1400/2002 is broader than the corresponding definition in Regulation 1475/95.[72]

11.41.

In order to qualify as a spare part, an article must meet one of the following tests: (a) either it replaces a component of a vehicle and is to be installed in or upon a motor vehicle; or (b) it is necessary for the use of a motor vehicle (with the exception of fuel).[73]

11.42.

A spare part is, by definition, a replacement part, that is, a part that replaces a component that was installed on the vehicle manufacturer's production line.[74] This implies that components that are supplied to the motor vehicle producer for first installation do not qualify as spare parts. Furthermore, the replacement part must be destined for installation in or upon a motor vehicle. This requirement may be problematic for parts that may also have end-uses for vehicles that are not covered by the Regulation (motorcycles, construction or earthmoving equipment, tractors). In order for those goods to qualify as spare parts, the Commission requires that it is reasonably certain that they are destined for installation in or upon a motor vehicle.[75] Both the nature of the vertical agreement and the parties to the agreement will be instrumental in

11.43.

---

[70] Art 4(1)(c).   [71] Reg 1400/2002, Art 1(1)(s).

[72] Reg 1475/95, Art 10(6); Explanatory Brochure 37, question 21; Notice pursuant to Article 19(3) of Council Regulation 17, *D'Ieteren—motor oils* [1989] OJ C119/14.

[73] In the definition, the word 'including' is used, thereby suggesting that the goods referred to in the second part of the definition are a subset of the goods covered by the first part of the definition. In view of the example of the lubricants referred to in the definition, this cannot, however, be accurate. Lubricants do not replace components of a motor vehicle. They are, at best, an article necessary for the use of a motor vehicle. We therefore assume that the word 'including' must be read to mean 'as well as'.

[74] Whether air conditioning, temperature control equipment, or a hi-fi system can qualify as a spare part will therefore in the first place depend on whether the relevant equipment was installed on the production line. The Commission seems to further require that equipment of this type must be integrated with other parts or systems of the vehicle (eg hi-fi controls integrated in the steering wheel) before it can qualify as a spare part. Explanatory Brochure 79, question 95.

[75] Explanatory Brochure 17.

determining whether such a reasonable certainty exists. For instance, vertical agreements for the supply of parts to motor vehicle repairers (even if the parts can be used on vehicles other than motor vehicles) may be deemed to concern 'spare parts'. Conversely, if the relevant goods are purchased by petrol filling stations, supermarket chains, or do-it-yourself stores, they will most likely not qualify as spare parts for block exemption purposes.[76]

11.44. An article that does not replace a motor vehicle component can only qualify as a spare part if it is necessary for the use of a motor vehicle. The necessity standard seems to be two-fold. It must be proven both:

— that the article is not a mere accessory that can be fitted in a motor vehicle, but is necessary for its use.[77] Reference can be made in this respect to problematic items such as hi-fi installations, and roof or bicycle racks; and
— that the article is destined to be installed in or upon a motor vehicle. This standard will again primarily concern double or multiple use items, such as lubricants, paint, screws, etc.[78]

11.45. Vertical agreements that concern goods that do not qualify as spare parts will be excluded from the scope of application of the Regulation, but can still benefit from the general regime included in Regulation 2790/99.[79]

Repair and maintenance services for motor vehicles

11.46. The concept of 'repair and maintenance services' will not normally give rise to interpretation difficulties. It is important to note, however, that the relevant services must concern motor vehicles in order to be covered by the block exemption. This implies that any restrictions that are imposed in respect of repair and maintenance work on other items (such as caravans, trailers, motorcycles, accessories, etc) cannot benefit from the block exemption. Such services can however qualify for exemption under Regulation 2790/99.

(6) *Territorial scope of application*

11.47. Regulation 1400/2002 applies throughout the EU, including the 10 new Member States that have recently joined.[80] The fact that the market conditions

---

[76] ibid.   [77] Explanatory Brochure 16, nn 34 and 79, question 95.
[78] Explanatory Brochure 17.
[79] The fact that in one and the same vertical agreement restrictions are included that concern both products covered by Reg 1400/2002 and products falling outside the Regulation's scope of application does not pose a problem. There is no reason to exclude the possibility that Reg 1400/2002 applies to a part of the vertical agreement and that the part not covered by the Regulation benefits from Reg 2790/99. This means, in effect, that two block exemption regulations can apply to the same vertical agreement.
[80] Act concerning the conditions of accession of the Czech Republic, the Republic of Estonia, the Republic of Cyprus, the Republic of Latvia, the Republic of Lithuania, the Republic of Hungary, the Republic of Malta, the Republic of Poland, the Republic of Slovenia and the Slovak

relating to motor vehicle distribution are quite different in some of these new Member States has not resulted in the Commission providing for a different regime. The territorial scope of the Regulation has furthermore been extended to cover the entire EEA.[81]

(7) *Application* ratione temporis

Regulation 1400/2002 entered into force on 1 October 2002[82] and contains two transitional regimes:

11.48.

— Agreements that were already in force on 30 September 2002 and that were compliant with Regulation 1475/95, continued to benefit from a block exemption up until 30 September 2003, even if the conditions of Regulation 1400/2002 were not met.[83] The main difficulty that presented itself during this transitional phase was whether vertical agreements that concerned exclusively authorized repair and maintenance work had to be brought into line with Regulation 1400/2002 as of 1 October 2002 or could benefit from a transitional regime up until 30 September 2003. The Commission pointed out that, as pure servicing agreements are not covered by Regulation 1475/95 (which imposes a mandatory link between sales and servicing), the networks of authorized repair shops had to comply with Regulation 1400/ 2002 as of its entry into force and therefore could not benefit from the one- year grace period.[84] As a result, Audi was required to implement a system of qualitative selective distribution with immediate effect.

— The application of the prohibition on the use of location clauses laid down in Article 5(2)(b) of the Regulation was suspended until 1 October 2005.[85]

Republic and the adjustments to the Treaties on which the European Union is founded [2003] OJ L236/33 (hereafter the 'Accession Act'), Art 2. A transitional regime is laid down in para 11 of Ch 5 (Competition policy) of Annex II to the Accession Act: List referred to in the Accession Act [2003] OJ L236/346, Art 20 which states as follows: '2. The prohibition laid down in Art 81(1) shall not apply to agreements existing at the date of accession for the Czech Republic, Estonia, Cyprus, Latvia, Lithuania, Hungary, Malta, Poland, Slovenia and Slovakia and which, by reason of accession, fall within the scope of Art 81(1) if, within six months from the date of accession, they are amended and thereby comply with the conditions laid down in the Regulation.' This implies that there was a transitional period of six months starting as of 1 May 2004, meaning that all distribution agreements should be in line with Reg 1400/2002 as of 1 November 2004. As a consequence, until 1 November 2004, Art 81(1) EC did not apply to the distribution agreements that were already in force on 1 May 2004, under the condition that these agreements had been brought into line with the block exemption no later than 1 November 2004. However, any new contract concluded in the new Member States after 1 May had to be in line with the Regulation as from its entry into force.

[81] Decision of the EEA Joint Committee 136/2002 of 27 September 2002 amending Annex IV (Competition) to the EEA Agreement [2002] OJ L336/38.

[82] Reg 1400/2002, Art 12(1).   [83] ibid, Art 10.

[84] Commission Press Release, IP/03/80, 20 January 2003 (Volkswagen and Audi) and Gambs (n 16 above) 53.

[85] Reg 1400/2002, Art 12(2) and Commission Press Release, IP 05/1208, 30 September 2005. The postponement of the ban on location clauses seems to have been the consequence

11.49. Regulation 1400/2002 expires on 31 May 2010.[86] Prior to the Regulation's expiry (and in any event, no later than 31 May 2008) the Commission will have to complete an evaluation report. This report will have to focus on the conditions set out in Article 81(3) EC.[87]

C. Distribution Formulas

11.50. The concept underlying Regulation 1400/2002 requires that motor vehicle producers and importers make a choice between a number of distribution formulas. This is, *inter alia*, due to the fact that the block exemption's applicability is linked to a market share limit and that these limits differ, depending on the distribution formula that is selected. Hence, depending on the market share level, certain distribution formulas may automatically be excluded. A second reason why it is important to distinguish between the different distribution formulas, is that many of the restrictions imposed by the block exemption are tailored towards a particular formula. For instance, while a restriction on active sales is not compatible with the block exemption in the context of selective distribution,[88] the same is not true if an exclusive distribution system is applied.[89] The analysis of the requirements imposed by the block exemption is therefore conducted by necessity within the context of a chosen distribution formula.

11.51. From the perspective of the market share limits imposed by Regulation 1400/2002, the following possibilities are available:

	Motor vehicles	Spare parts	After-sales
Qualitative selectivity[90]	no limit	no limit	no limit
Quantitative selectivity	40%[91]	30%	30%
Other formulas	30%	30%	30%

(1) Calculation of market shares

11.52. The calculation of the market shares presupposes that the relevant markets are defined and that the correct methodology for calculating the shares held on the properly defined markets is applied.

---

of pressure exerted by the European Parliament (J Clark, 'New Rules for Motor Vehicle Distribution and Servicing' (2002) 3 EC Competition Policy Newsletter 3, 5). For more details on location clauses, see para 11.204–11.211.

[86] Art 12(3).   [87] Art 11.   [88] Art 4(1)(d) and (e).   [89] Art 4(1)(b)(i).

[90] The absence of a market share limit for the application of the block exemption does not impair the possible application of Art 82 EC.

[91] This limit is reduced to 30% (to be calculated from the buyer's perspective) in the case of an exclusive supply obligation. The definition of an exclusive supply obligation is however quite narrow (Art 1(1)(e)).

(2) *Definition of relevant markets*

Notwithstanding the sector-specific nature of the block exemption and the **11.53**.
Commission's extensive experience with motor vehicle distribution (as witnessed by the two earlier block exemptions and a long list of—both formal and
informal—cases in the sector), Regulation 1400/2002 does not offer much
specific guidance on the relevant markets to be relied upon for the purposes of
calculating the market shares. The Explanatory Brochure[92] blames this on the
great number and variety of products that are covered by the block exemption.

The Commission's general approach towards market definition in the context of **11.54**.
Regulation 1400/2002 is based on the *Notice on the definition of the relevant market
for the purposes of Community competition law*.[93] It will further take into account the
decisions that have defined relevant markets in a precise manner[94] and the Vertical
Guidelines.[95] In the Explanatory Brochure,[96] the Commission illustrates the
application of the relevant principles, but hastens to add that these examples and
clarifications do not prejudge the approach it may adopt in future cases.

As the block exemption compels the parties to come up with a definition of the **11.55**.
relevant market(s) in order to be able to check its applicability, we will attempt
to make concrete proposals. It is obvious that these proposals cannot replace
thorough economic analysis of the issue (on a case-by-case basis), but the
indications provided by the Commission (albeit mostly not in the form of any
definitive decision on the matter) are sufficiently clear to be able to predict what
the parties may reasonably expect to be the Commission's starting position on
the issue of market definition. To put it differently, if the parties rely on the
proposals outlined below, they would in our view (taking account of the
indications provided) adopt a good faith interpretation of the Regulation and its
market share limits. If a company wishes to avail itself of a different (wider or
narrower) definition of the market, it would be well-advised to corroborate its
position with solid economic evidence.

(3) *Motor vehicles*

Regulation 1400/2002 hints at the fact that the relevant product markets are in **11.56**.
principle to be defined separately for new motor vehicles, spare parts, and the
provision of repair and maintenance services.[97] The Explanatory Brochure[98] adds

---

[92] Explanatory Brochure 70.   [93] [1997] OJ C372/5, 5–13 and Explanatory Brochure 70.
[94] This implies that the decisions in which market definition is addressed, but not decided in
detail (as such definition was not material to the outcome of the case), are of no direct use. This is
the case, for instance, for the decisions involving the definition of the passenger car market(s)
where the Commission has refrained to date from accepting a particular approach (*General Motors
v Daewoo Motors* (COMP/M2832) [2002] OJ C220/4, para 13 and references there and
DaimlerChrysler [2002] OJ L257/1, para 149).   [95] Explanatory Brochure 70.
[96] ibid.   [97] Art 8(1).   [98] Explanatory Brochure 71.

that, in line with the distinction which the Regulation operates between sales and servicing, the activity of selling new motor vehicles should, as a general rule, be examined separately.[99] Hence, it seems advisable to distinguish the relevant market(s) for motor vehicles from the markets for parts or after-sales servicing.[100]

11.57. In order to define the relevant product markets for the different types of new motor vehicle, regard should be given to the degree of demand substitutability (ie the extent to which a motor vehicle is regarded by the buyer as inter-changeable or substitutable, by reason of the product's characteristics, price and intended use).[101] Demand substitutability is assessed by measuring the reaction of buyers to a small but significant (5 to 10%) and not transitory increase in selling prices (the so-called 'SSNIP test').[102] Given the definition provided in Article 8(1)(a) of the Regulation, supply substitutability does not seem to be a factor which is to be taken into account.[103]

11.58. With regard to commercial vehicles, the Commission seems to have defined quite affirmatively the manner in which the market is to be split, albeit that the SSNIP test played almost no role in that definition. A cautious approach towards market definition would be as follows:

—Trucks and vans: light commercial vehicles,[104] light trucks (typically ranging between 3 and 5[105] tons GVW),[106] medium trucks (typically

---

[99] This also seems to be the approach which the Commission has adopted to conclude that Porsche was eligible for de *minimis* treatment in respect of its vehicle sales (Commission Press Release, IP/04/585, 3 May 2004).

[100] The Commission acknowledges correctly (Explanatory Brochure 71, footnote 185) the trend towards purchasing decisions based on the lifetime cost of a vehicle. This trend can be observed quite clearly in the commercial vehicle sector, where fleet operators no longer base their purchasing decisions on the price of the vehicle as such, but on the overall cost (including parts and repair/maintenance costs) they will incur during the life of the vehicle. This translates itself into novel purchasing formats, such as 'cost per kilometer' contracts. Depending on the pro-portion of buyers making their buying decisions on that basis, there may be reason to expand the scope of the relevant market beyond the vehicle itself and to include parts and even repair and maintenance services. Also, para 2.245 above.   [101] Reg 1400/2002, Art 8(1)(a).

[102] Explanatory Brochure 70.

[103] This approach is supported by F Verboven, who does not rely on supply substitutability 'given the large investment costs and time delay that is typically involved when developing and marketing new models of passenger cars' in F Verboven, *Quantitative Study on the Demand for New Cars to Define the Relevant Market in the Passenger Car Sector*, 17 September 2002, Catholic University Leuven 8, available at http://europa.eu.int/comm/competition/car_sector/distribu-tion/eval_reg_1475_95/studies/study01.pdf (hereafter 'Verboven Report').

[104] As defined in Reg 1400/2002, Art 1(1)(p). Also in merger cases, the Commission has considered light commercial vehicles as a sub-segment of the truck market: *Ford Motor Company Ltd v Polar Motor Group Ltd* (COMP/M3388) [2004] OJ C180/9; *General Motors v Daewoo Motors* (COMP/M2832) [2002] OJ C220/4; *Renault v Nissan* (Case IV/M1519) [1999] OJ C178/14 *and Ford v Mazda* (Case IV/M741) [1996] OJ C179/3.

[105] The upper limit of 5 tons is not fixed. Some manufacturers consider that vehicles within their range that go up to 6.9 tons GVW are to be considered as light trucks.

[106] GVW = Gross Vehicle Weight.

ranging between 5 and 16 tons GVW), heavy trucks (in excess of 16 tons GVW).[107]

— Buses:[108] city buses, intercity buses, coaches (touring buses).[109]

With regard to passenger cars, the position is substantially less clear. An indi- **11.59**
cation as to a possible market definition can be found in the segmentation used
by the Commission in its half-year reports on car prices ('the Car Price
Reports').[110] This segmentation has been assessed in a recent study commissioned by DG COMP.[111] The Verboven Report applies the SSNIP test on the
basis of car list prices[112] in five Member States (Germany, France, Italy, the
United Kingdom, and Belgium)[113] and concludes that there are five distinct
product markets: the subcompact market,[114] the compact market,[115] the
intermediate market,[116] the standard/luxury market,[117] and the sports

---

[107] *Renault/Volvo* (Case IV/M4) [1990] OJ C281/0, paras 9–10; *Renault/Nissan* (Case
IV/M1519) [1999] OJ C178/14, paras 21–2; *Volvo-Scania* (COMP/M1672) [2001] OJ
L143/74, paras 13–30 and *Volvo/Renault VI* (COMP/M1980) [2000] OJ C220/6, paras 10–16.
[108] While this approach may be applicable to most countries within the EU, it is not
appropriate for all. For instance, it is acknowledged that in the United Kingdom there is no
market for intercity buses and that there may be a need to consider the existence of separate
markets for doubledecker and medium buses (*Volvo/Scania* (COMP/M1672) [2001] OJ L143/
74, para 255, which refers to the advice of the Office of Fair Trading pertaining to the proposed
joint venture between the Mayflower Corporation plc and Henlys Group plc (Report under
section 125(4) of the Fair Trading Act 1973 of the Director General's advice, given on 24
November 2000, to the Secretary of State for Trade and Industry under section 76 of the Act)).
[109] *Volvo/Scania* (COMP/M1672) [2001] OJ L143/74, paras 214–30 and *Mercedes-Benz/
Kässbohrer* (Case IV/M477) [1995] OJ L211/1, paras 9–22.
[110] Factors that have influenced the segmentation proposed by the Commission include horse-
power, body and price (Explanatory Brochure 74). [111] Verboven Report (n 103 above).
[112] F Verboven acknowledges that list prices may differ from transaction prices (due to price
discounts and other benefits offered to the customers), but refers to the econometric literature on
passenger car demand to state that a consensus has emerged that list prices are informative for the
purposes of obtaining price elasticities provided that the econometric model is specified in a
sufficiently flexible way. Verboven Report (n 103 above) 16, footnote 7.
[113] The findings in the Verboven Report are therefore confined to these countries.
[114] This market corresponds to segments A and B in the Car Price Reports (eg Citroën C2,
Daihatsu Cuore, Fiat Panda, Renault Twingo, Seat Arosa, Citroën C3, Fiat Punto, Fiat Idea,
Ford Fiesta, Lancia Ypsilon, Mazda 2, Nissan Micra, Opel Corsa, Peugeot 206, Renault Clio,
Seat Ibiza, Skoda Fabia, Toyota Yaris, VW Polo).
[115] Corresponding with segment C in the Car Price Reports (eg Alfa Romeo 147, Audi A2,
Audi A3, Citroën Xsara, Citroën Xsara Picasso, Fiat Stilo, Fiat Stilo MW, Ford Focus, Honda
Civic, Mazda 3, Mitsubishi Space Star, Nissan Almera, Opel Astra, Peugeot 307, Renault
Mégane, Rover 25, Seat Cordoba, Seat León, Skoda Octavia, Suzuki Ignis, Toyota Corolla, VW
Touran, VW Golf).
[116] Corresponding with segment D in the Car Price Reports (eg Alfa Romeo 156, Audi A4,
BMW 318i, Citroën C5, Ford Mondeo, Honda Accord, Lancia Lybra, Mazda 6, Mercedes
C180, Nissan Primera, Opel Vectra, Renault Laguna, Rover 45, Saab 9–3, Seat Toledo, Skoda
Superb, Subaru Legacy, Toyota Avensis, Volvo S40, VW Passat).
[117] Corresponding with segments E and F in the Car Price Reports (eg Alfa Romeo 166, Audi
A6, BMW 520i, Mercedes E220, Opel Signum, Peugeot 607, Rover 75, Saab 9–5, Volvo S60,
Audi A8, BMW 735i, Lancia Thesis, Mercedes S350, Volvo S80).

market.[118] As a practical matter, we would suggest for the purposes of the block exemption, to rely on the findings in the Verboven Report and to do so even for the countries that were not within the scope of the study.[119]

11.60. There are two additional factors requiring careful consideration in order to determine whether they may have an impact on the pragmatic approach towards product market definition suggested here, namely the relevance of the level of trade at which the vertical agreement is concluded[120] and the existence of chains of substitution between products:[121]

— As to the level of trade, the issue is whether the product market definition will differ depending on whether the vertical agreement is to be situated at the wholesale level as opposed to the retail level. Even intuitively one would expect there to be a major difference.[122] Authorized dealers that will be expected by their customers to offer a particular range of motor vehicles will normally attach less importance to individual models, than to the scope of products that can be offered as a result of teaming up with a particular producer or importer. This assessment will typically be made in cases where a dealer switches brands.[123] While the Regulation seems to call for this type of analysis,[124] the Explanatory Brochure simplifies matters by stating that demand substitutability at the retail level must be deemed identical to demand substitutability at the wholesale level.[125] The consequence of this approach is that there will be an identical

---

[118] Corresponding with segment G in the Car Price Reports (eg Audi TTR, BMW X5, Citroën C8, Fiat Ulysse, Lancia Phedra, Land Rover, Mitsubishi Outlander, Peugeot 807, Range Rover, Renault Espace, Suzuki Grand Vitara, Volvo XC90).

[119] Verboven lends support to such an extension: '. . . , since the SSNIP results are similar for all countries [included in Verboven's investigation], one may conjecture that they would also apply to other European countries': Verboven Report (n 103 above) 35).

[120] Explanatory Brochure 70 and 71 (3).   [121] Explanatory Brochure 72 (5).

[122] In merger control case law, the Commission carefully distinguishes between the levels of trade.

[123] In cases where a dealer is terminated by a producer or importer, it will assess the range of alternative brands it may turn to. Dealers that have built up a customer base by presenting a full range of cars (typically including a larger car as the main car of the household and a smaller model as the second car) will seek producers having a similar range. It is on that basis that many terminated dealers for European brands have been seen to turn to producers such as Nissan, Daewoo, or Hyundai.

[124] Art 8(1)(a) requires indeed that demand substitutability be assessed from the perspective of the 'buyer', which at the wholesale level refers to the dealer, rather than the end-user.

[125] Explanatory Brochure 71 (4): 'For distribution of final goods, such as motor vehicles, or provision of repair and maintenance services to end-consumers, what is substitutable from the point of view of buyers which are active as retailers, such as authorised distributors or repairers who are members of the distribution system, will normally be determined by the preference of end-users. If different motor vehicles are not substitutable for end-users, they will be deemed not to be substitutable for distributors who retail them' and Explanatory Brochure 75: 'The product range includes several car models, which are mainly purchased by consumers, whose individual preferences for a particular type of car determine those of the authorised distributor'. The Verboven Report (n 103 above) 24 proceeds on the same assumption: '. . . assuming that the wholesale-level demand coincides with the retail-level demand'. This approach is criticized in legal literature: Automotive Sector Groups of HB and LWWK (n 11 above) 259–60.

product market definition regarding new motor vehicles, irrespective of the level of trade at which the vertical agreement is to be situated. Hence, taking into consideration the clarification offered in the Explanatory Brochure, there is no need to change the pragmatic approach towards product market definition suggested above on account of the level of trade involved.

— Both in the general description and the examples offered in the Explanatory Brochure,[126] the Commission clearly suggests that a chain of substitution may require several product segments (or candidate product markets) to be grouped into a single product market.[127] The Verboven Report would not lend support to a market definition based on a chain of substitution argument. In fact, it suggests that, rather than broadening the market definition beyond the segment level, it is conceivable to apply even narrower product market definitions.[128] For simplicity, however, the Verboven Report concludes[129] that 'it is reasonable to define the relevant product markets within each country at the segment level'.

In order to enable motor vehicle producers, importers, and dealers to efficiently assess whether they comply with the market share limits set forth in Regulation 1400/2002, we propose to stick to the product market definition outlined above and not to take account of the level of trade or chain of substitution arguments in order to refine these markets. In borderline cases (ie where the precise market share level approaches or slightly exceeds one of the limits)[130] a more sophisticated analysis may be called for. At such time, a solid and more detailed assessment (also taking account of different specifications and price levels within the range of a given model) will have to be conducted. **11.61.**

As to the relevant geographic market, the only safe assumption is to proceed on the basis of national market definitions. The Commission refers in this respect to the fact that 'distributors actually purchase on a national basis, wide differences in price and market penetration exist among Member States and parallel trading is minor'.[131] Also on other occasions the Commission has made it clear that it considers the relevant markets still to be divided along national **11.62.**

---

[126] Explanatory Brochure 72(5) and 74–5.

[127] The justification for combining several segments seems to be based on the price overlap between products at the higher end of one segment and the lower end of the next segment (Explanatory Brochure 74). There are certainly two possible approaches to such a situation. The first one (which seems to be proposed in the Explanatory Brochure) is to combine the complete segments into a single product market. The second approach would be to shift the higher-end products of the lower segment into the next segment, ie not to combine segments, but to shift products to a different level depending on their specification and price levels. If the volumes of the products for which the overlap exists are rather low, we fail to understand on what basis the first approach could be justified. [128] Verboven Report (n 103 above) 34.

[129] ibid.

[130] Which, in addition to the market share levels set forth in Reg 1400/2002, Art 3, may also be the 5% threshold for *de minimis* purposes. [131] Explanatory Brochure 75.

boundaries.[132] The Verboven Report[133] relies likewise on national markets. Hence, while a sophisticated analysis may be advisable in critical cases, the most pragmatic course of action is to rely on national geographic markets for assessing market share levels for the purposes of Regulation 1400/2002.

(4) Spare parts

11.63. The definition of the market(s) for spare parts is very complex. The Explanatory Brochure leaves the possibility open that spare parts are included within another market[134] (ie the markets for new motor vehicles[135] or for repair and maintenance services).[136] The overall position of the Commission seems to be, however, that there is in any event a separate market for brand-specific parts.[137] This market is to be distinguished from that or those consisting of non-brand specific parts (ie mostly parts that are used in unsophisticated repair and maintenance work and for which several alternatives are typically available).[138]

11.64. As to the relevant geographic market, a cautious and pragmatic approach is to rely on national territories. While little guidance is offered in this respect by the Commission, there is some indication in the Explanatory Brochure that, at the retail level, national markets are likely to be retained and that, at the wholesale level, the geographic market may be broader.[139]

(5) Repair and maintenance services

11.65. In the context of the *Audi* cases,[140] the Commission has confirmed its position that the relevant market is that for the repair and maintenance services for the

---

[132] As to vehicle retail, the Commission has recently stated that 'in previous vehicle retail cases, the Commission has left open whether these markets are regional, national or European-wide in scope, although a tendency towards a more European market can be taken into account due to the effects of the new block exemption for vertical agreements in the motor vehicle sector. Previous cases have however not ruled out the existence of markets that are narrower than national, specifically for the retail sale of vehicles to end customers.' *Ford Motor Company Ltd/Polar Motor Group Ltd* (COMP/M3388) [2004] OJ C180/9, para 10, with reference to *VW/Hahn + Lang* (COMP/M3352) [2004] OJ C56/6; *Inchape/IEP* (Case IV/M182) [1992] OJ C21/0; *Toyota Motor Corp/Walter Frey/Toyota France* (Case IV/M326) [1993] OJ C187/4; and *Ford/Jardine* (Case IV/M1435) [1999] OJ C73/9. For the truck markets: *Volvo/Scania* (COMP/M1672) [2001] OJ L143/74, paras 31–70 as confirmed by *Volvo/Renault VI* (COMP/M1980) [2000] OJ C220/6, paras 23 (heavy trucks) and 25 (medium trucks). As to the bus markets: *Volvo/Scania* (COMP/M1672) [2001] OJ L143/74, paras 231–59 as confirmed by *Volvo/Renault VI* (COMP/M1980) [2000] OJ C220/6, para 28.   [133] Verboven Report (n 103 above) 11 *et seq* and 33.

[134] Automotive Sector Groups of HB and LWWK (n 11 above) 261.

[135] This could be the case if the customer assesses the lifetime costs of the vehicle at the time of the initial purchase (Explanatory Brochure 71, footnote 185, also n 100 above).

[136] In the context of maintenance contracts, certain parts may be automatically included in the price (namely, those requiring replacement after certain time intervals) and for other parts a specific price list may be agreed.   [137] Explanatory Brochure 71, footnote 187 and Monti (n 13 above).

[138] Explanatory Brochure 71 (2) and footnote 186.   [139] ibid, footnote 189.

[140] Commission Press Release, IP/03/80, 20 January 2003 and *VW-Audi:/VW-Audi Vertriebszentren* (Case IV/M3198) [2003] OJ C206/15.

vehicles of a given brand and that the relevant geographic markets are still national.[141] Again, while there may be merit in reviewing this approach in a litigation context, the Commission's firm position on this point makes it advisable to structure after-sales networks on that basis.

(6) Calculation method

The methodology for calculating market shares will differ depending on the nature of the relevant product market. There are, however, a number of general principles that apply in all instances: **11.66**.

— Market shares are calculated on the basis of data relating to the preceding calendar year.[142]
— The market share includes retail sales made by the supplier through directly-operated sales points.[143]
— Account is not only taken of the sales by the supplier and purchases by the buyer that are parties to the vertical agreement, but also of the sales and purchases of their connected undertakings. In other words, the data at group level is relevant and not the data of the individual parties to the vertical agreement concerned.[144]
— If the market share limits of 30% and 40% are initially not exceeded, but the market shares subsequently rise above the limits, the block exemption may continue to apply under certain conditions for a maximum period of two calendar years.[145]

With regard to the markets for new motor vehicles, Article 8(1)(a) of Regulation 1400/2002 proposes a volume-based approach. It is only if volume data is not available that value data can be used.[146] With its preference for volume data, the Commission deviates from its standard value-based approach.[147] As statistics are typically kept on a volume and not on a value basis, it is clear that the Commission has selected a calculation method that coincides with industry practice.[148] **11.67**.

The Regulation refers to volumes 'sold by the supplier'. In the case of standard dealer agreements (ie vertical agreements at retail level) this implies that the sales by the importers to their network should in principle be taken in order to measure market shares. This information is not readily available. While a producer or importer most likely has precise information on its own sales to the network, the same information is normally not available for any of the competing brands. The Explanatory Brochure seems to accept therefore that the market shares may also **11.68**.

---

[141] Gambs (n 16 above) 54.   [142] Reg 1400/2002, Art 8(2)(a).
[143] ibid, Art 8(2)(b) and Explanatory Brochure 75.
[144] Reg 1400/2002, Art 1(2) and Explanatory Brochure 22.
[145] Reg 1400/2002, Art 8(2)(c), (d), and (e).   [146] ibid, Art 8(1), *in fine*.
[147] Reg 2790/99, Art 9(1). cf paras 2.249–2.251.   [148] *Opel* [2001] OJ L59/3, para 11.

be calculated on the basis of public data on vehicle registrations in the individual Member States.[149] It is obvious that, in doing so, sales volumes are measured at a different level than that at which the importer and the dealers interact.[150] The assumption seems to be that the volumes at the two levels will be sufficiently close so as to justify that the market shares are calculated in this manner.

11.69. The calculation of the market shares must be conducted within each geographic market for all the brands owned by the companies concerned.[151] As the same group frequently owns a number of brands and these brands are often distributed through distinct networks,[152] it would be inaccurate to limit the market share calculation to the brand involved in a given vertical agreement. If other brands of the same group are also part of the same relevant product and geographic market, the volumes of such other brands must be added for the purposes of the market share calculation. This means that, even if the volume represented by the individual brands does not exceed a market share limit stated in Article 3 of the Regulation, the limit will still be deemed to be exceeded if all of the brands of the same group combined exceed the limit.

11.70. With regard to the market(s) for spare parts, Article 8(1)(b) of the Regulation advances a value-based approach, with the possibility to switch to volume-based data if value data is not available. It is the value of the goods 'sold by the supplier' that must be taken as the basis for calculation. Contrary to the markets for new motor vehicles where registration statistics are readily available, we are not aware of similarly reliable databases covering spare parts. This is probably more a theoretical, than a practical problem. The Commission takes the view that brand-specific parts constitute (a) separate relevant product market(s) and that it may be assumed that the relevant market shares in any event exceed the limit of 30%.[153] If that view is accurate, there is no need to research for refined information as the producers have no other choice but to work with qualitative selective distribution.

11.71. In respect of repair and maintenance services, the Regulation adopts a peculiar calculation method that presumably serves to achieve a particular policy objective. The objective is that producers open up their after-sales networks by being compelled to rely on qualitative selective distribution.[154] This will only be the case if the relevant market share exceeds 30%. In order to ensure that this limit is likely to be exceeded, Article 8(1)(c) of the Regulation stipulates that the market share

---

[149] Explanatory Brochure 75.

[150] Which means, for instance, that parallel traded vehicles may be included, which were not sold by the supplier in the market concerned.　　　　[151] Explanatory Brochure 22.

[152] eg the Mercedes Benz, Smart, Jeep, and Chrysler brands within the DaimlerChrysler group; the Volkswagen and Audi brands within the Volkswagen group; the Ford, Mazda, Jaguar, Volvo, and Land Rover brands within the Ford Europe group; the Opel, Saab, and Daewoo brands within the GM group; Peugeot and Citroën within the PSA group; Fiat and Alfa Romeo within the Fiat group.　　　　[153] Monti (n 13 above).

[154] Without referring to complex market share issues or hinting at the possibility that in certain cases the market share limit will not be exceeded, Mr Monti (n 13 above) stated in

must be calculated 'on the basis of the value of the contract services sold by the members of the supplier's distribution network together with any other [interchangeable or substitutable] services sold by these members . . .'.[155] Hence, for the purposes of calculating the market shares that are relevant for the choice of the distribution formula in the relationship between producer/importer and the after-sales network, the turnover achieved by the after-sales network (ie at the retail level) is taken.[156] It is possible (at least in theory) that the producer/importer does not earn any turnover in respect of the services provided by its after-sales network (eg if the authorized workshop purchases its parts requirements elsewhere) but is nevertheless confronted with a high market share.

While the approach adopted in the Regulation for the purposes of calculating **11.72.** market shares has been questioned in legal literature,[157] the Commission seems to leave producers little choice other than to assume that the market shares on the market for repair and maintenance services will be higher than the 30% limit.[158] Both in *Audi*[159] and *Porsche*,[160] the Commission considered the limit exceeded and hence required that these producers implemented a qualitative selective after-sales network if they wished to comply with the block exemption. Producers that wish to implement a different distribution formula will therefore face a considerable burden of proof.

(7) Distribution formulas: general overview of possibilities

As stated above, the distribution formula that may be chosen under the Reg- **11.73.** ulation is subject to certain market share limits not being exceeded. There is one

absolute terms: 'The first area where we will see substantial changes and which is perhaps the most important for the consumer is servicing and repair. *Under the regulation, manufacturers will no longer be able to set limits on the numbers of authorised repairers [. . .] Furthermore, independent repair shops will also be able to join the network, so long as they meet the basic quality criteria [. . .].'* (emphasis added). Also Tsoraklidis (n 4 above) 33.

[155] In this context, account must be taken of the fact that the market for repair and maintenance services will often be deemed brand-specific so that after-sales services regarding other brands will not automatically be deemed substitutable or interchangeable; Explanatory Brochure 31 and Commission Press Release, IP/03/80, 20 January 2003 (re: Audi).

[156] This calculation method was introduced in the draft text of Reg 1400/2002 after the draft regulation had been published in the *Official Journal*. The version of 6 May 2002 highlighting the changes introduced to the draft regulation published in OJ C67 on 16 March 2002 is available at http://europa.eu.int/comm/competition/car_sector/distribution/new.pdf.

[157] Automotive Sector Groups of HB and LWWK (n 11 above) 260.

[158] C Aronica, 'Le contenu du Règlement automobile dans le domaine de la réparation et de l'entretien automobile' (2002) 239 Petites Affiches 20, 21 and C Schlenger and O Hinrichs, 'Kfz-Vertrieb (Verordnung Nr. 1400/2002)' in C Liebscher, E Flohr, and A Petsche (eds), *Handbuch der EU Gruppenfreistellungsverordnungen* (Verlag CH Beck—Manz'sche Verlags- und Universitätsbuchhandlung Wien, 2003) 532.

[159] *Audi* (COMP/F-2/38.554 Po/*Audi: Deutschland*); European Commision, *XXXIIIrd Report on Competition Policy* (2003), paras 155–7 Commission Press Release, IP/03/80, 20 January 2003.

[160] *Porsche*, not yet reported, European Commission, *Report on Competition Policy—Volume 1 (2004)* Commission Press Release, IP/04/585, 3 May 2004.

exception that is that qualitative selective distribution may always be chosen as it is not subject to any market share limit.[161] Hence, for all possible products and services that are covered by the block exemption (including spare parts), qualitative selectivity will always be an option. With regard to the distribution of new motor vehicles, quantitative selectivity may be applied up to a limit of 40%.[162] Other distribution formulas, as well as the distribution of spare parts or repair and maintenance services by means of a quantitative selective network, are subject to a limit of 30%.[163] In the exceptional case where the vertical agreement imposes an exclusive supply obligation on the supplier,[164] a market share limit of 30% will apply and the relevant market share must be calculated from the perspective of the buyer (ie the buyer's share of the market in which it purchases the contract goods or services).[165]

11.74. Taking into account both the market share parameters set forth in the Regulation and the attitude the Commission is likely to adopt in respect of market definition, the standard possibilities[166] offered by the block exemption as to distribution formulas can be summarized as follows:

— **New motor vehicles**: exclusive distribution (up to 30%)—quantitative selective distribution (up to 40%)—qualitative selective distribution (no limit)—non-exclusive/non-selective distribution (up to 30%).

— **Spare parts**: qualitative selective distribution.

— **Repair and maintenance services**: qualitative selective distribution.

11.75. If a given vertical agreement covers several relevant geographic markets or several relevant product markets and it meets the market share limits for some and exceeds them for others, the block exemption will remain applicable for those markets where the market share requirements are met.[167] For the other markets, the parties will be compelled to conduct their own self-assessment as to whether Article 81(3) EC is applicable, but they cannot rely on the block exemption.

11.76. While the Commission seems to leave little or no room for combining different distribution formulas in respect of spare parts or repair and maintenance services,

---

[161] Reg 1400/2002, Art 3(1), third subparagraph.
[162] ibid, Art 3(1), second subparagraph.   [163] ibid, Art 3(1), first subparagraph.
[164] This situation will indeed be rather exceptional in the motor vehicle sector as an exclusive supply obligation is defined as 'any direct or indirect obligation causing the supplier to sell the contract goods or services only to one buyer inside the common market for the purposes of a specific use or resale' (ibid, Art 1(1)(e)). A typical scenario would be one where a producer appoints a single importer for the whole of the Community and accepts not to supply any other company within the Community. The fact that a producer accepts to supply only one importer in a given Member State (eg in certain of the new Member States) is not sufficient. The exclusive supply obligation must concern a single buyer for the whole of the Community.   [165] ibid, Art 3(2).
[166] With that we mean the possibilities that are most likely to be in line with the Commission's expectations and from which companies probably can only deviate if they conduct a thorough market and economic analysis to justify their alternative approach.
[167] Explanatory Brochure 22.

that possibility does exist for the distribution of new motor vehicles. Generally speaking, there are two ways in which such a combination can be set up. The first is that where certain motor vehicles (for instance, the luxury brand of the producer) are sold via qualitative or quantitative selectivity and the other brands are marketed via an exclusive distribution scheme. This approach does not pose any real problems. The second and more complicated manner of combining formulas is that where, for the same products in one geographic area, quantitative selectivity is used and in another, exclusive distribution is applied.[168] The Regulation renders this combination quite unattractive.[169] Exclusive distributors cannot be prevented from reselling to independent traders that are located within the area where selective distribution is used. This implies in practice that the authorized dealers within that area will be confronted with traders that do not meet the quality criteria and have not invested to meet these criteria. The ensuing free-rider problem is obvious. Furthermore, the selective dealer himself will not be allowed to sell to these independent traders within his area, as it is an essential condition of selective distribution that an authorized dealer undertakes not to sell to unauthorized distributors. The combination of exclusivity and selectivity is therefore bound to create tension within the network.

(8) Distribution formulas: definition

Given their importance from the perspective of the applicability of the block exemption, it is crucial to have a solid understanding of the precise definition of the various distribution formulas.   **11.77**.

Selective distribution: general

Regulation 1400/2002 offers a general definition of a 'selective distribution system'. The constituent elements of this definition will have to be met in the case of both qualitative and quantitative selective distribution. This concept covers:[170]   **11.78**.

> a distribution system where the supplier undertakes to sell the contract goods or services, either directly or indirectly, only to distributors or repairers selected on the basis of specified criteria and where these distributors or repairers undertake not to sell such goods or services to unauthorised distributors or independent repairers, without prejudice to the ability to sell spare parts to independent repairers or the obligation to provide independent operators with all technical information, diagnostic equipment, tools and training required for the repair and maintenance of motor vehicles or for the implementation of environmental protection measures.

---

[168] Schlenger and Hinrichs (n 158 above) 532.
[169] Frequently Asked Questions (n 17 above) 6, question 11; Creutzig (n 11 above) 1126, and van Couter and Bogaert (n 11 above) 466, para 15.   [170] Reg 1400/2002, Art 1(1)(f).

11.79 Having regard to this definition, the essential features of a selective system encompass:

— *An obligation of the supplier to sell the contract goods only to authorized distributors or repairers*: This implies, on the one hand, that the supplier may not sell the contract goods or services to independent (ie unauthorized) traders and, on the other hand, that the supplier retains the freedom to sell other goods or services (eg second-hand cars) to such independent traders.

— *Direct or indirect sales*: The supplier does not have to assume the supply obligation itself, but may involve a third party for ensuring the necessary supplies to the selective network.

— *Selection on the basis of specified criteria*: At the time of the selection of the authorized dealer or repairer, specified criteria must be in place on the basis of which its application is assessed. The issue of the selection criteria will be discussed in further detail below.[171]

— *An obligation of the authorized dealers or repairers not to sell to unauthorized dealers or repairers*: The authorized dealers or repairers must be subject to a contractual obligation not to sell to traders that are not within the selective network. The fact that in practice the authorized dealers or repairers respect this principle, but are not contractually required to do so, is insufficient.

11.80. The definition contains limited and specified exceptions to the selectivity obligations (ie the obligations not to sell outside the network). These exceptions are logical as they relate to hardcore restrictions:

— The first exception concerns the supply of spare parts to independent repairers. This is a mandatory exception as far as the members of the selective network are concerned.[172] The exception is most likely not formulated sufficiently precisely in the definition, as the supplies to independent repairers must only be allowed in cases where such repairers use the relevant parts for the repair or maintenance of a vehicle. In order to maintain consistency throughout the Regulation, it seems necessary to read this additional condition into the definition. A second important observation is that this exception may not be construed as an implicit obligation for the supplier (ie the motor vehicle producer or importer) to supply parts to independent repairers. Such a direct supply obligation is not provided for in the Regulation. Hence, from the perspective of the producer or the importer, the exception must be understood to mean that no infringement of the selectivity requirement is committed if they supply independent repairers, but that there is no obligation to do so.[173]

---

[171] Para 11.83 below.   [172] Reg 1400/2002, Art 4(1)(i).
[173] This is so because neither Art 4(1), nor Art 4(2), qualify the refusal of a producer or importer to supply parts to independent repairers as a hardcore restriction.

—The second exception concerns the hardcore provision dealing with giving access to independent operators to certain technical information, equipment and tools.[174] This obligation is applicable to the supplier (ie the producer or the importer) and not to the authorized dealers or repairers. Hence, with regard to this exception, the reverse situation applies. The exception is mandatory for the supplier, but not for the network members. However, if the supplier were to delegate the relevant obligation to the network (or were to involve the network in the fulfilment of this obligation), this does not pose a problem from the perspective of the selectivity requirement. Conversely, the supplier may impose an obligation on its network members not to become involved in granting the access rights and to reserve the performance of the access obligations to itself.

Qualitative selective distribution

According to Article 1(1)(h) of the Regulation, qualitative selective distribution consists of: **11.81**.

> A selective distribution system where the supplier uses criteria for the selection of distributors or repairers which are only qualitative in nature, are required by the nature of the contract goods or services, are laid down uniformly for all distributors or repairers applying to join the distribution system, are not applied in a discriminatory manner, and do not directly limit the number of distributors or repairers.

Qualitative selective distribution will normally not be caught by the prohibition of Article 81(1) EC[175] and if it is (or if specific restrictions of competition are imposed on the network members), the block exemption will apply without any market share limit.   **11.82**.

The essential features of qualitative selectivity are therefore the following: **11.83**.

— *The selection must be based only on criteria of a qualitative nature and no criteria may be relied upon that directly limit the number of distributors or repairers*: Qualitative criteria will typically be performance-related in nature (such as an obligation to employ specialists, to design the retail space according to the manufacturer's directives, to provide after-sales servicing according to certain standards, to meet certain stock requirements and standards for advertising).[176]

An obvious example of a quantitative criterion that directly limits the number of authorized network members is the limitation of the network to a fixed number of participants.[177] For other examples that have been given in the

---

[174] ibid, Art 4(2).   [175] Evaluation Report (n 7 above) para 14.   [176] ibid.
[177] For an example, cf the judgment of the French *Cour de Cassation* of 28 June 2005, *DaimlerChrysler France v Grémeau*. DaimlerChrysler had appointed only one authorized distributor within a well-defined urban area (consisting of 500,000 inhabitants). This criterion was considered objective and precise and furthermore corresponded to a geographic and economic logic.

past (such as the imposition of quantitative sales targets)[178] it is much more difficult to determine whether they *directly* limit the number of network players.

The Commission has suggested that qualitative criteria will be deemed to directly limit the number of players if they 'have no function other than to limit the number of operators that can meet them'.[179] In the Frequently Asked Questions[180] a substantially broader definition is given of qualitative criteria that are deemed to directly limit the number of authorized repairers. The test there seems to be that if the supplier imposes requirements that do not allow a degree of flexibility as to how a defined result (in terms of quality and time limits) is achieved and if such requirements unnecessarily increase the cost of providing a service, they are no longer characterized as qualitative and will be deemed quantitative in nature. In its Frequently Asked Questions,[181] DG COMP has provided a list of concrete examples of qualitative criteria in the after-sales context which it recharacterizes as quantitative. These examples demonstrate that the Commission's initial indication that it would not define 'what criteria are permitted or how a carmaker should organise his network'[182] probably no longer holds true and that DG COMP is prepared to give a very restrictive interpretation to this condition.[183] It remains to be seen whether DG COMP's approach will withstand scrutiny by the Court of Justice or the national courts.[184]

Apart from this issue, it is not a matter of debate that any applicant that meets the relevant qualitative criteria will have to be allowed into the network. Any other approach would be tantamount to a (direct) quantitative limitation of the network.[185]

— *The qualitative criteria must be required by the nature of the contract goods or services*: The most delicate interpretation issue to date pertaining to this condition has been whether or not a proper condition for the appointment of a spare parts distributor is that it must qualify as an authorized workshop. *Prima facie* this requirement would seem to be legitimate. According to the Regulation, authorized spare parts distributors may be required to supply independent repairers only if they use the parts for repair or maintenance purposes.[186] Under such circumstances, it would seem a reasonable request that the authorized parts distributors have repair and maintenance experience

---

[178] Evaluation Report (n 7 above) para 14.   [179] Monti (n 13 above).
[180] Frequently Asked Questions (n 17 above) 7, question 12.   [181] ibid.
[182] Commission Press Release, IP/02/1073, 17 July 2002.
[183] This observation applies in particular to the requirement that the limitation must be *direct*. The Frequently Asked Questions seems to have written this requirement out of the Regulation.
[184] On the scope of judicial review by national courts, cf the judgment of the French *Cour de Cassation* of 28 June 2005, *DaimlerChrysler France v Grémeau*. The Court stated that national courts are required—even *ex officio*—to analyse the selection criteria, their objective nature as well as their implementation.   [185] Explanatory Brochure 61, question 74.
[186] Reg 1400/2002, Art 4(1)(i).

and are able to advise these independent repairers on the use of the parts in a particular repair or maintenance setting. DG COMP takes a radically different view and states 'that there is nothing in the nature of a spare part that requires it to be sold exclusively by firms that are authorised to repair vehicles of the make in question'.[187] This approach fits within the stated aim of creating separate authorized spare parts distribution networks,[188] but the fate of this interpretation of the Regulation will probably be decided in future case law of the Court of Justice or the national courts.

— *The criteria must be uniformly laid down for all applicants*: This condition implies, *inter alia*, that the supplier must disclose the quality criteria so that all possible candidates can know the standards they have to meet to be admitted.[189]

— *The criteria must be applied in a non-discriminatory manner*: This condition has raised quite some questions in the context of the implementation of the Regulation by the sector. The main issue is whether a producer/importer is required to work with one and the same set of criteria throughout the Community or whether different sets of criteria may be used and, if so, under which circumstances. The Explanatory Brochure[190] confirms that different criteria may be used depending on whether the network member is located in a rural as opposed to an urban area. The Frequently Asked Questions[191] state more generally that different sets of criteria may be used provided that all (potential) network members 'that are in similar situations' are subject to identical criteria.[192] A further example is given, namely that large workshops may be required to meet different criteria to small ones.

Quantitative selective distribution

Quantitative selective distribution is defined as:[193] 'A selective distribution system where the supplier uses criteria for the selection of distribution or repairers which directly limit their number'. **11.84**

Guidance on the interpretation of this definition (in particular as to the type of criteria that must be deemed to limit directly the number of network members) has been given in paragraph 11.83 above with respect to qualitative selective distribution. **11.85**

Distribution formulas other than selective distribution

For the purposes of the application of the block exemption, there is no need to define in detail any other possible distribution formulas. With two limited **11.86**

---

[187] Frequently Asked Questions (n 17 above) 9, question 16.   [188] Monti (n 13 above).
[189] Explanatory Brochure 61, question 73.   [190] Explanatory Brochure 54, question 54.
[191] Frequently Asked Questions (n 17 above) 9, question 14.
[192] If a particular criterion is dropped for certain categories of applicants, it may require careful consideration whether this undermines the statement that the relevant criterion is still required by the nature of the contract goods or services for the other categories of applicants that are, or remain, subject to the criterion.   [193] Reg 1400/2002, Art 1(1)(g).

exceptions, all of the distribution formulas that do not qualify as selective distribution (eg sole distribution, shared exclusivity, various types of non-exclusive distribution) are treated in the same manner under the Regulation.

11.87 The two exceptions are the following:

(1) If the distribution formula includes an exclusive supply obligation (as defined very restrictively in Article 1(1)(e) of the Regulation),[194] the market share limit of 30% must be calculated by reference to the share that the buyer's purchases represent on the relevant market.[195]

(2) The restriction of active sales is exempted only if it relates to territories or customer groups that have been reserved to the supplier or allocated on an exclusive basis by the supplier to a particular distributor or repairer. The distribution formula that renders restrictions on active sales compatible with the Regulation is subject to strict conditions and cannot be characterized as a standard exclusive distribution formula.[196]

D. Conditions of the Block Exemption

(1) General

11.88. Article 3 of Regulation 1400/2002 stipulates certain conditions that must be met in order to benefit from the block exemption. The legal effect of the failure to comply with these conditions is the same as that resulting from the inclusion of a hardcore restriction listed in Article 4 of the Regulation: the benefit of the block exemption is lost for the entire vertical agreement. While the legal effect may be the same, conditions and hardcore restrictions are of a completely different nature. Hardcore restrictions are *per se* restrictions of competition that, even for companies with a low market share, will normally not be eligible for an exemption.[197] Conditions are not intended to avoid a specific restrictive practice as such, but rather aim at creating the circumstances within which the Commission feels comfortable to extend a block exemption:[198] the block

---

[194] 'Any direct or indirect obligation causing the supplier to sell the contract goods or services only to one buyer inside the common market for the purposes of a specific use or for resale' (ibid, Art 1(1)(e)). [195] ibid, Art 3(2).

[196] The fairly complex conditions which such a distribution formula must meet, are described in detail in para 11.118 below.

[197] Reg 1400/2002, Art 4(1) and (2) and Explanatory Brochure 28–9.

[198] While DG COMP does not exclude the possibility that vertical agreements not meeting the relevant conditions may be eligible for an individual exemption, it requires the parties to prove specifically that the absence of the contractual protection offered by the conditions does not undermine the passing on to consumers of the benefits and cost savings of the distribution formula chosen (Explanatory Brochure 25, question 8).

exemption is granted only to players not exceeding a particular market presence (market share limit) and provided that the dealers or repairers can act sufficiently independently from the producer. All of the conditions, with the exception of the market share limit are indeed aimed at promoting dealer independence. As discussed above,[199] dealer independence is perceived by the Commission as a necessary ingredient to enhance intra-brand competition.

One of the most important conditions, namely the market share limit,[200] has been discussed separately given its importance for the selection of the appropriate distribution formula.[201] We will therefore limit the discussion of Article 3 to the other conditions: the transfer rights of the dealer and the repairer (Article 3(3)), principles governing term and termination (Article 3(4) and (5)) and dispute resolution mechanisms (Article 3(6)). **11**.89.

(2) Transfer rights

Article 3(3) renders the block exemption conditional upon the fact that: **11**.90.

> the vertical agreement concluded with a distributor or repairer provides that the supplier agrees to the transfer of the rights and obligations resulting from the vertical agreement to another distributor or repairer within the distribution system and chosen by the former distributor or repairer.

This condition must be met by all vertical agreements to which a distributor or a repairer is a party.[202] It is irrelevant whether the agreement concerns the supply of new motor vehicles, spare parts, or repair and maintenance services. It also does not matter whether the supplier is a supplier of new motor vehicles, as parts suppliers are also subject to the relevant condition.

Mixed messages have been given to justify the inclusion of this condition in the Regulation. One aim would be to strengthen dealer independence 'by allowing them to realise the value that they have built up by giving them the freedom to sell their businesses to other dealers authorised to sell the same brand'.[203] The link between dealer independence and the right to realize value by selling to fellow dealers is not straightforward. We assume that this condition anticipates the restructuring that will take place in the sector[204] and the Commission's hope that dealer independence (and increased intra-brand competition) will emerge if dealerships are combined and the creation of cross-border dealerships is facilitated.[205] **11**.91.

---

[199] Paras 11.09–11.12 above.   [200] Reg 1400/2002, Art 3(1) and (2).
[201] Paras 11.51 *et seq* above.   [202] Explanatory Brochure 25, question 9.
[203] Explanatory Brochure 13.
[204] Commission Press Release, IP/02/1392, 30 September 2002 and Martinez Lopez (n 5 above) 59.
[205] Clark (n 85 above) 3–4. Reg 1400/2002, recital 10 suggests that the condition will 'foster market integration and [. . .] allow distributors or authorised repairers to seize additional business opportunities'.

11.92. This condition raises a number of fairly complex interpretation issues. The first of these issues concerns the requirements that the transferee must meet in order to be able to benefit from this transfer regime. While Article 3(3) is noncommittal on whether an authorized dealer can sell to an authorized repairer and *vice versa*, recital 10[206] provides that the transferee must be an undertaking of the same type as the transferor. This implies that an authorized dealer is not entitled to avail itself of the transfer clause to pass his rights and obligations on to a company that is authorized only as a repairer and not as a dealer.[207] It is only in the field of activity where the acquirer has already been admitted to the network, that it can benefit from a presumption that it meets the criteria imposed by the supplier in respect of the business operations of the selling network member.[208] This implies also that if a company has been authorized both as a dealer and a repairer, it will be able to take over any possible network member.[209]

11.93. Another interpretation question is whether it suffices that the purchasing dealer or repairer is admitted to one of the authorized networks of the same group or whether the dealer or repairer must have been authorized for the specific brand concerned. The reference in Article 3(3) that the distributor or repairer must be part of the distribution system suggests that the latter interpretation is correct.[210] Hence, an authorized VW dealer will not be able to avail itself of Article 3(3) when contemplating a transfer to an authorized Audi dealer.

11.94. As stated earlier,[211] a supplier is not required to apply the same quality criteria throughout the EEA. The question therefore arises whether the favourable presumption underlying Article 3(3) also applies if the acquirer is active in a territory where lower admission standards are set. The Explanatory Brochure[212] suggests that this is the case. In other words, even in such a context, the selling network member and the acquirer will have the benefit of the regime of Article 3(3). This obviously does not mean that the acquirer will be entitled to lower the standards of the acquired business to the level of its existing business. The acquirer will be bound by the contractual obligations contained in the vertical agreement that is transferred, including the quality standards.

11.95. It is not necessary that the company that acquires an authorized dealership or workshop is identical to the company that is already a network member. It suffices that the acquiring entity is part of the same group as the existing network member. This results from Article 1(2) of the Regulation.

---

[206] Certain authors have questioned the binding character of the Recitals of Reg 1400/2002: Makhlouf and Malaurie-Vignal (n 19 above) 11, note 9.

[207] Explanatory Brochure 26, question 10 and at 58, question 66.

[208] ibid, question 10.   [209] Explanatory Brochure 64, question 83.

[210] J Creutzig, 'Vertrieb und Betreuung neuer Kraftfahrzeuge im 21. Jahrhundert—Fragen und Antworten zur Kfz-GVO 1400/2002' (2002) 42/56 Betriebs-Berater 2133.

[211] Para 11.83 above.   [212] Explanatory Brochure 26, question 10.

A special case is that of the transfer of a dealership or workshop that is under termination. The Explanatory Brochure[213] clarifies that the transfer rights also apply in such a scenario. It is obvious, however, that the termination is unaffected by the transfer and that the acquirer will lose the benefit of the vertical agreement upon its termination.[214]   **11.96**.

As to the exact scope of the object of the transfer, Article 3(3) refers to 'the rights and obligations resulting from the vertical agreement'. These rights and obligations are of a contractual nature. It is unclear whether Article 3(3) must be interpreted as going beyond these contractual rights and extend further to concern the physical assets of the dealership or the shares of the company that has been appointed as an authorized dealer or workshop. The language of Article 3(3) does not directly support such an extension. On the other hand, it could be argued that the transfer of the contractual rights and obligations does not make much sense if the assets or the shares cannot also benefit from the free transfer rights.[215] This is not a merely theoretical question. Motor vehicle producers that wish to vertically integrate will be interested in established dealer or workshop locations and assets, and may want to have pre-emptive rights on such assets or shares. In its Frequently Asked Questions[216] DG COMP has spelled out that such pre-emptive rights are not compatible with Article 3(3), but it has unfortunately not specified the scope of the transfer rights. With its reference to 'dealership' and 'repairership' DG COMP also seems to include the assets (and possibly even the shares). The question as to how such an interpretation can be reconciled with the specific wording of Article 3(3) remains, however, open.   **11.97**.

The practical implications of Article 3(3) include the following: **11.98**.

— Standard change of ownership clauses, whereby a change in ownership is subject to the supplier's prior consent, are no longer possible.[217] Such clauses must in any event be limited to the cases where no intra-network transfer is involved. It seems logical that the same applies to change of management clauses, to the extent that they can be used to veto the transfer of a dealer or workshop agreement.

---

[213] Explanatory Brochure 58, question 64.

[214] ibid, question 65. This does not exclude the possibility, for instance, that the acquiring dealer or workshop elects to use the transferred workshop as an additional outlet or even to move its entire workshop activities to that location.

[215] Since the location clause had to be dropped (as of 1 October 2005) an existing network member has, in any event, the possibility to open up new authorized outlets so that taking over of a vertical agreement (without the related assets or shares) will not be of any value. This possibility already existed prior to 1 October 2005 for authorized workshops (Reg 1400/2002, Art 5(3)).

[216] Frequently Asked Questions (n 17 above) 11, question 20. This is one of many examples where an interpretation is given to the Regulation that regulates, in a very detailed manner, the contractual relationship between the parties.   [217] Explanatory Brochure 57, footnote 135.

— DG COMP[218] accepts an obligation to inform the supplier in advance of the intention to transfer, but such a notice requirement may not delay the transfer. It is suggested that an advance notice of four weeks before the transfer becomes effective is acceptable.

(3) Term and termination

11.99. Article 3(5) of the Regulation stipulates as a condition certain term and termination requirements. These requirements apply only to vertical agreements between suppliers of new motor vehicles and distributors or authorized repairers. The scope of this condition is therefore more limited than in the case of Article 3(3).[219] The profile of both parties to the vertical agreement is relevant.[220]

11.100. Vertical agreements that are subject to Article 3(5) of the Regulation must be concluded:

— for a fixed term of at least five years, with an obligation to give a notice of non-renewal of at least six months; or

— for an indefinite term, with an obligation for both parties to give a notice of regular termination of at least two years. This notice requirement of two years is reduced to one year[221]

   (i) if the supplier is obliged by law or special agreement to pay appropriate compensation on termination of the agreement, or

   (ii) if the termination is necessary to re-organize the whole or a substantial part of the network.[222]

11.101. Article 3(5) does not affect the possibility of terminating the vertical agreement for serious breach, provided that such a possibility is available under the applicable law.[223] In such a scenario, there will be no need to respect any notice requirement pursuant to Article 3(5) of the Regulation.

11.102. Article 3(4) of the Regulation adds certain formalities that must be complied with in the case of termination. Vertical agreements concluded with a distributor or repairer must provide 'that a supplier who wishes to give notice of termination of

---

[218] Frequently Asked Questions (n 17 above) 11, question 20.
[219] Explanatory Brochure 25, question 9.
[220] The concept of 'supplier of new motor vehicles' is not free from questions of interpretation. Art 3(5) refers to vertical agreements entered into with authorized repairers. The concept must therefore probably be understood to cover vertical agreements entered into by a distributor or an authorized repairer with a supplier of new motor vehicles or a company of the same group—Reg 1400/2002, Art 1(2)— irrespective of whether the supplier effectively supplies new motor vehicles in the context of the vertical agreement concerned.
[221] It is to be noted that the new entrant exception that applied under Reg 1475/95, Art 5(2)(2) second indent has not been retained in Reg 1400/2002.
[222] Explanatory Brochure 58, question 68 and Evaluation Report (n 7 above) para 251.
[223] Explanatory Brochure 59, question 69.

an agreement must give such notice in writing and must include detailed, objective, and transparent reasons for the termination, in order to prevent a supplier from ending a vertical agreement with a distributor or repairer because of practices which may not be restricted under the Regulation.'[224]

The scope of this condition is broader than that of Article 3(5). Article 3(4) applies **11.103**. to all vertical agreements to which a distributor or repairer is a party but, unlike Article 3(5), does not require that the other party must be a supplier of new motor vehicles.[225] The Explanatory Brochure[226] specifies further that the formalities of Article 3(4) must only be complied with in cases of termination and not in the case of non-renewal of an agreement that has been entered into for a fixed term. This means in practice that the formalities must be adhered to in all cases of termination of an agreement of an indefinite term and all cases where an agreement entered into for a fixed term is terminated prior to the expiry of its stated term.

The function of the formalities imposed by Article 3(4) is quite specific. It must **11.104**. render it possible to verify whether it is the case that the termination was intended as a punishment of a dealer or repairer for the fact that it engaged in pro-competitive behaviour that is intended by the block exemption. Any suggestion that the function of Article 3(4) is broader (for instance, that it must be able to justify the termination) is inaccurate.[227] For example, if a vertical agreement has been entered into for an indefinite term and is terminated by means of a two-year notice and if applicable law does not impose any requirement to justify such a termination (a case of ordinary termination), no importance may be attached to the reasons given in the notice letter other than to verify whether the terminated dealer or repairer is sanctioned for having engaged in pro-competitive behaviour. It would be incorrect to interpret the block exemption in such a way that it imposes, as a matter of contract law, formalities that may influence the legal validity of the given termination.[228]

(4) Dispute resolution

Article 3(6) of the Regulation renders the application of the block exemption **11.105**. dependent upon the fulfilment of the condition that 'the vertical agreement

---

[224] The Explanatory Brochure (59, question 70) provides that 'in order to be covered by the Regulation, a supplier who wishes to terminate a dealer agreement must give detailed, objective and transparent reasons in writing'. This however, is not what Art 3(4) requires. Art 3(4) requires that the vertical agreement provides for these formalities as a condition for the applicability of the block exemption. Whether or not the supplier complies with these formalities may have consequences as a matter of contract law, but it is not a condition in the Regulation. As long as the agreement requires these formalities, the condition of Art 3(4) is met.

[225] Explanatory Brochure 25, question 9.   [226] Explanatory Brochure 60, question 71.

[227] Consider the suggestion contained in the Explanatory Brochure (Explanatory Brochure 59, question 70) to this effect.

[228] In view of this, the possibility to refer to arbitration the issue of whether the termination of an agreement is justified by the reasons given in the notice (Reg 1400/2002, Art 3(6)(g)) must be

provides for each of the parties the right to refer disputes concerning the fulfilment of their contractual obligations to an independent expert or arbitrator'. The scope of Article 3(6) is broader than that of any of the other conditions discussed above.[229] This condition must be met by all vertical agreements that fall within the field of application of the block exemption. It is immaterial whether or not an authorized dealer or repairer is a party to the agreement. Likewise, Article 3(6) is not confined to cases where suppliers of new motor vehicles are involved.

11.106. Such a dispute resolution provision is not new. It was also provided for in Regulation 1475/95. This procedure has been used very seldom.[230] The reason for keeping such a mechanism in Regulation 1400/2002 is that DG COMP believes that 'the effectiveness of the provisions on arbitration may lie in the fact that they offer the possibility of threatening the other partner with a call for arbitration' and that 'the possibility of recourse to a third party has generally led to more serious and balanced negotiations between dealers and manufacturers'.[231]

11.107. Article 3(6) lists issues which can usefully be referred to arbitration. These issues include supply obligations, the setting or attainment of sales targets, the implementation of stock requirements, the implementation of an obligation to provide or use demonstration vehicles, the conditions for the sale of different brands, the issue of whether the prohibition to operate out of an unauthorized place of establishment limits the ability of a distributor of trucks and buses to expand its business and the issue of whether the termination of an agreement is justified by the reasons given in the notice. These are however examples as Article 3(6) makes it clear that the dispute mechanism should cover all possible disputes pertaining to the fulfilment of contractual obligations in the context of a vertical agreement.

---

interpreted carefully. In cases where reasons must be given as a matter of contract law, the arbitration may assess whether these reasons can justify the termination. In all other cases, the arbitration should be limited to the question of whether the reasons invoked are inaccurate and whether the real reasons pertain to the pro-competitive behaviour of the dealer or repairer. The legal consequences of an arbitral finding that the grounds given for the termination were inaccurate and that in fact the dealer or workshop has been sanctioned for pro-competitive conduct, are unclear. If the termination is valid as a matter of contract law (because applicable contract law does not require any stated reasons for a case of ordinary termination), it is far from self-evident that the arbitrators would be entitled to award damages or to order the suspension of the termination. B Mathieu, 'La rupture du contrat du distributeur dans le nouveau règlement d'exemption automobile' (2002) 239 Petites Affiches 27, 29 (the author suggests that damages could be awarded on the basis of the theory of abuse of rights); Creutzig (n 210 above) 2147 (the author suggests that, in the absence of reasons for the termination or if the records are not objective and transparent, the termination would be null and void); Makhlouf and Malaurie-Vignal (n 19 above) 8 (these authors suggest that applicable national law will determine the legal consequences) and Schlenger and Hinrichs (n 158 above) 537 (these authors predict that the determination of the legal consequences of non-compliance with the justification requirement is bound to give rise to conflicts).

[229] Explanatory Brochure 25, question 9.
[230] Evaluation Report (n 7 above) 91, para 279: 'Very few cases of intervention by an arbitrator are recorded by car manufacturers and dealers'. [231] ibid.

The parties enjoy quite some flexibility as to the manner in which the dispute **11.108.** resolution procedure is to be set up, provided that it is done by common accord and not unilaterally by one of the parties.[232] Furthermore, Article 3(6) is without prejudice to each party's right to make an application to a national court.[233] This means in our view that, unless the vertical agreement provides otherwise, each party may bring a dispute directly before a court and they are not required to first apply the arbitration or third party expert procedure. The condition included in Article 3(6) requires that the vertical agreement includes a dispute settlement procedure and that each party can avail itself of that procedure if it so wishes. It does not require the prior application of the procedure before a case can be brought before the normal courts.

E. Hardcore Restrictions

(1) General

Article 4 of Regulation 1400/2002 contains the so-called blacklist, ie the list of **11.109.** hardcore restrictions that render the block exemption inapplicable to the vertical agreement as a whole. These are regarded as extremely serious restrictions by DG COMP and as a result they will not be able to benefit from any *De Minimis* treatment.[234] Further, they are unlikely to be eligible for an individual exemption.[235]

Article 4 lists four categories of restrictions: **11.110.**

(1) hardcore restrictions concerning the sale of new motor vehicles, repair and maintenance services or spare parts;
(2) hardcore restrictions only concerning the sale of new motor vehicles;
(3) hardcore restrictions only concerning the sale of repair and maintenance services and of spare parts;
(4) the obligation of a supplier of motor vehicles to provide independent operators access to technical information and certain equipment.

The introductory sentence to the first three parts is identical: 'The exemption **11.111.** shall not apply to vertical agreements which, directly or indirectly, in isolation or in combination with other factors under the control of the parties, have as their object [...]':

— The reference to 'directly or indirectly' underscores that it is not only outright prohibitions that are covered by the blacklist. Also, if the pro-competitive behaviour that is intended by Article 4 is prevented or restricted

---

[232] Explanatory Brochure 56, question 61.
[233] For criticism of the absence of a clear choice between arbitration and ordinary court proceedings, Automotive Sector Groups of HB and LWWK (n 11 above) 264 *et seq.*
[234] Paras 11.28–11.30 above. [235] Explanatory Brochure 12 and 29.

in an indirect manner, the block exemption will cease to apply. Typical examples[236] of such indirect means are limitations (eg of supplies of vehicles),[237] financial incentives or disincentives, pressures or obstacles to certain activities or transactions (eg delays in making available certificates of conformity).[238]

— If several factors are combined to demonstrate that an infringement of the blacklist has been committed, only the factors that are under the control of the parties may be taken into account.

— Of considerable importance is that the vertical agreement must have a hardcore restriction as its object. Hence, if the effect of a given vertical agreement is the same as a hardcore restriction, but the agreement did not have such a restriction as its object, there will be no infringement of Article 4.[239] Conversely, there will be no need to demonstrate the actual or potential effects of a restriction. It suffices that the agreement had the object of implementing a hardcore restriction.

(2) Hardcore restrictions concerning the sale of new motor vehicles, repair and maintenance services, or spare parts

11.112. The first category of hardcore restrictions is largely based on the blacklist included in Regulation 2790/99. To the extent that the provisions raise identical or similar interpretation or application questions, reference is made to the description of the relevant provision of Regulation 2790/99.

Vertical price fixing

11.113. Article 4(1)(a) blacklists:

> the restriction of the distributor's or repairer's ability to determine its sale price, without prejudice to the supplier's ability to impose a maximum sale price or to recommend a sale price, provided that this does not amount to a fixed or minimum sale price as a result of pressure from, or incentives offered by, any of the parties.

The fixing of actual selling prices or minimum prices amounts to a hardcore restriction. This includes interference on the part of the supplier with the level of the discounts that a dealer or repairer will grant.[240] The supplier is however entitled to issue recommended prices (provided that they are non-binding) and to impose (genuine) maximum resale prices. Vertical price fixing has

---

[236] Explanatory Brochure 20, question 6 and 29, question 11.
[237] Explanatory Brochure 41, footnote 85.   [238] ibid, question 28.
[239] Regarding the distinction between 'object' and 'effect', see paras 5.04–5.09 above.
[240] Explanatory Brochure 43, question 32.

traditionally been a point of attention in the sector[241] and has recently caused the Commission to impose considerable fines on Volkswagen.[242]

11.114. The price setting mechanisms in the motor vehicle business are quite sector-specific.[243] Suppliers typically start price calculations for motor vehicles from the recommended retail price. The dealer price is the recommended retail price minus a so-called dealer discount or margin and, in order to arrive at the importer price, a further importer margin will be deducted. The use of the recommended retail price in this manner does not pose a problem as long as the dealer remains free to apply a lower price (ie to pass on part of the dealer margin). In the repair business, prices for the work performed are typically calculated by multiplying the time spent by an hourly rate (the so-called labour rate). In order to avoid vertical price-fixing problems, suppliers should not set minimum levels of labour rates, nor of the time to be spent on a particular repair job. The imposition of maxima in respect of both parameters is, however, lawful.

Territorial and customer restrictions

11.115. The general principle underlying Regulation 1400/2002 is that no territorial or customer restrictions may be imposed on a distributor or repairer, unless they are specifically provided for in Article 4. The fact that Article 4(1)(b) focuses only on restrictions imposed on a distributor or repairer implies that any restriction of competition resulting from the imposition of territorial or customer restrictions on the supplier[244] benefits from the block exemption. Hence, standard clauses in which the supplier confines his direct sales rights to particular territories or specific categories of customers (eg fleet customers or governmental authorities) are valid.[245]

11.116. Both as to territorial and customer restrictions, the position under the block exemption differs, depending upon whether selective distribution or non-selective distribution is involved. It is important to emphasize that Article 4 blacklists

---

[241] *Bayerische Motoren Werke AG* [1975] OJ L29/1, 6.

[242] *Volkswagen II* [2001] OJ L262/14.

[243] Evaluation Report (n 7 above), paras 95–100, 182, 188–9, 255–66, and 311; Verboven Report (n 103 above) Ch 1.3.1, 53–6, Ch 2.3.2, 75–6, Ch 2.6.2, 112, and Ch 7, 86–7, and Andersen, *Study on the Impact of Possible Future Legislative Scenarios For Motor Vehicle Distribution on All Parties Concerned*, 3 December 2001, Ch III.3.6, 167 *et seq* available at http://europa.eu.int/comm/competition/car_sector/distribution/eval_reg_1475_95/ studies/impact_legislative_scenarios/ (hereafter 'Andersen Report'). It is important to note that, to our knowledge, the price setting methodology applied in the car industry has never been challenged by the European competition authorities. The absence of criticism in the *Opel* decision, where the methodology is summarized in explicit terms (*Opel* [2001] OJ L59/1, paras 43–44 and 123), illustrates the Commission's tacit acceptance of the said methodology.

[244] *Bayerische Motoren Werke AG* [1975] OJ L29/1, 5.

[245] This does not mean, however, that the supplier is entitled to reserve these territories or customers to himself by preventing his dealers from making sales (even passive sales) in such territories or to such customers.

restrictions imposed by the supplier on a distributor or repairer. This means, however, that if a distributor or repairer decides itself (without being subject to any restriction imposed by the supplier) not to sell in certain territories or to certain customers, then there is no blacklist issue.[246]

11.117. The vast majority of the cases brought by the Commission in respect of the motor vehicle sector concern restrictions on cross-border trade.[247] The level of the fines imposed in these cases underscores the importance attached by the Commission to unrestricted cross-border trade in motor vehicles. These cases illustrate furthermore that infringements of Article 4(1)(b) will in principle not be eligible for an individual exemption.

Territorial restrictions

11.118. The possibilities under the block exemption to impose territorial restraints are the following:

— Active sales[248] into a particular territory can only be restricted or prohibited in order to protect an exclusive distributor[249] or repairer.[250] The conditions that must be met in order to render the imposition of such a restriction or prohibition lawful are the same as under Regulation 2790/99.[251] These conditions are quite strict and imply that, if in certain territories selective distribution is used while in others exclusive distribution is used, the entire network (including the members of the selective distribution system) will have to be subject to the restriction or prohibition on active sales in respect of the territory of the exclusive distributor(s).

— In a selective distribution system, the restriction or prohibition of active or passive sales into a given territory is blacklisted. There is a very limited exception. In the context of the selective distribution of new passenger cars or light commercial vehicles, an authorized dealer may be prevented from operating out of an unauthorized place of establishment. As of 1 October 2005, the dealer must however be entitled to establish additional sales or delivery outlets.[252] A selective distribution system for new trucks and buses

---

[246] Evaluation Report (n 7 above) 24, footnote 86 and Explanatory Brochure 41, question 26.
[247] *Volkswagen I* [1998] OJ L124/60; *Opel* [2001] OJ L59/1; *Volkswagen II* [2001] OJ L262/14 and *DaimlerChrysler* [2002] OJ L257/1.
[248] This concept is to be defined in the same way as under Reg 2790/99; Explanatory Brochure 30, question 12. Also paras 5.46 and 5.47 above.
[249] Reg 1400/2002, Art 4(1)(b)(i).
[250] As DG COMP proceeds on the assumption that the market share limit of 30% will almost always be exceeded in respect of (brand-specific) repair and maintenance services, the reference to exclusive distribution for repair and maintenance may be somewhat theoretical (at least in respect of the producers/importers of new motor vehicles). Also paras 11.71 and 11.72 above.
[251] Paras 5.61–5.85 above.
[252] Reg 1400/2002, Arts 4(1)(d), 5(2)(b), and 12(2) and Commission Press Release, IP 05/1208, 30 September 2005. For more details on location clauses, see paras 11.204–11.211.

may include a location clause. This means that an authorized dealer can be prevented from operating out of an unauthorized place of establishment.[253] Apart from this limited exception, active or passive sales into other territories cannot be subjected to any restriction.

— Irrespective of the distribution system that is used (selective or non-selective), restrictions on passive sales into particular territories by dealers or repairers will never be covered by the block exemption.[254]

Customer restrictions

The position in respect of customer restrictions is slightly more complex: **11.119**.

— Restrictions on active sales may be imposed in respect of exclusive customer groups reserved to the supplier or allocated by the supplier to another distributor or repairer.[255] The conditions that must be met in order to render such restrictions lawful are the same as in the context of Regulation 2790/99 and hence, the same as with respect to restrictions on active sales into particular territories under Regulation 1400/2002.[256]

— Apart from such restrictions on active sales to certain customer groups, no customer restriction may be imposed in the context of a non-selective distribution network. This means, *inter alia*, that a distributor or repairer must be able to sell to independent traders, even if such traders are located within an area where a selective distribution system is operated.[257]

— In the context of a selective distribution system (and within the markets where selective distribution is applied), the members of the network may be prevented from selling new motor vehicles and spare parts to unauthorized distributors.[258] In fact, such a restriction must be imposed, as it is an inherent feature of any selective distribution system. In the absence of such a restriction, the system does not qualify as selective distribution.[259] Somewhat in the same spirit, cross-supplies between network members may not be restricted, even if the distributors or repairers operate at different levels of trade.[260]

— A distributor operating at the wholesale level may be prevented from selling to end-users.[261] This means that a wholeseller may be required to confine its operations to the wholesale level.

---

[253] Reg 1400/2002, Art 4(1)(e).   [254] ibid, recital 13.   [255] ibid, Art 4(1)(b).

[256] Para 11.118 above. For more details on restrictions on active sales to certain customer groups within the context of Reg 2790/99, see paras 5.86–5.94 above.

[257] Explanatory Brochure 47, question 40.   [258] Reg 1400/2002, Art 4(1)(b)(iii).

[259] Definition of selective distribution contained in Reg 1400/2002, Art 1(1)(f).

[260] ibid, Art 4(1)(c) and Explanatory Brochure 55, question 58. This implies that it is not possible to oblige a member of a selective distribution network to purchase exclusively from the supplier as this would mean in effect that cross-supplies are eliminated.

[261] Reg 1400/2002, Art 4(1)(b)(ii).

—A buyer that is supplied with components for the purposes of incorporation may be prevented from supplying these components to customers who would use them to manufacture the same type of goods as those produced by the supplier.[262] In the context of motor vehicles, it is not entirely clear what practical purpose is served by allowing this type of restriction.

Practical implications

11.120. The impact of the prohibition on territorial and customer restrictions (with the limited exceptions outlined above) is quite far-reaching and affects a wide variety of practices in the motor vehicle business.

Prohibition of registration requirement

11.121. It is not possible to link any advantage (such as rebates granted to customers or bonuses awarded to dealers or repairers) to the relevant motor vehicle being registered within a given Member State. A registration requirement is assimilated to a restriction on sales to customers located in another Member State and as such is incompatible with the block exemption.[263]

Repair, warranty, free servicing, recall

11.122. In order not to breach Article 4(1)(b), a supplier must impose an obligation on all its authorized repairers to repair all vehicles of the relevant brand, to honour warranties, perform free servicing, and recall work irrespective of the place where the vehicle was purchased within the EEA.[264] However, if the local authorized repairer is unable to fix a problem, it may still be necessary that the car is brought back to the dealer that has sold it.[265]

11.123. The Regulation does not require manufacturers to have a single European warranty database, but the absence of such a database may not subject a customer that has purchased his vehicle abroad to any special charge, nor require that he submits additional documentation. The manufacturer's warranty must be valid under the same conditions in all Member States.[266]

Ordering and delivery systems

11.124. There is no requirement that the ordering and delivery systems be the same or that the delivery times be identical throughout the Community. However, the

---

[262] ibid, Art 4(1)(b)(iv).
[263] Explanatory Brochure 43, question 33 and at 47, question 41.
[264] Reg 1400/2002, recital 17 and Explanatory Brochure 43, question 34.
[265] Explanatory Brochure 44, question 35.
[266] Frequently Asked Questions (n 17 above) question 1. This does not mean, however, that a manufacturer must offer exactly the same warranty in all Member States. It is possible that the warranty period is longer in one Member State than it is in another or that the scope of the warranty is broader in some Member States. However, to the extent that it is technically possible,

supply of vehicles by the supplier to an authorized dealer must be conducted in the same manner (eg as to price and delivery times) irrespective of whether or not a local customer is involved.[267] This implies also that, in the case of shortage, the supplier may not discriminate between dealers who also sell to non-local customers and may therefore have to implement a 'first come, first served' system.[268]

Sales targets

Sales targets fixed for areas that are smaller than the Community do not neces- **11.125.** sarily pose a problem under the Regulation.[269] However, such sales targets may not be used to limit supplies to dealers (so that they are indirectly restricted in their ability to sell throughout the Community).[270] DG COMP accepts furthermore, that the failure to meet a sales target (even for an area smaller than the Community) may be a ground for the termination of the dealer agreement.[271]

Bonuses on cross-supplies

The requirement that cross-supplies between members of a selective distribu- **11.126.** tion system may not be hampered or restricted poses practical problems in respect of bonus payments. DG COMP takes the view that cross-supplies between network members must also count for bonus calculation purposes, but that, in such a case, the subsequent resale of the vehicle to the end-user may be excluded from the bonus calculation.[272]

Intermediaries

Intermediaries are purchasing agents that buy new motor vehicles on behalf of a **11.127.** named consumer, but are not part of the distribution network, nor operate as an independent reseller.[273] The Commission attaches considerable importance to the role of intermediaries as it expects them to facilitate cross-border purchases.[274] Two notices issued by the Commission in respect of the role of intermediaries under the previous block exemption regulations[275] have been

---

the warranty obtained in one Member State should be honoured by the authorized repairer network in all other Member States.

[267] Explanatory Brochure 47, question 41 and at 55, question 59, and Monti (n 13 above).
[268] ibid.
[269] The position explicitly taken in the Explanatory Brochure (Explanatory Brochure 48, question 43) on this issue is difficult to reconcile with Tsoraklidis' observation that 'sales targets, and therefore bonus calculation, will now be set for the whole EU, instead of confined to allocated territories' (n 4 above) 32. While the observation on bonuses is undoubtedly accurate, the same would not seem to be true for the reference to sales targets.
[270] Reg 1400/2002, recital 16 and Explanatory Brochure 48, question 43.
[271] Frequently Asked Questions (n 17 above) 5, question 9.   [272] ibid, question 8.
[273] Explanatory Brochure 45.   [274] Explanatory Brochure 13.
[275] Commission Notice concerning Regulation (EEC) No 123/85 of 12 December 1984 on the application of Article 85(3) of the Treaty to certain categories of motor vehicle distribution and

abolished as they contained certain limitations on the activities of intermediaries. DG COMP is now reluctant to accept restrictions on the activities of
intermediaries and tests any such restrictions on the basis of Article 4(1)(b) of
the Regulation. For instance, suppliers may in principle request that their
dealers obtain a copy of the mandate signed by the consumer, but no more.[276]
Only in exceptional cases (eg where the supplier may have good reasons to
suspect that the intermediary operates as a disguised independent trader) may
additional formalities be imposed by the supplier[277] (such as a signed declaration that the intermediary will not resell the vehicle).[278]

Leasing companies

11.128. Leasing companies qualify as normal end-users (and hence not as independent
resellers), unless the leasing contracts provide for a transfer of ownership or an
option to purchase the vehicle prior to the expiry of the contract.[279] A leasing
company does not lose its status of end-user if it does not yet have a customer at
the time when it purchases a new motor vehicle[280] or if it buys cars in large
quantities.[281] Somewhat surprisingly, DG COMP allows suppliers to impose
more checks and formalities regarding leasing companies than in the case
of intermediaries to ensure that a leasing company will not resell a vehicle when
new (including a written declaration that the leasing company will not resell
the vehicle).[282] A leasing company may not, however, be requested to provide
copies of the leasing agreements to the dealer or the supplier.[283]

(3) Hardcore restrictions only concerning the sale of new motor vehicles

11.129. Article 4 lists two hardcore restrictions that only concern the sale of new motor
vehicles.

Availability clause

11.130. Article 4(1)(f) of the Regulation blacklists any restriction 'of the distributor's
ability to sell any new motor vehicle which corresponds to a model within its

---

servicing agreements [1985] OJ C17/4 and the Information from the Commission—Clarification
of the activities of motor vehicle intermediaries [1991] OJ C329/20.
  [276] Explanatory Brochure 46, question 39.
  [277] The dealer, who has a contractual obligation in a selective distribution system not to sell to
unauthorized traders, has more freedom in requesting additional evidence. However, the dealer
may not be put under pressure from the supplier to engage in systematic checks (Explanatory
Brochure 46, question 39). [278] Frequently Asked Questions (n 17 above) 2, questions 3 and 4.
  [279] Reg 1400/2002, Art 1(1)(w). [280] Explanatory Brochure 51, question 49.
  [281] Explanatory Brochure 47.
  [282] Explanatory Brochure 50, question 47. Compare also: Explanatory Brochure 42, question
29, where DG COMP does not provide a clear answer to the same question when consumers are
involved. [283] Explanatory Brochure 50, question 48.

contract range'. The objective of this provision is to enable consumers to take advantage of price differentials that exist throughout the Community.[284] The provision is intended to foster market integration and intra-brand competition.

It is incorrect to say that the availability clause has simply been carried forward **11.131.** from Regulation 1475/95.[285] A number of the restrictions on the use of the availability clause that were previously included in Article 5(1)(2)(d) of Regulation 1475/95 have either been deleted or relaxed:

— Under Regulation 1475/95 a supplier was only required to sell a corresponding vehicle to a dealer if the latter needed such a vehicle for the purpose of performing a contract of sale concluded with a final customer in the Community. Under Regulation 1400/2002, the availability clause applies irrespective of whether the dealer has already contracted with a particular customer or not.[286] This implies, for instance, that a dealer is free to stock corresponding vehicles in order to be able to meet the future demand of customers from other Member States.

— Also, the requirement that the corresponding vehicle had to be marketed by the manufacturer (or with its consent) in the Member State where the vehicle was to be registered has been dropped. This previously meant that in practice a Belgian dealer had to be supplied with a Danish model, provided that the vehicle was to be registered by the customer in Denmark. This condition no longer applies. It is now perfectly possible that a Belgian dealer requests to be supplied with a Danish model which can then be registered by the customer in Italy.

— Previously, in the context of Regulation 1475/95, the availability clause applied only to passenger cars. The scope of Article 4(1)(f) now extends to all new motor vehicles (including trucks and buses).

A motor vehicle will be deemed to correspond to a model within the contract **11.132.** range if it meets the following conditions:

— it is the subject of a distribution agreement with another undertaking within the distribution system set up by the manufacturer or with his consent;[287]
— the vehicle must be manufactured or assembled in volume by the manufacturer;[288]

---

[284] Explanatory Brochure 40.

[285] Explanatory Brochure 40 and Commission Press Release, IP/02/1073, 17 July 2002.

[286] Schlenger and Hinrichs (n 158 above) 540.

[287] It may be assumed that only the distribution network within the EEA is envisaged, so that vehicles that are made available outside the EEA do not fall within the scope of application of the availability clause. The language included in Reg 1475/95 to secure this territorial limitation has (probably inadvertently) been dropped in Reg 1400/2002.

[288] Thereby excluding from the scope of Art 4(1)(f) special models that are produced on a limited scale (eg special editions).

— the vehicle must be identical in relation to body style, drive-line, chassis, and type of motor to a vehicle within the dealer's contract range.[289] The consequence of this requirement is that a right-hand-drive version of a given model that is within the dealer's contract range will qualify as a corresponding model to the left-hand-drive version.

11.133. In order to avoid an infringement of Article 4(1)(f), dealers should be supplied with corresponding vehicles in exactly the same manner as the vehicles within their contract range. Any difference in treatment will have to be objectively justifiable. This implies that there should be no delays other than those strictly necessary to make the relevant supply.[290] Importantly, the price charged to the dealer for the corresponding vehicle should be the same as that applicable to the model within the contract range. Only additional costs in producing or delivering the vehicle (that can be objectively established) can justify the imposition of a surcharge.[291] This implies that the supplier is not entitled to simply charge the dealer the price that it charges to the dealers in the country where the corresponding vehicle is part of the contract range.

Subcontracting repair and maintenance services

11.134. One of the essential features of Regulation 1475/95 was that a dealer had to perform both a distribution role and also provide repair and maintenance services. Article 4(1)(g) of Regulation 1400/2002 alters this mandatory link between sales and servicing by allowing a dealer to focus on distribution activities and to subcontract the provision of after-sales services. The link between sales and after-sales is therefore not entirely severed, but it is reorganized.[292] A dealer that focuses on sales activities, may still be required to assume after-sales responsibility vis-à-vis customers,[293] but will be entitled to subcontract the physical performance of the work to an authorized repairer.

11.135. The policy objective of this provision may be clear in theory, but it is not so in practice. It is suggested that allowing dealers to specialize in vehicle distribution might be a particularly attractive option for dealers who wish to sell new vehicles

---

[289] This means that if a dealer does not normally sell a particular model, it cannot rely on the availability clause to obtain a model that is distributed elsewhere in the EEA; Explanatory Brochure 42, question 30.

[290] Giving preference to cars within the contract range as opposed to corresponding models is therefore not justified. [291] Explanatory Brochure 43, question 31.

[292] Tsoraklidis (n 4 above) 32. Certain authors emphasize that the nature of the subcontracting relationship remains unclear (Giroudet-Demay (n 16 above) 15).

[293] The Regulation does not make it entirely clear to what extent a dealer that confines its activities to distributing cars may still be required to assume responsibility for requests for servicing from its customers. For instance, the reference to subcontracting in Art 4(1)(g) suggests that a selling dealer may be required by the supplier (if the customer so wishes) to take contractual responsibility for servicing work performed by an authorized repairer. Also Explanatory Brochure 44, question 36 and AD Wendel, 'Die neue GVO Nr. 1400/2002 vom 31.07.2002—Automobilvertrieb seit dem 01.10.2002' (2002) 12 Wettbewerb in Recht und Praxis 1395, 1407.

from different manufacturers.[294] Reality shows however, that dealer margins in respect of vehicle sales are under pressure and that most dealers are dependent on their after-sales business in order to remain profitable.[295] This provision would fit perfectly in a situation where the Commission actively promotes the use of supermarkets or supermarket-like distribution outlets. However, the manufacturer is allowed to exclude this type of distribution channel within the context of a quantitative selective distribution system. As a consequence, this type of distribution cannot occur against the will of the manufacturer.

It would also seem that there is not a genuine demand from the market to have   **11.136.**
sales-only outlets. In this respect, the position is different from that of work-shop-only settings. While the market has demonstrated the need to have workshops that do not engage in selling activities,[296] the same is not true for pure sales outlets. One of the few exceptions is the so-called diplomat and military sales channels, which are often pure sales outlets (without workshop capabilities) located close to military bases or places with a high concentration of expatriates.[297] While these sales outlets did not fit well within Regulation 1475/95, they can now benefit from Regulation 1400/2002.

The type of servicing work that can be subcontracted to an authorized repairer   **11.137.**
includes the honouring of warranties, free servicing, and recall work.[298] It is not entirely clear to what extent a dealer should be entitled to outsource only a part of the after-sales work (eg the more complicated) whilst retaining the other part. As the after-sales network of a producer will typically be set up as a qualitative selective system, it seems unlikely that a dealer can meet the necessary quality requirements if it is not able to perform all of the after-sales work that is typically required from an authorized repairer. Hence, a dealer that subcontracts part of the repair and maintenance work, risks no longer qualifying as an authorized repairer.

The question then arises whether or not the dealer can perform such work acting in   **11.138.**
the capacity of an independent repairer. In other words, is it possible to combine an authorized distribution outlet with an independent (ie non-authorized) workshop that engages in brand-specific repair and maintenance work? The Explanatory Brochure states that this is allowed.[299] This position is not necessarily imposed by the Regulation and, in practice, leads to a somewhat confusing distribution model:

—A selling dealer must be entitled to subcontract repair and maintenance work, but he may be required to do so only to an authorized repairer (Article

---

[294] Explanatory Brochure 56.   [295] Evaluation Report (n 7 above) paras 95 and 235.
[296] ibid, para 224.
[297] These sales outlets present specific characteristics (eg in terms of language capability and knowledge pertaining to export formalities and tax free purchasing) in order to be able to meet the typical needs of such expatriate customers.   [298] Reg 1400/2002, recital 21.
[299] Explanatory Brochure 57, question 62.

4(1)(g)). Thus, the Regulation accepts that an authorized distributor may be prevented from subcontracting after-sales servicing to an independent workshop. This is logical and consistent with the need not to undermine the selective nature of the supplier's after-sales network. In that context it is difficult to understand (and even to reconcile with the text of Article 4(1)(g)) that an authorized distributor should be entitled to engage in brand-specific repair and maintenance work whilst not being an authorized workshop. The concept underlying the Regulation seems to be that an authorized distributor either qualifies as an authorized workshop (and therefore becomes part of the authorized network) or that he confines his business to distribution activities and subcontracts after-sales work to a member of the authorized repair and maintenance network.

— The policy objective underlying Article 4(1)(g) is to allow dealers to specialize in vehicle distribution (with the possibility of representing multiple brands).[300] The reorganization of the link between sales and after-sales is therefore intended as an opportunity for new entrants who will not be required to perform after-sales activity.[301] Hence, the new players which the Regulation hopes to attract are pure sales outlets that do not engage in, nor wish to invest in, brand-specific repair and maintenance work. By preventing such pure sales outlets from engaging in brand-specific after-sales work the stated objective is not lost.

— Most importantly, the position that is defended in the Explanatory Brochure creates serious free-rider problems. An authorized distribution outlet will have all of the brand-specific signage of an authorized network member. If such an outlet engages in brand-specific repair and maintenance work in an independent capacity, its status as an independent workshop will be almost impossible for customers to discern.[302] Hence, without making the investments required from an authorized workshop, the authorized distributor will have the 'look and feel' of an authorized workshop. Furthermore, in its capacity as an independent workshop, the workshop will be entitled to avail itself of the information rights (including the supply of relevant equipment) guaranteed in Article 4(2) of the Regulation. As Article 4(2) is based on positive discrimination towards independent repairers,[303] the authorized distributor will benefit from optimal flexibility in planning his investments.[304] In a regulatory context, where DG COMP pushes after-sales

---

[300] Explanatory Brochure 56.   [301] Tsoraklidis (n 4 above) 32.

[302] The fact that he will not be able to engage in warranty work (and may have to subcontract such work) will in practice not pose a problem and can easily be handled and organized by the workshop.   [303] Para 11.176 below.

[304] There will be no need for the distributor to obtain and pay for all the relevant information and equipment up front. The distributor will purchase the same according to its needs of the moment.

services into a qualitative selective distribution system, the creation of such free-rider problems is difficult to defend.

In view of the foregoing, it should be possible to prevent an authorized dis-   **11**.**139**. tribution outlet that decides not to become an authorized workshop from engaging in brand-specific repair and maintenance work. Such a restriction appears not to be blacklisted in the Regulation and it is consistent with both the language of the Regulation and the objectives and economics underlying the distribution model chosen by the Commission in respect of after-sales servicing.

Finally, if an authorized distributor elects to subcontract after-sales servicing,   **11**.**140**. the supplier may 'require the distributor to give end users the name and address of the authorised repairer or repairers in question before the conclusion of a sales contract'. Furthermore, if any of these authorized repairers are not in the vicinity of the distributor's sales outlet,[305] the distributor may be required to 'tell end users how far the repair shop or repair shops in question are from the sales outlet'. According to Article 4(1)(g), these obligations to give information may only be imposed on the distributor 'provided that similar obligations are imposed on distributors whose repair shop is not on the same premises as the sales outlet'. Thus, the failure to comply with this last condition makes it a hardcore restriction to impose such obligations (as to the location of the authorized repair shop to which after-sales work is subcontracted by the distributor).[306]

(4) Hardcore restrictions only concerning the sale of repair and maintenance services and of spare parts

The Regulation blacklists a number of restrictions that concern only after-sales   **11**.**141**. services and the distribution of spare parts. The underlying objective is clearly to inject additional competition in both areas.

Workshop-only scenario

Somewhat similar to the requirement that distributors must be able to confine   **11**.**142**. their business to sales activities,[307] is that Article 4(1)(h) blacklists 'the restriction of the authorised repairer's ability to limit its activities to the provision of repair and maintenance services and the distribution of spare parts'. This means that an authorized workshop cannot also be required by the supplier to become an authorized distribution outlet. An authorized repairer must be able to limit

---

[305] For a critical comment pertaining to this concept, Creutzig (n 11 above) 1129.
[306] This is one of many examples where the Regulation is prescriptive on points of detail and attaches very severe consequences (ie automatic and complete loss of the benefit of the block exemption) to the failure to comply with points that, from a competition law perspective, have minor (if any) importance.   [307] Reg 1400/2002, Art 4(1)(g).

its business to pure servicing work and have the freedom not to be engaged in any sales activities.[308]

11.143. Past experience demonstrates that the sector perceives a clear need to work with workshops (that are not distributing vehicles).[309] It is expected that this need will increase, as suppliers are expected to reduce the number of their authorized distributors.[310] The qualitative selective distribution formula (that *de facto* is imposed by the Regulation in respect of after-sales servicing) will enable those terminated dealers to remain within the network as authorized workshops.[311]

11.144. The drafting of Article 4(1)(h) suggests that a workshop may be required to perform both repair and maintenance work and parts distribution. Hence, a supplier seems to be entitled to refuse scenarios whereby a workshop could refuse to engage in parts distribution. The opposite, however, does not seem to apply. DG COMP takes the view that for brand-specific parts a qualitative selective distribution system will most probably be required (due to the 30% market share limit) and that the requirement to be an authorized workshop does not serve as a valid quality criterion in such a context.[312]

Supply of spare parts to independent repairers

11.145. Article 4(1)(i) blacklists 'the restriction of the sales of spare parts for motor vehicles by members of a selective distribution system to independent repairers which use these parts for the repair and maintenance of a motor vehicle'. This requirement is certainly not new. It dates back to the *BMW* decision and has been included in both of the previous block exemption regulations.[313]

11.146. The blacklisted provision concerns only sales by members of a selective distribution system and not the members of an exclusive distribution system. While possibly being somewhat theoretical,[314] the differences between the two distribution formulas, in respect of the sale of parts outside the network, can be summarized as follows:

— Selective parts distributors must be able to engage in both the active and passive sales of parts to independent repairers. Exclusive distributors can be

---

[308] Different from Art 4(1)(g), there is no need for an authorized workshop to team up with an authorized distribution outlet as a subcontractor or in any other co-operation formula.
[309] Evaluation Report (n 7 above) para 224.　　　　　　　　　[310] ibid, para 91.
[311] Tsoraklidis (n 4 above) 33 and Commission Press Release, IP/03/80, 20 January 2003 (Volkswagen and Audi). The increase in the number of authorized workshops may, however, have an impact on the profitability of the workshops, and the impact may be enhanced further by the longer service intervals that apply (Evaluation Report (n 7 above) para 117).　　　[312] Para 11.83.
[313] Reg 1475/95, Art 3(10)(b); Reg 123/85, Art 3(1)(b); and *Bayerische Motoren Werke AG* [1975] OJ L29/1, 8.
[314] Given DG COMP's position that brand-specific parts distribution most likely qualifies only for qualitative selective distribution.

prevented (provided the conditions of Article 4(1)(b) are met) from engaging in active sales of parts.[315]

— Selective distributors may be prevented from selling (both actively and passively) to independent parts distributors or traders or to independent repairers that use the parts for other purposes than the repairing or maintaining of a motor vehicle. Exclusive distributors cannot be restricted as to the customers (including traders) to whom they may sell parts.

The fact that the independent repairer uses the parts solely for repair and maintenance purposes is not sufficient. The parts must be used for the repair and maintenance of a motor vehicle. The wording of this additional condition has at least two implications: **11.147.**

— It is sufficient that repair and maintenance work on a motor vehicle is involved. The brand or model of the vehicle is immaterial. This may be important in scenarios where the same parts are used on different brands or models (eg where different car producers use the same components).
— If the part can and will be used by the independent repairer to service a vehicle other than a motor vehicle, then the supply must not be admitted pursuant to the block exemption.

Direct supplies by producers of parts, equipment, or tooling

Article 4(1)(j) of the Regulation blacklists: **11.148.**

> the restriction agreed between a supplier of original spare parts or spare parts of matching quality, repair tools or diagnostic or other equipment and a manufacturer of motor vehicles, which limits the supplier's ability to sell these goods or services to authorised or independent distributors or to authorised or independent repairers or end users.

This means in practical terms that a manufacturer of motor vehicles may not limit access to the authorized network by producers of parts, equipment, or tooling. This was already one of the aims underlying Regulation 1475/95.[316] Furthermore, access may not be limited in respect of independent distributors or repairers. The relevant producers must also be able to sell to end-users (eg fleet customers). **11.149.**

This provision uses a number of concepts that have a specific meaning in the Regulation and are also used in other provisions of the block exemption: **11.150.**

Original spare parts

These are 'parts which are of the same quality as the components used for the assembly of a motor vehicle and which are manufactured according to the **11.151.**

---

[315] Explanatory Brochure 81, question 100.
[316] Evaluation Report (n 7 above) para 52.

specifications and production standards provided by the vehicle manufacturer for the production of components and spare parts for the motor vehicle in question'.[317] Spare parts that are produced on the same production line as these components match the definition.[318] The Regulation contains a rebuttable presumption, namely that parts qualify as original spare parts if the parts manufacturer certifies that the parts match the quality of the components used for the assembly of the vehicle in question and have been manufactured according to the specifications and production standards of the vehicle manufacturer.[319] While the block exemption does not spell this out, the rebuttable presumption applies not only if the parts manufacturer is also the producer of the components which are supplied to, and used by, the vehicle manufacturer for the purposes of assembling the motor vehicle, but also to companies that are charged by the motor vehicle producer with the production of spare parts. In the latter case, even if they do not produce the corresponding components for first installation, they can still benefit from the rebuttable presumption.[320]

Spare parts of matching quality[321]

11.152. These are parts made by an undertaking which can certify at any moment that they match the quality of the components which are or were used for the assembly of the motor vehicle in question.[322] The type of certification which the parts producer must be prepared and able to issue is the same as in the case of original spare parts.[323]

11.153. No specific definition is given in the Regulation of repair tools or diagnostic or other equipment that is referred to in Article 4(1)(j).

11.154. One of the most important consequences of Article 4(1)(j) is that the block exemption will not apply to clauses in supply agreements between a motor vehicle producer and a parts/component producer in furtherance of which the latter must supply all parts and components to the motor vehicle manufacturer. This situation raises a number of questions of practical importance:

— The first question is whether the inapplicability of the block exemption resulting from an infringement of Article 4(1)(j) is limited to the agreement between the motor vehicle producer and the parts producer or extends also to other agreements (such as distribution agreements or agreements with authorized workshops). Article 4(1) starts by stating that 'the exemption shall not apply to vertical agreements which ... have as their object ...' This

---

[317] Reg 1400/2002, Art 1(1)(t).   [318] ibid.
[319] ibid, Art 1(1)(t). As to the manner in which a parts producer can issue certifications: Explanatory Brochure 82, question 101.   [320] Explanatory Brochure 79, question 97.
[321] This concept dates back to the 1974 *BMW* decision. The Evaluation Report (n 7 above) para 248, estimates that approximately 5 to 20% of a network's requirements are represented by parts of matching quality.   [322] Reg 1400/2002, Art 1(1)(u) and Explanatory Brochure 79.
[323] Explanatory Brochure 82, question 102.

language suggests that the consequences of an infringement of Article 4(1)(j) will be limited to the supply arrangement between the motor vehicle producer and the parts producer.

— The second question is whether the principle reflected in Article 4(1)(j) extends to all supply agreements between motor vehicle producers and parts producers. It is clear that Article 4(1)(j) applies only to supply agreements that fall within the scope of application of the block exemption. However, an important category of such agreements does not do so, namely the supply agreements that imply the passing on of intellectual property rights from the car producer to the parts manufacturer.[324] Such agreements will have to be assessed outside the framework of the Regulation and are therefore not subject to Article 4(1)(j).[325]

Freedom of distributors or repairers to source parts from third parties

Article 4(1)(k) blacklists: **11.155**.

> the restriction of a distributor's or authorised repairer's ability to obtain original spare parts or spare parts of matching quality from a third undertaking of its choice and to use them for the repair or maintenance of motor vehicles, without prejudice to the ability of a supplier of new motor vehicles to require the use of original spare parts supplied by it for repairs carried out under warranty, free servicing and vehicle recall work.

This is one of the central provisions in the block exemption aimed at opening up the parts market.

This blacklisted provision implies that: **11.156**.

— An authorized distributor or repairer may not be limited in its ability to purchase original spare parts, or parts of matching quality, from the source of its choice. Therefore, a provision requiring a distributor or repairer to purchase all or part of its requirements of such parts from the motor vehicle producer or its importer qualifies as a hardcore restriction.

— An authorized distributor or repairer may be required to use only original spare parts for the purposes of conducting warranty, free servicing, and vehicle recall work and, furthermore, to purchase such parts only from the vehicle producer or its importer.[326]

---

[324] This situation must be distinguished from that envisaged in the Explanatory Brochure 83, question 104, where the vehicle manufacturer requires that the intellectual property rights developed by the parts producer are passed on the vehicle manufacturer.

[325] With respect to agreements of this nature and the issue of supply-back obligations, see Ch 8 above. However, the impact of Art 4(1)(k) will be that exclusive supply-back obligations in supply agreements falling outside the scope of the block exemption will be problematic as they are likely to cause the block exemption to be inapplicable to the agreements with the authorized distributors and repairers.

[326] This exception is logical as these types of service works are paid for entirely by the motor vehicle producer or its importer. See also Explanatory Brochure 63, question 78.

11.157. One of the surprising changes, when comparing to Regulation 1475/95, is that an obligation to inform customers of the type of parts used is no longer automatically in conformity with the block exemption. Under Regulation 1475/95[327] such an obligation was whitelisted.[328] DG COMP now takes the view[329] that it will be a hardcore restriction:

> if the supplier uses an obligation on the repairer to inform its customers on the use of original spare parts or of spare parts of matching quality as a means to directly or indirectly restrict the right of the authorised repairer to purchase and use such spare parts. In particular, it may not use such an obligation to create the impression in the mind of consumers that these parts are of lesser quality than the original spare parts supplied by the vehicle manufacturer.[330]

It is important to note that the imposition of an information obligation is not, as such, contrary to Article 4(1)(k). There seems to be an additional burden of proof in order to challenge such an obligation ('as a means to directly or indirectly' and 'use . . . to create the impression'). It remains to be seen whether this burden of proof will not be reversed in practice, so that it will be for the party imposing the information obligation to prove that it did not pursue the aims referred to above.

11.158. It is not entirely clear whether the hardcore restriction contained in Article 4(1)(k) is limited to situations where the distributor or repairer intends to use the original spare parts or parts of matching quality only for repair and maintenance purposes (and hence, not to distribute them). The more likely interpretation is that this reading is too narrow. Given the impossibility of imposing a non-compete obligation in respect of parts,[331] as well as the language used in Article 4(1)(k), it seems likely that no sourcing restriction may be imposed, even where the distributor or repairer intends to distribute the parts concerned.

Trademark or logo of component supplier

11.159. Article 4(1)(l) of the Regulation blacklists:

> the restriction agreed between a manufacturer of motor vehicles which uses components for the initial assembly of motor vehicles and the supplier of such components which limits the latter's ability to place its trade mark or logo effectively and in an easily visible manner on the components supplied or on spare parts.

---

[327] Art 4(1)(8)–(9).

[328] This meant that it did not normally amount to a restriction of competition and, even if it did, that it benefited from the block exemption (Reg 1475/95, Art 4(2)).

[329] Most likely as a result of certain reactions received from parts distributors. Evaluation Report (n 7 above) 83.   [330] Explanatory Brochure 62, question 77.

[331] Reg 1400/2002, Art 5(1)(a).

The aim of this provision is undoubtedly to make it easier for potential **11.160**. purchasers of spare parts to find a way to identify alternative suppliers. At the same time, this requirement will facilitate the proof that the parts qualify as original spare parts.

F. Mandatory Access to Technical Information, Training, Tools, and Diagnostic and Other Equipment

The Regulation expands on the information obligation already contained in **11.161**. Article 6(1)(12) of Regulation 1475/95. This expansion concerns not only the beneficiaries of the information, but also the scope of the information and the items that have to be made available. In doing so the Commission addresses concerns expressed by the independent players on the aftermarket.[332] In addition to imposing qualitative selective distribution on the aftermarket (which is expected to increase competition between authorized workshops), the radical expansion of the rights of independent after-sales operators reflects the Commission's determination to enhance competition by having more players possessing equal resources to compete in the after-sales market.

The mandatory access requirement seems to have general application, meaning **11.162**. that the failure to comply with the obligation renders the block exemption inapplicable to all possible types of vertical agreements that may fall within the scope of application of the block exemption. Hence, if a supplier refuses to grant access, he will no longer be able to avail himself of the block exemption. This sanction must probably be applied with an element of reason. It should not be that because a supplier has a discussion with an individual operator or even a group of operators regarding certain specific aspects of the access rights, that the application of the block exemption should automatically be endangered. Such an approach would eliminate any fair and balanced discussion on the practical implementation of the access rights.

(1) Object of the access rights

Article 4(2) of Regulation 1400/2002 specifies that access must be given 'to any **11.163**. technical information, diagnostic and other equipment, tools, including any relevant software, or training required for the repair and maintenance of . . . motor vehicles or for the implementation of environmental protection measures'. In essence, three broad categories can be distinguished here:

---

[332] Evaluation Report (n 7 above) paras 294 *et seq.*

Technical information

11.164. The access rights concern all information needed to carry out repair and maintenance on a motor vehicle.[333] It includes the information needed for the unrestricted use of the electronic control and diagnostic systems of a motor vehicle, the programming of these systems in accordance with the supplier's standard procedures, the relevant repair and training instructions, and the information required for the use of diagnostic and servicing tools and equipment.[334] There are certain (albeit limited) exceptions to the technical information that has to be made available. The Commission accepts that it may be legitimate to withhold access to technical information that may enable a third party to bypass or disarm on-board anti-theft devices, to recalibrate electronic devices, or to tamper with devices which, for instance, limit the speed of a vehicle.[335] However, if there are less restrictive means than a flat refusal to provide technical information in order to protect against theft, recalibration or tampering, such means will have to be employed.[336]

Training

11.165. This concept consists of all possible types of technical training that are made available by the supplier to its authorized workshops. It may include on-line training or training where the mechanic has to be present in person.[337]

Tools and equipment

11.166. The tools and equipment that are made available to the authorized workshops must also be made available to the independent operators on the aftermarket. The supplier is also not entitled to prevent a producer of such tools and equipment from selling directly to such independent operators.[338]

(2) Beneficiaries

11.167. Article 4(2) of Regulation 1400/2002 defines the beneficiaries of the access rights as 'undertakings which are directly or indirectly involved in the repair and maintenance of motor vehicles'. It refers in particular to:[339]

— independent repairers (ie workshops that have not applied to be, or may have been refused from becoming a member of the authorized network);

---

[333] Explanatory Brochure 66, question 86. Non-technical information (such as management training) is not covered by Art 4(2) (ibid, footnote 169).
[334] Reg 1400/2002, Art 4(2), second subparagraph. The explicit reference to this type of technical information comes as no surprise as it concerns one of the areas where independent operators deemed Reg 1475/95 not to have worked well (Evaluation Report (n 7 above) 94, para 294).
[335] Reg 1400/2002, recital 26.   [336] ibid and Explanatory Brochure 68, question 94.
[337] Explanatory Brochure 66, question 88.   [338] Reg 1400/2002, Art 4(1)(j).
[339] Whilst in practice this list is probably fairly complete, it is not intended to be exhaustive.

— manufacturers of repair equipment or tools;
— independent distributors of spare parts (who must also have the right to resell such information in order to ensure that a purchaser of spare parts has, at the same location, access to the technical information concerning the use of the spare part);[340]
— publishers of technical information;[341]
— automobile clubs;[342]
— roadside assistance operators;
— operators offering inspection and testing services;
— operators offering training for repairers.

The linking of the object of the access rights to the profile of the beneficiaries raises **11.168**. fairly complex questions. Access must be given to technical information, equipment, tooling, and training 'required for the repair and maintenance of [the motor vehicles of the supplier]'. In most cases, it is obvious that the objectives of the independent operator will be met if he obtains exactly the same type of information as the authorized workshops. However, for some independent operators the position is different. For instance, manufacturers of repair equipment and tools may have needs for both information and tools that go beyond what is made available to the authorized workshops. However, as the access rights are expressly defined in terms of information and tools/equipment required for the repair and maintenance, it would seem difficult to extend the scope of the access rights to information and tools needed to produce tools and equipment.

(3) Party subject to the obligation

Article 4(2) makes it clear that the obligation to grant access to information, **11.169**. training, tools, and equipment is incumbent upon 'the supplier of motor vehicles'. It is obvious that the supplier can delegate this obligation, for instance to a national importer or even a company that is charged specifically with the task of distributing the relevant information.[343]

There is no obligation for the supplier of motor vehicles to allow its authorized **11.170**. distributors or workshops to supply the necessary access to independent

---

[340] Explanatory Brochure 67, question 93.
[341] ibid, question 92 and Evaluation Report (n 7 above) 95, para 295. The redistribution of technical information via publishers raises some delicate questions; for instance, regarding payment. It is unfortunate that the Explanatory Brochure does not provide any guidance in this respect. It is difficult to conceive that a publisher of technical information would be entitled to pay the same price for the information as an independent workshop and then be entitled to market the same information without making any additional payment to the supplier of motor vehicles. Royalty-based formulas that imply a fair payment per copy sold of the technical information should be compatible with Reg 1400/2002, Art 4(2).
[342] Evaluation Report (n 7 above) 95, para 297.
[343] Explanatory Brochure 65, question 85.

operators. Therefore, a supplier is entitled to impose an obligation on its network not to engage in any such types of exchange with the independent operators.

11.171. This allocation of tasks in Article 4(2) is logical. On the one hand, it assists in ensuring a consistent and coherent application of the access rights and, on the other hand, it renders it easier to enforce the obligation (by precisely specifying the party responsible).

(4) Conditions

11.172. The Regulation specifies that access must be given 'in a non-discriminatory, prompt and proportionate way' and that the information 'must be provided in a usable form'.[344] If an item is protected by an intellectual property right or qualifies as know-how, access may not be withheld in a manner that violates Article 82 EC.[345]

11.173. These conditions have quite serious implications on the manner in which the access rights have to be organized:

Non-discrimination

11.174. This condition implies in practice that an independent operator must be treated in the same manner as if he were an authorized workshop. The price charged for a given item may not be higher.[346] The format in which the information and training are provided must (at least) amount to the same as that which is made available to the authorized workshops. For instance, it will not be possible to reserve technical assistance via telephone or Internet to the authorized network and not to make the same accessible to independent operators.[347]

Prompt

11.175. This condition implies that access is given upon request and without undue delay.[348] In practice, access will have to be granted to the independent operators as quickly as information, training, or equipment/tooling is made available to the authorized workshops and it will not be possible to ensure that all of the authorized workshops are informed, trained, or supplied with tools and equipment first, before access is granted to the independent operators.[349] Where resources are limited (ie in the context of the organization of training courses), a 'first come, first served' procedure may have to be implemented.

---

[344] Reg 1400/2002, Art 4(2), third subparagraph.   [345] ibid.
[346] Explanatory Brochure 66, question 89 and Commission Press Release, MEMO/02/174, 17 July 2002.   [347] Explanatory Brochure 66, question 86.
[348] Reg 1400/2002, recital 26.   [349] Explanatory Brochure 67, question 91.

Proportionate

The proportionality standard must be linked to the use that the independent 11.176. operator intends to make of the relevant item and this seems to have a number of implications:

(i) an independent operator cannot be required to buy more than he needs (which may mean that the supplier can be forced to create smaller information packages than those ordinarily made available to the authorized network);[350]

(ii) the price charged for the technical information should not discourage access to it by failing to take into account the extent to which the independent operator uses it;[351] and

(iii) the format in which the information is made available may not require the independent operator to invest in expensive equipment so that, in effect, it is no longer worthwhile for him to seek access to the information.[352]

While authorized workshops will typically be required to purchase all of the information issued by the motor vehicle producer, the proportionality condition injects into the after-sales market a degree of positive discrimination, to the benefit of the independent operators.

G. Specific Conditions

Article 5 of the Regulation lists certain specific conditions. These are formulated 11.177. negatively, ie that obligations infringing upon the specific conditions do not benefit from the block exemption. The legal consequences of such an infringement are, however, limited to that. Contrary to infringements of the general conditions (Article 3) or the hardcore restrictions (Article 4), non-compliance with Article 5 does not have any consequences beyond the specific obligation or restriction concerned.[353]

---

[350] Explanatory Brochure 66, question 90. For instance, if the information provided to the authorized network covers all models, it may be necessary to provide the independent operators with information packages that are limited to individual models. On the other hand, it would be unreasonable to translate the proportionality condition into a right to receive tailor-made packages. Suppliers should have the right to compile blocks of technical information covering all aspects of given repair jobs (eg describing all the steps to be completed in order to conduct a certain engine repair task).

[351] Reg 1400/2002, recital 26. This condition will enter into play only if the price which an independent operator would have to pay is prohibitively high when compared to his needs. The basic principle for the Commission seems to be that of non-discrimination (ie the same price being charged to both the authorized and the independent repairers). Hence, to the extent that suppliers break down the technical information between the different models and/or the different repair jobs, there should be less need to take account of the use made by the independent repairer.

[352] Consider the requirement in Art 4(2) that the information must be provided 'in a usable form'.

[353] Provided that the relevant obligations can be severed from the rest of the agreement (Explanatory Brochure 30). This is, however, a matter of national contract law and not of

11.178. DG COMP states that obligations that do not comply with Article 5 may still be able to benefit from an individual exemption: 'By placing vertical agreements in the motor vehicle sector under a more demanding legal framework [than Regulation 2790/99], the Regulation indicates that obligations contrary to Article 5 may raise serious competition concerns that can only be assessed in an individual examination'.[354] Guidance for such assessment can be found in the Vertical Guidelines.[355]

11.179. The specific conditions included in Article 5 essentially concern various types of non-compete obligations and location clauses. As regards both of these types of restriction, the Regulation represents a revolutionary change in approach. While non-compete obligations were still automatically exempted (without conditions) in Regulation 123/85[356] and could *de facto* be imposed under Regulation 1475/95 (by means of various exempted restrictions that could be placed on the conditions under which competing brands could be handled), such obligations are simply no longer eligible for a block exemption under the current regime. A U-turn on this issue has been achieved. Similarly, location clauses could benefit from a block exemption under Regulations 123/85 and 1475/95 (as part of the possibility to restrict active sales outside the dealer territory),[357] but now receive generally negative treatment in a selective distribution context[358] and are subject to very strict conditions in a non-selective distribution context.[359]

(1) Non-compete obligations

11.180. Article 5(1) in combination with Article 1(1)(b) of the Regulation lists a wide variety of non-compete restrictions. Each of these restrictions will be discussed separately below.

(2) Standard non-compete obligation

11.181. Article 5(1)(a) specifies that the exemption shall not apply to 'any direct or indirect non-compete obligation'. The definition of this concept encompasses the standard non-compete obligation, that is 'any direct or indirect[360] obligation

---

Community competition law. See in this respect the Communication from the Commission: Notice—Guidelines on the application of Article 81(3) of the Treaty [2004] OJ C101/97, para 41 (and references made there to Case 56/65 *Société Technique Minière* [1966] ECR 337, para 9 and Case 319/82 *Kerpen & Kerpen* [1983] ECR 4173, paras 11 and 12).

[354] Explanatory Brochure 34, question 17.   [355] ibid.
[356] Reg 123/85, Art 3(3).   [357] ibid, Art 3(8) and Reg 1475/95, Art 3(8).
[358] For the various scenarios, see paras 11.204–11.211 below.
[359] Location restrictions will have to meet the same criteria as any other restriction on active sales in order to be able to benefit from the block exemption. See definition of 'active sales' (Explanatory Brochure 30, question 12).
[360] The double use of the words 'direct and indirect' in Arts 1(1)(b) and 5(1)(a) is unnecessary.

causing the buyer not to manufacture, purchase, sell or resell goods or services which compete with the contract goods or services'.[361]

Depending on the scope of the vertical agreement, this provision may concern new motor vehicles, repair and maintenance services, and/or spare parts. The scope of the provision is confined to goods or services that compete with the contract goods or services. This means in practice that the relevant goods or services must be part of the same relevant market as the contract goods or services.[362] **11.182.**

Only limited restrictions on the way in which multi-brand dealers sell competing goods or services may be imposed: **11.183.**

Brand-specific areas

The requirement that the supplier's vehicles are sold in brand-specific areas is considered acceptable from the perspective of Article 5(1)(a).[363] DG COMP is however quite severe in its stance as to the manner in which such a separation can be implemented.[364] This requirement must be implemented (and may therefore have to be relaxed) in such a manner that dealers retain a real and exercisable opportunity to sell brands of competing suppliers.[365] **11.184.**

Separate showrooms

Contrary to Regulation 1475/95, it is no longer compatible with the block exemption to require that competing brands are sold in separate showrooms.[366] Such a restriction can however be imposed in respect of different brands from the same manufacturer.[367] **11.185.**

---

[361] Given the increased emergence of car boulevards (with rows of dealerships of competing brands), the imposition of a standard non-compete obligation would not seem necessary in order to stimulate inter-brand competition. In fact, in the *BMW* decision (*Bayerische Motoren Werke AG* [1975] OJ L29/1, 7), the possibility for manufacturers to impose a non-compete obligation was justified by reference to the increased inter-brand competition that was likely to be expected from such a restriction. The main objective underlying Art 5(1)(a) is therefore most probably the creation of more dealer independence; the expectation is that dealers that handle several competing brands will be less inclined to avoid intra-brand competition or to comply with restrictions imposed by the supplier on intra-brand competition. L Idot (n 26 above); Arhel (n 26 above) 15; and Schlenger and Hinrichs (n 158 above) 533. As to the experience in the US with multi-branding, see Evaluation Report (n 7 above) para 105.

[362] However, as a result of Art 5(1)(b) and (c) the scope of the non-compete obligation is extended beyond the relevant market: see para 11.192–11.196 below.

[363] Reg 1400/2002, recital 27 and Art 1(1)(b).

[364] Explanatory Brochure 52, question 51.

[365] ibid and Frequently Asked Questions (n 17 above) 3, question 5.

[366] Explanatory Brochure 32, question 14.

[367] Frequently Asked Questions (n 17 above) 4, question 6. For instance, as Volkswagen and Audi are part of the same group, it is compatible with the block exemption if the Volkswagen group requires from its network that the two brands are sold in separate showrooms.

Brand-specific personnel

11.186. The need to have brand-specific personnel for different brands will be deemed as qualifying as a non-compete obligation, unless the distributor decides to have such brand-specific personnel and the supplier pays the additional costs involved.[368] Hence, a decision to work with brand-specific personnel will have to come from the dealer and cannot be imposed by the supplier. As to the reimbursement of the costs, no advantages in excess of the actual costs incurred in having such extra personnel may be paid.[369]

Display of full range

11.187. It is permissible to impose an obligation to display the full range of models.[370] However, such an obligation will have to be relaxed if it has a negative impact on the dealer's ability to represent or display competing brands.[371]

Separate entrances

11.188. The need to have separate entrances for the different brands is considered incompatible with the block exemption.[372]

Separate reception desks

11.189. The need to have separate reception desks is not *per se* a problem under the block exemption, but this requirement may have to be relaxed or dispensed with entirely if there is a shortage of space.[373]

Corporate identity

11.190. The imposition of standard CI requirements is not *per se* unlawful, but the conditions may have to be relaxed to the extent that they constitute a barrier to the dealer taking on additional brands.[374]

11.191. The treatment of non-compete obligations under the block exemption will not be influenced by the fact that the supplier extends trade loans to the dealer or provides the dealer with premises or land. Unlike the position under Regulation

---

[368] Reg 1400/2002, Art 1(1)(b). This provision is clearly inspired by the policy objective of increasing dealer independence and would seem to have little to do with enhancing inter-brand competition. Natural rivalry between competing sales teams seems to be a better guarantee for inter-brand competition than all brands being sold by the same team. See also Creutzig (n 210 above) 2142.   [369] Explanatory Brochure 32, question 14.
[370] Reg 1400/2002, recital 27 and Explanatory Brochure 32, question 14.
[371] Frequently Asked Questions (n 17 above) 3, question 5.
[372] Explanatory Brochure 52, question 52.
[373] Frequently Asked Questions (n 17 above) 3, question 5.
[374] Explanatory Brochure 52, question 52 and Frequently Asked Questions (n 17 above) 3, question 5.

2790/99,[375] such efforts or investments on the part of the supplier are irrelevant to the assessment of non-compete obligations under the block exemption.

(3) *Extended non-compete obligations*

Article 5(1)(a) is limited to competing products or services; that is to say **11.192.** products or services that are part of the same relevant market. As the definition of the relevant market in the present context is relatively narrow,[376] the scope of the prohibition on standard non-compete obligations is also limited. This is clearly not what the Commission had in mind and therefore it has expanded the scope of the prohibition to also include restrictions on the handling of non-competing products or services.

Article 5(1)(b) prohibits 'any direct or indirect[377] obligation limiting the ability **11.193.** of an authorised repairer to provide repair and maintenance services for vehicles from competing suppliers'. The addition of this provision to Article 5 is a direct consequence of the relevant market for after-sales services being deemed brand-specific. In order to allow authorized repairers to repair vehicles of different brands, the specific condition regarding non-compete obligations had to be complemented.[378] It is to be noted that the vehicles to which Article 5(1)(b) applies are those 'from competing suppliers'. This does not mean that the vehicles must be competing; it means that the suppliers must be competing. A practical example may demonstrate the difference. If model A1 of supplier X and model B of supplier Y are competing products, the authorized workshop appointed by Y must be able to render after-sales services to model A1. If supplier X also has a model A2 which is not in competition with any model of supplier Y, the workshop must also be allowed to service model A2. While A2 and B are not competing models, X and Y are competing suppliers.

Article 5(1)(c) deprives the block exemption of 'any direct or indirect obligation **11.194.** causing the members of a distribution system not to sell motor vehicles or spare parts of particular competing suppliers or not to provide repair and maintenance services for motor vehicles of particular competing suppliers'. Whilst it is suggested that this provision is tailored towards selective distribution systems,[379] it does not however, contain any limitation to that effect. It must therefore be assumed that Article 5(1)(c) applies to all distribution formulas covered by the block exemption.

---

[375] Paras 6.20–6.23 above.   [376] Paras 11.53 *et seq* above.
[377] For examples of indirect restrictions in the areas of parts stocking and the provision of information to the supplier, Explanatory Brochure 63, question 78 and Frequently Asked Questions (n 17 above) 10, question 19.   [378] Explanatory Brochure 31.
[379] Reg 1400/2002, recital 29.

11.195 With regard to the difference between competing products and competing suppliers, reference can be made to the discussion of Article 5(1)(b). Article 5(1)(c) adds, however, that 'particular competing suppliers' must be concerned. This suggests that it is possible for a supplier to require that its network does not distribute any non-competing motor vehicles or parts, as long as the supplier does not confine this requirement to particular (ie specified) competing suppliers. For instance, a French car producer may require its network to confine its business to competing models (ie models competing with the contract goods), but it may not stipulate that its network should refrain from taking on board non-competing models from any of the other French producers.

11.196 Finally, Article 5(1)(c) refers to motor vehicles and not to new motor vehicles. This suggests that the principle reflected in Article 5(1)(c) is not confined to new motor vehicles, but may also encompass second-hand cars.

(4) Quasi non-compete obligations

11.197. The definition of a non-compete obligation is not confined to standard non-competition restrictions, but extends also to 'any direct or indirect obligation on the buyer to purchase from the supplier or from another undertaking designated by the supplier more than 30% of the buyer's total purchases of the contract goods, corresponding goods or services and their substitutes on the relevant market, calculated on the basis of the value of its purchases in the preceding calendar year' (Article 1(1)b).

11.198. This figure of 30% is substantially lower than the corresponding figure of 80% in Regulation 2790/99.[380] The choice of the 30% level is inspired by the objective of ensuring that network members should be able to buy and sell goods from at least three different suppliers.[381] This does not, however, mean that network members are obliged to sell two or more brands. If they decide (without being restricted by the supplier) to confine their business to a single brand, this is perfectly compatible with the Regulation. However, if they wish to extend their business to other brands, they must be able to do so and a supplier cannot prevent such a move by imposing purchase obligations extending beyond the 30% level.

11.199. In the context of a selective distribution network, a supplier will not be entitled to oblige its network members to purchase all or part of its requirements from that supplier. As cross-supplies within the selective network cannot be restricted,[382] a dealer must be entirely free to source from other network members (even for the total of the 30% level imposed by the supplier).[383]

---

[380] Paras 6.08–6.12 above.   [381] Explanatory Brochure 32, question 13.
[382] Reg 1400/2002, Art 4(1)(c).
[383] Explanatory Brochure 31 and Frequently Asked Questions (n 17 above) 4, question 7.

As to the calculation of the 30% level, the following must be taken into account: **11.200**.

— the calculation is based on the value (and hence not on the volume) of the purchases;
— the purchases to be taken into account are those of the buyer, including the purchases of the other members of the group to which the buyer belongs;[384]
— the relevant purchases include the contract goods, the corresponding goods and all of their substitutes;[385]
— the purchases of the preceding calendar year (not the financial year) must be taken into account.

One of the areas where the quasi non-compete obligation has had an immediate **11.201**. impact is on the bonus schemes applied in the sector. These schemes were often based on the attainment of certain purchase levels. The relevant volumes were fixed on an annual basis and therefore in most cases exceeded the 30% limit of Article 5(1)(a) *juncto* Article 1(1)(b) of the Regulation.[386] The reduction of the annual volumes in the bonus schemes to a level below 30% would not make much commercial sense (certainly not for the leading brand of a given dealer). One possible way of keeping a (meaningful) bonus scheme in place would be to reduce the reference periods (eg to a quarterly basis). However, such a scheme would only be compatible with the Regulation if the bonus calculation makes a fresh start at the end of any such reference period.

(5) Post-term non-compete obligation

Article 5(1)(d) prohibits the application of the block exemption to 'any direct or **11.202**. indirect obligation causing the distributor or authorised repairer, after termination of the agreement, not to manufacture, purchase, sell or resell motor vehicles or not to provide repair or maintenance services.' So, in relation to a terminated network member, it will not be possible to impose any type of post-term non-compete obligation. This principle covers standard non-competition restrictions, as well as extended or quasi-non-compete obligations.

(6) Leasing services

The block exemption is denied to 'any direct or indirect obligation causing the **11.203**. retailer not to sell leasing services relating to contract goods or corresponding goods'. The dealer must be able to engage in leasing services himself, through a leasing company connected with the dealer or as an agent of a leasing company of his choice.[387]

---

[384] Reg 1400/2002, Art 1(2).
[385] Hence, the calculation must be conducted within a given relevant market.
[386] Explanatory Brochure 31. [387] Explanatory Brochure 50.

(7) Location clauses

11.204. The concept of location clauses covers a variety of restrictions, including the obligation not to change premises without the supplier's prior consent or the obligation to seek the supplier's consent for the opening of additional outlets. Location clauses are subject to a somewhat complex regime in the context of the Regulation. The following distinctions can be made:

Passenger cars and light commercial vehicles[388]

11.205. It is compatible with the block exemption to require a dealer not to alter his primary location (ie the location which he occupies at the time the dealer agreement is entered into or any subsequent location to which this outlet has moved to afterwards with the supplier's consent).[389] A member of a selective distribution system must however be free to open *additional* sales or delivery outlets.[390] The opening of such outlets may not be subjected to the requirement of prior consent or approval of the supplier.[391]

11.206. Sales outlets are outlets that include a showroom and all necessary infrastructures required to sell new motor vehicles.[392] Sales outlets will normally have to meet all of the qualitative criteria that are imposed on dealerships in the area where the sales outlet is located.[393] Delivery outlets are places where vehicles sold elsewhere are handed over to the end-customer and may include the necessary office space, a storage facility, or an area to prepare the cars for delivery.[394] A supplier may not require that a delivery outlet meets all the qualitative criteria of a dealership or sales outlet, but he may request that the delivery outlet meets the criteria imposed on other delivery outlets in the area concerned.[395]

11.207. The opening of additional outlets will not necessitate the conclusion of a new agreement.[396] However, if the qualitative requirements applicable in the area where the new outlets are located differ from those that govern the main outlet, it may be wise for the parties to supplement the dealer agreement so that there can be no misunderstanding as to the standards which are to be met. It will be the responsibility of the supplier (ie the party with which the dealer has entered into a dealer agreement) to ensure that the necessary cars are supplied to the new outlets. The manner in which this is organized is immaterial as long as the new outlets do not encounter problems in obtaining the cars needed.

---

[388] For a definition of a light commercial vehicle, Reg 1400/2002, Art 1(1)(p).
[389] Explanatory Brochure 54, question 55.
[390] Reg 1400/2002, Arts 4(1)(d) and 5(2)(b).
[391] The validity of such a requirement in an exclusive distribution system will be dependent upon whether it is possible to impose a restriction on active sales on the dealer concerned. It would seem to be possible, however, in any non-selective system to prevent a dealer changing his primary location without the supplier's consent. Also Explanatory Brochure 54, question 55.
[392] Explanatory Brochure 53, question 53.   [393] Explanatory Brochure 54, question 56.
[394] Explanatory Brochure 53, question 53.   [395] Explanatory Brochure 54, question 54.
[396] ibid, question 56.

Trucks and buses[397]

The Regulation allows suppliers of trucks and buses to impose location **11.208.**
restrictions on their dealers.[398] The dealers may be required not to change any of
their sales locations, nor to open additional sales or delivery outlets without the
prior consent of the supplier.[399]

Repair and maintenance

The most stringent regime as regards location restrictions applies to authorized **11.209.**
workshops. Such workshops may not be subject 'to any direct or indirect
obligation as to [their] place of establishment . . . where selective distribution is
applied'.[400] This means in practice that in the context of a selective distribution
system, authorized workshops must be free to change their initial or primary
location and to open additional outlets wherever they deem appropriate.[401] No
prior consent of the supplier with regard to any such change or initiative may be
imposed. This regime applies not only to the repair and maintenance of passenger cars and light commercial vehicles, but also to trucks and buses.

This is, in all likelihood, one of the most remarkable provisions of the Reg- **11.210.**
ulation. The Commission acknowledges that consumers prefer a dense after-
sales network and it is familiar with the problems encountered by producers in
finding suitable workshops in remote (often rural) locations.[402] From that
perspective, the policy choice not to extend the treatment of Article 5(2)(b) to
after-sales services, but to allow workshops even to change their primary location is surprising. It is striking that in none of the Commission commentaries
on the Regulation, is this difference in treatment properly justified. We believe
that the regime of Article 5(2)(b) would have been the more balanced one,
guaranteeing on the one hand increased intra-brand competition and on the
other hand that no network coverage problems can occur in remote areas.

Spare parts

To the extent that authorized repairers also distribute spare parts, Article 5(3) is **11.211.**
applicable. However, Article 5 would not seem to address the question of
distributors of spare parts that do not engage in after-sales services. As DG
COMP takes the view that producers may have to apply a qualitative selective

---

[397] For the reasons underlying the difference in treatment compared to passenger cars and
light commercial vehicles: Explanatory Brochure 53.
[398] Commercial vehicles that exist in versions both below and above 3.5 tons, will not qualify
for treatment as trucks and buses with regard to location clauses. Explanatory Brochure 33,
question 16. [399] Reg 1400/2002, Art 4(1)(e) and Explanatory Brochure 33, question 16.
[400] Reg 1400/2002, Art 5(3). [401] Explanatory Brochure 62, question 75.
[402] Monti (n 13 above) and M Malaurie-Vignal, 'Présentation et commentaire du Règlement
N° 1400/2002 du 31 juillet 2002' (2002) 239 Petites Affiches 3, 5.

distribution system in respect of parts distribution, such distributors are likely to emerge and their number is likely to increase. At the retail level, location clauses applied to such distributors are governed by Article 4(1)(d) of the Regulation and are hence blacklisted. At the wholesale level the same outcome may apply via Article 4(1)(b) of the Regulation, whereby a location clause may qualify as a restriction of the territory into which the distributor may sell the contract goods.

H. Non-Application and Withdrawal

11.212. Regulation 1400/2002 includes the classic procedural provisions. Article 6(1) describes the powers of the Commission to withdraw the benefit of the block exemption in certain specific circumstances:[403]

> The Commission may withdraw the benefit of this Regulation, pursuant to Article 7(1) of Regulation No 19/65/EEC, where it finds in any particular case that vertical agreements to which this Regulation applies nevertheless have effects which are incompatible with the conditions laid down in Article 81(3) of the Treaty, and in particular:
>
> (a) where access to the relevant market or competition therein is significantly restricted by the cumulative effect of parallel networks of similar vertical restraints implemented by competing suppliers or buyers, or
> (b) where competition is restricted on a market where one supplier is not exposed to effective competition from other suppliers, or
> (c) where prices or conditions of supply for contract goods or for corresponding goods differ substantially between geographic markets, or
> (d) where discriminatory prices or sales conditions are applied within a geographic market.[404]

11.213. Article 6(2) offers a similar possibility of withdrawal to the national competition authorities in certain individual cases.

11.214. Article 7 creates an option for the Commission to disapply the Regulation in accordance with Article 1*bis* of Regulation 19/65, to vertical agreements containing specific restraints relating to a market where there are parallel networks of similar vertical restraints.[405]

---

[403] Explanatory Brochure 35, question 18.
[404] Reg 19/65, Art 7 has been repealed by the regulation incorporating decentralization (Council Regulation (EC) No 1/2003 of 16 December 2002 on the implementation of the rules on competition laid down in Articles 81 and 82 of the Treaty [2003] OJ L1/1, Art 40), and has been replaced with a more or less identical Art 29.
[405] Explanatory Brochure 35, question 19.

APPENDICES

APPENDIX 1

Commission Regulation (EC) No 2790/1999 of 22 December 1999 on the application of Article 81(3) of the Treaty to categories of vertical agreements and concerted practices

([1999] OJ L336/21)

THE COMMISSION OF THE EUROPEAN COMMUNITIES,

Having regard to the Treaty establishing the European Community,

Having regard to Council Regulation No 19/65/EEC of 2 March 1965 on the application of Article 85(3) of the Treaty to certain categories of agreements and concerted practices,[1] as last amended by Regulation (EC) No 1215/1999,[2] and in particular Article 1 thereof,

Having published a draft of this Regulation,[3]

Having consulted the Advisory Committee on Restrictive Practices and Dominant Positions,

Whereas:

(1) Regulation No 19/65/EEC empowers the Commission to apply Article 81(3) of the Treaty (formerly Article 85(3)) by regulation to certain categories of vertical agreements and corresponding concerted practices falling within Article 81(1).

(2) Experience acquired to date makes it possible to define a category of vertical agreements which can be regarded as normally satisfying the conditions laid down in Article 81(3).

(3) This category includes vertical agreements for the purchase or sale of goods or services where these agreements are concluded between non-competing undertakings, between certain competitors or by certain associations of retailers of goods; it also includes vertical agreements containing ancillary provisions on the assignment or use of intellectual property rights; for the purposes of this Regulation, the term 'vertical agreements' includes the corresponding concerted practices.

(4) For the application of Article 81(3) by regulation, it is not necessary to define those vertical agreements which are capable of falling within Article 81(1); in the individual assessment of agreements under Article 81(1), account has to be taken of several factors, and in particular the market structure on the supply and purchase side.

(5) The benefit of the block exemption should be limited to vertical agreements for which it can be assumed with sufficient certainty that they satisfy the conditions of Article 81(3).

(6) Vertical agreements of the category defined in this Regulation can improve economic efficiency within a chain of production or distribution by facilitating better coordination between the participating undertakings; in particular, they can lead to a reduction in the transaction and distribution costs of the parties and to an optimisation of their sales and investment levels.

---

[1] OJ 36, 6.3.1965, p. 533/65.   [2] OJ L 148, 15.6.1999, p. 1.
[3] OJ C 270, 24.9.1999, p. 7.

(7) The likelihood that such efficiency-enhancing effects will outweigh any anti-competitive effects due to restrictions contained in vertical agreements depends on the degree of market power of the undertakings concerned and, therefore, on the extent to which those undertakings face competition from other suppliers of goods or services regarded by the buyer as interchangeable or substitutable for one another, by reason of the products' characteristics, their prices and their intended use.

(8) It can be presumed that, where the share of the relevant market accounted for by the supplier does not exceed 30%, vertical agreements which do not contain certain types of severely anti-competitive restraints generally lead to an improvement in production or distribution and allow consumers a fair share of the resulting benefits; in the case of vertical agreements containing exclusive supply obligations, it is the market share of the buyer which is relevant in determining the overall effects of such vertical agreements on the market.

(9) Above the market share threshold of 30%, there can be no presumption that vertical agreements falling within the scope of Article 81(1) will usually give rise to objective advantages of such a character and size as to compensate for the disadvantages which they create for competition.

(10) This Regulation should not exempt vertical agreements containing restrictions which are not indispensable to the attainment of the positive effects mentioned above; in particular, vertical agreements containing certain types of severely anti-competitive restraints such as minimum and fixed resale-prices, as well as certain types of territorial protection, should be excluded from the benefit of the block exemption established by this Regulation irrespective of the market share of the undertakings concerned.

(11) In order to ensure access to or to prevent collusion on the relevant market, certain conditions are to be attached to the block exemption; to this end, the exemption of non-compete obligations should be limited to obligations which do not exceed a definite duration; for the same reasons, any direct or indirect obligation causing the members of a selective distribution system not to sell the brands of particular competing suppliers should be excluded from the benefit of this Regulation.

(12) The market-share limitation, the non-exemption of certain vertical agreements and the conditions provided for in this Regulation normally ensure that the agreements to which the block exemption applies do not enable the participating undertakings to eliminate competition in respect of a substantial part of the products in question.

(13) In particular cases in which the agreements falling under this Regulation nevertheless have effects incompatible with Article 81(3), the Commission may withdraw the benefit of the block exemption; this may occur in particular where the buyer has significant market power in the relevant market in which it resells the goods or provides the services or where parallel networks of vertical agreements have similar effects which significantly restrict access to a relevant market or competition therein; such cumulative effects may for example arise in the case of selective distribution or non-compete obligations.

(14) Regulation No 19/65/EEC empowers the competent authorities of Member States to withdraw the benefit of the block exemption in respect of vertical agreements having effects incompatible with the conditions laid down in Article 81(3), where such effects are felt in their respective territory, or in a part thereof, and where such territory has the characteristics of a distinct geographic market; Member States should ensure that the exercise of this power of withdrawal does not prejudice the uniform application throughout the common market of the Community competition rules or the full effect of the measures adopted in implementation of those rules.

(15) In order to strengthen supervision of parallel networks of vertical agreements which have similar restrictive effects and which cover more than 50% of a given market, the Commission may declare this Regulation inapplicable to vertical agreements containing specific restraints relating to the market concerned, thereby restoring the full application of Article 81 to such agreements.

(16) This Regulation is without prejudice to the application of Article 82.

(17) In accordance with the principle of the primacy of Community law, no measure taken pursuant to national laws on competition should prejudice the uniform application throughout the common market of the Community competition rules or the full effect of any measures adopted in implementation of those rules, including this Regulation,

HAS ADOPTED THIS REGULATION:

Article 1

For the purposes of this Regulation:

(a) 'competing undertakings' means actual or potential suppliers in the same product market; the product market includes goods or services which are regarded by the buyer as inter-changeable with or substitutable for the contract goods or services, by reason of the products' characteristics, their prices and their intended use;

(b) 'non-compete obligation' means any direct or indirect obligation causing the buyer not to manufacture, purchase, sell or resell goods or services which compete with the contract goods or services, or any direct or indirect obligation on the buyer to purchase from the supplier or from another undertaking designated by the supplier more than 80% of the buyer's total purchases of the contract goods or services and their substitutes on the relevant market, calculated on the basis of the value of its purchases in the preceding calendar year;

(c) 'exclusive supply obligation' means any direct or indirect obligation causing the supplier to sell the goods or services specified in the agreement only to one buyer inside the Community for the purposes of a specific use or for resale;

(d) 'selective distribution system' means a distribution system where the supplier undertakes to sell the contract goods or services, either directly or indirectly, only to distributors selected on the basis of specified criteria and where these distributors undertake not to sell such goods or services to unauthorised distributors;

(e) 'intellectual property rights' includes industrial property rights, copyright and neighbouring rights;

(f) 'know-how' means a package of non patented practical information, resulting from experience and testing by the supplier, which is secret, substantial and identified: in this context, 'secret' means that the know how, as a body or in the precise configuration and assembly of its components, is not generally known or easily accessible; 'substantial' means that the know-how includes information which is indispensable to the buyer for the use, sale or resale of the contract goods or services; 'identified' means that the know-how must be described in a sufficiently comprehensive manner so as to make it possible to verify that it fulfils the criteria of secrecy and substantiality;

(g) 'buyer' includes an undertaking which, under an agreement falling within Article 81(1) of the Treaty, sells goods or services on behalf of another undertaking.

Article 2

(1) Pursuant to Article 81(3) of the Treaty and subject to the provisions of this Regulation, it is hereby declared that Article 81(1) shall not apply to agreements or concerted practices entered into between two or more undertakings each of which operates, for the purposes of the agreement, at a different level of the production or distribution chain, and relating to the conditions under which the parties may purchase, sell or resell certain goods or services ('vertical agreements'). This exemption shall apply to the extent that such agreements contain restrictions of competition falling within the scope of Article 81(1) ('vertical restraints').

(2) The exemption provided for in paragraph 1 shall apply to vertical agreements entered into between an association of undertakings and its members, or between such an association and

its suppliers, only if all its members are retailers of goods and if no individual member of the association, together with its connected undertakings, has a total annual turnover exceeding € 50 million; vertical agreements entered into by such associations shall be covered by this Regulation without prejudice to the application of Article 81 to horizontal agreements concluded between the members of the association or decisions adopted by the association.

(3) The exemption provided for in paragraph 1 shall apply to vertical agreements containing provisions which relate to the assignment to the buyer or use by the buyer of intellectual property rights, provided that those provisions do not constitute the primary object of such agreements and are directly related to the use, sale or resale of goods or services by the buyer or its customers. The exemption applies on condition that, in relation to the contract goods or services, those provisions do not contain restrictions of competition having the same object or effect as vertical restraints which are not exempted under this Regulation.

(4) The exemption provided for in paragraph 1 shall not apply to vertical agreements entered into between competing undertakings; however, it shall apply where competing undertakings enter into a non-reciprocal vertical agreement and:

(a) the buyer has a total annual turnover not exceeding € 100 million, or
(b) the supplier is a manufacturer and a distributor of goods, while the buyer is a distributor not manufacturing goods competing with the contract goods, or
(c) the supplier is a provider of services at several levels of trade, while the buyer does not provide competing services at the level of trade where it purchases the contract services.

(5) This Regulation shall not apply to vertical agreements the subject matter of which falls within the scope of any other block exemption regulation.

Article 3

(1) Subject to paragraph 2 of this Article, the exemption provided for in Article 2 shall apply on condition that the market share held by the supplier does not exceed 30% of the relevant market on which it sells the contract goods or services.

(2) In the case of vertical agreements containing exclusive supply obligations, the exemption provided for in Article 2 shall apply on condition that the market share held by the buyer does not exceed 30% of the relevant market on which it purchases the contract goods or services.

Article 4

The exemption provided for in Article 2 shall not apply to vertical agreements which, directly or indirectly, in isolation or in combination with other factors under the control of the parties, have as their object:

(a) the restriction of the buyer's ability to determine its sale price, without prejudice to the possibility of the supplier's imposing a maximum sale price or recommending a sale price, provided that they do not amount to a fixed or minimum sale price as a result of pressure from, or incentives offered by, any of the parties;
(b) the restriction of the territory into which, or of the customers to whom, the buyer may sell the contract goods or services, except:
   — the restriction of active sales into the exclusive territory or to an exclusive customer group reserved to the supplier or allocated by the supplier to another buyer, where such a restriction does not limit sales by the customers of the buyer,
   — the restriction of sales to end users by a buyer operating at the wholesale level of trade,
   — the restriction of sales to unauthorised distributors by the members of a selective distribution system, and

— the restriction of the buyer's ability to sell components, supplied for the purposes of incorporation, to customers who would use them to manufacture the same type of goods as those produced by the supplier;

(c) the restriction of active or passive sales to end-users by members of a selective distribution system operating at the retail level of trade, without prejudice to the possibility of prohibiting a member of the system from operating out of an unauthorised place of establishment;

(d) the restriction of cross-supplies between distributors within a selective distribution system, including between distributors operating at different level of trade;

(e) the restriction agreed between a supplier of components and a buyer who incorporates those components, which limits the supplier to selling the components as spare parts to end-users or to repairers or other service providers not entrusted by the buyer with the repair or servicing of its goods.

Article 5

The exemption provided for in Article 2 shall not apply to any of the following obligations contained in vertical agreements:

(a) any direct or indirect non-compete obligation, the duration of which is indefinite or exceeds five years. A non-compete obligation which is tacitly renewable beyond a period of five years is to be deemed to have been concluded for an indefinite duration. However, the time limitation of five years shall not apply where the contract goods or services are sold by the buyer from premises and land owned by the supplier or leased by the supplier from third parties not connected with the buyer, provided that the duration of the non-compete obligation does not exceed the period of occupancy of the premises and land by the buyer;

(b) any direct or indirect obligation causing the buyer, after termination of the agreement, not to manufacture, purchase, sell or resell goods or services, unless such obligation:
   — relates to goods or services which compete with the contract goods or services, and
   — is limited to the premises and land from which the buyer has operated during the contract period, and
   — is indispensable to protect know-how transferred by the supplier to the buyer, and provided that the duration of such non-compete obligation is limited to a period of one year after termination of the agreement; this obligation is without prejudice to the possibility of imposing a restriction which is unlimited in time on the use and disclosure of know-how which has not entered the public domain;

(c) any direct or indirect obligation causing the members of a selective distribution system not to sell the brands of particular competing suppliers.

Article 6

The Commission may withdraw the benefit of this Regulation, pursuant to Article 7(1) of Regulation No 19/65/EEC, where it finds in any particular case that vertical agreements to which this Regulation applies nevertheless have effects which are incompatible with the conditions laid down in Article 81(3) of the Treaty, and in particular where access to the relevant market or competition therein is significantly restricted by the cumulative effect of parallel networks of similar vertical restraints implemented by competing suppliers or buyers.

Article 7

Where in any particular case vertical agreements to which the exemption provided for in Article 2 applies have effects incompatible with the conditions laid down in Article 81(3) of the Treaty in the territory of a Member State, or in a part thereof, which has all the characteristics of a distinct geographic market, the competent authority of that Member State may withdraw the benefit of application of this Regulation in respect of that territory, under the same conditions as provided in Article 6.

Article 8

(1) Pursuant to Article 1a of Regulation No 19/65/EEC, the Commission may by regulation declare that, where parallel networks of similar vertical restraints cover more than 50% of a relevant market, this Regulation shall not apply to vertical agreements containing specific restraints relating to that market.

(2) A regulation pursuant to paragraph 1 shall not become applicable earlier than six months following its adoption.

Article 9

(1) The market share of 30% provided for in Article 3(1) shall be calculated on the basis of the market sales value of the contract goods or services and other goods or services sold by the supplier, which are regarded as interchangeable or substitutable by the buyer, by reason of the products' characteristics, their prices and their intended use; if market sales value data are not available, estimates based on other reliable market information, including market sales volumes, may be used to establish the market share of the undertaking concerned. For the purposes of Article 3(2), it is either the market purchase value or estimates thereof which shall be used to calculate the market share.

(2) For the purposes of applying the market share threshold provided for in Article 3 the following rules shall apply:

    (a) the market share shall be calculated on the basis of data relating to the preceding calendar year;

    (b) the market share shall include any goods or services supplied to integrated distributors for the purposes of sale;

    (c) if the market share is initially not more than 30% but subsequently rises above that level without exceeding 35%, the exemption provided for in Article 2 shall continue to apply for a period of two consecutive calendar years following the year in which the 30% market share threshold was first exceeded;

    (d) if the market share is initially not more than 30% but subsequently rises above 35%, the exemption provided for in Article 2 shall continue to apply for one calendar year following the year in which the level of 35% was first exceeded;

    (e) the benefit of points (c) and (d) may not be combined so as to exceed a period of two calendar years.

Article 10

(1) For the purpose of calculating total annual turnover within the meaning of Article 2(2) and (4), the turnover achieved during the previous financial year by the relevant party to the vertical agreement and the turnover achieved by its connected undertakings in respect of all goods and services, excluding all taxes and other duties, shall be added together.

For this purpose, no account shall be taken of dealings between the party to the vertical agreement and its connected undertakings or between its connected undertakings.

(2) The exemption provided for in Article 2 shall remain applicable where, for any period of two consecutive financial years, the total annual turnover threshold is exceeded by no more than 10%.

Article 11

(1) For the purposes of this Regulation, the terms 'undertaking', 'supplier' and 'buyer' shall include their respective connected undertakings.

(2) 'Connected undertakings' are:

   (a) undertakings in which a party to the agreement, directly or indirectly:
      — has the power to exercise more than half the voting rights, or
      — has the power to appoint more than half the members of the supervisory board, board of management or bodies legally representing the under taking, or
      — has the right to manage the undertaking's affairs;
   (b) undertakings which directly or indirectly have, over a party to the agreement, the rights or powers listed in (a);
   (c) undertakings in which an undertaking referred to in (b) has, directly or indirectly, the rights or powers listed in (a);
   (d) undertakings in which a party to the agreement together with one or more of the undertakings referred to in (a), (b) or (c), or in which two or more of the latter under-takings, jointly have the rights or powers listed in (a);
   (e) undertakings in which the rights or the powers listed in (a) are jointly held by:
      — parties to the agreement or their respective connected undertakings referred to in (a) to (d), or
      — one or more of the parties to the agreement or one or more of their connected undertakings referred to in (a) to (d) and one or more third parties.

(3) For the purposes of Article 3, the market share held by the undertakings referred to in paragraph 2(e) of this Article shall be apportioned equally to each undertaking having the rights or the powers listed in paragraph 2(a).

Article 12

(1) The exemptions provided for in Commission Regulations (EEC) No 1983/83,[4] (EEC) No 1984/83[5] and (EEC) No 4087/88[6] shall continue to apply until 31 May 2000.

(2) The prohibition laid down in Article 81(1) of the EC Treaty shall not apply during the period from 1 June 2000 to 31 December 2001 in respect of agreements already in force on 31 May 2000 which do not satisfy the conditions for exemption provided for in this Regulation but which satisfy the conditions for exemption provided for in Regulations (EEC) No 1983/83, (EEC) No 1984/83 or (EEC) No 4087/88.

Article 13

This Regulation shall enter into force on 1 January 2000. It shall apply from 1 June 2000, except for Article 12(1) which shall apply from 1 January 2000.

This Regulation shall expire on 31 May 2010.

This Regulation shall be binding in its entirety and directly applicable in all Member States.

---

[4] OJ L 173, 30.6.1983, p. 1.   [5] OJ L 173, 30.6.1983, p. 5.
[6] OJ L 359, 28.12.1988, p. 46.

APPENDIX 2

Commission Notice—Guidelines on Vertical Restraints

(2000/C 29101)

I. INTRODUCTION

1. Purpose of the Guidelines

(1) These Guidelines set out the principles for the assessment of vertical agreements under Article 81 of the EC Treaty. What are considered vertical agreements is defined in Article 2(1) of Commission Regulation (EC) No 2790/1999 of 22 December 1999 on the application of Article 81(3) of the Treaty to categories of vertical agreements and concerted practices[1] (Block Exemption Regulation) (see paragraphs 23 to 45). These Guidelines are without prejudice to the possible parallel application of Article 82 of the Treaty to vertical agreements. The Guidelines are structured in the following way:

— Section II (paragraphs 8 to 20) describes vertical agreements which generally fall outside Article 81(1);

— Section III (paragraphs 21 to 70) comments on the application of the Block Exemption Regulation;

— Section IV (paragraphs 71 to 87) describes the principles concerning the withdrawal of the block exemption and the disapplication of the Block Exemption Regulation;

— Section V (paragraphs 88 to 99) addresses market definition and market share calculation issues;

— Section VI (paragraphs 100 to 229) describes the general framework of analysis and the enforcement policy of the Commission in individual cases concerning vertical agreements.

(2) Throughout these Guidelines the analysis applies to both goods and services, although certain vertical restraints are mainly used in the distribution of goods. Similarly, vertical agreements can be concluded for intermediate and final goods and services. Unless otherwise stated, the analysis and arguments in the text apply to all types of goods and services and to all levels of trade. The term 'products' includes both goods and services. The terms 'supplier' and 'buyer' are used for all levels of trade.

(3) By issuing these Guidelines the Commission aims to help companies to make their own assessment of vertical agreements under the EC competition rules. The standards set forth in these Guidelines must be applied in circumstances specific to each case. This rules out a mechanical application. Each case must be evaluated in the light of its own facts. The Commission will apply the Guidelines reasonably and flexibly.

(4) These Guidelines are without prejudice to the interpretation that may be given by the Court of First Instance and the Court of Justice of the European Communities in relation to the application of Article 81 to vertical agreements.

2. Applicability of Article 81 to vertical agreements

(5) Article 81 of the EC Treaty applies to vertical agreements that may affect trade between Member States and that prevent, restrict or distort competition (hereinafter referred to as 'vertical

---

[1] OJ L 336, 29.12.1999, p. 21.

restraints').[2] For vertical restraints, Article 81 provides an appropriate legal framework for assessment, recognising the distinction between anti-competitive and pro-competitive effects: Article 81(1) prohibits those agreements which appreciably restrict or distort competition, while Article 81(3) allows for exemption of those agreements which confer sufficient benefits to out-weigh the anti-competitive effects.

(6) For most vertical restraints, competition concerns can only arise if there is insufficient inter-brand competition, i.e. if there is some degree of market power at the level of the supplier or the buyer or at both levels. If there is insufficient inter-brand competition, the protection of inter- and intra-brand competition becomes important.

(7) The protection of competition is the primary objective of EC competition policy, as this enhances consumer welfare and creates an efficient allocation of resources. In applying the EC competition rules, the Commission will adopt an economic approach which is based on the effects on the market; vertical agreements have to be analysed in their legal and economic context. However, in the case of restrictions by object as listed in Article 4 of the Block Exemption Regulation, the Commission is not required to assess the actual effects on the market. Market integration is an additional goal of EC competition policy. Market integration enhances com-petition in the Community. Companies should not be allowed to recreate private barriers between Member States where State barriers have been successfully abolished.

II. VERTICAL AGREEMENTS WHICH GENERALLY FALL OUTSIDE ARTICLE 81(1)

1. Agreements of minor importance and SMEs

(8) Agreements which are not capable of appreciably affecting trade between Member States or capable of appreciably restricting competition by object or effect are not caught by Article 81(1). The Block Exemption Regulation applies only to agreements falling within the scope of appli-cation of Article 81(1). These Guidelines are without prejudice to the application of the present or any future 'de minimis' notice.[3]

(9) Subject to the conditions set out in points 11, 18 and 20 of the 'de minimis' notice con-cerning hardcore restrictions and cumulative effect issues, vertical agreements entered into by undertakings whose market share on the relevant market does not exceed 10% are generally considered to fall outside the scope of Article 81(1). There is no presumption that vertical agreements concluded by undertakings having more than 10% market share automatically infringe Article 81(1). Agreements between undertakings whose market share exceeds the 10% threshold may still not have an appreciable effect on trade between Member States or may not constitute an appreciable restriction of competition.[4] Such agreements need to be assessed in their legal and economic context. The criteria for the assessment of individual agreements are set out in paragraphs 100 to 229.

(10) As regards hardcore restrictions defined in the 'de minimis' notice, Article 81(1) may apply below the 10% threshold, provided that there is an appreciable effect on trade between Member States and on competition. The applicable case-law of the Court of Justice and the Court of

---

[2] See *inter alia* judgment of the Court of Justice of the European Communities in Joined Cases 56/64 and 58/64 *Grundig-Consten v Commission* [1966] ECR 299; Case 56/65 *Technique Minière v Maschinenbau Ulm* [1966] ECR 235; and of the Court of First Instance of the European Communities in Case T–77/92 *Parker Pen v Commission* [1994] ECR II 549.

[3] See Notice on agreements of minor importance of 9 December 1997, OJ C 372, 9.12.1997, p. 13.

[4] See judgment of the Court of First Instance in Case T–7/93 *Langnese-Iglo v Commission* [1995] ECR II-1533, paragraph 98.

First Instance is relevant in this respect.[5] Reference is also made to the particular situation of launching a new product or entering a new market which is dealt with in these Guidelines (paragraph 119, point 10).

(11) In addition, the Commission considers that, subject to cumulative effect and hardcore restrictions, agreements between small and medium-sized undertakings as defined in the Annex to Commission Recommendation 96/280/EC[6] are rarely capable of appreciably affecting trade between Member States or of appreciably restricting competition within the meaning of Article 81(1), and therefore generally fall outside the scope of Article 81(1). In cases where such agreements nonetheless meet the conditions for the application of Article 81(1), the Commission will normally refrain from opening proceedings for lack of sufficient Community interest unless those undertakings collectively or individually hold a dominant position in a substantial part of the common market.

2. Agency agreements

(12) Paragraphs 12 to 20 replace the Notice on exclusive dealing contracts with commercial agents of 1962.[7] They must be read in conjunction with Council Directive 86/653/EEC.[8]

Agency agreements cover the situation in which a legal or physical person (the agent) is vested with the power to negotiate and/or conclude contracts on behalf of another person (the principal), either in the agent's own name or in the name of the principal, for the:

— purchase of goods or services by the principal, or
— sale of goods or services supplied by the principal.

(13) In the case of genuine agency agreements, the obligations imposed on the agent as to the contracts negotiated and/or concluded on behalf of the principal do not fall within the scope of application of Article 81(1). The determining factor in assessing whether Article 81(1) is applicable is the financial or commercial risk borne by the agent in relation to the activities for which he has been appointed as an agent by the principal. In this respect it is not material for the assessment whether the agent acts for one or several principals. Non-genuine agency agreements may be caught by Article 81(1), in which case the Block Exemption Regulation and the other sections of these Guidelines will apply.

(14) There are two types of financial or commercial risk that are material to the assessment of the genuine nature of an agency agreement under Article 81(1). First there are the risks which are directly related to the contracts concluded and/or negotiated by the agent on behalf of the principal, such as financing of stocks. Secondly, there are the risks related to market-specific investments. These are investments specifically required for the type of activity for which the agent has been appointed by the principal, i.e. which are required to enable the agent to conclude and/or negotiate this type of contract. Such investments are usually sunk, if upon leaving that particular field of activity the investment cannot be used for other activities or sold other than at a significant loss.

(15) The agency agreement is considered a genuine agency agreement and consequently falls outside Article 81(1) if the agent does not bear any, or bears only insignificant, risks in relation to the contracts concluded and/or negotiated on behalf of the principal and in relation to market-specific investments for that field of activity. In such a situation, the selling or purchasing function forms part of the principal's activities, despite the fact that the agent is a separate undertaking. The principal thus bears the related financial and commercial risks and the agent does not exercise

---

[5] See judgment of the Court of Justice in Case 5/69 *Völk v Vervaecke* [1969] ECR 295; Case 1/71 *Cadillon v Höss* [1971] ECR 351 and Case C–306/96 *Javico v Yves Saint Laurent* [1998] ECR I–1983, paragraphs 16 and 17. [6] OJ L 107, 30.4.1996, p. 4.
[7] OJ 139, 24.12.1962, p. 2921/62.   [8] OJ L 382, 31.12.1986, p. 17.

an independent economic activity in relation to the activities for which he has been appointed as an agent by the principal. In the opposite situation the agency agreement is considered a non-genuine agency agreement and may fall under Article 81(1). In that case the agent does bear such risks and will be treated as an independent dealer who must remain free in determining his marketing strategy in order to be able to recover his contract- or market-specific investments. Risks that are related to the activity of providing agency services in general, such as the risk of the agent's income being dependent upon his success as an agent or general investments in for instance premises or personnel, are not material to this assessment.

(16) The question of risk must be assessed on a case-by-case basis, and with regard to the economic reality of the situation rather than the legal form. Nonetheless, the Commission considers that Article 81(1) will generally not be applicable to the obligations imposed on the agent as to the contracts negotiated and/or concluded on behalf of the principal where property in the contract goods bought or sold does not vest in the agent, or the agent does not himself supply the contract services and where the agent:

— does not contribute to the costs relating to the supply/purchase of the contract goods or services, including the costs of transporting the goods. This does not preclude the agent from carrying out the transport service, provided that the costs are covered by the principal;
— is not, directly or indirectly, obliged to invest in sales promotion, such as contributions to the advertising budgets of the principal;
— does not maintain at his own cost or risk stocks of the contract goods, including the costs of financing the stocks and the costs of loss of stocks and can return unsold goods to the principal without charge, unless the agent is liable for fault (for example, by failing to comply with reasonable security measures to avoid loss of stocks);
— does not create and/or operate an after-sales service, repair service or a warranty service unless it is fully reimbursed by the principal;
— does not make market-specific investments in equipment, premises or training of personnel, such as for example the petrol storage tank in the case of petrol retailing or specific software to sell insurance policies in case of insurance agents;
— does not undertake responsibility towards third parties for damage caused by the product sold (product liability), unless, as agent, he is liable for fault in this respect;
— does not take responsibility for customers' non-performance of the contract, with the exception of the loss of the agent's commission, unless the agent is liable for fault (for example, by failing to comply with reasonable security or anti-theft measures or failing to comply with reasonable measures to report theft to the principal or police or to communicate to the principal all necessary information available to him on the customer's financial reliability).

(17) This list is not exhaustive. However, where the agent incurs one or more of the above risks or costs, then Article 81(1) may apply as with any other vertical agreement.

(18) If an agency agreement does not fall within the scope of application of Article 81(1), then all obligations imposed on the agent in relation to the contracts concluded and/or negotiated on behalf of the principal fall outside Article 81(1). The following obligations on the agent's part will generally be considered to form an inherent part of an agency agreement, as each of them relates to the ability of the principal to fix the scope of activity of the agent in relation to the contract goods or services, which is essential if the principal is to take the risks and therefore to be in a position to determine the commercial strategy:

— limitations on the territory in which the agent may sell these goods or services;
— limitations on the customers to whom the agent may sell these goods or services;
— the prices and conditions at which the agent must sell or purchase these goods or services.

(19) In addition to governing the conditions of sale or purchase of the contract goods or services by the agent on behalf of the principal, agency agreements often contain provisions which

concern the relationship between the agent and the principal. In particular, they may contain a provision preventing the principal from appointing other agents in respect of a given type of transaction, customer or territory (exclusive agency provisions) and/or a provision preventing the agent from acting as an agent or distributor of undertakings which compete with the principal (non-compete provisions). Exclusive agency provisions concern only intra-brand competition and will in general not lead to anti-competitive effects. Non-compete provisions, including post-term non-compete provisions, concern inter-brand competition and may infringe Article 81(1) if they lead to foreclosure on the relevant market where the contract goods or services are sold or purchased (see Section VI.2.1).

(20) An agency agreement may also fall within the scope of Article 81(1), even if the principal bears all the relevant financial and commercial risks, where it facilitates collusion. This could for instance be the case when a number of principals use the same agents while collectively excluding others from using these agents, or when they use the agents to collude on marketing strategy or to exchange sensitive market information between the principals.

III. Application of the Block Exemption Regulation

1. Safe harbour created by the Block Exemption Regulation

(21) The Block Exemption Regulation creates a presumption of legality for vertical agreements depending on the market share of the supplier or the buyer. Pursuant to Article 3 of the Block Exemption Regulation, it is in general the market share of the supplier on the market where it sells the contract goods or services which determines the applicability of the block exemption. This market share may not exceed the threshold of 30% in order for the block exemption to apply. Only where the agreement contains an exclusive supply obligation, as defined in Article 1(c) of the Block Exemption Regulation, is it the buyer's market share on the market where it purchases the contract goods or services which may not exceed the threshold of 30% in order for the block exemption to apply. For market share issues see Section V (paragraphs 88 to 99).

(22) From an economic point of view, a vertical agreement may have effects not only on the market between supplier and buyer but also on markets downstream of the buyer. The simplified approach of the Block Exemption Regulation, which only takes into account the market share of the supplier or the buyer (as the case may be) on the market between these two parties, is justified by the fact that below the threshold of 30% the effects on downstream markets will in general be limited. In addition, only having to consider the market between supplier and buyer makes the application of the Block Exemption Regulation easier and enhances the level of legal certainty, while the instrument of withdrawal (see paragraphs 71 to 87) remains available to remedy possible problems on other related markets.

2. Scope of the Block Exemption Regulation

(i) Definition of vertical agreements

(23) Vertical agreements are defined in Article 2(1) of the Block Exemption Regulation as 'agreements or concerted practices entered into between two or more undertakings each of which operates, for the purposes of the agreement, at a different level of the production or distribution chain, and relating to the conditions under which the parties may purchase, sell or resell certain goods or services'.

(24) There are three main elements in this definition:

— the agreement or concerted practice is between two or more undertakings. Vertical agreements with final consumers not operating as an undertaking are not covered; more generally, agreements with final consumers do not fall under Article 81(1), as that article applies only to agreements between undertakings, decisions by associations of undertakings and concerted practices. This is without prejudice to the possible application of Article 82 of the Treaty;

— the agreement or concerted practice is between undertakings each operating, for the purposes of the agreement, at a different level of the production or distribution chain. This means for instance that one undertaking produces a raw material which the other undertaking uses as an input, or that the first is a manufacturer, the second a wholesaler and the third a retailer. This does not preclude an undertaking from being active at more than one level of the production or distribution chain;

— the agreements or concerted practices relate to the conditions under which the parties to the agreement, the supplier and the buyer, 'may purchase, sell or resell certain goods or services'. This reflects the purpose of the Block Exemption Regulation to cover purchase and distribution agreements. These are agreements which concern the conditions for the purchase, sale or resale of the goods or services supplied by the supplier and/or which concern the conditions for the sale by the buyer of the goods or services which incorporate these goods or services. For the application of the Block Exemption Regulation both the goods or services supplied by the supplier and the resulting goods or services are considered to be contract goods or services. Vertical agreements relating to all final and intermediate goods and services are covered. The only exception is the automobile sector, as long as this sector remains covered by a specific block exemption such as that granted by Commission Regulation (EC) No 1475/95.[9] The goods or services provided by the supplier may be resold by the buyer or may be used as an input by the buyer to produce his own goods or services.

(25) The Block Exemption Regulation also applies to goods sold and purchased for renting to third parties. However, rent and lease agreements as such are not covered, as no good or service is being sold by the supplier to the buyer. More generally, the Block Exemption Regulation does not cover restrictions or obligations that do not relate to the conditions of purchase, sale and resale, such as an obligation preventing parties from carrying out independent research and development which the parties may have included in an otherwise vertical agreement. In addition, Articles 2(2) to (5) directly or indirectly exclude certain vertical agreements from the application of the Block Exemption Regulation.

(ii) Vertical agreements between competitors

(26) Article 2(4) of the Block Exemption Regulation explicitly excludes from its application 'vertical agreements entered into between competing undertakings'. Vertical agreements between competitors will be dealt with, as regards possible collusion effects, in the forthcoming Guidelines on the applicability of Article 81 to horizontal cooperation.[10] However, the vertical aspects of such agreements need to be assessed under these Guidelines. Article 1(a) of the Block Exemption Regulation defines competing undertakings as 'actual or potential suppliers in the same product market', irrespective of whether or not they are competitors on the same geographic market. Competing undertakings are undertakings that are actual or potential suppliers of the contract goods or services or goods or services that are substitutes for the contract goods or services. A potential supplier is an undertaking that does not actually produce a competing product but could and would be likely to do so in the absence of the agreement in response to a small and permanent increase in relative prices. This means that the undertaking would be able and likely to undertake the necessary additional investments and supply the market within 1 year. This assessment has to be based on realistic grounds; the mere theoretical possibility of entering a market is not sufficient.[11]

(27) There are three exceptions to the general exclusion of vertical agreements between competitors, all three being set out in Article 2(4) and relating to non-reciprocal agreements.

---

[9] OJ L 145, 29.6.1995, p. 25.   [10] Draft text published in OJ C 118, 27.4.2000, p. 14.
[11] See Commission Notice on the definition of the relevant market for the purposes of Community competition law, OJ C 372, 9.12.1997, p. 5, at paras. 20–24, the Commission's Thirteenth Report on Competition Policy, point 55, and Commission Decision 90/410/EEC in Case No IV/32.009—*Elopak/Metal Box-Odin*, OJ L 209, 8.8.1990, p. 15.

Non-reciprocal means, for instance, that while one manufacturer becomes the distributor of the products of another manufacturer, the latter does not become the distributor of the products of the first manufacturer. Non-reciprocal agreements between competitors are covered by the Block Exemption Regulation where (1) the buyer has a turnover not exceeding € 100 million, or (2) the supplier is a manufacturer and distributor of goods, while the buyer is only a distributor and not also a manufacturer of competing goods, or (3) the supplier is a provider of services operating at several levels of trade, while the buyer does not provide competing services at the level of trade where it purchases the contract services. The second exception covers situations of dual distribution, i.e. the manufacturer of particular goods also acts as a distributor of the goods in competition with independent distributors of his goods. A distributor who provides specifications to a manufacturer to produce particular goods under the distributor's brand name is not to be considered a manufacturer of such own-brand goods. The third exception covers similar situations of dual distribution, but in this case for services, when the supplier is also a provider of services at the level of the buyer.

(iii) Associations of retailers

(28) Article 2(2) of the Block Exemption Regulation includes in its application vertical agreements entered into by an association of undertakings which fulfils certain conditions and thereby excludes from the Block Exemption Regulation vertical agreements entered into by all other associations. Vertical agreements entered into between an association and its members, or between an association and its suppliers, are covered by the Block Exemption Regulation only if all the members are retailers of goods (not services) and if each individual member of the association has a turnover not exceeding € 50 million. Retailers are distributors reselling goods to final consumers. Where only a limited number of the members of the association have a turnover not significantly exceeding the € 50 million threshold, this will normally not change the assessment under Article 81.

(29) An association of undertakings may involve both horizontal and vertical agreements. The horizontal agreements have to be assessed according to the principles set out in the forthcoming Guidelines on the applicability of Article 81 to horizontal cooperation. If this assessment leads to the conclusion that a cooperation between undertakings in the area of purchasing or selling is acceptable, a further assessment will be necessary to examine the vertical agreements concluded by the association with its suppliers or its individual members. The latter assessment will follow the rules of the Block Exemption Regulation and these Guidelines. For instance, horizontal agreements concluded between the members of the association or decisions adopted by the association, such as the decision to require the members to purchase from the association or the decision to allocate exclusive territories to the members have to be assessed first as a horizontal agreement. Only if this assessment is positive does it become relevant to assess the vertical agreements between the association and individual members or between the association and suppliers.

(iv) Vertical agreements containing provisions on intellectual property rights (IPRs)

(30) Article 2(3) of the Block Exemption Regulation includes in its application vertical agreements containing certain provisions relating to the assignment of IPRs to or use of IPRs by the buyer and thereby excludes from the Block Exemption Regulation all other vertical agreements containing IPR provisions. The Block Exemption Regulation applies to vertical agreements containing IPR provisions when five conditions are fulfilled:

— the IPR provisions must be part of a vertical agreement, i.e. an agreement with conditions under which the parties may purchase, sell or resell certain goods or services;
— the IPRs must be assigned to, or for use by, the buyer;
— the IPR provisions must not constitute the primary object of the agreement;
— the IPR provisions must be directly related to the use, sale or resale of goods or services by the buyer or his customers. In the case of franchising where marketing forms the object of the

exploitation of the IPRs, the goods or services are distributed by the master franchisee or the franchisees;

— the IPR provisions, in relation to the contract goods or services, must not contain restrictions of competition having the same object or effect as vertical restraints which are not exempted under the Block Exemption Regulation.

(31) These conditions ensure that the Block Exemption Regulation applies to vertical agreements where the use, sale or resale of goods or services can be performed more effectively because IPRs are assigned to or transferred for use by the buyer. In other words, restrictions concerning the assignment or use of IPRs can be covered when the main object of the agreement is the purchase or distribution of goods or services.

(32) The first condition makes clear that the context in which the IPRs are provided is an agreement to purchase or distribute goods or an agreement to purchase or provide services and not an agreement concerning the assignment or licensing of IPRs for the manufacture of goods, nor a pure licensing agreement. The Block Exemption Regulation does not cover for instance:

— agreements where a party provides another party with a recipe and licenses the other party to produce a drink with this recipe;

— agreements under which one party provides another party with a mould or master copy and licenses the other party to produce and distribute copies;

— the pure licence of a trade mark or sign for the purposes of merchandising;

— sponsorship contracts concerning the right to advertise oneself as being an official sponsor of an event;

— copyright licensing such as broadcasting contracts concerning the right to record and/or the right to broadcast an event.

(33) The second condition makes clear that the Block Exemption Regulation does not apply when the IPRs are provided by the buyer to the supplier, no matter whether the IPRs concern the manner of manufacture or of distribution. An agreement relating to the transfer of IPRs to the supplier and containing possible restrictions on the sales made by the supplier is not covered by the Block Exemption Regulation. This means in particular that subcontracting involving the transfer of know-how to a subcontractor[12] does not fall within the scope of application of the Block Exemption Regulation. However, vertical agreements under which the buyer provides only specifications to the supplier which describe the goods or services to be supplied are covered by the Block Exemption Regulation.

(34) The third condition makes clear that in order to be covered by the Block Exemption Regulation the primary object of the agreement must not be the assignment or licensing of IPRs. The primary object must be the purchase or distribution of goods or services and the IPR provisions must serve the implementation of the vertical agreement.

(35) The fourth condition requires that the IPR provisions facilitate the use, sale or resale of goods or services by the buyer or his customers. The goods or services for use or resale are usually supplied by the licensor but may also be purchased by the licensee from a third supplier. The IPR provisions will normally concern the marketing of goods or services. This is for instance the case in a franchise agreement where the franchisor sells to the franchisee goods for resale and in addition licenses the franchisee to use his trade mark and know-how to market the goods. Also covered is the case where the supplier of a concentrated extract licenses the buyer to dilute and bottle the extract before selling it as a drink.

(36) The fifth condition signifies in particular that the IPR provisions should not have the same object or effect as any of the hardcore restrictions listed in Article 4 of the Block Exemption

---

[12] See Notice on subcontracting, OJ C 1, 3.1.1979, p. 2.

Regulation or any of the restrictions excluded from the coverage of the Block Exemption Regulation by Article 5 (see paragraphs 46 to 61).

(37) Intellectual property rights which may be considered to serve the implementation of vertical agreements within the meaning of Article 2(3) of the Block Exemption Regulation generally concern three main areas: trade marks, copyright and know-how.

Trade mark

(38) A trade mark licence to a distributor may be related to the distribution of the licensor's products in a particular territory. If it is an exclusive licence, the agreement amounts to exclusive distribution.

Copyright

(39) Resellers of goods covered by copyright (books, software, etc.) may be obliged by the copyright holder only to resell under the condition that the buyer, whether another reseller or the end user, shall not infringe the copyright. Such obligations on the reseller, to the extent that they fall under Article 81(1) at all, are covered by the Block Exemption Regulation.

(40) Agreements under which hard copies of software are supplied for resale and where the reseller does not acquire a licence to any rights over the software but only has the right to resell the hard copies, are to be regarded as agreements for the supply of goods for resale for the purpose of the Block Exemption Regulation. Under this form of distribution the licence of the software only takes place between the copyright owner and the user of the software. This may take the form of a 'shrink wrap' licence, i.e. a set of conditions included in the package of the hard copy which the end user is deemed to accept by opening the package.

(41) Buyers of hardware incorporating software protected by copyright may be obliged by the copyright holder not to infringe the copyright, for example not to make copies and resell the software or not to make copies and use the software in combination with other hardware. Such use-restrictions, to the extent that they fall within Article 81(1) at all, are covered by the Block Exemption Regulation.

Know-how

(42) Franchise agreements, with the exception of industrial franchise agreements, are the most obvious example where know-how for marketing purposes is communicated to the buyer. Franchise agreements contain licences of intellectual property rights relating to trade marks or signs and know-how for the use and distribution of goods or the provision of services. In addition to the licence of IPR, the franchisor usually provides the franchisee during the life of the agreement with commercial or technical assistance, such as procurement services, training, advice on real estate, financial planning etc. The licence and the assistance are integral components of the business method being franchised.

(43) Licensing contained in franchise agreements is covered by the Block Exemption Regulation if all five conditions listed in point 30 are fulfilled. This is usually the case, as under most franchise agreements, including master franchise agreements, the franchisor provides goods and/or services, in particular commercial or technical assistance services, to the franchisee. The IPRs help the franchisee to resell the products supplied by the franchisor or by a supplier designated by the franchisor or to use those products and sell the resulting goods or services. Where the franchise agreement only or primarily concerns licensing of IPRs, such an agreement is not covered by the Block Exemption Regulation, but it will be treated in a way similar to those franchise agreements which are covered by the Block Exemption Regulation.

(44) The following IPR-related obligations are generally considered to be necessary to protect the franchisor's intellectual property rights and are, if these obligations fall under Article 81(1), also covered by the Block Exemption Regulation:

(a) an obligation on the franchisee not to engage, directly or indirectly, in any similar business;

(b) an obligation on the franchisee not to acquire financial interests in the capital of a competing undertaking such as would give the franchisee the power to influence the economic conduct of such undertaking;

(c) an obligation on the franchisee not to disclose to third parties the know-how provided by the franchisor as long as this know-how is not in the public domain;

(d) an obligation on the franchisee to communicate to the franchisor any experience gained in exploiting the franchise and to grant it, and other franchisees, a non-exclusive licence for the know-how resulting from that experience;

(e) an obligation on the franchisee to inform the franchisor of infringements of licensed intellectual property rights, to take legal action against infringers or to assist the franchisor in any legal actions against infringers;

(f) an obligation on the franchisee not to use know-how licensed by the franchisor for purposes other than the exploitation of the franchise;

(g) an obligation on the franchisee not to assign the rights and obligations under the franchise agreement without the franchisor's consent.

(v) Relationship to other block exemption regulations

(45) Article 2(5) states that the Block Exemption Regulation does 'not apply to vertical agreements the subject matter of which falls within the scope of any other block exemption regulation'. This means that the Block Exemption Regulation does not apply to vertical agreements covered by Commission Regulation (EC) No 240/96[13] on technology transfer, Commission Regulation (EC) No 1475/1995[14] for car distribution or Regulations (EEC) No 417/85[15] and (EEC) No 418/85[16] exempting vertical agreements concluded in connection with horizontal agreements, as last amended by Regulation (EC) No 2236/97[17] or any future regulations of that kind.

3. Hardcore restrictions under the Block Exemption Regulation

(46) The Block Exemption Regulation contains in Article 4 a list of hardcore restrictions which lead to the exclusion of the whole vertical agreement from the scope of application of the Block Exemption Regulation. This list of hardcore restrictions applies to vertical agreements concerning trade within the Community. In so far as vertical agreements concern exports outside the Community or imports/re-imports from outside the Community see the judgment in Javico v Yves Saint Laurent. Individual exemption of vertical agreements containing such hardcore restrictions is also unlikely.

(47) The hardcore restriction set out in Article 4(a) of the Block Exemption Regulation concerns resale price maintenance (RPM), that is agreements or concerted practices having as their direct or indirect object the establishment of a fixed or minimum resale price or a fixed or minimum price level to be observed by the buyer. In the case of contractual provisions or concerted practices that directly establish the resale price, the restriction is clear cut. However, RPM can also be achieved through indirect means. Examples of the latter are an agreement fixing the distribution margin, fixing the maximum level of discount the distributor can grant from a prescribed price level, making the grant of rebates or reimbursement of promotional costs by the supplier subject to the observance of a given price level, linking the prescribed resale price to the resale prices of competitors, threats, intimidation, warnings, penalties, delay or suspension of deliveries or contract terminations in relation to observance of a given price level. Direct or indirect means of achieving price fixing can be made more effective when combined with measures to identify price-cutting distributors, such as the implementation of a price monitoring system, or the obligation on

---

[13] OJ L 31, 9.2.1996, p. 2. [14] OJ L 145, 29.6.1995, p. 25.
[15] OJ L 53, 22.2.1985, p. 1. [16] OJ L 53, 22.2.1985, p. 5.
[17] OJ L 306, 11.11.1997, p. 12.

retailers to report other members of the distribution network who deviate from the standard price level. Similarly, direct or indirect price fixing can be made more effective when combined with measures which may reduce the buyer's incentive to lower the resale price, such as the supplier printing a recommended resale price on the product or the supplier obliging the buyer to apply a most-favoured-customer clause. The same indirect means and the same 'supportive' measures can be used to make maximum or recommended prices work as RPM. However, the provision of a list of recommended prices or maximum prices by the supplier to the buyer is not considered in itself as leading to RPM.

(48) In the case of agency agreements, the principal normally establishes the sales price, as the agent does not become the owner of the goods. However, where an agency agreement falls within Article 81(1) (see paragraphs 12 to 20), an obligation preventing or restricting the agent from sharing his commission, fixed or variable, with the customer would be a hardcore restriction under Article 4(a) of the Block Exemption Regulation. The agent should thus be left free to lower the effective price paid by the customer without reducing the income for the principal.[18]

(49) The hardcore restriction set out in Article 4(b) of the Block Exemption Regulation concerns agreements or concerted practices that have as their direct or indirect object the restriction of sales by the buyer, in as far as those restrictions relate to the territory into which or the customers to whom the buyer may sell the contract goods or services. That hardcore restriction relates to market partitioning by territory or by customer. That may be the result of direct obligations, such as the obligation not to sell to certain customers or to customers in certain territories or the obligation to refer orders from these customers to other distributors. It may also result from indirect measures aimed at inducing the distributor not to sell to such customers, such as refusal or reduction of bonuses or discounts, refusal to supply, reduction of supplied volumes or limitation of supplied volumes to the demand within the allocated territory or customer group, threat of contract termination or profit pass-over obligations. It may further result from the supplier not providing a Community-wide guarantee service, whereby all distributors are obliged to provide the guarantee service and are reimbursed for this service by the supplier, even in relation to products sold by other distributors into their territory. These practices are even more likely to be viewed as a restriction of the buyer's sales when used in conjunction with the implementation by the supplier of a monitoring system aimed at verifying the effective destination of the supplied goods, e.g. the use of differentiated labels or serial numbers. However, a prohibition imposed on all distributors to sell to certain end users is not classified as a hardcore restriction if there is an objective justification related to the product, such as a general ban on selling dangerous substances to certain customers for reasons of safety or health. It implies that also the supplier himself does not sell to these customers. Nor are obligations on the reseller relating to the display of the supplier's brand name classified as hardcore.

(50) There are four exceptions to the hardcore restriction in Article 4(b) of the Block Exemption Regulation. The first exception allows a supplier to restrict active sales by his direct buyers to a territory or a customer group which has been allocated exclusively to another buyer or which the supplier has reserved to itself. A territory or customer group is exclusively allocated when the supplier agrees to sell his product only to one distributor for distribution in a particular territory or to a particular customer group and the exclusive distributor is protected against active selling into his territory or to his customer group by the supplier and all the other buyers of the supplier inside the Community. The supplier is allowed to combine the allocation of an exclusive territory and an exclusive customer group by for instance appointing an exclusive distributor for a particular customer group in a certain territory. This protection of exclusively allocated territories or customer groups must, however, permit passive sales to such territories or customer groups. For

---

[18] See, for instance, Commission Decision 91/562/EEC in Case No IV/32.737—*Eirpage*, OJ L 306, 7.11.1991, p. 22, in particular point (6).

the application of Article 4(b) of the Block Exemption Regulation, the Commission interprets 'active' and 'passive' sales as follows:

— 'Active' sales mean actively approaching individual customers inside another distributor's exclusive territory or exclusive customer group by for instance direct mail or visits; or actively approaching a specific customer group or customers in a specific territory allocated exclusively to another distributor through advertisement in media or other promotions specifically targeted at that customer group or targeted at customers in that territory; or establishing a warehouse or distribution outlet in another distributor's exclusive territory.

— 'Passive' sales mean responding to unsolicited requests from individual customers including delivery of goods or services to such customers. General advertising or promotion in media or on the Internet that reaches customers in other distributors' exclusive territories or customer groups but which is a reasonable way to reach customers outside those territories or customer groups, for instance to reach customers in non-exclusive territories or in one's own territory, are passive sales.

(51) Every distributor must be free to use the Internet to advertise or to sell products. A restriction on the use of the Internet by distributors could only be compatible with the Block Exemption Regulation to the extent that promotion on the Internet or sales over the Internet would lead to active selling into other distributors' exclusive territories or customer groups. In general, the use of the Internet is not considered a form of active sales into such territories or customer groups, since it is a reasonable way to reach every customer. The fact that it may have effects outside one's own territory or customer group results from the technology, i.e. the easy access from everywhere. If a customer visits the web site of a distributor and contacts the distributor and if such contact leads to a sale, including delivery, then that is considered passive selling. The language used on the website or in the communication plays normally no role in that respect. Insofar as a web site is not specifically targeted at customers primarily inside the territory or customer group exclusively allocated to another distributor, for instance with the use of banners or links in pages of providers specifically available to these exclusively allocated customers, the website is not considered a form of active selling. However, unsolicited e-mails sent to individual customers or specific customer groups are considered active selling. The same considerations apply to selling by catalogue. Notwithstanding what has been said before, the supplier may require quality standards for the use of the Internet site to resell his goods, just as the supplier may require quality standards for a shop or for advertising and promotion in general. The latter may be relevant in particular for selective distribution. An outright ban on Internet or catalogue selling is only possible if there is an objective justification. In any case, the supplier cannot reserve to itself sales and/or advertising over the Internet.

(52) There are three other exceptions to the second hardcore restriction set out in Article 4(b) of the Block Exemption Regulation. All three exceptions allow for the restriction of both active and passive sales. Thus, it is permissible to restrict a wholesaler from selling to end users, to restrict an appointed distributor in a selective distribution system from selling, at any level of trade, to unauthorised distributors in markets where such a system is operated, and to restrict a buyer of components supplied for incorporation from reselling them to competitors of the supplier. The term 'component' includes any intermediate goods and the term 'incorporation' refers to the use of any input to produce goods.

(53) The hardcore restriction set out in Article 4(c) of the Block Exemption Regulation concerns the restriction of active or passive sales to end users, whether professional end users or final consumers, by members of a selective distribution network. This means that dealers in a selective distribution system, as defined in Article 1(d) of the Block Exemption Regulation, cannot be restricted in the users or purchasing agents acting on behalf of these users to whom they may sell. For instance, also in a selective distribution system the dealer should be free to advertise and sell with the help of the Internet. Selective distribution may be combined with exclusive distribution

provided that active and passive selling is not restricted anywhere. The supplier may therefore commit itself to supplying only one dealer or a limited number of dealers in a given territory.

(54) In addition, in the case of selective distribution, restrictions can be imposed on the dealer's ability to determine the location of his business premises. Selected dealers may be prevented from running their business from different premises or from opening a new outlet in a different location. If the dealer's outlet is mobile ('shop on wheels'), an area may be defined outside which the mobile outlet cannot be operated.

(55) The hardcore restriction set out in Article 4(d) of the Block Exemption Regulation concerns the restriction of cross-supplies between appointed distributors within a selective distribution system. This means that an agreement or concerted practice may not have as its direct or indirect object to prevent or restrict the active or passive selling of the contract products between the selected distributors. Selected distributors must remain free to purchase the contract products from other appointed distributors within the network, operating either at the same or at a different level of trade. This means that selective distribution cannot be combined with vertical restraints aimed at forcing distributors to purchase the contract products exclusively from a given source, for instance exclusive purchasing. It also means that within a selective distribution network no restrictions can be imposed on appointed wholesalers as regards their sales of the product to appointed retailers.

(56) The hardcore restriction set out in Article 4(e) of the Block Exemption Regulation concerns agreements that prevent or restrict end-users, independent repairers and service providers from obtaining spare parts directly from the manufacturer of these spare parts. An agreement between a manufacturer of spare parts and a buyer who incorporates these parts into his own products (original equipment manufacturer (OEM)), may not, either directly or indirectly, prevent or restrict sales by the manufacturer of these spare parts to end-users, independent repairers or service providers. Indirect restrictions may arise in particular when the supplier of the spare parts is restricted in supplying technical information and special equipment which are necessary for the use of spare parts by users, independent repairers or service providers. However, the agreement may place restrictions on the supply of the spare parts to the repairers or service providers entrusted by the original equipment manufacturer with the repair or servicing of his own goods. In other words, the original equipment manufacturer may require his own repair and service network to buy the spare parts from it.

4. Conditions under the Block Exemption Regulation

(57) Article 5 of the Block Exemption Regulation excludes certain obligations from the coverage of the Block Exemption Regulation even though the market share threshold is not exceeded. However, the Block Exemption Regulation continues to apply to the remaining part of the vertical agreement if that part is severable from the non-exempted obligations.

(58) The first exclusion is provided in Article 5(a) of the Block Exemption Regulation and concerns non-compete obligations. Non-compete obligations are obligations that require the buyer to purchase from the supplier or from another undertaking designated by the supplier more than 80% of the buyer's total purchases during the previous year of the contract goods and services and their substitutes (see the definition in Article 1(b) of the Block Exemption Regulation), thereby preventing the buyer from purchasing competing goods or services or limiting such purchases to less than 20% of total purchases. Where for the year preceding the conclusion of the contract no relevant purchasing data for the buyer are available, the buyer's best estimate of his annual total requirements may be used. Such non-compete obligations are not covered by the Block Exemption Regulation when their duration is indefinite or exceeds five years. Non-compete obligations that are tacitly renewable beyond a period of five years are also not covered by the Block Exemption Regulation. However, non-compete obligations are covered when their duration is limited to five years or less, or when renewal beyond five years requires

explicit consent of both parties and no obstacles exist that hinder the buyer from effectively terminating the non-compete obligation at the end of the five year period. If for instance the agreement provides for a five-year non-compete obligation and the supplier provides a loan to the buyer, the repayment of that loan should not hinder the buyer from effectively terminating the non-compete obligation at the end of the five-year period; the repayment needs to be structured in equal or decreasing instalments and should not increase over time. This is without prejudice to the possibility, in the case for instance of a new distribution outlet, to delay repayment for the first one or two years until sales have reached a certain level. The buyer must have the possibility to repay the remaining debt where there is still an outstanding debt at the end of the non-compete obligation. Similarly, when the supplier provides the buyer with equipment which is not relationship-specific, the buyer should have the possibility to take over the equipment at its market asset value at the end of the non-compete obligation.

(59) The five-year duration limit does not apply when the goods or services are resold by the buyer 'from premises and land owned by the supplier or leased by the supplier from third parties not connected with the buyer'. In such cases the non-compete obligation may be of the same duration as the period of occupancy of the point of sale by the buyer (Article 5(a) of the Block Exemption Regulation). The reason for this exception is that it is normally unreasonable to expect a supplier to allow competing products to be sold from premises and land owned by the supplier without his permission. Artificial ownership constructions intended to avoid the five-year limit cannot benefit from this exception.

(60) The second exclusion from the block exemption is provided for in Article 5(b) of the Block Exemption Regulation and concerns post-term non-compete obligations. Such obligations are normally not covered by the Block Exemption Regulation, unless the obligation is indispensable to protect know-how transferred by the supplier to the buyer, is limited to the point of sale from which the buyer has operated during the contract period, and is limited to a maximum period of one year. According to the definition in Article 1(f) of the Block Exemption Regulation the know-how needs to be 'substantial', meaning 'that the know-how includes information which is indispensable to the buyer for the use, sale or resale of the contract goods or services'.

(61) The third exclusion from the block exemption is provided for in Article 5(c) of the Block Exemption Regulation and concerns the sale of competing goods in a selective distribution system. The Block Exemption Regulation covers the combination of selective distribution with a non-compete obligation, obliging the dealers not to resell competing brands in general. However, if the supplier prevents his appointed dealers, either directly or indirectly, from buying products for resale from specific competing suppliers, such an obligation cannot enjoy the benefit of the Block Exemption Regulation. The objective of the exclusion of this obligation is to avoid a situation whereby a number of suppliers using the same selective distribution outlets prevent one specific competitor or certain specific competitors from using these outlets to distribute their products (foreclosure of a competing supplier which would be a form of collective boycott).[19]

5. No presumption of illegality outside the Block Exemption Regulation

(62) Vertical agreements falling outside the Block Exemption Regulation will not be presumed to be illegal but may need individual examination. Companies are encouraged to do their own assessment without notification. In the case of an individual examination by the Commission, the latter will bear the burden of proof that the agreement in question infringes Article 81(1). When appreciable anti-competitive effects are demonstrated, undertakings may substantiate efficiency

---

[19] An example of indirect measures having such exclusionary effects can be found in Commission Decision 92/428/EEC in Case No IV/33.542—*Parfum Givenchy* (OJ L 236, 19.8.1992, p. 11).

claims and explain why a certain distribution system is likely to bring about benefits which are relevant to the conditions for exemption under Article 81(3).

6. No need for precautionary notification

(63) Pursuant to Article 4(2) of Council Regulation No 17 of 6 February 1962, First Regulation implementing Articles 85 and 86 of the Treaty,[20] as last amended by Regulation (EC) No 1216/1999,[21] vertical agreements can benefit from an exemption under Article 81(3) from their date of entry into force, even if notification occurs after that date. This means in practice that no precautionary notification needs to be made. If a dispute arises, an undertaking can still notify, in which case the Commission can exempt the vertical agreement with retroactive effect from the date of entry into force of the agreement if all four conditions of Article 81(3) are fulfilled. A notifying party does not have to explain why the agreement was not notified earlier and will not be denied retroactive exemption simply because it did not notify earlier. Any notification will be reviewed on its merits. This amendment to Article 4(2) of Regulation No 17 should eliminate artificial litigation before national courts and thus strengthen the civil enforceability of contracts. It also takes account of the situation where undertakings have not notified because they assumed the agreement was covered by the Block Exemption Regulation.

(64) Since the date of notification no longer limits the possibility of exemption by the Commission, national courts have to assess the likelihood that Article 81(3) will apply in respect of vertical agreements falling within Article 81(1). If such likelihood exists, they should suspend proceedings pending adoption of a position by the Commission. However, national courts may adopt interim measures pending the assessment by the Commission of the applicability of Article 81(3), in the same way as they do when they refer a preliminary question to the Court of Justice under Article 234 of the EC Treaty. No suspension is necessary in respect of injunction proceedings, where national courts themselves are empowered to assess the likelihood of application of Article 81(3).[22]

(65) Unless there is litigation in national courts or complaints, notifications of vertical agreements will not be given priority in the Commission's enforcement policy. Notifications as such do not provide provisional validity for the execution of agreements. Where undertakings have not notified an agreement because they assumed in good faith that the market share threshold under the Block Exemption Regulation was not exceeded, the Commission will not impose fines.

7. Severability

(66) The Block Exemption Regulation exempts vertical agreements on condition that no hardcore restriction, as set out in Article 4, is contained in or practised with the vertical agreement. If there are one or more hardcore restrictions, the benefit of the Block Exemption Regulation is lost for the entire vertical agreement. There is no severability for hardcore restrictions.

(67) The rule of severability does apply, however, to the conditions set out in Article 5 of the Block Exemption Regulation. Therefore, the benefit of the block exemption is only lost in relation to that part of the vertical agreement which does not comply with the conditions set out in Article 5.

8. Portfolio of products distributed through the same distribution system

(68) Where a supplier uses the same distribution agreement to distribute several goods/services some of these may, in view of the market share threshold, be covered by the Block Exemption Regulation while others may not. In that case, the Block Exemption Regulation applies to those goods and services for which the conditions of application are fulfilled.

---

[20] OJ 13, 21.2.1962, p. 204/62.   [21] OJ L 148, 15.6.1999, p. 5.
[22] Case C–2347/89 *Delimitis v Henninger Bräu* [1991] ECR I–935, at paragraph 52.

(69) In respect of the goods or services which are not covered by the Block Exemption Regulation, the ordinary rules of competition apply, which means:

— there is no block exemption but also no presumption of illegality;

— if there is an infringement of Article 81(1) which is not exemptable, consideration may be given to whether there are appropriate remedies to solve the competition problem within the existing distribution system;

— if there are no such appropriate remedies, the supplier concerned will have to make other distribution arrangements.

This situation can also arise where Article 82 applies in respect of some products but not in respect of others.

9. Transitional period

(70) The Block Exemption Regulation applies from 1 June 2000. Article 12 of the Block Exemption Regulation provides for a transitional period for vertical agreements already in force before 1 June 2000 which do not satisfy the conditions for exemption provided in the Block Exemption Regulation, but which do satisfy the conditions for exemption under the Block Exemption Regulations which expired on 31 May 2000 (Commissions Regulations (EEC) No 1983/83, (EEC) No 1984/83 and (EEC) No 4087/88). The Commission Notice concerning Regulations (EEC) Nos 1983/83 and 1984/83 also ceases to apply on 31 May 2000. The latter agreements may continue to benefit from these outgoing Regulations until 31 December 2001. Agreements of suppliers with a market share not exceeding 30% who signed with their buyers non-compete agreements with a duration exceeding five years are covered by the Block Exemption Regulation if on 1 January 2002 the non-compete agreements have no more than five years to run.

IV. WITHDRAWAL OF THE BLOCK EXEMPTION AND DISAPPLICATION OF THE BLOCK EXEMPTION REGULATION

1. Withdrawal procedure

(71) The presumption of legality conferred by the Block Exemption Regulation may be withdrawn if a vertical agreement, considered either in isolation or in conjunction with similar agreements enforced by competing suppliers or buyers, comes within the scope of Article 81(1) and does not fulfil all the conditions of Article 81(3). This may occur when a supplier, or a buyer in the case of exclusive supply agreements, holding a market share not exceeding 30%, enters into a vertical agreement which does not give rise to objective advantages such as to compensate for the damage which it causes to competition. This may particularly be the case with respect to the distribution of goods to final consumers, who are often in a much weaker position than professional buyers of intermediate goods. In the case of sales to final consumers, the disadvantages caused by a vertical agreement may have a stronger impact than in a case concerning the sale and purchase of intermediate goods. When the conditions of Article 81(3) are not fulfilled, the Commission may withdraw the benefit of the Block Exemption Regulation under Article 6 and establish an infringement of Article 81(1).

(72) Where the withdrawal procedure is applied, the Commission bears the burden of proof that the agreement falls within the scope of Article 81(1) and that the agreement does not fulfil all four conditions of Article 81(3).

(73) The conditions for an exemption under Article 81(3) may in particular not be fulfilled when access to the relevant market or competition therein is significantly restricted by the cumulative effect of parallel networks of similar vertical agreements practised by competing suppliers or buyers. Parallel networks of vertical agreements are to be regarded as similar if they contain restraints producing similar effects on the market. Similar effects will normally occur when

vertical restraints practised by competing suppliers or buyers come within one of the four groups listed in paragraphs 104 to 114. Such a situation may arise for example when, on a given market, certain suppliers practise purely qualitative selective distribution while other suppliers practise quantitative selective distribution. In such circumstances, the assessment must take account of the anti-competitive effects attributable to each individual network of agreements. Where appropriate, withdrawal may concern only the quantitative limitations imposed on the number of authorised distributors. Other cases in which a withdrawal decision may be taken include situations where the buyer, for example in the context of exclusive supply or exclusive distribution, has significant market power in the relevant downstream market where he resells the goods or provides the services.

(74) Responsibility for an anti-competitive cumulative effect can only be attributed to those undertakings which make an appreciable contribution to it. Agreements entered into by undertakings whose contribution to the cumulative effect is insignificant do not fall under the prohibition provided for in Article 81(1)[23] and are therefore not subject to the withdrawal mechanism. The assessment of such a contribution will be made in accordance with the criteria set out in paragraphs 137 to 229.

(75) A withdrawal decision can only have ex nunc effect, which means that the exempted status of the agreements concerned will not be affected until the date at which the withdrawal becomes effective.

(76) Under Article 7 of the Block Exemption Regulation, the competent authority of a Member State may withdraw the benefit of the Block Exemption Regulation in respect of vertical agreements whose anti-competitive effects are felt in the territory of the Member State concerned or a part thereof, which has all the characteristics of a distinct geographic market. Where a Member State has not enacted legislation enabling the national competition authority to apply Community competition law or at least to withdraw the benefit of the Block Exemption Regulation, the Member State may ask the Commission to initiate proceedings to this effect.

(77) The Commission has the exclusive power to withdraw the benefit of the Block Exemption Regulation in respect of vertical agreements restricting competition on a relevant geographic market which is wider than the territory of a single Member State. When the territory of a single Member State, or a part thereof, constitutes the relevant geographic market, the Commission and the Member State concerned have concurrent competence for withdrawal. Often, such cases lend themselves to decentralised enforcement by national competition authorities. However, the Commission reserves the right to take on certain cases displaying a particular Community interest, such as cases raising a new point of law.

(78) National decisions of withdrawal must be taken in accordance with the procedures laid down under national law and will only have effect within the territory of the Member State concerned. Such national decisions must not prejudice the uniform application of the Community competition rules and the full effect of the measures adopted in implementation of those rules.[24] Compliance with this principle implies that national competition authorities must carry out their assessment under Article 81 in the light of the relevant criteria developed by the Court of Justice and the Court of First Instance and in the light of notices and previous decisions adopted by the Commission.

(79) The Commission considers that the consultation mechanisms provided for in the Notice on cooperation between national competition authorities and the Commission[25] should be used to avert the risk of conflicting decisions and duplication of procedures.

---

[23] Judgment in the *Delimitis* Case.
[24] Judgment of the Court of Justice in Case 147/68 *Walt Wilhelm and Others v Bundeskartellamt* [1969] ECR 1, paragraph 4, and judgment in *Delimitis*.
[25] OJ C 313, 15.10.1997, p. 3, points 49 to 53.

2. Disapplication of the Block Exemption Regulation

(80) Article 8 of the Block Exemption Regulation enables the Commission to exclude from the scope of the Block Exemption Regulation, by means of regulation, parallel networks of similar vertical restraints where these cover more than 50% of a relevant market. Such a measure is not addressed to individual undertakings but concerns all undertakings whose agreements are defined in the regulation disapplying the Block Exemption Regulation.

(81) Whereas the withdrawal of the benefit of the Block Exemption Regulation under Article 6 implies the adoption of a decision establishing an infringement of Article 81 by an individual company, the effect of a regulation under Article 8 is merely to remove, in respect of the restraints and the markets concerned, the benefit of the application of the Block Exemption Regulation and to restore the full application of Article 81(1) and (3). Following the adoption of a regulation declaring the Block Exemption inapplicable in respect of certain vertical restraints on a particular market, the criteria developed by the relevant case-law of the Court of Justice and the Court of First Instance and by notices and previous decisions adopted by the Commission will guide the application of Article 81 to individual agreements. Where appropriate, the Commission will take a decision in an individual case, which can provide guidance to all the undertakings operating on the market concerned.

(82) For the purpose of calculating the 50% market coverage ratio, account must be taken of each individual network of vertical agreements containing restraints, or combinations of restraints, producing similar effects on the market. Similar effects normally result when the restraints come within one of the four groups listed in paragraphs 104 to 114.

(83) Article 8 does not entail an obligation on the part of the Commission to act where the 50% market-coverage ratio is exceeded. In general, disapplication is appropriate when it is likely that access to the relevant market or competition therein is appreciably restricted. This may occur in particular when parallel networks of selective distribution covering more than 50% of a market make use of selection criteria which are not required by the nature of the relevant goods or discriminate against certain forms of distribution capable of selling such goods.

(84) In assessing the need to apply Article 8, the Commission will consider whether individual withdrawal would be a more appropriate remedy. This may depend, in particular, on the number of competing undertakings contributing to a cumulative effect on a market or the number of affected geographic markets within the Community.

(85) Any regulation adopted under Article 8 must clearly set out its scope. This means, first, that the Commission must define the relevant product and geographic market(s) and, secondly, that it must identify the type of vertical restraint in respect of which the Block Exemption Regulation will no longer apply. As regards the latter aspect, the Commission may modulate the scope of its regulation according to the competition concern which it intends to address. For instance, while all parallel networks of single-branding type arrangements shall be taken into account in view of establishing the 50% market coverage ratio, the Commission may nevertheless restrict the scope of the disapplication regulation only to non-compete obligations exceeding a certain duration. Thus, agreements of a shorter duration or of a less restrictive nature might be left unaffected, in consideration of the lesser degree of foreclosure attributable to such restraints. Similarly, when on a particular market selective distribution is practised in combination with additional restraints such as non-compete or quantity-forcing on the buyer, the disapplication regulation may concern only such additional restraints. Where appropriate, the Commission may also provide guidance by specifying the market share level which, in the specific market context, may be regarded as insufficient to bring about a significant contribution by an individual undertaking to the cumulative effect.

(86) The transitional period of not less than six months that the Commission will have to set under Article 8(2) should allow the undertakings concerned to adapt their agreements to take account of the regulation disapplying the Block Exemption Regulation.

(87) A regulation disapplying the Block Exemption Regulation will not affect the exempted status of the agreements concerned for the period preceding its entry into force.

V. Market Definition and Market Share Calculation Issues

1. Commission Notice on definition of the relevant market

(88) The Commission Notice on definition of the relevant market for the purposes of Community competition law[26] provides guidance on the rules, criteria and evidence which the Commission uses when considering market definition issues. That Notice will not be further explained in these Guidelines and should serve as the basis for market definition issues. These Guidelines will only deal with specific issues that arise in the context of vertical restraints and that are not dealt with in the general notice on market definition.

2. The relevant market for calculating the 30% market share threshold under the Block Exemption Regulation

(89) Under Article 3 of the Block Exemption Regulation, it is in general the market share of the supplier that is decisive for the application of the block exemption. In the case of vertical agreements concluded between an association of retailers and individual members, the association is the supplier and needs to take into account its market share as a supplier. Only in the case of exclusive supply as defined in Article 1(c) of the Block Exemption Regulation is it the market share of the buyer, and only that market share, which is decisive for the application of the Block Exemption Regulation.

(90) In order to calculate the market share, it is necessary to determine the relevant market. For this, the relevant product market and the relevant geographic market must be defined. The relevant product market comprises any goods or services which are regarded by the buyer as interchangeable, by reason of their characteristics, prices and intended use. The relevant geographic market comprises the area in which the undertakings concerned are involved in the supply and demand of relevant goods or services, in which the conditions of competition are sufficiently homogeneous, and which can be distinguished from neighbouring geographic areas because, in particular, conditions of competition are appreciably different in those areas.

(91) For the application of the Block Exemption Regulation, the market share of the supplier is his share on the relevant product and geographic market on which he sells to his buyers.[27] In the example given in paragraph 92, this is market A. The product market depends in the first place on substitutability from the buyers' perspective. When the supplied product is used as an input to produce other products and is generally not recognisable in the final product, the product market is normally defined by the direct buyers' preferences. The customers of the buyers will normally not have a strong preference concerning the inputs used by the buyers. Usually the vertical restraints agreed between the supplier and buyer of the input only relate to the sale and purchase of the intermediate product and not to the sale of the resulting product. In the case of distribution of final goods, what are substitutes for the direct buyers will normally be influenced or determined by the preferences of the final consumers. A distributor, as reseller, cannot ignore the preferences of final consumers when he purchases final goods. In addition, at the distribution level the vertical restraints usually concern not only the sale of products between supplier and buyer, but also their resale. As different distribution formats usually compete, markets are in general not defined by the

---

[26] OJ C 372, 9.12.1997, p. 5.

[27] For example, the Dutch market for new replacement truck and bus tyres in the *Michelin* case (Case 322/81 *Nederlandsche Banden-Industrie Michelin v Commission* [1983] ECR 3461), the various meat markets in the Danish slaughter-house case: Commission Decision 2000/42/EC in Case No IV/M.1313—*Danish Crown/Vestjyske Slagterier*, OJ L 20, 25.1.2000, p. 1.

form of distribution that is applied. Where suppliers generally sell a portfolio of products, the entire portfolio may determine the product market when the portfolios and not the individual products are regarded as substitutes by the buyers. As the buyers on market A are professional buyers, the geographic market is usually wider than the market where the product is resold to final consumers. Often, this will lead to the definition of national markets or wider geographic markets.

(92) In the case of exclusive supply, the buyer's market share is his share of all purchases on the relevant purchase market.[28] In the example below, this is also market A.

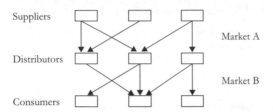

(93) Where a vertical agreement involves three parties, each operating at a different level of trade, their market shares will have to be below the market share threshold of 30% at both levels in order to benefit from the block exemption. If for instance, in an agreement between a manufacturer, a wholesaler (or association of retailers) and a retailer, a non-compete obligation is agreed, then the market share of both the manufacturer and the wholesaler (or association of retailers) must not exceed 30% in order to benefit from the block exemption.

(94) Where a supplier produces both original equipment and the repair or replacement parts for this equipment, the supplier will often be the only or the major supplier on the after-market for the repair and replacement parts. This may also arise where the supplier (OEM supplier) subcontracts the manufacturing of the repair or replacement parts. The relevant market for application of the Block Exemption Regulation may be the original equipment market including the spare parts or a separate original equipment market and after-market depending on the circumstances of the case, such as the effects of the restrictions involved, the lifetime of the equipment and importance of the repair or replacement costs.[29]

(95) Where the vertical agreement, in addition to the supply of the contract goods, also contains IPR provisions—such as a provision concerning the use of the supplier's trademark—which help the buyer to market the contract goods, the supplier's market share on the market where he sells the contract goods is decisive for the application of the Block Exemption Regulation. Where a franchisor does not supply goods to be resold but provides a bundle of services combined with IPR provisions which together form the business method being franchised, the franchisor needs to take account of his market share as a provider of a business method. For that purpose, the franchisor needs to calculate his market share on the market where the business method is exploited, which is the market where the franchisees exploit the business method to provide goods or services to end users. The franchisor must base his market share on the value of the goods or

---

[28] For an example of purchase markets, see Commission Decision 1999/674/EC in Case No IV/M.1221—*Rewe/Meinl*, OJ L 274, 23.10.1999, p. 1.

[29] See for example *Pelikan/Kyocera* in XXV Report on Competition Policy, point 87, and Commission Decision 91/595/EEC in Case No IV/M.12—*Varta/Bosch*, OJ L 320, 22.11.1991, p. 26, Commission Decision in Case No IV/M.1094—*Caterpillar/Perkins Engines*, OJ C 94, 28.3.1998, p. 23, and Commission Decision in Case No IV/M.768—*Lucas/Varity*, OJ C 266, 13.9.1996, p. 6. See also *Eastman Kodak Co v Image Technical Services, Inc et al*, Supreme Court of the United States, No 90 1029. See also point 56 of the Commission Notice on the definition of relevant market for the purposes of Community competition law.

services supplied by his franchisees on this market. On such a market the competitors may be providers of other franchised business methods but also suppliers of substitutable goods or services not applying franchising. For instance, without prejudice to the definition of such market, if there was a market for fast-food services, a franchisor operating on such a market would need to calculate his market share on the basis of the relevant sales figures of his franchisees on this market. If the franchisor, in addition to the business method, also supplies certain inputs, such as meat and spices, then the franchisor also needs to calculate his market share on the market where these goods are sold.

3. The relevant market for individual assessment

(96) For individual assessment of vertical agreements not covered by the Block Exemption Regulation, additional markets may need to be investigated besides the relevant market defined for the application of the Block Exemption Regulation. A vertical agreement may not only have effects on the market between supplier and buyer but may also have effects on downstream markets. For an individual assessment of a vertical agreement the relevant markets at each level of trade affected by restraints contained in the agreement will be examined:

(i) For 'intermediate goods or services' that are incorporated by the buyer into his own goods or services, vertical restraints generally have effects only on the market between supplier and buyer. A non-compete obligation imposed on the buyer for instance may foreclose other suppliers but will not lead to reduced in-store competition downstream. However, in cases of exclusive supply the position of the buyer on his downstream market is also relevant because the buyer's foreclosing behaviour may only have appreciable negative effects if he has market power on the downstream market.

(ii) For 'final products' an analysis limited to the market between supplier and buyer is less likely to be sufficient since vertical restraints may have negative effects of reduced inter-brand and/or intra-brand competition on the resale market, that is on the market downstream of the buyer. For instance, exclusive distribution may not only lead to foreclosure effects on the market between the supplier and the buyer, but may above all lead to less intra-brand competition in the resale territories of the distributors. The resale market is in particular important if the buyer is a retailer selling to final consumers. A non-compete obligation agreed between a manufacturer and a wholesaler may foreclose this wholesaler to other manufacturers but a loss of in-store competition is not very likely at the wholesale level. The same agreement concluded with a retailer may however cause this added loss of in-store inter-brand competition on the resale market.

(iii) In cases of individual assessment of an 'after-market', the relevant market may be the original equipment market or the after-market depending on the circumstances of the case. In any event, the situation on a separate after-market will be evaluated taking account of the situation on the original equipment market. A less significant position on the original equipment market will normally reduce possible anti-competitive effects on the after-market.

4. Calculation of the market share under the Block Exemption Regulation

(97) The calculation of the market share needs to be based in principle on value figures. Where value figures are not available substantiated estimates can be made. Such estimates may be based on other reliable market information such as volume figures (see Article 9(1) of the Block Exemption Regulation).

(98) In-house production, that is production of an intermediate product for own use, may be very important in a competition analysis as one of the competitive constraints or to accentuate the market position of a company. However, for the purpose of market definition and the calculation of market share for intermediate goods and services, in-house production will not be taken into account.

(99) However, in the case of dual distribution of final goods, i.e. where a producer of final goods also acts as a distributor on the market, the market definition and market share calculation need to include the goods sold by the producer and competing producers through their integrated distributors and agents (see Article 9(2)(b) of the Block Exemption Regulation). 'Integrated distributors' are connected undertakings within the meaning of Article 11 of the Block Exemption Regulation.

VI. Enforcement Policy in Individual Cases

(100) Vertical restraints are generally less harmful than horizontal restraints. The main reason for treating a vertical restraint more leniently than a horizontal restraint lies in the fact that the latter may concern an agreement between competitors producing identical or substitutable goods or services. In such horizontal relationships the exercise of market power by one company (higher price of its product) may benefit its competitors. This may provide an incentive to competitors to induce each other to behave anti-competitively. In vertical relationships the product of the one is the input for the other. This means that the exercise of market power by either the upstream or downstream company would normally hurt the demand for the product of the other. The companies involved in the agreement therefore usually have an incentive to prevent the exercise of market power by the other.

(101) However, this self-restraining character should not be over-estimated. When a company has no market power it can only try to increase its profits by optimising its manufacturing and distribution processes, with or without the help of vertical restraints. However, when it does have market power it can also try to increase its profits at the expense of its direct competitors by raising their costs and at the expense of its buyers and ultimately consumers by trying to appropriate some of their surplus. This can happen when the upstream and downstream company share the extra profits or when one of the two uses vertical restraints to appropriate all the extra profits.

(102) In the assessment of individual cases, the Commission will adopt an economic approach in the application of Article 81 to vertical restraints. This will limit the scope of application of Article 81 to undertakings holding a certain degree of market power where inter-brand competition may be insufficient. In those cases, the protection of inter-brand and intra-brand competition is important to ensure efficiencies and benefits for consumers.

1. The framework of analysis

1.1. Negative effects of vertical restraints

(103) The negative effects on the market that may result from vertical restraints which EC competition law aims at preventing are the following:

  (i)   foreclosure of other suppliers or other buyers by raising barriers to entry;
  (ii) reduction of inter-brand competition between the companies operating on a market, including facilitation of collusion amongst suppliers or buyers; by collusion is meant both explicit collusion and tacit collusion (conscious parallel behaviour);
  (iii) reduction of intra-brand competition between distributors of the same brand;
  (iv) the creation of obstacles to market integration, including, above all, limitations on the freedom of consumers to purchase goods or services in any Member State they may choose.

(104) Such negative effects may result from various vertical restraints. Agreements which are different in form may have the same substantive impact on competition. To analyse these possible negative effects, it is appropriate to divide vertical restraints into four groups: a single branding group, a limited distribution group, a resale price maintenance group and a market partitioning group. The vertical restraints within each group have largely similar negative effects on competition.

(105) The classification into four groups is based upon what can be described as the basic components of vertical restraints. In paragraphs 103 to 136, the four different groups are

analysed. In 137 to 229, vertical agreements are analysed as they are used in practice because many vertical agreements make use of more than one of these components.

Single branding group

(106) Under the heading of 'single branding' come those agreements which have as their main element that the buyer is induced to concentrate his orders for a particular type of product with one supplier. This component can be found amongst others in non-compete and quantity-forcing on the buyer, where an obligation or incentive scheme agreed between the supplier and the buyer makes the latter purchase his requirements for a particular product and its substitutes only, or mainly, from one supplier. The same component can be found in tying, where the obligation or incentive scheme relates to a product that the buyer is required to purchase as a condition of purchasing another distinct product. The first product is referred to as the 'tied' product and the second is referred to as the 'tying' product.

(107) There are four main negative effects on competition: (1) other suppliers in that market cannot sell to the particular buyers and this may lead to foreclosure of the market or, in the case of tying, to foreclosure of the market for the tied product; (2) it makes market shares more rigid and this may help collusion when applied by several suppliers; (3) as far as the distribution of final goods is concerned, the particular retailers will only sell one brand and there will therefore be no inter-brand competition in their shops (no in-store competition); and (4) in the case of tying, the buyer may pay a higher price for the tied product than he would otherwise do. All these effects may lead to a reduction in inter-brand competition.

(108) The reduction in inter-brand competition may be mitigated by strong initial competition between suppliers to obtain the single branding contracts, but the longer the duration of the non-compete obligation, the more likely it will be that this effect will not be strong enough to compensate for the reduction in inter-brand competition.

Limited distribution group

(109) Under the heading of 'limited distribution' come those agreements which have as their main element that the manufacturer sells to only one or a limited number of buyers. This may be to restrict the number of buyers for a particular territory or group of customers, or to select a particular kind of buyers. This component can be found amongst others in:

— exclusive distribution and exclusive customer allocation, where the supplier limits his sales to only one buyer for a certain territory or class of customers;
— exclusive supply and quantity-forcing on the supplier, where an obligation or incentive scheme agreed between the supplier and the buyer makes the former sell only or mainly to one buyer;
— selective distribution, where the conditions imposed on or agreed with the selected dealers usually limit their number;
— after-market sales restrictions which limit the component supplier's sales possibilities.

(110) There are three main negative effects on competition: (1) certain buyers within that market can no longer buy from that particular supplier, and this may lead in particular in the case of exclusive supply, to foreclosure of the purchase market, (2) when most or all of the competing suppliers limit the number of retailers, this may facilitate collusion, either at the distributor's level or at the supplier's level, and (3) since fewer distributors will offer the product it will also lead to a reduction of intra-brand competition. In the case of wide exclusive territories or exclusive customer allocation the result may be total elimination of intra-brand competition. This reduction of intra-brand competition can in turn lead to a weakening of inter-brand competition.

Resale price maintenance group

(111) Under the heading of 'resale price maintenance' (RPM) come those agreements whose main element is that the buyer is obliged or induced to resell not below a certain price, at a certain price or not above a certain price. This group comprises minimum, fixed, maximum and

recommended resale prices. Maximum and recommended resale prices, which are not hardcore restrictions, may still lead to a restriction of competition by effect.

(112) There are two main negative effects of RPM on competition: (1) a reduction in intra-brand price competition, and (2) increased transparency on prices. In the case of fixed or minimum RPM, distributors can no longer compete on price for that brand, leading to a total elimination of intra-brand price competition. A maximum or recommended price may work as a focal point for resellers, leading to a more or less uniform application of that price level. Increased transparency on price and responsibility for price changes makes horizontal collusion between manufacturers or distributors easier, at least in concentrated markets. The reduction in intra-brand competition may, as it leads to less downward pressure on the price for the particular goods, have as an indirect effect a reduction of inter-brand competition.

Market partitioning group

(113) Under the heading of 'market partitioning' come agreements whose main element is that the buyer is restricted in where he either sources or resells a particular product. This component can be found in exclusive purchasing, where an obligation or incentive scheme agreed between the supplier and the buyer makes the latter purchase his requirements for a particular product, for instance beer of brand X, exclusively from the designated supplier, but leaving the buyer free to buy and sell competing products, for instance competing brands of beer. It also includes territorial resale restrictions, the allocation of an area of primary responsibility, restrictions on the location of a distributor and customer resale restrictions.

(114) The main negative effect on competition is a reduction of intra-brand competition that may help the supplier to partition the market and thus hinder market integration. This may facilitate price discrimination. When most or all of the competing suppliers limit the sourcing or resale possibilities of their buyers this may facilitate collusion, either at the distributors' level or at the suppliers' level.

1.2. Positive effects of vertical restraints

(115) It is important to recognise that vertical restraints often have positive effects by, in particular, promoting non-price competition and improved quality of services. When a company has no market power, it can only try to increase its profits by optimising its manufacturing or distribution processes. In a number of situations vertical restraints may be helpful in this respect since the usual arm's length dealings between supplier and buyer, determining only price and quantity of a certain transaction, can lead to a sub-optimal level of investments and sales.

(116) While trying to give a fair overview of the various justifications for vertical restraints, these Guidelines do not claim to be complete or exhaustive. The following reasons may justify the application of certain vertical restraints:

(1) To 'solve a "free-rider" problem'. One distributor may free-ride on the promotion efforts of another distributor. This type of problem is most common at the wholesale and retail level. Exclusive distribution or similar restrictions may be helpful in avoiding such free-riding. Free-riding can also occur between suppliers, for instance where one invests in promotion at the buyer's premises, in general at the retail level, that may also attract customers for its competitors. Non-compete type restraints can help to overcome this situation of free-riding.

For there to be a problem, there needs to be a real free-rider issue. Free-riding between buyers can only occur on pre-sales services and not on after-sales services. The product will usually need to be relatively new or technically complex as the customer may otherwise very well know what he or she wants, based on past purchases. And the product must be of a reasonably high value as it is otherwise not attractive for a customer to go to one shop for information and to another to buy. Lastly, it must not be practical for the supplier to impose on all buyers, by contract, effective service requirements concerning pre-sales services.

Free-riding between suppliers is also restricted to specific situations, namely in cases where the promotion takes place at the buyer's premises and is generic, not brand specific.

(2) To 'open up or enter new markets'. Where a manufacturer wants to enter a new geographic market, for instance by exporting to another country for the first time, this may involve special 'first time investments' by the distributor to establish the brand in the market. In order to persuade a local distributor to make these investments it may be necessary to provide territorial protection to the distributor so that he can recoup these investments by temporarily charging a higher price. Distributors based in other markets should then be restrained for a limited period from selling in the new market. This is a special case of the free-rider problem described under point (1).

(3) The 'certification free-rider issue'. In some sectors, certain retailers have a reputation for stocking only 'quality' products. In such a case, selling through these retailers may be vital for the introduction of a new product. If the manufacturer cannot initially limit his sales to the premium stores, he runs the risk of being de-listed and the product introduction may fail. This means that there may be a reason for allowing for a limited duration a restriction such as exclusive distribution or selective distribution. It must be enough to guarantee introduction of the new product but not so long as to hinder large-scale dissemination. Such benefits are more likely with 'experience' goods or complex goods that represent a relatively large purchase for the final consumer.

(4) The so-called 'hold-up problem'. Sometimes there are client-specific investments to be made by either the supplier or the buyer, such as in special equipment or training. For instance, a component manufacturer that has to build new machines and tools in order to satisfy a particular requirement of one of his customers. The investor may not commit the necessary investments before particular supply arrangements are fixed.

However, as in the other free-riding examples, there are a number of conditions that have to be met before the risk of under-investment is real or significant. Firstly, the investment must be relationship-specific. An investment made by the supplier is considered to be relationship-specific when, after termination of the contract, it cannot be used by the supplier to supply other customers and can only be sold at a significant loss. An investment made by the buyer is considered to be relationship-specific when, after termination of the contract, it cannot be used by the buyer to purchase and/or use products supplied by other suppliers and can only be sold at a significant loss. An investment is thus relationship-specific because for instance it can only be used to produce a brand-specific component or to store a particular brand and thus cannot be used profitably to produce or resell alternatives. Secondly, it must be a long-term investment that is not recouped in the short run. And thirdly, the investment must be asymmetric; i.e. one party to the contract invests more than the other party. When these conditions are met, there is usually a good reason to have a vertical restraint for the duration it takes to depreciate the investment. The appropriate vertical restraint will be of the non-compete type or quantity-forcing type when the investment is made by the supplier and of the exclusive distribution, exclusive customer allocation or exclusive supply type when the investment is made by the buyer.

(5) The 'specific hold-up problem that may arise in the case of transfer of substantial know-how'. The know-how, once provided, cannot be taken back and the provider of the know-how may not want it to be used for or by his competitors. In as far as the know-how was not readily available to the buyer, is substantial and indispensable for the operation of the agreement, such a transfer may justify a non-compete type of restriction. This would nor- mally fall outside Article 81(1).

(6) 'Economies of scale in distribution'. In order to have scale economies exploited and thereby see a lower retail price for his product, the manufacturer may want to concentrate the resale of his products on a limited number of distributors. For this he could use exclusive distribution,

quantity forcing in the form of a minimum purchasing requirement, selective distribution containing such a requirement or exclusive purchasing.

(7) 'Capital market imperfections'. The usual providers of capital (banks, equity markets) may provide capital sub-optimally when they have imperfect information on the quality of the borrower or there is an inadequate basis to secure the loan. The buyer or supplier may have better information and be able, through an exclusive relationship, to obtain extra security for his investment. Where the supplier provides the loan to the buyer this may lead to non-compete or quantity forcing on the buyer. Where the buyer provides the loan to the supplier this may be the reason for having exclusive supply or quantity forcing on the supplier.

(8) 'Uniformity and quality standardisation'. A vertical restraint may help to increase sales by creating a brand image and thereby increasing the attractiveness of a product to the final consumer by imposing a certain measure of uniformity and quality standardisation on the distributors. This can for instance be found in selective distribution and franchising.

(117) The eight situations mentioned in paragraph 116 make clear that under certain conditions vertical agreements are likely to help realise efficiencies and the development of new markets and that this may offset possible negative effects. The case is in general strongest for vertical restraints of a limited duration which help the introduction of new complex products or protect relationship-specific investments. A vertical restraint is sometimes necessary for as long as the supplier sells his product to the buyer (see in particular the situations described in paragraph 116, points (1), (5), (6) and (8)).

(118) There is a large measure of substitutability between the different vertical restraints. This means that the same inefficiency problem can be solved by different vertical restraints. For instance, economies of scale in distribution may possibly be achieved by using exclusive distribution, selective distribution, quantity forcing or exclusive purchasing. This is important as the negative effects on competition may differ between the various vertical restraints. This plays a role when indispensability is discussed under Article 81(3).

1.3. General rules for the evaluation of vertical restraints

(119) In evaluating vertical restraints from a competition policy perspective, some general rules can be formulated:

(1) For most vertical restraints competition concerns can only arise if there is insufficient inter-brand competition, i.e. if there exists a certain degree of market power at the level of the supplier or the buyer or both. Conceptually, market power is the power to raise price above the competitive level and, at least in the short term, to obtain supra-normal profits. Companies may have market power below the level of market dominance, which is the threshold for the application of Article 82. Where there are many firms competing in an unconcentrated market, it can be assumed that non-hardcore vertical restraints will not have appreciable negative effects. A market is deemed unconcentrated when the HHI index, i.e. the sum of the squares of the individual market shares of all companies in the relevant market, is below 1000.

(2) Vertical restraints which reduce inter-brand competition are generally more harmful than vertical restraints that reduce intra-brand competition. For instance, non-compete obligations are likely to have more net negative effects than exclusive distribution. The former, by possibly foreclosing the market to other brands, may prevent those brands from reaching the market. The latter, while limiting intra-brand competition, does not prevent goods from reaching the final consumer.

(3) Vertical restraints from the limited distribution group, in the absence of sufficient inter-brand competition, may significantly restrict the choices available to consumers. They are particularly harmful when more efficient distributors or distributors with a different distribution format are foreclosed. This can reduce innovation in distribution and denies consumers the particular service or price-service combination of these distributors.

(4)   Exclusive dealing arrangements are generally worse for competition than non-exclusive arrangements. Exclusive dealing makes, by the express language of the contract or its practical effects, one party fulfil all or practically all its requirements from another party. For instance, under a non-compete obligation the buyer purchases only one brand. Quantity forcing, on the other hand, leaves the buyer some scope to purchase competing goods. The degree of foreclosure may therefore be less with quantity forcing.

(5)   Vertical restraints agreed for non-branded goods and services are in general less harmful than restraints affecting the distribution of branded goods and services. Branding tends to increase product differentiation and reduce substitutability of the product, leading to a reduced elasticity of demand and an increased possibility to raise price. The distinction between branded and non-branded goods or services will often coincide with the distinction between intermediate goods and services and final goods and services.

Intermediate goods and services are sold to undertakings for use as an input to produce other goods or services and are generally not recognisable in the final goods or services. The buyers of intermediate products are usually well-informed customers, able to assess quality and therefore less reliant on brand and image. Final goods are, directly or indirectly, sold to final consumers who often rely more on brand and image. As distributors (retailers, wholesalers) have to respond to the demand of final consumers, competition may suffer more when distributors are foreclosed from selling one or a number of brands than when buyers of intermediate products are prevented from buying competing products from certain sources of supply.

The undertakings buying intermediate goods or services normally have specialist departments or advisers who monitor developments in the supply market. Because they effect sizeable transactions, search costs are in general not prohibitive. A loss of intra-brand competition is therefore less important at the intermediate level.

(6)   In general, a combination of vertical restraints aggravates their negative effects. However, certain combinations of vertical restraints are better for competition than their use in isolation from each other. For instance, in an exclusive distribution system, the distributor may be tempted to increase the price of the products as intra-brand competition has been reduced. The use of quantity forcing or the setting of a maximum resale price may limit such price increases.

(7)   Possible negative effects of vertical restraints are reinforced when several suppliers and their buyers organise their trade in a similar way. These so-called cumulative effects may be a problem in a number of sectors.

(8)   The more the vertical restraint is linked to the transfer of know-how, the more reason there may be to expect efficiencies to arise and the more a vertical restraint may be necessary to protect the know-how transferred or the investment costs incurred.

(9)   The more the vertical restraint is linked to investments which are relationship-specific, the more justification there is for certain vertical restraints. The justified duration will depend on the time necessary to depreciate the investment.

(10) In the case of a new product, or where an existing product is sold for the first time on a different geographic market, it may be difficult for the company to define the market or its market share may be very high. However, this should not be considered a major problem, as vertical restraints linked to opening up new product or geographic markets in general do not restrict competition. This rule holds, irrespective of the market share of the company, for two years after the first putting on the market of the product. It applies to all non-hardcore vertical restraints and, in the case of a new geographic market, to restrictions on active and passive sales imposed on the direct buyers of the supplier located in other markets to intermediaries in the new market. In the case of genuine testing of a new product in a limited territory or with a limited customer group, the distributors appointed to sell the new product on the test market

can be restricted in their active selling outside the test market for a maximum period of 1 year without being caught by Article 81(1).

1.4. Methodology of analysis

(120) The assessment of a vertical restraint involves in general the following four steps:

(1) First, the undertakings involved need to define the relevant market in order to establish the market share of the supplier or the buyer, depending on the vertical restraint involved (see paragraphs 88 to 99, in particular 89 to 95).

(2) If the relevant market share does not exceed the 30% threshold, the vertical agreement is covered by the Block Exemption Regulation, subject to the hardcore restrictions and conditions set out in that regulation.

(3) If the relevant market share is above the 30% threshold, it is necessary to assess whether the vertical agreement falls within Article 81(1).

(4) If the vertical agreement falls within Article 81(1), it is necessary to examine whether it fulfils the conditions for exemption under Article 81(3).

1.4.1. Relevant factors for the assessment under Article 81(1)

(121) In assessing cases above the market share threshold of 30%, the Commission will make a full competition analysis. The following factors are the most important to establish whether a vertical agreement brings about an appreciable restriction of competition under Article 81(1):

(a) market position of the supplier;
(b) market position of competitors;
(c) market position of the buyer;
(d) entry barriers;
(e) maturity of the market;
(f) level of trade;
(g) nature of the product;
(h) other factors.

(122) The importance of individual factors may vary from case to case and depends on all other factors. For instance, a high market share of the supplier is usually a good indicator of market power, but in the case of low entry barriers it may not indicate market power. It is therefore not possible to provide strict rules on the importance of the individual factors. However the following can be said:

Market position of the supplier

(123) The market position of the supplier is established first and foremost by his market share on the relevant product and geographic market. The higher his market share, the greater his market power is likely to be. The market position of the supplier is further strengthened if he has certain cost advantages over his competitors. These competitive advantages may result from a first mover advantage (having the best site, etc.), holding essential patents, having superior technology, being the brand leader or having a superior portfolio.

Market position of competitors

(124) The same indicators, that is market share and possible competitive advantages, are used to describe the market position of competitors. The stronger the established competitors are and the greater their number, the less risk there is that the supplier or buyer in question will be able to foreclose the market individually and the less there is a risk of a reduction of inter-brand competition. However, if the number of competitors becomes rather small and their market position (size, costs, R&D potential, etc.) is rather similar, this market structure may increase the risk of collusion. Fluctuating or rapidly changing market shares are in general an indication of intense competition.

Market position of the buyer

(125) Buying power derives from the market position of the buyer. The first indicator of buying power is the market share of the buyer on the purchase market. This share reflects the importance

of his demand for his possible suppliers. Other indicators focus on the market position of the buyer on his resale market including characteristics such as a wide geographic spread of his outlets, own brands of the buyer/distributor and his image amongst final consumers. The effect of buying power on the likelihood of anti-competitive effects is not the same for the different vertical restraints. Buying power may in particular increase the negative effects in case of restraints from the limited distribution and market partitioning groups such as exclusive supply, exclusive distribution and quantitative selective distribution.

Entry barriers

(126) Entry barriers are measured by the extent to which incumbent companies can increase their price above the competitive level, usually above minimum average total cost, and make supra-normal profits without attracting entry. Without any entry barriers, easy and quick entry would eliminate such profits. In as far as effective entry, which would prevent or erode the supra-normal profits, is likely to occur within one or two years, entry barriers can be said to be low.

(127) Entry barriers may result from a wide variety of factors such as economies of scale and scope, government regulations, especially where they establish exclusive rights, state aid, import tariffs, intellectual property rights, ownership of resources where the supply is limited due to for instance natural limitations,[30] essential facilities, a first mover advantage and brand loyalty of consumers created by strong advertising. Vertical restraints and vertical integration may also work as an entry barrier by making access more difficult and foreclosing (potential) competitors. Entry barriers may be present at only the supplier or buyer level or at both levels.

(128) The question whether certain of these factors should be described as entry barriers depends on whether they are related to sunk costs. Sunk costs are those costs that have to be incurred to enter or be active on a market but that are lost when the market is exited. Advertising costs to build consumer loyalty are normally sunk costs, unless an exiting firm could either sell its brand name or use it somewhere else without a loss. The more costs are sunk, the more potential entrants have to weigh the risks of entering the market and the more credibly incumbents can threaten that they will match new competition, as sunk costs make it costly for incumbents to leave the market. If, for instance, distributors are tied to a manufacturer via a non-compete obligation, the foreclosing effect will be more significant if setting up its own distributors will impose sunk costs on the potential entrant.

(129) In general, entry requires sunk costs, sometimes minor and sometimes major. Therefore, actual competition is in general more effective and will weigh more in the assessment of a case than potential competition.

Maturity of the market

(130) A mature market is a market that has existed for some time, where the technology used is well known and widespread and not changing very much, where there are no major brand innovations and in which demand is relatively stable or declining. In such a market negative effects are more likely than in more dynamic markets.

Level of trade

(131) The level of trade is linked to the distinction between intermediate and final goods and services. As indicated earlier, negative effects are in general less likely at the level of intermediate goods and services.

Nature of the product

(132) The nature of the product plays a role in particular for final products in assessing both the likely negative and the likely positive effects. When assessing the likely negative effects, it is

---

[30] See Commission Decision 97/26/EC (Case No IV/M.619—*Gencor/Lonrho*), (OJ L 11, 14.1.1997, p. 30).

important whether the products on the market are more homogeneous or heterogeneous, whether the product is expensive, taking up a large part of the consumer's budget, or is inexpensive and whether the product is a one-off purchase or repeatedly purchased. In general, when the product is more heterogeneous, less expensive and resembles more a one-off purchase, vertical restraints are more likely to have negative effects.

Other factors

(133) In the assessment of particular restraints other factors may have to be taken into account. Among these factors can be the cumulative effect, i.e. the coverage of the market by similar agreements, the duration of the agreements, whether the agreement is 'imposed' (mainly one party is subject to the restrictions or obligations) or 'agreed' (both parties accept restrictions or obligations), the regulatory environment and behaviour that may indicate or facilitate collusion like price leadership, pre-announced price changes and discussions on the 'right' price, price rigidity in response to excess capacity, price discrimination and past collusive behaviour.

1.4.2. Relevant factors for the assessment under Article 81(3)

(134) There are four cumulative conditions for the application of Article 81(3):

— the vertical agreement must contribute to improving production or distribution or to promoting technical or economic progress;
— the vertical agreement must allow consumers a fair share of these benefits;
— the vertical agreement must not impose on the undertakings concerned vertical restraints which are not indispensable to the attainment of these benefits;
  the vertical agreement must not afford such undertakings the possibility of eliminating competition in respect of a substantial part of the products in question.

(135) The last criterion of elimination of competition for a substantial part of the products in question is related to the question of dominance. Where an undertaking is dominant or becoming dominant as a consequence of the vertical agreement, a vertical restraint that has appreciable anticompetitive effects can in principle not be exempted. The vertical agreement may however fall outside Article 81(1) if there is an objective justification, for instance if it is necessary for the protection of relationship-specific investments or for the transfer of substantial know-how without which the supply or purchase of certain goods or services would not take place.

(136) Where the supplier and the buyer are not dominant, the other three criteria become important. The first, concerning the improvement of production or distribution and the promotion of technical or economic progress, refers to the type of efficiencies described in paragraphs 115 to 118. These efficiencies have to be substantiated and must produce a net positive effect. Speculative claims on avoidance of free-riding or general statements on cost savings will not be accepted. Cost savings that arise from the mere exercise of market power or from anti-competitive conduct cannot be accepted. Secondly, economic benefits have to favour not only the parties to the agreement, but also the consumer. Generally the transmission of the benefits to consumers will depend on the intensity of competition on the relevant market. Competitive pressures will normally ensure that cost-savings are passed on by way of lower prices or that companies have an incentive to bring new products to the market as quickly as possible. Therefore, if sufficient competition which effectively constrains the parties to the agreement is maintained on the market, the competitive process will normally ensure that consumers receive a fair share of the economic benefits. The third criterion will play a role in ensuring that the least anti-competitive restraint is chosen to obtain certain positive effects.

2. Analysis of specific vertical restraints

(137) Vertical agreements may contain a combination of two or more of the components of vertical restraints described in paragraphs 103 to 114. The most common vertical restraints and

combinations of vertical restraints are analysed below following the methodology of analysis developed in paragraphs 120 to 136.

2.1. Single branding

(138) A non-compete arrangement is based on an obligation or incentive scheme which makes the buyer purchase practically all his requirements on a particular market from only one supplier. It does not mean that the buyer can only buy directly from the supplier, but that the buyer will not buy and resell or incorporate competing goods or services. The possible competition risks are foreclosure of the market to competing suppliers and potential suppliers, facilitation of collusion between suppliers in case of cumulative use and, where the buyer is a retailer selling to final consumers, a loss of in-store inter-brand competition. All three restrictive effects have a direct impact on inter-brand competition.

(139) Single branding is exempted by the Block Exemption Regulation when the supplier's market share does not exceed 30% and subject to a limitation in time of five years for the non-compete obligation. Above the market share threshold or beyond the time limit of five years, the following guidance is provided for the assessment of individual cases.

(140) The 'market position of the supplier' is of main importance to assess possible anti-competitive effects of non-compete obligations. In general, this type of obligation is imposed by the supplier and the supplier has similar agreements with other buyers.

(141) It is not only the market position of the supplier that is of importance but also the extent to and the duration for which he applies a non-compete obligation. The higher his tied market share, i.e. the part of his market share sold under a single branding obligation, the more significant foreclosure is likely to be. Similarly, the longer the duration of the non-compete obligations, the more significant foreclosure is likely to be. Non-compete obligations shorter than one year entered into by non-dominant companies are in general not considered to give rise to appreciable anti-competitive effects or net negative effects. Non-compete obligations between one and five years entered into by non-dominant companies usually require a proper balancing of pro- and anti-competitive effects, while non-compete obligations exceeding five years are for most types of investments not considered necessary to achieve the claimed efficiencies or the efficiencies are not sufficient to outweigh their foreclosure effect. Dominant companies may not impose non-compete obligations on their buyers unless they can objectively justify such commercial practice within the context of Article 82.

(142) In assessing the supplier's market power, the 'market position of his competitors' is important. As long as the competitors are sufficiently numerous and strong, no appreciable anti-competitive effects can be expected. It is only likely that competing suppliers will be foreclosed if they are significantly smaller than the supplier applying the non-compete obligation. Foreclosure of competitors is not very likely where they have similar market positions and can offer similarly attractive products. In such a case foreclosure may however occur for potential entrants when a number of major suppliers enter into non-compete contracts with a significant number of buyers on the relevant market (cumulative effect situation). This is also a situation where non-compete agreements may facilitate collusion between competing suppliers. If individually these suppliers are covered by the Block Exemption Regulation, a withdrawal of the block exemption may be necessary to deal with such a negative cumulative effect. A tied market share of less than 5% is not considered in general to contribute significantly to a cumulative foreclosure effect.

(143) In cases where the market share of the largest supplier is below 30% and the market share of the five largest suppliers (concentration rate (CR) 5) is below 50%, there is unlikely to be a single or a cumulative anti-competitive effect situation. If a potential entrant cannot penetrate the market profitably, this is likely to be due to factors other than non-compete obligations, such as consumer preferences. A competition problem is unlikely to arise when, for instance, 50 companies, of which none has an important market share, compete fiercely on a particular market.

(144) 'Entry barriers' are important to establish whether there is real foreclosure. Wherever it is relatively easy for competing suppliers to create new buyers or find alternative buyers for the product, foreclosure is unlikely to be a real problem. However, there are often entry barriers, both at the manufacturing and at the distribution level.

(145) 'Countervailing power' is relevant, as powerful buyers will not easily allow themselves to be cut off from the supply of competing goods or services. Foreclosure which is not based on efficiency and which has harmful effects on ultimate consumers is therefore mainly a risk in the case of dispersed buyers. However, where non-compete agreements are concluded with major buyers this may have a strong foreclosure effect.

(146) Lastly, 'the level of trade' is relevant for foreclosure. Foreclosure is less likely in case of an intermediate product. When the supplier of an intermediate product is not dominant, the competing suppliers still have a substantial part of demand that is 'free'. Below the level of dominance a serious foreclosure effect may however arise for actual or potential competitors where there is a cumulative effect. A serious cumulative effect is unlikely to arise as long as less than 50% of the market is tied. When the supplier is dominant, any obligation to buy the products only or mainly from the dominant supplier may easily lead to significant foreclosure effects on the market. The stronger his dominance, the higher the risk of foreclosure of other competitors.

(147) Where the agreement concerns supply of a final product at the wholesale level, the question whether a competition problem is likely to arise below the level of dominance depends in large part on the type of wholesaling and the entry barriers at the wholesale level. There is no real risk of foreclosure if competing manufacturers can easily establish their own wholesaling operation. Whether entry barriers are low depends in part on the type of wholesaling, i.e. whether or not wholesalers can operate efficiently with only the product concerned by the agreement (for example ice cream) or whether it is more efficient to trade in a whole range of products (for example frozen foodstuffs). In the latter case, it is not efficient for a manufacturer selling only one product to set up his own wholesaling operation. In that case anti-competitive effects may arise below the level of dominance. In addition, cumulative effect problems may arise if several suppliers tie most of the available wholesalers.

(148) For final products, foreclosure is in general more likely to occur at the retail level, given the significant entry barriers for most manufacturers to start retail outlets just for their own products. In addition, it is at the retail level that non-compete agreements may lead to reduced in-store inter-brand competition. It is for these reasons that for final products at the retail level, significant anti-competitive effects may start to arise, taking into account all other relevant factors, if a non-dominant supplier ties 30% or more of the relevant market. For a dominant company, even a modest tied market share may already lead to significant anti-competitive effects. The stronger its dominance, the higher the risk of foreclosure of other competitors.

(149) At the retail level a cumulative foreclosure effect may also arise. When all companies have market shares below 30% a cumulative foreclosure effect is unlikely if the total tied market share is less than 40% and withdrawal of the block exemption is therefore unlikely. This figure may be higher when other factors like the number of competitors, entry barriers etc. are taken into account. When not all companies have market shares below the threshold of the Block Exemption Regulation but none is dominant, a cumulative foreclosure effect is unlikely if the total tied market share is below 30%.

(150) Where the buyer operates from premises and land owned by the supplier or leased by the supplier from a third party not connected with the buyer, the possibility of imposing effective remedies for a possible foreclosure effect will be limited. In that case intervention by the Commission below the level of dominance is unlikely.

(151) In certain sectors the selling of more than one brand from a single site may be difficult, in which case a foreclosure problem can better be remedied by limiting the effective duration of contracts.

(152) A so-called 'English clause', requiring the buyer to report any better offer and allowing him only to accept such an offer when the supplier does not match it, can be expected to have the same effect as a non-compete obligation, especially when the buyer has to reveal who makes the better offer. In addition, by increasing the transparency of the market it may facilitate collusion between the suppliers. An English clause may also work as quantity-forcing. Quantity-forcing on the buyer is a weaker form of non-compete, where incentives or obligations agreed between the supplier and the buyer make the latter concentrate his purchases to a large extent with one supplier. Quantity-forcing may for example take the form of minimum purchase requirements or non-linear pricing, such as quantity rebate schemes, loyalty rebate schemes or a two-part tariff (fixed fee plus a price per unit). Quantity-forcing on the buyer will have similar but weaker foreclosure effects than a non-compete obligation. The assessment of all these different forms will depend on their effect on the market. In addition, Article 82 specifically prevents dominant companies from applying English clauses or fidelity rebate schemes.

(153) Where appreciable anti-competitive effects are established, the question of a possible exemption under Article 81(3) arises as long as the supplier is not dominant. For non-compete obligations, the efficiencies described in paragraph 116, points 1 (free riding between suppliers), 4, 5 (hold-up problems) and 7 (capital market imperfections) may be particularly relevant.

(154) In the case of an efficiency as described in paragraph 116, points 1, 4 and 7, quantity forcing on the buyer could possibly be a less restrictive alternative. A non-compete obligation may be the only viable way to achieve an efficiency as described in paragraph 116, point 5 (hold-up problem related to the transfer of know-how).

(155) In the case of a relationship-specific investment made by the supplier (see efficiency 4 in paragraph 116), a non-compete or quantity forcing agreement for the period of depreciation of the investment will in general fulfil the conditions of Article 81(3). In the case of high relationship-specific investments, a non-compete obligation exceeding five years may be justified. A relationship-specific investment could, for instance, be the installation or adaptation of equipment by the supplier when this equipment can be used afterwards only to produce components for a particular buyer. General or market-specific investments in (extra) capacity are normally not relationship-specific investments. However, where a supplier creates new capacity specifically linked to the operations of a particular buyer, for instance a company producing metal cans which creates new capacity to produce cans on the premises of or next to the canning facility of a food producer, this new capacity may only be economically viable when producing for this particular customer, in which case the investment would be considered to be relationship-specific.

(156) Where the supplier provides the buyer with a loan or provides the buyer with equipment which is not relationship-specific, this in itself is normally not sufficient to justify the exemption of a foreclosure effect on the market. The instances of capital market imperfection, whereby it is more efficient for the supplier of a product than for a bank to provide a loan, will be limited (see efficiency 7 in paragraph 116). Even if the supplier of the product were to be the more efficient provider of capital, a loan could only justify a non-compete obligation if the buyer is not prevented from terminating the non-compete obligation and repaying the outstanding part of the loan at any point in time and without payment of any penalty. This means that the repayment of the loan should be structured in equal or decreasing instalments and should not increase over time and that the buyer should have the possibility to take over the equipment provided by the supplier at its market asset value. This is without prejudice to the possibility, in case for example of a new point of distribution, to delay repayment for the first one or two years until sales have reached a certain level.

(157) The transfer of substantial know-how (efficiency 5 in paragraph 116) usually justifies a non-compete obligation for the whole duration of the supply agreement, as for example in the context of franchising.

(158) Below the level of dominance the combination of non-compete with exclusive distribution may also justify the non-compete obligation lasting the full length of the agreement. In the latter case, the non-compete obligation is likely to improve the distribution efforts of the exclusive distributor in his territory (see paragraphs 161 to 177).

(159) **Example of non-compete**

The market leader in a national market for an impulse consumer product, with a market share of 40%, sells most of its products (90%) through tied retailers (tied market share 36%). The agreements oblige the retailers to purchase only from the market leader for at least four years. The market leader is especially strongly represented in the more densely populated areas like the capital. Its competitors, 10 in number, of which some are only locally available, all have much smaller market shares, the biggest having 12%. These 10 competitors together supply another 10% of the market via tied outlets. There is strong brand and product differentiation in the market. The market leader has the strongest brands. It is the only one with regular national advertising campaigns. It provides its tied retailers with special stocking cabinets for its product.

The result on the market is that in total 46% (36% + 10%) of the market is foreclosed to potential entrants and to incumbents not having tied outlets. Potential entrants find entry even more difficult in the densely populated areas where foreclosure is even higher, although it is there that they would prefer to enter the market. In addition, owing to the strong brand and product differentiation and the high search costs relative to the price of the product, the absence of in-store inter-brand competition leads to an extra welfare loss for consumers. The possible efficiencies of the outlet exclusivity, which the market leader claims result from reduced transport costs and a possible hold-up problem concerning the stocking cabinets, are limited and do not outweigh the negative effects on competition. The efficiencies are limited, as the transport costs are linked to quantity and not exclusivity and the stocking cabinets do not contain special know-how and are not brand specific. Accordingly, it is unlikely that the conditions for exemption are fulfilled.

(160) **Example of quantity forcing**

A producer X with a 40% market share sells 80% of its products through contracts which specify that the reseller is required to purchase at least 75% of its requirements for that type of product from X. In return X is offering financing and equipment at favourable rates. The contracts have a duration of five years in which repayment of the loan is foreseen in equal instalments. However, after the first two years buyers have the possibility to terminate the contract with a six-month notice period if they repay the outstanding loan and take over the equipment at its market asset value. At the end of the five-year period the equipment becomes the property of the buyer. Most of the competing producers are small, twelve in total with the biggest having a market share of 20%, and engage in similar contracts with different durations. The producers with market shares below 10% often have contracts with longer durations and with less generous termination clauses. The contracts of producer X leave 25% of requirements free to be supplied by competitors. In the last three years, two new producers have entered the market and gained a combined market share of around 8%, partly by taking over the loans of a number of resellers in return for contracts with these resellers.

Producer X's tied market share is 24% (0.75 × 0.80 × 40%). The other producers' tied market share is around 25%. Therefore, in total around 49% of the market is foreclosed to potential entrants and to incumbents not having tied outlets for at least the first two years of the supply contracts. The market shows that the resellers often have difficulty in obtaining loans from banks and are too small in general to obtain capital through other means like the issuing of shares. In addition, producer X is able to demonstrate that concentrating his sales on a limited number of resellers allows him to plan his sales better and to save transport costs. In the light of the 25% non-tied part in the contracts of producer X, the real possibility for early termination of the contract, the recent entry of new producers and the fact that around half the resellers are not tied, the quantity forcing of 75% applied by producer X is likely to fulfil the conditions for exemption.

2.2. *Exclusive distribution*

(161) In an exclusive distribution agreement the supplier agrees to sell his products only to one distributor for resale in a particular territory. At the same time the distributor is usually limited in his active selling into other exclusively allocated territories. The possible competition risks are mainly reduced intra-brand competition and market partitioning, which may in particular facilitate price discrimination. When most or all of the suppliers apply exclusive distribution this may facilitate collusion, both at the suppliers' and distributors' level.

(162) Exclusive distribution is exempted by the Block Exemption Regulation when the supplier's market share does not exceed 30%, even if combined with other non-hardcore vertical restraints, such as a non-compete obligation limited to five years, quantity forcing or exclusive purchasing. A combination of exclusive distribution and selective distribution is only exempted by the Block Exemption Regulation if active selling in other territories is not restricted. Above the 30% market share threshold, the following guidance is provided for the assessment of exclusive distribution in individual cases.

(163) The market position of the supplier and his competitors is of major importance, as the loss of intra-brand competition can only be problematic if inter-brand competition is limited. The stronger the 'position of the supplier', the more serious is the loss of intra-brand competition. Above the 30% market share threshold there may be a risk of a significant reduction of intra-brand competition. In order to be exemptable, the loss of intra-brand competition needs to be balanced with real efficiencies.

(164) The 'position of the competitors' can have a dual significance. Strong competitors will generally mean that the reduction in intra-brand competition is outweighed by sufficient inter-brand competition. However, if the number of competitors becomes rather small and their market position is rather similar in terms of market share, capacity and distribution network, there is a risk of collusion. The loss of intra-brand competition can increase this risk, especially when several suppliers operate similar distribution systems. Multiple exclusive dealerships, i.e. when different suppliers appoint the same exclusive distributor in a given territory, may further increase the risk of collusion. If a dealer is granted the exclusive right to distribute two or more important competing products in the same territory, inter-brand competition is likely to be substantially restricted for those brands. The higher the cumulative market share of the brands distributed by the multiple dealer, the higher the risk of collusion and the more inter-brand competition will be reduced. Such cumulative effect situations may be a reason to withdraw the benefit of the Block Exemption Regulation when the market shares of the suppliers are below the threshold of the Block Exemption Regulation.

(165) 'Entry barriers' that may hinder suppliers from creating new distributors or finding alternative distributors are less important in assessing the possible anti-competitive effects of exclusive distribution. Foreclosure of other suppliers does not arise as long as exclusive distribution is not combined with single branding.

(166) Foreclosure of other distributors is not a problem if the supplier which operates the exclusive distribution system appoints a high number of exclusive distributors in the same market and these exclusive distributors are not restricted in selling to other non-appointed distributors. Foreclosure of other distributors may however become a problem where there is 'buying power' and market power downstream, in particular in the case of very large territories where the exclusive distributor becomes the exclusive buyer for a whole market. An example would be a supermarket chain which becomes the only distributor of a leading brand on a

national food retail market. The foreclosure of other distributors may be aggravated in the case of multiple exclusive dealership. Such a case, covered by the Block Exemption Regulation when the market share of each supplier is below 30%, may give reason for withdrawal of the block exemption.

(167) 'Buying power' may also increase the risk of collusion on the buyers' side when the exclusive distribution arrangements are imposed by important buyers, possibly located in different territories, on one or several suppliers.

(168) 'Maturity of the market' is important, as loss of intra-brand competition and price discrimination may be a serious problem in a mature market but may be less relevant in a market with growing demand, changing technologies and changing market positions.

(169) 'The level of trade' is important as the possible negative effects may differ between the wholesale and retail level. Exclusive distribution is mainly applied in the distribution of final goods and services. A loss of intra-brand competition is especially likely at the retail level if coupled with large territories, since final consumers may be confronted with little possibility of choosing between a high price/high service and a low price/low service distributor for an important brand.

(170) A manufacturer which chooses a wholesaler to be his exclusive distributor will normally do so for a larger territory, such as a whole Member State. As long as the wholesaler can sell the products without limitation to downstream retailers there are not likely to be appreciable anti-competitive effects if the manufacturer is not dominant. A possible loss of intra-brand competition at the wholesale level may be easily outweighed by efficiencies obtained in logistics, promotion etc, especially when the manufacturer is based in a different country. Foreclosure of other wholesalers within that territory is not likely as a supplier with a market share above 30% usually has enough bargaining power not to choose a less efficient wholesaler. The possible risks for inter-brand competition of multiple exclusive dealerships are however higher at the wholesale than at the retail level.

(171) The combination of exclusive distribution with single branding may add the problem of foreclosure of the market to other suppliers, especially in case of a dense network of exclusive distributors with small territories or in case of a cumulative effect. This may necessitate application of the principles set out above on single branding. However, when the combination does not lead to significant foreclosure, the combination of exclusive distribution and single branding may be pro-competitive by increasing the incentive for the exclusive distributor to focus his efforts on the particular brand. Therefore, in the absence of such a foreclosure effect, the combination of exclusive distribution with non-compete is exemptable for the whole duration of the agreement, particularly at the wholesale level.

(172) The combination of exclusive distribution with exclusive purchasing increases the possible competition risks of reduced intra-brand competition and market partitioning which may in particular facilitate price discrimination. Exclusive distribution already limits arbitrage by customers, as it limits the number of distributors and usually also restricts the distributors in their freedom of active selling. Exclusive purchasing, requiring the exclusive distributors to buy their supplies for the particular brand directly from the manufacturer, eliminates in addition possible arbitrage by the exclusive distributors, who are prevented from buying from other distributors in the system. This enhances the possibilities for the supplier to limit intra-brand competition while applying dissimilar conditions of sale. The combination of exclusive distribution and exclusive purchasing is therefore unlikely to be exempted for suppliers with a market share above 30% unless there are very clear and substantial efficiencies leading to lower prices to all final consumers. Lack of such efficiencies may also lead to withdrawal of the block exemption where the market share of the supplier is below 30%.

(173) The 'nature of the product' is not very relevant to assessing the possible anti-competitive effects of exclusive distribution. It is, however, relevant when the issue of possible efficiencies is discussed, that is after an appreciable anti-competitive effect is established.

(174) Exclusive distribution may lead to efficiencies, especially where investments by the distributors are required to protect or build up the brand image. In general, the case for efficiencies is strongest for new products, for complex products, for products whose qualities are difficult to judge before consumption (so-called experience products) or of which the qualities are difficult to judge even after consumption (so-called credence products). In addition, exclusive distribution may lead to savings in logistic costs due to economies of scale in transport and distribution.

(175) **Example of exclusive distribution at the wholesale level**

In the market for a consumer durable, A is the market leader. A sells its product through exclusive wholesalers. Territories for the wholesalers correspond to the entire Member State for small Member States, and to a region for larger Member States. These exclusive distributors take care of sales to all the retailers in their territories. They do not sell to final consumers. The wholesalers are in charge of promotion in their markets. This includes sponsoring of local events, but also explaining and promoting the new products to the retailers in their territories. Technology and product innovation are evolving fairly quickly on this market, and pre-sale service to retailers and to final consumers plays an important role. The wholesalers are not required to purchase all their requirements of the brand of supplier A from the producer himself, and arbitrage by wholesalers or retailers is practicable because the transport costs are relatively low compared to the value of the product. The wholesalers are not under a non-compete obligation. Retailers also sell a number of brands of competing suppliers, and there are no exclusive or selective distribution agreements at the retail level. On the European market of sales to wholesalers A has around 50% market share. Its market share on the various national retail markets varies between 40% and 60%. A has between 6 and 10 competitors on every national market: B, C and D are its biggest competitors and are also present on each national market, with market shares varying between 20% and 5%. The remaining producers are national producers, with smaller market shares. B, C and D have similar distribution networks, whereas the local producers tend to sell their products directly to retailers.

On the wholesale market described above, the risk of reduced intra-brand competition and price discrimination is low. Arbitrage is not hindered, and the absence of intra-brand competition is not very relevant at the wholesale level. At the retail level neither intra- nor inter-brand competition are hindered. Moreover, inter-brand competition is largely unaffected by the exclusive arrangements at the wholesale level. This makes it likely, if anti-competitive effects exist, that the conditions for exemption are fulfilled.

(176) **Example of multiple exclusive dealerships in an oligopolistic market**

In a national market for a final product, there are four market leaders, who each have a market share of around 20%. These four market leaders sell their product through exclusive distributors at the retail level. Retailers are given an exclusive territory which corresponds to the town in which they are located or a district of the town for large towns. In most territories, the four market leaders happen to appoint the same exclusive retailer ('multiple dealership'), often centrally located and rather specialised in the product. The remaining 20% of the national market is composed of small local producers, the largest of these producers having a market share of 5% on the national market. These local producers sell their products in general through other retailers, in particular because the exclusive distributors of the four largest suppliers show in general little interest in selling less well-known and cheaper brands. There is strong brand and product differentiation on the market. The four market leaders have large national advertising campaigns and strong brand images, whereas the fringe producers do not advertise their products at the national level. The market is rather mature, with stable demand and no major product and technological innovation. The product is relatively simple.

In such an oligopolistic market, there is a risk of collusion between the four market leaders. This risk is increased through multiple dealerships. Intra-brand competition is limited by the territorial exclusivity. Competition between the four leading brands is reduced at the retail level, since one retailer fixes the price of all four brands in each territory. The multiple dealership implies that, if one producer cuts the price for its brand, the retailer will not be eager to transmit this price cut to the final consumer as it would reduce its sales and profits made with the other brands. Hence, producers have a reduced interest in entering into price competition with one another. Inter-brand price competition exists mainly with the low brand image goods of the fringe producers. The possible efficiency arguments for (joint) exclusive distributors are limited, as the product is relatively simple, the resale does not require any specific investments or training and advertising is mainly carried out at the level of the producers.

Even though each of the market leaders has a market share below the threshold, exemption under Article 81(3) may not be justified and withdrawal of the block exemption may be necessary.

(177) **Example of exclusive distribution combined with exclusive purchasing**

Manufacturer A is the European market leader for a bulky consumer durable, with a market share of between 40% and 60% in most national retail markets. In every Member State, it has about seven competitors with much smaller market shares, the largest of these competitors having a market share of 10%. These competitors are present on only one or two national markets. A sells its product through its national subsidiaries to exclusive distributors at the retail level, which are not allowed to sell actively into each other's territories. In addition, the retailers are obliged to purchase manufacturer A's products exclusively from the national subsidiary of manufacturer A in their own country. The retailers selling the brand of manufacturer A are the main resellers of that type of product in their territory. They handle competing brands, but with varying degrees of success and enthusiasm. A applies price differences of 10% to 15% between markets and smaller differences within markets. This is translated into smaller price differences at the retail level. The market is relatively stable on the demand and the supply side, and there are no significant technological changes.

In these markets, the loss of intra-brand competition results not only from the territorial exclusivity at the retail level but is aggravated by the exclusive purchasing obligation imposed on the retailers. The exclusive purchase obligation helps to keep markets and territories separate by making arbitrage between the exclusive retailers impossible. The exclusive retailers also cannot sell actively into each other's territory and in practice tend to avoid delivering outside their own territory. This renders price discrimination possible. Arbitrage by consumers or independent traders is limited due to the bulkiness of the product.

The possible efficiency arguments of this system, linked to economies of scale in transport and promotion efforts at the retailers' level, are unlikely to outweigh the negative effect of price discrimination and reduced intra-brand competition. Consequently, it is unlikely that the conditions for exemption are fulfilled.

2.3. Exclusive customer allocation

(178) In an exclusive customer allocation agreement, the supplier agrees to sell his products only to one distributor for resale to a particular class of customers. At the same time, the distributor is usually limited in his active selling to other exclusively allocated classes of customers. The possible competition risks are mainly reduced intra-brand competition and market partitioning, which may in particular facilitate price discrimination. When most or all of the suppliers apply exclusive customer allocation, this may facilitate collusion, both at the suppliers' and the distributors' level.

(179) Exclusive customer allocation is exempted by the Block Exemption Regulation when the supplier's market share does not exceed the 30% market share threshold, even if combined with

other non-hardcore vertical restraints such as non-compete, quantity-forcing or exclusive purchasing. A combination of exclusive customer allocation and selective distribution is normally hardcore, as active selling to end-users by the appointed distributors is usually not left free. Above the 30% market share threshold, the guidance provided in paragraphs 161 to 177 applies mutatis mutandis to the assessment of exclusive customer allocation, subject to the following specific remarks.

(180) The allocation of customers normally makes arbitrage by the customers more difficult. In addition, as each appointed distributor has his own class of customers, non-appointed distributors not falling within such a class may find it difficult to obtain the product. This will reduce possible arbitrage by non-appointed distributors. Therefore, above the 30% market share threshold of the Block Exemption Regulation exclusive customer allocation is unlikely to be exemptable unless there are clear and substantial efficiency effects.

(181) Exclusive customer allocation is mainly applied to intermediate products and at the wholesale level when it concerns final products, where customer groups with different specific requirements concerning the product can be distinguished.

(182) Exclusive customer allocation may lead to efficiencies, especially when the distributors are required to make investments in for instance specific equipment, skills or know-how to adapt to the requirements of their class of customers. The depreciation period of these investments indicates the justified duration of an exclusive customer allocation system. In general the case is strongest for new or complex products and for products requiring adaptation to the needs of the individual customer. Identifiable differentiated needs are more likely for intermediate products, that is products sold to different types of professional buyers. Allocation of final consumers is unlikely to lead to any efficiencies and is therefore unlikely to be exempted.

(183) **Example of exclusive customer allocation**

A company has developed a sophisticated sprinkler installation. The company has currently a market share of 40% on the market for sprinkler installations. When it started selling the sophisticated sprinkler it had a market share of 20% with an older product. The installation of the new type of sprinkler depends on the type of building that it is installed in and on the use of the building (office, chemical plant, hospital etc.). The company has appointed a number of distributors to sell and install the sprinkler installation. Each distributor needed to train its employees for the general and specific requirements of installing the sprinkler installation for a particular class of customers. To ensure that distributors would specialise the company assigned to each distributor an exclusive class of customers and prohibited active sales to each others' exclusive customer classes. After five years, all the exclusive distributors will be allowed to sell actively to all classes of customers, thereby ending the system of exclusive customer allocation. The supplier may then also start selling to new distributors. The market is quite dynamic, with two recent entries and a number of technological developments. Competitors, with market shares between 25% and 5%, are also upgrading their products.

As the exclusivity is of limited duration and helps to ensure that the distributors may recoup their investments and concentrate their sales efforts first on a certain class of customers in order to learn the trade, and as the possible anti-competitive effects seem limited in a dynamic market, the conditions for exemption are likely to be fulfilled.

2.4. Selective distribution

(184) Selective distribution agreements, like exclusive distribution agreements, restrict on the one hand the number of authorised distributors and on the other the possibilities of resale. The difference with exclusive distribution is that the restriction of the number of dealers does not depend on the number of territories but on selection criteria linked in the first place to the nature of the product. Another difference with exclusive distribution is that the restriction on resale is not a restriction on active selling to a territory but a restriction on any sales to non-authorised

distributors, leaving only appointed dealers and final customers as possible buyers. Selective distribution is almost always used to distribute branded final products.

(185) The possible competition risks are a reduction in intra-brand competition and, especially in case of cumulative effect, foreclosure of certain type(s) of distributors and facilitation of collusion between suppliers or buyers. To assess the possible anti-competitive effects of selective distribution under Article 81(1), a distinction needs to be made between purely qualitative selective distribution and quantitative selective distribution. Purely qualitative selective distribution selects dealers only on the basis of objective criteria required by the nature of the product such as training of sales personnel, the service provided at the point of sale, a certain range of the products being sold etc.[31] The application of such criteria does not put a direct limit on the number of dealers. Purely qualitative selective distribution is in general considered to fall outside Article 81(1) for lack of anti-competitive effects, provided that three conditions are satisfied. First, the nature of the product in question must necessitate a selective distribution system, in the sense that such a system must constitute a legitimate requirement, having regard to the nature of the product concerned, to preserve its quality and ensure its proper use. Secondly, resellers must be chosen on the basis of objective criteria of a qualitative nature which are laid down uniformly for all potential resellers and are not applied in a discriminatory manner. Thirdly, the criteria laid down must not go beyond what is necessary.[32] Quantitative selective distribution adds further criteria for selection that more directly limit the potential number of dealers by, for instance, requiring minimum or maximum sales, by fixing the number of dealers, etc.

(186) Qualitative and quantitative selective distribution is exempted by the Block Exemption Regulation up to 30% market share, even if combined with other non-hardcore vertical restraints, such as non-compete or exclusive distribution, provided active selling by the authorised distributors to each other and to end users is not restricted. The Block Exemption Regulation exempts selective distribution regardless of the nature of the product concerned. However, where the nature of the product does not require selective distribution, such a distribution system does not generally bring about sufficient efficiency enhancing effects to counterbalance a significant reduction in intra-brand competition. If appreciable anti-competitive effects occur, the benefit of the Block Exemption Regulation is likely to be withdrawn. In addition, the following guidance is provided for the assessment of selective distribution in individual cases which are not covered by the Block Exemption Regulation or in the case of cumulative effects resulting from parallel networks of selective distribution.

(187) The market position of the supplier and his competitors is of central importance in assessing possible anti-competitive effects, as the loss of intra-brand competition can only be problematic if inter-brand competition is limited. The stronger the position of the supplier, the more problematic is the loss of intra-brand competition. Another important factor is the number of selective distribution networks present in the same market. Where selective distribution is applied by only one supplier in the market which is not a dominant undertaking, quantitative selective distribution does not normally create net negative effects provided that the contract goods, having regard to their nature, require the use of a selective distribution system and on condition that the selection criteria applied are necessary to ensure efficient distribution of the goods in question. The reality, however, seems to be that selective distribution is often applied by a number of the suppliers in a given market.

---

[31] See for example judgment of the Court of First Instance in Case T–88/92 *Groupement d'achat Édouard Leclerc v Commission* [1996] ECR II–1961.

[32] See judgments of the Court of Justice in Case 31/80 *L'Oréal v PVBA* [1980] ECR 3775, paragraphs 15 and 16; Case 26/76 *Metro I* [1977] ECR 1875, paragraphs 20 and 21; Case 107/82 *AEG* [1983] ECR 3151, paragraph 35; and of the Court of First Instance in Case T–19/91 *Vichy v Commission* [1992] ECR II–415, paragraph 65.

(188) The position of competitors can have a dual significance and plays in particular a role in case of a cumulative effect. Strong competitors will mean in general that the reduction in intra-brand competition is easily outweighed by sufficient inter-brand competition. However, when a majority of the main suppliers apply selective distribution there will be a significant loss of intra-brand competition and possible foreclosure of certain types of distributors as well as an increased risk of collusion between those major suppliers. The risk of foreclosure of more efficient distributors has always been greater with selective distribution than with exclusive distribution, given the restriction on sales to non-authorised dealers in selective distribution. This is designed to give selective distribution systems a closed character, making it impossible for non-authorised dealers to obtain supplies. This makes selective distribution particularly well suited to avoid pressure by price discounters on the margins of the manufacturer, as well as on the margins of the authorised dealers.

(189) Where the Block Exemption Regulation applies to individual networks of selective distribution, withdrawal of the block exemption or disapplication of the Block Exemption Regulation may be considered in case of cumulative effects. However, a cumulative effect problem is unlikely to arise when the share of the market covered by selective distribution is below 50%. Also, no problem is likely to arise where the market coverage ratio exceeds 50%, but the aggregate market share of the five largest suppliers (CR5) is below 50%. Where both the CR5 and the share of the market covered by selective distribution exceed 50%, the assessment may vary depending on whether or not all five largest suppliers apply selective distribution. The stronger the position of the competitors not applying selective distribution, the less likely the foreclosure of other distributors. If all five largest suppliers apply selective distribution, competition concerns may in particular arise with respect to those agreements that apply quantitative selection criteria by directly limiting the number of authorised dealers. The conditions of Article 81(3) are in general unlikely to be fulfilled if the selective distribution systems at issue prevent access to the market by new distributors capable of adequately selling the products in question, especially price discounters, thereby limiting distribution to the advantage of certain existing channels and to the detriment of final consumers. More indirect forms of quantitative selective distribution, resulting for instance from the combination of purely qualitative selection criteria with the requirement imposed on the dealers to achieve a minimum amount of annual purchases, are less likely to produce net negative effects, if such an amount does not represent a significant proportion of the dealer's total turnover achieved with the type of products in question and it does not go beyond what is necessary for the supplier to recoup his relationship-specific investment and/or realise economies of scale in distribution. As regards individual contributions, a supplier with a market share of less than 5% is in general not considered to contribute significantly to a cumulative effect.

(190) 'Entry barriers' are mainly of interest in the case of foreclosure of the market to non-authorised dealers. In general entry barriers will be considerable as selective distribution is usually applied by manufacturers of branded products. It will in general take time and considerable investment for excluded retailers to launch their own brands or obtain competitive supplies elsewhere.

(191) 'Buying power' may increase the risk of collusion between dealers and thus appreciably change the analysis of possible anti-competitive effects of selective distribution. Foreclosure of the market to more efficient retailers may especially result where a strong dealer organisation imposes selection criteria on the supplier aimed at limiting distribution to the advantage of its members.

(192) Article 5(c) of the Block Exemption Regulation provides that the supplier may not impose an obligation causing the authorised dealers, either directly or indirectly, not to sell the brands of particular competing suppliers. This condition aims specifically at avoiding horizontal collusion to exclude particular brands through the creation of a selective club of brands by the leading suppliers. This kind of obligation is unlikely to be exemptable when the CR5 is equal to or above

50%, unless none of the suppliers imposing such an obligation belongs to the five largest suppliers in the market.

(193) Foreclosure of other suppliers is normally not a problem as long as other suppliers can use the same distributors, i.e. as long as the selective distribution system is not combined with single branding. In the case of a dense network of authorised distributors or in the case of a cumulative effect, the combination of selective distribution and a non-compete obligation may pose a risk of foreclosure to other suppliers. In that case the principles set out above on single branding apply. Where selective distribution is not combined with a non-compete obligation, foreclosure of the market to competing suppliers may still be a problem when the leading suppliers apply not only purely qualitative selection criteria, but impose on their dealers certain additional obligations such as the obligation to reserve a minimum shelf-space for their products or to ensure that the sales of their products by the dealer achieve a minimum percentage of the dealer's total turnover. Such a problem is unlikely to arise if the share of the market covered by selective distribution is below 50% or, where this coverage ratio is exceeded, if the market share of the five largest suppliers is below 50%.

(194) Maturity of the market is important, as loss of intra-brand competition and possible foreclosure of suppliers or dealers may be a serious problem in a mature market but is less relevant in a market with growing demand, changing technologies and changing market positions.

(195) Selective distribution may be efficient when it leads to savings in logistical costs due to economies of scale in transport and this may happen irrespective of the nature of the product (efficiency 6 in paragraph 116). However, this is usually only a marginal efficiency in selective distribution systems. To help solve a free-rider problem between the distributors (efficiency 1 in paragraph 116) or to help create a brand image (efficiency 8 in paragraph 116), the nature of the product is very relevant. In general the case is strongest for new products, for complex products, for products of which the qualities are difficult to judge before consumption (so-called experience products) or of which the qualities are difficult to judge even after consumption (so-called credence products). The combination of selective and exclusive distribution is likely to infringe Article 81 if it is applied by a supplier whose market share exceeds 30% or in case of cumulative effects, even though active sales between the territories remain free. Such a combination may exceptionally fulfil the conditions of Article 81(3) if it is indispensable to protect substantial and relationship-specific investments made by the authorised dealers (efficiency 4 in paragraph 116).

(196) To ensure that the least anti-competitive restraint is chosen, it is relevant to see whether the same efficiencies can be obtained at a comparable cost by for instance service requirements alone.

(197) **Example of quantitative selective distribution:**

In a market for consumer durables, the market leader (brand A), with a market share of 35%, sells its product to final consumers through a selective distribution network. There are several criteria for admission to the network: the shop must employ trained staff and provide pre-sales services, there must be a specialised area in the shop devoted to the sales of the product and similar hi-tech products, and the shop is required to sell a wide range of models of the supplier and to display them in an attractive manner. Moreover, the number of admissible retailers in the network is directly limited through the establishment of a maximum number of retailers per number of inhabitants in each province or urban area. Manufacturer A has 6 competitors in this market. Its largest competitors, B, C and D, have market shares of respectively 25, 15 and 10%, whilst the other producers have smaller market shares. A is the only manufacturer to use selective distribution. The selective distributors of brand A always handle a few competing brands. However, competing brands are also widely sold in shops which are not member of A's selective distribution network. Channels of distribution are various: for instance, brands B and C are sold in most of A's selected shops, but also in other shops providing a high quality service and in hypermarkets. Brand D is mainly sold in high service shops. Technology is evolving quite rapidly in this market, and the main suppliers maintain a strong quality image for their products through advertising.

In this market, the coverage ratio of selective distribution is 35%. Inter-brand competition is not directly affected by the selective distribution system of A. Intra-brand competition for brand A may be reduced, but consumers have access to low service/low price retailers for brands B and C, which have a comparable quality image to brand A. Moreover, access to high service retailers for other brands is not foreclosed, since there is no limitation on the capacity of selected distributors to sell competing brands, and the quantitative limitation on the number of retailers for brand A leaves other high service retailers free to distribute competing brands. In this case, in view of the service requirements and the efficiencies these are likely to provide and the limited effect on intra-brand competition the conditions for exempting A's selective distribution network are likely to be fulfilled.

(198) **Example of selective distribution with cumulative effects:**

On a market for a particular sports article, there are seven manufacturers, whose respective market shares are: 25%, 20%, 15%, 15%, 10%, 8% and 7%. The five largest manufacturers distribute their products through quantitative selective distribution, whilst the two smallest use different types of distribution systems, which results in a coverage ratio of selective distribution of 85%. The criteria for access to the selective distribution networks are remarkably uniform amongst manufacturers: shops are required to have trained personnel and to provide pre-sale services, there must be a specialised area in the shop devoted to the sales of the article and a minimum size for this area is specified. The shop is required to sell a wide range of the brand in question and to display the article in an attractive manner, the shop must be located in a commercial street, and this type of article must represent at least 30% of the total turnover of the shop. In general, the same dealer is appointed selective distributor for all five brands. The two brands which do not use selective distribution usually sell through less specialised retailers with lower service levels. The market is stable, both on the supply and on the demand side, and there is strong brand image and product differentiation. The five market leaders have strong brand images, acquired through advertising and sponsoring, whereas the two smaller manufacturers have a strategy of cheaper products, with no strong brand image.

In this market, access by general price discounters to the five leading brands is denied. Indeed, the requirement that this type of article represents at least 30% of the activity of the dealers and the criteria on presentation and pre-sales services rule out most price discounters from the network of authorised dealers. As a consequence, consumers have no choice but to buy the five leading brands in high service/high price shops. This leads to reduced inter-brand competition between the five leading brands. The fact that the two smallest brands can be bought in low service/low price shops does not compensate for this, because the brand image of the five market leaders is much better. Inter-brand competition is also limited through multiple dealership. Even though there exists some degree of intra-brand competition and the number of retailers is not directly limited, the criteria for admission are strict enough to lead to a small number of retailers for the five leading brands in each territory.

The efficiencies associated with these quantitative selective distribution systems are low: the product is not very complex and does not justify a particularly high service. Unless the manufacturers can prove that there are clear efficiencies linked to their network of selective distribution, it is probable that the block exemption will have to be withdrawn because of its cumulative effects resulting in less choice and higher prices for consumers.

2.5. Franchising

(199) Franchise agreements contain licences of intellectual property rights relating in particular to trade marks or signs and know-how for the use and distribution of goods or services. In addition to the licence of IPRs, the franchisor usually provides the franchisee during the life of the

agreement with commercial or technical assistance. The licence and the assistance are integral components of the business method being franchised. The franchisor is in general paid a franchise fee by the franchisee for the use of the particular business method. Franchising may enable the franchisor to establish, with limited investments, a uniform network for the distribution of his products. In addition to the provision of the business method, franchise agreements usually contain a combination of different vertical restraints concerning the products being distributed, in particular selective distribution and/or non-compete and/or exclusive distribution or weaker forms thereof.

(200) The coverage by the Block Exemption Regulation of the licensing of IPRs contained in franchise agreements is dealt with in paragraphs 23 to 45. As for the vertical restraints on the purchase, sale and resale of goods and services within a franchising arrangement, such as selective distribution, non-compete or exclusive distribution, the Block Exemption Regulation applies up to the 30% market share threshold for the franchisor or the supplier designated by the franchisor.[33] The guidance provided earlier in respect of these types of restraints applies also to franchising, subject to the following specific remarks:

1) In line with general rule 8 (see paragraph 119), the more important the transfer of know-how, the more easily the vertical restraints fulfil the conditions for exemption.
2) A non-compete obligation on the goods or services purchased by the franchisee falls outside Article 81(1) when the obligation is necessary to maintain the common identity and reputation of the franchised network. In such cases, the duration of the non-compete obligation is also irrelevant under Article 81(1), as long as it does not exceed the duration of the franchise agreement itself.

(201) **Example of franchising**:

A manufacturer has developed a new format for selling sweets in so-called fun shops where the sweets can be coloured specially on demand from the consumer. The manufacturer of the sweets has also developed the machines to colour the sweets. The manufacturer also produces the colouring liquids. The quality and freshness of the liquid is of vital importance to producing good sweets. The manufacturer made a success of its sweets through a number of own retail outlets all operating under the same trade name and with the uniform fun image (style of lay-out of the shops, common advertising etc.). In order to expand sales the manufacturer started a franchising system. The franchisees are obliged to buy the sweets, liquid and colouring machine from the manufacturer, to have the same image and operate under the trade name, pay a franchise fee, contribute to common advertising and ensure the confidentiality of the operating manual prepared by the franchisor. In addition, the franchisees are only allowed to sell from the agreed premises, are only allowed to sell to end users or other franchisees and are not allowed to sell other sweets. The franchisor is obliged not to appoint another franchisee nor operate a retail outlet himself in a given contract territory. The franchisor is also under the obligation to update and further develop its products, the business outlook and the operating manual and make these improvements available to all retail franchisees. The franchise agreements are concluded for a duration of 10 years.

Sweet retailers buy their sweets on a national market from either national producers that cater for national tastes or from wholesalers which import sweets from foreign producers in addition to selling products from national producers. On this market the franchisor's products compete with other brands of sweets. The franchisor has a market share of 30% on the market for sweets sold to retailers. Competition comes from a number of national and international brands, sometimes

---

[33] See also [Case 107/82] *AEG* [1983] ECR 3151, paragraph 35; and of the Court of First Instance in Case T–19/91 *Vichy v Commission* [1992] ECR II–415, paragraph 65. See also paragraphs 89 to 95, in particular paragraph 95.

produced by large diversified food companies. There are many potential points of sale of sweets in the form of tobacconists, general food retailers, cafeterias and specialised sweet shops. On the market for machines for colouring food the franchisor's market share is below 10%.

Most of the obligations contained in the franchise agreements can be assessed as being necessary to protect the intellectual property rights or maintain the common identity and reputation of the franchised network and fall outside Article 81(1). The restrictions on selling (contract territory and selective distribution) provide an incentive to the franchisees to invest in the colouring machine and the franchise concept and, if not necessary for, at least help to maintain the common identity, thereby offsetting the loss of intra-brand competition. The non-compete clause excluding other brands of sweets from the shops for the full duration of the agreements does allow the franchisor to keep the outlets uniform and prevent competitors from benefiting from its trade name. It does not lead to any serious foreclosure in view of the great number of potential outlets available to other sweet producers. The franchise agreements of this franchisor are likely to fulfil the conditions for exemption under Article 81(3) in as far as the obligations contained therein fall under Article 81(1).

2.6. Exclusive supply

(202) Exclusive supply as defined in Article 1(c) of the Block Exemption Regulation is the extreme form of limited distribution in as far as the limit on the number of buyers is concerned: in the agreement it is specified that there is only one buyer inside the Community to which the supplier may sell a particular final product. For intermediate goods or services, exclusive supply means that there is only one buyer inside the Community or that there is only one buyer inside the Community for the purposes of a specific use. For intermediate goods or services, exclusive supply is often referred to as industrial supply.

(203) Exclusive supply as defined in Article 1(c) of the Block Exemption Regulation is exempted by Article 2(1) read in conjunction with Article 3(2) of the Block Exemption Regulation up to 30% market share of the buyer, even if combined with other non-hardcore vertical restraints such as non-compete. Above the market share threshold the following guidance is provided for the assessment of exclusive supply in individual cases.

(204) The main competition risk of exclusive supply is foreclosure of other buyers. The market share of the buyer on the upstream purchase market is obviously important for assessing the ability of the buyer to 'impose' exclusive supply which forecloses other buyers from access to supplies. The importance of the buyer on the downstream market is however the factor which determines whether a competition problem may arise. If the buyer has no market power downstream, then no appreciable negative effects for consumers can be expected. Negative effects can however be expected when the market share of the buyer on the downstream supply market as well as the upstream purchase market exceeds 30%. Where the market share of the buyer on the upstream market does not exceed 30%, significant foreclosure effects may still result, especially when the market share of the buyer on his downstream market exceeds 30%. In such cases withdrawal of the block exemption may be required. Where a company is dominant on the downstream market, any obligation to supply the products only or mainly to the dominant buyer may easily have significant anti-competitive effects.

(205) It is not only the market position of the buyer on the upstream and downstream market that is important but also the extent to and the duration for which he applies an exclusive supply obligation. The higher the tied supply share, and the longer the duration of the exclusive supply, the more significant the foreclosure is likely to be. Exclusive supply agreements shorter than five years entered into by non-dominant companies usually require a balancing of pro- and anti-competitive effects, while agreements lasting longer than five years are for most types of investments not considered necessary to achieve the claimed efficiencies or the efficiencies are not sufficient to outweigh the foreclosure effect of such long-term exclusive supply agreements.

(206) The market position of the competing buyers on the upstream market is important as it is only likely that competing buyers will be foreclosed for anti-competitive reasons, i.e. to increase their costs, if they are significantly smaller than the foreclosing buyer. Foreclosure of competing buyers is not very likely where these competitors have similar buying power and can offer the suppliers similar sales possibilities. In such a case, foreclosure could only occur for potential entrants, who may not be able to secure supplies when a number of major buyers all enter into exclusive supply contracts with the majority of suppliers on the market. Such a cumulative effect may lead to withdrawal of the benefit of the Block Exemption Regulation.

(207) Entry barriers at the supplier level are relevant to establishing whether there is real foreclosure. In as far as it is efficient for competing buyers to provide the goods or services themselves via upstream vertical integration, foreclosure is unlikely to be a real problem. However, often there are significant entry barriers.

(208) Countervailing power of suppliers is relevant, as important suppliers will not easily allow themselves to be cut off from alternative buyers. Foreclosure is therefore mainly a risk in the case of weak suppliers and strong buyers. In the case of strong suppliers the exclusive supply may be found in combination with non-compete. The combination with non-compete brings in the rules developed for single branding. Where there are relationship-specific investments involved on both sides (hold-up problem) the combination of exclusive supply and non-compete i.e. reciprocal exclusivity in industrial supply agreements is usually justified below the level of dominance.

(209) Lastly, the level of trade and the nature of the product are relevant for foreclosure. Foreclosure is less likely in the case of an intermediate product or where the product is homogeneous. Firstly, a foreclosed manufacturer that uses a certain input usually has more flexibility to respond to the demand of his customers than the wholesaler/retailer has in responding to the demand of the final consumer for whom brands may play an important role. Secondly, the loss of a possible source of supply matters less for the foreclosed buyers in the case of homogeneous products than in the case of a heterogeneous product with different grades and qualities.

(210) For homogeneous intermediate products, anti-competitive effects are likely to be exemptable below the level of dominance. For final branded products or differentiated intermediate products where there are entry barriers, exclusive supply may have appreciable anti-competitive effects where the competing buyers are relatively small compared to the foreclosing buyer, even if the latter is not dominant on the downstream market.

(211) Where appreciable anti-competitive effects are established, an exemption under Article 81(3) is possible as long as the company is not dominant. Efficiencies can be expected in the case of a hold-up problem (paragraph 116, points 4 and 5), and this is more likely for intermediate products than for final products. Other efficiencies are less likely. Possible economies of scale in distribution (paragraph 116, point 6) do not seem likely to justify exclusive supply.

(212) In the case of a hold-up problem and even more so in the case of scale economies in distribution, quantity forcing on the supplier, such as minimum supply requirements, could well be a less restrictive alternative.

(213) **Example of exclusive supply:**

On a market for a certain type of components (intermediate product market) supplier A agrees with buyer B to develop, with his own know-how and considerable investment in new machines and with the help of specifications supplied by buyer B, a different version of the component. B will have to make considerable investments to incorporate the new component. It is agreed that A will supply the new product only to buyer B for a period of five years from the date of first entry on the market. B is obliged to buy the new product only from A for the same period of five years. Both A and B can continue to sell and buy respectively other versions of the component elsewhere. The market share of buyer B on the upstream component market and on the downstream final goods market is 40%. The market share of the component supplier is 35%. There are two other component suppliers with around 20–25% market share and a number of small suppliers.

Given the considerable investments, the agreement is likely to fulfil the conditions for exemption in view of the efficiencies and the limited foreclosure effect. Other buyers are foreclosed from a particular version of a product of a supplier with 35% market share and there are other component suppliers that could develop similar new products. The foreclosure of part of buyer B's demand to other suppliers is limited to maximum 40% of the market.

(214) Exclusive supply is based on a direct or indirect obligation causing the supplier only to sell to one buyer. Quantity forcing on the supplier is based on incentives agreed between the supplier and the buyer that make the former concentrate his sales mainly with one buyer. Quantity forcing on the supplier may have similar but more mitigated effects than exclusive supply. The assessment of quantity forcing will depend on the degree of foreclosure of other buyers on the upstream market.

2.7. Tying

(215) Tying exists when the supplier makes the sale of one product conditional upon the purchase of another distinct product from the supplier or someone designated by the latter. The first product is referred to as the tying product and the second is referred to as the tied product. If the tying is not objectively justified by the nature of the products or commercial usage, such practice may constitute an abuse within the meaning of Article 82.[34] Article 81 may apply to horizontal agreements or concerted practices between competing suppliers which make the sale of one product conditional upon the purchase of another distinct product. Tying may also constitute a vertical restraint falling under Article 81 where it results in a single branding type of obligation (see paragraphs 138 to 160) for the tied product. Only the latter situation is dealt with in these Guidelines.

(216) What is to be considered as a distinct product is determined first of all by the demand of the buyers. Two products are distinct if, in the absence of tying, from the buyers' perspective, the products are purchased by them on two different markets. For instance, since customers want to buy shoes with laces, it has become commercial usage for shoe manufacturers to supply shoes with laces. Therefore, the sale of shoes with laces is not a tying practice. Often combinations have become accepted practice because the nature of the product makes it technically difficult to supply one product without the supply of another product.

(217) The main negative effect of tying on competition is possible foreclosure on the market of the tied product. Tying means that there is at least a form of quantity-forcing on the buyer in respect of the tied product. Where in addition a non-compete obligation is agreed in respect of the tied product, this increases the possible foreclosure effect on the market of the tied product. Tying may also lead to supra-competitive prices, especially in three situations. Firstly, when the tying and tied product are partly substitutable for the buyer. Secondly, when the tying allows price discrimination according to the use the customer makes of the tying product, for example the tying of ink cartridges to the sale of photocopying machines (metering). Thirdly, when in the case of long-term contracts or in the case of after-markets with original equipment with a long replacement time, it becomes difficult for the customers to calculate the consequences of the tying. Lastly, tying may also lead to higher entry barriers both on the market of the tying and on the market of the tied product.

(218) Tying is exempted by Article 2(1) read in conjunction with Article 3 of the Block Exemption Regulation when the market share of the supplier on both the market of the tied product and the market of the tying product does not exceed 30%. It may be combined with other non-hardcore vertical restraints such as non-compete or quantity forcing in respect of the

---

[34] Judgment of the Court of Justice in Case C–333/94 P *Tetrapak v Commission* [1996] ECR I–5951, paragraph 37.

tying product, or exclusive purchasing. Above the market share threshold the following guidance is provided for the assessment of tying in individual cases.

(219) The market position of the supplier on the market of the tying product is obviously of main importance to assess possible anti-competitive effects. In general this type of agreement is imposed by the supplier. The importance of the supplier on the market of the tying product is the main reason why a buyer may find it difficult to refuse a tying obligation.

(220) To assess the supplier's market power, the market position of his competitors on the market of the tying product is important. As long as his competitors are sufficiently numerous and strong, no anti-competitive effects can be expected, as buyers have sufficient alternatives to purchase the tying product without the tied product, unless other suppliers are applying similar tying. In addition, entry barriers on the market of the tying product are relevant to establish the market position of the supplier. When tying is combined with a non-compete obligation in respect of the tying product, this considerably strengthens the position of the supplier.

(221) Buying power is relevant, as important buyers will not easily be forced to accept tying without obtaining at least part of the possible efficiencies. Tying not based on efficiency is therefore mainly a risk where buyers do not have significant buying power.

(222) Where appreciable anti-competitive effects are established, the question of a possible exemption under Article 81(3) arises as long as the company is not dominant. Tying obligations may help to produce efficiencies arising from joint production or joint distribution. Where the tied product is not produced by the supplier, an efficiency may also arise from the supplier buying large quantities of the tied product. For tying to be exemptable, it must, however, be shown that at least part of these cost reductions are passed on to the consumer. Tying is therefore normally not exemptable when the retailer is able to obtain, on a regular basis, supplies of the same or equivalent products on the same or better conditions than those offered by the supplier which applies the tying practice. Another efficiency may exist where tying helps to ensure a certain uniformity and quality standardisation (see efficiency 8 in paragraph 116). However, it needs to be demonstrated that the positive effects cannot be realised equally efficiently by requiring the buyer to use or resell products satisfying minimum quality standards, without requiring the buyer to purchase these from the supplier or someone designated by the latter. The requirements concerning minimum quality standards would not normally fall within Article 81(1). Where the supplier of the tying product imposes on the buyer the suppliers from which the buyer must purchase the tied product, for instance because the formulation of minimum quality standards is not possible, this may also fall outside Article 81(1), especially where the supplier of the tying product does not derive a direct (financial) benefit from designating the suppliers of the tied product.

(223) The effect of supra-competitive prices is considered anti-competitive in itself. The effect of foreclosure depends on the tied percentage of total sales on the market of the tied product. On the question of what can be considered appreciable foreclosure under Article 81(1), the analysis for single branding can be applied. Above the 30% market share threshold exemption of tying is unlikely, unless there are clear efficiencies that are transmitted, at least in part, to consumers. Exemption is even less likely when tying is combined with non-compete, either in respect of the tied or in respect of the tying product.

(224) Withdrawal of the block exemption is likely where no efficiencies result from tying or where such efficiencies are not passed on to the consumer (see paragraph 222). Withdrawal is also likely in the case of a cumulative effect where a majority of the suppliers apply similar tying arrangements without the possible efficiencies being transmitted at least in part to consumers.

2.8. Recommended and maximum resale prices

(225) The practice of recommending a resale price to a reseller or requiring the reseller to respect a maximum resale price is—subject to the comments in paragraphs 46 to 56 concerning

RPM—covered by the Block Exemption Regulation when the market share of the supplier does not exceed the 30% threshold. For cases above the market share threshold and for cases of withdrawal of the block exemption the following guidance is provided.

(226) The possible competition risk of maximum and recommended prices is firstly that the maximum or recommended price will work as a focal point for the resellers and might be followed by most or all of them. A second competition risk is that maximum or recommended prices may facilitate collusion between suppliers.

(227) The most important factor for assessing possible anti-competitive effects of maximum or recommended resale prices is the market position of the supplier. The stronger the market position of the supplier, the higher the risk that a maximum resale price or a recommended resale price leads to a more or less uniform application of that price level by the resellers, because they may use it as a focal point. They may find it difficult to deviate from what they perceive to be the preferred resale price proposed by such an important supplier on the market. Under such circumstances the practice of imposing a maximum resale price or recommending a resale price may infringe Article 81(1) if it leads to a uniform price level.

(228) The second most important factor for assessing possible anti-competitive effects of the practice of maximum and recommended prices is the market position of competitors. Especially in a narrow oligopoly, the practice of using or publishing maximum or recommended prices may facilitate collusion between the suppliers by exchanging information on the preferred price level and by reducing the likelihood of lower resale prices. The practice of imposing a maximum resale price or recommending resale prices leading to such effects may also infringe Article 81(1).

2.9. Other vertical restraints

(229) The vertical restraints and combinations described above are only a selection. There are other restraints and combinations for which no direct guidance is provided here. They will however be treated according to the same principles, with the help of the same general rules and with the same emphasis on the effect on the market.

APPENDIX 3

Commission Regulation (EC) No 1400/2002 of 31 July 2002 on the application of Article 81(3) of the Treaty to categories of vertical agreements and concerted practices in the motor vehicle sector

([2002] OJ L203/30)

THE COMMISSION OF THE EUROPEAN COMMUNITIES,

Having regard to the Treaty establishing the European Community,

Having regard to Council Regulation No 19/65/EEC of 2 March 1965 on the application of Article 85(3) of the Treaty to certain categories of agreements and concerted practices,[1] as last amended by Regulation (EC) No 1215/1999,[2] and in particular Article 1 thereof,

Having published a draft of this Regulation,[3]

Having consulted the Advisory Committee on Restrictive Practices and Dominant Positions,

Whereas:

(1) Experience acquired in the motor vehicle sector regarding the distribution of new motor vehicles, spare parts and after sales services makes it possible to define categories of vertical agreements which can be regarded as normally satisfying the conditions laid down in Article 81(3).

(2) This experience leads to the conclusion that rules stricter than those provided for by Commission Regulation (EC) No 2790/1999 of 22 December 1999 on the application of Article 81(3) of the Treaty to categories of vertical agreements and concerted practices[4] are necessary in this sector.

(3) These stricter rules for exemption by category (the exemption) should apply to vertical agreements for the purchase or sale of new motor vehicles, vertical agreements for the purchase or sale of spare parts for motor vehicles and vertical agreements for the purchase or sale of repair and maintenance services for such vehicles where these agreements are concluded between non-competing undertakings, between certain competitors, or by certain associations of retailers or repairers. This includes vertical agreements concluded between a distributor acting at the retail level or an authorised repairer and a (sub)distributor or repairer. This Regulation should also apply to these vertical agreements when they contain ancillary provisions on the assignment or use of intellectual property rights. The term 'vertical agreements' should be defined accordingly to include both such agreements and the corresponding concerted practices.

(4) The benefit of the exemption should be limited to vertical agreements for which it can be assumed with sufficient certainty that they satisfy the conditions of Article 81(3).

(5) Vertical agreements falling within the categories defined in this Regulation can improve economic efficiency within a chain of production or distribution by facilitating better coordination between the participating undertakings. In particular, they can lead to a reduction in the

---

[1] OJ 36, 6.3.1965, p. 533/65. [2] OJ L 148, 15.6.1999, p. 1.
[3] OJ C 67, 16.3.2002, p. 2. [4] OJ L 336, 29.12.1999, p. 21.

transaction and distribution costs of the parties and to an optimisation of their sales and investment levels.

(6) The likelihood that such efficiency-enhancing effects will outweigh any anti-competitive effects due to restrictions contained in vertical agreements depends on the degree of market power held by the undertakings concerned and therefore on the extent to which those undertakings face competition from other suppliers of goods or services regarded by the buyer as interchangeable or substitutable for one another, by reason of the products' characteristics, prices or intended use.

(7) Thresholds based on market share should be fixed in order to reflect suppliers' market power. Furthermore, this sector-specific Regulation should contain stricter rules than those provided for by Regulation (EC) No 2790/1999, in particular for selective distribution. The thresholds below which it can be presumed that the advantages secured by vertical agreements outweigh their restrictive effects should vary with the characteristics of different types of vertical agreement. It can therefore be presumed that in general, vertical agreements have such advantages where the supplier concerned has a market share of up to 30% on the markets for the distribution of new motor vehicles or spare parts, or of up to 40% where quantitative selective distribution is used for the sale of new motor vehicles. As regards after sales services it can be presumed that, in general, vertical agreements by which the supplier sets criteria on how its authorised repairers have to provide repair or maintenance services for the motor vehicles of the relevant make and provides them with equipment and training for the provision of such services have such advantages where the network of authorised repairers of the supplier concerned has a market share of up to 30%. However, in the case of vertical agreements containing exclusive supply obligations, it is the market share of the buyer which is relevant for determining the overall effects of such vertical agreements on the market.

(8) Above those market share thresholds, there can be no presumption that vertical agreements falling within the scope of Article 81(1) will usually give rise to objective advantages of such a character and magnitude as to compensate for the disadvantages which they create for competition. However, such advantages can be anticipated in the case of qualitative selective distribution, irrespective of the supplier's market share.

(9) In order to prevent a supplier from terminating an agreement because a distributor or a repairer engages in pro-competitive behaviour, such as active or passive sales to foreign consumers, multi-branding or subcontracting of repair and maintenance services, every notice of termination must clearly set out in writing the reasons, which must be objective and transparent. Furthermore, in order to strengthen the independence of distributors and repairers from their suppliers, minimum periods of notice should be provided for the non-renewal of agreements concluded for a limited duration and for the termination of agreements of unlimited duration.

(10) In order to foster market integration and to allow distributors or authorised repairers to seize additional business opportunities, distributors or authorised repairers have to be allowed to purchase other undertakings of the same type that sell or repair the same brand of motor vehicles within the distribution system. To this end, any vertical agreement between a supplier and a distributor or authorised repairer has to provide for the latter to have the right to transfer all of its rights and obligations to any other undertaking of its choice of the same type that sell or repairs the same brand of motor vehicles within the distribution system.

(11) In order to favour the quick resolution of disputes which arise between the parties to a distribution agreement and which might otherwise hamper effective competition, agreements should only benefit from exemption if they provide for each party to have a right of recourse to an independent expert or arbitrator, in particular where notice is given to terminate an agreement.

(12) Irrespective of the market share of the undertakings concerned, this Regulation does not cover vertical agreements containing certain types of severely anti-competitive restraints (hardcore restrictions) which in general appreciably restrict competition even at low market shares and

which are not indispensable to the attainment of the positive effects mentioned above. This concerns in particular vertical agreements containing restraints such as minimum or fixed resale prices and, with certain exceptions, restrictions of the territory into which, or of the customers to whom, a distributor or repairer may sell the contract goods or services. Such agreements should not benefit from the exemption.

(13) It is necessary to ensure that effective competition within the common market and between distributors located in different Member States is not restricted if a supplier uses selective distribution in some markets and other forms of distribution in others. In particular selective distribution agreements which restrict passive sales to any end user or unauthorised distributor located in markets where exclusive territories have been allocated should be excluded from the benefit of the exemption, as should those selective distribution agreements which restrict passive sales to customer groups which have been allocated exclusively to other distributors. The benefit of the exemption should also be withheld from exclusive distribution agreements if active or passive sales to any end user or unauthorised distributor located in markets where selective distribution is used are restricted.

(14) The right of any distributor to sell new motor vehicles passively or, where relevant, actively to end users should include the right to sell such vehicles to end users who have given authorisation to an intermediary or purchasing agent to purchase, take delivery of, transport or store a new motor vehicle on their behalf.

(15) The right of any distributor to sell new motor vehicles or spare parts or of any authorised repairer to sell repair and maintenance services to any end user passively or, where relevant, actively should include the right to use the Internet or Internet referral sites.

(16) Limits placed by suppliers on their distributors' sales to any end user in other Member States, for instance where distributor remuneration or the purchase price is made dependent on the destination of the vehicles or on the place of residence of the end users, amount to an indirect restriction on sales. Other examples of indirect restrictions on sales include supply quotas based on a sales territory other than the common market, whether or not these are combined with sales targets. Bonus systems based on the destination of the vehicles or any form of discriminatory product supply to distributors, whether in the case of product shortage or otherwise, also amount to an indirect restriction on sales.

(17) Vertical agreements that do not oblige the authorised repairers within a supplier's distribution system to honour warranties, perform free servicing and carry out recall work in respect of any motor vehicle of the relevant make sold in the common market amount to an indirect restriction of sales and should not benefit from the exemption. This obligation is without prejudice to the right of a motor vehicle supplier to oblige a distributor to make sure as regards the new motor vehicles that he has sold that the warranties are honoured and that free servicing and recall work is carried out, either by the distributor itself or, in case of subcontracting, by the authorised repairer(s) to whom these services have been subcontracted. Therefore consumers should in these cases be able to turn to the distributor if the above obligations have not been properly fulfilled by the authorised repairer to whom the distributor has subcontracted these services. Furthermore, in order to allow sales by motor vehicle distributors to end users throughout the common market, the exemption should apply only to distribution agreements which require the repairers within the supplier's network to carry out repair and maintenance services for the contract goods and corresponding goods irrespective of where these goods are sold in the common market.

(18) In markets where selective distribution is used, the exemption should apply in respect of a prohibition on a distributor from operating out of an additional place of establishment where he is a distributor of vehicles other than passenger cars or light commercial vehicles. However, this prohibition should not be exempted if it limits the expansion of the distributor's business at the

authorised place of establishment by, for instance, restricting the development or acquisition of the infrastructure necessary to allow increases in sales volumes, including increases brought about by Internet sales.

(19) It would be inappropriate to exempt any vertical agreement that restricts the sale of original spare parts or spare parts of matching quality by members of the distribution system to independent repairers which use them for the provision of repair or maintenance services. Without access to such spare parts, these independent repairers would not be able to compete effectively with authorised repairers, since they could not provide consumers with good quality services which contribute to the safe and reliable functioning of motor vehicles.

(20) In order to give end users the right to purchase new motor vehicles with specifications identical to those sold in any other Member State, from any distributor selling corresponding models and established in the common market, the exemption should apply only to vertical agreements which enable a distributor to order, stock and sell any such vehicle which corresponds to a model within its contract range. Discriminatory or objectively unjustified supply conditions, in particular those regarding delivery times or prices, applied by the supplier to corresponding vehicles, are to be considered a restriction on the ability of the distributor to sell such vehicles.

(21) Motor vehicles are expensive and technically complex mobile goods which require repair and maintenance at regular and irregular intervals. However, it is not indispensable for distributors of new motor vehicles also to carry out repair and maintenance. The legitimate interests of suppliers and end users can be fully satisfied if the distributor subcontracts these services, including the honouring of warranties, free servicing and recall work, to a repairer or to a number of repairers within the supplier's distribution system. It is nevertheless appropriate to facilitate access to repair and maintenance services. Therefore, a supplier may require distributors who have subcontracted repair and maintenance services to one or more authorised repairers to give end users the name and address of the repair shop or shops in question. If any of these authorised repairers is not established in the vicinity of the sales outlet, the supplier may also require the distributor to tell end users how far the repair shop or shops in question are from the sales outlet. However, a supplier can only impose such obligations if he also imposes similar obligations on distributors whose own repair shop is not on the same premises as their sales outlet.

(22) Furthermore, it is not necessary, in order to adequately provide for repair and maintenance services, for authorised repairers to also sell new motor vehicles. The exemption should therefore not cover vertical agreements containing any direct or indirect obligation or incentive which leads to the linking of sales and servicing activities or which makes the performance of one of these activities dependent on the performance of the other; this is in particular the case where the remuneration of distributors or authorised repairers relating to the purchase or sale of goods or services necessary for one activity is made dependent on the purchase or sale of goods or services relating to the other activity, or where all such goods or services are indistinctly aggregated into a single remuneration or discount system.

(23) In order to ensure effective competition on the repair and maintenance markets and to allow repairers to offer end users competing spare parts such as original spare parts and spare parts of matching quality, the exemption should not cover vertical agreements which restrict the ability of authorised repairers within the distribution system of a vehicle manufacturer, independent distributors of spare parts, independent repairers or end users to source spare parts from the manufacturer of such spare parts or from another third party of their choice. This does not affect spare part manufacturers' liability under civil law.

(24) Furthermore, in order to allow authorised and independent repairers and end users to identify the manufacturer of motor vehicle components or of spare parts and to choose between competing spare parts, the exemption should not cover agreements by which a manufacturer of motor vehicles limits the ability of a manufacturer of components or original spare parts to place

its trade mark or logo on these parts effectively and in a visible manner. Moreover, in order to facilitate this choice and the sale of spare parts, which have been manufactured according to the specifications and production and quality standards provided by the vehicle manufacturer for the production of components or spare parts, it is presumed that spare parts constitute original spare parts, if the spare part producer issues a certificate that the parts are of the same quality as the components used for the assembly of a motor vehicle and have been manufactured according to these specifications and standards. Other spare parts for which the spare part producer can issue a certificate at any moment attesting that they match the quality of the components used for the assembly of a certain motor vehicle, may be sold as spare parts of matching quality.

(25) The exemption should not cover vertical agreements which restrict authorised repairers from using spare parts of matching quality for the repair or maintenance of a motor vehicle. However, in view of the vehicle manufacturers' direct contractual involvement in repairs under warranty, free servicing, and recall operations, agreements containing obligations on authorised repairers to use original spare parts supplied by the vehicle manufacturer for these repairs should be covered by the exemption.

(26) In order to protect effective competition on the market for repair and maintenance services and to prevent foreclosure of independent repairers, motor vehicle manufacturers must allow all interested independent operators to have full access to all technical information, diagnostic and other equipment, tools, including all relevant software, and training required for the repair and maintenance of motor vehicles. Independent operators who must be allowed such access include in particular independent repairers, manufacturers of repair equipment or tools, publishers of technical information, automobile clubs, roadside assistance operators, operators offering inspection and testing services and operators offering training for repairers. In particular, the conditions of access must not discriminate between authorised and independent operators, access must be given upon request and without undue delay, and the price charged for the information should not discourage access to it by failing to take into account the extent to which the independent operator uses it. A supplier of motor vehicles should be required to give independent operators access to technical information on new motor vehicles at the same time as such access is given to its authorised repairers and must not oblige independent operators to purchase more than the information necessary to carry out the work in question. Suppliers should be obliged to give access to the technical information necessary for re-programming electronic devices in a motor vehicle. It is, however, legitimate and proper for them to withhold access to technical information which might allow a third party to bypass or disarm on-board anti-theft devices, to recalibrate electronic devices or to tamper with devices which for instance limit the speed of a motor vehicle, unless protection against theft, re-calibration or tampering can be attained by other less restrictive means. Intellectual property rights and rights regarding know-how including those which relate to the aforementioned devices must be exercised in a manner which avoids any type of abuse.

(27) In order to ensure access to and to prevent collusion on the relevant markets and to give distributors opportunities to sell vehicles of brands from two or more manufacturers that are not connected undertakings, certain specific conditions are attached to the exemption. To this end, the exemption should not be accorded to non-compete obligations. In particular, without prejudice to the ability of the supplier to require the distributor to display the vehicles in brand-specific areas of the showroom in order to avoid brand confusion, any prohibition on sales of competing makes should not be exempted. The same applies to an obligation to display the full range of motor vehicles if it makes the sale or display of vehicles manufactured by undertakings which are not connected impossible or unreasonably difficult. Furthermore, an obligation to have brand-specific sales personnel is considered to be an indirect non-compete obligation and therefore should not be covered by the exemption, unless the distributor decides to have brand-specific sales personnel and the supplier pays all the additional costs involved.

(28) In order to ensure that repairers are able to carry out repairs or maintenance on all motor vehicles, the exemption should not apply to any obligation limiting the ability of repairers of motor vehicles to provide repair or maintenance services for brands of competing suppliers.

(29) In addition, specific conditions are required to exclude certain restrictions, sometimes imposed in the context of a selective distribution system, from the scope of the exemption. This applies in particular to obligations which have the effect of preventing the members of a selective distribution system from selling the brands of particular competing suppliers, which could easily lead to foreclosure of certain brands. Additional conditions are necessary in order to foster intra-brand competition and market integration within the common market, to create opportunities for distributors and authorised repairers who wish to seize business opportunities outside their place of establishment, and to create conditions which allow the development of multi-brand distributors. In particular a restriction on operating out of an unauthorised place of establishment for the distribution of passenger cars and light commercial vehicles or the provision of repair and maintenance services should not be exempted. The supplier may require additional sales or delivery outlets for passenger cars and light commercial vehicles or repair shops to comply with the relevant qualitative criteria applicable for similar outlets located in the same geographic area.

(30) The exemption should not apply to restrictions limiting the ability of a distributor to sell leasing services for motor vehicles.

(31) The market share limitations, the fact that certain vertical agreements are not covered, and the conditions provided for in this Regulation, should normally ensure that the agreements to which the exemption applies do not enable the participating undertakings to eliminate competition in respect of a substantial part of the goods or services in question.

(32) In particular cases in which agreements which would otherwise benefit from the exemption nevertheless have effects incompatible with Article 81(3), the Commission is empowered to withdraw the benefit of the exemption; this may occur in particular where the buyer has significant market power on the relevant market on which it resells the goods or provides the services or where parallel networks of vertical agreements have similar effects which significantly restrict access to a relevant market or competition thereon; such cumulative effects may for example arise in the case of selective distribution. The Commission may also withdraw the benefit of the exemption if competition is significantly restricted on a market due to the presence of a supplier with market power or if prices and conditions of supply to motor vehicle distributors differ substantially between geographic markets. It may also withdraw the benefit of the exemption if discriminatory prices or sales conditions, or unjustifiably high supplements, such as those charged for right hand drive vehicles, are applied for the supply of goods corresponding to the contract range.

(33) Regulation No 19/65/EEC empowers the national authorities of Member States to withdraw the benefit of the exemption in respect of vertical agreements having effects incompatible with the conditions laid down in Article 81(3), where such effects are felt in their territory, or in a part thereof, and where such territory has the characteristics of a distinct geographic market; the exercise of this national power of withdrawal should not prejudice the uniform application throughout the common market of the Community competition rules or the full effect of the measures adopted in implementation of those rules.

(34) In order to allow for better supervision of parallel networks of vertical agreements which have similar restrictive effects and which cover more than 50% of a given market, the Commission should be permitted to declare the exemption inapplicable to vertical agreements containing specific restraints relating to the market concerned, thereby restoring the full application of Article 81(1) to such agreements.

(35) The exemption should be granted without prejudice to the application of the provisions of Article 82 of the Treaty on the abuse by an undertaking of a dominant position.

(36) Commission Regulation (EC) No 1475/95 of 28 June 1995 on the application of Article 85(3) of the Treaty to certain categories of motor vehicle distribution and servicing agreements[5] is applicable until 30 September 2002. In order to allow all operators time to adapt vertical agreements which are compatible with that regulation and which are still in force when the exemption provided for therein expires, it is appropriate for such agreements to benefit from a transition period until 1 October 2003, during which time they should be exempted from the prohibition laid down in Article 81(1) under this Regulation.

(37) In order to allow all operators within a quantitative selective distribution system for new passenger cars and light commercial vehicles to adapt their business strategies to the non-application of the exemption to location clauses, it is appropriate to stipulate that the condition set out in Article 5(2)(b) shall enter into force on 1 October 2005.

(38) The Commission should monitor the operation of this Regulation on a regular basis, with particular regard to its effects on competition in motor vehicle retailing and in after sales servicing in the common market or relevant parts of it. This should include monitoring the effects of this Regulation on the structure and level of concentration of motor vehicle distribution and any resulting effects on competition. The Commission should also carry out an evaluation of the operation of this Regulation and draw up a report not later than 31 May 2008.

HAS ADOPTED THIS REGULATION:

Article 1

Definitions

(1) For the purposes of this Regulation:

(a) 'competing undertakings' means actual or potential suppliers on the same product market; the product market includes goods or services which are regarded by the buyer as inter-changeable with or substitutable for the contract goods or services, by reason of the products' characteristics, their prices and their intended use;

(b) 'non-compete obligation' means any direct or indirect obligation causing the buyer not to manufacture, purchase, sell or resell goods or services which compete with the contract goods or services, or any direct or indirect obligation on the buyer to purchase from the supplier or from another undertaking designated by the supplier more than 30% of the buyer's total purchases of the contract goods, corresponding goods or services and their substitutes on the relevant market, calculated on the basis of the value of its purchases in the preceding calendar year. An obligation that the distributor sell motor vehicles from other suppliers in separate areas of the showroom in order to avoid confusion between the makes does not constitute a non-compete obligation for the purposes of this Regulation. An obligation that the distributor have brand-specific sales personnel for different brands of motor vehicles constitutes a non-compete obligation for the purposes of this Regulation, unless the distributor decides to have brand-specific sales personnel and the supplier pays all the additional costs involved;

(c) 'vertical agreements' means agreements or concerted practices entered into by two or more undertakings, each of which operates, for the purposes of the agreement, at a different level of the production or distribution chain;

(d) 'vertical restraints' means restrictions of competition falling within the scope of Article 81(1), when such restrictions are contained in a vertical agreement;

(e) 'exclusive supply obligation' means any direct or indirect obligation causing the supplier to sell the contract goods or services only to one buyer inside the common market for the purposes of a specific use or for resale;

---

[5] OJ L 145, 29.6.1995, p. 25.

(f) 'selective distribution system' means a distribution system where the supplier undertakes to sell the contract goods or services, either directly or indirectly, only to distributors or repairers selected on the basis of specified criteria and where these distributors or repairers undertake not to sell such goods or services to unauthorised distributors or independent repairers, without prejudice to the ability to sell spare parts to independent repairers or the obligation to provide independent operators with all technical information, diagnostic equipment, tools and training required for the repair and maintenance of motor vehicles or for the implementation of environmental protection measures;

(g) 'quantitative selective distribution system' means a selective distribution system where the supplier uses criteria for the selection of distributors or repairers which directly limit their number;

(h) 'qualitative selective distribution system' means a selective distribution system where the supplier uses criteria for the selection of distributors or repairers which are only qualitative in nature, are required by the nature of the contract goods or services, are laid down uniformly for all distributors or repairers applying to join the distribution system, are not applied in a discriminatory manner, and do not directly limit the number of distributors or repairers;

(i) 'intellectual property rights' includes industrial property rights, copyright and neighbouring rights;

(j) 'know-how' means a package of non-patented practical information, derived from experience and testing by the supplier, which is secret, substantial and identified; in this context, 'secret' means that the know-how, as a body or in the precise configuration and assembly of its components, is not generally known or easily accessible; 'substantial' means that the know-how includes information which is indispensable to the buyer for the use, sale or resale of the contract goods or services; 'identified' means that the know-how must be described in a sufficiently comprehensive manner so as to make it possible to verify that it fulfils the criteria of secrecy and substantiality;

(k) 'buyer', whether distributor or repairer, includes an undertaking which sells goods or services on behalf of another undertaking;

(l) 'authorised repairer' means a provider of repair and maintenance services for motor vehicles operating within the distribution system set up by a supplier of motor vehicles;

(m) 'independent repairer' means a provider of repair and maintenance services for motor vehicles not operating within the distribution system set up by the supplier of the motor vehicles for which it provides repair or maintenance. An authorised repairer within the distribution system of a given supplier shall be deemed to be an independent repairer for the purposes of this Regulation to the extent that he provides repair or maintenance services for motor vehicles in respect of which he is not a member of the respective supplier's distribution system;

(n) 'motor vehicle' means a self propelled vehicle intended for use on public roads and having three or more road wheels;

(o) 'passenger car' means a motor vehicle intended for the carriage of passengers and comprising no more than eight seats in addition to the driver's seat;

(p) 'light commercial vehicle' means a motor vehicle intended for the transport of goods or passengers with a maximum mass not exceeding 3.5 tonnes; if a certain light commercial vehicle is also sold in a version with a maximum mass above 3.5 tonnes, all versions of that vehicle are considered to be light commercial vehicles;

(q) the 'contract range' means all the different models of motor vehicles available for purchase by the distributor from the supplier;

(r) a 'motor vehicle which corresponds to a model within the contract range' means a vehicle which is the subject of a distribution agreement with another undertaking within the distribution system set up by the manufacturer or with his consent and which is:
— manufactured or assembled in volume by the manufacturer, and
— identical as to body style, drive-line, chassis, and type of motor to a vehicle within the contract range;

(s) 'spare parts' means goods which are to be installed in or upon a motor vehicle so as to replace components of that vehicle, including goods such as lubricants which are necessary for the use of a motor vehicle, with the exception of fuel;

(t) 'original spare parts' means spare parts which are of the same quality as the components used for the assembly of a motor vehicle and which are manufactured according to the specifications and production standards provided by the vehicle manufacturer for the production of components or spare parts for the motor vehicle in question. This includes spare parts which are manufactured on the same production line as these components. It is presumed, unless the contrary is proven, that parts constitute original spare parts if the part manufacturer certifies that the parts match the quality of the components used for the assembly of the vehicle in question and have been manufactured according to the specifications and production standards of the vehicle manufacturer;

(u) 'spare parts of matching quality' means exclusively spare parts made by any undertaking which can certify at any moment that the parts in question match the quality of the components which are or were used for the assembly of the motor vehicles in question;

(v) 'undertakings within the distribution system' means the manufacturer and undertakings which are entrusted by the manufacturer or with the manufacturer's consent with the distribution or repair or maintenance of contract goods or corresponding goods;

(w) 'end-user' includes leasing companies unless the leasing contracts used provide for a transfer of ownership or an option to purchase the vehicle prior to the expiry of the contract.

(2) The terms 'undertaking', 'supplier', 'buyer', 'distributor' and 'repairer' shall include their respective connected undertakings.

'Connected undertakings' are:

(a) undertakings in which a party to the agreement, directly or indirectly:
  (i) has the power to exercise more than half the voting rights, or
  (ii) has the power to appoint more than half the members of the supervisory board, board of management or bodies legally representing the undertaking, or
  (iii) has the right to manage the undertaking's affairs;

(b) undertakings which directly or indirectly have, over a party to the agreement, the rights or powers listed in (a);

(c) undertakings in which an undertaking referred to in (b) has, directly or indirectly, the rights or powers listed in (a);

(d) undertakings in which a party to the agreement together with one or more of the undertakings referred to in (a), (b) or (c), or in which two or more of the latter undertakings, jointly have the rights or powers listed in (a);

(e) undertakings in which the rights or the powers listed in (a) are jointly held by:
  (i) parties to the agreement or their respective connected undertakings referred to in (a) to (d), or
  (ii) one or more of the parties to the agreement or one or more of their connected undertakings referred to in (a) to (d) and one or more third parties.

Article 2

Scope

(1) Pursuant to Article 81(3) of the Treaty and subject to the provisions of this Regulation, it is hereby declared that the provisions of Article 81(1) shall not apply to vertical agreements where they relate to the conditions under which the parties may purchase, sell or resell new motor vehicles, spare parts for motor vehicles or repair and maintenance services for motor vehicles.

The first subparagraph shall apply to the extent that such vertical agreements contain vertical restraints.

The exemption declared by this paragraph shall be known for the purposes of this Regulation as 'the exemption'.

(2) The exemption shall also apply to the following categories of vertical agreements:

(a) vertical agreements entered into between an association of undertakings and its members, or between such an association and its suppliers, only if all its members are distributors of motor vehicles or spare parts for motor vehicles or repairers and if no individual member of the association, together with its connected undertakings, has a total annual turnover exceeding € 50 million; vertical agreements entered into by such associations shall be covered by this Regulation without prejudice to the application of Article 81 to horizontal agreements concluded between the members of the association or decisions adopted by the association;

(b) vertical agreements containing provisions which relate to the assignment to the buyer or use by the buyer of intellectual property rights, provided that those provisions do not constitute the primary object of such agreements and are directly related to the use, sale or resale of goods or services by the buyer or its customers. The exemption shall apply on condition that those provisions do not contain restrictions of competition relating to the contract goods or services which have the same object or effect as vertical restraints which are not exempted under this Regulation.

(3) The exemption shall not apply to vertical agreements entered into between competing undertakings.

However, it shall apply where competing undertakings enter into a non-reciprocal vertical agreement and:

(a) the buyer has a total annual turnover not exceeding €100 million, or

(b) the supplier is a manufacturer and a distributor of goods, while the buyer is a distributor not manufacturing goods competing with the contract goods, or

(c) the supplier is a provider of services at several levels of trade, while the buyer does not provide competing services at the level of trade where it purchases the contract services.

Article 3

General conditions

(1) Subject to paragraphs 2, 3, 4, 5, 6 and 7, the exemption shall apply on condition that the supplier's market share on the relevant market on which it sells the new motor vehicles, spare parts for motor vehicles or repair and maintenance services does not exceed 30%.

However, the market share threshold for the application of the exemption shall be 40% for agreements establishing quantitative selective distribution systems for the sale of new motor vehicles.

Those thresholds shall not apply to agreements establishing qualitative selective distribution systems.

(2) In the case of vertical agreements containing exclusive supply obligations, the exemption shall apply on condition that the market share held by the buyer does not exceed 30% of the relevant market on which it purchases the contract goods or services.

(3) The exemption shall apply on condition that the vertical agreement concluded with a distributor or repairer provides that the supplier agrees to the transfer of the rights and obligations resulting from the vertical agreement to another distributor or repairer within the distribution system and chosen by the former distributor or repairer.

(4) The exemption shall apply on condition that the vertical agreement concluded with a distributor or repairer provides that a supplier who wishes to give notice of termination of an agreement must give such notice in writing and must include detailed, objective and transparent

reasons for the termination, in order to prevent a supplier from ending a vertical agreement with a distributor or repairer because of practices which may not be restricted under this Regulation.

(5) The exemption shall apply on condition that the vertical agreement concluded by the supplier of new motor vehicles with a distributor or authorised repairer provides

(a) that the agreement is concluded for a period of at least five years; in this case each party has to undertake to give the other party at least six months' prior notice of its intention not to renew the agreement;

(b) or that the agreement is concluded for an indefinite period; in this case the period of notice for regular termination of the agreement has to be at least two years for both parties; this period is reduced to at least one year where:

  (i) the supplier is obliged by law or by special agreement to pay appropriate compensation on termination of the agreement, or

  (ii) the supplier terminates the agreement where it is necessary to re-organise the whole or a substantial part of the network.

(6) The exemption shall apply on condition that the vertical agreement provides for each of the parties the right to refer disputes concerning the fulfilment of their contractual obligations to an independent expert or arbitrator. Such disputes may relate, inter alia, to any of the following:

(a) supply obligations;

(b) the setting or attainment of sales targets;

(c) the implementation of stock requirements;

(d) the implementation of an obligation to provide or use demonstration vehicles;

(e) the conditions for the sale of different brands;

(f) the issue whether the prohibition to operate out of an unauthorised place of establishment limits the ability of the distributor of motor vehicles other than passenger cars or light commercial vehicles to expand its business, or

(g) the issue whether the termination of an agreement is justified by the reasons given in the notice.

The right referred to in the first sentence is without prejudice to each party's right to make an application to a national court.

(7) For the purposes of this Article, the market share held by the undertakings referred to in Article 1(2)(e) shall be apportioned equally to each undertaking having the rights or the powers listed in Article 1(2)(a).

Article 4

Hardcore restrictions

(Hardcore restrictions concerning the sale of new motor vehicles, repair and maintenance services or spare parts)

(1) The exemption shall not apply to vertical agreements which, directly or indirectly, in isolation or in combination with other factors under the control of the parties, have as their object:

(a) the restriction of the distributor's or repairer's ability to determine its sale price, without prejudice to the supplier's ability to impose a maximum sale price or to recommend a sale price, provided that this does not amount to a fixed or minimum sale price as a result of pressure from, or incentives offered by, any of the parties;

(b) the restriction of the territory into which, or of the customers to whom, the distributor or repairer may sell the contract goods or services; however, the exemption shall apply to:

  (i) the restriction of active sales into the exclusive territory or to an exclusive customer group reserved to the supplier or allocated by the supplier to another distributor or repairer, where such a restriction does not limit sales by the customers of the distributor or repairer;

447

(ii) the restriction of sales to end users by a distributor operating at the wholesale level of trade;

(iii) the restriction of sales of new motor vehicles and spare parts to unauthorised distributors by the members of a selective distribution system in markets where selective distribution is applied, subject to the provisions of point (i);

(iv) the restriction of the buyer's ability to sell components, supplied for the purposes of incorporation, to customers who would use them to manufacture the same type of goods as those produced by the supplier;

(c) the restriction of cross-supplies between distributors or repairers within a selective distribution system, including between distributors or repairers operating at different levels of trade;

(d) the restriction of active or passive sales of new passenger cars or light commercial vehicles, spare parts for any motor vehicle or repair and maintenance services for any motor vehicle to end users by members of a selective distribution system operating at the retail level of trade in markets where selective distribution is used. The exemption shall apply to agreements containing a prohibition on a member of a selective distribution system from operating out of an unauthorised place of establishment. However, the application of the exemption to such a prohibition is subject to Article 5(2)(b);

(e) the restriction of active or passive sales of new motor vehicles other than passenger cars or light commercial vehicles to end users by members of a selective distribution system operating at the retail level of trade in markets where selective distribution is used, without prejudice to the ability of the supplier to prohibit a member of that system from operating out of an unauthorised place of establishment;

(Hardcore restrictions only concerning the sale of new motor vehicles)

(f) the restriction of the distributor's ability to sell any new motor vehicle which corresponds to a model within its contract range;

(g) the restriction of the distributor's ability to subcontract the provision of repair and maintenance services to authorised repairers, without prejudice to the ability of the supplier to require the distributor to give end users the name and address of the authorised repairer or repairers in question before the conclusion of a sales contract and, if any of these authorised repairers is not in the vicinity of the sales outlet, to also tell end users how far the repair shop or repair shops in question are from the sales outlet; however, such obligations may only be imposed provided that similar obligations are imposed on distributors whose repair shop is not on the same premises as their sales outlet;

(Hardcore restrictions only concerning the sale of repair and maintenance services and of spare parts)

(h) the restriction of the authorised repairer's ability to limit its activities to the provision of repair and maintenance services and the distribution of spare parts;

(i) the restriction of the sales of spare parts for motor vehicles by members of a selective distribution system to independent repairers which use these parts for the repair and maintenance of a motor vehicle;

(j) the restriction agreed between a supplier of original spare parts or spare parts of matching quality, repair tools or diagnostic or other equipment and a manufacturer of motor vehicles, which limits the supplier's ability to sell these goods or services to authorised or independent distributors or to authorised or independent repairers or end users;

(k) the restriction of a distributor's or authorised repairer's ability to obtain original spare parts or spare parts of matching quality from a third undertaking of its choice and to use them for the repair or maintenance of motor vehicles, without prejudice to the ability of a supplier of new motor vehicles to require the use of original spare parts supplied by it for repairs carried out under warranty, free servicing and vehicle recall work;

(l) the restriction agreed between a manufacturer of motor vehicles which uses components for the initial assembly of motor vehicles and the supplier of such components which limits the latter's ability to place its trade mark or logo effectively and in an easily visible manner on the components supplied or on spare parts.

(2) The exemption shall not apply where the supplier of motor vehicles refuses to give independent operators access to any technical information, diagnostic and other equipment, tools, including any relevant software, or training required for the repair and maintenance of these motor vehicles or for the implementation of environmental protection measures.

Such access must include in particular the unrestricted use of the electronic control and diagnostic systems of a motor vehicle, the programming of these systems in accordance with the supplier's standard procedures, the repair and training instructions and the information required for the use of diagnostic and servicing tools and equipment.

Access must be given to independent operators in a non-discriminatory, prompt and proportionate way, and the information must be provided in a usable form. If the relevant item is covered by an intellectual property right or constitutes know-how, access shall not be withheld in any abusive manner.

For the purposes of this paragraph 'independent operator' shall mean undertakings which are directly or indirectly involved in the repair and maintenance of motor vehicles, in particular independent repairers, manufacturers of repair equipment or tools, independent distributors of spare parts, publishers of technical information, automobile clubs, roadside assistance operators, operators offering inspection and testing services and operators offering training for repairers.

Article 5

Specific conditions

(1) As regards the sale of new motor vehicles, repair and maintenance services or spare parts, the exemption shall not apply to any of the following obligations contained in vertical agreements:

(a) any direct or indirect non-compete obligation;

(b) any direct or indirect obligation limiting the ability of an authorised repairer to provide repair and maintenance services for vehicles from competing suppliers;

(c) any direct or indirect obligation causing the members of a distribution system not to sell motor vehicles or spare parts of particular competing suppliers or not to provide repair and maintenance services for motor vehicles of particular competing suppliers;

(d) any direct or indirect obligation causing the distributor or authorised repairer, after termination of the agreement, not to manufacture, purchase, sell or resell motor vehicles or not to provide repair or maintenance services.

(2) As regards the sale of new motor vehicles, the exemption shall not apply to any of the following obligations contained in vertical agreements:

(a) any direct or indirect obligation causing the retailer not to sell leasing services relating to contract goods or corresponding goods;

(b) any direct or indirect obligation on any distributor of passenger cars or light commercial vehicles within a selective distribution system, which limits its ability to establish additional sales or delivery outlets at other locations within the common market where selective distribution is applied.

(3) As regards repair and maintenance services or the sale of spare parts, the exemption shall not apply to any direct or indirect obligation as to the place of establishment of an authorised repairer where selective distribution is applied.

Article 6

Withdrawal of the benefit of the Regulation

(1) The Commission may withdraw the benefit of this Regulation, pursuant to Article 7(1) of Regulation No 19/65/EEC, where it finds in any particular case that vertical agreements to which this Regulation applies nevertheless have effects which are incompatible with the conditions laid down in Article 81(3) of the Treaty, and in particular:

(a) where access to the relevant market or competition therein is significantly restricted by the cumulative effect of parallel networks of similar vertical restraints implemented by competing suppliers or buyers, or

(b) where competition is restricted on a market where one supplier is not exposed to effective competition from other suppliers, or

(c) where prices or conditions of supply for contract goods or for corresponding goods differ substantially between geographic markets, or

(d) where discriminatory prices or sales conditions are applied within a geographic market.

(2) Where in any particular case vertical agreements to which the exemption applies have effects incompatible with the conditions laid down in Article 81(3) of the Treaty in the territory of a Member State, or in a part thereof, which has all the characteristics of a distinct geographic market, the relevant authority of that Member State may withdraw the benefit of application of this Regulation in respect of that territory, under the same conditions as those provided in paragraph 1.

Article 7

Non-application of the Regulation

(1) Pursuant to Article 1a of Regulation No 19/65/EEC, the Commission may by regulation declare that, where parallel networks of similar vertical restraints cover more than 50% of a relevant market, this Regulation shall not apply to vertical agreements containing specific restraints relating to that market.

(2) A regulation pursuant to paragraph 1 shall not become applicable earlier than one year following its adoption.

Article 8

Market share calculation

(1) The market shares provided for in this Regulation shall be calculated

(a) for the distribution of new motor vehicles on the basis of the volume of the contract goods and corresponding goods sold by the supplier, together with any other goods sold by the supplier which are regarded as interchangeable or substitutable by the buyer, by reason of the products' characteristics, prices and intended use;

(b) for the distribution of spare parts on the basis of the value of the contract goods and other goods sold by the supplier, together with any other goods sold by the supplier which are regarded as interchangeable or substitutable by the buyer, by reason of the products' characteristics, prices and intended use;

(c) for the provision of repair and maintenance services on the basis of the value of the contract services sold by the members of the supplier's distribution network together with any other services sold by these members which are regarded as interchangeable or substitutable by the buyer, by reason of their characteristics, prices and intended use.

If the volume data required for those calculations are not available, value data may be used or vice versa. If such information is not available, estimates based on other reliable market information may be used. For the purposes of Article 3(2), the market purchase volume or the market purchase value respectively, or estimates thereof shall be used to calculate the market share.

(2) For the purposes of applying the market share thresholds of 30% and 40% provided for in this Regulation the following rules shall apply:

(a) the market share shall be calculated on the basis of data relating to the preceding calendar year;

(b) the market share shall include any goods or services supplied to integrated distributors for the purposes of sale;

(c) if the market share is initially not more than 30% or 40% respectively but subsequently rises above that level without exceeding 35% or 45% respectively, the exemption shall continue to apply for a period of two consecutive calendar years following the year in which the market share threshold of 30% or 40% respectively was first exceeded;

(d) if the market share is initially not more than 30% or 40% respectively but subsequently rises above 35% or 45% respectively, the exemption shall continue to apply for one calendar year following the year in which the level of 30% or 40% respectively was first exceeded;

(e) the benefit of points (c) and (d) may not be combined so as to exceed a period of two calendar years.

Article 9

Turnover calculation

(1) For the purposes of calculating total annual turnover figures referred to in Article 2(2)(a) and 2(3)(a) respectively, the turnover achieved during the previous financial year by the relevant party to the vertical agreement and the turnover achieved by its connected undertakings in respect of all goods and services, excluding all taxes and other duties, shall be added together. For this purpose, no account shall be taken of dealings between the party to the vertical agreement and its connected undertakings or between its connected undertakings.

(2) The exemption shall remain applicable where, for any period of two consecutive financial years, the total annual turnover threshold is exceeded by no more than 10%.

Article 10

Transitional period

The prohibition laid down in Article 81(1) shall not apply during the period from 1 October 2002 to 30 September 2003 in respect of agreements already in force on 30 September 2002 which do not satisfy the conditions for exemption provided for in this Regulation but which satisfy the conditions for exemption provided for in Regulation (EC) No 1475/95.

Article 11

Monitoring and evaluation report

(1) The Commission shall monitor the operation of this Regulation on a regular basis, with particular regard to its effects on:

(a) competition in motor vehicle retailing and in after sales servicing in the common market or relevant parts of it;

(b) the structure and level of concentration of motor vehicle distribution and any resulting effects on competition.

(2) The Commission shall draw up a report on this Regulation not later than 31 May 2008 having regard in particular to the conditions set out in Article 81(3).

Article 12

Entry into force and expiry

(1) This Regulation shall enter into force on 1 October 2002.

(2) Article 5(2)(b) shall apply from 1 October 2005.

(3) This Regulation shall expire on 31 May 2010.

This Regulation shall be binding in its entirety and directly applicable in all Member States.

INDEX